*Jefferson's principles are sources of light
because they are not made up of pure reason,
but spring out of aspiration, impulse, vision, sympathy.
They burn with the fervor of the heart....*

—Woodrow Wilson

Also by Alf J. Mapp, Jr.

*The Virginia Experiment: The Old Dominion's Role in the Making of America

*Frock Coats and Epaulets: Psychological Portraits of Confederate Military and
 Political Leaders

America Creates Its Own Literature

Just One Man

*The Golden Dragon: Alfred the Great and His Times

*Thomas Jefferson: A Strange Case of Mistaken Identity

Co-author

Chesapeake Bay in the American Revolution

Constitutionalism: Founding and Future

Portsmouth: A Pictorial History

Also Available from Madison Books

THOMAS JEFFERSON IN 1805   Painted by Rembrandt Peale shortly before Jefferson's second inauguration as President, the portrait shows him nearing his sixty-second birthday, at the height of his political career. Courtesy of The New-York Historical Society, New York City.

THOMAS JEFFERSON PASSIONATE PILGRIM

The Presidency

The Founding of the

University

and

The Private Battle

ALF J. MAPP, JR.

Madison Books

Lanham • New York • London

Published by Madison Books
4720 Boston Way
Lanham, Maryland 20706

Distributed by National Book Network

The paper used in this publication meets the minimum
requirements of American National Standard for
Information Sciences—Permanence of Paper for
Printed Library Materials, ANSI Z39.48–1984. ⊗ ™
Manufactured in the United States of America.

Library of Congress Cataloging-in-Publication Data

Mapp, Alf J. (Alf Johnson), 1925-
Thomas Jefferson : passionate pilgrim : the presidency,
the founding of the University, and the private battle /
Alf J. Mapp, Jr.
p.   cm.
Includes bibliographical references and index.
1. Jefferson, Thomas, 1743-1826.
2. Presidents—United States—Biography.
3. University of Virginia—History.
I. Title.
E332.M29   1990
973.4' 6' 092—dc20   [B]   90-19614 CIP
ISBN 0–8191–8053–X (cloth : alk. paper)
ISBN 1–56833–020–0 (paper : alk. paper)

To
RAMONA HARTLEY MAPP

Table of Contents

List of Illustrations

Acknowledgment

This acknowledgment, like that for *Thomas Jefferson: A Strange Case of Mistaken Identity,* must begin with an expression of appreciation to Jefferson himself. Few persons of international importance have left so voluminous a file of personal correspondence in addition to priceless public archives. Once again, too, I am grateful for his varied interests and lively style that for me made the pursuit of his thoughts an enterprise of unflagging enthusiasm.

My special appreciation goes to those people who have helped me directly in research and in preparation of the manuscript. Important among these are staff members of the Hughes Library of Old Dominion University; the Library of Congress, Washington, D.C., which provided me a study room and valuable cooperation, especially Bruce Martin (director of research facilities), and Dr. Marilyn K. Parr (a remarkably efficient senior researcher in American history, who not only was of great help in locating sources but also read the unpublished manuscript); the Norfolk (Va.) Public Library, especially Peggy Haile, assistant head librarian of the Sargeant Room; the Portsmouth (Va.) Public Library, especially Dean Burgess (director), and William A. Brown, II, and Susan H. Burton; the library of the Virginia Historical Society, especially Frances Pollard; the Virginia State Library; the Earl Gregg Swem Library of the College of William and Mary, the library of the University of South Carolina; and the Alderman Library of the University of Virginia. Appreciation is due Mrs. J. Carrol Melton for the gift of research materials preserved in her family.

I am grateful for the extraordinary hospitality of Melba Meador and Howard Messner, who made their home available as our residence when I was researching at the Library of Congress.

I have consulted with experts whose help is acknowledged in the annotation. Special thanks, however, should go to Virginius Dabney, a Pulitzer Prize-winning editor, author, and historian, who read the entire manuscript before publication. As the author of *Virginia: the New Dominion, The Jefferson Scandals,* and *Mr. Jefferson's University,* he was extraordinarily well versed in many aspects of the subject of this biography and his native state.

A research leave of one semester from Old Dominion University helped me to meet my deadline for this volume.

It is a pleasure to express appreciation to Charles Lean, managing editor and later assistant publisher of Madison Books, who initiated plans for publication of this volume. His sensitivity, intelligence, enthusiasm, and generous availability made work with him a pleasant experience.

Finally, and in largest measure, my gratitude goes out to my wife, Ramona Hartley Mapp, for the skill, knowledge, and patience that she brought to the typing and indexing of this work and to an important part of the research. Her keen perceptions were a constant stimulus when we visited sites related to Jefferson's life and when I needed to talk about research in progress. In the acknowledgments for *Thomas Jefferson: A Strange Case of Mistaken Identity* I said of her, "She is a part of everything I do of any importance." I did not think that statement ever could be truer than at that time. But, to my amazement, it is even truer now as I dedicate to her *Thomas Jefferson: Passionate Pilgrim*.

Alf J. Mapp, Jr.
Willow Oaks
Portsmouth, Virginia

I

THE GREAT EXPERIMENT

WHEN A TALL, lanky Virginian stood in the Senate Chamber of the United States Capitol on March 4, 1801, and swore that he, Thomas Jefferson, would defend the Constitution of the United States, the proceedings must have had a comforting air of stability. No one had been more vigilant than this fifty-seven-year-old statesman in guardianship of constitutional guarantees to the people of the United States and to the states which comprised the Union. Even the informality of his walk from the boardinghouse where he lived to the site of his inauguration bespoke a confidence both in the people he would serve and in the continuity of democratic government. It was as if the pomp surrounding the carriage rides of Washington to his two inaugurations and John Adams to his one had been rendered unnecessary by growing popular acceptance of the federal government as an essential institution. Golden epaulets were not necessary when power rested securely on the shoulders of a new President, and boisterous trumpets were not needed to clear the path for the Chief Magistrate of a well-established republic. The sense of security was increased when those near enough to the President heard him, rising above factionalism, declare: "We have called by different names brethren of the same principle. We are all republicans; we are all federalists."

Actually, the government was not nearly so stable as the ceremonies in the Senate Chamber might make it seem, and the conciliatory words of the new President could assuage but did not completely obliterate the fears of many of his fellow citizens.

Jefferson was too proud to answer the charge of some New England preachers that, in the new administration, chaste churches would be converted to temples of prostitution or even to comment on their advice to the faithful that they hide their Bibles to thwart confiscation by the Arch Atheist. He seldom deigned to reply to those Federalists in every state who charged that he would make the United States a satellite of France. He did nothing to allay fears that he would welcome foreign-born intellectuals to American shores and made no effort to conceal his liking for French cuisine, a sure sign to some that he had been corrupted by his experience in Paris as United States Minister. Jefferson's delight in such Virginia staples as cornbread was not completely reassuring; a man even partially weaned from his native victuals might well have found alien nutriment for the spirit as well.

Even though the tone and content of Jefferson's inaugural address were reassuring to some Federalist leaders such as John Marshall, his cousin but also a political foe, the less sophisticated were not so easily comforted. And, while a great many ordinary Americans saw Jefferson as the protector as well as the articulator of their freedom, there were enough erratic and exhibitionistic Republicans to give a bad name in some quarters to a President who wore the same label.

Quite apart from fears fanned by factional strife, the government certainly was not impregnably bedded in immovable rock. Not only was the administration brand new; the republic itself was only twelve years old. This span seemed short indeed to people who had declared their independence from a government to which they had yielded obedience for centuries, declaring in a document written by the man now newly inaugurated President that it was not only the right, but the duty, of the people "to alter or to abolish" any government that no longer served the purposes for which it had been created.

If one looked beyond the traditional trappings of the Senate Chamber where the tall man took the oath of office, even the physical symbols of government were more suggestive of transition or impermanence than of stability. The Capitol, whose exterior revealed its unfinished state, had no counterpart to its Senate Chamber to shelter the deliberations of the House of Representatives. The more popular branch of the legislature was assigned a strictly temporary wing, and even this was still under construction. It was called the oven because of its circular structure. The term acquired peculiar aptness on warm days and, of course, in all seasons invited wisecracks about its being the source of half-baked ideas.

Even Jefferson's official residence was unfinished. The barnlike character of the bare-walled East Room was such that Abigail Adams had used it for her washroom. Heraldic pennants adorned the palaces of some European rulers; snow-white linens and colorful waistcoats, coats, and petticoats hung once a week in the home of America's Chief Magistrate. When the President complained about leaks under his roof he did not refer to the unauthorized emissions of news but the quite literal pouring of rain through numerous places in the ceilings.

No real street, not even the "good gravel road" advocated by Jefferson, linked the unfinished Executive Mansion with the unfinished Capitol. Around these structures, incomplete and distinguished from ruins chiefly by their rawness, stretched bogs, wastes, and wilderness. No wonder some people thought the whole capital city a very tentative business. Soon after Jefferson's inauguration one prominent Federalist reported to another that the new President was working hard "to induce a continuance of the government at Washington."[1] The reporter thought that these efforts would succeed, but he was not sure.

The inchoate character of the new federal city and of the federal government itself did not depress Jefferson. The man who for years had been building, unbuilding, and rebuilding his own Monticello to accord with his changing dreams had little right to complain of the unfinished state of his physical surroundings. But there was more than mere acquiescence in Jefferson's cheerful acceptance of the state of flux in which he found both the government and its capital. Though a cherisher of the traditions of Western civilization and of the architectural forms of antiquity, he was also a lover of beginnings. Though sometimes skeptical of things in the short run, he was an optimistic long-range planner. As a devotee of the Enlightenment, he believed that humanity and its institutions were improvable. Unlike patriots such as Patrick Henry, who had been ready to celebrate the end of the Revolution when Cornwallis surrendered at Yorktown in 1781 and quite certain that it was over when the Treaty of Paris was signed in 1783, Jefferson saw the winning of independence as only the prelude to the real revolution: reform in the institutions through which Americans would work out their destiny.

Coming to the presidency in a capital and a government generally regarded as finished would have offered to him a dreary prospect. Instead of this he had the opportunity to build for the future, judiciously drawing upon the best from the past to meet the challenges of the present and the demands of posterity. Dr. Joseph Priestley, the controversial clergyman and revered scientist, was one of the few correspondents to whom Jefferson confided the combination of religious faith and secular hope that sustained him. To his friend, in this first year of the nineteenth century, the new President exuberantly wrote: "We can no longer say there is nothing new under the sun. For this whole chapter in the history of man is new. The great extent of our Republic is new."[2]

II

A REASONABLE REVOLUTIONIST

J EFFERSON'S INAUGURAL address, a masterpiece of eloquence, furnished argument for all whose expectations, for good or ill, had been raised by his controversial career and further heightened by the vituperative campaign of 1800. Partisan nerves had been additionally exacerbated by the accidental tie between Jefferson and Aaron Burr in the electoral college, which had caused the election to be thrown into the House of Representatives, rendering the result uncertain until election of Jefferson on the thirty-sixth ballot. Now Jefferson's statements in his inaugural address, delivered in a voice unequal to the acoustics of the Senate Chamber, had been carried far and wide by newspapers, furnishing, in cold print, items for lively debate in the parlors, taverns, crossroads stores, countinghouses, and blacksmith shops of America.

The most impressive thing about the address was its conciliatory tone, not only in its statement about all alike being Federalists and Republicans, but in more specific passages, such as his assertion: "All, too, will bear in mind this sacred principle, that though the will of the majority is in all cases to prevail, that will to be rightful must be reasonable; that the minority possess their equal rights, which equal law must protect, and to violate would be oppression." This statement was welcome to Federalists who feared reprisals for their own persecutions and to Republicans who welcomed the opportunity to demonstrate moral superiority, but it was frustrating to some other Republicans who hungered for vengeance. Likewise reassuring to some and disturbing to others was the new President's declaration: "If there be any among us who would wish to dissolve this Union or to change its republican form, let them stand undisturbed as monuments of the safety with which error of opinion may be tolerated where reason is left free to combat it."

Jefferson had spoken of the need to encourage agriculture and "its hand-maid" commerce. No one was surprised and many, particularly in the South, were pleased at the reference to agriculture. Some were pleased by the recognition of commerce but others resented its relegation to handmaid status. Still others complained that there was no specific reference to industry and were not reassured by speculation that the President thought of commerce as embracing industry.

Some who feared that Jefferson would involve the United States in the quarrels of France were encouraged by his saying that America's ocean barriers could enable her to escape the quarrels of the Old World.

Many who feared the growth of federal power, especially in the Adams administration, cheered his assertion that the federal government should deal chiefly with foreign affairs, including defense, and leave domestic affairs to the states. He advocated "a wise and frugal government which shall restrain men from injuring one another, shall leave them otherwise free to regulate their own pursuits of industry and improvement, and shall not take from the mouth of labor the bread it has earned. This is the sum of good government. . . ."

The Federalist followers of Alexander Hamilton believed in strengthening the central government and using its powers to foster industry and commerce—when necessary, by direct federal intervention. They saw Jefferson's attitude as one likely to undermine the movement toward national prosperity advanced in the administrations of Washington and Adams.

Both the fears and the enthusiasms stirred by Jefferson's inaugural utterances were lessened by strong skepticism. Would the new President continue to be so distrustful of federal power when he himself was wielding it? When he saw opportunities to advance pet projects by executive intervention, would he still define the functions of government in negative terms? And would he be able to tolerate public criticism of himself as easily as he had tolerated criticism of others? Even on the local level, Americans had seen opposition leaders alter their philosophies when they became incumbents.

Time would be necessary to test the new President's loyalty to his stated ideals. This early in his administration, some cynics thought, even he probably still believed his own inaugural rhetoric.

The degree of consistency between the President's views and his actions, however, was soon revealed in one matter. Hamilton had said that government should be the business of the well bred, well educated, and affluent; Jefferson, on the other hand, had professed his faith that a peculiar wisdom resided in the people, especially those who tilled the soil, and had said that confidence should be placed in one's fellow citizens solely with regard to their actions and not to their birth. Was Jefferson going to call plowmen to abandon their furrows that they might follow the intricate paths of statecraft?

The first chosen member of Jefferson's cabinet was indeed a farmer. To the demanding post of Secretary of State he called that prominent Orange County, Virginia, farmer James Madison. Of course, Madison lived in Montpelier, one of the Old Dominion's great mansions, and was a powerful member of its plantocracy. Also, he had received a superb education at Princeton and an even more impressive one subsequently in his private studies. This farmer was a fully qualified member of any elite defined in Hamiltonian terms of breeding, education, and affluence. Jefferson gloried in his own occupation as a farmer; evidently when he thought of farmers in government he thought of people very much like himself.

To the second major cabinet position, Secretary of the Treasury, Jefferson appointed a man whose background was far more exotic than Madison's but equally elite. Albert Gallatin was a native of Switzerland and a scion of its ancient nobility. His heavy accent was a constant reminder of his origins in the French canton and therefore an irritant to Francophobe Federalists. His large Roman nose and the black hair framing his gleaming bald pate gave him a Mediterranean look that many Americans of northern European ancestry found decidedly alien. In addition to these external characteristics, his spirited and effective leadership of Republicans in the House of Representatives in the acrimonious sessions during the recent crisis with France had made him the peculiar object of Federalist fear and hatred. Some saw his appointment to the cabinet as "a violent outrage on the virtue and respectability" of the nation.[1] Fully anticipating the reaction to his choice of a Treasury Secretary, Jefferson waited until Congress had recessed. An interim appointment did not immediately require senatorial consent.

Jefferson rounded out his cabinet and placated some New Englanders by appointing General Henry Dearborn as Secretary of War and Levi Lincoln as Attorney General. He was frustrated in his attempts to secure a suitable Secretary of the Navy, but the incumbent, Benjamin Stoddert, agreed to serve until Jefferson could make other arrangements. Now at the half-century mark, Dearborn had been a physician in his native New Hampshire before joining the provincial forces in the Revolution and serving from Bunker Hill to Yorktown. His military experience embraced Quebec, Saratoga, Valley Forge, and Monmouth, and his remarkably comprehensive journal revealed that the order of his mind matched the valor of his spirit. Two terms as a Republican congressman had acquainted him with the civil processes of government. In New England he had the respect of Federalists as well as Republicans.

Lincoln also had the respect of both parties, especially in his own state of Massachusetts. He had only recently been elected to Congress. Before Madison's arrival to take his post, Lincoln had filled in as Secretary of State as well as assuming the office of Attorney General.

Hardly less important than the fact that the new cabinet included four honest men, two of them brilliant and two of them able, was the fact that their relationships with each other were harmonious. Jefferson, who craved harmony in all working relationships, would not be cursed with the kind of strife-torn cabinet that had plagued Washington when Jefferson himself was a cabinet member.

Among the cabinet secretaries and their chief there was philosophical as well as personal harmony. All were dedicated to reform but constrained by common sense and the lessons of history. Jefferson soon was referring privately to the events of 1800 as the second of "two revolutions," and nearly a score of years later would pronounce the changes inaugurated then "as real a revolution in the principles of our government as that of 1776 was in its form";[2] but less than four weeks after taking office he confided his agreement with Solon that "no more good must be attempted than the nation can bear."[3] Ever the pragmatist in support of his ideals, he principally hoped "to reform the waste of public money, and thus drive away the vultures who prey on it, and improve some little on old routines." Anticipating the dictum that politics is the science of the possible, he ventured to hope that "some new fences for securing constitutional rights may, with the aid of a good legislature, perhaps be attainable."[4]

In his advocacy of both revolution and restraint, Jefferson was troubled by no sense of paradox. The revolution was to be one of mood and attitude; the results would be evident at least as much in things refrained from as in things initiated. In his belief that a President's most important mission was to help the nation achieve a revolution of the spirit, Jefferson anticipated such philosophically disparate successors as Theodore Roosevelt, Woodrow Wilson, Franklin D. Roosevelt, John F. Kennedy, and Ronald Reagan.

As envisioned by Jefferson, this spiritual revolution was not to be a punitive expedition. He cultivated harmony in the nation as well as in the cabinet. Having declared in his inaugural address, "We are all republicans; we are all federalists," he seemed determined to prove that this was at least as true of himself as of the mass of citizens. Indeed, he not only sought to demonstrate his devotion to the philosophical principles of republicanism and federalism but also to amalgamate policies advocated by the contending parties that flourished the capitalized labels of Republican and Federalist. To this task he brought the considerable diplomacy of a man who had resolved early in life that whenever possible he would "take things by the smooth handle" and later had honed his skills in the chancelleries of Europe. Jefferson presented to his antagonists a front like the leather-bound shields of his Anglo-Saxon antecedents, yielding on the surface but firm underneath.

Jefferson's statement that, except for reforming "the waste of public money," he might "improve some little on old routines" might have suggested to some that he would be content to preside over a caretaker government. Indeed, he seemed at first to depart little from his own personal routine, his self-chosen role of country gentleman taking an intelligent interest in public affairs, passing the problems of the nation and the world around a civilized table between the hors d'oeuvre and the dessert. There were some in Washington who assumed that he was a dilettante.

Not until fifteen days after his inauguration did Jefferson leave Conrad's boardinghouse to move into the President's House. There, more than the unfinished state of the mansion was reminiscent of Monticello. The President left Washington on April 1 for his Albemarle County home, but soon after he returned April 29 the Madisons arrived in the capital, spending the first three weeks of May in the President's House. Jefferson entertained daily, eschewing crowded levees in favor of a table set for a dozen or fewer. With the sly wit of "the great little Madison," the warm charm of the clever Dolley, and the European sophistication of Gallatin, the company was the kind to which Jefferson was accustomed in his private home. His Washington residence was not atop a mountain, but, located on the fringe of the nation's capital village, it sometimes seemed as remote as his Virginia house. To his son-in-law Thomas Mann Randolph, Jefferson wrote: "We find this a very agreeable country residence. Good society, and enough of it, and free from the noise, the heat, the stench, and the bustle of a close built town."[5]

One thing in addition to its not being in Albemarle County kept Jefferson's new residence from being completely agreeable. His daughters were not with him, and there was no prospect that they would join him for many months. The nearest to a family member after departure of the Madisons for their own quarters was Meriwether Lewis, a twenty-seven-year-old native of Jefferson's home county who served as the President's private secretary. Captain Lewis lived in the President's House, and Jefferson had a paternal affection for him reminiscent of his relationship with William Short, who had been his secretary in Paris.

For those alert enough to spot them—or enjoying the great advantage of hindsight—there were clues that Jefferson would be more than a caretaker. The man who had instigated both the Virginia and Kentucky Resolutions opposing the Alien and Sedition Acts when he was supposedly living in retirement as a country squire was not likely to pass up opportunities to determine the course of events when he was President. When the President appointed Lewis he said he valued his experiences in the army and in the West.[6]. Though Jefferson, being a poor traveler, had only once ventured more than fifty miles through the rugged terrain west of his birthplace, he had reiterated at various stages of his career his faith in the importance of the West to the development of the United States. During the American Revolution he had voiced a "peculiar confidence in the men from the western side of the mountains."[7] Since Jefferson penned his own letters, it was obvious that the new secretary's duties would not be what the title implied. It was almost equally obvious that Jefferson planned for Lewis a mission suited to his military and Western experience.

This supposition gained added significance when Jefferson, sifting rumors from many sources, concluded in mid-May that Spain would probably cede Louisiana to France.[8] By the Treaty of San Lorenzo, negotiated in 1795 by Thomas Pinckney along lines devised by Jefferson when he had been Secretary of State, American interests affected by Spain's possession of Louisiana and the Floridas were effectively protected. The right of United States citizens to unrestricted navigation of the Mississippi was recognized. American traders were even allowed to deposit their goods custom-free at New Orleans preparatory to reloading on oceangoing ships. United States security was dependent on this arrangement. That security would be shattered if control of Louisiana passed from a war-weary Spain to a France now headed by a First Consul who was King in all but name, Napoleon Bonaparte, a humorless genius driven by an imperial appetite for conquest. The United States might find it impossible to avoid a critical confrontation with its oldest ally. Secretary of State Madison asked American Ministers in Europe to investigate the reports of a Franco-Spanish treaty in the making.[9]

While Jefferson was pondering the possibilities of conflict with France, another state declared war on the United States. The Pasha of Tripoli on May 14 signaled his declaration by having the flagpole of the American consulate chopped down. He was angry because the United States paid a higher tribute to his neighbor the Dey of Algiers as the price of protection for American commerce than it paid to him. Jefferson had despised the payment of protection money to the pirate states of the Barbary Coast when he had been Minister to France and as Secretary of State, but in Washington's administration and later in Adams' the United States followed the example of older and more powerful states in meekly submitting to blackmail. Now that Jefferson himself was President, he could make a difference. Even before the cutting down of the American flag, threats from Tripoli had caused him to send four armed vessels to the Mediterranean under Commodore Richard Dale. The Commodore, a Virginian who had been a trusted lieutenant of John Paul Jones, was instructed to show proper respect for friendly powers but to do what was necessary to protect American shipping.[10]

Before returning to American shores, the naval squadron blockaded Tripoli. Dale's schooner *Enterprise*, without losing a single man, captured a Tripolitan warship, disarmed it, and sent it back to its home port. Jefferson's swift and decisive response to Barbary belligerence surprised some who had ridiculed his strict constructionism and scorned his supposed pacifism. He had not appealed to Congress for authority. He acknowledged that, under the Constitution, the President could not take military action against a foreign power solely on his own initiative except in defense of the United States. But he concluded that one line of his country's defense was in the Mediterranean.

Jefferson had learned from vexatious experience as Governor of Virginia in the Revolution. Frustrated by a state Constitution adopted by men who had deliberately weakened the executive because of the bitter lessons of colonial tyranny, Governor Jefferson had scrupulously kept within the bounds of specifically accorded authority. He had not ventured a sortie into the gray areas of undefined responsibility even when emergencies demanded executive boldness. The legislature, prompted by his enemies and by the need for a scapegoat, had investigated his conduct. Though handsomely exonerated and generously praised in a resolution of the Assembly, he smarted a little, even as President, with every remembrance of his embarrassment as Governor. Jefferson the President would not only be a much less strict constructionist than Jefferson the Governor; he would also be much more flexible than Jefferson the presidential candidate.

Even so, the President was not bold enough for his old adversary Alexander Hamilton, who, writing in the *New York Evening Post* under the protection of an assumed name, charged Jefferson with cowardice.[11] He believed that the President should have boldly asserted the Chief Executive's prerogative to respond as he saw fit to a declaration of war from any nation without waiting for a corresponding declaration by Congress.

United States policy toward Tripoli was still the subject of lively debate at year's end, with every prospect of continuing to be for many months as the war dragged on. Even within the generally harmonious cabinet there was sharp disagreement. Robert Smith, a Baltimore lawyer whom Jefferson had persuaded to serve as Secretary of the Navy, argued for continued use of American frigates in the Mediterranean, while Secretary of the Treasury Gallatin insisted that such a policy might overtax the fragile economy of the young republic. Gallatin's argument gained force from the fact that the President had proclaimed discharge of the public debt to be the linchpin of his domestic policy and also had promised to lower taxes. Nevertheless, Jefferson supported Smith, saying that the cost of maintaining an American squadron in the Mediterranean was not much greater than that of keeping it in United States coastal waters.

Meanwhile, there had been an important development in United States relations with France. Ever since the efforts of French Ambassador Edmond Genet to embroil the United States in France's war with England had caused President Washington and then Secretary of State Jefferson to demand his removal, United States dealings with its sister republic had been unhappy. Incidents on the high seas exacerbated the trouble. Defying Hamilton and other Federalist warhawks, President Adams had made earnest overtures to stabilize Franco-American relations by a new treaty. The result was the drafting of an agreement known as the Convention of 1800, which the United States Senate approved subject to minor changes. These alterations had been made and Adams had ratified the document, but the French had not responded when Jefferson began his term. Not until July 31 did Bonaparte ratify the agreement on behalf of his government and then with a minor proviso of his own. Thus, undramatically, full diplomatic intercourse was restored between the two nations.

At the moment of signing, Jefferson was not holding his breath to see what Napoleon would do. He was on his way back to Monticello, having left Washington the day before. Jefferson was the first President to have a "summer White House."[12] He believed that the heat and humidity of the capital in summer were unhealthful and vowed that he would not remain in those miasmic surroundings when he could transact the business of his office just as efficiently from his cool mountaintop. Nevertheless, what had happened in Paris would protect Jefferson, upon his return to Washington in the fall, from heat generated from another source. The Franco-American quarrel which had plagued his two predecessors with divisions at home as well as conflict abroad could be buried—at least unless and until France obtained Louisiana.

Monticello in August was idyllic. In the warm days successive blue ridges of the western mountains stretched away into the distance like ocean waves. Cool nights gave a promise of autumn. Best of all, his family had congregated there to be with him. "Papa" and "Grand Papa" were much sweeter terms of address than "Mr. President." Maria Eppes, the younger daughter, was there with her child. Martha Randolph, the daughter who looked like him, had all five of her children. Both daughters were pregnant. Little Virginia Jefferson Randolph was born August 22. Francis Eppes was born September 20, exactly one week before his grandfather left Monticello to return to Washington. Before leaving, Jefferson had had members of his family and a number of friends inoculated against smallpox—still a bold step though one Jefferson personally had taken many years before.

The pain of leaving Monticello was mitigated by his finding Washington remarkably tranquil. Reduction of tension over Franco-American relations was further promoted in November, when it was learned in the United States that Great Britain and France had signed preliminary articles of peace. Jefferson rejoiced that the federal government would be able to reduce expenditures for defense and that he would be able to make good his promise of tax relief for the people.[13]

Though some Republicans thought that Jefferson's policies were too conservative, most were delighted with his stewardship. And even many Federalists, once they discovered that the tall, shambling President did not leave cloven hoofprints in the earth, were content to accept his leadership until the next presidential election. Exceptions were the people of a few areas in New England, notably New Haven, Connecticut. Merchants of that city had addressed a remonstrance to the President during the summer, protesting his ousting of a Federalist from the post of Collector of the Port and the offering of the position as a sinecure to a seventy-seven-year-old Republican in failing health.

Jefferson reminded the merchants of the public usefulness of the late Benjamin Franklin at a still more advanced age. He declared that the Republicans, having been favored with the confidence of a majority of the voters, deserved proportionate representation in desirable offices even if it meant removal of unoffending Federalists. He asked, "If a due participation of office is a matter of right, how are vacancies to be obtained? Those by death are few, by resignation none." This sentence has often been misquoted as "Few die and none resign." The President demanded: "Can any other mode than that of removal be proposed? This is a painful office; but it is made my duty, and I meet it as such." When he had remedied the imbalance he would "return with joy to that state of things when the only questions concerning a candidate shall be: is he honest? is he capable? is he faithful to the Constitution?"[14]

Jefferson ousted a few other Federalist officeholders in Connecticut, enough to show that he would not change his policies because of the remonstrance. The man who preferred always to "take things by the smooth handle" would not refrain from using a needed tool simply because its only handle was rough.

The seventh Congress of the United States convened December 7 and the next day received the first of Jefferson's annual State of the Union messages. Despite his eloquent persuasiveness with individuals and small groups, his attempts at public speaking to large groups were almost as painful to them as to him. So he abandoned his predecessors' practice of appearing before Congress in person and sent a written message instead. In it he stressed that opportunities for national development and the easing of burdensome taxes were presented by the new reign of peace in the Western world. He did not sound belligerent about anything. Still, he had been removing some of the Federalist marshals and attorneys who owed their offices to Adams' "midnight appointments" under the Judiciary Act, passed by the preceding Congress. These names appeared on a private list which Jefferson headed "Attorneys and Marshals removed for high Federalism, and Republicans appointed as a protection to Republican suitors in courts entirely Federal and going all lengths in party spirit." To the Congress, Jefferson, who could be as guarded in public comment as he was reckless in private correspondence, simply said: "The judiciary system of the United States, and especially that portion of it recently erected, will of course present itself to the contemplation of the Congress."

The portion of the judiciary system "recently erected" was that provided for in February 1801, when the Federalist-dominated Congress had created sixteen circuit courts to free the Supreme Court Justices from their extra roles as circuit riders. The plan had merit. Judicial minds were more likely to wander when their owners' aging bones had been subjected to long rides over rough roads; overlong pummeling in the saddle made even the most acute less sensitive to logic pounded home by the rhetoricians of the courtroom. But in Jefferson's view any advantages of the so-called reform were outweighed by the fact that passage of the act had enabled Adams to pack a middle level of the federal court system with judges whose Federalism could block the Republican measures of his own administration.

Jefferson knew that loyal legislators were eager to follow his understated cue. It was not essential for him as President, any more than it had been necessary for him as party leader, to be obviously in the forefront of every project that he undertook for the good of the republic.

III

THE BATTLE IS JOINED

AS THE NEW year of 1802 began, Jefferson not only continued to direct movements from behind the scenes as he had when leader of the opposition party, but he even used the same human instruments to accomplish his purposes. In response to the President's hint in his address to the Congress that the "judiciary system of the United States" would "of course present itself to the contemplation" of that body, Senator John Breckinridge of Kentucky introduced a resolution for repeal of the Judiciary Act of the previous Congress. As a Kentucky state legislator in 1798, he had introduced far-reaching resolutions secretly authored by Jefferson himself—the famous Kentucky Resolutions, which protested as unconstitutional the Alien and Sedition Acts of the Adams administration. Breckinridge's motion for repeal of the Judiciary Act was seconded by Stevens Thomson Mason of Virginia, a faithful supporter of Jefferson and now the Senate's majority leader.

Prospects for passage of the Senate resolution were reasonably good. Republicans enjoyed an edge in that body, even though it was slight enough to be imperiled by absences. The House was much more secure: there Republicans outnumbered Federalists 69 to 36.

Republican leaders in both houses charged that an attack by the Supreme Court on the presidency made repeal of the Judiciary Act imperative. They referred to the action of the six-member court on December 21 in granting a preliminary motion to show cause why a writ of mandamus should not be served upon the Secretary of State, instructing him to deliver commissions as Justices of the Peace in the District of Columbia to William Marbury and others appointed by Adams in the last days of his administration.

Federalists replied that the Supreme Court's action was a necessary one in response to the high-handedness of the Jefferson administration. Marbury's persistence, and the opportunity that it afforded Jefferson's political enemies, eventually made that obscure aspirant to judicial dignity more famous than most Supreme Court Justices. Marbury was one of the so-called "midnight appointees" of President Adams under the Judiciary Act designed to enable him to pack the federal courts, high and low, with true-blue Federalists to thwart Republican designs. The fact that virtually all judicial appointments were for long terms and some were for "life and good behavior" raised the hopes of Adams and his supporters that Federalist dominance could be insured in the judiciary long after it ended in the executive and legislature. Adams' appointment of Marbury was one of forty-two rushed to the Senate on March 2, 1801, two days before Jefferson's inauguration, and approved by that Federalist-controlled body on the last day of its existence before reconstitution under Republican leadership. As the clock ticked off the final hours of the Adams administration, the commission was returned to him. He signed it, and John Marshall, as acting Secretary of State, countersigned it, sealed it, and left it on the State Department desk. There it lay when Madison moved in as Secretary of State.

Jefferson asserted that all the "midnight appointments" undelivered before the change of administration were "nullities" and instructed Madison to withhold Marbury's and the rest. The Secretary of State was happy to comply. He and virtually all the Republican philosophers, especially those in Virginia, believed that repeal of the Judiciary Act was imperative and saw the Marbury case and the Marshall court's action in it as an effort to thwart repeal. John Taylor of Caroline, who shared Jefferson's agrarian philosophy and distrust of big government, was consulted in the matter by both Breckinridge and Wilson Cary Nicholas, also an agent of Jefferson's in the Kentucky Resolutions. Taylor had not only urged repeal of the Judiciary Act but had confided his hopes for further action—genuine "constitutional reform." It was necessary to thwart the "monarchists" who "deprecate political happiness." He added, "All my hopes upon this question rest, I confess, with Mr. Jefferson."[1] Many of Taylor's ideas, and even some of his expressions, on judicial reform glowed in the rhetoric of Breckinridge's speeches in the Senate debate. There were gleams of Jefferson too in the Kentuckian's words—perhaps drawn from communications of earlier years, but almost certainly burnished in recent conversation.

Jefferson's influence was more obviously exerted through a statistical compendium he had attached to his message to Congress. It was designed to show that the federal judiciary was inefficient and overloaded with jurists, at great expense to the taxpayer. Republican Senators found much ammunition in these "facts" until one Federalist legislator after another pointed out numerous omissions of cases. Senator Uriah Tracy of Connecticut asserted that there were in all five or six hundred such omissions. Jefferson's supporters correctly contended that these figures were grossly exaggerated, but the President's own revised statistics revealed his original omission of eighty-two cases instituted and ninety pending. Such inaccuracies were common in political exchanges, but the admission of error must have been painful to a man whose reports as Secretary of State had been marvels of detailed accuracy and whose mathematical computations even during his quotidian migraines had been reliable within thousandths of one percent.

Two months of turbulence marked the Senate debates. Some of the nation's best minds were reduced to mere gristmills for invective. Others, in the heat of emotion, voiced sentiments that would haunt them in later contests. "Why are we here?" asked New York's Gouverneur Morris, one of the fiercest Federalists. "To save the people from their most dangerous enemy; to save them from themselves."

More effective was the argument of his Federalist colleague Jeremiah Mason of Massachusetts that the Constitution was subverted when an office could be eliminated to get rid of an occupant with a lifetime appointment. At this point some of the less dedicated Republicans wavered.

Most of the arguments were not that logical. Rasping voices of anger exacerbated frayed nerves. Equally abrasive was the crunching of those who devoured apples with a ferocity suggesting that each piece of fruit was surrogate for an opponent. When patrician little Vice President Aaron Burr assumed his place as President of the Senate, replacing a President Pro Tem, the offending chompers hastily stuffed their apples into their pockets.[2]

When the bill was reported out of committee on January 22 Jefferson wrote his son-in-law John Wayles Eppes, "Our friends have not yet learned to draw well together, and there has been some danger of a small section of them, aided by the Feds, carrying a question against the larger section." But, characteristically, he was ultimately optimistic: "They have seen, however, that this practice would end in enabling the Feds to carry everything as they please by joining whichever section of Republicans they chose; and they will avoid this rock."[3]

From the Federalist side, Delaware's James A. Bayard forecast three days later that the Senate balloting was likely to be a tie which would place Burr in the dilemma of casting the decisive vote—either with his own Republican Party or with the Federalists who had secretly supported his candidacy in the presidential race with Jefferson.

Bayard's prophecy was fulfilled January 26, when the bill was moved for its third reading. The vote was 15 to 15. Gouverneur Morris hoped that Burr, rankling over Jefferson's failure to consult him on a series of federal appointments in New York, would cast his vote with the Federalists in revenge. He was not the only one to hold his breath as the Vice President, in a calmly modulated voice, announced his support of the Republican resolution.

The battle in the Senate was not won yet. When the bill came up for final vote, the absence or apostasy of a single member could reverse the outcome. On February 3, when the moment arrived, the Republicans won 16 to 15.

Morris thought back to the January day when Burr's vote had saved the Republican measure on its third reading. The memory festered. About six months later he would write: "There was a moment when the Vice-President might have arrested the measure by his vote, and that vote would, I believe, have made him President at the next election; but there is a tide in the affairs of men which he suffered to go by."[4]

The fight in the House of Representatives was spirited but anticlimactic. With a large Republican majority in that chamber, Jefferson's anxiety was not that his party might fail in the balloting but that lengthy debates might delay action. To his son-in-law Thomas Mann Randolph he wrote: "The H. of R. have now been a week debating the judiciary law, and scarcely seem to be yet on the threshold of it. I begin to apprehend a long session; however, I believe all material matters recommended in the first day's message will prevail. The majority begins to draw better together than at first. Still there are some wayward freaks which now and then disturb the operations."[5] Repeal of the Judiciary Act carried March 3, 59 to 32.

One important by-product of the legislative struggle was its effect on Burr's career. Though the Vice President had cast the decisive vote with his party on the crucial third reading, he had sided with the Federalists in another tie-breaking vote on the following day. The effect of this vote—a move to recommit the bill for judicial reform on the grounds that the whole judicial system needed revision—was later circumvented by the Republicans' parliamentary maneuvering. But the Republicans tended to remember Burr's ineffectual gesture toward the Federalists far more vividly than his very real help to themselves in the previous day's balloting. Many were determined never to reward him with national office.

Thinking to exploit the gap between Burr's cadre of determinedly loyal followers and the great mass of Republicans, Federalist leaders invited him to attend their annual Washington's birthday banquet. Making the most of the moment's potential for drama, Burr toasted "the union of all honest men." The Republicans saw this move as a bid for Federalist support. Thus the Vice President alienated some Republicans still willing to give him the benefit of the doubt. He gained no ground with the Federalists. Alexander Hamilton, retired from public office but not from leadership of the Federalist Party, had decided long before that his fellow New Yorker could not be trusted.

So Jefferson worked to lower taxes and simultaneously reduce the national debt, pondered reports of a Franco-Spanish treaty that threatened American navigation of the Mississippi and at the same time dreamed of ways to win for his country the lands west of that natural boundary, used naval power to defy Tripoli's demand for tribute, weighed the conflicts between the nation's needs and the virtues of strict constructionism as well as the conflicting demands of his positions as national magistrate and party leader, directed repeal of the Judiciary Act, and sifted through lists of friends and strangers to make appointments to the most elevated and the most humble offices. And amid all these cares and considerations, he still responded to public service demands from the state that he always called "my country."

One call for advice was prompted by the attempts of his friend Governor James Monroe and the Virginia legislature to deal with the problem of slavery— one to which Jefferson had devoted many hours of agonized thought. He had denounced slavery in the Declaration of Independence and had been chagrined when New England delegates representing slave-trading constituencies joined with South Carolinians and Georgians to delete the denunciation. He had been pleased two years later when Virginia became the first state in modern history to make the importation of slaves a criminal offense. His optimism grew in 1782 when the Virginia General Assembly enacted a law to encourage individual owners to free their slaves. But Gabriel's Insurrection, a slave attempt in 1800 to capture the state arsenal in Richmond and the state capitol and massacre large numbers of white citizens, ended all moves toward abolition of slavery in Virginia. Two slaves revealed the plot, and a mighty storm that flooded roads and swept away bridges further frustrated the rebellion. Many white Virginians believed that they had been spared by divine intervention but that next time God would expect them to help themselves. The Virginia Abolition Society quickly faded away. Virginians now feared the slaves but feared free Negroes even more.

The Virginia General Assembly considered the selection of some place outside the Commonwealth to which free Negroes as well as slaves convicted of crimes could be deported. When Governor Monroe sought Jefferson's advice in the matter, the President suggested Sierra Leone, in Africa, as a suitable dumping ground.[6] As that country was a British colony, he eventually instructed Rufus King, the American Minister to England, to submit the proposition to his Majesty's government. Regarding convicted blacks, Jefferson wrote, "Observe that they are not felons or common malefactors but persons guilty of what the safety of society obliges us to treat as a crime, but which their feelings may represent as a far different shape."[7]

In another matter affecting his home state, Jefferson urged a cherished plan of his as a program for advocacy by his son-in-law John Eppes. This was Jefferson's design for dividing the state into "hundreds," or "captaincies," for the more efficient and economical administration of "police, justice, elections, musters, schools, and many other essential things. . . . there is not a single political measure for our state which I have so much at heart. The captain or head borough would be there what the sergeants are in an army: the finger of execution."[8] Jefferson's logic was impeccable regarding the abstract virtues of his plan, but Eppes, as one just beginning a political career, seems to have eschewed the honor of being standard-bearer for a program likely to raise the hackles of officeholders in his own county and all others in the Commonwealth.

In a letter to Charles Willson Peale, the eminent portraitist and museum founder, Jefferson told of another project he dreamed of for Virginia: the establishment of a "general university . . . on the most extensive and liberal scale that our circumstances would call for and our faculties meet."[9]

A personal project in Virginia was always in his mind and heart. Work continued on his mountaintop home in Albemarle County. He once said, "All my wishes end where I hope my days will end, at Monticello." His personal fortune seemed likely to end there too. The many alterations of plan as he built and rebuilt through the years, together with the elegance of his dinners both there and in Washington, added tremendously to his expenses. If Jefferson lived in republican simplicity, as he fondly believed, then simplicity came with a surprisingly high price tag. His annual salary as President was $25,000, a considerable sum in those days, but his personal expenses for his first year in office totaled $33,624.84. His tobacco crops and nail factory, in that same year, brought him profits of $3,507.33. As he himself meticulously recorded, on March 4, 1802, exactly one year after his inauguration, he wound up with a deficit of $5,117.51.[10]

Runaway expenses were not the only reason that thoughts of his beloved Monticello were not completely relaxing. Much as he longed to have his family with him, he had to admit that their lives were not the idyll that he had hoped for. At the end of his first year as President, he was aware of deficits not revealed on the financial balance sheet.

At this time he wrote to Maria, his younger daughter. In childhood, her traumatic separation from her father when he sailed for France as United States Minister, and the equally traumatic experience later of being torn from her Aunt Eppes, who had become a second mother, had reinforced whatever tendency to shyness she already had. Now she seemed to be becoming a recluse. Jefferson thought back to his own time of withdrawal from the world after the death of this young woman's mother. "I can speak from experience on this subject," he wrote. "From 1793 to 1797 I remained closely at home, saw none but those who came there, and at length became very sensible of the ill effect it had upon my mind, and of its direct and irresistible tendency to render me unfit for society and uneasy when necessarily engaged in it. I felt enough of the effect of withdrawing from the world then to see that it led to an anti-social and misanthropic state of mind which severely punishes him who gives in to it: and it will be a lesson I shall never forget as to myself."[11]

There was unhappiness also in the home of the older daughter, Martha. Her husband, Thomas Mann Randolph, Jr., suffered, as he had off and on for years, from some mysterious malady as well as a deep-seated melancholy. Admittedly, his depressed finances were enough to account for his depressed mind, but even in times of relative prosperity he had been troubled by the vapors. He was well educated, personable, and able. The people of his district talked of sending him to Congress. Unfortunately, he seemed to have much less talent for handling his private affairs than for dealing with public matters.

Jefferson, as far as was feasible in his own straitened circumstances, had extended financial help to his son-in-law. But that aid was not enough, and Randolph now talked of leaving Virginia and starting over on a cotton plantation in Mississippi.

Such talk was alarming to Jefferson. He was even closer to Martha than to Maria, and his parental love had always been possessive and all-encompassing. Only two months after her marriage in 1790, Martha had written to her father: ". . . I assure you, my dear Papa, my happiness can never be complete without your company. Mr. Randolph omits nothing that can in the least contribute to it. I have made it my study to please him in every thing and do consider all other objects as secondary to that *except* my love for you."[12]

The acutely intelligent and sensitive Randolph must have realized that he was second in his wife's affections. Moreover, he knew that, however far his abilities might carry him, to most people he would always be Mr. Jefferson's son-in-law. Randolph seems to have felt a strong filial affection for Jefferson and in various crises he leaned on him, but at other times he must have felt threatened by the patriarch's "relentless love."[13] Jefferson persuaded Randolph that the Natchez area, where he proposed to settle, was too dangerous because of an unhealthful climate and the threat of Indians and Spaniards. But, full of concern for the young couple, this man who wished to end his days at Monticello proposed a compromise. If they must move south, perhaps they should not move quite so far away. "In fact," he wrote, "I should be delighted to own a cotton estate in Georgia, and go and pass every winter under the orange trees of that country."[14]

While Jefferson wrestled with his many problems, foreign and (in both senses of the word) domestic, there were other distractions. From all over the United States—indeed, from all over the Western world—people, by letter and in person, sought information and opinions from the President of the United States, the leader of the Republican Party, the author of the Declaration of Independence and of the Statute of Virginia for Religious Freedom. They called upon America's leading writer, its principal architect, one of its foremost historians, one of its respected anthropologists, its pioneer paleontologist, and the President of the American Philosophical Society. All were seeking one man named Thomas Jefferson.

Actually, answering inquiries on intellectual subjects—as when Jefferson as Virginia's Revolutionary Governor wrote the *Notes on Virginia* in reply to a French diplomat's questions, seemed to provide relief from problems of state.

When Jefferson in March 1802 came to the end of his first year as President, he had dealt with, or at least adumbrated, within the preceding twelve months every major problem or achievement of his two administrations.

He had anticipated that Spain would cede Louisiana to France. The threat to the United States implicit in French control of the Mississippi claimed Jefferson's attention early, and he foresaw the necessity of dealing with Napoleon in some way to obviate this threat. He saw that the fate of America was bound up with the vast Louisiana Territory. When Jefferson appointed Meriwether Lewis his personal secretary, saying at the time that he valued his experience in the army and in the West, he foreshadowed one of history's most famous expeditions of exploration. Whether or not the President originally envisioned training the young officer to be a Western explorer, subsequent events made it clear that Jefferson soon began preparing him for that role. Lewis certainly was not burdened with what usually are considered secretarial duties.[15]

Jefferson's military expedition against Tripoli was the start of a long campaign to free American commerce from blackmail and terrorism by the Barbary States. Also, the President's swift response to Tripolitan aggression, without waiting to appeal to Congress, signaled that he would depart from his strict constructionism when convinced that the national welfare could not wait on parliamentary delays.

Jefferson's behind-the-scenes management of repeal of the Judiciary Act and his refusal to deliver commissions to some recipients of his predecessor's "midnight appointments" to the bench challenged the Federalists and Chief Justice John Marshall to a contest of wills and ingenuity that would continue through the rest of his presidency. That struggle would do more to define the relationships among the three branches of the federal government than any other event after the ratification of the Constitution.

An expression of "esteem and approbation" from the Baptists of Danbury, Connecticut, near the end of Jefferson's first year as President gave him the opportunity to reiterate a constitutional principle which he had continuously advocated and supported since the writing of his Statute of Virginia for Religious Freedom in 1777, nine years before its enactment into law. In words much quoted through the years by lawyers, legislators, and editorialists, Jefferson told the Danbury Baptists:

> Believing with you that religion is a matter which lies solely between man and his God, that he owes account to none other for his faith or his worship, that the legislative powers of government reach actions only, and not opinions, I contemplate with sovereign reverence that act of the whole American people which declared that their legislature should "make no law respecting an establishment of religion, or prohibiting the free exercise thereof," thus building a wall of separation between church and state.[16]

So strongly did Jefferson adhere to this principle that he even refrained from proclaiming days of thanksgiving, fasting, or prayer, as had been the custom of his predecessors. President Jefferson would have disapproved his own action as a 31-year-old revolutionary in 1774 in calling for a day of fasting and prayers "to inspire us with firmness in support of our rights."

Jefferson was at least as concerned with practice as with theory. In his first year as President, he effectively curbed spending and lowered taxes, setting a pattern of managing the nation's finances most successfully while failing miserably with his own.

In this year also, Jefferson dreamed of the founding of a great university in Virginia. And he continued to change and add to his beloved Monticello.

He was painfully concerned with the problems of his two daughters and of a son-in-law whose maladjustment became increasingly obvious.

And amid all these varied activities and concerns he continued to pursue knowledge and ideas with the avidity of his youth.

He also, as at virtually every stage of his career, delighted in congenial company. When he was sixteen he had written to one of his legal guardians, arguing that going to college at William and Mary would be an economy rather than an expense. "In the first place," he argued, "as long as I stay at the mountains the loss of one fourth of my time is inevitable, by company's coming here and detaining me from school. And likewise my absence will in a great measure put a stop to so much company, and by that means lessen the expenses of the estate in housekeeping."[17] If he had attracted company as a private citizen, he obviously was even more sought after as President, despite the fact that he antagonized members of the diplomatic establishment by deliberate disregard of protocol in seating. The unwritten laws of Virginia hospitality had compelled Jefferson as a private citizen to entertain hordes of strangers, some quite dull, simply because (by accident or design) their travels had brought them near his home at sunset. As President he was under still greater compulsion to entertain many people whom he found unattractive.

Any boredom on formal occasions was offset by the pleasure of small, informal dinner parties where ideas passed as freely as food and wine. A guest at one of these was Dr. Samuel Latham Mitchill, an intellectual Republican Congressman who wrote about it to his wife back home in New York. He described the President as "tall in stature and rather spare in flesh. His dress and manners are very plain; he is grave, or rather sedate, but without any tincture of pomp, ostentation, or pride, and occasionally can smile, and both hear and relate humorous stories as well as any other man of social feelings."[18] The physician noted some books lying on the mantel as if for easy reference: a volume of the French *Encyclopedia* in the original, Tacitus with facing texts of Latin and Spanish, and a volume of Plato. The wide range of the President's intellect was well known. But Dr. Mitchill was in for a surprise when he discussed with his host something from the doctor's own field—inoculation for smallpox. He talked, said the doctor, "with the intelligence of a physician." Before the evening was over, Dr. Mitchill experienced added proof of Jefferson's sense of humor as the President led him in fascination through the windings of a gravely delivered anecdote to a patently ridiculous conclusion.

Anyone following Jefferson closely from his inauguration March 4, 1801, to the conclusion of his first year in office on March 4, 1802, would have seen him engaged with virtually all the major public and private concerns of his life. What remained in doubt—to friends, foes, and curious observers of no special commitment—was the degree of success with which he would pursue his objectives.

IV

LONELY LABOR AND
PUBLIC SCANDAL

THE GREENING of trees outside the Executive Mansion signaled the renewal of nature as Jefferson in March 1802 began his second year as President. He himself did not feel renewed. Next month he would be fifty-nine—elderly by the standards of his day. His animation and capacity for long hours of hard work kept others from thinking of him as old, but a hidden problem nudged him toward thoughts of mortality.

Near the end of the preceding year he had confided to Dr. Benjamin Rush a physical weakness that convinced him he would not be cursed with too long a life. He did not, however, believe death was imminent. Without labeling or describing his complaint, he wrote, "It will probably give me as many years as I wish and without pain or debility."[1] His letter made clear that the distinguished Philadelphia physician was his only confidant in this matter.

The ensuing correspondence between the two men revealed that Jefferson's affliction was diarrhea.[2] He had suffered from it at least as early as 1774, when an attack had frustrated his journey to Williamsburg to present "A Summary View of the Rights of British America" to the Virginia Convention. The heat, a possible infection, the emotional trauma of defying the Crown—or perhaps a combination of two or all three of these—could have been responsible for the ailment that prevented Jefferson from presenting his resolutions in person. Whatever the basic cause of Jefferson's condition, he now concluded on empirical evidence that it was aggravated by eating fish.[3]

A clue to his mood of disenchantment was furnished by his reply a little earlier to a young poet sending him his epic for comment. "Of all men living," Jefferson wrote, "I am the last who should undertake to decide as to the merits of poetry. In earlier life I was fond of it, and easily pleased. But as age and cares advanced, the powers of fancy have declined. . . . So much has my relish for poetry deserted me that at present I cannot read even Virgil with pleasure. . . . The very feelings to which it is addressed are among those I have lost."[4]

Characteristically, however, Jefferson was touched, rather than weighed down, by somber thoughts. Most of his thoughts on health seem to have been directed toward constructive action. Dr. Benjamin Waterhouse of Boston was America's pioneer in the Jenner method of inoculation against smallpox, and his proselyting made him one of the most controversial characters in America. Jefferson aligned himself with the doctor. The President's concern was an old one. One of the principal reasons for his visiting Philadelphia at the age of 23 was to be inoculated against smallpox. The process of variolation then in use was a far more dangerous one than the Jenner method. For that method, as practiced by Dr. Waterhouse, Jefferson now became the nation's principal lay crusader. Thanks to Jefferson's personal efforts, the Massachusetts physician was ". . . convinced that the matter commences its career in Virginia . . . under more favorable circumstances than it has in any other state in the Union." Such zeal in a chief of state is reminiscent of Peter the Great's enthusiasm for western dentistry that led him personally to pull the offending molar of any courtier with a toothache. Jefferson not only had his own family and his people, as he called his slaves, inoculated with virus obtained from Dr. Waterhouse; the President seems to have personally vaccinated a large number of people from a central Virginia neighborhood stricken by smallpox.[5] The protective scratches on their arms were made by the hand that had penned the Declaration of Independence.

Of course, Jefferson was serving the people in ways more customary for a Chief Executive. And, if his thoughts occasionally turned toward mortality, he could take some comfort in the place he was winning in history by his actions as President. Granted, his self-written epitaph would suggest that he did not regard his presidency as one of his three greatest achievements. By that reckoning, two of the three—the Declaration of Independence and the Statute of Virginia for Religious Freedom—were already behind him. The third—the founding of a university—was still a dream. But Jefferson had seen in historical perspective the administrations of his two predecessors and he must have applied the historical measuring stick to his own.

Probably no early achievement of his presidency gave him more satisfaction than the repeal on March 8 of the Judiciary Act passed by the Federalist Congress that had expired in March 1801. He believed that he and his supporters had saved the nation's judicial system from domination for years to come by Federalists appointed specifically because of their political philosophy. He believed that in so doing his administration had not only given a better opportunity for a fair trial to many individuals but also had made it less likely that a Federalist judiciary would thwart the reforms proposed by a Republican Executive and Congress recently chosen by the people. Jefferson said, "We have restored our Judiciary to what it was while justice and not Federalism was its object."[6]

Jefferson was pleased that the new Judiciary Act, headed for passage in April, provided for six circuits instead of three, with a Justice of the Supreme Court residing in each and sharing the circuit court bench twice a year with the resident district judges. The Supreme Court thus would be brought closer to the people.

In Jefferson's eyes another benefit from repeal of the old Judiciary Act and enactment of the new was the saving of money by the elimination of superfluous judgeships. This and many other economies made possible repeal of internal taxes on April 6.

Jefferson also derived satisfaction from the successful completion of business initiated by President Adams and John Marshall when Marshall had been Secretary of State. They had instructed Rufus King, United States Minister to the Court of St. James', to negotiate a convention respecting American debts to British creditors. Jay's Treaty in 1794 had acknowledged United States responsibility for prerevolutionary American debts and had referred the problem to joint commissions. Despite Republican officeseekers, Jefferson had not replaced King and had instructed him to continue negotiations. This commonsense and statesmanlike policy had resulted in a convention including a provision for United States payment of a lump sum of $600,000. This convention was reported to the Senate on March 29. There it met with an overwhelmingly favorable reception—something that would not have been predicted by most Americans a little earlier. Republican legislators no longer indulged in excesses of Anglophobia and Francomania. When Jefferson looked to Europe, the pale, brooding face of Napoleon scowled in the foreground. Shortly after his inauguration, the President had told Edward Thornton, the young British chargé d'affaires, that there was "nothing in the present government" of France "which would naturally incline him to show the smallest undue partiality to it at the expense of Great Britain or indeed of any other country." Admittedly, he might have been partial to "*republican* France," but "that was long over."[7]

Now, in the anxious spring of 1802, Joseph Hale, an ardent Boston Federalist, reassured Rufus King about the Republicans in general and their chief in particular: "The sect and even the philosopher openly inveigh against Bonaparte . . . . One source of apprehension is therefore removed, and at present there is not much reason to fear that we shall be thrown into the arms of France, should the present European armistice end."[8] One of Jefferson's chief lieutenants, Senator Wilson Cary Nicholas, was more emphatic: "I do not believe that any event would produce more or greater mischievous consequences to the United States than a rupture with Great Britain."[9]

In another event Jefferson took even greater pleasure than most men in his position would. On April 30 he signed an act of Congress authorizing a convention to form a constitution for a new state. To Kentucky and Tennessee, the two states west of the Appalachians at the start of his administration, would be added a third, Ohio. Jefferson's satisfaction with this development was enhanced by his enthusiasm for the West and his romantic faith in those who lived close to nature.

Ohio's movement toward statehood had begun with its attainment of territorial status, and it would have become a state in or about 1802 even if someone else had been President. But Jefferson, more than anyone else, was the father of the process by which Western territories achieved statehood. On March 1, 1784 when Congress officially accepted Virginia's generous cession of her Western lands to the United States, a committee headed by Jefferson proposed a plan for government of those lands. Jefferson's plan was adopted and, though never implemented, it provided the basis for the Northwest Ordinance of 1787.

One of the great documents of political history, it provided for territorial governments and outlined an orderly process by which, consistent with population growth, communities could attain the status of partially self-governing entities with bicameral legislatures and eventually emerge as new states "on an equal footing with the original states in all respects whatsoever." Frustrated in his attempts to deal with slavery where it already existed, Jefferson rejoiced that the ordinance prohibited involuntary servitude in the territories except as punishment for crime. Freedom of religion and right of trial by jury were guaranteed. Public support of education was provided.

Just as Jefferson regarded the New World as a place for fresh beginnings free from the trammels of old inequities, so did he look upon the American West as offering more opportunities for democratic experiment than the Atlantic littoral with its historic ties to Europe. Much credit should go to Jefferson and his associates—some of whom do not loom large in history—for the work that culminated in the Northwest Ordinance. It would be difficult to find in modern annals a comparably enlightened provision for the integration of developing territories into an established government.

Jefferson had another reason for welcoming the admission of Ohio. Its leadership, like that of the two trans-Appalachian states already in the Union, was Republican. On its way to statehood, Kentucky had passed from being a Virginia colony to being a Virginia county. Though native Virginians eventually were a minority, they were a disproportionately influential one. Republicans had spearheaded the movement for statehood in Tennessee. These states were led by Jeffersonians, and their loyalty was intensified by Jefferson's understanding of their problems. While the population of Ohio was not so predominantly Southern as that of the other two transmontane states, its leadership resided principally in the southern tier, where loyalty to the President and his party was strong. Jefferson could be grateful for this fact both as an enlightened statesman depending on Republican support for what he believed to be badly needed reforms and as a politician reluctant to become embroiled in fights but, once involved, fiercely determined upon victory.

Jefferson's hold on Ohio was further strengthened by the way he dealt with a problem related to its transition from territory to state. General Arthur St. Clair, Governor of the Northwest Territory from its inception, seemed to think that he owned the office. He fought the movement toward statehood with all the vehemence of a homesteader threatened with eviction. His resistance took forms not countenanced by many of his fellow Federalists in Washington. He acted as if the territorial legislature were a juvenile debating society whose fun and games interfered with the adult business of government. Legislative leaders charged the Governor with unlawful exercise of power.

Jefferson considered the bill of complaints serious enough to justify removal of St. Clair. But the Governor's long service would soon come to an end. Gallatin urged forbearance and Jefferson himself adhered to his "smooth handle" philosophy. So the President simply directed Secretary of State Madison to send the old General a reprimand. Far from chastened, the Governor appeared before the Ohio Constitutional Convention to declare null the enabling act passed by the Congress of the United States. On Jefferson's orders, St. Clair was dismissed. More than ever, the people of Ohio regarded Jefferson as their champion. Before long Ohioans would augment Republican forces in both houses of Congress and would improve the chances of Republican candidates for President.

When the seventh Congress ended on May 3, Jefferson did not linger at his scene of triumph. Two days later he was on the road to Monticello. He missed his family and friends in Albemarle. He missed the misty mountains rolling away to the west like the waves of a blue ocean. And he missed the white spray of dogwood. He missed the mansion that was his own creation—that had grown in complexity as he himself had grown in sophistication.

On May 30 Jefferson was back in Washington and badly in need of all the fortification of spirit gained on his trip home. He faced perplexing problems of the gravest kind, and the nation's short history furnished no precedents for dealing with some of them.

Even before the seventh Congress concluded, Jefferson had written to Robert Livingston, the American Minister to France, about a problem always in the background of the President's thoughts when it was not in the foreground. So confidential were the contents of this letter that the President entrusted it to his old friend Du Pont de Nemours, then returning to France on a visit, with instructions to deliver it personally to Livingston. If any accident should befall Du Pont, his wife was to hand-deliver the letter to the American minister. Enclosed with the instructions to Livingston was a cipher for use in future correspondence.

This letter was far more colorful and boldly assertive than Secretary of State Madison's official missive to Livingston, of which Du Pont was also the bearer. Jefferson gave the Frenchman permission to read his letter but asked him to seal it immediately afterwards. Probably Jefferson hoped his old friend, without divulging the actual contents of the President's message, would convey to his countrymen the drift of official thinking in Washington.

Jefferson wrote that free navigation of the Mississippi was essential to the security of the United States. Self-preservation must take precedence over sentimental ties and old hostilities. No Parisian protestations of friendship would make the United States acquiesce in French control of New Orleans. By "placing herself in that door" France would assume "the attitude of defiance." Friendship between the two countries would be at an end, and the United States would be forced to look elsewhere for an ally. "The day that France takes possession of New Orleans," Jefferson said, "fixes the sentence which is to restrain her forever within her low water mark. It seals the union of two nations who in conjunction can maintain exclusive possession of the ocean. From that moment we must marry ourselves to the British fleet and nation."[10]

Jefferson had been reducing the United States Navy, but he was prepared to reverse this policy. "We must, " he said, "turn all our attentions to a maritime force, for which our resources place us" at a great advantage.

As soon as hostilities between England and France reopened in Europe—as surely they would—the United States would eject the French from New Orleans. Then the Americans and British in unison would drive the French from the New World.

There was one way for France to prevent this succession of reverses: by ceding New Orleans to the United States as soon as Spain ceded it to France. Jefferson's letter to Livingston implied as much.[11] His conversations with Thornton had already made that fact clear. In conversation, Jefferson had made the same point with L. A. Pinchon, the French chargé.[12] The President was courteous and friendly in talking with the Frenchman, but Jefferson made sure that France and the United States would not drift into war because of French misunderstanding of the measure of American tolerance.

A week after entrusting him with the letter to Livingston, Jefferson wrote Du Pont a letter spelling out more clearly what he expected from France.[13] Relying on the Frenchman's enthusiasm for the United States and broad international view of many issues, the President was unsparingly frank. He said that it would be necessary for France to cede the Floridas as well as New Orleans. Though people disagreed as to the boundary between West Florida and East Florida, it was generally agreed that the Floridas embraced both the present state of Florida and coastal areas of the present states of Alabama and Mississippi. Jefferson assumed that they would be included with Spain's cession of the Louisiana Territory to France. Ceding both the Floridas and New Orleans to the United States would eliminate the immediate necessity for forming an alliance with the British.

But this move would not be sufficient for America's longtime security. Only the departure of the French from North America could accomplish that. Bonaparte had dispatched troops to St. Domingo to overthrow Toussaint L'Ouverture. That task should keep them occupied for a while, but, if and when they completed it, where would they go? To Louisiana? The United States could find no comfort in their presence on its doorstep.

Ordinarily the most diplomatic of men except when dealing with his own children, Jefferson in this instance badly underestimated the emotional strength of Du Pont's attachment to his native land. The President's words about the French being unwelcome had an unanticipated effect. The distinguished Frenchman could not have been galvanized into a more rigid posture of patriotism if Jefferson had broken out the tricolor and ordered a band to play the *Marseillaise*.

Du Pont granted full weight to Jefferson's assertion that "this affair of Louisiana" had "produced more uneasy sensations through the body of the nation" than anything else since the American Revolution. When the President said that he wanted the French to be aware of the "inevitable consequences of their taking possession of Louisiana," Du Pont understood that he was threatening war. Though the Frenchman had once been a political prisoner in his native land and afterwards a political refugee in the United States, he had also been a member of the States General, and, with the shift of regimes, his return was welcomed by powerful people in Paris. A welter of conflicting emotions made

Du Pont more painfully aware of the tragedy of war between France and the United States than most people in either nation. But, however angry he might be with some of his countrymen for their actions, he resented from the depths of his Gallic soul what he apparently regarded as the arrogance of the American President. It had caught him off guard because Jefferson was his cherished friend and Du Pont had believed him to be one of the most enlightened people on earth.

Now Du Pont issued his own warning. If his initial reaction had been anger, he had it under control by the time he replied to the President's letter. He began disarmingly by admitting the validity of the President's major premise—that free navigation of the Mississippi was a necessity. But what made the Americans trust the British? Why should anyone suppose that navigation of the Mississippi would be less free with the French occupying its banks than with Spain in control? United States officials had said that French occupation of parts of North America would be a threat to Mexico as well as the United States. But wasn't it true that Americans coveted Mexico for themselves?

France, Du Pont insisted, could be trusted to guarantee free navigation of the Mississippi. But if the United States would not be satisfied with a guarantee from France and was bent on securing strategic lands, it should stop demanding cessions by France and offer Paris a sufficient sum for New Orleans and the Floridas—and make the offer before the transfer from Spain to France. As for the Louisiana Territory, that vast area west of the Mississippi equal in size to the present American republic, there was only one thing for the United States to do: forget about it.[14]

Jefferson hastened to reply that he had not meant to threaten France but to give friendly warning. "It is as if I foresaw a storm tomorrow and advised my friend not to embark on the ocean today. My foreseeing it does not make me the cause of it, nor can my admonition be a threat, the storm not being produced by my will. It is in truth our friendship for France which renders us so uneasy at seeing her take a position which must bring us into collision."[15]

He said that his present desire was to make the Mississippi River the western boundary of the United States. This was one way of saying that he intended for the United States to possess both New Orleans and the Floridas. The subtle-minded Du Pont was also sure to see that the President's statement involved a good bit of sophistry. It spoke of desires for the present but not for the future.

One thing Jefferson did not have a desire for was conquest. The United States was prepared to buy both New Orleans and the Floridas when they passed into French hands. He did not believe, however, that the United States would be able to afford a price exceeding the spoliation claims—compensation for losses through French seizure of American ships—awarded under the convention ratified in 1801.

He tried to soften his earlier comments about a British alliance by saying, "It would only be better than to have no friend."

Perhaps as much to honor Du Pont with a sense of being in his confidence as for any other reason, Jefferson asked him to show this letter to Livingston.

The President also addressed to Livingston a note[16] in which he said that he had trespassed on the Secretary of State's territory in his previous letter to the Minister. This may have been a literal statement of Jefferson's reconsidered view, or it may have been a way of conveying his wishes to the diplomat without giving them the rigidity of official instructions. He said that he had no desire to conquer Mexico and was not eager for war with France. Madison's instructions were as valid as ever. Livingston should point out to the French the serious consequences if they should assume control of the mouth of the Mississippi, and he should ferret out the price at which New Orleans and the Floridas could be purchased. The instructions stopped short of authorizing the Minister to make an offer.

As Jefferson, in the heat and humidity of a Washington July, anxiously awaited the sound of gunfire from Europe that might be echoed in the American West, he found himself the target of a sniper much nearer home. At this time James T. Callender, a journalist with whom Jefferson had heretofore had scant association, launched a campaign that would make the President to many of his countrymen a symbol of unbridled sexual indulgence.

Callender was a Scotsman who had fled to the United States in the 1790s to escape trial for sedition. At that time many Republicans regarded being in trouble with the British government as one of the best possible character references. A lively master of invective, Callender quickly found a place on the staff of the *Philadelphia Gazette*, a Republican newspaper. Over the next several years, he moved from one journal to another, always attacking the Federalists. He charged that President John Adams was "a British spy" and even that George Washington was "a scandalous hypocrite" who for personal gain had "authorized the robbery and ruin of his own army."[17]

Jefferson as Vice President once called on Callender at a Philadelphia printing office where the Scotsman was employed. Presumably he thanked him for his exertions on behalf of the Republican Party. Shortly afterwards Callender, in the guise of recording history, made it. In his *History of the Year 1796*, he wrote that Secretary of the Treasury Alexander Hamilton had embezzled from the public funds. The charge was false, but, in order to prove it so, Hamilton had to reveal the titillating details of his backstairs romance with the wife of a Treasury employee.

Jefferson did not drop Callender after this incident. He did not embrace him socially, but from time to time he lent or gave money to the perpetually impecunious journalist. There is no reason to think that Jefferson was tolerant of Callender's writings about the private sexual lives of his victims, but he was tolerant of other outrageous attacks on Federalist foes. In this respect, Jefferson was like many politicians and all too many true statesmen who, even though a man is doing a work which they themselves would not stoop to, believe that nevertheless it is a work that needs to be done.

As a writer for the *Richmond Examiner*, a Republican newspaper edited by one of Jefferson's friends, Callender in 1799 began publishing an anti-Federalist tract called *The Prospect Before Us*. Jefferson saluted the first installment: "Such papers cannot fail to produce the best effects."[18] The work became progressively abusive and the writer was indicted and tried under the Sedition Act. At the conclusion of a trial in Richmond presided over by the ardently Federalist Justice Samuel Chase, Callender was fined $200 and sentenced to nine months in jail.

Jefferson and other Republicans believed the Sedition Act to be unconstitutional, so political principle and party passion ran in the same conduit. They gave unreserved support to the imprisoned journalist. Callender corresponded with Jefferson from what the writer called a "den of wretchedness and horror."[19]

When Jefferson became President, he pardoned all persons convicted under the Sedition Act and promised remission of Callender's fine. As the bureaucratic process proved slow, Jefferson personally paid fifty dollars of the sum. Less than overwhelmed by the President's generosity, Callender asked appointment as postmaster in Richmond as compensation for his services to the Republican cause. When Jefferson stopped answering the persistent man's letters, the journalist "intimated that he was in possession of things which he could and would make use of . . . [and] he received the fifty dollars not as a charity but a due, in fact as hush money."[20]

As all of Callender's attempts to gain a federal job were frustrated, he made good his threats. In February 1802 he became copublisher of the Richmond *Recorder*, a pro-Federalist newspaper, and began attacking the Republican administration with the vehemence that he had formerly reserved for its enemies. Before summer's end he was writing that the President's reputation would be sounder if that gentleman had been beheaded before he could deliver his inaugural address. Ironically, at the very time that the President was being harassed by Callender's editorial attacks he was embarrassed by Federalist newspapers' revelations of his earlier gifts to the now notorious journalist.

Callender's reputation was such that his endorsement could not help any man's image, but even a villain can raise doubts about others. And the journalist now conducted against Jefferson the greatest smear campaign the United States had yet known. He reported that in 1768 the Virginian had attempted to seduce a friend's wife. There was a germ of truth in the accusation. This was the incident arising out of Jefferson's promise to his neighbor John Walker to check regularly on his wife, Betsey, while official business took the husband out of the colony. Jefferson had failed to perceive that precise moment at which Mrs. Walker's personal attractions became a stronger motivation for neighborly visits than the obligations to her husband. No one loved to pay compliments more than Jefferson. The polite language of gallantry became a declaration of infatuation.[21] Callender's charge about Jefferson and Mrs. Walker became an oft repeated Federalist chorus. The President did not deign to answer publicly but eventually he wrote Robert Smith, his Secretary of the Navy: "I plead guilty to one of their charges, that when young and single I offered love to a handsome lady. I acknowledge its incorrectness. It is the only one founded on truth among all their allegations against me."[22]

What Jefferson meant by the phrase "offered love" we cannot know. It could be interpreted to mean, in more modern phraseology, that he propositioned her. On the other hand, it could mean that he attempted to kiss or caress her. Or to offer love could even be simply to proffer one's heart.

Callender's other charges appealed even more strongly to Federalist fancy. He wrote that Jefferson maintained at Monticello a "Congo harem," the queen of which was a "black Venus" named Sally Hemings. Soon the journalist was referring to her familiarly as "Dusky Sally" and "Black Sal."[23] The lubricious appeal of these stories was particularly strong in the Northeast, where blacks were regarded as exotic. Callender's accounts were not only reprinted but heavily embroidered, enlivened with sensuous accounts of welcoming "mahogany" arms that eventually became welcoming "mahogany" thighs.

Thomas Moore, the famous Irish poet, wrote:

> The weary statesman for repose has fled
>   From halls of council to his Negro's shed
> Where blest he woos some black Aspasia's grace
>   And dreams of freedom in his slave's embrace.[24]

An American versifier admonished:

> Resume thy shells and butterflies,
> Thy beetles' heads and lizards' thighs,
> The state no more controul:
> Thy tricks with Sooty Sal give o'er:
> Indulge thy body, Tom, no more;
> But try to save thy *soul*.[25]

Rhymes ricocheted down the corridors of months and years, begetting ever more distorted echoes. Even the pubescent William Cullen Bryant got into the act. The precocious 13-year-old won Federalist applause for writing:

> Go, wretch, resign the presidential chair,
> Disclose thy secret features foul or fair . . .
> Go scan, Philosophist, thy ****** charms,
> And sink supinely in her sable arms;
> But quit to abler hands the helm of state,
> Nor image ruin on thy country's fate![26]

Only three years later, at the age of sixteen, the poet earned immortality with his somberly majestic "Thanatopsis." Later renouncing his family's Federalism, he became a Democratic editor preaching Jeffersonian principles and is said to have regretted the juvenile effusion that first brought him notoriety.

The charge that Sally Hemings was Jefferson's mistress was lent a specious credence by the undeniable fact that some of her children resembled Jefferson and other members of his family. This resemblance was not surprising in the light of confessions of paternity by Jefferson's nephews Peter and Samuel Carr. Ellen Randolph, Jefferson's granddaughter, particularly resented Samuel's hedonism, calling him "the most notorious good-natured Turk that ever was master of a black seraglio kept at other men's expense."[27] Not so widely circulated was the information that Sally Hemings was the half-sister of Jefferson's wife.[28]

A proud and sensitive man, Jefferson was assuredly angered, frustrated, and depressed by the ugly rumors published in numerous journals and the crude jests exchanged at tavern tables by guffawing drinkers to the accompaniment of winks, leers, and elbow digs in the ribs. But nothing induced him to depart from his established practice of refusing to comment on any personal criticism of himself.

Jefferson did not abandon his reticence even when Callender widened the scope of his calumnies by reporting that the President had in effect stolen by paying off a private debt in depreciated money. This charge, however, gained little currency. Larceny could not compete with lubricity as a fascinating subject for libel.

Jefferson left Washington for Monticello on July 21, 1802. Quitting the capital for his summer stay on the mountaintop must have been an even greater blessing than in the past. He had said from the first that he would not remain in Washington at the height of its heat and humidity. He was acutely sensitive to these discomforts and believed them injurious to his health. But leaving Washington now was especially important to his mental health. He had to escape the miasma of gossip that infected the environs of Foggy Bottom.

The President did not, however, leave the work of his office behind him. He continued to spend up to fourteen hours a day at his desk. Messages from Washington normally arrived within two or three days. The world's alarums seemed a little muted by the time they reached his mountaintop, but they were just as real.

The most notable during this particular stay at Monticello was the news that Morocco had declared war on the United States. The Americans were still at war with Tripoli, and other Barbary states were threatening to go to war in defense of their sovereign right to piracy.

With the President and the Secretary of State both out of town, Treasury Secretary Gallatin was apprehensive that Navy Secretary Smith would take some precipitate action or by letter persuade the President to do something risky and costly. Soon Jefferson could count on a daily letter expressing Gallatin's perturbation.[29]

The President approved ordering the frigate *John Adams* to the Mediterranean, but later delayed its sailing upon a report that Morocco's uncertain sovereign had declared peace. Smith argued that the Mediterranean situation was too volatile to justify detaining the frigate. Jefferson conferred with Madison and then ordered the vessel to sail.

By now the year was well into September and the Barbary crisis appeared to be cooling in pace with the weather in the Blue Ridge Mountains. Jefferson was busy reconstructing Monticello according to his revised plans, and there was every reason to believe that portions of the interior would be exposed to winter's rains and sleets and snows. A vivid picture of how it was in September is given by Mrs. William Thornton, wife of the designer of the national Capitol. She, her husband, and her mother were staying with James and Dolley Madison and accompanied them on a visit to Jefferson. Arriving at the base of the mountain after dark, Dr. and Mrs. Thornton and some other guests abandoned their carriages to complete the journey on foot. White flashes of lightning lit the three-quarters of a mile climb to the summit, abruptly disclosing the separate identities of trees increasingly agitated by a rising wind. The party barely beat the thunderstorm to the house.

Mrs. Thornton hardly had time to rejoice on reaching shelter before discovering that it seemed of a very temporary sort. By the feeble light of a single lantern the guests crossed a floor of loose planks to the dining room, whose only illumination came from the adjacent tea room beyond a large arch. The guests sat down to tea, some in the smaller room, some in the shadowy large one. As one agitated by the hazards of both outdoor and indoor walking on this stormy night, and with the critical eye of an architect's spouse, Mrs. Thornton found her surroundings "irregular and unpleasant." More disillusion-ment awaited her. "When we went to bed, we had to mount a little ladder of a staircase about two feet wide and very steep into rooms with the beds fixed up in recesses in the walls—the windows small and square, turning on pivots. Everything has a whimsical and droll appearance."[30]

The narrow stairs and recessed beds were not temporary inconveniences but features which Jefferson was determined to include in the final version of his house. He regarded as conspicuous waste the grand staircases that distin-guished many mansions and went to the opposite extreme in conservation of space. The recessed beds were also space savers, as was his own bed, which could be raised or lowered in the passageway between his bedroom and his study.

Having leveled the mountaintop to provide a building site for Monticello, Jefferson planned the home as a capstone for the mountain. His newer plan, with a dome replacing the more conventional roof of his original sketches, was even more conformable to this ideal. Temporary discomforts were tolerable even to this comfort-loving man because he carried in his mind and heart the image of the Monticello that was to be. Its red brick matching the red soil, it rose like a natural excrescence from his beloved mountain.

When autumn touched the landscape with fire, and little red and yellow flames glowed in the dusky groves and licked at the hillsides as if they were the source of the smoky blue haze, Jefferson had to go back to the gritty strife of Washington. Bidding farewell to his children on October 1, he returned on October 4 to the empty rooms of the President's House.[31]

But this time there was a difference. His daughters had promised that they would join him before long. Of course, for Jefferson, in matters of the affec-tions—whether as in early years, he was parted from an adored wife or a passionately loved sweetheart or, as now, from his idolized and idolizing children—any separation was long.

While Jefferson, impatiently awaiting his family's arrival, busied himself with vexing problems and tedious routine, he received one day a very satisfying reward: official notification of his election to the Institut National de France. The institute was the foremost society of arts and sciences in France, and France was then in the forefront of learning and creative culture in the Western world. Only reservedly and cautiously did it look beyond French borders for members, and political prominence was no qualification. It was precisely the kind of honor that Jefferson most cherished.

In an informal letter from Du Pont de Nemours he had been apprised earlier that the distinction was coming his way. In nominating him, Du Pont had said that Jefferson not only stood foremost in the world in the category of moral and political philosophy, but in "other branches of learning" was equaled by "few men in Europe."[32] Since Jefferson had been elected before Du Pont's nomination was received, the Frenchman's declaration served no practical purpose, but it must have delighted the President to receive such an encomium from one he so much admired as scholar and friend.

It was ironic that this much prized award should have been bestowed on Jefferson at a time when he agonized over the possibilities of war with France. But elected along with Jefferson, despite the apparent imminence of bloody battles between the French and the English, was Sir Joseph Banks, Britain's great explorer-naturalist and the president of its Royal Society. The election of Jefferson and Banks at such a time was heartening evidence that the empire of the mind did not balk at national borders.

As President of the United States, however, Jefferson worried a great deal about national borders. His belief that his country's boundaries must be extended westward for the sake of its security received disturbing confirmation in the last week of November. It was then that he learned that in mid-October the Spanish Intendant had closed the deposit at New Orleans. This action violated the Treaty of San Lorenzo of 1795, for which Jefferson himself had laid the groundwork before his retirement as Secretary of State.

Even Jefferson, with all his prescient study of the Louisiana problem, had not foreseen that Spain would act so peremptorily, particularly at a time when she was preparing to part with the territory. Now, even before Napoleon assumed control of New Orleans, Americans were denied the right to deposit their goods custom-free in the port before exportation. This development underlined the threat to free navigation of the Mississippi if Louisiana became the property of imperialist France.

Just about the time that Jefferson received the bad news about New Orleans, he had the joy of welcoming his daughters and two grandchildren, Thomas Jefferson Randolph and Ellen Wayles Randolph. For a while their visit had been in doubt. Maria, seemingly apprehensive, had urged delay, but Martha would not hear of it. In a letter to Martha, the President had furnished an itinerary prepared with his usual meticulousness. It included information on roads and taverns and provided for four days of travel over the 120-mile route, longer than he himself usually took. According to plan, the President's secretary, Captain Meriwether Lewis, who performed almost any task except the nominal one, met them en route at Strode's Tavern with another carriage and fresh horses. Now, at the end of each day's annoyances and tribulations, Jefferson could relax with those he loved best.

The young women brightened not only their father's house but Washington society as well. Even the Rev. Manasseh Cutler, Federalist Congressman from Massachusetts and thundering pulpit orator, who seemed to identify the Republicans of Jefferson's administration with the publicans and sinners of the New Testament, admitted: "They appeared well-accomplished women—very delicate and tolerably handsome."[33]

Maria's beauty impressed people even more than her shyness. Much later a fellow Virginian wrote as if still under her spell: "Her complexion was exquisite; her features all good, and so arranged as to produce an expression such as I never beheld in any other countenance: sweetness, intelligence, tenderness, beauty were exquisitely blended. . . . Her eye, fine blue, had an expression that cannot I think be described."[34] Margaret Bayard Smith, wife of the publisher of the *National Intelligencer*, informed a friend: "Mrs. Eppes is beautiful, simplicity and timidity personified when in company, but when alone with you of communicative and winning manners."[35]

Maria's timidity may have been the reflection of a fullblown inferiority complex. Many years later her niece Ellen Randolph Coolidge wrote that Maria "undervalued and disregarded her own beauty . . . . saying that people only praised her for that because they could not praise her for better things." She "sometimes mourned over the fear that her father *must* prefer her sister's society, and *could* not take the same pleasure in hers."[36]

In this connection it is interesting that Mrs. Smith, after praising Maria Eppes' beauty, wrote that Martha Randolph was "rather homely, a delicate likeness of her father, but still more interesting than Mrs. E. She is really one of the most lovely women I have ever met with, her countenance beaming with intelligence, benevolence, and sensibility, and her conversation fulfills all her countenance promises. Her manners, so frank and affectionate, that you know her at once, and feel perfectly at your ease with her."[37]

Six-year-old Ellen Randolph drew attention in her own right. Mrs. Smith found her "singularly and extravagantly fond of poetry" and pronounced her "without exception one of the finest and most intelligent children I have ever met with."[38] The words were reminiscent of Abigail Adams' description of Ellen's Aunt Maria at age nine: "She is a child of the quickest sensibility, and the maturest understanding, that I have ever met with for her years. . . . Books are her delight."[39]

Jefferson's namesake, ten-year-old Thomas Jefferson Randolph, was not a model of deportment, but he was notably enterprising. Without parental permission he rode with the coachman in one of the presidential vehicles to the Navy Yard, where he received salutes, was treated to a collation, and otherwise was made an honored guest. When he returned to the President's House and told of his triumph, his mother scolded him but his grandfather could not conceal an amusement bordering on delight. Taking advantage of the conflicting responses of his elders, the boy "skulked away."[40]

Boyish escapades were far more diverting than congressional schemes. The conversation of loving daughters was much more congenial than the arguments of Federalist delegations or even insistent Republicans. Poetry probably regained its charms for Jefferson when he heard it from the lips of a precocious granddaughter. Altogether he was much happier than he had been a short while before.

Jefferson's cheerfulness was reflected in his second annual message to Congress. Like his address of the year before, it was sent to the legislators and not delivered in person. Republican simplicity has been assigned as a reason for departure from the procedure of Washington and Adams, but if Jefferson had been a masterful orator he might have continued the practice of personal appearances. The tenor of the message, consistently adhered to throughout, was accurately reflected in its first sentence:

> Another year has come around, and finds us still blessed with peace and friendship abroad; law, order and religion at home; good affection and harmony with our Indian neighbors; our burdens lightened, yet our income sufficient for the public wants, and the produce of the year great beyond example.[41]

The President conceded that some European nations continued to discriminate against the United States carrying trade, but the remedy should lie in "friendly discussion." If this did not prove sufficient, Congress could decide upon the wisdom of retaliation or, in the President's euphemistic phrase, "countervailing inequalities."

If any members were lulled into inattention as one of their officers intoned these innocuous paragraphs, they must have sprung alert at mention of Louisiana. If so, they must have subsided again as they learned that the President said only that retrocession of the territory to France, if it should occur, would effect "a change in the aspect of our foreign relations."

The Chief Executive acknowledged hostilities between the United States and Tripoli but quite accurately reported that the war had become uneventful. He acknowledged also that agreements about boundaries would have to be reached with the Indians.

Then the President got to what he wanted to say: "It is with pleasure I inform you that the receipts of external duties for the last twelve months have exceeded those of any former year." The administration had simultaneously met all expenses of the government and reduced the public debt by $5,500,000—a huge sum in those days. As a fillip, he could report a surplus in the Treasury. He proudly asserted that the rigorous economies of the administration had made foreseeable eventual eradication of the "moral canker" of public debt.

A hint that the world was less than perfect was implicit in his concluding remarks. Jefferson had reduced the navy as part of his economy plan, but he now said that some small vessels might be added. The emphasis, though, was still on "the saving of what we already possess." He proposed construction in the Washington Navy Yard of a dock in which ships could be "laid up dry and under cover from the sun." "Thus, for a sum scarcely exceeding the cost of one new vessel," many ships could be saved. He had conceived a dry dock, utilizing the principle of canal locks to lift vessels to higher levels that could be drained of water.

The address reflected the President's commitment to optimism and his determination to avoid needless friction. It also exhibited the tendency of most Chief Executives in times of prosperity to emphasize economic benefits and gloss over dangers. Jefferson did, however, have a better excuse than most. If the Louisiana question became the subject of heated debate, old animosities toward France might be stirred again and United States attempts to negotiate a settlement with Napoleon might be frustrated. And there could be no denial that the economic achievements of the administration were impressive, a tribute to Jefferson's dedication to a principle and Gallatin's skill in implementing it.

The President's message placated the Federalists. Senator William Plumer of New Hampshire was representative. While complaining that the President acted "with an ill grace" when he "boasted of the fullness of the Treasury when at the same time he condemned those federal laws by which the money was collected," the Senator nevertheless pronounced the message "an excellent one." He said it was "calculated to soothe the angry passions and quiet the fears of the people."[42]

But it did not have this effect on some of the President's own party. Two days after the reading of the President's message, his distant cousin John Randolph of Roanoke, one of the most prominent Republican Congressmen, challenged the secrecy of the administration's proceedings in regard to Louisiana. Randolph had been elected to Congress at the age of twenty-six in a campaign in which he had had to debate with Patrick Henry. By the time he threw down the gauntlet to Jefferson, he was Republican floor leader of the United States House of Representatives, and chairman of its powerful Ways and Means Committee, having been elected to both positions the year before at the age of twenty-eight.

Even if Randolph had not held such important positions of leadership, he would have commanded the attention of the House when he rose to move that all documents relating to the United States' right of deposit at New Orleans and its closure be submitted to Congress by the administration. Even before he revealed his subject, his signal that he wished the floor would have been sufficient to gain the notice of the most confirmed daydreamer in the house. The youthful Congressman commenced some of his more understated performances by striding alone into the chamber, booted and spurred, propping his tall, reed-thin frame against one of the architectural columns, idly toying with his riding crop as he warmed to his subject.

In startling contrast to his macho entrance was his piping voice, suggestive of a boy soprano. It was reported that a prepuberty bout with scarlet fever had made him impotent. It was also said that he had once pursued on horseback, firing a brace of pistols all the while, a man rash enough to suggest that he was a eunuch. Fears of the truthfulness of the second story discouraged inquiries about the first.

His more dramatic entrances were unforgettable. Then, too, he would stride into the chamber booted and spurred and carrying his riding crop but he would also be followed by a pack of yelping hounds.

One might marvel that such a man would be taken seriously, much less elevated to two of the three highest offices in the gift of the House while he was still in his twenties and only two years after his debut as a member. But Randolph was notable for much more than eccentricity. The piping voice, ludicrous when first heard, assumed a seductive, flutelike musicality as he proceeded. Listeners ceased to speculate about his sex as they succumbed to fascination with his eloquence, erudition, and savage wit.

The incongruity of the smooth, boyish face atop the tall, emaciated figure riveted all eyes. Moving from insouciance to spontaneous indignation, he quoted from first one classic and then another. If anyone accused him of taking the phrases out of context, he was quite capable of quoting accurately page after page of context. Before his twelfth birthday he had been thoroughly familiar with a tremendous variety of works including Shakespeare, Voltaire, Cervantes, Plutarch, *Gil Blas*, and *Orlando Furioso*.[43] His voracious self-education had been followed by formal studies at Princeton, Columbia, and William and Mary.

He did not have to use quotations as a substitute for native wit. He had already created some that were clever and some memorable merely for being outrageous, and he would originate many more. He described his cousin Edmund Randolph as "the chameleon on the aspen, always trembling, always changing." He said of a secretive politician that he "rowed to his object with muffled oars." To a slaveowner exuding pity for the suffering Greeks while oblivious to the ragged little blacks near her steps, he exclaimed, "Madam, the Greeks are at your door!" Referring to two opponents, Robert Wright and John Rea (Ray), he said the House presented two anomalies, "a Wright always wrong and a Ray without light."[44]

Impoliticly, he proclaimed: "I am an aristocrat; I love liberty, I hate equality." He further testified to his faith in breeding: "The bad blood *will* show in some part of the four-mile heat." He himself came from a long line of winners, including the royalty of both Europe and America, William the Conqueror and Edward I, and also the Emperor Powhatan and the Princess Pocahontas. Like his kinsmen Thomas Jefferson and John Marshall, he was related by a complex system of intermarriages to a large proportion, perhaps a majority, of Virginia notables. His home, Roanoke, looked out on one side to an English garden, and on another to the wilderness that had been home to his Indian ancestors.

One memorable saying of Randolph's expressed a philosophy that spelled trouble for Jefferson: "Asking one of the States to surrender part of her sovereignty is like asking a lady to surrender part of her chastity." In 1798 Randolph had ardently supported the Virginia Resolutions written by James Madison at Jefferson's instigation and adopted by the Virginia General Assembly. He agreed vehemently with Jefferson's and Madison's contention that the federal government acted unconstitutionally whenever it exercised powers not specifically granted to it in the Constitution. He supported the Virginia Resolutions' declaration that each state, in its sovereignty, had "an equal right to judge for itself" whether an infraction had been committed and what "mode and measure of address" were appropriate.

He was still inflexibly dedicated to the same principles, and he conceded no exceptions, no possibilities of modification. And though he was floor leader of his President's party, he was determined to learn the details of the Chief Executive's maneuverings to meet the crisis of New Orleans and to expose to the nation any failure to protect American rights or any action exceeding constitutional authority.

The President, on the other hand, was moving toward greater flexibility in judging what was constitutional and what was not. Recently, when a proposal was before the Congress to build a series of piers in the Delaware River, he had felt compelled to assert his conviction that the use of federal funds for that or any other internal improvement would be unconstitutional. But he suggested that the cause was not hopeless. If these piers could be used by the United States Navy, the necessary appropriation could be classified as a defense expenditure. "A power to provide and maintain a navy," he said, "is a power to provide receptacles for it and places to cover and preserve it."[45]

It might seem paradoxical that this argument should be advanced by one alarmed by Hamilton's advocacy of the doctrine of implied powers. But Jefferson's interpretation was not something suddenly devised to meet the exigencies of the moment. In August 1787, when some had insisted that Congress lacked the power to enforce levies on the states, he had argued that no express grant of authority was necessary. "When two parties make a compact," he had said, "there results to each a power of compelling the other to execute it."[46]

Many Federalists were quick to think that Randolph had launched an attack on the President. Some Republicans then, and some historians of later times, believed that the Congressman performed a friendly act in moving the resolution for an investigation. They argued that Randolph beat the Federalists to the draw and insured by the language of his resolution that the scope of the investigation would be restricted to matters pertaining directly to New Orleans, thus allowing the President to proceed secretly to obtain the best possible settlement regarding the Louisiana Territory.

Whatever Randolph's intent, however, the move signaled an inevitable conflict between the President and the Republican floor leader. In his struggle with the judiciary Jefferson was opposed by a Randolph cousin, John Marshall. Now, in his struggle with the legislature, he was sure to be opposed by another Randolph cousin.

Jefferson and John Randolph were much alike. Both geniuses represented the highest intellectual flowering of the Virginia plantocracy. Each was devoted to his concept of the public good and to the ideal of liberty. But the two were doomed to disagree. Jefferson had a strong streak of pragmatism, which he placed in the service of his ideals. Randolph was dedicated to holy abstractions. Jefferson would compromise, at least for a while, on almost everything except principles. But he could not carry on a true dialogue with Randolph, nor could any of his less principled followers. Randolph was impervious alike to the temptations of corruption and to any logic but his own.

A struggle between the two men could be costly to both and to the nation they sought to serve. Though Jefferson had the more capacious and disciplined mind, they were equally brilliant in resourceful argument. Jefferson had the advantage of much greater maturity and experience. But he was no orator, whereas Randolph was perhaps the most accomplished public speaker in the United States since Patrick Henry. Jefferson's breadth of view made him a greater statesman, but Randolph's ideological narrowness spared him from draining doubts. He could apply to every question the litmus of his ideology. The narrowness that restricted his value as a statesman was one of his greatest strengths as a political combatant.

V

WONDERFUL YEAR

THE PRESIDENT who didn't hold levees was holding one to celebrate New Year's Day 1803.[1] Senators, Congressmen, and diplomats wearing broad bright ribbons and glittering decorations paid their respects to the tall Chief Magistrate and his two daughters. Joining them were Washington residents of varied backgrounds, for, according to custom established by the first President, all who left their calling cards at the President's house were subsequently invited to a reception. Some of Jefferson's callers had seen him at times in threadbare garments, but tonight his hair was heavily powdered and, as on other special occasions, his dark-suited dapperness recalled the dress of his Parisian days. His costume doubtless had been subjected to the loving inspection of his daughters. Many of the guests probably suspected as much but did not surmise the strong possibility that the President had urged his sartorial advice upon them. As a widower he had regularly purchased clothing for them when they were growing up, and, as in the case of almost everything he undertook, he had made himself quite knowledgeable in feminine fashion. Jefferson never ceased to guide his children in any matter significant to him, and now it was important to him that all Washington should see how wonderful they were.

Four days later Martha and Maria left Washington for their respective homes. Jefferson took the Georgetown ferry across the Potomac with them and rode on horseback beside the carriage for a few miles through the Virginia countryside. Then, giving each a hundred dollars for expenses, he sadly told them goodbye and his coach rolled away with them. John, a slave who waited on table at the President's House, was the driver. The condition of the road was appalling, and Jefferson was acutely anxious as he turned back to Washington.

His anxiety heightened a few days later when he heard that his daughters had had to take shelter in a house unsuitable for ladies. Ten days passed, instead of the usual five or six, before he received word of their safe arrival. It came in a letter from Maria telling of her worries about him. "The pain of seeing you turn back alone after having experienced so many happy hours, my dear Papa, in the little room to us endeared by your sitting in it always, and the recollection of the heavy expense this journey has been to you, for indeed it must be in all immense, made my heart ache. . . . How much do I think of you at the hours which we have been accustomed to be with you alone, my dear Papa, and how much pain it gives me to think of the unsafe and solitary manner in which you sleep upstairs."[2]

She closed: "Adieu, dearest and most beloved of fathers. I feel my inability to express how much I love and revere you. But you are the first and dearest to my heart."

So Jefferson returned to his lonely labors, consoled by the professions of love on which his heart fed. There were other consolations; some of his most vexing problems were also pregnant with great opportunities. He would certainly not languish in boredom during 1803. His political acumen and sense of history told him that this year could be one of the most important in the life of the United States—could determine for generations the physical shape of the nation, the scope of its influence, and even its chance of survival. If disasters were to be averted and opportunities realized, the President must be energetic and resourceful.

Jefferson acted decisively in January to deal with two of these problems, negotiations with France over Louisiana and the related matter of exploring the great West of which Louisiana was a part. In February his contest with the Supreme Court resulted in a history-making decision in the case of *Marbury* v. *Madison*.

1

Jefferson was a master of the art of timing so essential to political success. The Federalist resolution demanding submission to Congress of the President's papers relating to Louisiana was finally defeated on January 6, 1803. On that very day the President sent to the Senate his nomination of James Monroe as Minister Extraordinary to the French government to negotiate concerning Louisiana. He would also be authorized to negotiate with the Spanish, if their involvement necessitated conversations with Madrid.

Jefferson had foreseen the crisis to be precipitated by French acquisition of New Orleans and of all of Louisiana, had analyzed the problem, and had instructed United States diplomats to put out feelers regarding the possibilities. But these activities could not be publicized. Westerners, those most directly threatened, were alarmed. Jefferson had long had a special relationship with these people. As early as 1781 he had said that he had a "peculiar confidence in the men from the western side of the mountains."[3] They had reciprocated, and his efforts to help them attain statehood had intensified their loyalty. The ties remained but were frayed by gnawing fears that the President was not active enough in dealing with the problems of the closing of the deposit at New Orleans. The Kentucky legislature had sent a memorial on the subject to both the President and the Congress. Madison told Jefferson that similar declarations were being drafted all over the West. The special appointment of Monroe was intended to provide reassuring evidence of the President's concern.

Monroe was a good symbol. He shared Jefferson's sympathy for Western interests. But there were other reasons for choosing him. After classes at William and Mary, he had studied law in Jefferson's office and was a Jefferson protégé. His personal loyalty to the President was strong enough to include both dedicated service and the frank telling of unpleasant truths. Jefferson's confidence in him was complete: he once said that Monroe could be turned inside out without revealing any serious blemish. A former member of both the House of Representatives and the Senate, Monroe would have firsthand knowledge of the ways of the Congress. Having just completed a successful term as Governor of Virginia, he enjoyed high prestige in Republican circles. In Washington's administration he had served as United States Minister to France. True, he had been recalled in what Federalists were pleased to call "disgrace," but it was pleasing to Jefferson to send back to Paris the old friend rejected by the Federalists.

Above all, Monroe should be helpful to United States Minister Robert R. Livingston in negotiating with France for purchase of New Orleans and other territory at the mouth of the Mississippi and to Charles Pinckney, United States Minister in Madrid, in obtaining the Floridas from Spain. Besides, if the American diplomats were forced to act in some matters before there was time to consult with the President, Monroe, better than anyone else except Madison, would know the President's mind.

Livingston had been acting under double-barreled instructions from Jefferson. First he was to talk with Charles-Maurice de Talleyrand, Napoleon's wily Foreign Minister, in an effort to prevent the retrocession if it had not yet taken place. As Jefferson had feared, the march of events had already made the transfer from Spain to France a *fait accompli*. Livingston's remaining task was to pursue the second objective—trying to purchase New Orleans and, if possible, adjacent territory.

He was repeatedly frustrated in his efforts to deal face to face with Talleyrand. The Frenchman, however, had fed the American diplomat tantalizing suggestions that France soon might offer the United States a great opportunity. When Livingston learned that the Spanish Governor had revoked the United States right of deposit at New Orleans, he concluded that Talleyrand had been tantalizing him into immobility and suspected that Bonaparte was responsible for the Spanish official's action. This development might signal the realization of American fears that France would close the Mississippi to United States commerce.

A bold-featured, imposing man of considerable political experience, Livingston was a skilled negotiator. New York State's first Chancellor, or Chief Justice, he had been a prominent member of the Continental Congress and had served with Jefferson on the committee appointed to draft the Declaration of Independence. Taking his cue from the President, he leaked the news that United States leaders were considering a *rapprochement* with Great Britain as perhaps the best move for national security.

Jefferson and Livingston were not paranoid in their fears that Bonaparte's government contemplated using control of the Mississippi to stunt the growth of the United States as a world power. Talleyrand believed that, despite the

American Revolution, the Americans were so closely tied to the mother country that the United States and Great Britain were natural allies. In 1798, when the Frenchman had drafted instructions to Guillemardet, French Minister to Madrid, outlining an appeal to Spain for retrocession, he had warned that the Americans obviously meant to rule in their own continent and meddle in Europe as well. "Moreover," he said, "their conduct ever since the moment of their independence is enough to prove this truth: the Americans are devoured by pride, ambition, and cupidity; the mercantile spirit of the city of London ferments from Charleston to Boston. . . ."[4]

As Talleyrand had been rebuffed only a few months before in his effort to solicit a bribe of $250,000 from American negotiators, one is tempted to conclude that he regarded American reluctance on that occasion as evidence of excessive love of money.

Talleyrand had an answer to the American threat: "There are no other means of putting an end to the ambition of the Americans than that of shutting them up within the limits which Nature seems to have traced for them; but Spain is not in a condition to do this great work alone. She cannot, therefore, hasten too quickly to engage the aid of a preponderating Power, yielding to it a small part of her immense domains in order to preserve the rest.

"Let the Court of Madrid cede these districts to France," he urged, "and from that moment the power of America is bounded by the limit which it may suit the interests and the tranquility of France and Spain to assign her. The French Republic, mistress of these two provinces [Louisiana and the Floridas], will be a wall of brass forever impenetrable to the combined efforts of England and America."

Talleyrand's views remained unchanged. But the government that he served was now an empire rather than a republic, and one man made the big decisions. If Napoleon were convinced of the necessity for bottling up the United States, he could act immediately and with more finality than the former Directory.

But events in another part of the New World were claiming Bonaparte's attention. What was happening in the West Indian island of St. Domingo could have a great deal to do with his decision on New Orleans and Louisiana. Half the island[5] had at least nominally belonged to France, half to Spain. The Spanish half was one of the areas to be ceded to France under the Treaty of San Ildefonso. In actuality the French part of the island had been engulfed in civil strife since the fall of the monarchy in 1792 as Creole aristocrats struggled to retain dominance in the face of assaults by two much more numerous groups— mulattoes and full-blooded Negroes. A former slave, Toussaint L'Ouverture, obtained power by providing guidance for the blacks and courting the Creoles. He further cemented the support of the whites by encouraging the mass of blacks to return to their usual labors. Too busy with his Egyptian campaign to become embroiled in civil turmoil on a Caribbean island, Napoleon confirmed Toussaint's self-conferred rank of general.

When Toussaint learned that the Spanish half of the island was to be transferred to France, he seized that territory before arrival of the occupying French forces. In July 1801 he had himself proclaimed Governor for life.

The new Governor wore out six horses and six secretaries in a day. His phenomenal energy and decisiveness invited comparison with the attributes of the world's foremost man of action. And Toussaint worked to heighten the resemblance, wearing fancy uniforms like Napoleon, strutting like the Corsican, surrounding himself with nouveau-regal grandeur suggestive of the Little Corporal's palace.

Napoleon was not amused. As a practical matter, he knew that St. Domingo, his Caribbean base, must be completely under his control before he began to occupy the Louisiana Territory. Though Napoleon had once proclaimed to the people of St. Domingo, "Remember, brave Negroes, that France alone recognizes your liberty and your equal rights,"[6] he now told his Council of State that the security of civilization demanded obliteration of the "new Algiers" growing in the Caribbean.[7] Josephine, a product of the French colonial Creole aristocracy, fed his prejudices. Exacerbating Napoleon's impatience to crush the "Bonaparte of the Antilles" was the realization that the melodramatic posturings of his imitator were causing people to laugh at the original. He would not tolerate this "gilded African."[8]

When the French Minister of Marine sent Toussaint warnings that he was exhausting Napoleon's patience, the black dictator said that he dealt only with sovereigns, not with valets.[9]

Napoleon flattered Toussaint into a false sense of security that caused him to isolate himself still further from his own people and to neglect every means of escape. Then Bonaparte sent to St. Domingo a French fleet accompanied by a Spanish squadron. Toussaint thought that he was France's faithful ally against Great Britain. But even in the troubled state of Franco-British relations, Napoleon took care to inform the English of his intentions so they would not become unduly alarmed. He explained: "In the course which I have taken of annihilating the black government at Santo Domingo, I have been less guided by considerations of commerce and finance than by the necessity of stifling in every part of the world every kind of germ of disquiet and trouble; but it could not escape me that Santo Domingo, even after being reconquered by the whites, would be for many years a weak point which would need the support of peace and the mother country."[10] If the French government had recognized the power of the Negroes in Santo Domingo, he said, "the scepter of the New World would sooner or later have fallen into the hands of the blacks."[11]

The two great Western powers, so soon to be at war, understood each other in this instance. Britain acquiesced.

To capture Toussaint and subdue the blacks, Napoleon sent ten thousand men under the command of his brother-in-law, General Charles V. E. Leclerc. Bonaparte also sent a reassuring message to Toussaint: "If you are told that these forces are destined to ravish your liberty, answer: The Republic has given us liberty, the Republic will not suffer it to be taken from us! . . . We have conceived esteem for you and we take pleasure in recognizing and proclaiming the great services you have rendered to the French people. If their flag floats over St. Domingo, it is to you and to the brave blacks that they owe it."[12]

Jefferson observed the approaching crisis in St. Domingo with mixed feelings. An easy triumph of French arms in the island would give France the outpost from which she could extend her control over the Louisiana Territory. On the other hand, he reportedly had told L. A. Pichon, the French chargé in Washington, that neither the United States nor Great Britain was eager for St. Domingo to become "another Algiers."[13] Indeed, it is quite possible that when Napoleon used that phrase in communicating with the British he had gotten it from Jefferson by way of Pichon. Though the duel of the gingham dog and calico cat had not yet been recorded, such a mutually consuming fight is what Jefferson would have liked to see on the disputed island.

Leclerc arrived at Santo Domingo early in 1802 prepared to shed blood to protect Western civilization, secure a French springboard to the North American mainland, safeguard his country's access to West Indian sugar and coffee, and end the "Negro travesty"[14] on the great First Consul of France.

By June, Bonaparte received word that Leclerc had completely subdued the island's blacks. Betrayed by one of his black generals, Toussaint trustingly placed himself in the hands of his French idol's brother-in-law. Leclerc shipped him back to imprisonment and an early death in a French dungeon.

Bonaparte's dreams of empire in the Western Hemisphere were freshly stimulated by this initial success, but began to fade with reports of attrition of his forces by black guerrillas and by tropical diseases to which the Africans were immune. In January 1803 news reached Paris that Leclerc himself was dead. Napoleon exclaimed: "Damn sugar! Damn coffee! Damn colonies!"[15]

Monroe arrived in Paris before Bonaparte recovered his taste for sugar, coffee, or colonies. The time for bargaining over New Orleans and adjacent territory was better than it had been at any time since Napoleon first determined that New Orleans must be his and cast covetous eyes on the virgin acres that stretched beyond. Livingston had been doing as well as could have been expected, patiently maintaining communication with the French Foreign Ministry, accurately informing his own government, and fanning French fears of an Anglo-American alliance. But, while the New Yorker read French well, he lacked Monroe's fluency in speaking the language, and such mastery now seemed likely to become more important. Livingston's deafness, no insuperable difficulty when listening to familiar American accents, was a serious impediment to communication in Paris, making the Virginian's help desirable. Besides, if a French offer should present great opportunities, a bold response would be easier if the American Minister could share the decision with a plenipotentiary who was one of the President's most trusted friends.

All of these good reasons put together, however, were not sufficient to make Livingston welcome the appointment of Monroe. The Minister wrote to Madison: "I cannot wish, sir, that my fellow citizens should . . . be led to believe, from Mr. Monroe's appointment, that I had been negligent to their interests, or too delicate on any of the great points entrusted to my care. I trust that a communication of my notes to some of them would show that I had gone as far as it was possible for me to go, and perhaps further than my instructions would justify."[16]

Livingston's sensitivity on the point had been abraded by Talleyrand's suggestion that negotiations be delayed since Monroe could be expected to replace the New Yorker in the discussions.

If Napoleon had lost his taste for empire building in the New World, then his ferocious energies must be directed to conquest of his chief rival in the Old. Forces that might be sent to St. Domingo could be used in Europe against Great Britain. But of course it would be utterly reckless to be implacable about Louisiana and thus drive the United States into an alliance with Great Britain. So, Napoleon spoiled Talleyrand's Easter holiday by telling him that the First Consul had decided to sell Louisiana to the United States.

The Foreign Minister, together with Napoleon's brothers Joseph and Lucien, argued against the transaction. But Napoleon was adamant. He would not even consider the alternative of retroceding the lands to Spain. Sale to the Americans would be financially profitable, and Bonaparte needed more money for his war with the British. Besides, placing the vast western territory in American hands could create future problems for the British. Accordingly, on April 11, Talleyrand asked the two American envoys whether their government would be interested in buying all of Louisiana.

Ironically, Jefferson's administration had just reduced its hopes. On March 2 Madison had instructed the two American envoys to propose that France cede to the United States the Floridas, New Orleans, and all lands east of the Mississippi but retain all lands west of the river. The navigation of the Mississippi "from its source to the ocean" would be free alike to France and the United States. Residents of the lands ceded by France would become United States citizens with full rights. The United States would pay for the ceded lands a sum to be arrived at by negotiation. Madison confided to the envoys that President Jefferson was prepared to pay as much as fifty million livres if he had to. "Every struggle, however, is to be made against such an augmentation of the price, that will consist with an ultimate acquiescence."[17]

The federal government was prepared to make other concessions. Rather than resort to war it would accept a part of the island of New Orleans and give up completely on the Floridas if rights of deposit and free navigation were guaranteed.

Despite Jefferson's rhetoric of 1787 that "the tree of liberty must be refreshed from time to time with the blood of patriots and tyrants,"[18] he was determined to avoid by every honorable means the shedding of American patriots' blood in a quarrel with the tyrant Napoleon. When Spain disavowed her Intendant's action in closing the deposit at New Orleans, the President gloried, "By a reasonable and peaceable process, we have obtained in 4 months what would have cost us 7 years of war, 100,000 human lives, 100 millions of additional debt."[19] He rejoiced that he had not "seized New Orleans as our Federal maniacs wished."[20]

Jefferson's activities in Washington had skillfully complemented Livingston's in Paris in bringing Napoleon to the point of parting with Louisiana. So shrewdly had the President played his role at state dinners that the letters of French Chargé Pichon to his home government were filled with revelations of subtle evidence that Jefferson's administration was moving secretly toward alliance with Britain. The President had no idea how well he had succeeded. While sure that his policies were sound, he confessed that he did not "count with confidence on obtaining New Orleans from France for money."[21]

Already Napoleon had brought into the negotiations one likely to be more sympathetic toward his thoughts of parting with Western territory, his Finance Minister, François Barbé-Marbois. This was the same Barbé-Marbois who, as a young Secretary of Legation in an embattled America in 1780, had sent to Jefferson questions about Virginia that elicited from the war-harassed Governor a book-length masterpiece, the famous *Notes on Virginia*. Jefferson had said that he was obliged to the Frenchman "for making me much better acquainted with my own country than I ever was before."

Bonaparte told Barbé-Marbois on April 10 that he was considering the transfer. "I can scarcely say that I cede it to them," he acknowledged, "for it is not yet in our possession. If, however, I leave the least time to our enemies, I shall only transmit an empty title to those Republicans whose friendship I seek. They ask of me only one town in Louisiana, but I already consider the colony as entirely lost. And it appears to me that in the hands of this growing power [the United States] it will be more useful to the policy, and even the commerce, of France than if I should attempt to keep it."[22]

The next day Bonaparte was all decision. "I renounce Louisiana," he told Barbé-Marbois. "It is not only New Orleans that I cede; it is the whole colony, without reserve. . . . I direct you to negotiate the affair. Have an interview this very day with Mr. Livingston."[23]

Talleyrand's question—"Would the United States wish to have the whole of Louisiana?"—caught Livingston off guard. Whether because of difficulties imposed by his deafness and weak French or his long concentration on more limited goals, or a combination of the three factors, Livingston answered, "No." The United States, he said, wanted only New Orleans and the Floridas. A moment later he said that his government might be interested in land above the Arkansas River.[24]

Talleyrand pressed: What would the United States "give for the whole"? Flustered, Livingston snatched a figure out of the air: 20 million livres.

Not an acceptable sum, said the Foreign Minister. Monsieur Livingston should think about the matter and answer again tomorrow.

The American replied that Mr. Monroe had already landed in France and was due in Paris the day after tomorrow. The two United States envoys would have to consult before another offer could be made.

Before Livingston fell asleep that night he repeatedly replayed his conversation with Talleyrand. In no version did he stick to the lines he had originally spoken. Perhaps he had lost an opportunity for his country. Even if he had not, perhaps he had delayed that opportunity so that Monroe, who had done nothing so far, might walk in just in time to claim the major credit.[25]

The next day he hurried to the Foreign Ministry. Talleyrand was polite but impassive. His manners were as meticulous as his grooming. The countenance that betrayed no emotion in the face of Napoleon's tirades—that would remain unmoved even when his royal master publicly called him a silk stocking filled with excrement and while the man behind the courtier's mask plotted his revenge[26]—revealed nothing now. When Livingston tried to resume the conversation of the day before, he was handicapped because he could not make a larger offer without consulting Monroe. Talleyrand did not wish the American to trouble himself on that account. He himself had been talking without authorization by the government of France. He had merely voiced a question that had flitted through his mind.[27]

Returning to his own quarters in great frustration, Livingston found a note from Monroe, who was already in the capital. He wished to call in the morning.

The visit was a tense one, with Livingston fearing that Monroe would steal credit from him and Monroe suspecting that Livingston was trying to shut him out of the negotiations. Nevertheless, they busily pored over the relevant documents.

When they quit their labors for dinner, Livingston—by a "coincidence" not reassuring to Monroe—discovered Barbé-Marbois walking in the garden and invited him to join them. The Virginian's resentment boiled when the American Minister and the Frenchman went into another room, leaving Monroe at the table. He was not soothed when his host returned to tell him that he had agreed to a conference with Barbé-Marbois at the Frenchman's house at eleven o'clock at night. Monroe was not included.

When Livingston came back, he brought confirmation that Talleyrand had not been merely talking off the top of his head and that Napoleon himself was the author of the offer to sell the Louisiana Territory. The price would be 1 million francs. Actually it would be much more because the United States would be expected to pay the spoliation claims of its own citizens, a total of 25 million francs.

When told this, Livingston said, he had feigned surprise and declared such an expenditure out of the question. What the United States really wanted, he had said, was New Orleans and the Floridas. For those it would pay 10 million francs. Barbé-Marbois had insisted on a bid for the entire territory, implying that 85,000 francs, 60,000 for the land and 25,000 for the spoliation claims, just might be acceptable.

The two Americans' roles in the negotiation were not clearly defined. Livingston was the American Minister but Monroe was the Minister Extraordinary and had conferred much more recently with the President and Secretary of State. The Virginian assumed leadership. He instructed Livingston to make no actual offer. But he might suggest, Monroe said, that the United States might be willing to buy the Louisiana Territory for 10 million francs if France would give up all claims to the Floridas and back American claims to them against the Spaniards. Such an offer might well be viewed as colossal impudence. The sum of 10 million francs was precisely what Livingston had just offered for the comparatively small regions east of the Mississippi. But Monroe gambled that Napoleon, on the eve of war with the British, was eager to divest himself of New World responsibilities.

In the following week both Americans met with Barbé-Marbois and other

Frenchmen. The French seemed to regard the Americans' bold tactics as juvenile impudence. There were signs that Bonaparte's resistance might be hardening.

Actually, Napoleon was wavering on the whole idea of selling Louisiana. Talleyrand, tactfully, and Napoleon's brothers Joseph and Lucien, bluntly, tried to deflect Bonaparte from any plan to part with the great Western territory. Even the First Consul's bathtub was not a refuge from his brothers' importunities. They burst in upon him and berated him for thinking about betraying the national interest.[28]

The air was heavy with the scent of cologne in the First Consul's bath, but it did not sweeten his disposition.

"I flatter myself," Lucien ventured, "that the Chambers will not give their consent."

"You flatter yourself!" said Napoleon, And then, half murmuring to himself, "That is precious, in truth."

"And I too flatter myself as I have already told the First Consul," said Joseph.

"And what did I answer?" Napoleon demanded.

"That you would do without the Chambers," Joseph said.

"Precisely! That is what I have taken the great liberty to tell Mr. Joseph, and what I now repeat to the Citizen Lucien. . . . I shall do without the consent of anyone whomsoever. Do you understand?"

Joseph stepped closer to the tub. "And you will do well, my dear brother," he said, "not to expose your project to parliamentary discussion; for I declare to you that if necessary I will put myself first at the head of the opposition which will not fail to be made against you."

With an angry laugh Napoleon retorted, "You will have no need to lead the opposition, for I repeat that there will be no debate, for the reason that the project which has not the fortune to meet your approval, conceived by me, negotiated by me, shall be ratified and executed by me alone. Do you comprehend? By me, who laugh at your opposition!"

"Good!" Joseph yelled, "I'll tell you, General, that you, I, and all of us, if you do what you threaten, may prepare ourselves soon to go and join the poor innocent devils whom you so legally, humanely, and especially with such justice, have . . . [sentenced]."

Raising himself, Napoleon shouted, "You are insolent! I ought ————." Then he threw himself back, smacking the water with a force that drenched Joseph and Lucien.

The valet, silent through the whole discussion, fell fainting to the floor.

Joseph left to change his clothes, but Lucien continued to talk as Napoleon dried off and dressed. The First Consul was calmer, perhaps mollified by enjoyment of his brothers' dripping state.

But the argument soon returned to its angry pitch. "If I were not your brother," said Lucien, "I would be your enemy."

"My enemy!" exclaimed the First Consul, advancing as if to strike him. "You my enemy! I would break you, look, like this box!" He hurled his snuffbox to the floor.

Even a naked Napoleon was more than a match for Joseph and Lucien arrayed in uniforms of state. Beneath their bemedaled elegance they were only his brothers and even in the nude, he, the great Napoleon, was clothed in majesty. The arrogance of a nation half a world away was more tolerable than impudence in his own family. Besides, he was impatient to get to the business of fighting England and of creating obstructions to her imperialist ambitions in North America. Napoleon dismissed his brothers and their advice.

For many years historians believed that Joseph and Lucien had been inspired by patriotism to risk a confrontation with their high-tempered brother, but we now know that they had been bribed by British interests.[29]

Next negotiations were slowed by another cause—Monroe's untimely illness. Monroe continued to guide Livingston, but the New Yorker had to carry the burden of the conferences with the French.

The Americans were anxious about making a purchase not authorized by their government. But consultation with Washington would consume months and such a lengthy delay might cost them the opportunity to obtain a monumental bargain from the mercurial Napoleon. Under these circumstances, Livingston does not seem to have chafed at sharing responsibility with Monroe.

The illness that kept Monroe from participating in the actual conferences could have been used by the French as an excuse for delay. The Virginian knew that the French were eager to reach agreement when, on April 27, Barbé-Marbois accompanied Livingston to Monroe's quarters. The Finance Minister presented an official proposal embodying the original terms of 100 million francs and 20 million more for the spoliations. He obviously had carefully planned for psychological effect. As the Americans reiterated that the price was unacceptable, the Frenchman confided that he thought so too. He then pulled from his pocket another proposal, saying this one was his own. He hoped that, if the Americans accepted it, his own government would. This one provided for payment of 80 million francs by the United States, and the sum for spoliation would be included in the total. The Americans agreed to consider it.[30]

Later, Livingston prepared a counterproposal, pressing for further advantages. Monroe considered it "very loosely drawn" but, in his illness, did not attempt to edit it.

Two days later, when Monroe was a little stronger, he and Livingston called on Barbé-Marbois with the new proposition. The Finance Minister firmly refused it, and the Americans agreed to the proposal that he had described as his own.

Several days later Monroe was ushered into Napoleon's presence. The lanky Virginian towered above the First Consul. But mesmerizing fires burned in the dark eyes that punctuated Bonaparte's pale face, and one knew at once that he was energy incarnate. "Our affairs should be settled," he said.

And settled they were in record time. The next day a treaty in French ceding Louisiana to the United States was signed. The price was 60 million francs. English-language copies were signed several days later. A little later the United States signed a convention agreeing to settle its spoliation claims against France for 20 million francs, and make restitution to its own citizens.

Then the United States won the opportunity to acquire, for 80 million francs or approximately $15 million in its own currency, the vast territory between Canada and Mexico which stretched westward from the great Father of Waters to the towering Rockies. At the stroke of a pen the United States won the chance to double its size at a price of about $18 a square mile.

Whether it actually would remained problematical. The boundaries of the territory were conjectural. The treaty defined them as "the same extent that is now in the hands of Spain." That reference raised another sticking point: France was offering to sell lands not yet in her possession and which a treaty with Spain forbade France to sell even after acquisition. The American negotiators also worried about what Jefferson would do. He had written and talked much about the necessity of adhering to the Constitution. Nothing in the Constitution seemed to provide for the President to acquire territory from a foreign power without the consent of Congress. Yet any delay might forever cost the United States the opportunity to acquire the Western lands.

Livingston repeatedly pressed Talleyrand for a definition of the eastern boundaries of the territory and was repeatedly told, "I do not know." At length the American asked, "Then you mean that we shall construe it our own way?" The Frenchman replied: "I can give you no direction. You have made a noble bargain for yourselves, and I suppose you will make the most of it."[31]

Other questions brought from Talleyrand the disturbing opinion that the Floridas were not included. There was slight consolation in the information that Napoleon would support the United States in negotiations to obtain them from Spain. Even this minuscule reassurance was further diminished by the First Consul's unwillingness to put his pledge into writing. Livingston and Monroe would have been incensed if they could have overheard Napoleon tell Barbé-Marbois, "If an obscurity did not already exist, it would perhaps be good policy to put one there."[32]

Extracting an amazing amount of assurance from paltry materials, Livingston and Monroe wrote Madison that it was "incontrovertible that West Florida is comprised in the cession of Louisiana."[33]

American worries that France had no right to sell the Louisiana Territory were soon justified. Learning of the secret agreement with the United States, Spain protested to France that it was not only premature but a violation of the Franco-Spanish treaty. Furthermore, Spain's Ambassador told Talleyrand, the pact with the Americans "deranges from top to bottom the whole colonial system of Spain, and even of Europe."[34]

Napoleon, never mated to truth, said that he had acted as he had because the Spanish had broken their promise to him to sustain the Intendant at New Orleans in denying Americans the right of deposit. By reversing her own colonial representative and restoring that privilege to Americans, Spain had made all of Louisiana less valuable to France.[35]

Much worse from the American standpoint was the word in Paris that Napoleon already regretted the terms of his bargain with the United States. Bonaparte said that the United States had been granted for the payment of spoliations an amount four times the actual sum. French ratification of the agreement, he now insisted, should not have been handed to Livingston and

Monroe but sent to the French Minister in Washington to hold until it could be exchanged for the United States ratification. He also warned that failure to meet a single deadline of the treaty would void the entire agreement.

Livingston bypassed Secretary of State Madison to warn Jefferson directly that he must not only adhere rigidly to the prescribed schedule but also prevent even the most minute change in the ratification. "Be assured," he said, "that the slightest pretense will be seized to undo the work." He also instructed Jefferson, "We must as far as we can soothe the young Conqueror whose will knows no resistance."[36]

In the humidity of a Washington June, Jefferson impatiently—and at times not too hopefully—awaited word of the negotiations in Paris. Sometimes he thought his two envoys might be able to purchase New Orleans and the Floridas. At other times he was not even sure they would be able to obtain the port city alone. Obtaining anything more than New Orleans and the Floridas seemed impossible.

Vexations of the flesh were added to those of the spirit. Avoiding fish did not cure his diarrhea. He decided that horseback riding helped—and it may have if only because the outdoor exercise reduced the tensions of office. For a man who so liked to be liked, dealing with officeseekers, a business sure to offend more people than it pleased, was painful. And anxieties over the negotiations with Bonaparte denied him peace.

Even thoughts of Monticello, which ordinarily led to tranquility, now were involved with matters that fretted him. Acting through an agent in an effort to conceal his own interest in acquiring four acres from a neighbor whose property adjoined his own, Jefferson found it difficult to make the payments. The neighbor, one Bennett Henderson, sued. Furthermore, he dammed a stream that had powered Jefferson's mill and built a canal to direct other waters from the mill wheel.

This problem underlined Jefferson's financial plight. Not only was there the burden of past debts, but for the year ending March 4, 1803, his income from all sources—his salary as President, his crops, his rents, and his nailery—amounted to $26,446.99, or $1,273.93 less than his debts for the same period.[37]

When Jefferson received the treaty early in July, its astonishing provisions drove smaller subjects from his mind. His problems were suddenly magnified but so were his opportunities. He was seized with uncertainty but galvanized with excitement. Whether the Floridas were securely within the document's provisions was somewhat doubtful despite the assurances of Livingston and Monroe. But New Orleans was definitely included and so—wonder of wonders—was the whole of the Louisiana Territory.

Personally, and through Madison, Jefferson had told Livingston and Monroe to negotiate for New Orleans and the Floridas. The United States, he had said, would be justified in paying up to $2 million. Instead of what he had modestly hoped for, he was offered a land as big as the United States itself. With this addition, the American republic would stretch from the Atlantic to the Pacific. Into the resulting empire Great Britain would fit eighteen times with room to spare. But the price was almost as staggering as the magnitude of the property. No longer was $2 million the figure; it would have to be $16 million.

On the other hand even that sum would be a bargain price for so rich and promising a piece of real estate.

Then, though, there was the disturbing uncertainty about whether the Floridas really were included. If Jefferson did push the purchase of Louisiana, the representatives of the Western states probably would go along because of their anxiety about the Mississippi. If there was doubt about getting the Floridas, however, there might be a cooling of the Southern ardor for acquisition. On the other hand, if Jefferson hesitated, with Bonaparte reportedly looking for an excuse to break the agreement, a great opportunity might be lost forever.

But he almost had to hesitate. He was the mastermind of the Virginia and Kentucky Resolutions that had so forcefully attacked federal assumption of powers not granted in the Constitution. To friend and foe alike he was the nation's foremost symbol of the philosophy of strict construction. He was also its most dedicated practitioner of governmental economy. To purchase the Louisiana Territory he would have to approve the most stupendous expenditure in the history of the republic and act without specific constitutional authorization.

His quandary was broken in upon by the protestations and importunities of Senators and Congressmen. Most seemed to be contradicting their own oft-stated philosophical convictions. Republicans, because of their concern with the frontier and their assumption that the new states to be formed would be Republican, called upon the President to seize the opportunity. Federalists shared the same assumption and were stirred by it to a frenzy of opposition. Ironically, though most of them had been broad constructionists, they now raised questions of constitutional propriety.

Jefferson, though indicating at least partial agreement with Gallatin's argument that the Constitution indirectly conferred the power to acquire new lands, still felt uncomfortable without direct constitutional authorization. He therefore proposed to the cabinet an amendment to the Constitution. He submitted to them two separate drafts, each of which provided specifically for the incorporation of the Louisiana Territory into the United States and conferred upon the federal government jurisdictional powers comparable to those exercised in the Northwest Territory.[38]

It soon became obvious that delaying the purchase until an amendment could be obtained would doom the entire enterprise. At a cabinet meeting on July 16 the President and the department heads agreed that it would be necessary to act first and then obtain congressional ratification. The President would convene Congress on October 17 to secure approval.

At least partly to placate Congress, and perhaps also partly because of his fears of too frequent resort to broad construction of the Constitution, Jefferson included a special provision in the amendment that he proposed. This was that no new state should be created in the area north of the Arkansas River's mouth, and no land grants issued for that territory except to the Indians in exchange for lands presently occupied by them, before specific authorization by another constitutional amendment. On Madison's advice, he added a proviso that Florida, when "rightfully obtained," should also become part of the United States.

Perhaps, in addition to his other reasons for proposing these provisions, Jefferson wished to commit the federal government to a policy of national expansion. In a few months he would confide his hope that when the United States was fully populated east of the Mississippi, "We may lay off a range of states on the western bank from the head to the mouth, and so, range after range, advancing compactly as we multiply."[39]

Senator Wilson Cary Nicholas of Virginia urged the President not to call for supportive constitutional amendments after the fact, as to do so would be tantamount to admitting that the administration had exceeded its constitutional authority. Nicholas insisted on a generous interpretation that gave the President every power to act in adding territory to the United States.[40] Jefferson liked and admired Nicholas, but the Senator's advice in this instance had no influence on the President. Its chief significance was in eliciting from Jefferson not only an explanation of the practical difficulties of his position but also a memorable statement of his theories of constitutional government.

First Jefferson said, "Whatever Congress shall think it necessary to do, should be done with as little debate as possible, and particularly so far as respects the constitutional difficulty." Then he discussed the broad context of the problem:

> When an instrument admits two constructions, the one safe, the other dangerous, the one precise, the other indefinite, I prefer that which is safe and precise. I had rather ask an enlargement of power from the nation where it is found necessary, than to assume it by a construction which would make our powers boundless. Our peculiar security is in possession of a written Constitution. Let us not make it a blank paper by construction.[41]

He foresaw, however, that the Constitution would not be adequate for all exigencies if it were left unaltered as the years passed. "Let us go on then perfecting it," he said, "by adding, by way of amendment to the Constitution, those powers which time and trial show are still wanting. . . ."

But Jefferson was no ideologue. Although he told Nicholas, "I confess then I think it important in the present case to set an example against broad construction by appealing for new power to the people," he added: "If, however, our friends shall think differently, certainly I shall acquiesce with satisfaction, confiding that the good sense of our country will correct the evil of [broad] construction when it shall produce ill effects."

Events within one week made it advisable for the President to abandon his original plan for a constitutional amendment and to demonstrate that capacity for compromise to which he had alluded in correspondence with Nicholas. The Marqués de Casa Yrujo, Spanish Minister to the United States, wrote Secretary of State Madison that the King of Spain was surprised to learn of French negotiations with the United States over Louisiana, as the French had promised never to sell the territory and in fact had no right to sell it.

Jefferson feared that Spain intended to deliver New Orleans to the United States as a sop while holding fast to the rest of Louisiana.[42] Madison counseled reassuringly that Spain probably sought only to gain some advantage from the United States in return for consent to the purchase or might even be maneuvering to contest the boundaries of the territory without seriously attempting to nullify the sale. But Jefferson was not easily reassured on this point. He had the Secretary of State ask the American Consul in New Orleans to report on the strength of Spanish forces in the area.

Jefferson's anxiety was increased when Madison received a second letter from Yrujo strongly reasserting the claims of the first and protesting additionally that the sale by France was illegal because the French had never fulfilled their obligations under the Treaty of San Ildefonso. With the President's approval, the Secretary of State temperately rejected Spanish claims that the sale was void but did not enter into any discussion of French conduct. Madison's letter pointedly reminded Yrujo that earlier the Spanish government had officially notified the American Minister in Madrid that Spain had retroceded Louisiana to France and that the United States should negotiate with Napoleon on any matters concerning the territory.

Jefferson was still taking no chances on the seriousness of Spanish intentions. On October 4 he met with the Secretaries of State, Treasury, and War, and they agreed with him that the United States should prepare immediately to use armed force if it should prove necessary. American forces in the Mississippi Territory were alerted for combat readiness although their commanders were told to avoid alarming actions.

If the President had thought earlier that "whatever Congress shall think it necessary to do should be done with as little debate as possible," the difficulties with Spain rendered promptness even more imperative. The message that Jefferson sent to Congress on October 17 did not press for an amendment to the Constitution.[43] This was no time to suggest that the administration's actions might have been unconstitutional and to open a full-scale debate on the philosophical premises of the Constitution. Jefferson simply presented to Congress the *fait accompli* of the treaty, saying that now it was necessary only for the Senate to exercise its constitutional power of ratification and for the House to provide the funds necessary for purchase. Acquisition of the Louisiana Territory would increase the public debt by $13 million. Jefferson had already greatly reduced federal expenditures and he now proposed a particularly sharp reduction in naval funds. If rigorous economy were practiced, the growing wealth of the nation, increasing with its population, should take care of the interest and eventually the principal of the debt without the levying of new taxes. He believed that, even with the threat of conflict with Spain, defense expenditures could be reduced because, as he wrote Benjamin Rush, the two greatest European powers would soon be entirely occupied in fighting each other. He hoped England would destroy France's power of "tyrannizing . . . over the earth" and France would end England's power to "tyrannize . . . over" the waters.[44]

Jefferson watched the ensuing congressional debates with concern but certainly not with paralyzing anxiety. To friends the President had explained earlier that he must first conclude the treaty and then in effect say to Congress: "I pretend no right to bind you. You may disavow me, and I must get out of the scrape as best I can. I thought it my duty to risk myself for you." But, he said, Congress would have to ratify his actions, "casting behind them metaphysical subtleties." And, he said, "We shall not be disavowed by the nation, and their act of indemnity will confirm and not weaken the Constitution, by more strongly marking out its lines."[45] This "metaphysical" President, as he had shown before in dealing with the Barbary pirates, could be bolder in pursuit of national goals than some who proudly called themselves "hardheaded" men.

In the Senate debate, Virginia's Senator John Taylor of Caroline, one of America's principal strict constructionists, echoed publicly his President's private reasoning. "I have no doubt our envoys had no authority to make such a treaty and that it is a violation of the Constitution," he said, "but I will, like an attorney who exceeds the authority delegated to him by his client, vote to ratify it and then throw myself on the people for pardon."[46] When the formal vote on the treaty was taken in the Senate on October 20, every Federalist present but one voted against it, but ratification rolled in on a Republican tide, 24 to 7.

Now it remained for the House to provide means to implement the annexation made possible by Senate ratification. One might have supposed that action in the House of Representatives, where the Republican majority was even more vehement than in the Senate, would be even swifter and more decisive than in the upper chamber. Such was not the case. The House did not even begin the debate on the treaty until October 24, four days after the Senate had ratified it. And then the initiative came from Federalist opponents rather than Republican supporters. The challenge was issued by Representative Gaylord Griswold of New York when he moved that the President be called upon to furnish the House all documents "tending to ascertain whether the United States have, in fact, acquired any title to the province of Louisiana by the treaties with France." Spain could not have hoped for better cooperation.

As Republican majority leader, John Randolph led the fight against the motion. As many of his party remained more loyal to Republican precedents than to the Republican label, he saw his majority melt steadily until the motion was blocked by a vote of only 59 to 57.

When debate began on the treaty proper, Griswold questioned the constitutionality of the provision for attainment of citizenship by residents of Louisiana. Federalists feared the potential addition of the predominantly Republican Western population to the national electorate.

Randolph taunted Griswold with trying to block the treaty after having earlier advocated that the United States seize New Orleans by force. "Can a nation acquire by force," he demanded, "what she cannot acquire by treaty?"

The Federalists now urged strict construction while the Republicans argued for a broad interpretation. It was as though the Federalists and Republicans had emerged from the cloakrooms with switched scripts.

The situation became even more confused when the House received a Senate motion to grant the President authority to take possession of Louisiana, using armed forces in the process, and to direct the civil, judicial, and military administration of the new territory pending permanent provisions by Congress. The most vehement opponent of this motion was the majority leader of the President's own party—John Randolph himself. Drawing himself up to his full, willowy height, he shrilled: "If we give this power out of our hands, . . . the Executive branch, with a small minority of either house, may prevent its resumption."

The Federalists quickly moved to strike the grant of authority. A freshman Representative, Jefferson's son-in-law John Eppes, reminded the House of the danger of permitting anarchy for even a short time. What powers might move to fill the vacuum? But another Republican replied that he had rather accept that risk than act "against the Constitution or principles that have long been respected."

Understandably worried, Jefferson did not reproach Randolph but sent him the French originals of the treaty, saying that he did so lest there be doubts about the English translation. Randolph replied that he did not need them and continued to fight the Senate motion. But eventually, despite Randolph, the motion carried.

The House provided the means for the annexation made possible by Senate ratification of the treaty. The next day, October 29, Jefferson ordered five hundred regulars and one thousand volunteers from the territory to assume possession of Louisiana. He also called for six thousand volunteers from Kentucky and Tennessee.

Impressed with American determination abetted by Napoleon's resolve, Spain rather surlily yielded New Orleans and Louisiana to France. On December 20, 1803, in ceremonies at New Orleans, the French tricolor was lowered and another red, white, and blue ensign, the flag of the United States, was raised amid thunderous cheers.

Anticipating the event, Jefferson had boasted to his old friend John Page that the United States would have more cultivable land than any other civilized nation.[47] He dreamed of a national destiny appropriate to his country's new dimensions.

2

As early as November 1802, when Spain still exercised sovereignty over Louisiana, Jefferson had asked the Spanish Minister, the Marqués de Casa Yrujo, if Spain would "take it badly" if the United States sent a small party into the territory to "explore the course of the Missouri River." To satisfy constitutional requirements, the President said, congressional authorization would have to be in the name of promotion of commerce, though "in reality it would have no other view than the advancement of the geography."[48]

The President's informal, seemingly confidential approach was not unusual in his dealings with the Spanish envoy. John Adams' Secretary of State, Timothy Pickering, had asked for Yrujo's dismissal, but Jefferson, on becoming President, had requested his retention and thereby had won a friend. Nevertheless, the Marqués considered it his duty to protect Spanish interests in the territory as long as it still belonged to Spain. He told the President that "an expedition of this nature could not fail to give umbrage to our government."[49]

Jefferson, according to the Spaniard's report to Madrid, replied that he did not see why the Spanish "should have the least fear." The purpose of the expedition would be "to observe the territories which are found between 40° and 60° from the mouth of the Missouri to the Pacific Ocean" and add fresh discoveries to those made in 1793 by Alexander Mackenzie. Especially it would be desirable to discover whether a Northwest Passage existed—a continuous waterway to the South Sea or at least one interrupted only by short portages.[50]

Yrujo argued that the question had already been settled by Spanish, French, British, and other explorations. The legendary Northwest Passage was precisely that. A "considerable cordillera" lay athwart the route to the Pacific, and Indians questioned by Mackenzie had said that they knew of no navigable river flowing from the mountains to the Pacific. Actually, the Spaniard had exaggerated negative aspects of the available information. The Marqués assured his government that "this account of the useless and fruitless attempts, it seems to me, calmed [the President's] spirit."[51]

The diplomat, however, was not completely confident of the sedative effect of his words. He added to his report: "The President has been all his life a man of letters, very speculative and a lover of glory, and it would be possible he might attempt to perpetuate the fame of his administration not only by the measures of frugality and economy which characterize him, but also by discovering or at least attempting to discover the way by which the Americans may some day extend their population and their influence up to the coasts of the South Sea."

This report was written in December 1802. On January 31, 1803, the Minister confessed to his government that the President had "communicated his design to the Senate, which has already taken a step toward the execution."[52] If a portrait by Gilbert Stuart is to be trusted, the Marqués, with his lifted eyebrows and uptilted nose and chin, could have been typecast as the complacent dandy in a Restoration comedy. Certainly his complacency was unshaken by the latest developments in Washington. Despite the Senate's initiative in support of the President, Yrujo was sure that its "good judgement" would perceive no such advantages in an expedition as the President conceived. The Senators, he said, were aware that such an undertaking "might offend one of the European nations." He thought it probable that "the project will not proceed."

Actually, Jefferson's plans were much farther advanced than the Spaniard supposed. The President had submitted the proposal in a secret message to

Congress on January 18 requesting a $2,500 appropriation for an expedition to ascend the Missouri River to its source and proceed from there to the Pacific. Officially, the expedition would be "for the purpose of extending the external commerce of the United States."[53] Jefferson said that the valuable fur trade now moving from the Missouri country to the Pacific over northern routes frozen in the winter and involving numerous portages could be moved across the United States instead of Canada if a southern route were discovered. The boost for commerce on the Mississippi would be great. In fact, discovery of such a route would open the West to commerce moving along the Ohio, the Susquehanna, the Potomac, and the James. Moved by patriotism, cupidity, and a modicum of intellectual curiosity, the House quickly passed the appropriation and the Senate promptly concurred.

Actually, Jefferson's motivation was threefold: to gain for the United States Britain's immensely profitable Canadian fur trade, to promote development of the Louisiana Territory as an integral part of the United States, and to add to the sum of human knowledge. Doubtless these purposes were never completely separate in his mind.

In his book *Voyages from Montreal* Mackenzie had urged the necessity for vigorous efforts to find a water route to the northwest coast of North America before the Americans did, so that Britain could claim for herself "the entire command of the fur trade of North America" from "48° north to the Pole." England could accomplish this purpose "by opening this intercourse between the Atlantic and Pacific Oceans, and forming regular establishments through the interior and at both extremes, as well as along the coasts and islands."[54] Such action on Britain's part would block not only the commercial, but also the political, ambitions of the United States. It is easy to see why Jefferson could not wait for completion of the Louisiana Purchase before obtaining authorization for the exploratory expedition.

On June 20, about two months after the signing of the Louisiana Treaty in Paris but nearly four months before its submission to the United States Senate, Jefferson issued to Meriwether Lewis formal instructions for conduct of the expedition.[55]

"The object of your mission," the President wrote, "is to explore the Missouri River, and such principal streams of it as, by its course and communication with the waters of the Pacific Ocean, may offer the most direct and practicable water communication across this continent for the purposes of commerce." Ancillary to this assignment were the tasks of obtaining precise information about the branches of the river and the topography of adjacent lands. Jefferson asked many questions about "the soil and face of the country"; its flora, fauna, and minerals; its climate; and its Indian inhabitants, including their numbers, their relations with other tribes, their languages and traditions, diseases and remedies, laws and customs, and "articles of commerce they may need or furnish." He added, "It will be useful to acquire what knowledge you can of the state of morality, religion, and information among them, as it may better enable those who endeavor to civilize and instruct them to adapt their measures to the existing notions and practices of those on whom they are to operate."

He admonished: "In all your intercourse with the natives treat them in the most friendly and conciliatory manner which their own conduct will admit. . . . Make them acquainted with. . . our wish to be neighborly, friendly, and useful to them, and of our dispositions to a commercial intercourse with them; confer with them on the points most convenient as mutual emporiums, and the articles of most desirable interchange for them and us."

Jefferson believed that the aborigines might benefit from some of the arts of civilization, but also that they were fellow beings deserving respect, knowledgeable about their own needs, and capable of teaching some lessons to white people. He occupied a middle ground between fellow litterateurs who saw the Indians as noble savages untainted by civilization and other political leaders who saw them as brutes fit for exploitation. Jefferson remembered sitting at dinner with Indian chiefs in his father's home and, as a student at William and Mary, listening transfixed to the oratory of the great sachem Outassete.[56] Of the oratory of a Mingo chief, he had written in *Notes on Virginia*, "I may challenge the whole orations of Demosthenes and Cicero, and of any more eminent orator, if Europe has furnished any more eminent, to produce a single passage superior to the speech of Logan."[57]

Jefferson's battery of questions suggests that he sought a report as detailed as his own *Notes on Virginia*, a work whose completeness as well as insightfulness had captured the admiration of Europe's principal intellects. The leaders of the Missouri expedition would be covering a vaster territory than Jefferson had described in his book and would have to make their notes amid untold hardships and dangers. But there would be two of them whereas he had written his book alone and as Governor in days of British invasion, when his saddle was the Commonwealth's seat of government.

Though the instructions for the expedition bore the stamp of Jefferson's far-ranging and insatiable intellect, the enterprise's mingling of scholarly concerns with commercial aspirations was not unique in its time.

The late J. Christopher Herold, discussing ideas prevalent in the Western world in the early years of the nineteenth century, wrote: "Although the heroic era of discoveries was long past, the earth was now beginning to be explored systematically. Captain Cook's last expedition, with its carefully selected personnel and equipment, had set an example to the later explorers. Alexander von Humboldt's exploration of the South American continent was entirely scientific in character; the observations made by him and his French companion Bonpland were equally valuable to meteorology, geology, botany, and zoology. Even Bonaparte's Egyptian campaign . . . yielded important scientific, ethnological, and archaeological information. Mungo Park explored the totally unknown interior of central Africa; the Lewis and Clark expedition, due to Jefferson's initiative, opened up the North American continent to United States expansionism and at the same time made contributions to physical geography and ethnology. It was by no means accidental that the first systematic hypothesis of the origin of the earth, James Hutton's *Theory of the Earth*, should appear about that time, in 1795."[58]

Meriwether Lewis was an extraordinarily appropriate choice for the leader of Jefferson's expedition. A captain of the First Infantry, U.S.A., he had been on detached duty since Jefferson's inauguration, serving officially as the President's secretary. Actually, as we have seen, he had lived in the Executive Mansion, where his studies in preparation for his career as explorer of the Louisiana Territory had been carefully supervised by the President himself. Jefferson, who relied much on familiar blood lines in both horses and people, was reassured by the fact that Lewis sprang from an old Virginia family in his own county of Albemarle. He had known the young man personally for most of his twenty-nine years.

Lewis's preparation for his historic role had begun long before his service in Jefferson's administration. His military experience was a great asset. And he had long anticipated such an opportunity. As early as 1793 he had sought inclusion in a more modest attempt at westward exploration. Besides having acquired the wilderness skills expected of a good frontiersman and the boating skills of a competent riverman, he had trained in Philadelphia, then the center of scientific investigation in the United States, in botany, zoology, and celestial navigation. He also was a student of diplomatic and commercial factors affecting development of his native continent. Added to these qualifications was a passionate devotion to abstract reasoning and philosophical contemplation that enabled him to communicate to Jefferson the combination of factual and speculative knowledge on which the President so avidly fed.[59]

No one is ideally cast for any complexly demanding role. For all his virtues of mind and character, Lewis often had to fight private battles with depression. Sometimes outbursts of temper punctuated his usually friendly demeanor.

Lewis had a Virginia friend whose qualities complemented his own. William Clark, younger brother of General George Rogers Clark, conqueror of the Northwest Territory in the Revolution, was a frontier soldier of equable temperament and an engagingly outgoing personality. Though less abstractly intellectual than Lewis, he had a quick and active intelligence and great practical competence in many things. He could not match Lewis's mastery of celestial navigation, but he excelled him in the actual handling of boats and was an expert engineer and geographer. And while Lewis carried in his head the panoply of diplomatic and economic considerations lending international significance to the projected expedition, Clark was unequaled in trading and negotiating with the Indians. Lewis asked Jefferson to name Clark to coequal command of the expedition.

The President feared trouble from a divided command, but Lewis pleaded and Jefferson acquiesced. He tried to commission Clark a captain, but the soldier emerged from a tangle of War Department red tape as a second lieutenant in the Corps of Artillerists. Even in those times the federal bureaucracy thwarted the intentions of Chief Executives. Neither Jefferson nor Lewis, however, was easily turned from the accomplishment of a set purpose. Clark functioned as coequal head of the expedition and signed orders as "captain."

Bernard DeVoto, a distinguished scholar of Western exploration, says: "The two agreed and worked together with a mutuality unknown elsewhere in the history of exploration and rare in any kind of human association. . . . Both were men of great intelligence, of distinguished intelligence. The entire previous history of North American exploration contains no one who could be called their intellectual equal."[60]

Lewis left Washington for Louisville, Kentucky, where he joined Clark. Together they proceeded to St. Louis, arriving in December. Encamping at the mouth of Wood River on the eastern side of the Mississippi, they prepared to spend the winter in planning and training for the expedition. Their party consisted of nine young Kentuckians, fourteen volunteers from the United States Army, two French watermen, an interpreter and hunter, and Clark's black servant. The two captains, like their President, realized that their force had the opportunity to make history on a scale seldom attained by such a mere handful of men.

3

Despite Jefferson's enthusiasm for the Lewis and Clark expedition, his attention in 1803 was often drawn to another small group of men whose history-making potential was great—the Supreme Court under the leadership of Chief Justice Marshall. Jefferson himself spent a great deal of time searching and exploring—for precedents in the law and in history to aid him in meeting the challenge of *Marbury* v. *Madison*.[61]

Ever since William Marbury had instituted suit in the Supreme Court against Secretary of State Madison for failure to deliver President Adams' "midnight appointment" of the plaintiff as a justice of peace, Marshall too had done a good deal of worrying and searching. Jefferson had been enraged by his predecessor's attempt to pack the judiciary with Federalists in the last hours of his administration. Marshall was an avowed Federalist and had been Adams' Secretary of State. The Chief Justice was animated both by partisan zealotry and an intense devotion to the principle of an independent judiciary. The contest between the executive and judicial branches was aggravated by the long-standing rivalry between the President and the Chief Justice—Virginia cousins who embodied antipodal philosophies.

In pleading Marbury's case, Charles Lee, former Attorney General of the United States, argued that the Supreme Court had the authority to issue a writ of mandamus requiring the administration to deliver the appointment. He then argued that justice demanded issuance of such a writ because, once the appointment had been granted, the officers of the succeeding administration had no legal right to withhold it from the appointee.

Marshall was convinced that Marbury had a vested right to the appointment and that failure to release it was an unlawful act. But the case was far from simple. If the Court issued a writ of mandamus commanding the Secretary of State to deliver the commission to Marbury, the President would surely instruct his Secretary to disregard the order. Who then could compel the President to obey? Rather than asserting judicial dignity, such action by the Court would demonstrate judicial impotence. Yet even if conscience permitted Marshall to rule that Marbury did not have a vested right, he would then be saying that Jefferson had been right all along in the controversy—and such a decision would be unthinkable.

Tension was high on February 24, 1803, when Marshall delivered the opinion of the Court. The Chief Justice's rumpled appearance in everyday life frequently made him an unprepossessing figure but, clothed in the majesty of his judicial robes, he had a long-faced, broad-browed dignity that was imposing. From his elevated seat, he peered with a penetrating gaze that many attorneys found unnerving. He once privately cited as a requisite for judicial success "the ability to look a lawyer straight in the eyes for two hours and not hear a damned word he says."[62]

In his usually deliberate manner Marshall first addressed himself to the question of whether Marbury was entitled to the commission. He asserted on behalf of the Court that Marbury indeed had a right and asked, "Is it to be contended that the heads of departments are not amenable to the laws of their country?" He thus summoned in support of his position the ancient English principle that even the sovereign does not stand above the law.

Spectators noted with rising excitement that the Chief Justice seemed to be inviting a head-on collision with the President. This impression was strengthened when Marshall asked rhetorically whether Marbury was entitled to remedy under the law and concluded that he was.

Finally, the Chief Justice addressed the question of whether the proper remedy was a writ of mandamus from the Supreme Court. A collision appeared inevitable. Then Marshall abruptly swerved. "The province of the court," he said, "is, solely, to decide on the rights of individuals, not to inquire how the executive, or executive officers, perform duties in which they have a discretion. Questions in their nature political, or which are, by the Constitution and laws, submitted to the executive, can never be made in this court."

Astonishment prevailed among all not originally privy to the Chief Justice's deliberations. It took awhile for people to comprehend what he had accomplished.

The first shrewd move by Marshall in rendering the opinion of the Court was to reverse the order in which the attorney for the plaintiff had addressed the questions involved. Charles Lee had first considered whether the Court had the authority to issue a writ of mandamus ordering delivery of the appointment. Marshall had put off this question to the last. In this way, even though he asserted that the Court had no jurisdiction in the case, he would still be able to discuss the questions of the applicant's right to the commission and of his right to legal remedy. Thus, without having to undertake the frustrating procedure of ordering the Executive to grant the commission, he was able to portray the Republican President and Secretary of State as lawbreakers.

This accomplishment was a shrewd one. But Marshall had gone beyond it to a monumental achievement. He had declared that, despite acts of Congress seeming to empower the Court to act in such cases, the judiciary in fact had no jurisdiction. What appeared superficially to be a modest renunciation of authority was really a tremendous assumption of dominion. The Chief Justice had just asserted a sweeping power of judicial review—the authority to set aside, as unconstitutional, legislation passed by the Congress.

Marshall concluded "that a law repugnant to the Constitution is void, and that courts, as well as other departments, are bound by that instrument." The concept enunciated by Marshall was not completely new. The justices of Virginia's counties of Northampton and Accomack in 1766 had declared the Stamp Act void and therefore unconstitutional.[63] Edmund Pendleton, presiding justice of the court in Caroline County, Virginia, and later Virginia's highest judge, refused to rule on any contentions arising out of the Stamp Act, saying that it was not law, owing to "want of power (I mean constitutional authority) in the Parliament to pass it."[64] The Virginia and Kentucky Resolutions instigated by Jefferson in 1798 asserted the right of state legislatures to declare acts of Congress unconstitutional.

When Marshall rendered the Court's decision in *Marbury* v. *Madison* his enunciation of the concept of judicial review of congressional acts stirred far less contention than his implied criticism of Madison and Jefferson. Hardly anyone—not even Jefferson—seems at the time to have believed that Marshall was laying claim for the Supreme Court to a monopoly of the process by which an act of Congress could be declared unconstitutional. What could bar exercise of the same right by the President?

4

However much Americans—including the extraordinarily prescient Jefferson—failed to appreciate the full ramifications of events in 1803, they knew it to be an *annus mirabilis*. Any year would be an extraordinary one in United States history that saw, besides an epic struggle between a giant President and a giant Chief Justice, the peaceful doubling of United States territory by acquisition of all lands between the Mississippi and the Rockies, north to Canada and south to Mexico, and that saw also the launching of an exploration of those lands that, if successful, would be a major achievement of the human mind and spirit. Small wonder that, with such a trinity of events in the forefront, Americans took little note of the activities of their countryman Robert Fulton, who, in the same year in distant France, launched on the Seine a ship propelled by steam.

VI

PRIVATE LOSS AND
PUBLIC TRIUMPH

WOULD JEFFERSON be a candidate for election to a second term as President? With the start of the new year of 1804 the question gained special urgency—partly because it was indeed the election year and partly because of a proposed amendment to the Constitution.

The reform, eagerly sought by the Republicans and vehemently opposed by most Federalists, was designed to prevent a recurrence of the situation that had nearly cost Jefferson the presidency in the election of 1800. The Constitution provided that each presidential elector should vote for two persons without distinguishing one as the choice for President and the other as the selection for Vice President. The person receiving the most votes would be elected to the higher office and the one emerging second from the balloting would be named to the lower. Federalists who hated and feared Jefferson more than any other American had voted in 1801 for his running mate, Aaron Burr, preferring as President a troublesome devil rather than Satan himself. Through a combination of circumstances, their strategy had resulted in a tie between Jefferson and Burr and the election had been thrown into the House of Representatives. Not until February 17, 1801, and then only after thirty-six ballots, did the House declare Jefferson the victor. The inauguration was only two weeks distant.

The electoral system had been devised by men who hoped to avoid the formation of political parties and did not envision the selection of tickets of candidates. With the existence of parties the original system was too easily manipulated to serve partisan interest.

Shortly after the confusion of the 1800 election Jefferson's supporters pressed for a corrective amendment and secured passage in the House by the necessary two-thirds majority but failed in the Senate by a single vote. In two subsequent sessions the matter was proposed but deferred. Pressure was renewed in the fall of 1803 and, with the deadline for effective action uncomfortably near, both chambers of Congress voted on December 12 to propose an amendment for ratification by the states. It provided that the electors should "name in their ballots the person voted for as President, and in distinct ballots the person voted for as Vice President." In 1804 Republicans and Federalists, in the legislatures of several states, fought over ratification as vigorously as had their counterparts in the national legislature.

Early in January, Pennsylvania's Governor Thomas McKean wrote the President that Pennsylvania had ratified. In his reply Jefferson predicted that the Federalists would continue their fierce opposition on other fronts. "They know," he said, "that if it [the amendment] prevails, neither a President or Vice President can ever be made but by the fair vote of the majority of the nation." And the Federalists, he said, were not a majority party. He said that he desired reform for personal as well as public reasons. He wanted no mistaking the import of the mandate in the next presidential election. His next words revealed that, despite his talk about longing to return to Monticello, he would be a candidate for reelection. "The abominable slanders of my political enemies have obliged me to call for that verdict from my country in the only way it can be obtained; and if obtained, it will be my sufficient voucher to the rest of the world and to posterity, and leave me free to seek, at a definite time, the repose I sincerely wished to have retired to now."[1]

Jefferson was incensed by the role newspapers had played in disseminating the slanders. His enchantment with the press had not survived the stresses of his own political career. In 1787 he had written to Edward Carrington, "The basis of our government being the opinion of the people, the very first object should be to keep that right; and were it left to me to decide whether we should have a government without newspapers, or newspapers without government, I should not hesitate a moment to prefer the latter." By October 1798, when he was drafting the Kentucky Resolutions, his enthusiasm for the press had tempered to a more qualified admiration. He asserted that, in framing the Constitution of the United States, the people had "manifested their determination to retain to themselves the right of judging how far the licentiousness of speech and of the press may be abridged without lessening their useful freedom, and how far those abuses which cannot be separated from their use should be tolerated, rather than the use being destroyed."[2]

In 1804, with the contest for reelection looming, he complained of "the late abuses of the press" but still insisted that "Freedom of the press" was "the most effectual" avenue to truth.[3]

McKean had been prominently mentioned as a possible running mate—a term that Jefferson would have abhorred. He still maintained that men should stand for office, not run for it. McKean himself, however, would doubtless have been perfectly acceptable to Jefferson. The President regarded him as a friend, and the Pennsylvania Governor could have attracted Northern support. But McKean had made clear that he was not interested in the position. In his letter to McKean the President said that he himself did not even ask whose names were being put forward for the vice presidency. Jefferson seems often to have convinced himself that he was as far above the fray of ordinary politics as Monticello was above some of the storms that flashed and rolled through the valley below. In truth, he did not need to ask who was competing for "the public favor." Aside from hints in the newspapers there were plenty of people to tell him, plenty to seek his endorsement by guarded indirection.

Not the most subtle seeker was incumbent Aaron Burr. He had called upon the President to assure him that he originally had accepted his office in the hope of promoting Jefferson's reputation and being near one "whose company and conversation had always been fascinating." Burr did not want the President to be misled by the machinations of the Clintons and the Livingstons, the Vice President's principal enemies in his own state. Despite all these people, Burr insisted, his own devotion to Jefferson remained undiminished. He now craved some expression of approbation from the President, not with the idea of promoting his candidacy for reelection but to protect his reputation if, for the good of the party, he should decline to be a candidate. Jefferson said that, as a matter of policy, he didn't even allow people to talk to him about the election. In the time-honored way of officeholders, he promised to consider what Burr had said. In his private memorandum on the meeting, he registered continued distrust of the New Yorker.[4]

Earlier Jefferson had assured an anxious George Clinton that he had given no credence to reports that Clinton had spoken ill of him at a gathering in Burr's home. Now the President received a letter in which Clinton expressed gratitude for his confidence and esteem. Amid the perfunctory pleasantries was Clinton's declaration that his age and ill health would prevent him from being a candidate for reelection as Governor of New York, but he hinted that he would be available for service as Vice President of the United States. The prestige of the vice presidency had not yet descended to the level which would cause one of its occupants, John Nance Garner, to describe it as worth less than "a pitcher of warm spit." But it had sunk a good deal since the days when John Adams had wondered aloud about what form of address could express the full dignity of the position, even while he lamented that it occasionally required his association with "the common major generals, simple bishops, earls and barons" and "common trash of ambassadors, envoys, and ministers plenipotentiary."[5] Jefferson's own reluctance to travel to Philadelphia to take the vice presidential oath in 1797, saying at first that the matter could be taken care of very easily at Monticello without public ceremony, had contributed to the downgrading of the office.[6]

Caucusing in Philadelphia on February 25, 1804, the Republican members of Congress unanimously nominated Jefferson for reelection as President. In the balloting for Vice President, George Clinton was first in a field of six, garnering more than three times as many votes as his nearest competitor, John Breckinridge.[7] The Kentuckian urged his supporters to close ranks behind the Easterner and thus discouraged any possible Western challenge to the caucus's right to speak for all Republicans. The party government which Washington had warned against had already become a reality. Now its machinery was developing with the naturalness of an organic process. But nothing was left to chance. A committee to promote the success of the ticket was charged primarily with the task of preventing an accidental tie between Jefferson and Clinton if the Twelfth Amendment were not ratified before the general election.

But all was not unity among Republicans everywhere. The party machinery in New York would be dominated by the victor in its approaching gubernatorial election and, though Morgan Lewis was the nominee of the Republican caucus in that state, Burr was the choice of a rival group. Burr's Republican adherents were greatly outnumbered by Morgan's, but many Federalists were talking of forming a coalition with Burr in an effort to thwart Jefferson's reelection. Moreover, efforts to form such a coalition supposedly were under way in six other states.

Some Northern Federalists plotted an even bolder scheme if Burr could be made Governor of New York. They advocated secession of the five New England states and New York and New Jersey. If Burr were in the saddle in New York, he could ensure the participation of that state, which would become the "center" of a "permanent union." Federalist advocates of secession included three Connecticut men, Roger Griswold, James Hillhouse, and Uriah Tracy, generally regarded as among the most effective leaders of their party in the Congress. The most rabid of the group was Timothy Pickering of Massachusetts, Adjutant General and Quartermaster General of the Continental Army in the Revolution, formerly Postmaster General of the United States, Secretary of War, and Secretary of State, and since 1803 a United States Senator.[8]

Any movement led by such men as these four New Englanders had to be taken seriously. Jefferson himself had admitted that there was nothing in the Constitution forbidding secession. His own Virginia had made its ratification of the document contingent upon the right to secede, and the representatives of other states would not have acquiesced in the granting of a unique privilege to the Old Dominion.

To George Cabot, Pickering wrote, "Mr. Jefferson's plan of destruction has been gradually advancing. . . . The principles of our Revolution point to the remedy—a separation."[9] He was even more unrestrained when he wrote Rufus King: "I am disgusted with the men who now rule, and with their measures. . . . The cowardly wretch at their head, while, like a Parisian revolutionary monster, prating about humanity, would feel an infernal pleasure in the utter destruction of his opponents." Bridling at the fact that the Constitution provided for popular representation on the basis of the number of all free persons plus three-fifths of the slaves, he demanded, "Without a separation, can those states [of the Northeast] ever rid themselves of Negro Presidents and Negro Congresses, and regain their just weight in the political balance?"[10]

The campaign for reelection promised to be a nasty one. Previous rumors about Jefferson's supposed dalliance with a female slave were warmed over for the contest, and some Federalists threatened to reveal information about his overtures to a married woman.

Jefferson had long adhered to a policy of ignoring personal gossip. He would answer attacks on his policies but refuse to discuss slurs on his character.

In this spring of 1804, however, he had trouble concentrating on any phase of the election. And when he thought of Congress it was mainly to wish fervently for its early adjournment. He was deeply worried about Maria. This delicate younger daughter was pregnant and "nearing her time." She did not enjoy the robust health of her older sister, Martha, who a few months earlier had given birth to her seventh child, a daughter named Mary. At first, the President's worry had been small, and his concern was more for Maria's state of mind than for her physical condition. Two years before he had gently reproved Maria for "a willingness to withdraw from society more than is prudent," saying he could "speak from experience," and citing his days as a recluse after the death of his wife. Now, by the standards of the day, confinement was inevitable. It was all the more isolating because her father and her husband, Congressman John Wayles Eppes, must remain in Washington until Congress adjourned. Jefferson, hoping to keep his daughter from feeling too sorry for herself, had made a clumsy attempt at jocularity. In the winter he had written of her approaching delivery, "You are prepared to meet it with courage, I hope. Some female friend of your Mama's (I forget who) used to say it was no more than a knock of the elbow."[11]

Martha wrote to her father of her own concern: "Maria's spirits are bad, partly occasioned by her situation which precludes everything like comfort or cheerfulness and partly from the prospect of Congress not rising till April," probably after the birth. "I hope we shall do as well as if Mr. Eppes was here but certainly her mind would be more at ease could he be with her."[12] Maria's anxiety was increased by the fact that her two-year-old son, Francis, always a delicate child, was having "dreadful fits."

In February Maria wrote her husband, her "best beloved of my soul," that she was daily growing worse. An early adjournment of Congress, permitting his return home, would help her more than anything else. In any event, she anticipated "so sweet an addition" to the family as to make all the agony worthwhile.[13]

Jefferson had written her of his hopes for early adjournment but also of his hopes that she would demonstrate "the resources of a courage not requiring the presence of anybody." But his letter had been fond and even playful. He had received the gift of two beautiful bantams from Algiers. He was sure that Congress would adjourn before the end of March and he would be with Maria and her family, and they could begin leveling the peak of Pantops so that Maria and Mr. Eppes and the children could live very near Monticello. Besides a big house, there could be a chicken house for the exotic Algerians and their progeny.[14]

Though extremely fatigued, Maria summoned the energy to write her father when she heard that the celebrated portraitist Fevret de Saint-Memin would be in Washington. Jefferson had promised his daughters that he would sit for a Saint-Memin portrait at the first opportunity. "If you did but know," Maria said, "what a source of pleasure it would be to us while so much separated from you to have so excellent a likeness of you, you would not I think refuse us. It is what we have always most wanted all our lives and the certainty with which he takes his likenesses makes this one request I think not unreasonable."[15]

Just five days after writing this message, Maria gave birth to a baby girl. Mistakenly assuming from the report he received that all was well with the mother, Jefferson sent her a joyful letter of congratulations. Only a week later did he learn that Maria was still quite ill. Without waiting for adjournment, Mr. Eppes set out for home in a winter storm that delayed him greatly and at times forced him to proceed on foot. Jefferson wrote to Martha with deepened concern but comforted himself with the hope that Mr. Eppes' return to Maria would "render her spirits triumphant over her physical debility."[16]

Jefferson's anxiety mounted until he received from Eppes news that the baby was in excellent health and that Maria, her fever gone and pain vanished, seemed well on the way to recovery. Maria had lost her milk, but the durable Martha had enough for her child and Maria's too.[17]

Jefferson answered with his old exuberance and his old habit of prescribing for his children. He recommended that the patient be given light food and cordial wines. "The sherry at Monticello is old and genuine and the Pedro Ximenes much older still and stomachic. Her palate and stomach will be the best arbiters between them." He himself hoped to be home on April 1. Couldn't Maria and her family be there then? "The house, its contents, and appendages and servants," he wrote Mr. Eppes, "are as freely subjected to you as to myself and I hope you will make it your home till we can get you fixed at Pantops."[18]

Congress adjourned March 27, but the President was not able to leave Washington until April 1. He arrived at Monticello on April 4, and five days later wrote James Madison: "I found my daughter Eppes at Monticello, whither she had been brought on a litter by hand, so weak as barely to be able to stand, her stomach so disordered as to reject almost everything she took into it, a constant small fever and an imposthume rising in her breast." The imposthume had broken, but a second abscess might form. Then Jefferson retreated into the clipped style of communication that he used when fearful for his loved ones: "Her spirits and confidence are favorably affected by my being with her and aid the effects of regimen."[19]

Four days later he reported to Madison: "My daughter exhibits little change. No new imposthume has come on, but she rather weakens. Her fever is small and constant." In the same letter he wrote: "Our spring is remarkably uncheery. A northwest wind has been blowing three days."

On the morning of April 17, between eight and nine o'clock, Maria died. Toward sunset, some of the family later recalled, Martha found her father all alone with a Bible in his hands. When Jefferson wrote to Madison on April 23, saying that he would be a little late in returning to Washington, his style was so reserved as almost to obscure the meaning: "On the 17th instant our hopes and fears here took their ultimate form. I had originally intended to have left this [place] towards the end of the present week. But a desire to see my family in a state of more composure before we separate will keep me somewhat longer."[20] Madison, as Secretary of State, would inform the other department heads.

According to his family, Jefferson spent hours of self-imposed isolation after Maria's death. No one can presume to know his thoughts, but he would have been either more, or less, than human if he had not reflected solemnly on his admonitions to his dying daughter to lift her spirits by determined effort. If he recalled having written her about childbirth being "no more than a knock on the elbow," the recollection must have been tinged with bitter irony.

Unusually tactful and understanding in his dealings with most people, he had often lacked these qualities in dealing with his younger daughter. Obviously he had loved her dearly, but, even more than with Martha, he had been unduly afraid of pampering her. He had seemed to have little appreciation of the stress he had imposed upon her when he insisted that she join him in Paris during his service as United States Minister, tearing the child away from the Aunt Eppes who had become a second mother after loss of the girl's own mother. Once the normally sensitive Jefferson had written the seven-year-old a list of demanding instructions, concluding, "I hope you are a very good girl, . . . that you never suffer yourself to be angry with anybody, that you give your playthings to those who want them. . . . Remember too as a constant charge not to go out without your bonnet because it will make you very ugly and then we should not love you so much. If you will always practice these lessons we shall continue to love you as we do now, and it is impossible to love you more."[21] Jefferson had always been afraid that too much indulgence, too much coddling, would encourage this frail daughter to retreat from the responsibilities of life. Somehow, through all his anxious admonitions, she had sensed the strength of his love and returned it with fervor. Her last note to him, written from her deathbed, had begged for a portrait of him, the thing that she had "always most wanted."

After Jefferson was back in Washington, he replied to a letter of condolence from former Governor John Page, a college mate and one of the most cherished companions of his youth. In the old days Jefferson had written to him about adolescent loves and infatuations, apparently with greater freedom than to anyone else. Paraphrasing the biblical account of the widow's mite, Jefferson now said, "Others may lose of their abundance, but I, of my want, have lost even the half of all I had. My evening prospects now hang on the slender thread of a single life." That thread, of course, was Martha. "Perhaps I may be destined to see even this last cord of parental affection broken!" Death had made of the habitations of his friends a "field of slaughter." Then he added: "We have, however, the traveler's consolation. Every step shortens the distance we have to go; the end of our journey is in sight, the bed wherein we are to rest, and to rise in the midst of the friends we have lost."

This time, though, he was not disposed to withdraw from society as he had after his wife's death. "We have not many summers to live," he told Page. "While fortune places us then within striking distance, let us avail ourselves of it, to meet and talk over the tales of other times."[22]

Shortly before writing to Page, Jefferson had received a remarkable letter from Martha in which she declared:

No apology can be necessary for writing lengthily to you about your self. I hope you are not yet to learn that no subject on earth *is* or *ever can be* so dear and interesting to me. I speak so entirely without an exception that I do not hesitate to declare if my other duties could possibly interfere with my devotion to you I should not feel a scruple in sacrificing them, to a sentiment which has literally "grown with my growth and strengthened with my strength," and which no subsequent attachment has in the

smallest degree weakened. It is truly the happiness of my life to think that
I can dedicate the remainder of it to promote yours. It is a subject however
upon which I ought never to write for no pen on earth can do justice to
the feelings of my heart.[23]

Jefferson's remarks about his prospects hanging "on the slender thread of
a single life" did not indicate a lack of interest in his grandchildren. He
continued to show a lively concern for Martha's children and to John Eppes he
wrote, "While I live, both of the children will be to me the dearest of all pledges;
and I should consider it as increasing our misfortune should we have less of
your society." And Jefferson was going ahead with his plans for Pantops.
Someday it would belong to young Francis.[24]

Jefferson was finding solace of another sort—in creative activity. Before
Maria's death the President had purchased a new invention, the polygraph, from
the multitalented Charles Willson Peale. The inventor had asked the President
to let him know any ways in which he found the machine wanting. Jefferson
was delighted to have a device that would make copies of his letters as he wrote
the originals. Just a week after Maria's death he wrote Peale: "Your polygraph
gave me so much satisfaction that I thought it worthwhile to bestow some time
in contriving one entirely suited to my own convenience: it was therefore the
subject of my meditations on the road [from Monticello to Washington], and on
my arrival here I made the drawings which I now send you."[25] Over a period of
months, Jefferson, working with Peale, converted the polygraph from a promising but fragile mechanism to one of great practicality. He also gave it a new
name—the "portable secretary."

Through Peale came another intellectual distraction to tear Jefferson from
his grief. The Philadelphian and two other members of the American Philosophical Society brought to see him Baron Alexander von Humboldt, the celebrated
natural scientist, explorer, and polymath. Already on his way to becoming the
most famous European of his time with the exception of Napoleon and possibly
Goethe, Humboldt had just returned from his great scientific expedition to
South America. Jefferson had just sent Meriwether Lewis and William Clark into
the American West on a similar fact-finding expedition. No wonder the President
and the German scholar had been eager to meet.

Jefferson entertained at a dinner which Peale pronounced "very elegant"
even by Philadelphia standards. But the chief feast was of conversation—
principally on natural history, anthropology, and the progress of invention.[26]
Jefferson always maintained that he had never found better talk anywhere than
in Williamsburg. And in Washington he had the frequent privilege of talking
with two fellow geniuses, Madison and Gallatin. Even so, he reveled in opportunities to converse with Old World luminaries. From 1784 through most of
1789, he had rejoiced in the stimulating salons of Paris. With great relish he now
enjoyed one of the most brilliant intellectual products of German culture.
Humboldt later wrote: "I have had the good fortune to see the first Magistrate
of this great republic living with the simplicity of a philosopher who received
me with that profound kindness that makes for a lasting friendship."[27] Indeed,

these two giants of the Enlightenment corresponded for nearly twenty-one years.

With all his enthusiasm for new acquaintances, Jefferson still relied for emotional support principally on family ties and long-nourished friendships. Therefore, the moment must have been emotion-charged when he opened a letter of condolence from Abigail Adams.

Once Abigail and John Adams had been among Jefferson's dearest friends. John had insisted that Jefferson, not he, prepare the principal draft of the Declaration of Independence, protesting, "You can write ten times better than I can."[28] The two men had served together as envoys in Europe and had consulted in strictest confidence on matters of public concern. Together they had toured the gardens of England. When Jefferson was in London, the Adams residence was his home. In France young John Quincy Adams spent so much time with the Virginian that the elder John told Jefferson, "He appeared to me to be almost as much your boy as mine."[29] When Jefferson was in Paris and the Adamses were in London, they kept up a steady correspondence. Jefferson especially appreciated the wit and pungency of Abigail's letters. Jefferson and Abigail were always shopping for each other in their respective capitals. On at least one occasion he bought shoes for her.[30] Once she called Jefferson "one of the choice ones of the earth."[31] After the Adamses left Paris following a long stay she wrote Jefferson that she had been loath to leave because of "the increasing pleasure and intimacy which a longer acquaintance with a respected friend promised," and because she hated "to leave behind . . . the only person with whom my [husband] could associate with perfect freedom and unreserve."[32] Later she had received little Maria with maternal warmth upon the child's first arrival in Europe and had scolded Jefferson for failure to comprehend the trauma of the child's experience. Abigail wrote Jefferson, "She is the favorite of every creature in the house."[33] The Adamses had commissioned a portrait of Jefferson so that they would have the comfort of his likeness when he was far away.

But political differences during and after Adams' presidency had severed communication between the Massachusetts family and their Virginia friend. A beleaguered Chief Executive found it impossible to view charitably the leader of a group pledged to unseat him. And the First Lady shifted from adoration to antipathy. For Jefferson, who, even more than most people, liked to be liked, the loss of friendship was especially painful. His heart leaped at the prospect of reconciliation.

"Had you been no more than the private inhabitant of Monticello," Abigail wrote, "I should ere this time have addressed you, with that sympathy which a recent event has awakened in my bosom. But reasons of various kinds withheld my pen, until the powerful feelings of my heart have burst through the restraint, and called upon me to shed the tear of sorrow over the departed remains of your beloved and deserving daughter, an event which I most sincerely mourn. The attachment which I formed for her when you committed her to my care upon her arrival in a foreign land has remained with me to this hour. . . . The tender scene of her separation from me rose to my recollection, when she clung around my neck and wet my bosom with her tears, saying, 'O! now I have learnt to love you, why will they tear me from you?' "[34]

Mrs. Adams robbed her condolences of considerable warmth when she said that, until Maria's death, she had not "conceived of any event in this life which could call forth feelings of mutual sympathy" with Jefferson. Still cooler was her concluding sentence: "That you may derive comfort and consolation in this day of your sorrow and affliction from that only source calculated to heal the wounded heart—a firm belief in the being, perfections, and attributes of God—is the sincere and ardent wish of her who once took pleasure in subscribing herself your friend."

Before replying, Jefferson transmitted the letter to Eppes so that the widower might read the tribute to his beloved Maria. In an accompanying message, the President noted the cool conclusion but nevertheless interpreted Mrs. Adams' letter as "proof that our friendship is unbroken on her part."[35]

Jefferson told her in a letter of June 13 that the "affectionate sentiments" she had expressed had "awakened in [him] sensibilities natural to the occasion." He said that whenever he and Maria had met again after long separation one of her first questions had always been about Mrs. Adams. "The friendship with which you honored me," he said, "has ever been valued and fully reciprocated; and though events have been passing which might be trying to some minds, I never believed yours to be of that kind, nor felt that my own was. Neither my estimate of your character, nor the esteem founded in that, have ever been lessened for a single moment, although doubts whether it would be acceptable may have forbidden manifestation of it."[36]

Jefferson's next comment was probably intended at least as much for John Adams as for Abigail: "Mr. Adams' friendship and mine began at an earlier date. It accompanied us through long and important scenes. The different conclusions we had drawn from our political reading and reflections were not permitted to lessen mutual esteem, each party being conscious they were the result of an honest conviction in the other."

So far so good! But Jefferson could not resist adding: "One act of Mr. Adams' life, and one only, ever gave me a moment's personal displeasure. I did consider his last appointments to offices as personally unkind. They were from among my most ardent political enemies, from whom no faithful cooperation could ever be expected, and laid me under the embarrassment of acting through men whose views were to defeat mine; or to encounter the odium of putting others in their places. It seemed but common justice to leave a successor free to act by instruments of his own choice." Jefferson said that "after brooding over it for some little time" he "forgave it cordially and returned to the same state of esteem and respect for him which had so long subsisted."

Having vented his old resentment of Adams' "midnight appointments," Jefferson said, "I have thus, my dear Madam, opened myself to you without reserve, which I have long wished an opportunity of doing; and without knowing how it will be received, I feel relief from being unbosomed."

Mrs. Adams, in her first sentence, ended his suspense as to how his unbosoming would be received. If his letter "had contained no other sentiments and opinions than those which my letter of condolence could have excited, and which are expressed in the first page of your reply, our correspondence would have ended here; but you have been pleased to enter upon some subjects which call for a reply." In long paragraph after long paragraph, she defended her husband's "midnight appointments," and excoriated: "I have never felt any enmity towards you, Sir, for being elected President of the United States. But the instruments made use of, and the means which were practiced [in the campaign], have my utter abhorrence and detestation, for they were the blackest calumny and foulest falsehoods. . . . And now, Sir, I will freely disclose to you what has severed the bonds of former friendship, and placed you in a light very different from what I once viewed you in. One of the first acts of your administration was to liberate a wretch who was suffering the just punishment of the law due to his crimes for writing and publishing the basest libel, the lowest and vilest slander, which malice could invent, or calumny exhibit, against the character and reputation of your predecessor, of him for whom you profess the highest esteem and friendship, and whom you certainly knew incapable of such complicated baseness."[37]

The "wretch" was James Thomson Callender, who, among other things, had charged that John Adams as President had imported two mistresses, one from France and one from Germany. According to Callender's fantastic story, Adams had sent the German mistress back but had kept the French one. The Massachusetts statesman believed that this calumny had cost him the support of Pennsylvania and thus doomed his bid for reelection. The Pennsylvania Dutch, loyal to their Germanic origins, had not been as upset over the Chief Executive's supposed moral lapse as over the idea that he should prefer a French woman to a German one.

Abigail attacked Jefferson for complimenting Callender as a writer and giving him a "reward of 50 dollars." The so-called reward was Jefferson's gift of fifty dollars when the journalist was out of a job.[38] Eventually his importunities became too much for Jefferson, and, when he tried to brush him off, Callender turned upon Jefferson with all of the viciousness that he had shown to the Federalists. Callender drowned in the James River in July 1803,[39] but the rumors that he circulated lived on and took on new life with Jefferson's candidacy for reelection. Mrs. Adams was not sympathetic. She wrote, "The serpent you cherished and warmed, bit the hand that nourished him, and gave you sufficient specimens of his talents, his gratitude, his justice and his truth."

Mrs. Adams seemed to be ending the correspondence abruptly, dismissing any attempt at further communication by Jefferson. But was she really? She wrote: "There is one other act of your administration which I consider as personally unkind, and which your own mind will readily suggest to you, but as it neither affected character, or reputation, I forbear to state it." Whose curiosity would not have been piqued by such a statement? Abigail knew Jefferson well enough to know that he was one who had to know everything. The conclusion to this letter was not as cold as the ending of her first: "This letter is written in confidence—no eye but my own has seen what has passed. . . . Often have I wished to have seen a different course pursued by you. I bear no malice; I cherish no enmity. I would not retaliate if I could—nay, more in the true spirit of Christian charity, I would forgive, as I hope to be forgiven. And with that disposition of mind and heart, I subscribe the name of

Abigail Adams"

Jefferson was tantalized by Mrs. Adams' reference to the "personally unkind" act which she forbore to describe. He was intrigued by the revelation that John Adams knew nothing of this most recent letter. Besides, he was burning to reply to her charges against him.

And so, of course, he did.[40] Matching Mrs. Adams' reserve, he began: "Your favor of the 1st instant was duly received, and I would not again have intruded on you but to rectify certain facts which seem not to have been presented to you under their true aspect." He explained about Callender in detail, saying that his praise for the man's writing had been for his book *The Political Progress of Britain*, rather than for his gossip. "When he first began to write he told some useful truths in his coarse way; but nobody sooner disapproved of his writings than I did, or wished more that he would be silent. My charities to him were no more meant as encouragements to his scurrilities than those I give to the beggar at my door are meant as rewards for the vices of his life. . . . With respect to the calumnies and falsehoods which writers and printers at large published against Mr. Adams, I was as far from stooping to any concern or approbation of them as Mr. Adams was respecting those of Porcupine, Fenno, or Russell, who published volumes against me for every sentence vended by their opponents against Mr. Adams."

He got to the point. "You observe there has been one other act of my administration personally unkind, and suppose it will readily suggest itself to me. I declare on my honor, Madam, I have not the least conception what act is alluded to. I never did a single one with an unkind intention."

Nothing offensive there. But before making this statement, Jefferson had yielded to the temptation to reply in more provocative terms to Mrs. Adams' charge that he had liberated "a wretch who was suffering" for a libel against her husband. Jefferson wrote: "I discharged every person under punishment or prosecution under the Sedition Law, because I considered and now consider that law to be a nullity as absolute and as palpable as if Congress had ordered us to fall down and worship a golden image; and that it was as much my duty to arrest its execution in every stage as it would have been to have rescued from the fiery furnace those who should have been cast into it for refusing to worship their image. It was accordingly done in every instance without asking what the offenders had done, or against whom they had offended, but whether the pains they were suffering were inflicted under the pretended Sedition Law."

When Mrs. Adams replied,[41] she found it necessary to defend in provocative terms her husband's enforcement of the Sedition Law. But she gratified Jefferson's curiosity about his action which was supposedly "personally unkind." She wrote: "Soon after my eldest son's return from Europe, he was appointed by the district judge to an office into which no political concerns entered, personally known to you, and possessing all the qualifications, you yourself being judge, which you had designated for office. As soon as Congress gave the appointments to the President you removed him. This looked so particularly pointed that some of your best friends in Boston at that time expressed their regret that you had done so. I must do him the justice to say that I never heard an expression from him of censure or disrespect towards you in consequence of it. With pleasure I say that he is not a blind follower of any party." The injured young man was John Quincy Adams, who had once been almost as a son to Jefferson.

Before wishing the President "health and happiness," Abigail said, "I have written to you with the freedom and unreserve of a former friendship to which I would gladly return could all causes but mere difference of opinion be removed."

Someone of Jefferson's optimism in such matters would see Abigail's words as a hint of the possibility that the old friendship might be resumed. In his next letter[42] he was at pains to explain to her in circumstantial detail that the rejection of her son had come at a level below the President's office. "Had I known . . . , it would have been a real pleasure to me to have preferred him to some who were named in Boston in what were deemed the same line of politics. To this I should have been led by my knowledge of his integrity as well as my sincere dispositions towards yourself and Mr. Adams." But, in justification of his actions in other matters, Jefferson lectured her on the differences between the Federalists and the Republicans. When he had almost concluded the recital, he tactfully said: "I hope you will see these intrusions on your time to be what they really are, proofs of my great respect for you. I tolerate with the utmost latitude the right of others to differ from me in opinion without imputing to them criminality. I know too well the weakness and uncertainty of human reason to wonder at its different results. Both of our political parties, at least the honest portion of them, agree conscientiously in the same object, the public good, but they differ essentially in what they deem the means of promoting that good." Unfortunately he proceeded to elucidate these differences in a way not flattering to the Federalists.

Abigail replied[43] after an illness of three weeks: "When I first addressed you, I little thought of entering into a correspondence with you upon political topics. I will not, however, regret it, since it has led to some elucidations and brought on some explanations which place in a more favorable light occurrences which had wounded me. Having once entertained for you a respect and esteem founded upon the character of an affectionate parent, a kind master, a candid and benevolent friend, I could not suffer different political opinions to obliterate them from my mind, and I felt the truth of the observations that the heart is long, very long, in receiving the conviction that is forced upon it by reason." The next words must have leaped out at Jefferson: "Affection still lingers in the bosom. . . ." But she added, ". . . even after esteem has taken its flight."

Abigail accepted without question Jefferson's explanation that he had nothing to do with the removal of her son. But his criticism of the policies of her husband's administration rankled, and she said: "Here, sir, may I be permitted to pause and ask you whether, in your ardent zeal, and desire to rectify the mistakes and abuses as you may consider them, of the former administrations, you are not led into measures still more fatal to the constitution, and more derogatory to your honor, and independence of character? Pardon me, sir, if I say that I fear you are." And she argued vehemently.

And now Mrs. Adams, who had written nearly four months earlier about terminating the exchange of letters, concluded this missive on a note of firmness: "I will not, sir, any further intrude upon your time, but close this correspondence by my sincere wishes that you may be directed to that path which may terminate in the prosperity and happiness of the people over whom you are placed, by administering the government with a just and impartial hand. Be assured, sir, that no one will more rejoice in your success than

Abigail Adams."

Nearly a month later, on the morning of November 19, John Adams sat in his Quincy home with his round, bald head bent over the letters from Jefferson to Abigail and copies of her letters to the Virginian. Before putting them aside, he added a note of his own, addressed perhaps to posterity: "The whole of this correspondence was begun and conducted without my knowledge or suspicion. Last evening and this morning at the desire of Mrs. Adams I read the whole. I have no remarks to make upon it at this time and in this place.

J. Adams."[44]

Six years later Jefferson told his friend Dr. Benjamin Rush that it had pained him to be misunderstood by Mrs. Adams, but that, "yielding to an intimation in her last letter, I ceased from further explanation."[45]

While Jefferson and Abigail Adams indulged in epistolary fencing in the summer of 1804, a more deadly duel was fought between two other famous Americans. On April 25 Burr had lost his bid for the office of Governor of New York. Humiliated by defeat and raging at the epithets Alexander Hamilton had hurled at him in the campaign, Burr challenged his fellow New Yorker to a duel. In a confrontation on the heights of Weehawken, New Jersey, early on the morning of July 11, Hamilton was killed. As a political martyr, he was canonized in the deliberations of his Federalist followers. Warrants were issued for Burr's arrest in both New Jersey and New York, and he fled to Pennsylvania.

Jefferson and Hamilton had been philosophical antagonists since their service in Washington's cabinet, where the bitterness between them was exacerbated by rivalry for the regard of the President who was a father figure to them both. A streak of elitism in the Virginian and his willingness to enlarge the sphere of federal (and specifically executive) action in the pursuit of such objectives as the Louisiana Purchase kept him and Hamilton from a perfect political antithesis. But many Americans thought of Jefferson as the embodiment of agrarian democracy and Hamilton as the personification of business interests and centralized government. Hamilton had slandered Jefferson in published letters over a variety of pseudonyms, and the Virginian had described the New Yorker as "a man whose history, from the moment at which history can stoop to notice him, is a tissue of machinations against the liberty of the country which has not only received [him] and given him bread, but heaped its honors on his head."[46] But Hamilton in 1801, when Jefferson and Burr were rivals in balloting in the House of Representatives, told his followers that he would not be loath to have a part in Jefferson's "disappointment and mortification" but saw "no fair reason to suppose him capable of being corrupted," and therefore preferred him to Burr, whom he called "as unprincipled and dangerous a man as any country can boast."[47] Jefferson's correspondence with political allies suggests that he respected Hamilton much more than he did Burr. The President made no public statement about Hamilton's demise, and his available private correspondence shows him reporting the death without reference to the fact that it was a violent one.

Most historians think that, even without Hamilton's intervention, Burr would have been defeated. In any event, Burr's loss of the gubernatorial contest in New York and subsequent disgrace after the killing of Hamilton removed one possible threat to Jefferson's reelection. On September 25 the declaration that the Twelfth Amendment had been ratified removed the possibility that the wishes of the electorate might be thwarted by an accidental or contrived tie between the presidential and vice presidential candidates of the same party. Reports from the states made it obvious that, barring some completely unexpected occurrence, Jefferson would be reelected. The only thing in doubt was the size of the victory. Would he receive the massive mandate that he sought as an answer to critics and slanderers?

The Federalists had a strong ticket. Charles Cotesworth Pinckney, a fifty-eight-year-old South Carolinian, had served in the American Revolution as an aide to General Washington and as a Brigadier General. He had been a prominent member of the Constitutional Convention of 1787, arguing successfully for several provisions as well as vainly advocating a deadline of 1808 for the ending of the slave trade. As an American diplomat from whom French negotiators requested a bribe in the XYZ affair, he was apparently reliably quoted as saying, "No! No! Not a sixpence," a response soon magniloquently translated into "Millions for defense but not one cent for tribute." His patriotism was beyond question, but his nomination did hobble any Federalist efforts to revive the 1800 tactic of attacking Jefferson as contaminated by foreign influences. He had been educated in England both at Oxford and London's Middle Temple and in France at the academy in Caen. Rufus King, the Federalist nominee for Vice President, had been a Massachusetts member of the Congress under the Articles of Confederation and a United States Senator from New York. Service as Minister to Great Britain had increased his knowledge of foreign affairs.

The stature of the two Federalists and their bases of strength in Massachusetts, New York, and South Carolina led many observers to believe that, while a victory for Jefferson was virtually assured, it would not be a walkover. As returns filtered in week after week in the cumbersome system then prevailing, the magnitude of the prognosticators' error was revealed. He carried every state except Connecticut and Delaware, and Connecticut was lost by only a narrow margin. Even many Republicans found it almost inconceivable that they had triumphed in Massachusetts, home both of the moderate Federalist forces led by John Adams and of the erstwhile Northern Confederacy secessionists led by

Senator Timothy Pickering. The electoral vote was 162 to 14 in Jefferson's favor. And throughout the entire contest he is not believed to have made a single public reference to his opponent. Writing to a friend on December 13,[48] the President expressed particular satisfaction in the New England results. Regarding Massachusetts he was moved to biblical quotation: "This our brother was dead, and is alive again; and was lost, and is found." Surely Connecticut, the lone New England holdout, eventually would "dismount her oligarchy and fraternize with the great federated family." And his optimism was undimmed when he looked beyond American shores: "With England we are in cordial friendship; with France in the most perfect understanding; with Spain we shall always be bickering, but never at war."

Now that Jefferson had been so resoundingly vindicated, he had no desire for a third term. On January 6 he wrote to his old friend John Taylor, the political philosopher, that there was "but one circumstance which could engage my acquiescence in another election, to wit, such a division about a successor as might bring in a Monarchist."[49] He had abandoned his old idea that ideally the President would serve a single seven-year term and now believed that four-year terms were good. He hoped that his example, added to Washington's, of refusing to serve more than two terms would set a precedent respected by all their successors.

Though Jefferson eschewed a third term, he was happy to have a second one in which to advance projects initiated in the first. One of the most important was his plan for judicial reform. In February 1803, shortly before Chief Justice Marshall rendered his historic decision in *Marbury* v. *Madison*, the President had sent to the House of Representatives a communication leading to an equally important precedent. Jefferson had transmitted to the House certain complaints against Federal District Judge John Pickering of New Hampshire. The President said that, finding these matters not "within Executive cognizance," he was sending them to those in whom the Constitution had "confided a power of instituting proceedings of redress."[50] Pickering's offenses were numerous and serious. He had often been intoxicated on the bench, had badgered and denounced witnesses (sometimes in foul language), and had even refused to hear their testimony. He had actually refused some defendants the legally guaranteed right of appeal. Pickering was the most conspicuous of a number of Federalist judges whom Jefferson regarded as strangers to judicial objectivity. Many were complacent in the knowledge that their appointments were consti-tutionally for life "during good behavior." Replacing the Judiciary Act and declaring the "midnight appointments" null and void had been the first steps of judicial reform, but now, Jefferson believed, it was necessary to demonstrate to the Federalist-dominated judiciary that they did not live in sacred security. In sending to the House the charges against Pickering, the President was very discreetly inviting the chamber to consider impeachment.

On February 18, two weeks after receiving Jefferson's message, the House voted 45 to 8 to impeach the New Hampshire jurist. Impeachment proceedings in the Senate were conducted by Joseph Nicholson, John Randolph, and other Republican stalwarts with Aaron Burr, as Vice President, presiding. On March 12 the Senate voted, 19 to 7, that Pickering was guilty and, 20 to 6, that he should be removed from office for "high crimes and misdemeanors." Some Federalists complained at the time that Pickering was innocent by reason of insanity and many lawyers and historians since have agreed. But there was no constitutional provision for removing a federal judge because of mental incompetency.

Encouraged by this success, Jefferson went after bigger game: Samuel Chase, a Justice of the United States Supreme Court. Chase had been a signer of the Declaration of Independence but before the end of the Revolution had fallen from grace. Whether or not he was guilty, as Alexander Hamilton charged, of profiteering during the Revolution, his financial operations made patriots look askance. His performance as a Maryland judge was such that a majority of both houses of the legislature voted to remove him from the bench. But his prosecutors failed by a few votes to obtain the necessary two-thirds majority. He had recovered sufficiently in public esteem to be appointed to the Supreme Court by President Washington in 1796. His intelligence and forceful personality, and even the massive bulk of the white-maned jurist, gave him disproportionate influence on the court until Marshall became Chief Justice in 1801.

In those days, when members of the Supreme Court rode the circuit as presiding justices, Chase earned a reputation for bullying. When Chase presided in Richmond in the trial of James Callender, John Eppes found the judge "indecent and tyrannical."[51] In a charge to a Baltimore grand jury in May 1803, Chase said that "universal suffrage" would "rapidly destroy all protection of property and all security to personal liberty," causing "our republican constitution" to "sink into a mobocracy, the worst of all possible government." The allusion to the author of the Declaration of Independence was obvious when he said: "The modern doctrines by our late reformers that all men in a state of society are entitled to enjoy equal liberty and equal rights, have brought this mighty mischief upon us; and I fear that it will rapidly progress until peace and order, freedom and property, shall be destroyed."[52] Jefferson himself did not have unbounded faith in the wisdom of unlimited suffrage until education caught up with the enlargement of the electorate. Only a few weeks after the signing of the Declaration, he had opposed direct election of United States Senators, explaining to a friend, "I have ever observed that a choice by the people themselves is not generally distinguished for its wisdom."[53] But when such an opinion was voiced by a Federalist judge who disregarded individual liberty, Jefferson was incensed. And the ridicule of the Virginian's rhetoric did not engage his tolerance. To Joseph Nicholson, co-manager of the impeachment proceedings against Pickering, the President wrote: "Ought this seditious and official attack on the principles of our Constitution, and on the proceedings of a State, to go unpunished? And to whom so pointedly as yourself will the public look for the necessary measures? I ask these questions for your consideration; for myself it is better that I should not interfere."[54]

Despite this prodding from the President, Nicholson was reluctant to act. John Randolph, who felt no such compunctions, introduced in January 1804 a resolution for an inquiry into Chase's judicial conduct. The resolution was passed and resulted in a vote of 73 to 32 for impeachment. Trial by the Senate began January 2, 1805, almost exactly a year after Randolph had introduced his resolution in the lower chamber. Judge Chase requested time to prepare an answer to the charges and was given until February 4, 1805.

On that day, in an atmosphere reminiscent of the impeachment trial of Warren Hastings in Britain's Westminster Hall ten years before, Chase faced his accusers. The Senate Chamber was packed.[55] Members sat on the crimson-covered benches, Representatives sat in special seats, prominent federal officials and foreign diplomats occupied places of honor, women filled a special ladies' gallery, and other spectators crowded the outer rim. Even if Chase had not been the accused, his massive bulk, red face, and flowing white locks would have attracted special notice.

Presiding by virtue of his position as Vice President of the United States was little Aaron Burr, ironically a fugitive from justice in New York and New Jersey for the killing of Alexander Hamilton. The *New York Evening Post* quoted someone as saying that "it was the practice in courts of justice to arraign the *murderer* before the *Judge*, but now we behold the *Judge* arraigned before the *murderer*."[56]

Despite the pain of gout that drained his energy, Chase spent two and a half hours replying to the articles of impeachment. In answering the eighth, based on his charge to the grand jury in Baltimore, he defiantly asserted that accepting this article would subject "the liberty of speech on national concerns, and the tenure of the judicial office" to the "arbitrary will" of Congress.

When John Randolph opened for the prosecution three days later, the chamber was tense with expectation. Even those who had never heard him speak knew his reputation for dramatic eloquence and withering invective. But in the first few minutes all perceived that something was wrong. Though Randolph's voice was always high-pitched, it nevertheless was musical and had an almost hypnotic quality when he was in true form. Now he rambled and faltered. He apologized for illness and inadequate preparation. He confessed that he had lost his notes. He had another handicap he did not mention: he was not a lawyer and these proceedings required legal expertise more than eloquence. Chase was defended by a brilliant legal team headed by the redoubtable Robert G. Harper and Luther Martin, "the bulldog of Federalism." Martin, shabbily dressed, coarse in manners, and often ungrammatical, was an anomaly in that assemblage of men molded by eighteenth-century decorum. But the hammer blows of his intellect and brute force of his personality beat down the opposition. By the time the Senators voted on the indictments on March 1, 1805, they and the public had listened to a succession of celebrity witnesses. The most formidable was Chief Justice Marshall, who drew praise even from prosecutor Randolph. Burr announced: "The Sergeants-at-Arms will face the spectators and seize and commit to prison the first person who makes the smallest noise or disturbance."

Some spectators found the tension almost unbearable as the roll was called on each of the eight articles of impeachment. All thirty-four members of the Senate were in attendance, even Uriah Tracy, who had dragged himself from his sickbed and had to draw on smelling salts, or some similar olfactory stimulant, to keep from swooning. There would be no question about his vote. Tracy's ardent Federalism had drawn him for a time into Timothy Pickering's plot for Yankee secession. On one of the articles not a single Senator of either party voted guilty. On four others only a minority did. On three a majority voted to convict, but in each case the ballot was far short of the two-thirds vote required for conviction. Jefferson had rightly supposed that Chase would be most vulnerable in the matter of his instructions to the Baltimore jury. On the eighth and final article, which dealt with this matter, the vote for conviction was highest, 19 to 15. Six Republican Senators joined with their Federalist colleagues to acquit Chase on all counts.

So much for Jefferson's efforts to purge the judiciary through impeachment. From that time to our own there has been much speculation that, if Chase had been impeached, Jefferson would have encouraged the congressional prosecutors to go after Chief Justice Marshall himself. But nothing so far uncovered in Jefferson's correspondence supports this belief. And, as Dumas Malone pointed out, John Randolph, the chief prosecutor of Chase, not only addressed Marshall deferentially in the proceedings but continued to praise him through ensuing years.[57]

There can be no doubt, however, that Jefferson had hoped to scare some reprobate judges into better behavior and secure the removal of others whose actions he considered especially reprehensible. Now, just a few days before his second inauguration, he had to abandon one of his cherished projects for the second term. The lengthy proceedings in Congress had left unsolved for future generations the problem of dealing with a Supreme Court Justice who was unfit for any reason, physical, mental, or temperamental, but had committed no criminal act.

One problem, however, had been averted. At that early stage of the republic, a successful impeachment of a Supreme Court Justice innocent of criminal activity probably would have left the judicial branch of the federal government forever dependent on the legislative. Forrest McDonald has observed: "It was a victory for law and a defeat for democracy. The integrity of the federal judiciary was saved, and thereby the Constitution of the United States was saved also." With a nice note of irony, he added: "And the man most responsible was named Aaron Burr."[58]

The effects on Randolph's career were immediate. Some of his fellow Republicans charged that he had bungled the case for impeachment. Returning to the House in frustration, Randolph proposed a constitutional amendment empowering the President to remove federal judges upon recommendation of a simple majority of both houses of Congress. Nicholson, also frustrated, proposed empowering state legislatures to recall United States Senators at will. Both measures swept through the House on a tide of Republican fury. But the Senate let them die.

Some Republicans closely tied to the administration blamed Randolph for more than ineptness in the impeachment trial. They noted that the Federalist victory was made possible by six Republicans who voted with the winners. Five of the six were from Northern states. Some Republicans suggested—perhaps unfairly—that their deviant brethren had joined the opposition in protest against Randolph's role in subverting the Yazoo settlement, a matter in which the Northerners had a financial interest.

In 1795 the Georgia legislature had sold 35 million acres in the Yazoo River country of Mississippi and Alabama, but the next year, after revelation that Georgia legislators were among the shareholders, had rescinded the transaction. But in 1802, when Georgia ceded to the federal government the state's claims to Western lands, the Jefferson administration attempted a final settlement by granting 5 million acres to holders of Yazoo land warrants.

Congressional cooperation was taken for granted until Randolph rose in the House to protest "plunder of the public property" for the benefit of a "set of speculators." He asserted that Jefferson's Postmaster General, Gideon Granger, had lobbied for New England claimants to Yazoo lands and awarded mail contracts as bribes to Congressmen. Granger demanded an investigation to clear his name. Randolph sowed enough doubts to block the settlement. The Senator had been exhausted by his labors in the matter when he turned to the prosecution of Chase.

Randolph's actions in both the Yazoo affair and the impeachment proceedings displeased so many Republicans that they voted him out of his post as majority leader.

Jefferson remained untainted by any blame either for the proceedings against Chase or their unsuccessful conclusion. After all, he had uttered no word publicly about the matter. Some people noted that he had invited Burr, the presiding officer of the trial, to dine with him several times during the deliberations. But the New Yorker had presided fairly, and surely the President had the right to invite the Vice President to the Executive Mansion.

Jefferson conceded privately that impeachment was a "bungling way of removing judges." The attempt to remove Chase by this means was "a farce which will not be tried again."[59] Despite the shattering of his plans for purging the federal judiciary, Jefferson rallied with his customary optimism. Randolph would not be in a position to thwart him so much as before. Admittedly, some of the President's principal plans for his second administration were no longer intact. But he had emerged from the impeachment crisis with his personal popularity undiminished. Sustained by the popular mandate so convincingly demonstrated at the polls and by the laudatory comments that followed, he prepared to move forward on other fronts.

VII

'DESCENT INTO THE MAELSTROM'

THOMAS JEFFERSON'S second inaugural was not a matter of great excitement in Washington. The ceremony on Monday (most daily of days), March 4, 1805, followed by only three days the dramatic conclusion to the exhausting impeachment trial of Justice Chase. Two days before the inauguration, the President had been upstaged by the retiring Vice President. Aaron Burr, distrusted by a majority of Congress and bearing the onus of the arrest warrants of two states, had delivered a valedictory that wrung tears from his fellow Senators.[1] Four years before, the stark simplicity of Jefferson's walk from a boardinghouse to the capitol had been an impressive foil for the general excitement. This time his determinedly plain procession from the Executive Mansion to the Capitol, deprived of the backdrop of wildly enthusiastic spectators, was a low-key affair. He was cheered by warm admirers but he was no longer an unproven man producing a tension between exhilarating hopes and exaggerated fears.

Congress had adjourned after nine o'clock the night before, and so many of the weary members had headed for home that there was no quorum to witness Jefferson's inauguration. Of course, he had never been heard by a congressional quorum. His delivery, the curse of his public career, had rendered his words inaudible to most who had been present four years earlier. With his second inaugural address already in print in the *National Intelligencer*, there seemed no reason to delay departures from Washington in order to strain for an occasional word from the President's lips.

Those who did attend the second inauguration saw a man little changed from the one who had stood before them in 1801. The tall figure, large-boned but spare as ever, was clad in black. Black silk stockings covered his long calves. We have a good idea of the subtle changes in appearance after a full term as President. Jefferson had posed for his portrait more often than in any comparable period. In November he had sat for Saint-Mémin, as his now dead daughter had begged him to do. The results were pleasing to some of the family, but the artist's use of his prized physiognotrace in capturing the profile seems to have lent a heaviness to Jefferson's features not found in any other life portrait of him. The "Edgehill portrait," soon to be painted by Gilbert Stuart, shows the liveliness of eye often commented upon by contemporaries but has the same postal slot mouth with which that painter endowed Washington and other worthies. Fortunately, Jefferson posed for Rembrandt Peale, a recognized master of physiognomy, a few months before his first inauguration and about two months before his second. In the second portrait, the President appears to have aged a little more than four years, but he does not appear to be little more than a month short of his sixty-second birthday. There still were few wrinkles except for the parentheses framing the sensitive mouth and the faint crow's feet by the large, luminous hazel eyes. But the full, formerly reddish-brown eyebrows were frosted, matching his hair. And the jaws and chin, though still remarkably firm, were somewhat softened. The bold nose still seemed fresh from the sculptor's chisel, and ruddy spots of color still glowed through the thin skin near his high cheekbones.

The inaugural address was not as eloquent as the earlier one, with its famous declaration: "We are all republicans, we are all federalists." But it was spoken by a more confident Jefferson. This time he said, "Our fellow citizens have . . . pronounced their verdict, honorable to those who had served them, and consolatory to the friend of man, who believes he may be entrusted with his own affairs."[2] Before, Jefferson and Burr, through the vagaries of the electoral system, had been tied with eight votes more than Adams, and the contest had been resolved only after 36 ballots in the House of Representatives. This time Jefferson had triumphed 162 to 14 in the electoral college, and his party was in undisputed control of both houses of Congress.

He could not resist the temptation to oblique criticism of his adversaries. He did this in the guise of explaining that certain "crafty individuals" among the Indians resisted all government efforts to introduce improved methods of agriculture for fear that reform would drive them from leadership. "These persons," he said, "inculcate a sanctimonious reverence for the customs of their ancestors; that whatsoever they did, must be done through all time; that reason is a false guide, and to advance under its counsel, in their physical, moral, or political condition, is perilous innovation; that their duty is to remain as their Creator made them, ignorance being safety, and knowledge full of danger." Lest some miss the point, he added, "They, too, have their anti-philosophers, who find an interest in keeping things in their present state, who dread reformation, and exert all their faculties to maintain the ascendancy of habit over the duty of improving our reason and obeying its mandates."

After the ceremony a considerable concourse followed the President along Pennsylvania Avenue to the Executive Mansion. A. J. Foster, a young member of the British Minister's staff, was favorably impressed with Jefferson but deplored the number of "low persons"[3] in the procession. He looked askance at the mechanics who had marched from the Navy Yard and had formally saluted the President as leader of a country "where the honest industry of the mechanic is equally supported with the splendor of the wealthy." Jefferson had long since broadened his affection for tillers of the soil to include skilled industrial workers.

The President's reelection triumph, despite its massive scope, afforded him no immunity to savage criticism. Between his election and his oath taking,

Jefferson was savagely attacked in the *New-England Palladium*, a Boston newspaper whose publishers were printers to the state of Massachusetts. This was the same paper that in 1800 had proclaimed: "Should the infidel Jefferson be elected to the Presidency, the seal of death is that moment set on our holy religion, our churches will be prostrated, and some infamous prostitute, under the title of the Goddess of Reason, will preside in the sanctuaries now devoted to the worship of the Most High."[4] The Boston publication revived the old, baseless charge of cowardice during Jefferson's service as Governor in the Revolution. It branded him an atheist. Most illogically, it charged him with sponsoring James Callender, a known calumniator of public figures, and then cited the discredited journalist's writings as evidence that Jefferson had kept a slave mistress and had also laid siege to his neighbor's wife.

Demands by Republicans in the Massachusetts House of Representatives that the chamber express formal disapproval of the article or abrogate the state's contract with the publishers provoked a vindictive debate in which Federalists slandered the President's morals.

In his inaugural address, he had said, "The artillery of the press has been leveled against us, charged with whatsoever its licentiousness could devise. . . . he who has time renders a service to public morals and public tranquility in reforming these abuses by the salutary coercions of the law." But he concluded, "The public judgement will correct false reasonings and opinions on a full hearing of all parties, and no other definite line can be drawn between the inestimable liberty of the press and its demoralizing licentiousness."[5]

Jefferson held fast to his policy of outwardly ignoring any public criticism of his personal life, but the inward wear and tear on this sensitive man may well be imagined. More than most, he craved the approval and affection of his fellow creatures. Even though Jefferson specifically assured close friends that he was no atheist, he would not repudiate the charge in public.

The nearest he came was through the refutation implicit in such passages from public papers as the concluding paragraph of his inaugural address, in which he invoked "the favor of that Being in whose hands we are, . . . and to whose goodness I ask you to join with me in supplications. . . ."

The accusations of atheism are ironic in view of the fact that, when Jefferson was plagued by unjust criticisms, he sometimes found comfort in religion. During the winter of 1802–1803, when Federalists were saying that Jefferson had brought Thomas Paine back to America to "destroy religion," the President's thoughts were turned much to matters of faith. Impressed by Joseph Priestley's pamphlet *Socrates and Jesus*, Jefferson urged him to discuss the same subject "on a more extensive scale." He stressed the need to call attention to the sayings of Jesus which endeavored to bring people to "the principles of a pure deism, and juster notions of the attributes of God, to reform their moral doctrines to the standard of reason, justice and philanthropy, and to inculcate the belief of a future state."[6] He said that the teachings of Jesus should be separated from any corruptions that they had acquired through the zeal or ignorance of adherents in subsequent generations. Jefferson outlined the sort of work that he himself would attempt if public duties allowed him time for the task.

During this same period he mailed to Dr. Benjamin Rush a "Syllabus of an Estimate of the merit of the doctrines of Jesus, compared with those of others."[7] In this document Jefferson confessed that, although he had once valued the moral teachings of the Epicureans and Stoics above all others, and indeed still held them in high regard, he now realized that they were inferior to the precepts of Christ. The classical moralists, he said, had directed our attention inward to improving ourselves whereas the Nazarene had led our attention outward to the needs of others. Jefferson sent copies of the "Syllabus" to a few close friends, including the old friend of his boyhood, John Page, and to his own daughters.[8]

On January 29, 1804, Jefferson wrote to Priestley: "I rejoice that you have undertaken the task of comparing the moral doctrines of Jesus with those of the ancient philosophers. You are so much in possession of the whole subject that you will do it easier and better than any other person living."[9] Despite Jefferson's confidence in the superior qualifications of the clergyman-scientist, the President presumed to suggest the procedure: "I think you cannot avoid giving, as preliminary to the comparison, a digest of his moral doctrines, extracted in his own words from the evangelists, and leaving out everything relative to his personal history and character. It would be short and precious. With a view to do this for my own satisfaction, I had sent to Philadelphia to get two testaments (Greek) of the same edition, and two English with a design to cut out the morsels of morality, and paste them on the leaves of a book in the manner you describe as having pursued in forming your *Harmony*.[10] But I shall now get the thing done by better hands."

The "better hands" were stilled by death on February 6 before Priestley could receive Jefferson's letter. Two days before, the President had received two virtually identical English editions of the New Testament and two identical copies of a Greek-Latin edition, all of which he had ordered from a bookseller. Jefferson therefore took upon himself the task which he had contemplated before assigning it to Priestley. The President was too pressed for time to carry out his intention of creating a multilingual edition of the New Testament, but he did not abandon the idea for the future. Jefferson pored over the English Gospels, noting the verses from Matthew, Mark, Luke, and John that he wished to include in his version. Then for several evenings he cut the selected passages from his two testaments, the use of two books making it possible for him to preserve verses on the reverse side of ones already clipped out. He pasted the selected passages in double columns on 46 octavo sheets. The whole process took only several evenings. By March 10 he had had the volume professionally bound. Jefferson's celerity was made possible by the confidence with which he extracted "46 pages of pure and unsophisticated doctrines, such as were professed and acted on by the *unlettered* apostles, the apostolic fathers, and the Christians of the first century." He later wrote John Adams that the authentic sayings of Jesus were "as easily distinguishable as diamonds in a dunghill."[11]

Absorbed in the duties of his second administration, Jefferson found little time for further research into the essence of Christianity. But as slanders continued though the spring of 1805 and into the summer, with the angry replies of loyal followers drawing additional attention to the rumors, Jefferson often contemplated his faith. He planned eventually to organize his thoughts on paper.

Jefferson did not have the luxury of answering questions of morality solely in the abstract. Not only affairs of state demanded concrete answers. His endorsement was sought in many other matters. Just before the second inaugural he had received from Dr. Benjamin Waterhouse a letter that posed a hard question. One of the United States pioneers in Jennerian vaccination for smallpox, Dr. Waterhouse was a Harvard professor and one of a small number of physicians whom Jefferson strongly admired. In 1766, at the age of twenty-three, Jefferson had been inoculated against smallpox on a trip to Philadelphia. That was by the old, highly dangerous variolation process. He had hailed the advent of the Jennerian method in 1798 and had used his influence to promote it. He had even obtained from Dr. Waterhouse samples of living virus with which to inoculate the Jefferson family and their neighbors and friends. Now Dr. Waterhouse was launched upon another crusade and sought the President's support.

The physician enclosed a printed copy of a lecture which he had delivered at Harvard on the pernicious effects of tobacco and intoxicating beverages. The doctor's theories posited no threat to Jefferson's personal habits. He drank only moderately, confining his consumption of alcohol almost entirely to wine, and he did not smoke at all. But, despite his personal prejudice against tobacco and his early intention to avoid planting it, he had turned to tobacco cultivation on many occasions when he was heavily burdened with debt. To condemn nicotine would be to brand his own record as a planter and to invite the outrage of his neighbors and other Virginians financially dependent on tobacco culture.

The President replied[12] just five days after his inauguration. Acknowledging the threat to his own livelihood, he began with a quotation from Ovid's *The Remedy of Love*: "War, I see, is being prepared against me." But he felt compelled to testify that he was convinced of the dangers of tobacco and was "a friend neither to its culture nor consequences." He therefore hoped that the doctor would be able to curb "this organ of Virginia influence" as one would wish to eliminate anything inimical to "physical, moral, or political well being."

Thanking the President for his endorsement, Waterhouse praised him for its "Ciceronian" qualities. The Massachusetts physician said that, as a Federalist, he wished to assure the President that "the men among us most distinguished for talents, character, and years abhor[red] that odious vapor of calumny" being spread against the Jefferson administration. In fact, he had frequently told his more zealous Federalist brethren that their own calumniating spirit was a far greater threat to the republic than the "Virginia influence" which they so loudly deplored.[13]

Tired of criticisms on the domestic front, weary with schisms in his own party, and impatient with frustration in his attempts at judicial reform, yet buoyed by his reelection landslide, Jefferson turned his energies to foreign affairs. His success as Minister to France and Secretary of State, and especially as President in negotiating the Louisiana Purchase, encouraged him to play boldly for big stakes in the international arena. Forrest McDonald has well said: "The game was deadly dangerous: France and England were locked in a struggle for dominance of the Western world, and any nation that managed to be neither devoured nor reduced to puppet status could count itself blessed. And yet the opportunities were as great as the risks, as American commercial prosperity and the acquisition of Louisiana abundantly attested."[14]

The President's confidence in himself was well placed. As the same historian has said, "Thomas Jefferson was a wily and resourceful player in this perilous game, one of the most gifted of them all, even in an age that numbered Napoleon and Talleyrand, Pitt and Castlereagh, and Godoy and Metternich among the contestants."[15]

The first major foreign policy project of Jefferson's second term stemmed from his first and was rooted in the negotiations for the Louisiana Purchase. After all the argument about whether West Florida had been included in the territory obtained by the United States, Napoleon, in the summer of 1804, had flatly asserted that it absolutely had not. By this time Jefferson's protégé James Monroe, who had helped to conduct the original negotiations in Paris, was United States Minister to Great Britain. The President and Secretary of State Madison instructed Monroe to proceed to Madrid to confer with Charles Pinckney, United States Minister to Spain, on the means of acquiring West Florida from the Spanish. Jefferson believed that it was best at this time to act as if Napoleon's declaration had resulted from a sincere misunderstanding rather than any devious intent.

Leaving London in October, Monroe proceeded to Madrid, but by way of Paris so that he could appraise the situation there for himself. In France he learned that Napoleon was sticking by his contention that the French government, because of a previous agreement with Spain, had no right to sell West Florida. Robert Livingston, still United States Minister in France, said that Barbé-Marbois recently had said that the Americans might be able to gain both West Florida and East Florida through the good offices of the French government, obtainable by the payment of 60 million francs. The French diplomat knew of no other possible way.

Believing that the government of Napoleon was not so completely mercenary as Livingston assumed, Monroe wrote to Talleyrand offering no money but stressing the justice of the American claim. Weeks passed with no answer from the wily Foreign Minister but with rumors that fed the Virginian's optimism.

Talleyrand's answer came in an interview when he told Monroe concerning his prospects in Madrid, "You will have much difficulty to succeed there." A few days later Talleyrand's principal assistant was more specific: "Spain must cede territory, and . . . the United States must pay money."[16] Monroe still could not believe that Napoleon was aware of the unbecoming actions of his subordinates. He did conclude that Talleyrand and lesser figures, like the principals in the XYZ affair of 1797, were fishing for bribes. Convinced at least that further efforts in Paris would be fruitless, he left on December 8 for Madrid.

When Monroe reached Madrid on January 2, 1805, Pinckney, his bags already packed, was both physically and mentally ready to quit the capital. Spain had demanded recall of the American Minister and was on the point of breaking off diplomatic relations. Secretary of State Madison, who disapproved of Pinckney's threatening tactics, had given him "leave" to return. Monroe's late arrival after a leisurely progress by way of Paris was nevertheless timely. As a new American diplomat on the scene, he provided fresh options for negotiators whose intransigency had brought them to an ineluctable standoff. Monroe assured Pinckney that he would work with him in support of the same objectives that had engaged the South Carolinian, and Pinckney stayed on.

Though Monroe had been requested by Madison to smooth out the difficulties created by Pinckney's bellicosity, the two envoys joined in a peremptory demand addressed to Foreign Minister Cevallos. They called upon Spain to cede to the United States both of the Floridas and Texas as far as the Rio Colorado. Instead of exploding, as he might have, Cevallos played for time while soliciting French support.

By this time Livingston, who had (in Jefferson's words) "quarreled with every public agent with whom he had anything to do,"[17] had been replaced as Minister to France by General John Armstrong, a former United States Senator from New York. Monroe asked Armstrong to discreetly determine the likely French response. In March the General replied. He had discovered that Napoleon was hostile toward Americans for a variety of reasons ranging from insults in the American press to the contagious example of freedom in the prospering New World republic. In the event of conflict between Spain and the United States, France would undoubtedly side with Spain.[18]

The situation was complicated by the fact that, while Monroe was traveling from Paris to Madrid, Spain's Charles IV, who divided his time between praying and hunting and ruled without the hindrance of a parliament, had declared war against Great Britain. An optimistic American might be inclined to assume that war with England would make Spain eager to settle differences with her New World neighbor, the United States. Instead it made Spain even more dependent on the friendship of her powerful continental neighbor France. Even the ever hopeful Monroe had to admit failure.

The perilous state of relations between Spain and the United States was evident later, when the next American envoy to Madrid was greeted by Prince Godoy, who, without benefit of formal appointment, took his sovereign's place in both the Queen's bed and the King's Council. In 1795, by restoring the right of deposit of American traders in New Orleans, he had sought to propitiate the United States even at the risk of offending France.[19] But in 1805 he told the new American representative, George M. Erving: "You may choose either peace or war. 'Tis the same thing to me."[20]

In contrast to his leisurely progress from London to Madrid, Monroe's return to the British capital was hurried. On arrival, he found that he had quit one crisis for another. The tolerant, easygoing Henry Addington, Viscount Sidmouth, had been replaced as Prime Minister by William Pitt the Younger. Now in his forty-ninth year, Pitt was a slender, Saxon blond man of fine steel courage. The second son of the elder Pitt, the great Earl of Chatham, whom Americans had counted a friend during their pre-Revolutionary quarrels with the mother country, he had delivered at the age of 21 a maiden speech in Parliament that won from Edmund Burke the praise that he was "not a chip off the old block but the old block itself." He had become Prime Minister for the first time at the age of 24, having refused the office earlier, and had promoted good relations with the United States. Now this brilliant and strong-willed man had become Prime Minister again at a time when the Jefferson administration was looking earnestly toward England and seeing her in a different light.

In the summer of 1805, alarmed by Spanish hostility, Jefferson wrote Madison, "We should not permit ourselves to be found off our guard and friendless."[21] A short while later, echoing the President's promptings, Madison wrote his chief: "The more I reflect on the papers from Madrid, the more I feel the value of some eventual security for the active friendship of G. B. but the more I see at the same time the difficulty of obtaining it without a like security to her for ours."[22] The circumlocutory phrase softened the shared admission of these two American statesmen that an alliance with the old enemy might be necessary. On August 25 Jefferson wrote Madison, "I am thoroughly impressed with a belief of hostile and treacherous intentions against us on the part of France, and that we should lose no time in securing more than a neutral friendship from England."[23] Writing from Monticello, where Jefferson saw events with a simplicity sometimes enlightening and sometimes deceptive, the President had sent circular letters to his cabinet proposing seizure of West Florida. English support could be counted on because "the first wish of every Englishman's heart is to see us once more fighting by their sides against France."[24]

Unfortunately, there was strong evidence, climaxing at the time of Monroe's return to London, that Great Britain might not welcome an alliance on terms acceptable to the United States. Before leaving London for Madrid, Monroe had talked the Sidmouth ministry into readiness to deal with the United States but had felt no personal urgency and no pressure from Washington to accelerate the process. On his return to London the American Minister now had to deal with an unconvinced Pitt ministry. Though scrupulously preserving a technical neutrality between the warring Franco-Spanish alliance on one side and Great Britain on the other, Jefferson and Madison had spoken warm words of friendship to the Continental powers while maintaining a studied aloofness toward the British. The theory was that the cold shoulder would cause London to remove obstacles to good relations with the United States.

Before relinquishing to Monroe his post as Minister to London, Rufus King had obtained from his Majesty's government a "partial repudiation of the right of impressment of American seamen." But, sure that a far better agreement could be negotiated, the Jefferson administration scorned to accept the terms. Now Pitt was no longer so interested, as in his first ministry, in improving relations with the United States. Indeed, he suspected that Jefferson was incapable of "any great, vigorous, or persevering exertion"[25] and resolved to test his theory. He ordered the seizure of American ships sailing from the West Indies to France.

This policy was in accord with Britain's so-called Rule of 1756, adopted when she declared war on France but not enforced for the past decade. Monroe correctly evaluated the move as an "experiment" to disclose "what the United States will bear."[26]

The lesson was underlined for the American Minister on July 23, 1805, when Sir William Scott, England's renowned admiralty judge, rendered his historic prize-court decision in the case of the United States merchantman *Essex*. The vessel had sailed with a cargo from Martinique in the West Indies to London, but by way of Charleston, South Carolina. For some years American ships had been using this "broken voyage" device to get around the Rule of 1756, and Great Britain had tacitly accepted it. In London the *Essex* routinely presented customs house papers proving entrance at the port of Charleston, but the judge ruled that the voyage was illegal unless it could be proved that originally the South Carolina city, rather than London, had been the intended terminus.

Throughout the remainder of the summer and into the fall one American ship after another was seized by the British. The President was appalled one day to discover that the government had received no fewer than 781 appeals from American seamen impressed into the British navy. Letters from individual shipowners, merchants' groups, and seamen's relatives piled up. Petitions arrived from Charleston, Norfolk, Baltimore, Philadelphia, New York, and New-buryport, pleading for relief not only from seizures by the British, but in some cases by the French and Spanish as well.[27]

Every American overture to the British government met with seemingly endless delays. On October 18, Monroe wrote Madison: "On a review of the conduct of this government towards the United States, from the commencement of the war, I am inclined to think that the delay . . . is . . . part of a system, and that it is intended, as circumstances favor, to subject our commerce at present and hereafter to every restraint in their power."[28]

The Virginian thought that his usefulness in London was over. He urged Jefferson to abandon the delays of diplomatic maneuvering and send American soldiers into the parts of Texas claimed by the United States as well as into the Floridas.

Jefferson himself had often talked privately of marching into the Floridas. For years he had indulged in hyperbolic rhetoric on many issues, often counting on Madison to urge restraint. The practice was a form of self-indulgence that had little to do with his ultimate action in a given case. Jefferson saw Spain unyielding, with France supportive of Spanish intransigence and England more unfriendly to the United States than at any time since 1794. Whatever the differences among themselves, France, Spain, and Great Britain all seized American seamen and cargoes. Under these conditions Jefferson was too practical to invade disputed territory held by Spain.

But he was not ready to abandon hopes of acquiring both Floridas, especially the West Florida Gulf Coastal lands extending from the Florida peninsula to the Mississippi River. He was prepared to wait and to use the time to pave the way for future action. And he had not lost his optimism. Europe soon would be convulsed in a war of vast proportions. Under such circum-stances, it would be safer for the United States not to be bound by an alliance to any of the contending powers. With the nations of Europe completely occupied with each other, the United States might enjoy a respite of perhaps two years from their interference. This time could be used to strengthen itself for tasks ahead. If the United States, despite the most determined efforts at neutrality, should eventually be drawn into the war, it would not be compelled by terms of an alliance to remain in the struggle after its own ends had been achieved.[29]

Of course, as Jefferson himself was painfully aware, the nation would not be free of one kind of foreign interference: the disruption of its commerce on the high seas.

Into October, Jefferson had continued to nurse the hope that Britain might yet relax its policy toward American maritime commerce, although he was too realistic to count on it. But harsh experience killed the hope, as it had even earlier with Madison and Gallatin.

By this time, too, Napoleon, having been crowned Emperor of France the previous December, seemed now on his way to being the imperial master of a continent. He had occupied Hanover and Naples and afterwards had marched from conquest to conquest across Europe. One of his armies was reported poised on the Channel for invasion of England. The shadow of Napoleon, massive head thrust forward belligerently from the slouched shoulders, seemed to cover the map of Europe. It might be unwise to offend this titan by courting Britain.

By the same token it might be advantageous to be in the Emperor's good graces. This supposition was strongly supported by a message from General Armstrong in Paris. The United States diplomat had become acquainted with Daniel Parker, an American expatriate with a wide acquaintance not only among European bankers but also with shady politicians in France, the Netherlands, and Great Britain. Parker introduced Armstrong to certain members of Napoleon's government who assured him that, if the United States would repose its territorial aspirations in the hands of the Emperor, Bonaparte would arrange sale of the Floridas for a sum between seven and ten million dollars. Furthermore, firm friendship with France during her present struggle would earn a bonus for the Americans: extension of the Louisiana boundary 400 miles westward along the Gulf Coast. This gain would push the United States border as far west as the Colorado River, almost to the present site of Corpus Christi, Texas. Madison received Armstrong's report near the end of October.[30] The Secretary of State also received from Armstrong the informal advice that the United States should persist in its bellicose confrontation of Spain, thus adding force to Napoleon's anticipated argument to Madrid that it would be better to "get the proceeds of an honorable sale [of the Floridas] than to lose them by American cupidity and conquest."[31]

When Jefferson saw these messages, his optimism soared. Here was a chance to crown his second administration with a territorial gain comparable to the acquisition of Louisiana in his first. The Floridas and the Texas coast did not rival the Louisiana Territory in area. But when one considered the huge coastline involved and the convenience to Caribbean and South American ports, the immediate economic significance of the prospective gain might well exceed that of the earlier acquisition. A booming United States economy had provided a surplus in the Treasury. The federal government had both the opportunity and the means.

Of course, in 1797 agents of the United States, sent to Paris to negotiate a treaty, had recoiled in indignation when three French officials, designated as X, Y, and Z, had requested a large bribe. Correspondence regarding the affair had been submitted to Congress by President Adams and had infuriated Federalists and Republicans alike. Now, however, in the autumn of 1805, Jefferson told Madison that it was better to acquire territory by purchase than by war and that, as to who received the money, or any portion of it, "we need not care."[32] He seemed to regard the whole matter as a real estate deal, albeit a gigantic one, and the total price was the important thing, not the percentage earned by the agent.

The President, eager to pave the way for negotiations with the aid of France, decided upon a threefold policy: forceful confrontation with Britain as a protest against violations of American sovereignty on the high seas, some concessions to France as evidence of goodwill, and a request to Congress for funds for the deal. One leg of Jefferson's tripod—the stern policy toward England—was firm, braced by public opinion. The second was less reliable; the American people were not in a mood to appease France. The third leg was downright shaky; not many Congressmen would willingly jeopardize their careers to appropriate money for a deal with France. Their constituents would be incensed over the idea of lining the pockets of French politicians. The old rallying cry of "Millions for defense but not one cent for tribute" had become part of the cherished rhetoric of the republic.

To overcome these difficulties, Jefferson determined upon a risky course. Congress would soon convene and the President would send it his fifth annual message on December 3. This would be a public document for public perusal. But several days later he would send to Congress a second message intended only for the eyes of Congress. In this paper he would request funds for the deal with France. He would depend upon the patriotism—and in some cases the instinct for political self-preservation—of both Republicans and Federalists to keep the matter secret until an appropriate time for revelation.

In the public message of December 3,[33] Jefferson said that foreign relations had worsened markedly since the year before, when he had reported that the United States lived in harmony with the nations of Europe. Belligerents in the great power struggle were acting as pirates on the high seas and even in American waters, completely disregarding United States rights as a neutral. He singled out Spain as a particularly obnoxious offender. She was impeding American commerce with Mobile, denying compensation for spoliations, seizing American citizens in the disputed territory, and showing no desire to settle the question of Louisiana's boundaries.

If peaceful means failed, force was the only resort. It was only prudent, he said, that the United States should fortify its seaports, build more gunboats. Maybe a younger militia should be recruited so that, in the event of war, maturer men would not be torn from "the bosom of their families." He was ready, if Congress deemed it necessary, to build ships of the line carrying seventy-four guns. He thought it wise to raise the peacetime limits on numbers of seamen. These things would take money, but $4 million more of the public debt had been eliminated in the past year and the Treasury had a healthy surplus.

This message met with general approbation, as Jefferson had expected. Some Congressmen in both parties thought that the administration had tried appeasement long enough.

Three days later came the more doubtful part of the President's scheme—the secret message—by which he took Congress into his confidence, asking them to be partners in misleading the public for a time. Only thus, he reasoned with himself and members of his administration, could the nation's needs be met without bloodshed. On December 6, the Congress received behind closed doors the President's secret message telling of the opportunity to negotiate with Spain through Napoleon's agents. Jefferson was as candid with the Congress as he was secretive with the public. He requested a secret appropriation of $5 million to be used in obtaining territory from Spain with the help of France. This sum would supplement the secret appropriation of $2 million which the President had obtained from Congress in 1802 "to defray any expenses which may be incurred in relation to the intercourse between the United States and foreign nations."[34] The President had hoped to use the money to obtain New Orleans and West Florida, but the anticipated opportunity had not materialized and the funds had never been spent.

The House of Representatives, constitutionally charged with the origination of appropriations, assigned the President's request to a seven-member ad hoc committee chaired by John Randolph. In committee, and to the Secretary of the Treasury, the Secretary of State, and the President, the chairman attacked Jefferson's clandestine proposal as a "base prostration of the national character." The Chief Executive, he shrilled, could not make the Congress of the United States responsible for "delivering the public purse to the first cut-throat that demanded it."[35] While they did not all express themselves so vehemently, all but one—a first-term Congressman from Massachusetts—agreed with the stand. Even Joseph Nicholson, Jefferson's longtime friend and staunch supporter, agreed this time with the opposition.

One week, two weeks, three weeks passed with no action by the committee. While the President paced in frustration, Randolph even took off one week for a jaunt to Baltimore. Jefferson's proposal to win France's favor and bring England to compromise by twisting the British lion's tail suffered another big loss in credibility when news was received of Nelson's great victory at Trafalgar over the combined French and Spanish fleets. It was London's greatest naval triumph since the defeat of the Spanish Armada in 1588, and this achievement, unlike the earlier one, owed far less to the intervention of nature than to the skills of man. Britain would be mistress of the seas for the foreseeable future, and shipping off the Gulf Coast shores that Jefferson sought would be as vulnerable to a hostile England as any commerce off the coast of Europe itself.

The disappointment and painful suspense were made more bearable for Jefferson by the presence of his daughter Martha, who had joined him in the Executive Mansion about the time that he sent his two messages to Congress. In time of crisis, Jefferson, even more than most men, needed the comfort of family love. Martha idolized her father above all other people on earth. But in other ways, too, she was important to his well-being. She anticipated his needs with rare sensitivity, and she was an intelligent companion with whom he could discuss privately many things that worried him. In some ways she must have seemed a reincarnation of his beloved, long dead sister Elizabeth. Martha had her children with her and Jefferson was diverted by their gambols and by the opportunity to teach them some of the bits of knowledge that he found exciting. One granddaughter, Anne Cary, almost fifteen years old, could join distinguished table company as a young lady. Another grandchild was due in January, and Jefferson's solicitude for his pregnant daughter drew him from worries of state even more than her solicitude for him.[36]

The President's grandchildren surely were almost as delighted with their grandsire's special pet as he himself was. Jefferson had tamed a mockingbird so that the little creature, slimly elegant in its pearl gray vest and dark morning coat of feathers, would sit on his shoulder as he worked at his desk. The usually fastidious President, who would even wipe off a freshly groomed horse before mounting him, would hold a morsel of food in his lips for the bird to take directly into its beak.

Jefferson found diversion too in conversation with dinner guests. Ironically enough, one of the most pleasurable visits during this trying period was from a Federalist Senator from Massachusetts.[37] But this was a very special senator, not only because of his brilliance, but because he was John Quincy Adams, the son of dear friends now estranged from Jefferson. It was a delight to the Virginian to sit once again in animated conversation with the young man who, as an adolescent, had looked upon him as a second father.

It was good that Jefferson found relief in social pleasures because his anxieties about the ad hoc House committee proved justified. That group not only formally voted to reject the President's request for funds to acquire the Spanish lands, but in its report on January 3, 1806, boldly offered a substitute resolution to raise troops for defense "from Spanish inroad and insult, and to chastise the same."[38]

The President hoped that the committee was not truly representative of the Congress. On receipt of the ad hoc report, some Republicans in the House moved two substitute motions intended to meet Jefferson's request. One of these would provide an appropriation for "extraordinary expenses" in the conduct of foreign policy. The other would continue the "Mediterranean Fund," established in 1804 ostensibly in support of measures to "protect the commerce and seamen of the United States against the Barbary Powers." Gallatin's creative bookkeeping, however, had allowed the money to be applied to a variety of purposes without violating the letter of the law.

The acrimonious debate that followed revealed that Jefferson might not be able to depend on as many legislative troops as he had thought. The great shocker must have come when Randolph, in ten days of maneuvering, enlisted for the opposition a majority of Virginia's Republican Congressmen. One after the other, Southern Congressmen of the President's own party deserted his colors on this issue. A more wholesale flocking to the opposition seemed imminent when it became apparent that the dissenters were even more notable for their stature than for sheer numbers.

Jefferson put his powers as President and as party leader on the line to rescue his program.

When the vote came on January 16, fifty-four Congressmen voted against Jefferson's request but seventy-six voted for it. The occasion, however, was not one for unalloyed celebration. The fight had widened divisions within the President's party. Some of those who had supported him had done so grudgingly and with misgivings. It might be an exaggeration to say that Jefferson's victory was Pyrrhic, but he had begged so many favors and twisted so many arms that he had deprived himself of flexibility in maneuvering with the great powers. Those who had followed him in blind faith against their own convictions, or even simply to avoid a breach with the Chief Executive, would not take kindly to abandonment of a policy they had embraced so reluctantly.

Did Jefferson himself have misgivings? Strangely, although the bill passed the Senate with little difficulty and was signed by the President on February 13, only in mid-March did the Secretary of State send to General Armstrong a letter authorizing him to proceed with the plan to acquire the Spanish lands. Half a year had elapsed between the American Minister's original suggestion about acting through the French and his receipt of instructions to go ahead. Some of the delay had been legislative, but a good deal had been administrative. When Jefferson was very sure and very enthusiastic, he frequently moved himself and his administration with surprising rapidity.

To implement the new policy, the United States government must make some substantial concession to the French, indicating its firm commitment to friendship. The President and Congress did not have long to wonder what that might be. Napoleon and his agents called upon Washington to prohibit American trade with all portions of St. Domingo controlled by Negro insurgents. With the blessings of the administration, Senator George Logan of Pennsylvania introduced a bill to effect the prohibition.

Immediately, the Senate's Federalists and even some Republicans from the Northeastern maritime regions pointed out that most of St. Domingo was in the hands of the rebels and therefore a ban on commerce with the occupied ports of the island would mean an end to the most important part of America's foreign trade. Highhanded actions of the British and other belligerents had deprived the United States of most of the rest of its overseas trade. Idle ships would clog American harbors, and the nation's seamen and many of its merchants would be reduced to poverty. The government would inflict a wound upon itself; the stagnation would reduce federal revenues by hundreds of thousands of dollars, then a considerable sum. By meekly accepting Napoleon's conditions, it was argued, the United States would be joining those nations that had already surrendered their sovereignty to him.

A few argued that the United States, a nation dedicated to liberty, would be helping to defeat revolutionists engaged in the same kind of war for independence Americans themselves had waged. But with the Southern states dependent on slave labor and New England states profiting from the international slave trade, there were few Senators in a position to belabor this point without antagonizing influential constituents and appearing hypocritical to boot. The President himself, though a sincere foe of slavery, was no friend to slave insurrection. Randolph, who seemed always to be very sure what everyone should do, for once found himself in a quandary. He was opposed to the whole scheme for soliciting French aid, and the St. Domingo proposal was an integral part of it. On the other hand, as a slaveholder he was acutely aware that a successful slave rebellion in the Caribbean could be a signal for revolts in the United States. When the matter came to a vote, he abstained. His help was not needed. The administration won handily.[39] The President signed the measure February 28.

The Federalists in Congress had long been impatient to deal sternly with the British in retaliation for insults to American sovereignty on the high seas, and the Republicans too were now ready for this part of the administration's tripartite policy to acquire the Spanish lands. Everyone agreed that England should be taught a lesson but no one knew how to do it. So long as Pitt remained Prime Minister—and he was quite popular—there was no reason to suppose that Great Britain would be deflected from its maritime policy by anything but a successfully prosecuted war. Few Americans were so fanatical as to believe that the United States was in a position to wage such a fight. The United States Navy, cut back as an economy measure, was a good deal weaker than it had been several years before. The British navy was the strongest in the world. An ocean dominated by British sails yawned between the English seat of empire and the American republic. Everyone agreed that the greatest of cats, the British lion, should be belled. But no one knew how to proceed.

Some proposed an embargo, but fears that such a step might lead to war killed any enthusiasm for that course. Senator John Quincy Adams was a brilliant man, but his resolutions[40] condemning Britain's interference with American commerce, though duly adopted by his colleagues, served only to demonstrate American impotence.

A resolution calling for exclusion of all British imports had been introduced in the House of Representatives by Andrew Gregg of Pennsylvania. Few thought that it had much chance of passage, but Randolph seized the occasion to deliver a series of philippics against the administration. The former majority leader no longer enjoyed the popularity he had known earlier, but, as chairman of the Ways and Means Committee, he was a power to be reckoned with. Moreover, though Randolph's endorsement might do little to advance anyone's political fortunes on the national scene, his eloquence commanded attention and he was able to sow suspicion and discord. He made speeches about two hours long on two successive days. He continued his impassioned charges even after Gregg's resolution was shelved in favor of a less sweeping one introduced by Joseph Nicholson.

Randolph openly declared that his sympathies lay with the English in the Anglo-French wars. If he pleased some New England Federalists by this assertion he must have alienated them by his perfervid denunciations of merchants and shipowners who threatened to place the nation under the domination of its Atlantic seaports. His comments also worsened the conflict between agricultural Republicans from the South and West on one side and their commerce-oriented colleagues from the Northeast on the other. He heated a myriad of conflicts with the baleful fires of his eloquence without once bringing to the problem the cold light of logic. By turns charging the executive branch with undue influence in the legislature and then sneering at its supposed impotence, he lit up the sky with pyrotechnics that dimmed any mere lodestar of constancy. "There is no longer any cabinet!" he screamed. He explained that the Secretary of the Treasury was never consulted, and he implied that the President and Secretary of State decided everything between them. Anyone familiar with the assertive Gallatin should have found this charge unbelievable. But Randolph, praising the Treasury Secretary while roundly criticizing Madison, apparently was trying to provoke a quarrel between the two cabinet officers.

More opportunities for Randolph's divisive tactics were presented in March 1806, when the Senate sent to the House a bill providing for payment of the Yazoo claims. The administration had continued to favor payment. Randolph, leading the opposition, pronounced, "This bill . . . is the head of the divisions among the Republican Party; it is the secret and covert cause of the whole." He certainly did his part to give truth to his words. Ironically, the chief advocate, within the administration, of this measure which Randolph called "corrupt" was Gallatin, the one cabinet member for whom he professed admiration. The Congressman and his followers carried the day for rejection of the Senate bill.

One legacy of the debate was the fanning of rumors about division in the cabinet until the belief was widespread that Jefferson had alienated all of the department heads except Madison. Supposedly the Secretaries of War and Navy were actively working against their chief, while the Postmaster General plotted and the Secretary of the Treasury was on the point of resigning.[41] While making no public reply to these charges, Jefferson attempted to scotch them through letters to influential individuals. Representative was the note,[42] replying to one from William Duane, a newspaper editor, in which the President said: "There never was a more harmonious, a more cordial administration, nor ever a moment when it has been otherwise. And while differences of opinion have been always rare among us, I can affirm, that as to present matters, there was not a single paragraph in my message to Congress, or those supplementary to it, in which there was not an unanimity of concurrence in the members of the Administration."

Jefferson's note is interesting also as a revelation of his methods of working with his cabinet. "The fact is," he said, "that in ordinary affairs every head of a department consults me on those of his department, and where anything arises too difficult or important to be decided between us, the consultation becomes general. That there is an ostensible cabinet and a concealed one, a public profession and concealed counteraction, is false." The practice of which Jefferson was accused would become very near a reality in 1829, when Andrew Jackson suspended the practice of holding cabinet meetings and began conferences with an informal group of advisers who came to be known as the "Kitchen Cabinet."

To the cynical, Jefferson's picture of a harmonious cabinet may seem too good to be true, but correspondence between him and the department heads suggests that more cordiality existed among them than among their counterparts in either of the two preceding administrations. Indeed, in the roster of presidential administrations from Washington to our own times, Jefferson's would be among the tiny handful most notable for internal harmony. This happy circumstance resulted as much from Jefferson's avowed preference for "the smooth handle" as from his selection of able people who were philosophically compatible.

Jefferson needed all the cooperation he could obtain in the executive branch as trouble multiplied in the legislature and schisms widened in his party, which had survived earlier frustrations of defeat better than it now withstood the stresses of victory. Fortunately for the President, Randolph's verbal excesses soon alienated most of the Congressman's own following. On April 7 Randolph called for publication of Jefferson's confidential message on Spain. The proposal was disturbing but was counterbalanced by the Congressman's simultaneous declaration that he could no longer support the administration and would henceforth work against it. The President was relieved to have his opponent's role stripped of all ambiguity.

The Nicholson bill, passed over Randolph's opposition, was a compromise with antagonistic views—and with reality. Its sponsor doubtless was influenced by the anxiety of his brother-in-law Gallatin that a stringent embargo on British goods would deprive the federal government of annual tariffs amounting to $5 million. No prohibition would be placed on the importation of certain "necessary" goods that the United States could not produce. Coarse woolens, salt, and hardware were specifically exempted, as was another item, Jamaica rum, whose "necessity" might be debated by some. Beyond argument, however, was the fact that all were producers of substantial revenue. The limited effects of the measure were further vitiated by the fact that it would not become operative until November 16, 1806, and thus offered no impediment to full-scale importation in the spring and fall.

Though Randolph was unable to defeat Nicholson's bill, he denounced it, in much quoted language, as "a milk and water bill, a dose of chicken broth to be taken nine months hence. . . . It is too contemptible to be the object of consideration or to excite the feelings of the pettiest state in Europe."[43]

Certainly Great Britain would not be moved by it as long as Pitt was Prime Minister, nor were the British likely to oust him from office. But Pitt received a call more inexorable than the demands of the electorate. As arguments over the policy raged in the United States, word came that the redoubtable statesman had died on January 23. He had been succeeded by Lord Grenville, heading a coalition ministry with the pro-American Charles James Fox as Secretary of State. The abandonment of Pitt's maritime policy was virtually assured.

An event on the Continent also dramatically altered the milieu of decision. In the Battle of Austerlitz, Napoleon won a brilliant victory that compelled

Austria to sign an armistice and Russia to withdraw its troops under a truce. With Europe at his feet, the Emperor no longer needed the money that he had sought to raise by compelling Spain to sell the Floridas to the United States.

Events an ocean away had deprived the President's Spanish policy of its meaning. Yet, after twisting so many Congressmen's arms to gain his way, he could not now completely abandon that policy.

The situation was complicated by the activities of a "war party" within Republican ranks. It was further worsened by the fact that the bellicose faction's leader was Senator Samuel Smith of Maryland, brother to Secretary of the Navy Robert Smith. The Secretary himself encouraged the group. They advocated a large-scale shipbuilding program to increase the navy. They also insisted that, with this evidence of American determination in hand, Senator Smith be sent to London to negotiate a settlement of the maritime problem. Jefferson's supporters defeated the proposed navy buildup, but they could not prevent inclusion in Nicholson's bill of a provision for sending a special minister to London.

Jefferson knew that, if he attempted to placate the war faction of his party by naming Smith, he would be surrendering authority over his own foreign policy. He also had to face the fact that, although his relations with his cabinet had been unusually harmonious, his Secretary of the Navy was more a supporter of his brother's policies than of the President's. While the bill was still being debated, Jefferson revealed that he intended to appoint to the London mission William Pinkney. The snub to Senator Smith was the greater in that Pinkney was not only a fellow Marylander but also a Federalist. By his bold action the President signaled that he would make no concessions to the Smith faction and thus dealt a death blow to their organization while it was still in its infancy. In naming a Federalist under those circumstances, he also, without the slightest indication of weakness, partially disarmed the opposition party.

To score this double victory Jefferson did not have to appoint a mediocrity. William Pinkney was not yet a power on the national scene, but he already promised to become one of the country's ablest lawyers and he had an independent streak evidenced in 1788, when, as a member of the Maryland convention that ratified the Constitution of the United States, he voted against ratification. His appointment to the London mission was particularly appropriate in view of the fact that from 1796 to 1804 he had served as a United States Commissioner to treat with the British concerning capture of neutral ships in wartime.

Despite his success in dealing with the Smith problem and in containing the revolt led by John Randolph, Jefferson had reason to be greatly relieved when Congress adjourned April 21. At his second inauguration little more than a year earlier, after a sweeping victory, it had seemed unlikely that such a concatenation of international emergencies and intraparty problems would plague him in so short a time. Probably Henry Adams did not exaggerate in saying that "never before in the history of the government had a President been obliged to endure such public insults and outrage at the hands of friend and enemy alike."[44] French Chargé Turreau reported to Talleyrand, "Mr. Jefferson has worried himself so much with the movements of Congress that he has made himself ill."[45]

VIII

BUCCANEERS AND REBELS

PERHAPS NO insult hurled at Jefferson in 1806 by his American critics was more frustrating than the one dropped from the supercilious lips of the Marqués de Casa Yrujo, Spain's Minister to the United States. Quite apart from any quarrels with Madrid, the President had grown tired of Yrujo. Though Gilbert Stuart tended to paint similar postal slot mouths on his portraits of men, that of the grandee is decidedly different. The corners of his mouth are turned upward but, far from rendering his countenance more inviting, the expression recalls Ozymandias' "sneer of cold command." The most frustrating thing about the Spaniard's insult to Jefferson was that the President had a perfectly good answer but couldn't use it.

The Marqués, incensed by Jefferson's picture of Spanish belligerence in his annual message to Congress, sent the Secretary of State a missive blasting the President's words. Jefferson's modest sword rattling, of course, had not been intended to antagonize Spain but to justify the administration's request that Congress appropriate $2 million towards defraying any extraordinary expenses that might be incurred in the intercourse between the United States and foreign nations. Jefferson could not tell Yrujo that the request was intended to provide funds for purchasing New Orleans and rewarding Napoleon for pressuring Spain to acquiesce in the deal. He certainly could not tell him that the request was vaguely worded to keep the American people from knowing at that time what was known by Congress.

The insult of the criticisms in the Spaniard's letter was magnified by the Ambassador's releasing it to the Federalist press. In effect he had entered the domestic politics of the United States, conspiring with the President's political enemies.

When Yrujo returned to Washington after a sojourn in Philadelphia, Madison informed him that his remaining in the capital would be "dissatisfactory" to the President. Courteously but firmly, the Secretary's letter added, "Although he cannot permit himself to insist on your departure from the United States during an inclement season, he expects it will not be unnecessarily postponed after this obstacle has passed."[1]

The note was delivered to the grandee while he was dining with General

Louis Turreau, the French chargé, and probably did not aid the Spaniard's digestion. The next day he fired off a reply to Madison saying that he shared the President's desire that he leave the United States. But he asserted that he remained "in the full enjoyment of all my rights and privileges." And he said, "I intend remaining in the city . . . as long as it may suit the interest of the King my master or my own personal convenience."[2]

Though Jefferson believed that he had the power to expel foreign diplomats in the United States, neither he nor his resourceful cabinet could find any law justifying expulsion of the Spaniard. British Minister Merry supported Yrujo's defiance and French Chargé Turreau, who had tried to restrain Yrujo's rashness, now cautioned the President to refrain from precipitate action.[3] Siding with the administration, Senator John Quincy Adams introduced a measure to empower the President to expel ministers from foreign nations under certain circumstances. But the Massachusetts statesman confided to his diary, "The marquis's letters last published seem to have frightened many of them so that probably nothing will be done."[4]

After staying in Washington long enough to emphasize his defiance, the Marqués returned to the greater graces of Philadelphia. Frustrated in attempts to drive the Minister from the United States, Madison could resort only to refusing all communication with him.

A new player had recently arrived on the scene of Spanish-American contention, and Yrujo was quick to exploit the opportunity to embarrass the Jefferson administration. Francisco Miranda strode onto the Washington political stage like a grand opera star playing to a provincial audience.

Actually, this was a return engagement. The Venezuelan revolutionary had visited the United States in 1783, winning the friendship of Thomas Paine, Alexander Hamilton, and Washington himself. To them he had communicated his dream of liberating both South and Central America from Spanish rule. When Spanish agents thwarted him, he fled to England, and then to Germany, Austria, Italy, and Turkey. Finally he found his way to the Court of Catherine the Great of Russia, who took her measure of men in both the council chamber and the bedchamber. She found in Miranda qualities that compensated for his libertarian zeal. The Venezuelan, having known hardship as a soldier and as a prisoner of the Spanish government, found his pampered existence as a royal pet doubly delightful, and he lingered in St. Petersburg.

Later, counting on the French Revolution to divert the attention of Continental powers, he conceived the idea of a New World empire extending from the Mississippi Delta to Cape Horn, and in a trip to London sought the support of William Pitt. When he received no encouragement from the Prime Minister, he enrolled under the revolutionary banner of France. He narrowly escaped bullets, sabers, and the guillotine, and in 1798 was back in England pleading for a British attack on Spain's American colonies. When British leaders once again gave no support, he set out unaided to liberate Venezuela. After two frustrated attempts, he was in Washington, his hopes raised by the possibility of war between the United States and Spain.

For twenty-three years he had gone from capital to capital in two hemispheres, talking to world-famous leaders with a grandiosity more fascinating than convincing and dulcetly whispering his way into an incredible number of boudoirs. And along the whole tawdry, glittering trail, something at the core of him had remained unfalteringly true to the shining ideal of Latin American liberation. It was as though Don Juan and Don Quixote had ridden into town in the same skin.

Miranda came to the capital from New York, where, with the financial assistance of Aaron Burr's friends, he had acquired and armed the ship *Leander*, besides recruiting adventurers for a filibustering expedition to South America. Indeed, Burr's friends found Miranda so captivating that the former Vice President, himself a seductive talker and spinner of grandiose schemes, was reported to be "jealous."

In Washington, General Francisco de Miranda, as he was now known, was the guest of both Madison and Jefferson. There was nothing surprising in this fact, particularly as regarded the President. Jefferson entertained notables of every sort at the Executive Mansion and was a connoisseur of exotic strangers. The General's friendship with the two statesmen assumed a new complexion, however, when word was received in February that he had sailed for the West Indies. Rumor said that his true destination was Venezuela.

Realizing that his administration could be compromised, Jefferson asked Madison to ask the United States Attorney in New York whether the Venezuelan's operations in that state had violated federal laws. Unable to communicate directly with the administration, Yrujo prodded France's Turreau to protest the appearance of complicity. Turreau disliked Madison, and his delight in the Secretary's discomfiture was obvious in his report to the Spanish minister:

> I imparted to him my suspicions and yours. I sought his eyes and, what is rather rare, I met them. He was in a state of extraordinary prostration while I was demanding from him a positive explanation on the proceedings in question. It was with an effort that he broke silence, and at length answered me that the President had already anticipated my representations by ordering measures to be taken against the accomplices who remained in the country and against the culprits who should return. I leave you to judge whether I was satisfied by this answer, and I quitted him somewhat abruptly in order to address him in writing.[5]

Madison's consternation is understandable. For about four months the wooing of Napoleon and cultivation of the Emperor's envoy in Washington had been prime objects of the Secretary's diplomacy. French cooperation was needed to pressure Spain into selling the Floridas to the United States.

Madison's and Jefferson's embarrassment worsened. Showering rumors like sparks in his coruscating progress from Washington to New York, the General had burned a path across three states and ignited many brushfires in the process. Some newspapers reported that he said the United States government had agreed to look the other way while he outfitted his expedition. According to other accounts, he had claimed the active support of the administration.

The Secretary of State denied all allegations of complicity but Federalist newspapers gleefully pointed out that Madison had had several meetings with Miranda, and those who wanted to believe the rumors found that evidence enough. Yrujo warned his government of the Venezuelan's expedition, fanned some of the flames of rumor, and then sat back to enjoy his revenge.

As a result of the investigation ordered by Jefferson, a federal grand jury indicted Samuel G. Ogden, owner of the *Leander*, and William S. Smith, surveyor of the port of New York. Smith was John Adams' son-in-law and a friend and supporter of Burr. Pressed by Gallatin, Jefferson reluctantly removed Smith from office before the formal indictment. These actions and Madison's denials satisfied the Republicans but had little effect on the Federalists. Significantly, British Minister Merry, who was highly critical of the Jefferson administration, nevertheless believed that Miranda's solicitation of Jefferson and Madison had been "attended with no material result."[6] And John Quincy Adams wrote Smith, his own brother-in-law, concerning Miranda's claims of promises from the President and Secretary of State: "That he misunderstood or misrepresented their real intentions I have no doubt."[7]

Nevertheless, both houses of Congress received memorials from Ogden and Smith, begging legislative intervention to protect them from prosecution inasmuch as they had been "led into error by the conduct of the officers of the Executive government," who now sought scapegoats "in expiation of their own errors, or to deprecate the vengeance of foreign governments." This effort accomplished nothing in the Senate. The House, by a vote of 75 to 8, declared that it found no supporting evidence for the charge. By a vote of 70 to 13 it declared its belief that the memorials had been "presented at a time, and under circumstances, insidiously calculated to excite unjust suspicions."

So the Miranda affair did not wreck Jefferson's relations with Congress. And it did not precipitate war with Spain. Its chief negative effect was a further erosion of the public confidence which the President had enjoyed at the time of his reelection.

Jefferson did not know it, but, while Yrujo was expressing indignation over United States encouragement of plots against Spain, Spanish agents were rewarding United States citizens for cooperation against the government in Washington. Jefferson was unaware that one of his own appointees, one of the highest officers of the United States government, was at that very time betraying his country. That man was General James Wilkinson, Commanding General of the army and Jefferson's choice as Governor of the Louisiana Territory. A confidence man of the first water, Wilkinson had won the trust of two highly intelligent men who were much more suspicious of their fellows than the Virginian ever was. When an investigation, initiated in Washington's presidency, brought to his successor's attention reports that Wilkinson was a pensioner of Spain, John Adams assured the accused that he took no stock in such charges, saying, "I esteem your talents, I respect your services and feel an attachment to your person. . . ." Adams wrote that almost everyone coming from the Mississippi Territory, where Wilkinson was then on duty, said that the General was on Spain's payroll, but he explained: "They seem to be in such a temper that nobody escapes accusation."[8] The other brilliant skeptic duped by the General was Aaron Burr, who had entrusted him with secrets that could be the New Yorker's undoing.

As early as March 9, 1805, Turreau wrote to Talleyrand that Burr and Wilkinson were in league and included a shrewd analysis of each. Of the forty-eight-year-old General he said: "He has an amiable exterior. Though said to be well-informed in civil and political matters, his military capacity is small. Ambitious and easily dazzled, fond of show and appearances, he complains rather indiscreetly, and especially after dinner, of the form of his government, which leaves officers few chances of fortune, advancement, and glory, and which does not pay its military chiefs enough to support a proper style. He listened with pleasure, or rather with enthusiasm, to the details which I gave him in regard to the organization, the dress, and the force of the French army. My uniform, the order with which I am decorated, are objects of envy to him; and he seems to hold to the American service only because he can do no better. General Wilkinson is the most intimate friend, or rather the most devoted creature of Colonel Burr."[9]

Turreau told Talleyrand: "Mr. Burr's career is generally looked upon as finished; but he is far from sharing that opinion, and I believe he would rather sacrifice the interests of his country than renounce celebrity and fortune. Although Louisiana is still only a territory, it has obtained the right of sending a delegate to Congress. Louisiana is therefore to become the theatre of Mr. Burr's new intrigues; he is going there under the aegis of General Wilkinson."

By the summer of 1806 several people, at least, were telling Jefferson stories of Burr's and Wilkinson's duplicity. He had no doubt of the New Yorker's capacity for deceit but, ever disinclined to think the worst of those with whom he had ostensibly friendly relations, he preferred to suspend judgement on the General. In that summer of 1806, though, amid vexatious problems of state, he had a painful reminder that treachery could occur where little suspected. His devoted friend George Wythe died under mysterious circumstances. The kindly savant, founder of America's first school of law, had been Jefferson's teacher at William and Mary, had encouraged the youthful genius, repeatedly had gone with him to dine at the Governor's Palace with Governor Fauquier, and had lent Jefferson his Williamsburg home when the teacher was sent to the Continental Congress and the student to the House of Burgesses. When Jefferson's Declaration of Independence had been adopted in Philadelphia, his old teacher had been a proud signer. Later, still a professor at William and Mary, Wythe had claimed the privilege of writing the Latin citation when his former pupil was awarded an honorary doctorate.

The loss of this friend would have been troubling to Jefferson under any circumstances, but it was still more upsetting to learn that he had been poisoned and that the benevolent old man's nephew had been indicted for the murder. Amid his deathbed agonies, Wythe had changed his will, eliminating his nephew as beneficiary and substituting the young black boy who cared for him in his illness. The only witness to the poisoning was a female slave. Only the fact that a slave's testimony could not send a white person to his death prevented conviction of the nephew.[10]

A letter from Joseph Hamilton Daveiss, United States District Attorney for Kentucky, in January 1806 had excited Jefferson's suspicions of Wilkinson. Daveiss said that the General "has been for years, and now is, a pensioner of Spain." In evident reference to Burr, he added that "a very exalted magistrate of this country has lately drawn on Spain for his pension." If Jefferson required him to, he would reveal the identity of that official and of other Americans who were pensioners of Spain. In any event, if war with Spain should come, the President should "let neither the first nor second in command be appointed out of the western country."[11]

Jefferson sought Gallatin's advice. The Treasury Secretary said that Wilkinson was "extravagant and needy, and would not I think feel much delicacy in speculating on public money or public land. In both those respects he must be closely watched." But treason—Gallatin did not believe that the General would sink so low.[12]

Jefferson's request to Daveiss for further information was crossed by a second letter from Daveiss naming Burr. No surprise there, but there was also a long list that included Jefferson's longtime friend John Breckinridge and such other Republican stalwarts as Henry Clay and William Henry Harrison.[13] As part of such a list, the charge against Wilkinson lost its credibility. Daveiss was John Marshall's brother-in-law and a Federalist so devoted that he had taken as his middle name the surname of party chief Alexander Hamilton.[14] Partisan prejudice, or even political machinations, might account for his accusations.

Jefferson did not completely dismiss the possibility of trouble with Wilkinson, but it did take a back seat to a more pressing worry about Louisiana. Suppose Spain, still vehemently charging that France's cession of New Orleans to the United States was illegal, should attempt to retake the city by force. The President proposed to Congress that two million acres in the area be divided into 160-acre plots, every alternate one of which would be granted to a man who would contract to live on the land and farm it and to serve in the militia. Jefferson saw his plan as a far more democratic one than maintaining a large standing army. But New Hampshire's Senator William Plumer thought the President's plan smacked of "the feudal system" and a majority of his colleagues appeared to agree. For whatever reason, they tabled his proposal.

Still worse was the fate of his bill to classify the militia by age groups to put it into a better state of readiness; this measure was summarily voted down. Jefferson had proposed making militiamen between the ages of twenty-one and twenty-five liable to military service one year out of two anywhere in the United States or contiguous nations. Those between the ages of twenty-six and thirty-four could be required to serve for three months in their own state or an adjoining one while those over thirty-four or under twenty-one could not be required to serve outside their own states or for more than three months of any given year. The plan had to recommend it only common sense as opposed to the full weight of parochial pride and plume-hatted vainglory. Plumer reported that the President, tears welling in his eyes, protested, "The people expect I should provide for their defense but Congress refuse me the means."[15]

Jefferson's anxiety about defense brought him closer to the philosophy of the naval enthusiasts whom he had often antagonized. Thanks to the valor and ability of General William Eaton, Commodores Edward Preble and John Rodgers, and Captain Stephen Decatur, the Tripolitan War had ended in victory for the United States. The triumph solved an old problem but created a new one. By a law enacted March 25, 1804, the administration was required to reduce the navy to peacetime dimensions when the war with Tripoli ended. Commodore Rodgers thought the fleet should be kept at wartime strength in the Mediterranean for some months until the stability of the peace was assured. Jefferson agreed, but his cabinet insisted unanimously that the letter of the law must be obeyed. The President was not required to follow his cabinet, but he was required to follow the law. Still, he told Secretary of the Navy Robert Smith, he feared that abrupt reduction of American forces in the Mediterranean might invite a resumption of the war. Or "is it," he asked, "one of those cases where the Executive should hazard the doing good against law, and throw himself on his country for justification?"[16] Only in the Louisiana Purchase had he acted on this principle, although, as a diplomat in Europe in 1785, he had considered doing so.[17]

In the midst of his concerns over external and internal threats to national security, Jefferson received fresh news of the Burr conspiracy from a credible source. At Monticello on September 15 he received a letter from Colonel George Morgan, a respected citizen of Pennsylvania, and it was corroborated a few days later by one from John Nicholson of Herkimer, New York. En route west, according to Morgan, Burr had stopped at the colonel's farm and attempted to recruit his sons in a military adventure apparently tied in with dreams of an independent nation across the Mississippi free from a federal government that the Vice President considered contemptible. Jefferson wrote to both informants for more particulars of the "parricide propositions," promising to keep their roles confidential if they wished.[18]

A more shocking disclosure came October 20 in a letter[19] from Postmaster General Gideon Granger relaying testimony from General William Eaton. The General was a bitter Federalist foe of Republicanism and his military record included more than one charge of insubordination, but he had led a "horde of Americans, Greeks, Tripolitans and Arab camel-drivers," "even without water for days," across five hundred miles of desert to win for the United States the greatest land victory of the Tripolitan War.[20] His patriotism should be beyond question—always of course allowing for such anomalies as Benedict Arnold's turning traitor after his heroism at Saratoga. Eaton had told both Granger and Congressman Ely of Massachusetts that in the winter of 1805 Burr had offered him appointment, as second in command under General Wilkinson, of forces organized to separate the Western states from the Union. Burr may have conjectured that Eaton, vociferously disappointed by what he regarded as meager rewards for his services, would be as easily tempted as Arnold had been in a similar situation.

In three cabinet meetings over a period of four days Jefferson explored the problems of defense of the Southwest frontier raised by Spain's overt actions and Burr's clandestine ones. On May 6 Secretary of War Dearborn, acting on the President's instructions, had ordered General Wilkinson to move "with all practicable dispatch" from St. Louis to Orleans Territory to take command in that enclave in the Louisiana Territory. The General was instructed to repel any Spanish invasion east of the Sabine River (marking the western boundary of the present state of Louisiana) or on the American side of West Florida. Only two days before, Jefferson, who had provoked criticism for uniting civil and military authority when he appointed Wilkinson as Governor of Louisiana, had written to Senator Samuel Smith, "Not a single fact has appeared which occasions me to doubt that I could have made a fitter appointment than General Wilkinson."[21]

He soon had reason to doubt his optimistic estimate. Wilkinson had been ordered to Orleans Territory because its Governor, W. C. C. Claiborne, reported heightened military activity by the Spanish in Mobile. The General declined to hurry to his assigned post, pleading the illness of his wife (who did die) but also saying that his assessment of the situation differed from Claiborne's. In fact, nearly the entire summer passed before he left for Orleans.

In the meantime there had been many reports of dissatisfaction with him on the part of both Anglo-Americans and Creoles. Laussat, the French Prefect in Orleans, was as critical of Wilkinson in his reports to his government as Turreau had been in his dispatches from Washington. Laussat said the General was "a flighty, rattle-headed fellow, often drunk, who has committed a hundred impertinent follies."[22]

Now, in October 1806, Jefferson had to deal with a far graver problem in the Orleans area and on the Southwest border than he had anticipated. Not only was his chosen commander self-willed and incompetent; his patriotism was seriously in doubt. But while Wilkinson was, in Jefferson's words, under "very general suspicion of infidelity," Burr was, he believed, almost certainly guilty of plotting to sever the Western states from the rest of the nation, perhaps with the aid of the Spanish. The cabinet agreed with the President's plan to ask Governors and District Attorneys of those states to have Burr "strictly watched and, on his committing any overt act unequivocally, to have him tried for treason, misdemeanor, or whatever other offense" he might have committed.[23]

The officials would be instructed to keep Burr's followers under equally strict surveillance and, if they should prove guilty, to proceed against them in the same manner. No followers were named but, next to Burr himself, Wilkinson was the principal suspect in the whole affair. In view of suspicions of Wilkinson and of the General's flagrant disregard of orders to move quickly to Orleans, what action should be taken? The possibility that the American commander might deliver Orleans to the enemy was alarming, but so was the possibility that, if he were only tempted by Burr's blandishments but had not yet succumbed, any punitive action might cause him to embrace the Colonel as his savior. No one had a satisfactory answer to the President's dilemma. Decision was postponed.

At another meeting, Jefferson and his cabinet took three bold steps against

Burr. They unanimously agreed that two of the greatest heroes of the Tripolitan War, Edward Preble and Stephen Decatur, should be ordered to New Orleans; that additional gunboats be sent there if funds were available; that John Graham, Secretary of the Orleans Territory, replace Wilkinson as Governor of the Louisiana Territory and be empowered to arrest Burr if his transgressions warranted it. At their next meeting Jefferson and his cabinet took three steps backward, rescinding their arguments of the previous session because of the President's announcement that the latest dispatches from the West contained no report of questionable actions by Burr. Jefferson, however, had not ended his watchfulness. On November 3 he wrote his son-in-law Thomas Mann Randolph, "We give him all the attention our situation admits; as yet we have no legal proof of any overt act which the law can lay hold of."[24]

The arrival in Washington of a mysterious messenger on November 25 made Jefferson thankful that he had deferred action against both Burr and Wilkinson. The courier was Lieutenant Thomas A. Smith, a young officer who ostensibly had journeyed to the capital from the South to resign his commission. He carried, among other dispatches, a letter from Wilkinson to the President explaining that the bearer was a valuable man whose resignation should be rejected; the supposed resignation attempt was a device to send confidential messages to the President without exciting suspicion. As a further precaution, one of the letters was anonymous, though obviously, as was later acknowledged, it was from the General. According to this communication, a secret organization reaching southward and westward from New York to Louisiana was composed of eight thousand to ten thousand men scheduled to descend upon New Orleans about February 1 after a general rendezvous near the falls of the Ohio River no later than November 20. In contrast to all this specificity regarding movements, the anonymous writer professed to be ignorant of the identities of leaders of the enterprise. He did feel sure, however, that England would lend a hand to the conspirators.[25]

In a signed letter marked "confidential," Wilkinson commented on the "revelations" he had made anonymously. Maintaining the fiction that the un-signed communication was by a third party, he said that, although the writer did not say that United States territory was threatened by the conspiracy, he personally believed that "the revolt of this [Orleans] territory will be made an auxiliary step to the main design of attacking Mexico, to give it a new master in the place of promised liberty." Because of this menace, he said, he found it necessary to disregard the President's orders to stand firm against the Spaniards in the vicinity of the Sabine River and instead to compromise with them and then proceed swiftly to New Orleans "to be ready to defend that capital against usurpation and violence."[26]

On November 5 Wilkinson and Spanish Colonel Simon de Herrera reached an agreement creating a neutral zone between the Arroyo Hondo and the Sabine pending diplomatic determination of a permanent boundary. Arriving in New Orleans shortly afterward, Wilkinson wrote the President that "this deep, dark, wicked and widespread conspiracy" exceeded his original suspicions, but he would fight it with "indefatigable industry, incessant vigilance, and hardy courage." Just send him the necessary reinforcements. In defense of the beloved United States, "I shall glory to give my life."[27] One is reminded of Little Jack Horner exclaiming, "What a good boy am I!"

Wilkinson did not have that "lean and hungry look" that Shakespeare's Julius Caesar associated with plotting rebels nor was he of that dull tribe that his Lorenzo deemed obviously "fit for treasons, stratagems, and spoils." He was a well-fed, roundfaced man with large, sparkling eyes and full lips that seemed made for savoring life.[28] One could scarcely have found a less conspiratorial-looking figure than Wilkinson as, after writing to the President of the United States a pledge of sacrificial patriotism, he bent his sleek head to the task of composing a letter to the King of Spain's Viceroy in Mexico. The General had the honor to report that he had been privileged to serve his Catholic Majesty by frustrating the evil designs of an American citizen, Colonel Burr. Under these circumstances, his usual pension was inadequate. He was entitled to the sum of $110,000 in addition to reimbursement for what he had been "obliged to spend in order to sustain the cause of good government, order, and humanity."[29]

In citing Burr as the leader of the conspiracy, Wilkinson was franker with the Spanish Viceroy than with his own President. In one of his confidential letters to Jefferson he had written, "I have never in my whole life found myself in such circumstances of perplexity and embarrassment as at present; for I am not only uninformed of the prime mover and ultimate objects of this daring enterprise, but am ignorant of the foundation on which it rests, of the means by which it is to be supported, and whether any immediate or collateral *protection*, internal or external, is expected."[30]

But Jefferson was sure of "the prime mover," and so were others. District Attorney Daveiss sought an indictment of Burr in Lexington, Kentucky, on grounds that he had conspired to make war on the United States or Spain or both. Burr, almost always convincing to those who had seen little of him, appeared eloquently in his own behalf. Appearing also as counsel for Burr was a native Virginian not yet thirty years old who had studied under Jefferson's old law professor George Wythe and later moved to Kentucky to escape the too crowded competition of the Richmond bar. He was a thin, bony-faced grass-hopper of a man, all motion and electricity. When he began talking his magnetism was electric too and those packing the courtroom predicted a great future for this Henry Clay. The grand jury refused to return a true bill against Burr, and the spectators' cheers defied the gavel. The District Attorney tried again, and again the jury refused to indict. Convinced that Burr was a loyal Jeffersonian Republican victimized by Federalists, Lexington gave a public ball in his honor.

On December 9, five days after the Kentucky grand jury's final failure to indict Burr, the Colonel suffered a setback. Men acting on orders of Ohio Governor Edward Tiffin, who had obtained the authorization of the state legislature, seized ten of his boats on the Ohio River as well as others under construction.[31]

With less regard for legal niceties, a raiding party, drawing inspiration from Jefferson's November 27 proclamation[32] calling for seizure of the vessels and arms of "sundry persons" conspiring to wage war on Spain, descended on Blennerhassett's Island in the Ohio River in Wood County, Virginia (now West Virginia). The island was the home of one of Burr's chief lieutenants, Harman Blennerhassett, a romantic Irishman whose friends said that he "had all kinds of sense except common sense."[33] Lured into Burr's conspiracy by the promise of glory and his infatuation with the Colonel's beautiful daughter, Blennerhassett wrote indiscreetly for an Ohio newspaper, calling for secession of the Western states. His island became the center of operations for the expedition Burr was assembling.

Getting wind that the Wood County militia were on the way, Blennerhassett escaped downriver with some thirty men, slipping past the drunken and slumbering militia sentries. In the words of Albert Beveridge: "Next day . . . the militia invaded the deserted island and, finding the generously stocked wine cellar, restored their strength by drinking all the wine and whisky on the place. They then demonstrated their abhorrence of treason by breaking the windows, demolishing the furniture, tearing the pictures, trampling the flower-beds, burning the fences, and insulting Mrs. Blennerhassett."[34]

Still unaware of the President's proclamation, Burr hurried to Nashville. There Andrew Jackson, a former United States Senator who lived in a log cabin but dreamed of a mansion on the same site and perhaps some day one in Washington, had assembled a fleet of small boats for the New Yorker. Jackson was an ardent Jeffersonian and an intensely patriotic citizen of the United States, but his fiery spirit yearned for war with Spain. He was so deceived by Burr that he entrusted his own nephew to the Colonel as the expedition assembled.

The President's proclamation provided the opportunity Wilkinson sought. From New Orleans he had kept up a steady barrage of cliches designed to evidence his passionate patriotism: "The plot thickens. . . . What a situation has our country reached. Let us save it if we can. . . . Be you silent as the grave. . . . You are surrounded by secret agents. . . . The storm will probably burst in New Orleans, where I shall meet it and triumph or perish."[35] Jefferson's proclamation gave him the chance to give force to another saying: "Civil institutions must for a short period yield to the strong arm of military law."[36]

What tortures of anxiety Wilkinson must have suffered as, one after the other, Burr's followers were apprehended. The General himself had been a partner in the Colonel's imperial schemes, and New Orleans was full of people who knew it. The General proceeded to arrest them.

Two of those involved, Samuel Swartwout and Dr. Justus Erich Bollmann, were arrested and imprisoned without warrant and denied counsel. They were placed aboard a warship for delivery to Washington. When Swartwout, fearing that he was to be murdered, jumped into the river, an officer "drew up his file of six men and ordered them to shoot him." Only the wetness of the gunpowder saved the prisoner.[37]

When General John Adair, a former United States Senator and old comrade in arms of Wilkinson, rode unsuspecting into New Orleans, he was immediately arrested by a captain and one hundred soldiers. He could not look to Wilkinson for redress. Wilkinson had ordered his arrest. Adair was denied the opportunity to take his medicine with him and was transported "down the river twenty-five miles, loaded on the other side . . . and placed under a tent in a swamp." Wilkinson ordered the lieutenant in charge of Adair to resist "with force and arms" any civil officer presenting a writ of habeas corpus.[38]

During this reign of terror, Wilkinson continued in the pay of the Spanish government and remained their faithful correspondent.[39]

How was the General's tyranny viewed by the apostle of liberty in the President's office? Apparently Jefferson was not dismayed by the arrests and seizures of Swartwout, Bollmann, and Adair, nor of about sixty others, including the editor of the *Orleans Gazette*. Nor was he incensed at the rifling of a federal post office in Wilkinson's search for evidence, all of this in spite of the fact that the President so recently had had serious doubts about the General's own patriotism and trustworthiness.[40] Wilkinson had written the President that harsh measures were necessary because Burr commanded six or seven thousand men about to descend on New Orleans. The President told the General that Burr's army consisted of only eighty to one hundred borne down the Mississippi by boats manned by sixty oarsmen. Moreover, as he pointed out, the oarsmen had simply been employed for the transportation and were "not at all of [Burr's] party."[41]

Nevertheless, while denying the premises of Wilkinson's justification, Jefferson endorsed his actions, those contemplated as well as those already performed. "Your sending here Swartwout and Bollmann, and adding to them Burr, Blennerhassett, and Tyler, should they fall into your hands," he wrote, "will be supported by the public opinion." The President added a word of caution, but on pragmatic rather than moral grounds. Whether Jefferson's adjuration reflected his own uppermost consideration or simply that to which his correspondent would be most sensitive, we cannot know. He wrote, "I hope, however, you will not extend this deportation to persons against whom there is only suspicion, or shades of offense not strongly marked. In that case, I fear the public sentiment would desert you; because, [the people] seeing no danger here, violations of law are felt with strength."

The President went so far as to say that, although those unfamiliar with the General's conduct might be misled by the "malicious insinuation" of the press, those more knowledgeable "have not failed to strengthen the public confidence in you; and I can assure you that your conduct, as now known, has placed you on grounds extremely favorable with the public."

Anticipating a fire storm of criticism, not only from the opposition party but also from the Quids, erstwhile Republicans led by John Randolph, Jefferson wrote on the same day to Governor Claiborne: "On great occasions every good officer must be ready to risk himself in going beyond the strict line of law, when the public preservation requires it. . . . The Feds, and the little band of Quids in opposition, will try to make something of the infringement of liberty by the military arrest and deportation of citizens, but if it does not go beyond such offenders as Swartwout, Bollmann, Burr, Blennerhassett, Tyler, etc., they will be supported by the public approbation."[42] This from the leader of America's strict constructionists! Leonard Levy has noted the ironic fact that

"Years earlier, when writing the Declaration of Independence, Jefferson had thought that among George III's serious crimes were those making the 'Military independent of and superior to the Civil Power' and 'transporting us beyond Seas to be tried.' "[43]

Randolph, on January 18, 1807, introduced in the House of Representatives a resolution demanding from the President any information about an unlawful combination against the United States or any other nation, as well as a statement of what the President had done or had planned to do about such activity. Minus the demand for the Chief Executive's plans, the resolution was passed.[44]

Four days later Jefferson reported on the proceedings in New Orleans in a "Special Message to Congress."[45] He said that Burr was guilty "beyond question" of leading an expedition to attack New Orleans or Mexico. He had, he said, issued his proclamation upon receipt of the first reliable account of Burr's machinations, and that response had proved sufficient. The plot had been thwarted; the danger was past. General Wilkinson's stringent measures were consistent with "the honor of a soldier and fidelity of a good citizen."

Dispensing with the Senate rules by unanimous consent the next day, the upper chamber, without debate, passed a bill suspending the writ of habeas corpus for three months. Floor leader William B. Giles of Virginia and his lieutenants had the situation well in hand.

But the House was another story. Led by Randolph, and more surprisingly by the President's own son-in-law, John Eppes, the lower chamber rejected the Senate bill by a vote of 113 to 19. Jefferson was caught by surprise. Anticipating passage, he had instructed a United States Attorney to apply for a bench warrant against Bollmann and Swartwout. Most Republican Congressmen were still loyal to the President but they were even more loyal to certain principles of individual liberty. Some zealots introduced a bill making "further provision for securing the privilege of the writ of habeas corpus," but most Republicans considered it not so much a needed guarantee of rights as a rebuke to the President. For want of their support, it was killed.

The disagreement between the two chambers of Congress symbolized the growing rift in the Republican Party: between those who held that it was better to endanger the fabric of government than to violate the civil liberties of a single individual and those who argued that, in the interest of preserving the liberties of the greatest possible number of citizens, individual liberties must occasionally be sacrificed. Jefferson himself had begun his career on the high ground occupied by the first group, and he still thought of those heights as his home; but as President his zeal for judicial reform and his fear of designs to split the Union had led him several times to pitch his tent on the lower ground of compromise. He would not rebuild his philosophical shelter in the bottomlands, but in some emergencies he would camp out there.

News traveled slowly from the Western country. When Jefferson sent his special message to Congress on the alleged conspiracy, he did not know that Burr had been arrested in Mississippi Territory five days earlier. The little Colonel had been wearing "an old blanket-coat begirth with a leathern strap, to which a tin cup was suspended on the left and a scalping knife on the right."[46]

But the eyes that peered from under the "old white hat flopped over his face"[47] were the luminous jet orbs for which the fugitive was famous, and the elegance of his bearing belied his shabby habiliments.[48] Some said, too, that in animation he spoke with an eloquence that rendered disguise useless.

Confined to a frontier fort for two weeks before being sent east, Burr captivated his captors. The officers and the enlisted men found him equally entertaining. When the brother of the Captain commanding Burr's guards became ill, the prisoner revealed a surprising knowledge of the healing arts. Even clad in worn homespun, the little bantam proved irresistible to the officers' wives.[49]

The pampering ended abruptly with the start of the painful, thousand-mile journey to Washington through pelting rains and flooded wilderness. A large part of the route was only an Indian trail. Night after night the entire party lay down on the spongy ground and went to sleep to the howling of wolves.

Twelve days' travel brought them to South Carolina, where Burr's beautiful daughter Theodosia lived with her husband, Joseph Allston, one of its most influential citizens. Many South Carolinians were sympathetic to Burr. When the convoy passed some men standing in front of a tavern, he leaped from his horse, shouting, "I am Aaron Burr, under military arrest, and claim the protection of civil authorities."[50]

Nicholas Perkins, a brawny frontier lawyer who had been the first person to penetrate the Colonel's disguise, aimed a brace of pistols at him and commanded him to remount. When Burr refused, Perkins swept him up into the saddle as if he were a child. Tears welled in the prisoner's eyes as he resumed his journey, now flanked as well as preceded and followed by armed guards.

The Burr affair was the nexus of a conglomeration of problems, foreign and domestic, that encircled the President like a chorus of harpies. The Colonel's actions realized the worst of Jefferson's fears of Republican division and of national disunity. And, as those actions involved Great Britain, France, Spain, and Mexico, they also exacerbated the danger of war, economic even if not military and naval, with foreign powers.

Since 1803 American trade had been severely damaged and United States neutrality sorely tried by the harsh restrictions Britain and France each sought to impose upon the carrying trade of nonbelligerent nations in order to deprive the other of the material means of waging war. Experience as Secretary of State and a knowledge of history had taught Jefferson what to expect. The little American ship of state would be tossed about in the wakes of the mighty contenders. On April 18, 1802, he had written Robert Livingston, then representing the United States in Paris, "Nothing but Europe is seen, or supposed to have any weight in the affairs of nations."[51] But he saw, as many of his European counterparts did not, that a crisis in the vicinity of New Orleans could threaten the Old World as well as the New: ". . . this speck which now appears as an almost invisible point on the horizon, is the embryo of a tornado which will burst on the countries [?] on both shores of the Atlantic and involve in its effects their highest destinies."[52] Trevelyan said of William Pitt the Elder, "He alone of

British statesmen carried the map of the empire in his head and in his heart."[53] It might with equal justice be said of Jefferson that, almost alone among the statesmen of his time, he carried in his head the map of the Atlantic world. He was exhilarated and tortured by seeing much larger potentialities for both good and evil than were apparent to his contemporaries.

The Non-Importation Act passed by Congress to counter British violations of the rights of neutral commerce had been suspended on December 19, 1806, at the President's request. The administration intensified its efforts to solve the problem through diplomacy. James Monroe and William Pinkney, in London negotiating a treaty with Great Britain, threatened that the United States would enforce the Non-Importation Act if Britain did not cease the seizure of American seamen, authorize indemnity payments for seizure, and make other concessions.

The American diplomats abandoned their strong stance when Napoleon issued his Berlin Decree, proclaiming a blockade of Great Britain and announcing his "continental system," a Europe sufficient unto itself. Napoleon lacked the naval strength to isolate the United Kingdom, and he overreached himself in trying to make the Continent his private terrarium. But he could make trade with the British extremely costly. And his forbidding the United States to engage in that trade called for resistance and, to Monroe and Pinkney, seemed to make the United States a natural ally of the British. They therefore settled for what London was willing to offer.

The treaty reached the President on March 3, 1807, the day on which Congress adjourned. Jefferson and Madison had said earlier that no treaty would be acceptable unless it included an agreement on disputed matters concerning the impressment of American seamen. There was no such provision in this document. More disturbing to Jefferson than this omission was an addendum on which the British had insisted. It provided that the treaty would become effective only upon assurance that the United States would ignore the Berlin Decree. Jefferson saw such an agreement as an act of belligerence toward France. He rejected the treaty. Moreover, in an unprecedented exercise of executive power, he refused to submit the document to the Senate.[54]

What a traumatic session of the Congress it had been! He had been opposed by prominent members of his own party, even friends from his own state, even his own son-in-law. The international situation was such that the United States was forced to consider whether it would suffer a greater loss of dignity and material advantage by accepting insults from Britain or from France. Hope of changing these bitter alternatives had vanished with receipt of the treaty from London, and his disappointment had been deepened by the fact that one of the two chief United States negotiators had been one of his favorite proteges, James Monroe. Once an opponent of a strong navy, Jefferson now saw the necessity of increased naval strength and improved shore defenses if the United States was to have security in its own territorial waters, but Congress rebelled against the expense. A federal court had freed two men charged as coconspirators with Burr and there was no telling what a judicial system dominated by John Marshall would do with Burr himself.

Probably most wounding of all was the belief of some of his most loyal supporters that, in suspending the writ of habeas corpus and supporting military over civilian authority, he had betrayed his own principles of individual liberty. Confronted by a crisis, he had reacted as the British King and Parliament had at the prospect of rebellion in the American colonies. Like the Federalists that he had so scathingly condemned, he had attempted to make the courts the instruments of the Executive.

Why did Jefferson so relentlessly pursue Aaron Burr? Many historians have said that, even if Jefferson himself was unaware of the fact, he must have been driven by animosity toward an old political opponent. Virtually all seem to have overlooked another factor. Jefferson undoubtedly believed, as he said, that Burr was a traitor. Certainly, though scholars differ on the matter even today, there was abundant evidence to suggest that he was. Jefferson could not bring judicial objectivity to the case of a traitor. He had shown this in 1781 when he had pursued Benedict Arnold, with whom his acquaintance was at most limited, with all the fury of a personal vendetta. Jefferson, then Governor, had asked General J. P. G. Muhlenberg to select men "to seize and bring off this greatest of all traitors." The Governor would see that they were rewarded in the amount of 5,000 guineas among them. Jefferson crossed out one part of his original draft and omitted it from the final copy. It read in part: "I shall be sorry to suppose that any circumstance may put it out of their power to bring him off alive after they shall have taken him and of course oblige them to put him to death. Should this happen, however, and America be deprived of the satisfaction of seeing him exhibited as a public spectacle of infamy, and of vengeance, I must give my approbation to their putting him to death. . . . In event of his death, however, I must reduce the reward proposed to 2,000 guineas, in proportion as our satisfaction would be reduced."[55]

Still, how could President Jefferson, the great apostle of liberty, move to suspend the writ of habeas corpus? Many historians and biographers have asked the question. It is disappointing that Jefferson should have so acted, but it should not be so surprising to anyone with a knowledge of either history or human nature. Offenses against liberty have been committed throughout history by its zealous protectors. In the spring of 1807 the constitutional government of the United States was less than eighteen years old. The infant nation was threatened by the greatest land power in the world, the greatest sea power in the world, and other strong and hostile countries. A movement to divide the United States and found an empire was being led by a charismatic former Vice President. In these circumstances, Jefferson, unnecessarily and wrongly, sought suspension of the writ of habeas corpus and countenanced on United States territory the subordination of civil to military authority. Unfortunately, he was not the last American President to act so in a time of national crisis. Abraham Lincoln in 1861 "suspended the writ of habeas corpus and authorized army commanders to declare martial law in various areas behind the lines and to try civilians in military courts."[56] In World War II Franklin D. Roosevelt approved depriving United States citizens who were Japanese-Americans of their civil rights. Both Lincoln and Roosevelt, like Jefferson, were great defenders and advancers of civil rights.

After Congress adjourned, Jefferson was assailed by a massive migraine from which he found release for only an hour or so every day.[57] Who knows what inner wrestlings increased his torment as he lay alone in the dark for three weeks?

IX

THE 'LITTLE EMPEROR' AND THE BLIND GIANTS

WHEN JEFFERSON recovered from his three weeks of migraine torture following adjournment of Congress on March 3, 1807, there were still duties to be performed in Washington before he could quit the city. He longed for the day of departure. Some seven months before, he had written his daughter Martha: "Absence from you becomes more and more insupportable, and my confinement here more disgusting."[1] But he found consolation: "I have certainly great reasons for gratitude to my constituents. They have supported me as cordially as I could ever have expected; and if their affairs can preserve as steady a course for two years to come, and I can then carry into retirement the good will they have hitherto bestowed on me, the day of retirement will be the happiest I have now to come."

A few months later he had lost that comfort. Many of his supporters—and not just the little coterie surrounding John Randolph—had grown openly critical of the President. He still dreamed of retirement but was no longer confident of carrying with him the full measure of goodwill that he had hitherto enjoyed. Now he wrote to Martha: "The lonesomeness of this place is more intolerable than I ever found it. My daily rides too are sickening for want of some interest in the scenes I pass over: and indeed I look over the two ensuing years as the most tedious of my life."[2] By March 1807, though Jefferson undoubtedly still could command more support than any other politician in the United States, partly by virtue of his office and partly because of his personal image, even more of his following had eroded. Perhaps Jefferson had never been more eager to quit the capital than on April 7, when he left for Monticello.

He arrived home on April 11. Seven days later he explained to Jonathan Shoemaker, a miller, "Though I have been home a week, I have not had time to go to the mill, having a great deal of planting to do, and the season having burst upon us very suddenly after my arrival, and passing off very rapidly."[3] It was good that his farms made these demands upon him. Like Antaeus, he could be exhausted by conflict but repeatedly renewed his strength by contact with the earth. He had once written his daughter Martha, "There is not a sprig of grass that shoots uninteresting to me."[4] Trees were budding. Soon great white clouds of dogwood would be cascading down his beloved mountain.

His perspective improved. Some good things had been accomplished during the past year, some even with the cooperation of Congress. Jefferson's efforts to include in the Declaration of Independence a pledge to abolish slavery had been foiled by Deep Southern planters combined with New England politicians whose constituents had grown fat in the slave trade, but he had not abandoned the effort to chip away at the institution in more modest ways. Mindful of the approaching expiration of the Constitution's twenty-year moratorium on congressional action on slavery, the President had recommended a law, effective January 1, 1808, to abolish the slave trade. Virginia, in 1776, had become the first modern state of any kind—state of the Union or national state—to prohibit the importation of slaves from abroad. Other states of the Union had followed until, by 1806, South Carolina was the only one still permitting the traffic. She had banned the trade after 1786 but in 1804 had removed the prohibition. As pointed out by Forrest McDonald,[5] not all the congressional support of a federal ban was prompted by idealism. Some states of the upper South had the burden of too many slaves. If importation from overseas was forbidden, these states might find to the south a market for their surplus. But, whatever the mixed motives that made passage possible, a small reform had been achieved.

And Jefferson had planted the seeds of two needed extensions of the national government's authority: federal aid to public education and federal funding of internal transportation. Some saw in these proposals a contradiction to his Republican ideals and strict constructionist philosophy. But Jefferson did not find it even paradoxical that he was the proponent of these measures; precisely as a strict constructionist, he called for constitutional amendments to insure the constitutionality of these provisions. The Congress just adjourned had not been ready to take this step, but some future Congress would, either with or without amendments; better with, he thought.

Probably the most lasting accomplishment of the past year of his administration was one that certainly would not have come about except for his initiative. Meriwether Lewis and William Clark completed their transcontinental expedition.[6] Lewis had arrived in Washington on December 28 with enough news and specimens of flora and fauna to provide the sage of Monticello with materials for a lifetime of speculation. America had no more avid collector of facts and artifacts. And for natural curiosities his appetite was insatiable. Gradually his collection, increasing with the years, overflowed onto chairs in the foyer, so that the elegant lines of his own design were marred by the accumulation of objects and packing cases. Between Monticello's handsome portico and its beautiful dining room, a guest passed through a long hall that looked like the packing room of a museum of natural history.

Epic and odyssey were not too florid terms to be applied to the great adventure by Lewis and Clark. The two years of training for Lewis while he was officially Jefferson's secretary and the twenty-eight months of toil and danger for the two leaders and their followers had reaped handsome rewards for the nation. The twenty-three men had left the frontier settlement of St. Louis, a great fur-trading center, on the afternoon of May 14, 1804, proceeding up the Missouri River in two pirogues and a fifty-five-foot keelboat. With them was Lewis's Newfoundland dog, Scammon. As a pet lover, Lewis must have suffered later when, with food stores exhausted and game scarce, the expedition ate dogs furnished by friendly Indians. Some Easterners had suspected that a lost tribe of Israel and a colony of displaced Welshmen were to be found somewhere between the Missouri and the Pacific. Sober men—Jefferson among them— hoped for a water passage, interrupted only by short portages, between the Mississippi and the great western ocean. But this hope was not realized. Several barriers were in the way, chief among them the snowcapped Rocky Mountains. But the truth was as expansive as the frustrated dream. Prairies awaiting the plow rippled in the wind like the waves of the ocean and seemed as endless.

Two non-Caucasian members of the party played significant roles. York, Clark's black servant, was a giant whose courage matched his physical prowess. Sacajawea was the Indian wife of the expedition's interpreter. She has often been called the guide for the party, but, according to Clark, she indicated the way only once and on that occasion chose instead of the better path "an intolerable route" through swampy ground. But Clark testified to her great value as a "pilot" among the Indian tribes. "Janey," as the Captain insisted on calling her, proved a gifted diplomat and an expert on tribal protocol. She carried with her on the rigorous journey her infant, born a little before she joined the expedition, and the seventeen-year-old mother's fortitude proved an inspiration to the men. The explorers were doubly grateful for her presence when they came upon a tribe of fierce warriors. They proved to be the Shoshone, Sacajawea's own people, from whom she had been kidnapped four years before by the Hidatsa, and her brother was now the chief. She literally danced for joy. The reaction of Lewis and Clark was more restrained, but only a little less heartfelt.

Before meeting the Shoshone they had wintered in the country of the friendly Mandan Sioux (now North Dakota) in a fort of their own construction. It was there that they had hired Sacajawea's husband as interpreter and reaped her services in the bargain. In April 1805 they had sent sixteen men back to St. Louis with reports to the President and specimens for his cabinets and had pushed farther up the Missouri. They followed a tributary stream, which they named Jefferson, to its source in what is now Montana. With the aid of a guide and horses furnished by the Shoshone, they crossed the Continental Divide. In canoes that they themselves built, the expedition moved down the Clearwater, the Snake, and the Columbia. They built a fort on the Columbia's south bank (near the present Astoria, Oregon).

The high point of the expedition had been the glimpsing on November 15, 1806, of the great western sea. The journal entry for that day read, "O joy," in exuberant contrast to the report to the President: "In obedience to your orders we have penetrated the Continent of North America to the Pacific Ocean."

Remarkably, in their entire transit of the continent they had battled with Indians only once—when they encountered the Blackfeet, a tribe as dedicated to war as the ancient Spartans. Only one member of the party had been lost, apparently a victim of appendicitis.

Despite the herculean accomplishment, Jefferson was disappointed that Spaniards and unfriendly Indians had barred exploration of the Southwest. He also was frustrated by news that the Rockies were so formidable a barrier to commerce and that persistent intertribal wars of the West, as revealed by the explorers, would be an impediment to development.

Nevertheless, Jefferson was proud of the achievement of his two fellow Virginians. He saw that Lewis and Clark were awarded 1,600 acres apiece of public land. To each of their men went double pay and 320 acres.

Their achievement was great in practical promise. The mountain country, they discovered, was filled with beaver and otter. Americans using the Columbia River could transport pelts for the China trade much faster than the British moving through Montreal. The lands where buffalo grazed between the mountains and St. Louis could some day support great herds of cattle and sheep.

Lewis and Clark had behaved with wisdom as well as fortitude. Theirs had been a diplomatic tour among the aborigines as well as a commercial venture and a military and political expedition reinforcing United States claims to the West. Thanks to the interests of the President and to the qualifications of its two leaders, the expedition had also been a scientific one to gain knowledge of the topography, climate, and products of a vast territory awaiting development, and to add to the world's sum of knowledge. Both Lewis and Clark were highly intelligent and intellectually curious. To a good general education Lewis, as we have seen, had added two years of specialized training for the task of exploration. Some modern readers of quotations from Clark, misled by the eccentricity of his spelling, have thought of him as Lewis's frontier-wise but otherwise ignorant companion. Actually Clark was a man of some geographical knowledge with an aptitude for scientific illustration. The Lewis and Clark expedition was one of intellectual as well as physical discovery and in this respect was much closer to Captain James Cook's great Pacific explorations than to most searching by frontiersmen or naval navigators.

Of greatest immediate importance, perhaps, was dramatization of the fact that a great territory was open and available. On their return Lewis and Clark met trappers headed west.

It was good that Jefferson could find satisfaction in the great saga of the West in which he played a key part, by the Louisiana Purchase and by the Lewis and Clark expedition. And it is good that he could restore his spirits by the return to familiar farming tasks at Monticello. He needed all the comfort and refreshment he could obtain because on May 13, just thirty-two days after returning to Albemarle County, he headed back to Washington.[7]

In Washington he would daily be made aware of the many slanders and slurs about him that titillated readers in virtually every state. And he would find no relief in looking South to his own Virginia. Released on bail after commitment for a high misdemeanor, Burr was in Richmond awaiting a grand jury appearance scheduled for May 22. In those days Supreme Court Justices rode the circuit; in Richmond Federal Court the presiding judge would be none other than the Chief Justice himself, John Marshall, Jefferson's cousin and arch rival, already locked with him in a struggle between the judicial and executive branches of the government. In the interim between commitment and trial, Burr's chief counselor, John Wickham, the acknowledged leader of the Richmond bar, entertained together as dinner guests in his home both Burr and Marshall. As the Chief Justice's admiring biographer Albert J. Beveridge suggests,[8] Marshall probably did not know in advance that Burr would be present. On finding that to be the case, he may have remained rather than hurt his host's feelings by leaving abruptly. Even so, Marshall's remaining was a serious judicial indiscretion. Jefferson's feelings about the news may have been mixed— pleasure that the Chief Justice's conduct provided a good basis for attack by the Richmond *Enquirer* and other Republican newspapers and genuine concern that Marshall could not bring an unbiased mind to the proceedings.

The popularity Burr enjoyed in Richmond and the preferential treatment he received there is illustrated by what he wrote from his cell on July 3, 1807. Though the Colonel had complained of ill treatment elsewhere, he recorded on this occasion an amusing dialogue:

Jailer: "I hope, sir, that it would not be disagreeable to you if I should lock this door after dark."

Burr: "By no means. I should prefer it, to keep out intruders."

Jailer: "It is our custom, sir, to extinguish all lights at nine o'clock. I hope, sir, you will have no objection to conform to that."

Burr: "That, sir, I am sorry to say, is impossible, for I never go to bed till twelve, and always burn two candles."

Jailer: "Very well, sir, just as you please. I should have been glad if it had been otherwise; but, as you please, sir."

"While I have been writing," Burr added, "different servants have arrived with messages, notes, and inquiries, bringing oranges, lemons, pineapples, raspberries, apricots, cream, butter, ice and some ordinary articles."[9]

Prodded by Virginia's Senator William Branch Giles,[10] who believed that the administration was not doing enough to secure the conviction of Burr for a major crime, Jefferson said he was disappointed that the Colonel had been indicted only for a high misdemeanor rather than treason. He accused Marshall of using "tricks to force trials before it is possible to collect evidence." As he often did with the close-mouthed Madison and sometimes, less discreetly, with others, Jefferson said in his letter to Giles things that he would never say in a public pronouncement. He averred that the Federalists, presumably including the Chief Justice, were "mortified only that [Burr] did not separate the Union or overturn the government." Only a lack of confidence in the colonel's prospects, he suggested, had prevented them from joining him in an attempt to establish a monarchy.

Jefferson was quick to take offense at any hint of a slur from Marshall, and he was stung by the Chief Justice's statement from the bench that the executive branch had been too slow in collecting evidence. But the President was sure of his own objectivity. "If there ever had been an instance in this or the preceding Administrations, of Federal[ist] judges so applying principles of law as to condemn a Federal[ist] or acquit a Republican offender, I should have judged them in the present case with more charity."[11]

But he snatched a flower of hope from the nettle. "If a member of the Executive or Legislature does wrong," he said, "the day is never far distant when the people will remove him." No such remedy existed with the federal judiciary, whose members were appointed for life on "good behavior." In this case, even "impeachment is a farce which will not be tried again." But if the Chief Justice should do something truly outrageous, the people surely would be provoked to insist that their representatives correct this defect in the government. "They will see that one of the great coordinate branches of the government, setting itself in opposition to the other two, and to the commonsense of the nation, proclaims immunity to that class of offenders which endeavors to overturn the Constitution, and are themselves protected in it by the Constitution itself." He felt certain that the demand to amend the Constitution to curb the judiciary would be irresistible. "If [the Federalists'] protection of Burr produced this amendment, it will do more good than his condemnation would have done; . . . and if his punishment can be counted now for a useful amendment to the Constitution, I shall rejoice in it."

Jefferson's subsequent action—or inaction—in the Burr affair during legal proceedings in Richmond supports the sincerity of his declaration to Giles. Even those not disposed to go so far as Forrest McDonald in his statement that "Jefferson's handling of Burr's case was so moderate as to border on the negligent"[12] should acknowledge that any zeal Jefferson might have had to persecute Burr had evaporated by the time of the trial.

Certainly the President made no extraordinary efforts to secure the Colonel's conviction. Attorney General John Breckinridge, who had died in December 1806, had been replaced on January 20, 1807, by Caesar A. Rodney. After an initial appearance in Richmond, Rodney had to withdraw from the case because of ill health, leaving the prosecution to George Hay, the local District Attorney. Hay was assisted by Virginia's Lieutenant Governor Alexander McRae, no giant of the bar. By contrast, Burr had a formidable array of counselors. Besides the remarkably able and prestigious Wickham, there were former Governor Edmund Randolph, successively Attorney General and Secretary of State in Washington's cabinet; Benjamin Botts, another prominent Virginian; and Maryland's Luther Martin, the famed "Bulldog of Federalism." The only effort that Jefferson made toward paring these odds was to appoint as an assistant to the prosecution William Wirt, brilliant and promising, a master of perfervid oratory but still more widely known as the author of *The Letters of the British Spy* than as a formidable attorney.[13]

If Jefferson's zeal against Burr faded quickly, his animus against Marshall did not. The President foresaw that the Federalist defense attorneys would try to transform the proceedings against Burr into a trial of Jefferson himself, and he believed that the Chief Justice would abet their effort. Martin had not had a real go at Jefferson since the impeachment trial of Justice Samuel Chase, and his massive jaws ached for their prey. Besides, he had conceived a passion for the beautiful Theodosia Burr Alston and was determined to be top dog in her father's defense. Not only was there a strong social bond between Wickham and the Chief Justice, but Marshall chose as foreman of the grand jury John Randolph, who disliked Burr but hated Jefferson more. As foreman of the petit jury, Marshall appointed Colonel Edward Carrington, his own brother-in-law. Richmond, the milieu of the trial, was Marshall's home, where he was admired and even loved as a good neighbor as well as a great statesman.

But the spectators who packed the Hall of the House of Delegates, where the trial was being conducted, and overflowed into the rotunda were not all Richmonders. They had come from many parts of Virginia and far beyond. They were so numerous that sandboxes had been brought in to augment the brass cuspidors de rigueur in American public buildings of the period. Even so, the stately Houdon statue of Washington, the most valuable piece of sculpture in the United States, was in danger of acquiring brown spots on its creamy marble surface. The revered "father of his country" was certainly not a target for the milling patriots, but even in life the old General probably had never been in so much danger from random fire.

A namesake and future biographer of Washington was among them, a fastidious New Yorker, slim, handsome, delicate-featured, who had this very month celebrated his twenty-third birthday. Only recently returned from a stay of nearly two years in Europe, Washington Irving probably had not yet reaccustomed himself to all the spitting at public gatherings in his native land. He was practicing law in a desultory way, but his main interest now was *Salmagundi*, a magazine modeled after England's *Spectator*, which he was producing with the aid of his brother and a friend. His family was solidly Federalist and his Addisonian wit frequently was directed at President Jefferson. Now the young man was in Richmond to report on the Burr trial.

Winfield Scott, then a trim young lawyer and not the corpulent general of later years, stood on the large box lock of one of the chamber doors to see above the crowd.

Even professed Republicans had come to town to root for Burr and against Jefferson. One such attracted the attention of a spectator who recalled: "As I was crossing the court-house green, I heard a great noise of haranguing some distance off. Inquiring what it was, I was told it was a great blackguard from Tennessee, one Andrew Jackson, making a speech for Burr and damning Jefferson as a persecutor."[14]

Martin's performance must have pleased the most determined of Jefferson's enemies. He demanded that the President submit to the court any pertinent executive papers and, if need be, appear as a witness. With justice he charged that the President had prejudged the defendant in asserting, "of his guilt there can be no doubt." Then he shouted: "He has let slip the dogs of war, the hellhounds of persecution, to hunt down my friend. And would this President of the United States, who has raised all this absurd clamor, pretend to keep back the papers which are wanted for this trial, where life itself is at stake?"[15]

Hay conceded that it was possible to subpoena a President but insisted that no necessity for subpoenaing this one had been demonstrated. In any event, he argued, there was no justification for a *subpoena duces tecum* (literally, "under penalty you shall bring with you"), a writ commanding the recipient to appear in court with a designated document or documents.

Martin recalled that Jefferson, during the trial of Smith and Ogden for aiding and abetting Miranda, had ordered members of his cabinet to disregard the summons of a New York court. "Perhaps," he said, "the same farce may be repeated here."

After hearing extensive arguments the Chief Justice on June 13 ruled on the point. Speaking in a tone of solemn asseveration, he was most impressive, clothed in dignity as well as in the robes of the court. His luminous eyes seemed to concentrate the light of truth. Burr's equally luminous eyes stared into Marshall's. Many people had remarked on this strange quality of luminosity as the most distinguishing feature of each man. Some now thought it uncanny to see two such pairs of eyes in one room.[16]

"If upon my principle," said Marshall, "the President could be construed to stand exempt from the general provisions of the Constitution, it would be because his duties as chief magistrate demand his whole time for national objects. But it is apparent that this demand is not unremitting. . . ."

Marshall concluded: "It cannot be denied that to issue a subpoena to a person filling the exalted station of the chief magistrate is a duty which would be dispensed with much more cheerfully than it would be performed; but if it be duty the court can have no choice in the case."

The Chief Justice's ruling provoked a succession of letters from Jefferson to Hay. On June 20 the President wrote: "The leading feature of our Constitution is the independence of the Legislature, Executive, and Judiciary of each other; and none are more jealous of this than the Judiciary. But would the Executive be independent of the Judiciary if he were subjected to the *commands* of the latter, and to imprisonment for disobedience; if the smaller courts could bandy him from pillar to post, keep him constantly trudging from north to south and east to west, and withdraw him entirely from his executive duties?"[17]

One particular part of the Chief Justice's pronouncement rankled with Jefferson: "The Judge says '*it is apparent* that the President's duties as chief magistrate do not demand his whole time, and are not unremitting.' If he alludes to our annual retirement from the seat of government during the sickly season, he should be told that such arrangements are made for carrying on the public business, at and between the several stations we take, that it goes on as unremittingly there as if we were at the seat of government."

Jefferson was surely one of the most industrious people who ever served as President of the United States. He came to office with deeply ingrained habits of work. He always performed conscientiously not only his assigned duties but self-imposed ones as well. As a student at the College of William and Mary he had toiled far into the night, not just to complete assignments, which apparently he did with great speed, but to acquire the peripheral learning he was determined to make his. One of his schoolmates, returning from a night on the town, would regularly overturn young Tom's table of books. As a state legislator, he missed so much time from deliberations that the sergeant-at-arms was sent to arrest him and compel his attendance. But he was not relaxing; he resented the repetitiveness of the discussions that took time from the busy hours in his quarters where he prepared an almost incredible volume of legislation.[18] As President he carried on an amazingly large correspondence by hand on questions of science and history as well as matters of state, meanwhile turning the light of his intellect on a myriad of problems and opportunities awaiting the republic. At the start of his first term as President, he had announced his intentions of spending the warm months on his breeze-swept mountaintop, away from the heat and humidity of Washington, which depleted his energy and made him feel sick. But couriers with heavy saddlebags rode regularly up the little mountain to the man with the restless mind, and messages in his small, neat handwriting, duplicated for his files with the polygraph that his own inventiveness had improved, went out in energizing streams to Washington, Philadelphia, New York, London, Paris, Lisbon, Madrid, and dozens of other points. To suggest that he was vacationing was to invite his ire.

Jefferson never accepted Marshall's ruling, and no responsible person seriously suggested that the President be arrested and compelled to appear in court with relevant documents. The precedent he established has been useful to some of his successors in the presidency.

But Jefferson was not serene in his defiance. He saw himself always as a champion of human rights and he found it insufferable that Martin, with ungrammatical but undiminished force, should almost daily rail against him as the enemy of individual freedom. In a letter to a protégé, William Short, Jefferson implied that he sometimes envied John Adams' uninhibited explosions through the crust of decorum: "I have heard, indeed, that my predecessor sometimes decided things against his Council [cabinet] by dashing and trampling his wig on the floor. This only proves what you and I knew, that he had a better heart than head."[19] As Jefferson wore no wig, his nearest approach to emulation would have been tearing his hair out.

Once, as the heat of mid-June closed in on Richmond and tempers flared and Martin, reeking with alcohol, increased the venom of his denunciation, Jefferson wrote to Hay: "Shall we move to commit L. M. [Luther Martin] as *particeps criminis* with Burr?" He believed that a witness could "fix upon him [Burr] misprision of treason at least. And at any rate his evidence will put down this unprincipled and imprudent Federal bulldog, and add another proof that the most clamorous defenders of Burr are all his accomplices."[20]

Jefferson did not follow up his ill-advised suggestion. He was a man of strong emotions and sometimes harrowing sensitivity, but his hostility to others was likely to provoke temporary irritation rather than a sustained drive for vengeance.

The President's common sense, by no means crowded out by his passion for abstractions, told him that he had better concentrate on another participant in the trial. General Wilkinson was supposed to be the star witness for the prosecution, but he himself had barely escaped indictment along with Burr. The defense was busy discrediting Wilkinson, and his former close association with Burr and later fierce turning upon Burr's lieutenants in a high-handed exercise of martial law simplified their task.

Major James Bruff, an artillery officer under Wilkinson, was testifying that the General had sounded him out as a possible recruit for Burr's expedition. Though Bruff had not hitherto publicly denounced his superior officer, his testimony now represented no after-the-fact conversion. Three months before Burr was indicted, Bruff had traveled from St. Louis to Washington and confided to Secretary of War Dearborn that he believed Wilkinson to be a Spanish spy and a partner in Burr's treason.

Dearborn told Bruff that the President had been dubious about Wilkinson but that the General's effective way of dealing with the emergency at New Orleans had earned Jefferson's confidence. The President would surely back his appointee. Maybe later on, Dearborn said, there could be an inquiry.

Attorney General Rodney was more candid in his explanation to Bruff. He asked, "What would be the result if all your charges against General Wilkinson should be proven? Why, just what the Federalists and the enemies of the present Administration wish. It would turn the indignation of the people from Burr on Wilkinson. Burr would escape, and Wilkinson take his place."[21]

Jefferson and his cabinet were fully aware that conviction of Wilkinson, even if only in the court of public opinion, might not only enable Burr to escape justice but also would be a great blow to the prestige and popularity of the President who appointed him. Jefferson doubtless reflected in his pragmatic way that, however treasonable Wilkinson's intentions had been, he was not a man to remain wedded to a lost cause. His loyalty, at least temporarily, was almost guaranteed. Nevertheless, the President sought to encourage the General in his new role. "Your enemies," he wrote, "have filled the public ear with slanders and your mind with trouble. . . . The establishment of their guilt will let the world see what they ought to think of their clamors; it will dissipate the doubts of those who doubted for want of knowledge, and will place you on higher ground in the public estimate and public confidence."[22]

Jefferson went even beyond these words to an assertion still harder to justify. "No one," he said, "is more sensible than myself of the injustice which has been aimed at you. Accept, I pray you, my salutations and assurances of respect and esteem." Before we brand Jefferson a hypocrite, we should consider the possibility that he was neither the first nor the last beleaguered President to embrace as a hero some overbearing subordinate whose bold actions rescued the administration even at the expense of civil liberty. This reaction is more disturbing in Jefferson's case because of his uncommon dedication to individual freedom through most of his career.

Jefferson had won most of the early skirmishes. Witnesses had testified as he wanted them to, Wilkinson had escaped indictment, Burr had not, and the President's rejection of the Chief Justice's subpoenas had demonstrated Marshall's impotence on this issue. Observers remarked on the Chief Justice's monumental calm throughout the proceedings. Outward calm was characteristic of Marshall. Besides, this time he could be confident of ultimate victory. The Constitution provided that "no person shall be convicted of treason unless on the testimony of two witnesses to the same overt act, or on confession in open court." As the presiding judge, Marshall controlled the admission of evidence.

The case was by no means clear-cut, and Marshall was in a position to prevent anything that he regarded as a miscarriage of justice.

Blennerhassett, the Irishman whom Burr had flattered into joining in his imperial schemes, could have been an effective witness for the prosecution. Blaming the Colonel for all his troubles, he wrote privately, "The present trial cannot fail to furnish ample testimony, if not to the guilt, at least to the defect of every talent under the assumption of which this giddy adventurer has seduced so many followers of riper experience and better judgement than myself."[23] Jefferson apparently hoped that Blennerhassett could be persuaded to turn state's evidence.[24]

Blennerhassett had been too quick to call Burr's reputation lost. The Irishman had not counted on Burr's control and cheerful courtesy in the face of attack, nor on the exercise of skills in testimony that made him his own most effective attorney. Even Blennerhassett conceded, "Perhaps the little 'Emperor' at Cole's Creek may be forgotten in the attorney at Richmond."

Some of the government's principal witnesses proved less effective than expected, and some impaired their credibility by well-publicized conduct outside the courtroom. General William Eaton, who had early warned Jefferson of Burr's machinations and who testified that the Colonel had invited him to participate in a conspiracy, had, in Blennerhassett's words, "dwindled down in the eyes of this sarcastic town into a ridiculous mountebank, strutting about the streets under a tremendous hat, with a Turkish sash over colored clothes, when he is not tippling in the taverns, where he offers up with his libations the bitter effusions of his sorrows."[25]

"The bias of Judge Marshall," Hay wrote Jefferson, "is as obvious as if it was stamped upon his forehead. . . . His concern for Mr. Burr is wonderful. He told me many years ago, when Burr was rising in the estimation of the Republican Party, that he was as profligate in principle as he was desperate in fortune. I remember his words; they astonished me. Yet when the grand jury brought in their bill the Chief Justice gazed at him for a long time, without appearing conscious that he was doing so, with an expression of sympathy and sorrow as strong as the human countenance can exhibit without palpable emotion."[26]

Wilkinson needed all the support the administration could give him. Many people would have agreed with Blennerhassett's sarcastic comment in his diary that the General "exhibited the manner of a sergeant under a court-martial rather than the demeanor of an accusing officer confronted with his culprit. His perplexity and derangement, even upon his direct examination, has placed beyond all doubt 'his honor as a soldier and his fidelity as a citizen.' "[27]

Abruptly, on August 19, the defense moved to "arrest the evidence." Burr's counsel reminded the court that conviction for treason required, in the absence of confession, "the testimony of two witnesses to the same overt act" charged in the indictment. But, they pointed out, the prosecution had already admitted that Burr had been hundreds of miles from the scene of the alleged act of treason at the time of its execution. Now the District Attorney was preparing to introduce collateral testimony concerning acts perpetrated beyond the assigned jurisdiction of the court. On the grounds of irrelevance, the defense objected to the introduction of such additional evidence.

The argument between opposing counsel over the motion by defense raged ten days. Luther Martin, the bulldog that Jefferson had hoped to silence, talked for fourteen hours. Wickham delivered a much more restrained but powerful speech, one which one of the audience, Virginia's great future Senator Littleton W. Tazewell, remembered as "the greatest forensic effort of the American bar."

Replying for the defense, William Wirt made a four-hour speech apparently intended to induce Blennerhassett to turn state's evidence and testify against Burr. "Who is Blennerhassett?" he asked. "A native of Ireland, a man of letters, who fled from the storms of his own country to find quiet in ours. His history shows that war is not the natural element of his mind. If it had been, he never would have exchanged Ireland for America. So far is an army from furnishing the society natural and proper to Mr. Blennerhassett's character, that on his arrival in America he retired even from the population of the Atlantic States, and sought quiet and solitude in the bosom of our western forests." He pictured the happy life of the retiring scholar with his beautiful wife and his children, surrounded by books, the delights of music, and the glories of nature.

Wirt told of the invasion of this Eden by a subtle seducer. His voice throbbing, he exclaimed: "Yet this unfortunate man, thus deluded from his interest and his happiness, thus seduced from the paths of innocence and peace, thus confounded in the toils that were deliberately spread for him, and overwhelmed by the mastering spirit and genius of another—this man, thus ruined and undone, and made to play a subordinate part in this grand drama of guilt and treason, this man is to be called the principal offender, while he by whom he was thus plunged into misery is comparatively innocent, a mere accessory! . . . Sir, neither the human heart nor the human understanding will bear a perversion so monstrous and absurd! so shocking to the soul! so revolting to reason! Let Aaron Burr, then, not shrink from the high [destiny] which he has courted, and having already ruined Blennerhassett in fortune, character, and happiness forever, let him not attempt to finish the tragedy by thrusting that ill-fated man between himself and punishment!"[28]

The audience was deeply moved. Indeed, people throughout the nation were. Wirt's words, in that age of elocution, became a recitation second in popularity only to Patrick Henry's "Liberty or Death" speech. But Blennerhassett was not moved enough to speak out against the little Colonel.

In addressing the court, Hay referred to the impeachment of a judge and Martin seized upon the opportunity to suggest that the District Attorney's remark might have been intended as a threat to the court. "I do not know whether it were [sic] intended by this observation," he said, "that your honors should be apprehensive of an impeachment in case you should decide against the wishes of the government."

Though it was generally anticipated that Marshall would refuse to hear further evidence, there was tension in the courtroom on August 18 when he prepared to give his decision. In measured tones, the Chief Justice acknowledged that what he was about to say would undoubtedly provoke fierce condemnation. But he said: "No man is desirous of becoming the peculiar subject of calumny; no man, might he let the bitter cup pass from him without self-reproach, would drain it to the bottom; but if he has no choice in the case,—if there is no alternative presented to him but a dereliction of duty or the opprobrium of those who are denominated the world,—he merits the contempt as well as the indignation of his country who can hesitate which to embrace. . . ."

He then ruled that additional testimony, being irrelevant for the reasons cited by the defense, could not be admitted.

The next day Hay announced that the defense rested. The jury's verdict was, "Not guilty."

Jefferson's languishing zeal was revitalized. He wrote Hay: "The event has been what was evidently intended from the beginning of the trial; that is to say, not only to clear Burr, but to prevent the evidence from ever going before the world. But this latter case must not take place. It is now, therefore, more than ever indispensable that not a single witness be paid or permitted to depart until his testimony has been committed to writing. . . . These whole proceedings will be laid before Congress, that they may decide whether the defect has been in the evidence of guilt, or in the law, or in the application of the law, and that they may provide the proper remedy for the past and the future."[29]

The feeling is inescapable that, in looking to that future, Jefferson was concerned not only with laying his case before the elected representatives of the people but also with his own appearance at the bar of history. Before that bar, Burr, Marshall, and Jefferson all stand arraigned. Of course, Burr's guilt—if indeed he was guilty—incomparably exceeded that of the other two. But neither of the great Americans—Marshall or Jefferson—is seen at his best in the lurid lights of the Burr trial. Superficially alike in their long, lanky figures and in their membership in the Virginia elite, and indeed in their cousinhood, their common heritage from the great Randolph clan, they were alike in deeper and more significant ways although they had given their allegiance to opposing parties. Each was dedicated to the truth as he saw it, but the vision of each was distorted by the heat and dust of battle.

Marshall once admitted that he had read Alexander Pope with greater pleasure than he had Coke and Blackstone. He was familiar with the poet's description of humankind in *An Essay on Man*: "Created half to rise, and half to fall; / Great lord of all things, yet a prey to all; / Sole judge of truth, in endless error hurled; / The glory, jest, and riddle of the world!" In his more judicial moments, the Chief Justice was prepared to admit that man was an unstable compound. Jefferson acknowledged the fact too, especially under the proddings of James Madison. Though blessed with a more than common share of human benevolence and a rare share of intellect, Marshall and Jefferson conspicuously exemplified the contradictions of their species. Each could be firm for wisdom, obdurate for folly. Each was a son of the Enlightenment who could marshal formidable forces of logic in support of his insights or his prejudices, his convictions or his whims. Neither was the complete man of reason idealized by the Age of Reason. In that lay their weakness—and their strength.

X

THROUGH THE STORM

WHILE OPPOSING attorneys skirmished in the summer heat in the Virginia capitol designed by Jefferson, cannon shots that took American lives were fired off the Virginia capes. The shedding of American blood in American coastal waters on June 22, 1807, by a British naval ship told United States citizens that the greatest threat to their country was not Aaron Burr's dream of empire but instead the most powerful empire on earth.

The threat was not only to peace but to national sovereignty. It was ironic that it should have occurred in the same waters where, fewer than twenty-six years before, a victory of America's French allies over the British navy had led to a triumph at Yorktown widely hailed as guaranteeing the independence of the United States.

The trouble was rooted in the whole problem of British officers boarding United States vessels to search for deserters from their navy and sometimes, the Americans charged, seizing American seamen owing no allegiance to Britain. The charge that the British navy deliberately pursued the impressment of American sailors as a matter of imperial policy had long been a sticking point in treaty negotiations between the two nations. The problem was exacerbated by events of the spring and summer of 1807 centering on the port of Hampton Roads and the United States frigate *Chesapeake*.

In February British seamen had escaped from H. M. S. *Melampus* in the Captain's gig and, despite fire from the ship, had reached Norfolk. Three of them had enlisted aboard the *Chesapeake*. The British Consul in Norfolk had protested and David Erskine, British Minister to the United States, had demanded surrender of the three. Secretary of State Madison rejected the demand. Later, after investigation by an American officer, Madison said that he believed the men were American citizens.[1] On March 7 seamen aboard the British sloop *Halifax* seized the vessel's jolly boat and escaped to Norfolk, where five of them enlisted aboard the *Chesapeake*.[2] Irate British officers thought this insufferable conduct was becoming a habit.

The commander of the *Halifax*, already frustrated in his efforts to recover the men through action of the British Consul and even through personal application to the United States Navy, suddenly met two of them face to face on a Norfolk street. Why did they not return to duty? he demanded. One of them replied with a round of abusive oaths and the assertion that, now that he was in the land of liberty, he would do as he pleased.[3]

The infuriated officer and his comrades in Chesapeake Bay appealed to Admiral George Cranfield Berkeley, commander of British warships of the North American station. On his own authority, without waiting for permission from London, Berkeley on June 1, 1807, addressed a special order to all vessels in his command: "Whereas many seamen, subjects of his Britannic Majesty, and serving in his ships . . . while at anchor in the Chesapeake, deserted and entered on board the U. S. frigate the *Chesapeake*, and openly paraded in the streets of Norfolk, in sight of their officers, under the American flag, protected by the magistrates of the town and the recruiting officer belonging to the above-mentioned American frigate, . . . The captains and commanders of his Majesty's ships and vessels under my command are therefore hereby required and directed, in case of meeting with the American frigate *Chesapeake* at sea, and without the limits of the United States, to show to the captain of her this order, and to require to search his ship for the deserters."[4]

The Admiral's order was not extraordinarily bellicose. It provided that "if a similar demand shall be made by the American, he is to be permitted to search for any deserters from their service, according to the customs and usage of civilized nations on terms of peace and amity with each other." The potential for tragedy lay in the failure to define "the customs and usage of civilized nations" and to prescribe what a British officer should do if an American Captain should deny the right of search.

On the morning of June 22, after long delays because of bad weather, the *Chesapeake* sailed from Virginia's great anchorage of Hampton Roads under command of Commodore James Barron.[5] Many of the ship's crew were ill and were lying on deck to take advantage of the sun and fresh air. The gun-deck was "encumbered with lumber of one sort or another." Cables blocked some areas.

Watching from Lynnhaven Bay was the British frigate *Leopard*. Anchored nearby were his Majesty's ships *Bellona* and *Melampus*. After receiving signals from the *Bellona*, the *Leopard* put out to sea.

The *Leopard* followed the *Chesapeake*. About 3:30 p.m., when the two ships were about eight or ten miles southeast by east of Cape Henry, the *Leopard* signaled that she was carrying dispatches for the commodore. Barron signaled the ship to send its boat alongside and shortly afterwards received a British Lieutenant in the Commodore's cabin. The young officer handed the American a copy of Admiral Berkeley's order, together with a note from their own Captain Humphrey explaining "a hope that every circumstance . . . may be adjusted in a manner that the harmony subsisting between the two countries may remain undisturbed."

Barron's note in reply said, in part, "The officers that were on the recruiting service for this ship were particularly instructed by the government, through me, not to enter any deserters from his Britannic Majesty's ships, nor do I know of any being here. I am also instructed never to permit the crew of any ship that I command to be mustered by any other but their own officers. It is my disposition to preserve harmony, and I hope this answer to your dispatch will prove satisfactory."

Minutes after the Lieutenant left Barron's cabin, Captain Humphreys hailed the *Chesapeake* and, now very near, shouted, "Commodore Barron, you must be aware of the necessity I am under of complying with the orders of my commander-in-chief."

Trying to buy time, Barron, who had just ordered his own ship to prepare for action, shouted back through his trumpet, "I do not hear what you say." Captain Humphreys repeated his original words, and Barron—painfully aware of the cluttered state of his decks—again pretended not to understand.

The answer was a shot across the *Chesapeake*'s bow. A minute later came another.

Before the *Chesapeake*'s guns were ready for action, the American ship received a full broadside. Though wounded, Barron did not take cover. He repeatedly hailed the *Leopard*, hoping to gain a respite from fire while he sent instructions to his gunners.

After two more broadsides, a total of three in fifteen minutes, the hull of the *Chesapeake* had received twenty-two round shot, its sails were riddled, its rigging was cut, and its three masts were seriously damaged. Three Americans had been killed and eighteen wounded.

Barron ordered the flag to be lowered in surrender and as it was hauled down a Third Lieutenant aboard, using a live coal which he had brought in his fingers from the galley, fired for honor's sake the only shot from the *Chesapeake*. It hit its target.

British officers boarded the American frigate and took with them four sailors. Three were United States citizens who had deserted from the *Melampus*. The fourth man, dragged from hiding in a coal hole, was Jenkin Ratford, the British seaman who had cursed his captain on a Norfolk street.

Barron offered to surrender his ship as a prize of war. Captain Humphreys refused in a note that said, "I am ready to give you every assistance in my power, and do most sincerely deplore that any lives should have been lost in the execution of a service which might have been adjusted more amicably, not only with respect to ourselves but the nations to which we respectively belong."

What the British officer thought of as gallantry seemed to the Americans further insult. It increased the bitterness of their humiliation as the riddled *Chesapeake* crept back to Hampton Roads.

The people of the area were enraged. A protest meeting of Norfolk and Portsmouth citizens swelled beyond the confines of Norfolk's Town Hall and moved to a large church. Resolutions adopted expressed a determination to refuse all transactions with British ships of war. A subscription was inaugurated for the benefit of the wounded and the families of the dead. Support was pledged to the United States government in its efforts to obtain satisfaction for the losses sustained and the insult to national honor.[6]

The funeral in Norfolk on June 28 of a sailor who died of his wounds occasioned a procession of four thousand persons. Young men of the city formed a volunteer company for its defense, repairs were pushed on Fort Norfolk, and militia began arriving from Richmond and Petersburg.[7]

Commodore John E. Douglas, commander of his Majesty's fleet in Hampton Roads, feared that the resolution to suspend intercourse with British ships meant that he would be cut off from communication with the British Consul. In a message on July 3 to Norfolk's Mayor Richard E. Lee, he said, "I am determined, if this infringement is not immediately annulled, to prohibit every vessel bound either in or out of Norfolk, to proceed to their destination until I know the pleasure of my government. . . . You must be perfectly aware that the British flag never has [been] nor will be, insulted with impunity."[8]

The next day, the Fourth of July, Mayor Lee sent his reply: "The day on which this answer is written ought of itself to prove to the subjects of your sovereign that the American people are not to be intimidated by menace. . . . Seduced by the false show of security, they may be sometimes surprised and slaughtered while unprepared to resist a supposed friend; that delusive security is now however passed forever. . . . We do not seek hostility, nor shall we avoid it. We are prepared for the worst you may attempt, and will do whatever shall be judged proper to repel force whensoever your efforts shall render any act of ours necessary."[9] In conclusion, he informed him that letters addressed to the Consul had been duly forwarded.

Littleton Waller Tazewell, who personally delivered the Mayor's letter, warned Captain Douglas against sending "any of his officers or people on shore, for that if he did, the arm of the civil authority, I did not believe, would be able to protect them from the vengeance of the enraged people."[10]

On that same day Admiral Berkeley, from his base in Halifax, Nova Scotia, commended Captain Humphreys for his conduct in the *Chesapeake* incident. He urged him not to trouble himself about published criticisms in the United States, as "we must make allowances for the heated state of the populace in a country where law and every tie, both civil and religious, is treated so lightly."[11]

Although public indignation was focused in Hampton Roads, it erupted up and down the Atlantic Coast. DeWitt Clinton presided at a citizens' meeting in New York City which pledged to support the federal government "in whatever measures it may deem necessary to adopt in the present crisis" following "the dastardly and unprovoked attack." A partial exception to the general reaction was Boston, the great Federalist stronghold. After brief deliberation, the party's leaders decided not to call a public meeting.[12] But the Republican minority in the city met on July 10, and Federalist Senator John Quincy Adams joined them. They adopted a resolution to cooperate "in any measures, however serious," which the administration might adopt. Yielding to pressure from the rank and file, the Federalists met at Faneuil Hall on July 16 and unanimously adopted resolutions of support introduced by Senator Adams. Still, some prominent Federalists had remained at home and a Federalist newspaper had alienated many Bostonians by saying that the British had acted correctly.[13]

Jefferson did not believe that this was one of those times when the tree of liberty needed to be refreshed by the blood of tyrants. On June 25 he had received news of the *Leopard*'s attack, but cabinet members were absent from

Washington and he could not assemble a full meeting until July 2. He then read a proclamation he had drafted with Madison's help. The preamble was concilia- tory. Sounding more like the gracious host of Monticello than the President of the United States, Jefferson explained in the first sentence that the Americans had endeavored "by a regular discharge of their national and social duties, and by every friendly office their situation has admitted, to maintain, with all the belligerents, their accustomed relations of friendship, hospitality, and commer- cial intercourse." After deploring British violations of neutral rights not only in the case of the *Chesapeake* but also in a long series of earlier "breaches of hospitality," the document mildly observed:

> Hospitality under such circumstances ceases to be a duty: and a counte- nance of it, with such uncontrollable abuses, would tend only to multiply injuries and irritations, to bring a rupture between the two nations. This extreme result is equally opposed to the interests of both, as it was to assurances of the most friendly dispositions on the part of the British government, in the midst of which this outrage was committed. In this light the subject cannot but present itself to the government, and strengthen the motives to an honorable reparation of the wrong which has been done, and to that effectual control of its naval commanders, which alone can justify the government of the United States in the exercise of those hospitalities it is now constrained to discontinue.[14]

The remainder of the proclamation was specific and forceful. It ordered all armed ships of Great Britain to leave American waters "immediately." If any British vessels should ignore this command, United States citizens were forbid- den to furnish supplies to them or have any intercourse whatever with them. Only "a vessel forced by distress or charged with public dispatches" would be permitted within the jurisdiction of the United States.

The cabinet approved the proclamation as drafted, and the President issued it that day. There was little to oppose in its main provisions. The question was how it could be enforced against the world's greatest naval power. Also, even the successful exclusion of all British ships from waters the United States legally claimed as its own would not be a guarantee against repetition of such incidents as the one precipitating the immediate crisis. The *Chesapeake* and the *Leopard* had met well outside the three-mile limit.

Consulting with the cabinet, Jefferson made other decisions. He sent gunboats to vulnerable points and recalled all United States vessels from the Mediterranean. Barron had been Commodore of the Mediterranean Squadron, and the *Chesapeake* had been headed to that area. Jefferson sent instructions to James Monroe, the United States Minister in London, to demand: "(1) a disavowal of the act and of the principle of searching a public armed vessel; (2) a restoration of the men taken; (3) a recall of Admiral Berkeley."[15] He also ordered the Minister to communicate to the Russian government the facts of the *Chesapeake* and *Leopard* affair. Russia was an ally of Britain's in the war against Napoleon, and London might be willing to listen to the Czar. Alexander I had imbibed Rousseau's philosophy and talked much about the "rights of nations." Jefferson hoped that he would urge fairer treatment of neutral states.

Two days later the President and cabinet agreed that a call should be issued to Congress on August 24 to convene October 26. Both Robert Smith and Gallatin favored an earlier meeting, but they did not prevail.

Jefferson had no illusions about the effect of his words in his own country. "I imagine," he wrote John Page, "the ardor of our fellow citizens is scarcely satisfied by our proclamation."[16] But, even though many Americans wished for bolder and more precipitate action from their President, there was a tendency for most groups to coalesce in support of the administration. Before the end of the month the *National Intelligencer* said that there might never have been "so memorable an example of unanimity as that evinced by the United States at this interesting crisis."[17] Only in Boston did there seem to be heated criticism of the President's course, and there the complaint was not that the President had not gone far enough but that he had gone too far.

In ensuing months, the drama of the *Chesapeake* and *Leopard* played out in courts-martial on both sides. In proceedings presided over by Admiral Cochrane aboard H. M. S. *Belleisle* at Halifax on August 28, Jenkin Ratford paid dearly for the alleged crime of desertion, compounded as it was by insulting behavior to his Captain on a Norfolk street. He testified that he had hidden in the coal hole of the *Chesapeake* "for fear of the Americans making him fight against his country," and he threw himself upon the mercy of the court. He was hanged at the yardarm. Death sentences were meted out to the three men seized with him but were mitigated to five hundred lashes each, and even these gentler sentences were shortly remitted.[18] On the American side charges were preferred against Commodore Barron by six officers from the *Chesapeake*. He was relieved of his command and a Court of Naval Enquiry was appointed. At a general court martial assembled in Norfolk on January 4, 1808, and continued until February 8, he was adjudged guilty of "neglect, on the probability of an engagement, to clear his ship for action." He was suspended for five years without pay.[19] A festering quarrel between Barron and Commodore Stephen Decatur concerning Barron's surrender to the British would lead in 1820 to the killing of Decatur in a duel between the two.

But concern over the fate of individuals was dwarfed in the summer of 1807 by the dark thunderheads of war that towered off the Atlantic Coast. Some in port cities who remembered the devastation of British cannonades and naval raids in the American Revolution scanned the hazy horizon for hostile ships. For them the palpable mists of July and August lay upon the shore like a miasma of fear. Others, with shorter memories or more belligerent temperaments, longed for the storm of war to end the agony of waiting in those hot and humid days of inaction.

Danger flashed like the heat lightning of summer nights, and the low rumble of distant thunder reminded coast dwellers of the threat of cannonade. There were substantial reports of British commanders prowling the coast longing for orders to flatten American ports. From Britain came newspaper predictions of war. Some Americans called for war, and even some of the most responsible United States leaders demanded bold reprisals that invited war. No less a congressional leader than Joseph Nicholson wrote Gallatin: "The people are ready to submit to any deprivation, and if we withdraw ourselves within our own shell, and turn loose some thousands of privateers, we shall obtain in a little time an absolute renunciation of the right of search for the purposes of impressment." He feared that time and the spirit of resolve would be wasted in diplomatic efforts. "A parley will prove fatal," he warned, "for the merchants will begin to calculate. They rule us, and we should take them before their resentment is superseded by considerations of profit and loss." He hoped that diplomatic relations with Great Britain were already being broken off. "I trust in God," he said, "the [U.S.S.] *Revenge* is going out to bring Monroe and Pinkney home."[20]

Gallatin replied[21] that he had "not bestowed much thought" on what actions might or might not touch off hostilities, "having considered from the first moment war was a necessary result, and the preliminaries appearing to me but matters of form." He confessed that he was "not very sanguine as to the brilliancy of our exploits, the field where we can act without a navy being very limited." He was also "perfectly aware that a war, in a great degree passive and consisting of privations, will become very irksome to the people." Nevertheless, he felt "no apprehension of the immediate result. We will be poorer both as a nation and as a government, our debt and taxes will increase, and our progress in every respect be interrupted. But all those evils are not only not to be put in competition with the independence and honor of the nation; they are moreover temporary, and a very few years of peace will obliterate their effects."

Here, from one of the administration's most important figures, was resolution, determination after full consideration of the consequences rather than impulsive chauvinism. The naval inadequacy, to which he referred, was enough to give pause to any reasonably cautious person. But the question was how far the President himself was willing to go.

There were clues but they sent a mixed message. To Barnabas Bidwell, a Massachusetts Congressman whom Jefferson had encouraged to aspire to the Republican leadership of the House, the President declared that in dealing with England he was acting on three principles: "(1) to give that government an opportunity to disavow and make reparation; (2) to give ourselves time to get in the vessels, property, and seamen now spread over the ocean; (3) to do no act which might compromit Congress in their choice between war, nonintercourse, or any other measure."[22] He was equally cautious in a letter to Vice President Clinton,[23] stressing the third point of his policy because, "the power of declaring war being with the Legislative, the Executive should do nothing necessarily committing them to decide for war in preference of non-intercourse, which will be preferred by a great many." To several correspondents, he praised nonintercourse as a "peaceable means of repressing injustice, by making it the interest of the aggressor to do what is just, and abstain from future wrong."[24] Watching Jefferson for clues, just as closely as his countrymen, were the envoys of foreign nations. To them he sometimes presented a different picture, but it is difficult to tell whether it reflected his actual thinking or was an image assumed for diplomatic effect.

Both General Turreau, the French Minister, and David Erskine, his British counterpart, focused their powers of analysis on the President at a dinner for twenty at the Executive Mansion. Turreau, who had been out of town when the *Chesapeake* crisis developed, had hurried back because of the emergency. He wrote Foreign Minister Talleyrand a detailed account of the evening.[25] Dinner was past when the General arrived. The windows would have been open to take advantage of any breeze that might enliven the July night. Turreau found the company composed mostly of "new friends of the government." He recognized no one but Erskine and the British Secretary of Legation. The President greeted him even more warmly than usual but soon left him to return to a conversation with the British Minister which the Frenchman's arrival had interrupted. Later Jefferson came back and sat down by Turreau. Finally, all the American guests had gone and only Erskine and Turreau remained. The General thought the British minister was trying to outwait him. Certainly the Frenchman was determined to outstay Erskine.

At length the Englishman left, and the President spoke of the *Chesapeake* affair. According to Turreau, Jefferson said: "If the English do not give us the satisfaction we demand, we will take Canada, which wants to enter the union. And when, together with Canada, we shall have the Floridas, we shall no longer have any difficulties with our neighbors; and it is the only way of preventing them. I expected that the Emperor would return sooner to Paris—and then this affair of the Floridas would be ended."

Apparently Jefferson was taking the opportunity to push for the settlement of one old problem with France while reminding the French Minister that the two countries had a common enemy in England. According to Turreau, Jefferson next went so far as to ask "what were the means to employ in order to be able to defend the American harbors and coasts." The Minister replied that "the choice of means depended on local conditions" and advised the President to consult his own officers. According to Turreau, Jefferson exclaimed, "We have no officers!"

It is surprising that Jefferson should say such a thing. Probably he was flattering the French Minister and indicating confidence in the French government, by asking his advice about United States defense. It was not as farfetched as if he had asked the average foreign diplomat. Turreau had been one of Napoleon's Generals. But if Jefferson's purpose was to win the friendship of the Minister, his efforts were doomed. This man had avowed to Talleyrand on other occasions a distaste for President Jefferson, Secretary of State Madison, and the American people. Moreover, his domestic misery caused him to see the whole world through jaundiced eyes. By his own account a woman had saved his life during turbulent times in France and he had married her in gratitude. She proved to be a virago who made him so miserable that, even though he spoke no English and had no experience in diplomacy, he begged for the Washington appointment. While he was pining for the lost charms of Paris and almost wondered if escaping from his wife was worth the loss, that indefatigable woman showed up in Washington to share his roof. And according to the neighbors the rafters rang with their quarrels.[26]

Not only was Turreau unfriendly to the world in general and the American President in particular, but he would be especially indisposed to urge a settlement placing the Floridas under United States control. Two years earlier he had asked Napoleon to seize the Floridas because he believed that only France could "arrest these American enterprises and baffle their plan."[27] Jefferson had been a remarkably successful diplomat in Paris, but this was one Frenchman he could not charm.

"He treated twenty-seven different subjects in a conversation of half an hour," Turreau told Talleyrand. But the President "showed, as usual, no sort of distrust" in "this conversation of fits and starts," and the General was able to reach a conclusion: "Once for all, whatever may be the disposition of mind here, though everyone is lashing himself to take a warlike attitude, I can assure your Highness that the President does not want war, and that Mr. Madison dreads it still more. I am convinced that these two personages will do everything that is possible to avoid it, and that if Congress, which will be called together only when an answer shall have arrived from England, should think itself bound, as organ of public opinion, to determine on war, its intention will be [thwarted] by powerful intrigues, because the actual Administration has nothing to gain and everything to lose by war."[28]

Erskine, like Turreau, concluded that the administration did not want war, but he believed that war could come if his Majesty's government did not make a small concession to save the young republic's pride. "The ferment in the public mind," he reported to Britain's Foreign Secretary Canning,[29] "has not yet subsided and I am confirmed in the opinion . . . that this country will engage in war rather than submit to their national armed ships being forcibly searched on the high seas." But the situation was not hopeless. "Should his Majesty think fit to cause an apology to be offered to these States on account of the attack of his Majesty's ship *Leopard* on the United States frigate *Chesapeake*, it would have the most powerful effect not only on the minds of the people of this country, but would render it impossible for the Congress to bring on a war upon the other points of difference between his Majesty and the United States at present under discussion."

In London, while some British newspapers asserted that the *Leopard*'s firing upon the *Chesapeake* was perfectly justified and that the Americans should be taught a lesson, Monroe extracted from Canning an important concession. While the Foreign Secretary's reply was, as the American Minister said, "addressed in a rather harsh tone," it stressed "the earnest desire of his Majesty . . . to assure you that his Majesty neither does [maintain] nor has at any time maintained the pretension of a right to search ships of war in the national service of any state for deserters."[30]

Monroe sent Canning's letter to Washington with the comment that it might be "considered as conceding essentially the point desired," but with the warning that there was a strong war party in England. Undeterred by reverses in Northern Europe and the threat of further triumphs by Napoleon, this group was ready to move against the United States. "This party," he said, "is composed of the shipowners, the Navy, the East and West India merchants, and certain political characters of great consideration in the state. So powerful is this combination, that it is most certain that nothing can be obtained of the government on any point but what may be extorted by necessity. The dissenters to the north ought to inspire moderation, but, with respect to the northern powers, it seems to have produced directly the opposite effect."[31]

The "dissenters to the north" were far-reaching. Napoleon had soundly defeated the Russians at the battle of Friedland. The potbellied Little Emperor of France and Russia's tall, regal Alexander I, the storybook image of a monarch, met alone for three hours on a raft moored in the Niemen River opposite Tilsit while the two armies, and metaphorically the world, looked on but could not hear. They embraced like dear friends. Afterwards Napoleon wrote to Josephine, "If he were a woman, I think I would make him my mistress."[32] Other meetings followed in quick succession. As a result, Alexander removed his empire from the war against the French. With Austria and Prussia already knocked out by Bonaparte, Britain now stood alone. Soon France and Russia were allies. So much for Jefferson's hope that the Czar would intercede with Britain to protect the rights of neutrals.

England's leaders had visions of Napoleon augmenting his meager naval forces by the addition of Russian sea power and perhaps the bold seizure of neutral Denmark's navy. In a savage pre-emptive seizure, the British almost leveled Copenhagen and ran away with the entire Danish navy. If this was the way Britain treated a Continental neutral, what hope was there that she would respect American neutrality?

Madison, on September 20, wrote Jefferson: "You will find the British government renounces the pretension to search ships of war for deserters; but employs words which may possibly be meant to qualify the renunciation, or at least to quibble away the promised atonement." The Secretary of State was more than ever convinced of "the absolute necessity of a radical cure for the ills inflicted by British ships of war frequenting our waters."[33]

Nevertheless, Madison recommended that Canning's assurances be circulated unofficially. Even if a "radical" solution should be necessary, it was desirable to buy time to consider the options. Therefore there must be some quieting of the public clamor for immediate action. American newspapers began to carry stories that the British naval officers involved in the *Chesapeake* affair had acted without the direction or approval of their government. Public excitement subsided a little, but Jefferson knew that a single incident could make it flare at once into a consuming flame.

The President's anxiety was heightened by a message from a new source. David Humphreys, freshly arrived in New York from a trip to England, wrote Jefferson that recent publications in England seemed "calculated to prepare the public mind for a rupture with America."[34] Humphreys was a Federalist whom Jefferson had replaced with a Republican as Minister to Spain. But he was a patriot first and a partisan second, and he and Jefferson respected each other. When Jefferson was Secretary of State in 1790 and war threatened, he and

President Washington had sent Humphreys to Europe as a secret agent to communicate with American representatives in London, Lisbon, and Madrid.[35] Humphreys' words were not those of just another American returned from abroad.

One can imagine the feelings with which Jefferson read Humphreys' statement that a war with the United States would probably be more popular in Great Britain now than it had been in 1776. Jefferson's correspondent explained that not only would war be welcomed by naval officers, shipowners, and the zealous British foes of the revolutionary era, but now even former sympathizers anticipated it as "an almost inevitable event, and not very much to be depre-cated—at best, much less so than the loss of the smallest of their naval rights." They believed that American resistance to search and seizure threatened British naval superiority. And now, with Napoleon master of the European continent and commander of the world's greatest army, "To maintain the naval superiority or perish as a nation [was] the prevalent doctrine of the day." Humphreys believed that the conflict over searching ships of war could be settled in a way acceptable to the United States if Washington did not insist that merchant ships flying the American flag should enjoy the same immunity. But Madison had instructed Monroe to stand firm on this very point. Humphreys concluded that American security depended on "becoming in a great degree an armed and united people."

Jefferson's anxiety and uncertainty are indicated not only by his long delay in proposing decisive action but also by the frequency with which he discussed the crisis with members of Congress and the freedom with which he shared official information. He sent the legislators copies of his correspondence with Canning, together with relevant documents, but with no presidential recom-mendations. Jefferson usually played his cards close to the vest, especially in foreign policy. He had accomplished the momentous Louisiana Purchase largely through secret maneuvers. No American had longer and broader experience with foreign policy than Jefferson, and he usually was sure of what he wanted in this field. He sought the counsel of Madison and Gallatin in international matters, but his decisions were his own. He was especially reluctant to throw any vital question of national policy into either of those debating societies, the Senate or the House, until he had communicated his own preferences to a few influential members and obtained their promises of support. Now he talked and wrote about the power of decision belonging to Congress.[36]

In October, with Congress about to convene, the President could not much longer postpone a public stand. He favored an embargo and consulted with his cabinet about its provisions and implementation. Jefferson's first drafts of his message to Congress probably were influenced by Madison, who urged bold-ness. Both Gallatin and Secretary of the Navy Smith thought there was too much sword rattling in the President's paragraphs. The Navy Secretary's apprehension is understandable in light of the slender means with which he was expected to oppose the planet's greatest naval power. Gallatin's concern might have been more surprising to Jefferson. After all, the Treasury Secretary believed that war was inevitable. But so long as there was a shred of doubt, it was unwise to act precipitately and replace anxious belief with ugly certainty. But even if war was truly unavoidable, there were reasons for delay. More time should be provided to enable United States vessels in distant waters to return to home port. Furthermore, Gallatin believed that if war came the United States should immediately invade Canada. Most strategists think that winter is the worst season for launching such an enterprise, but Gallatin thought the best time for a Canadian campaign would be when frozen ports prevented the entrance of the British navy with men and supplies. Finally, he believed that if war should come the United States would stand better in the court of public opinion if it appeared to have exhausted all reasonable efforts for a peaceful solution, or better still if Britain were led to made the actual declaration.[37]

In November the President received a formal message from Canning admitting that the United States was entitled to reparations for depredations committed by H.M.S. *Leopard*, but insisting that earlier illegal acts were American and that their consequences must be dealt with first.

Jefferson saw the embargo as the middle way of the three possibilities of "war, embargo, or nothing."[38] And, though sensitive to questions of national honor, he concluded that it would be better not to compromise the policy of embargo by increasing the likelihood of war.

The President's message to Congress on October 27, therefore, was somewhat ambiguous in regard to the *Chesapeake* crisis. It said that "the love of peace" might not be enough to insure its continuance. "Whether a regular army is to be raised, and to what extent, must depend on the information so shortly expected." Far less equivocal were the President's comments on what he saw as a miscarriage of justice in the trial of Aaron Burr and his recommendation that Congress "inquire by what means more effectual" the national government might be protected "against destruction by treason."

Not until December 18 did the President send Congress a message dealing specifically with the maritime crisis and making definite recommendations. Unlike the earlier drafts, which had alarmed Smith and Gallatin, it was shorn of bristling rhetoric. It recommended an embargo but was free of trumpet calls.

More alarming than anything in the President's message were two foreign documents which he submitted with it. One was an announcement from Napoleon's government that his Berlin Decree forbidding trade in British goods with the European continent would henceforth be interpreted to include the United States. The days of special treatment for the Americans were over. Another document was a proclamation from King George III not only reasserting the right of impressment but saying that it would be applied to naval vessels as well as merchant ships. Jefferson let these materials speak for themselves. He presented no formal argument for an embargo but simply said that the need should be apparent.

It was not apparent to Gallatin. On the very day that Jefferson sent the embargo message to Congress, the Treasury Secretary told him that he would go along with it as a temporary measure but asserted: "In every point of view, privations, sufferings, revenue, effect on the enemy, politics at home, etc., I prefer war to a permanent embargo." He also said: "I think that we had better recommend [the embargo] with modifications, and at first for such a limited time as will afford us all time for reconsideration and, if we think proper, for an alteration in our course without appearing to retract."[39]

Jefferson asked Gallatin to come by the Executive Mansion before 10:30 a.m. to discuss the message before it reached Congress. The President did not change anything but, given his own philosophy, he probably was somewhat susceptible to an argument that Gallatin had used in his note: "Governmental prohibitions do always more mischief than had been calculated, and it is not without much hesitation that a statesman should hazard to regulate the concerns of individuals as if he could do it better than themselves."

Jefferson evidently was realistic in his assumption that the need for an embargo would be "apparent" to the Congress without an argument from him. Or perhaps one should say without additional argument. Doubtless his reasoning had been conveyed to its members in individual conversations, and events had worked their own conversion. By the time the President sent his message, many members were pressuring him to adopt the course he had already chosen. The Nicholson Non-Importation Act, passed in April 1806 and prohibiting importation from Great Britain of certain articles, had been suspended by Congress at Jefferson's urging. By coincidence, it had become effective automatically on December 14, just four days before the President's embargo message. While the act was deplored by some Northeastern Federalists and South Carolina's Senator Thomas Sumter, many people in the South and West complained that its scope was far too narrow. Despite the determined opposition of a handful of Federalists, a bill embodying the Embargo Act proposed by the President was brought to a vote in the Senate on the very day his message was received. It passed 22 to 6.

Jefferson's supporters realized that victory would not be that easily won in the House. Federalists were stronger in the lower chamber and its Republican members were divided on a variety of issues.

A major change had come with reorganization of the House at the beginning of the session. Nathaniel Macon, of North Carolina, Speaker since 1801, was not a candidate for reelection. He had once been one of Jefferson's closest allies in the Congress, but he had come under the spell of John Randolph and for the past year had associated with the Quids, the Republicans who complained that the President had departed from pure Republicanism. His identification with Randolph cost him so much support that he realized it would be futile to offer again as a candidate for the speakership. Joseph Bradley Varnum, of Massachusetts, was elected in his stead by a one-vote majority.

The new Speaker appointed George Washington Campbell of Tennessee to replace Randolph as chairman of the powerful House Ways and Means Committee. The Virginian had so dominated the committee's proceedings that the change was an important one. Gallatin, who believed that Randolph was the greatest master of finance in the chamber, said the change was "much against my wishes. . . . and will give me additional labor."[40]

We may safely assume that Jefferson did not share the Treasury Secretary's view. The President would not have been human if he had not been pleased to see his most eloquent denouncer replaced by a man who recently had declared that in history the reputation of Jefferson's defamers as compared with his record would be "like the feeble glow of the glow-worm before the splendid glory of the mid-day sun."[41]

The House debate took place on a new stage. After seven years in uncomfortable temporary quarters known as "the oven," the Representatives convened in their new chamber. The combined talents of Jefferson and Capitol architect Benjamin Latrobe had produced a room whose elegance and beauty, once the interior was complete, would equal those of Europe's greatest national assemblies. It was a graceful oval. Already the work of Italian sculptors lent a note of drama. Before the many months of foreign policy debates in the Jefferson administration had ended, the chamber would glow with crimson draperies anchored by the earth color of its fluted sandstone columns. The splendid ceiling frescoes would tempt the gaze of members upward and away from action on the floor. In secret session, in this operatic setting, the drama of debate raged Friday, Saturday, and Monday, with time off for the sabbath. On Friday, Randolph demanded the floor at the start and introduced a resolution calling for an embargo "on all shipping." The next day he astonished a House long accustomed to his tergiversations by denouncing in the strongest terms the very resolution he himself had introduced. Such a measure, he screamed, would toady to Napoleon and bring war with Great Britain. On Monday, December 21, at the close of general debate, various amendments were introduced and voted down. Most of the Southern and Western representatives stood with Jefferson. So did the New England and Pennsylvania Republicans. The embargo passed, 82 to 44.

The new House Chamber was an appropriate symbol for the legislation just adopted within its walls and for the thunderous pronouncements it sent forth in ensuing months to great and ancient states of the Old World. Soon it looked like the legislative hall of a mighty nation but in reality it was the elaborate creation of a feeble republic. Immediately on leaving the chamber, as if exiting a particularly convincing set, one entered a tunnel of rough boards. The Capitol, like the nation itself, promised to be great someday. Both were now incomplete structures. In many ways, the embargo, as an instrument of national policy, was much more a matter of theater than of substance.

To United States citizens the embargo forbade virtually all commerce, by land or sea, with other nations. Not only were United States ships forbidden to sail for foreign ports, but there was a provision to prevent American vessels ostensibly in coastwise trade from slipping away to foreign ports. Each such ship was required to post bond double the value of both the vessel itself and its cargo as insurance that its load would be relanded at an American port.

Technically, the act did not prohibit importation in foreign vessels, but another provision, for all practical purposes, interdicted such traffic. This was the proviso that foreign ships could not carry goods out of a United States port. If a ship crossing the ocean with a cargo bound for the United States could not return with another cargo, the operation would not be a profitable one.

Jefferson and the Congress were not alone in hoping that the Embargo Act would bring tyrants to heel. Though some shipowners, particularly in the Northeast, feared the embargo more than foreign impressment, most Americans who had convictions in the matter supported the act. Jefferson, whose support a short while before had been eroding rapidly even in his own party, enjoyed a new burst of popularity. In a surge of patriotism, most Americans of both parties rallied behind their President.

The young republic was naive in its assumption that, by withholding its goods and its trade, it could bring Great Britain, France, and the rest of Europe to the bargaining table. American insularity caused even astute citizens to exaggerate the western world's dependency on the United States. Their view was analogous to that of the London newspaper which, with the fury of the elements cutting off Great Britain from the mass of Europe, headlined: "Storm Rages in Channel; Continent Is Isolated."

While the embargo initially caused some inconvenience for British merchants and manufacturers, this effect was short-lived. The United States, except for a few shipowners successfully violating the law, had removed its own shippers from competition with their British rivals. The want of American raw materials was felt at first, but British importers soon turned to South American sources.

Some Americans were able to defy the embargo in ways that allowed them to continue to trade while depriving their government of tax revenues. The masters of some United States vessels at sea when the act became effective simply began carrying between foreign ports without approaching United States shores. The British government was hospitable to them. Smugglers were more active than at any time since the old pre-Revolutionary days when it was easy for a smuggler to see himself as an especially enterprising patriot. The traffic in British and United States goods flowed across the Canadian border through woodland paths and on dark nights via the Great Lakes. Goods moved, too, across the border with Spanish Florida.

Elaborate schemes were devised to elude the blockade. One of the most fantastic was hatched by a German who had fled his country at age seventeen for London, where he had learned English and prepared for life in the United States. He had settled in New York after coming to America in steerage in 1783. His ambition to be rich was fueled by a miserable childhood as the son of an impecunious butcher said to have been "much more at home in the beer-house than at his own fireside." By the time of the embargo, this stout, square-built, now middle-aged man was a prosperous fur trader, but not nearly so rich as he dreamed of being. Nor did he shine in elite society. Much more money would be necessary to transform his bad grammar into an appealing quaintness of speech.

While some of his fellow merchants moaned that the embargo was ruining them, he saw in it the opportunity of his life. He instructed one of his clerks to write a letter to the President, purportedly from "The Honorable Punqua Wingchong, a Chinese mandarin." This imaginary gentleman sought permission to charter a ship to pass through the blockade and return him to his native land, "where the affairs of his family, and particularly the funeral obsequies of his grandfather, require[d] his solemn attention." Jefferson, always a humanitarian and also eager to improve United States relations with China, instructed Gallatin to do the requisite paperwork and issue the necessary orders. The fur trader's ship was the one commissioned for the task, and it sailed with many "attendants" and box after box of the "mandarin's" baggage. The retinue, of course, was composed of the trader's employees, and the baggage consisted of goods in trade.

The speculator who foisted this scheme upon the administration was thus able to send a ship to China under federal protection and return through the blockade with a full cargo of Chinese manufactures. This venture rocketed him into such empyrean realms of riches that the narrator of Herman Melville's "Bartleby the Scrivener" insisted that the wily trader's very name "hath a rounded orbicular sound to it, and rings like unto bullion"—John Jacob Astor.[42] Thus Jefferson and Gallatin—both of whom feared the influence in the United States of great mercantile fortunes—unwittingly helped to transform a not too scrupulous trader into America's richest merchant and the founder of a family fortune that made its holders financial barons for generations.

The fate of most shippers was vastly different from Astor's. Port cities, not only in the Northeast but also in Hampton Roads and points south, stagnated. When trade on land ceases, the affected area sometimes reverts to forest. To an imaginative eye, embargo-stricken harbors must have presented an analogous phenomenon. The masts of idle ships, like a forest of naked trees, stretched across each anchorage. Eventually even these disappeared as their owners moved them to fresh water to escape worms. Shipyards were idled. Ship chandlers locked their shops. Merchants deriving their margin of profit from the purchases of shipyard workers or free-spending sailors suffered painful reverses.

How could Jefferson, who had compiled brilliant analyses of European economy during his service as an envoy and as Secretary of State, so miscalculate the effects of an embargo? We should remember that, even when the President requested that Congress pass the Embargo Act, he did not present any arguments for it. He simply made his recommendation, submitted pertinent documents, and said the need should be "apparent." On January 6, 1808, little more than a fortnight after the act became law, Jefferson explained to John Taylor of Caroline what he hoped to accomplish by it. Others had talked about bringing England to her knees or dealing a heavy blow to both Britain and France. Jefferson said nothing of these things in his letter[43] to the distinguished economist and political philosopher. Instead he wrote: "The embargo, keeping at home our vessels, cargoes, and seamen, saves us the necessity of making their capture the cause of immediate war: for if [they had been] going to England, France had determined to take them; if to any other place, England was to take them." He summarized: "Till they return to some sense of moral duty, therefore, we keep within ourselves. This gives time. Time may produce peace in Europe: peace in Europe removes all causes of difference till another European war: and by that time our debt may be paid, our revenues clear, and our strength increased."

Americans were entitled to ask what their President was doing to increase their naval and military strength while their economy was being weakened. In 1805 he had proposed to the Congress an act[44] providing "that every free, able-bodied, white male citizen of the United States of the age of 18 years and under the age of 45, whose principal occupation is not on the high sea or the tide-waters within the United States, shall be of the militia for the land service of the United States." An enrollment by names, ages, and districts was to be made without delay. As other men became eligible for military service, their names would be added. Those between 21 and 26 years of age would be "strictly trained to the exercises and maneuvers of a soldier, either of artillery, infantry, or cavalry." Any person refusing to report for assigned duty, or delaying entrance upon it, would be "arrested as a deserter either by the civil or military authority." In effect, the President was proposing to draft citizens into a national guard. Many members of Congress were quite willing to threaten Britain, France, and Spain, to talk of seizing Spanish Florida or Canada, and at every possible excuse to brandish the American flag as a weapon, but they threw up their hands in horror at the President's suggestion for building an army.

Jefferson drafted in September 1805, and submitted in final form in December, "A Bill for Establishing a Naval Militia."[45] This would provide "that every free, able-bodied, white male citizen of the United States of the age of 18 years and under the age of 45 years, whose principal occupation is on the high sea or on the tide-water within the United States shall be of the militia for the naval service of the United States and shall be exempt from the services of the land militia." Congress was in no mood to support this proposal.

Jefferson pointed out to the Congress, collectively and individually, that vital harbors of the United States were inadequately defended. In 1806 he requested cannon for land batteries and called for construction of gunboats. He said that the government already had materials for building ships of the line, and that such construction could begin if Congress saw fit. Congress turned down this idea of a naval militia but provided for the land batteries and gunboats. Representative John Dawson, of Virginia, introduced legislation calling for construction of six ships of the line but the measure won the support of less than one-third of the House.

It could be said that Jefferson had not supported this last proposal energetically. It has been suggested that he did not have strong convictions about it. But a letter[46] that the President wrote after the *Chesapeake* affair to Congressman Jacob Crowninshield, a former sea captain he had once asked to be Secretary of the Navy, suggests otherwise. "Building some ships of the line instead of our most indifferent frigates is not to be lost sight of. That we should have a squadron properly composed to prevent blockading our ports is indispensable. The Atlantic frontier, from members, wealth, and exposure to potent enemies, have a proportionate right to be defended with the Western frontier, for whom we keep up 3000 men." He counted on "bringing forward the measure therefore in a moderate form, placing it on the ground of comparative right," believing that "our nation, which is a just one, will come into it, notwithstanding the repugnance of some on the subject being first presented."

Jefferson, it seems clear, forbore pressuring the Congress on constructing ships of the line for fear that such insistence would build resistance. He depended on a growing climate of public opinion to move Congress toward the necessary measures.

The charge, often repeated since Jefferson's time, that he was never interested in building national defense, especially naval defense, is a gross exaggeration. His achievements in defense are certainly not notable among the accomplishments of his administration, but his advocacy in the field was far ahead of the commitment or understanding of the people's representatives in both houses of Congress. His usual method of accomplishing something for which automatic support was lacking was to plant suggestions among the nation's legislators and among those in the electorate who might influence them. He often got Congress or the public to demand that he do what he had already planned. If success could not be won through the force of public opinion, Jefferson was capable of acting covertly with bold independence and the support of a few trusted confreres—as, for instance, in the Louisiana Purchase and in some matters concerning the Lewis and Clark expedition. Planting suggestions proved too slow a process when the people were deeply concerned with the national debt and when their colonial experience had fastened upon them an almost visceral fear of standing armies and cannonading fleets. The only way of arousing sufficient public enthusiasm for defense was to whip the people into a war frenzy, which then almost surely would precipitate the United States into the bloody struggle which the President was working so hard to prevent. Jefferson's second method was not applicable here. Obviously, he could not secretly create a national militia, military or naval, and—leaving constitutional restrictions aside—he could not build and operate in secret a flotilla of ships of the line.

Jefferson did, however, make at least one major blunder in defense. He put too much faith in gunboats.

The President was convinced that the United States Navy must be strengthened. But he also feared that naval service was especially prone to create an officer caste roaming the oceans of the world and frequently out of touch with the lives and thoughts of the mass of their countrymen. Jefferson also believed, and Gallatin emphatically agreed with him, that a navy tended to extend a nation's frontiers of hostility. It carried the nation's armed presence to the shores of distant countries and tremendously enlarged the area of potential friction. The President's solution to this problem was to concentrate on the building of shallow-draft vessels about fifty feet in length and outfitted with both oars and sails. Each would have one or two cannon. Such boats, he argued, would have the advantage of maneuverability in defense of American harbors and the ability to take refuge in creeks, small rivers, and branches where enemy warships could not follow. On the other hand, not being suitable for transoceanic travel, they were not likely to be used where their officers would be tempted, or forced, into foreign adventures.[47]

These gunboats had the added advantages of economical and quick construction. Jefferson, as we have seen, did not believe that gunboats could eliminate the need for frigates, but he did believe that they could reduce the number of frigates needed. And he was impressed by the fact that 127 of the "mosquito boats" could be constructed for $500,000 to $600,000, less than the cost of two frigates.[48] Congress in the spring of 1806 authorized construction of fifty gunboats. Later the Senate cut out provisions for more gunboats in a harbor defense bill passed by the House. But late in 1807, a little before enactment of the embargo and under the pressure of crisis, the President's recommendation prevailed. His proposal for construction of 188 gunboats at an estimated cost of $852,000 cleared the Senate by a vote of 26 to 3 and the House by 111 to 19.

The record of gunboats in Jefferson's administration was inconclusive. Their chief value was in defense of harbors and inland waters in time of hostile invasion, and this threat did not materialize until Madison's presidency, at which time the government had few gunboats in operation. The record does suggest that a few more frigates would have benefited the country even at the expense of many gunboats, but it does not prove that no gunboats should have been built. In the time of power-driven craft, the mosquito boat would prove an effective instrument of war, but Jefferson's tiny, wind-driven craft were sometimes too vulnerable to both the enemy and the elements. When one of the boats was driven into a cornfield by a storm, some Federalists joked about its having found its natural element.

There is a widely held belief, strongly promoted by Henry Adams, a brilliant historian but sorely prejudiced against Jefferson in favor of his own ancestors, that faith in gunboats was a personal aberration which the Virginian foisted on the nation. The truth is that while John Randolph, whose judgment most had learned to distrust, ridiculed gunboats from the first, many people of prominent military or naval reputations supported the concept. Indeed, while the idea of the gunboat appealed to Jefferson's inventive mind, he was by no means its originator or even its first American proponent. Some gunboats had been authorized in Washington's administration, even though they had not been built. General James Wilkinson, an untrustworthy blowhard but nevertheless the nation's highest military officer, testified in Jefferson's presidency that "barges, galleys, or gunboats" in conjunction with "heavy movable batteries which may be expeditiously transferred from one part of a town or city to another by men and horses" would provide the "most economical, durable, and effectual means of defense."[49] More to the point, the able General Horatio Gates had said he believed gunboats to be "the most proper defense for large harbors that has hitherto been imagined." Commodore Samuel Barron, who had seen them in action in the Mediterranean, believed them "the most effectual means of defense within the bays and rivers." One of the nation's most respected naval officers, Captain Thomas Tingey, testified that their value was "obvious to every person capable of reflection."[50] They had already been introduced into the navies of Britain and France, both of which had been impressed with the Russians' effective use of them against a Turkish fleet in 1787.

Though Jefferson's gunboat proposals won the support of leading naval figures, his advocacy of a truly radical innovation drew only ridicule from the professionals. This was his call in 1802 for construction of a dry dock as an aid to the building and repair of warships. The Congress did not get around to an appropriation for such a purpose until 1823. The first drydocking in America was at the Gosport Navy Yard in Portsmouth, Virginia, in 1833.[51]

It can scarcely be emphasized too often that Jefferson had no desire to convert the United States Navy to gunboats to the exclusion of larger vessels. This canard was spread by Theodore Roosevelt in a poorly researched part of his generally valuable work *The Naval War of 1812*. The two Presidents—Jefferson and Roosevelt—had much in common: patrician backgrounds, education at distinguished universities, dedication to public service, devotion to literary and scholarly pursuits. But the conciliatory Jefferson and the aggressive Roosevelt had incompatible temperaments. Roosevelt was so far from appreciating his predecessor of exactly a century before that he called him the worst of American Presidents. Ironically, today the two, cheek by jowl, look out in monumental placidity from Mount Rushmore.

In considering the problems of defense, Jefferson pushed his countrymen in the right direction, though not always successfully. His mistakes were matters of emphasis within a generally sound framework. And his advocacy was necessarily within the constraints imposed by an important realization: arming at the cost of economic stability would not only ultimately deprive the young republic of its ability to wage war successfully but even of existence itself.

Frustrated in efforts to plug holes in United States defenses, the administration attempted to plug holes in the embargo. A supplementary act of January 9, 1808 exacted bonds from vessels engaged in fishing and whaling. An act approved March 12 required bonds from foreign ships in coastwise trade and extended control over American commerce far beyond anything suggested by the President's original request for an embargo. It put tight controls on movement of imported goods by land. Federalist Representative Barent Gardenier, of New York, railed against this feature and accused the sponsors of the original Embargo Act, and by implication the President, of being "sly" and "cunning." He called Jefferson the "Imperial Conqueror" to whom the members of the Congress had been delivered as captive slaves. Majority leader George Washington Campbell replied in such vigorous terms that Gardenier challenged him to a duel. The New Yorker was wounded. Jefferson always appreciated the loyalty of his sons-in-law, but, deploring dueling as "the most barbarous of appeals,"[52] he must have regretted deeply that John Eppes demonstrated his loyalty on this occasion by serving as Campbell's second. The participants being well known, this "affair of honor" attracted reams of publicity embarrassing the administration.

Jefferson's personal popularity nevertheless remained high. There was every indication that the embargo enjoyed majority support in most of the nation. The General Assembly of Virginia, despite the commonwealth's stake in the great port of Hampton Roads, addressed to the President resolutions avowing that they would "submit with pleasure to the privations arising from the energetic measure" and declared their willingness to make additional sacrifices for peace or honor. More surprising was a resolution of support from the legislators of Massachusetts which, though now in the Republican column, was a center of Federalist opposition to restrictions on shipping. Other resolutions of endorsement came from North Carolina, South Carolina, Maryland, Kentucky, Pennsylvania, New Hampshire, Georgia, and the Territory of Orleans. Though he did not receive a resolution from the New York legislature, he was sent enough messages from the state's bodies of lesser jurisdiction to indicate pockets of strong approval. He received some bitter complaints about the embargo, but there was comfort in the fact that most were anonymous.

Jefferson himself was confident of public support.[53] This success was doubly satisfying because it followed by a few months a period in which the press had vilified him for everything from richly imagined accounts of his rompings with naked slaves to much more substantive evidence of his carelessness about civil rights in the pursuit of Aaron Burr. The abrasive effect of this harassment is apparent in the reply Jefferson wrote on June 11, 1806, to John Norvell, a seemingly idealistic young man who had asked him by what course of reading one might prepare for participation in government and also how one might conduct a newspaper so as to make it most useful to society.[54]

Though saying that his "occupations" limited him to very short answers, this busy man, in reply to the first question, took time to list a few works and compare their merits. He suggested writings of Locke, Priestly, and Chapman. He named Adam Smith's *Wealth of Nations*, Say's *Political Economy*, and *The Federalist*, not being blinded by the fact that his old enemy Alexander Hamilton was one of the two principal coauthors. Despite his troubles with Britain, he recommended a study of British history "as we have employed some of the best materials of the British constitution in the construction of our own government." In evaluating histories of England, he lamented, "The elegant one of Hume seems intended to disguise and discredit the good principles of the government, and is so plausible and pleasing in its style and manner as to instil its errors and heresies insensibly into the minds of unwary readers." He recommended instead Baxter's derivative work, which he called "Hume's history republicanized." One of the works he most respected was by a woman, Catharine Macaulay, author of an eight-volume *History of England*.

Then Jefferson turned to the second question and the man of reason became a man of passion. Young Mr. Norvell, so eager to serve mankind through the powers of the press, must have been startled by this part of the letter: "To your request of my opinion of the manner in which a newspaper should be conducted so as to be most useful, I should answer, 'By restraining it to true facts and sound principles only.' Yet I fear such a paper would find few subscribers. It is a melancholy truth that a suppression of the press could not more completely deprive the nation of its benefits than is done by its abandoned prostitution to falsehood. Nothing can now be believed which is seen in a newspaper. Truth itself becomes suspicious by being put into that polluted vehicle."

He was, he insisted, in a position to know what he was talking about. "The real extent of this state of misinformation is known only to those who are in situations to confront facts within their knowledge with the lies of the day." And, in words now reminiscent of a later observation by Thoreau, he said: "I really look with commiseration over the great body of my fellow citizens, who, reading newspapers, live and die in the belief that they have known something of what has been passing in the world in their time; whereas the accounts they have read in newspapers are just as true a history of any other period of the world as of the present, except that the real names of the day are affixed to their labels."

Jefferson's denunciation of newspapers continued for some four hundred words, including such gems as "The man who never looks into a newspaper is better informed than he who reads them; inasmuch as he who knows nothing is nearer than he whose mind is filled with falsehoods and errors."

As a specific reform, he suggested that an editor might "divide his paper into four chapters, heading the 1st Truths, 2nd Probabilities, 3rd Possibilities, 4th Lies. The first chapter would be very short, as it would contain little more than authentic papers, and information from such sources, as the editor would be willing to risk his own reputation for their truth. The 2d would contain what, from a mature consideration of all circumstances, his judgement should con- clude to be probably true. This, however, should rather contain too little than too much. The 3d and 4th should be professedly for those readers who would rather have lies for their money than the blank paper they would occupy."

For the low quality of newspapers, Jefferson blamed the public even more than he did journalists. A reforming editor, he said, "would have to set his face against the demoralizing practice of feeding the public mind habitually on slander, and the depravity of taste which this nauseous aliment induces. Defa- mation is becoming a necessary of life; insomuch that a dish of tea in the morning or evening cannot be digested without this stimulant. Even those who do not believe these abominations, still read them with complacence to their auditors, and instead of the abhorrence and indignation which should fill a virtuous mind, betray a secret pleasure in the possibility that some may believe them, though they do not themselves. It seems to escape them, that it is not he who prints, but he who pays for printing a slander, who is its real author."

Jefferson feared that he might have been indiscreet in answering the young man so frankly. "These thoughts on the subjects of your letters," he said, "are hazarded at your request. Repeated instances of the publication of what has not been intended for the public eye, and the malignity with which political enemies torture every sentence from me into meanings imagined by their own wicked- ness only, justify my expressing a solicitude that this hasty communication may in nowise be permitted to find its way into the public papers. Not fearing these political bull-dogs, I yet avoid putting myself in the way of being baited by them, and do not wish to volunteer away that portion of tranquility which a firm execution of my duties will permit me to enjoy."

No matter how strong the provocation, Jefferson as President had adhered to his long practice of not replying to any charges against his personal character. From his public statements one might conclude that, serene in his general optimism and sure sense of rectitude, he had remained indifferent to the most scurrilous attacks. His letter to Norvell and some other personal communica- tions on the subject reveal the agony of this sensitive man.

The experience was made even more painful by his strong resistance to any invasion of his privacy. Even when prompted by adulation, such intrusions were disagreeable to him. When supporters in the North told him of his popularity in their region in the summer of 1807 and urged him to make a tour of the area, he thanked them but said: "I confess that I am not reconciled to the idea of a chief magistrate parading himself through the several states as an object of public gaze and in quest of an applause which, to be valuable, should be purely voluntary. I had rather acquire silent good will by a faithful discharge of my duties than owe expressions of it to my putting myself in the way of receiving them."[55]

Two days after replying to the invitation for a Northern tour, he wrote to Dr. Casper Wistar[56] of Philadelphia regarding opportunities for his grandson, Thomas Jefferson Randolph, to study in that city. The President digressed into his views of medicine, basically that healing could best be achieved by aiding natural processes rather than resorting too readily to medication, and by "keep[ing] alive the hope and spirits of the patient." After diplomatic reference to his trust in such proven practitioners as his correspondent, he said: "I believe we may safely affirm that the inexperienced and presumptuous band of medical tyros let loose upon the world destroys more of human life in one year than all the Robin Hoods, Cartouches, and Macheaths do in a century. It is in this part of medicine that I wish to see a reform, an abandonment of hypothesis for sober facts, the first degree of value set on clinical observation, and the lowest on visionary theories." He concluded by saying that although his observation might be worthless, "it has permitted me for a moment to abstract myself from the dry and dreary waste of politics, into which I have been impressed by the times on which I happened" and to indulge in those fields of intellectual speculation "where alone I should have served as a volunteer if left to my natural inclinations and partialities."

So, wearied with uncongenial tasks and burdened with memories of past libels, Jefferson took comfort in the resurgence of his popularity in the spring of 1808. But he did not trust that he would inevitably bask in public good will until the end of his administration. The reliable cure for the vexations of public life would be retirement from office. He was consoled by the fact that it was less than a year away.

It is good that Jefferson had philosophically braced himself for a change of fortune. Spring brought troubles flooding like the seasonal freshets in his native Blue Ridge Mountains.

The spring thaw quite literally was responsible for some of his difficulties. It freed New England ports of ice. Then the embargo really made a difference in the lives of the people. So long as Winter's own embargo had held the harbors in its frozen grip, federal prohibitions had made little difference. As merchants and shipowners counted their losses and humbler workers felt the pain of unemployment, resentment against the administration mounted. Smuggling suddenly increased in New England and upstate New York. One of the most influential New England Federalists, Senator Timothy Pickering of Massachusetts, called for nullification of the embargo by legislatures of the states most affected.

Pickering had led prominent Federalists in 1804 in an attempt to persuade the five New England states, New York, and New Jersey to secede from the Union and form a Northern Confederacy. He saw the embargo issue as an opportunity to breathe new life into his old scheme. He charged that Jefferson had fastened the embargo on the nation in obedience to orders from Napoleon. Such a claim, if believed, was enough to infuriate any American proud of his country's hard-won independence, but it was utterly maddening to New England's many Francophobes.

Pickering played a still more dangerous game. Erskine, Britain's young Minister to Washington, had grown to admire Jefferson and sympathize with the Americans. His dispatches to London repeatedly urged more conciliatory conduct toward the United States. In February, British Foreign Secretary Canning sent George Henry Rose as a special envoy to deal directly with Secretary Madison and President Jefferson on matters of contention between the two countries. As Henry Adams aptly said: "Rose came, not to conciliate, but to terrify. His apology was a menace." He arrived the day after Christmas 1807 and added nothing to the jollity of the season. Jefferson and Madison soon realized the virtual surrender of American independence would be the price of any peace negotiated through this man. They were also sure that he followed faithfully his instructions from Canning and accurately represented the disposition of His Majesty's government. On February 16 Madison and Rose acknowledged that further negotiations would be useless. But Pickering resumed where the properly constituted American authorities left off. He conferred repeatedly with Rose, assuring him that the Jefferson administration did not represent the views of the American people. He not only said that he and others wished to form a pro-British party in New England but actually called upon Rose to recommend that Canning remain adamant in his policy toward the United States.

Pickering's conduct violated the Logan Act of 1799, which prohibited unauthorized American citizens from negotiating with foreign powers in an attempt to influence their policies toward the United States. More important, his activities lent encouragement to hardliners in Britain. His words were printed there and he was hailed as a hero by English newspapers.

Pickering and other Federalist leaders were able to influence Massachusetts voters strongly in the March elections. The Federalists recaptured both houses of the legislature and almost succeeded in turning out Governor Sullivan, one of Jefferson's most enthusiastic supporters.

The most prominent casualty of the Federalist resurgence was John Quincy Adams. As a United States Senator he had crossed party lines to support the administration in the Yrujo affair, the suspension of habeas corpus, the *Chesapeake* crisis, and the embargo. In the last case, his constituents had been infuriated by his statement: "The President has recommended the measure on his high responsibility. I would not consider, I would not deliberate; I would act." In that time, when United States Senators were still elected by state Senates (as they would be until 1913), the Federalist majority in the Massachusetts upper chamber was determined to retire him in the most insulting way possible. They elected his successor on June 3, 1808, several months before the customary time. This action could not legally shorten the remainder of his term but it did express their eagerness to be rid of him. Five days later, he resigned. Adams was Boylston Professor of Rhetoric and Oratory at Harvard, and there was much laughter about sending the professor back to his books—merriment in which George Henry Rose joined from across the Atlantic when Pickering informed him of the Senator's fate. Governor Sullivan told Jefferson that the "principal object" of the Federalists appeared to be "the political, and even the personal, destruction of John Quincy Adams."[57] They believed that they had succeeded.

John Quincy Adams had to endure not only the hatred of erstwhile friends but the misunderstanding of his beloved parents. Their criticisms, he said, were "a test for my firmness, for my prudence, and for my filial reverence." The senior Adams had once written to his son, "You come into life with advantages which will disgrace you if your success is mediocre. And if you do not rise to the head not only of your profession, but of your country, it will be owing to your own laziness, slovenliness, and obstinacy." Both John and Abigail now saw their son as disgraced. "I would wish to please my parents," John Quincy said, "but my duty I *must* do. It is a law far above that of my mere wishes."[58]

Jefferson himself was sorely tried as he strove to do his duty. Even his most loyal supporters complicated problems created by his enemies. Governor Sullivan granted so many special permissions for the importation of flour and grain into Massachusetts that the effectiveness of the blockade was being undermined at the same time that Bay State merchants and shippers complained of its strictures. The President had to ask the Governor to curb his leniency and to give the administration an estimate of the state's future needs.[59] There was little comfort in Sullivan's excuse that he feared the outbreak of riots.

With negotiations with Britain having failed and the embargo of doubtful efficacy, it was painfully frustrating for Jefferson to have his defense budget reduced by the Congress. Before submitting it he had trimmed his requests below what he would have considered prudent except for the threat of economic ruin. National security had to be balanced delicately on the two frail props of insufficient funds and insufficient arms.

With Congress denying money even for what the President regarded as essential defense, he suffered excruciating embarrassment over a deficit of $50,000 incurred in providing what many members regarded as frills. The painful moment came when Jefferson submitted the report of the Surveyor of Public Buildings. The Surveyor had been allotted $65,000 and had spent $115,000. He was Benjamin Latrobe, appointed by Jefferson in 1803 to supervise the work on the Capitol begun by William Thornton and Stephen Hallet. A native of England educated in Germany, he was the architect and engineer responsible for construction of a penitentiary in Richmond, the Bank of Pennsylvania in Philadelphia, and that city's waterworks.

It has been said that Jefferson, as both an architect and a statesman, was in a unique position to mediate between the Congress and the Surveyor of Public

Buildings.[60] There may be something to the argument, but for Latrobe the situation was analogous to that of a general serving under a civilian official who has been a military professional and has great confidence in his own judgment. The two clashed on esthetic issues.

One argument was provoked by Jefferson's decision that panel lights should be placed in the dome of the House Chamber rather than adding for daylight illumination an architectural lantern or cupola as advocated by Latrobe. The President wrote: "It is with real pain I oppose myself to your passion for the lantern, and that in a matter of taste, I differ from a professor in his own art. But the object of the artist is lost if he fails to appeal to the general eye."[61] Jefferson was not insisting that he knew more about architecture than Latrobe, who had made it his chief pursuit, but that he knew better how to use the art in ways that pleased the public.

He did not, however, advocate capitulation to the lowest denominator of public taste. He adhered to ancient standards. "You know my reverence for the Grecian and Roman style of architecture," he told Latrobe. "I do not recollect ever to have seen in their buildings a single instance of a lantern, cupola, or belfry." Such devices, he believed, had been introduced solely to accommodate church bells. Whatever their origin, they were, in his view, examples of the degeneracy of "modern" architecture.

The central portion of the Capitol, he argued, should be in the style of the Pantheon without the introduction of features unknown to the Romans. Of course, Jefferson had modeled the Virginia State Capitol after the Roman temple at Nimes, but he had modified that design.[62] And in designing Monticello he was both traditional and innovative. But he was sure that he knew where to draw the line between innovation and tradition.

Even within the classical category, Jefferson insisted on his own choices. Latrobe preferred Doric columns and Jefferson demanded Corinthian.

Jefferson insisted on the ceiling panels to admit light, not only as an alternative to a lantern or cupola, but as a highly desirable feature in itself. He had fallen in love with the device when he first saw it in Paris' Halle aux Bleds on the same day in 1786 that he had fallen in love with the beautiful Maria Cosway. Her hair had shone golden in rays of light from such a panel.[63]

Latrobe had already said that a light-paneled dome would mean a leaking roof. His reply to the President's commands and admonitions was heavily sarcastic: "I am very sensible of the honor you do me in discussing with me the merits of the detail of the public building. I know well that *to you* it is my duty to obey implicitly or to resign my office: to myself it is my duty to maintain myself in a situation in which I can provide for my family by all honorable means."[64]

Latrobe said that he would install the glass panels in the dome even though he would be proceeding "diametrically contrary" to his own judgment, which told him condensation on the glass would drip on the Congressmen's heads. In following the President's orders, he said, he was motivated not by a desire to hold on to his job but rather by "gratitude and the highest esteem." Then he counteracted all the conciliatory effects of this declaration by warning Jefferson that esthetics "ought never to be at warfare with good sense."

Though Jefferson had given minute attention to Latrobe's plans for the Capitol, he had neither foreseen nor overseen the expenditures involved. One may easily imagine his anger when, after a working association marked by so much controversy, he discovered the necessity of reporting to the Congress a cost overrun of 56 percent. The members were already irritated by the inconveniences of what they regarded as a much too protracted process of building and renovation. Some were also weary of the President's chidings about economy. Though most now were disenchanted with John Randolph, they agreed with his statement that the period of crisis was "no time for a wanton waste of public money." In reporting the deficit, Jefferson told the Congress that he had been unaware of it until the total had already been incurred. While Jefferson's son-in-law Congressman Eppes was aiming at Latrobe rather than the President, he nevertheless greatly embarrassed the Chief Executive when he moved that the appropriation be recommitted and that an inquiry be instituted into the advisability of abolishing the office of Surveyor of the Public Buildings.

"The lesson of the last year has been a serious one," Jefferson wrote Latrobe. "It has done you great injury, and has been much felt by myself."[65] He was determined that in future the budget for building would not be exceeded by a single dollar. Fiscal irresponsibility, he admonished, was "so contrary to the principles of our government, which make the representatives of the people the sole arbiters of the public expense, and do not permit any work to be forced on them on a larger scale than their judgement deems adapted to the circumstances of the Nation."

Personal, as well as public, debt plagued Jefferson. His daughter Martha wrote that her husband, Thomas Mann Randolph, was trying to help out his sister, whose husband had sailed for England after losing all his property and being unable to pay his debts. She had started a boardinghouse in Richmond but so far had no boarders. Knowing that Thomas himself was beset with financial problems, Jefferson hoped that his son-in-law would not plunge himself into ruin in an effort to help his sister. The President wrote Martha: "I never in my life have been so disappointed as in my expectations that the office I am in would have enabled me from time to time to assist him in his difficulties. So far otherwise has it turned out that I have now the gloomy prospect of retiring from office loaded with serious debts, which will materially affect the tranquility of my retirement. However, not being apt to deject myself with evils before they happen, I nourish the hope of getting along."[66] He reminded her that he continued to count on the Randolphs' living with him at Monticello after his retirement from the presidency. When Martha replied, regretting the drain on his income when she and her family had lived in the Executive Mansion, Jefferson insisted that the burdensome time had not been then but was the present's "comfortless solitude."[67]

Health problems added to the President's troubles. His last full year in office had begun in physical pain. A Christmas Eve toothache had become so excruciating that he had feared he would have to cancel the 1808 New Year's reception, an annual open house for residents of the District of Columbia and any visitors who happened to be in town. He went through the ordeal although about that time he had a facial swelling the size of a pigeon's egg, had part of his jawbone removed afterward, and remained indoors for a month.[68] Not surprisingly, given his medical history and the pressures to which he was subjected, Jefferson said on April 3 that he had suffered for ten days the terrible migraine headaches that incapacitated him for hours at a time. Month after month, one physical indisposition after another reminded him of encroaching age.

Another factor added to his mental pain, and the pressure of it increased as the year progressed. Every day that brought Jefferson nearer to the time when he could pass the burden of office to a successor also brought him nearer to estrangement from a protégé who had become one of his most trusted friends. Madison and Monroe, the two people outside Jefferson's family in whom he most confided, both sought the presidency. Jefferson believed that his policies, and therefore the nation itself, would be safer under Madison's leadership. Monroe had great prospects but he could stand a little seasoning. The younger man could not understand the President's attitude and regarded his reasoning as a betrayal of friendship.

Even more than most decent people, Jefferson dreaded hurting the feelings of anyone but his bitterest enemies. His relationship with Monroe was close enough to make a breach distressing. Fifteen years younger than the President, Monroe at first had worshiped his older friend as a hero. But in 1782, when Jefferson, anxious for his ill wife, had refused to serve in the Virginia House of Delegates after being elected against his will, Monroe had boldly responded to him: "It is publicly said here that people of your county informed you they had frequently elected you in times of less difficulty and danger than the present to please you, but that now they had called you forth into public office to serve themselves."[69] Jefferson valued the honesty and fidelity of his outspoken young friend, who shared with him a background that included education at William and Mary and under George Wythe as well as devotion to republican ideals. Monroe had become his cherished neighbor in Albemarle County. As Virginia Congressmen the two had rented joint quarters in 1784 and hired a French servant. Like Jefferson, Monroe had been Minister to France and Governor of Virginia. As a negotiator along with Robert Livingston, Monroe was intimately associated with one of Jefferson's greatest achievements, the Louisiana Purchase.

Monroe had returned to the United States in 1807 after the failure of negotiations to end the impressment of American seamen by the British. His association with this unhappy business did not warm the public toward his presidential candidacy, and Monroe himself resented the fact that Jefferson had sent William Pinkney to help him in the fruitless effort.

Still, Monroe was a viable candidate. He was a Revolutionary War veteran, he had a strong base in his own state, his association with Jefferson was still a winning point with most Republicans, and the variety of his service (as state legislator, Congressman, Governor, United States Senator, and Minister to both France and Great Britain) was impressive. Even though his part in the failed negotiations over impressment reduced his electability, he almost certainly would have been Jefferson's choice as a successor if Madison had not been available.

Only three Republicans besides Jefferson himself had the broad and deep experience in both domestic and foreign affairs needed in the crisis-ridden presidency—Monroe, Madison, and Gallatin. Few persons served the United States as well as Gallatin, but his French accent and Continental ways inspired distrust in many Americans.

Madison was a native-born citizen with most of Monroe's advantages and none of his disadvantages. Though as Secretary of State slightly tainted with the failure of impressment negotiations with the British, he was not nearly so intimately involved in those discussions as Monroe. He had been a member of the Continental Congress, was more than anyone else the "Father of the Constitution," had argued effectively for its ratification in *The Federalist* and in the Virginia convention, had served in the United States House of Representatives and led Republican opposition to Hamilton's financial program, had been the strongest force except Jefferson (and indeed a more visible one than the Sage of Monticello) in fighting the Alien and Sedition Laws, and in both terms of Jefferson's administration had been his Secretary of State and principal prop. Jefferson valued also Madison's philosophical and brilliantly analytical mind, his unswerving but not uncritical loyalty, his extraordinary powers of quiet persuasion. Above all, he and Madison enjoyed a remarkable rapport such as each had with no other man.

Jefferson, as he had repeatedly announced, was determined not to serve again as Chief Executive. He believed that Madison, among all the members of his party, had the best chance to succeed him. He also believed that, of all who might be elected, he had the best chance to become a successful President.

Of course, there was no guarantee that any Republican but Jefferson himself could be elected. Even his popularity, while still impressive, had declined substantially since his triumph of 1804. Some thought he had been too temporizing with the British, and some believed he had been too assertive. The embargo had not only angered many Federalists who would never vote for a Republican anyway; it also had eroded Republican support for the administration.

Upon his return from his unsuccessful mission abroad, Monroe was upset by the criticism that he encountered on all sides. He protested to Jefferson that it had not been right to send Pinkney to Europe to assist him in negotiations already under way, that it had signaled a lack of confidence in his abilities. Interestingly, Monroe had thought Livingston was too sensitive when the New Yorker had made the same complaint over the Virginian's being sent to Paris to aid him in negotiations for the purchase of Louisiana. Now he said that never before had he been treated so badly.[70] Principally responsible, he thought, were Jefferson and Madison, the friends he had trusted. He listened to those who suggested that his diplomatic service was being minimized to reduce him as a rival to Madison as a presidential candidate.

Jefferson was distressed that his two friends were quarreling, that his party was being torn apart by the adherents of each, and that Monroe blamed him. Though the President favored Madison's candidacy, he was determined to remain neutral publicly. He believed that his own private choice would be that of most Republicans. His immediate concern was to reassure Monroe of his friendship. Jefferson had tried to do this earlier by assuring Monroe that he and Madison were "two principal pillars of my happiness."[71] But such declarations were not enough, especially when the President skirted the issues of Monroe's service in Europe and the administration's dismissal of the treaty the Virginian had helped to frame, leaving these matters to the Secretary of State. There was nothing unusual in a President's leaving the appropriate cabinet officer to deal with an envoy, but the practice was infuriating to Monroe when the Chief Executive was an old friend and the cabinet officer suddenly was his chief rival. Jefferson therefore now discussed the matters which he had avoided. He had sent Pinkney, he wrote Monroe, in response to congressional demand. As for the charge that he had ignored the treaty, it had reached his desk on the day Congress had adjourned. Analysis of it therefore was no longer urgent. He had always defended both Monroe and Pinkney against their critics.[72]

Monroe professed satisfaction with the President's reply and remarked on the comfort of having his doubts about their friendship settled, but entered into such a long explanation of his own actions as to leave in doubt the degree of his reassurance.[73] It is not surprising that during this period of strained relations Jefferson suffered many migraine attacks and several severe bouts of arthritis.

By September 1808 it was evident that Monroe had not been mollified for long by Jefferson's overtures. It was a time when the President needed both the aid and the comfort of every available friend. A month earlier one of his cabinet stalwarts, Gallatin, had told him, "The embargo is now defeated . . . by open violations, by vessels sailing without any clearances whatever; an evil which under the existing law we cannot oppose in any way but by cruisers."[74]

Monroe was not sympathetic. He had spent little time practicing law, he had been a planter in only the most negligible sense, and he was not a businessman. He was one of America's first professional politicians, perhaps the most prominent example of the breed in the early days of the Republic, and in every fiber of his being he yearned for his calling's highest reward. Fortunately, this ambitious man was ethical and humane. But his choler rose so at the threatened frustration of his desire that he saw through jaundiced eyes anyone who appeared to be standing in his way. To Joseph H. Nicholson he wrote: "Such is the state of our affairs, and such the compromitment of the Administration at home and abroad by its measures, that it seems likely that it will experience a great difficulty in extricating itself. . . . We are invited with great earnestness to give the incumbents all the support we can—by which is meant to give them our votes at the approaching election; but it is not certain that we could give effectual support to the person [Madison] in whose favor it is requested, or that it would be advisable in any view to yield it. . . . After what has passed, [the administration] has no right to suppose that we will, by a voluntary sacrifice, consent to bury ourselves in the same tomb with it."[75]

After Jefferson had made it clear that he would not even consider a third term, three Republican candidates had appeared: Madison, Monroe, and George Clinton. The New Yorker had the advantage of being Vice President. It was from the vice presidency that both Adams and Jefferson had ascended to the presidency. Moreover, Clinton had few enemies. But early in 1808 it was evident that his support did not equal that of either of the two Virginians. Nevertheless, he had the firm support of his own state and he could bring significant strength to anyone with whom he allied.

A Republican caucus in Richmond led by Edmund Randolph endorsed Monroe. This was not intended as a slap at Jefferson; the President had remained neutral in the contest. But most Republicans displeased with the embargo or other acts of the Jefferson administration were inclined to blame the Secretary of State more than the President. None doubted Madison's intelligence or his patriotism, but there were complaints that he was too theoretical. Monroe was considered more "down to earth."

The effect of Edmund Randolph's meeting was more than countered when a caucus of the General Assembly of Virginia was swept by Madison for President and Clinton for Vice President. But far from conceding to the opposition, Randolph and his associates published an attack on Madison's candidacy, charging that he had provided "moderation when energy was needed" and had compromised with Federalism when the country had viewed such compromises with "loathing and abhorrence."[76] John Randolph and John Taylor of Caroline were among notables supporting Monroe.

But as the choice of electors was reported in separate contests state by state, it became evident before the end of November that Madison would be the victor, not only in his party but in the nation. When electoral votes were totaled on December 7, Madison had 122 to 47 for Federalist candidate Charles Cotesworth Pinckney of South Carolina. In the race for Vice President, Clinton won 113 votes to 47 for New York's Rufus King. Moreover, despite some Federalist gains, the Republicans retained their majority in both the Senate and the House of Representatives.

Public disapproval of Jefferson's administration, while greater than in his first term, obviously had been much exaggerated by the Federalists, diehard "Old Republicans," and the press. Even amid his suffering as the target of abuse from many directions, Jefferson had believed this to be so.

People hurt in both their pride and their pocketbooks are likely to vote an incumbent government out of office. How then can we explain the triumph of Jefferson's party, including the election of his closest political associate as his successor? This was a time when the British navy was contemptuously insulting American sovereignty and the President had deliberately launched upon a policy that kept American ships in harbor and closed American factories.

The answer lies partly in the fact that a portion of the electorate saw the crisis with Britain as capable of diplomatic solution and admired the President's mixture of patience and firmness while a greater number believed the nation was on the edge of war and rallied to their leader. As for the embargo, it caused serious problems and it was unpopular, but it was never the unmitigated disaster that some of its critics then and since have painted it. It was not troublesome to all parts of the United States. Though Virginia's Hampton Roads was hard hit, one of the commonwealth's two United States Senators, William Branch Giles, said as late as November 1808 that Southerners as a whole went along with the policy because they did not much care who transported their agricultural products.[77] In the Northeast commerce was depressed, but this depression was somewhat mitigated by many violations. The reduction in imports nevertheless was sufficient to stimulate the growth of native manufacturers, especially in Pennsylvania and other middle states. Connecticut Senator James Hillhouse, also in November, noted with alarm that gains in manufacturing were reconciling some to losses in commerce.[78] In the Senator's own state, David Humphreys, the retired diplomat who had reported to Jefferson on British public opinion in 1807, was acquiring a national reputation as a manufacturer of fine cloth. The President himself was one of his customers.

In his eighth and final annual message to Congress, on November 8, Jefferson had proudly called attention to this industrial development. He noted the necessity for building up the armed forces and said that their increase had required arms difficult to procure "from abroad during the present situation and dispositions of Europe." To solve the problem, the administration had not only more than doubled the size of public factories but also had contracted with individual entrepreneurs and in effect subsidized their expansion. Additionally, he said, the suspension of foreign commerce "has impelled us to apply a portion of our industry and capital to internal manufactures and improvements. The extent of this conversion is daily increasing, and little doubt remains that the establishments formed and forming will—under the auspices of cheaper materials and subsistence, the freedom of labor from taxation with us, and of protecting duties and prohibitions—become permanent."[79]

In an earlier draft, Jefferson had boasted more extensively of industrial growth, but Gallatin had cautioned him that some shippers would be irritated by such a diapason of praise for prosperity gained at their expense.[80] Of course, the President, aware of discontent over the embargo, was looking for silver linings. Nevertheless there is no reason to doubt the sincerity of his hope that continued industrial growth would be a permanent legacy of the act. Jefferson had come a long way since the early days of his career, when he had seen agriculture as the natural occupation of man and industry as a corruption.

Jefferson had also come quite a way along another philosophical path. Looking ahead to the resumption of commerce with other nations, he foresaw "probable accumulation of the surpluses of revenue beyond what can be applied to the payment of the public debt." The question of what to do about this surplus, he said, "merits the consideration of Congress. Shall it lie unproductive in the public vaults? Shall the revenue be reduced? Or shall it rather be appropriated to the improvements of roads, canals, rivers, education, and other great foundations of prosperity and union, under the powers which Congress may already possess, or such amendment of the Constitution as may be approved by the States?"[81]

Jefferson knew well the impassioned opposition of the so-called Old Republicans to any assumption of new responsibilities by the federal government. He knew, too, that even some more moderate members of the party had troubling questions about any extension of central authority. He did not attempt to push Congress toward federal public works projects or federal support of public education. But he did attempt to nudge them toward more open-minded consideration of the possibilities. He did not assert that Congress definitely had the necessary powers to effect such changes; he only said that Congress *might* already possess the powers. And he ventured that, if such power was not believed to be existent, it could be conferred by a constitutional amendment "approved by the States." He described the projects that would benefit as "great foundations of prosperity and union" and suggested there might be others he had not named. Then he suggested that the period of watchful waiting imposed by the international crisis need not be wasted. "While uncertain of the course of things," he said, "the time may be advantageously employed in obtaining the powers necessary for a system of improvement, should that be thought best."

This declaration, low key as it was, dramatized something that should have been obvious for a long time to close observers of Jefferson. Though he remained dedicated to the essential tenets of his Republican faith, he could not be described accurately as diametrically opposed to Hamilton's vision of a nation grown strong partly through flexible use of federal power.

Partly because of his strong personal following and partly because his chief lieutenant would be his successor, Jefferson's influence with the legislative branch was still strong. This was demonstrated when those parts of the President's message dealing with the embargo and other foreign policy matters were referred to special committees in the Senate and House chaired by men who conferred with Gallatin. He quite evidently was in turn conferring with Madison and Jefferson. Some people expected Gallatin to be Madison's Secretary of State in an administration that would be an almost seamless continuation of Jefferson's eight years in office. Giles, who was chairman of the Senate committee, closely followed Gallatin's recommendations. His House counterpart, Tennessee's George W. Campbell, actually presented on behalf of his committee a report written by Gallatin. Much of this document echoed statements previously made by the President. For example, in discussing problems relating to France and Great Britain, it concluded that only two choices were available to the United States: "abject and degrading submission, or a continuance and enforcement of the present suspension of commerce."[82]

In the report presented to the House by Campbell, Gallatin submitted three resolutions. The first declared that the United States could not obey the commands of Britain and France without sacrificing its "rights, honor, and independence." Although it provoked extended debate, it ultimately met with overwhelming approval. The third resolution, calling in general terms for rapid strengthening of United States defenses, passed by an even larger margin. The second resolution asked that United States ports be closed to both French and British armed ships and that all imports from both countries be forbidden. This resolution, with its tighter requirements regarding France, introduced a more even-handed policy toward the two great European powers. Since it advocated not only a continuation but also an extension of restrictions on foreign commerce, it drew more opposition than either of the other two. Nevertheless, it passed in the most crucial of a series of votes, procedural and otherwise, by a comfortable 82 to 36. The Senate bill embodying Gallatin's suggestions passed on December 21 by a vote of 20 to 7. The final House bill, as distinguished from the earlier resolutions, was passed, after a long night of debate, shortly after daybreak on January 6, 1809. The numbers of the opposition were not equal to their vehemence. The vote was 71 to 32.

A superficial view of events in the Congress would lead to the conclusion that the administration envisioned no early end to the embargo and therefore was fastening it down as a permanent fixture. Such, however, was not the case. Jefferson still hoped that the British might make concessions that would permit the United States to lift the embargo. David Erskine, who longed for reconciliation between his government and the United States, encouraged the President to hope for an honorable accommodation.[83] Jefferson and Gallatin knew that lifting the embargo without any change in the American relations with Britain or France would signal submission and thus, in English and French eyes, obviate the need for concessions of any sort. Therefore the Jefferson administration sought and obtained legislation to make the policy more effective so that the United States could bargain from a position of strength.

Wavering could invite doom, but so could rash belligerence. Don Quixote was one of Jefferson's favorite characters in all literature. Certainly the President, astride the feeble Rosinante of the American defense establishment, had not so far lost a sense of proportion as to charge headlong against the two great giants on the international scene.

Jefferson, using diplomatic skills which had served him well as Minister to France, Secretary of State, and President, sought to convey to Erskine in informal conversation the impression that the United States would never yield on the issue of impressment but wished for friendly relations with the British. If only the British had been receptive to the very reasonable proposal submitted through Pinkney, the United States was ready to be a friend. Now, if France should lift its ban on neutral commerce on the high seas, the Americans would have to remove the embargo on trade with her. The United States then would find itself in friendly commerce with Napoleon at the same time that such relations with Britain were banned. The President seemed to find the situation ironic and a little sad. The Americans really did not prefer the French to their brothers in blood, culture, and language. If Britain had only recognized the necessity of the American stand on impressment, other issues could have been settled eventually, and meanwhile the two Anglo-Saxon nations might have "shoved along."

In his eagerness to promote a peaceful settlement, Erskine not only encouraged the Jefferson administration to hope for concessions from London but also led British Foreign Secretary Canning to anticipate a yielding by the United States. His intentions were beneficent, but in a potentially explosive situation he raised the hopes of each party past the confines of realism. Believing that the United States was on the verge of ending the embargo, Canning hardened his resistance to any concession.

On December 13 Jefferson wrote Thomas Mann Randolph that he believed the wish to lift the embargo before the Congress adjourned prevailed "with everybody but the Federalists."[84] He believed that the opposition party, particularly in the Northeast, wanted the unpopular measure as a rallying point. The Republicans had demonstrated that even on this issue they could outvote the Federalists in both houses of Congress. Jefferson had no worry on this score. He worried about the widening geographical schism in the United States. On New Year's Day 1809 he wore his usual public smile at the President's traditional public reception. But privately that day he confided to Randolph that he feared the life of the Republic was endangered by the "monarchists of the North."[85] The Massachusetts legislature, he said, was expected to call a convention soon to consider the advisability of secession by all states east of the Hudson. Once again, in a Northeast consistently outvoted by the rest of the nation, there rose a demand for formation of a Confederacy. Such a new nation, he was sure, would enjoy British protection.

Beleaguered Republicans in the disaffected area, he said, argued that the announcement of a precise date for ending the embargo would defuse the convention scheduled for a fortnight thence. Writing as if he were a mere onlooker, careful to avoid committing his successor's administration, Jefferson opined that such an announcement probably would be made. He believed that letters of marque and reprisal would be issued on the same day that the embargo ended. But he thought that this action also would draw the fire of Federalists. They feared that the licensing of private persons to seize foreign ships at sea in compensation for claims against the offending nation or its citizens would lead to war with England. He said, "We must save the Union but we wish to sacrifice as little as possible of the honor of the nation."

The threat of disunion was not merely hypothetical. He feared that, in the event of war with Great Britain, London would offer New England neutral status and with it full resumption of commerce. He also feared that New Englanders would find such an offer too tempting to resist. For years, when national policy had not been in accord with what its residents regarded as their interest, some of its most prominent political leaders had advocated secession.

On January 14 Jefferson wrote a Boston supporter of the embargo that the policy was strictly a temporary one.[86] About six weeks earlier Erskine had written the Foreign Secretary that the chief Republicans in Congress said that the embargo would soon be discontinued.[87] On January 7 a resolution providing for an extra session was introduced in the House. The purpose, of course, was to provide an opportunity for repeal of the embargo at a time deemed appropriate by the administration and Republican leaders in Congress.

On January 9, 1809, the President signed into law the Second Enforcement Act, which closed loopholes in the Embargo Act. Though this might seem a contradiction of Republican plans to end the embargo, it was of course perfectly in accord with Jefferson's idea of enforcing the act as rigorously as possible to the very end so as to bargain from strength. Only fifteen days later Wilson Cary Nicholas, Congressman from Jefferson's home district, introduced a resolution for repeal of the embargo and for defense of American vessels on the high seas.

In the course of debate he presented a second resolution, proposing June 1 as the date for repeal and the issuance of letters of marque and reprisal authorizing private action against nations seizing American seamen, cargoes, or ships or otherwise violating American maritime rights.

As the debate continued, Jefferson, in a kind of obituary for the embargo about to expire, wrote to Monroe: "There never has been a situation of the world before, in which such endeavors as we have made would not have secured our peace. It is probable there never will be such another. If we go to war now, I fear we may renounce forever the hope of seeing an end of our national debt."[88]

The President, however, had not yet given up all hope for a peaceful accommodation with either Britain or France in the time remaining before the June date which seemed probable for the embargo's demise. He wrote: "If, as is expected, Bonaparte should be successful in Spain, however every virtuous and liberal sentiment revolts at it, it may induce both powers to be more accommodating with us. England will see here their only asylum for her commerce and manufactures, worth more to her than her orders of council. And Bonaparte, having Spain at his feet, will look immediately to the Spanish colonies, and think our neutrality cheaply purchased by a repeal of the illegal parts of his decrees, with perhaps the Floridas thrown into the bargain. Should a change in the aspect of affairs in Europe produce this disposition in both powers, our peace and prosperity may be revived and long continue. Otherwise, we must again take the tented field, as we did in 1776 under more inauspicious circumstances."

There was one possibility—admittedly not a probability but a possibility nevertheless—full of hope: "If we can keep at peace eight years longer, our income, liberated from debt, will be adequate to any war, without new taxes or loans, and our position and increasing strength put us *hors d'insulte* from any nation."[89]

As the debate continued, Jefferson, who had so accurately predicted most congressional moves, was surprised by a sudden turn of events. On February 7 he wrote Thomas Mann Randolph: "I thought Congress had taken their ground firmly for continuing their embargo till June, and then war. But a sudden and unaccountable revolution of opinion took place the last week, chiefly among the New England and New York members, and in a kind of panic they voted the 4th of March for removing the embargo, and by such a majority as gave all reason to believe they would not agree either to war or non-intercourse. . . . The majority of Congress, however, has now rallied to the removing the embargo the 4th of March, non-intercourse with France and Great Britain, trade everywhere else, and continuing war-preparations."[90]

Another surprise awaited Jefferson. On February 7, the very day that he wrote to Randolph, the House voted down the Senate's proposal for letters of marque and reprisal. Thus congressional action assumed much more the aspect of capitulation to Britain and France than the President had anticipated. The House made one more change—a relatively insignificant one—changing the date of repeal to March 15. The House amendments were accepted by the

Senate on February 28, and the bill was signed by the President the next day. Jefferson was disappointed in the timing of repeal and, of course, in the failure to provide for letters of marque and reprisal. Though he was not quite so aloof from it all as he apparently pretended even to himself, he was not directly involved in efforts to influence the Congress and seems not to have suffered a sense of personal defeat. Certainly many Federalists thought he had no reason to. One of the most visible of them, Massachusetts Congressman Josiah Quincy, said in disgust: "Jefferson has triumphed. His intrigues have prevailed."[91]

A sense of personal defeat came much more strongly from Jefferson's efforts to help his friends in the last days of his presidency. The Congress was more willing to follow his lead in matters of national policy than in appointments.

He was severely wounded February 27, 1809, when the Senate not only rejected his nomination of William Short as Minister to Russia but did so unanimously. Short was a Jefferson protégé. He had been one of the bright young men who worshiped him. In 1784, when Jefferson accepted appointment as Minister to France, he offered Short the post of personal secretary. Already at twenty-five a member of the Executive Council of Virginia, Short replied without hesitation, "My determination is what it has long been, to accompany you in any capacity whatsoever."[92] He was as much a surrogate son as a secretary. Later, as Secretary of State, Jefferson defended Short's service as a United States Commissioner in Madrid.

Afterwards Short was Jefferson's favorite informant on affairs in France. He lingered in France because of Rosalie, Duchesse de la Rochefoucauld. Correspondence reveals that the two never consummated their romance but that she returned his affection. After the stoning to death of her husband in her presence and her own imprisonment by the revolutionists, she cited another call of duty that prevented her from going to America with Short. He wrote to her, "If you insist upon remaining with your grandmother—and I admit that her age and your devotion to her would demand it—I shall never again leave you, but shall ask permission of my government to remain in Paris."[93] In that decision lay part of the trouble when Jefferson submitted his nomination of Short as Minister to Russia. Some Senators said that he was no longer an American but a Frenchman. Some objected that it was not necessary to have a Minister in Russia at all. And then, Jefferson—eager to advance his protégé—had pushed too hard. He had given Short an *ad interim* appointment, and only in the last presidential communication to the Senate, after the appointee had served five months, did Jefferson reveal this fact and request confirmation. Ordinarily, the President was a consummate diplomat, privately and publicly, but at rare intervals his overeagerness in behalf of friends led him into manipulation that offended. This was such an instance.

Jefferson was even less discreet in his efforts to help a much older friend, John Page. After a distinguished public career climaxed by three terms as Governor of Virginia, Page lay on his deathbed haunted by debt. His beloved Rosewell, once the handsomest mansion in Virginia, was decaying. His fields were worn out by generations of tobacco culture. And the estate had suffered at the hands of inactive, incompetent, or untrustworthy overseers. Page was an intelligent man, skilled in the processes of government, a former president of the Philosophical Society of Williamsburg, an inventor, and a student of theology, mathematics, and the physical sciences. But Jefferson called him "the worst judge of man existing," and once wrote him, "I know your character to be much inclined to indulgence and confidence in others."[94] Page's too trusting nature had brought him to the brink of financial ruin.

John Page was Jefferson's age and had been his earliest close friend. They had been classmates at William and Mary and faithful correspondents when apart. It was to Page that Jefferson had imparted the frustrations of his teenaged crush on Rebecca Burwell. He had even asked his friend to intercede with her and had addressed to him coded correspondence about her and other early loves. When Jefferson was ready to leave the country because of disappointment in love, the two young men planned trips to Europe and Africa that they never took. Later the two worked together in behalf of the same political causes. Their friendship had survived easily a crisis when eager friends placed the two opposite each other in a gubernatorial contest that Jefferson won. Though Jefferson as a mature statesman was much closer to Madison than to Page, the boyhood companions remained cherished friends.

Jefferson agonized over the old friend harassed on his deathbed by financial problems and fearing even the loss of his family home. The President had rescued Page two years earlier, appointing him Commissioner of Loans for Virginia, but now his health prevented him from performing his duties. Jefferson proposed in a letter to Page that the office be transferred to his son Francis. The income, he explained, underlining the words he wished to emphasize, would be "*for your use*, with an understanding that it should afterwards continue with him for the *benefit of the family*. Or would you rather retain it in your own name, during your own life, with the probability . . . that he will succeed you for the same *family benefit*?"[95]

John Page appreciated the offer, but Francis rejected it. St. George Tucker, a distinguished attorney and former college mate of Page and Jefferson, wrote the President that a Thomas Taylor of Richmond had volunteered to take the position and give all the moluments to the Page family. Tucker thought Jefferson should know that the Richmond man was a Federalist who had given bail for Aaron Burr. Tucker said that a good Republican, young Benjamin Harrison, would accept the appointment if Taylor would perform all of the duties. This arrangement was acceptable to Taylor, and both he and Harrison were willing for all of the pay to go to Page's family.[96]

John Page, hurt by his sons' refusal to cooperate in this and other matters, wrote that he would rather the office be given to a friend than to "any *Son* I have."[97] He was one of the most beloved men in Virginia, and Bishop William Meade praised him as "a most affectionate domestic character." It was sad that, wherever the fault might lie, John Page in his dying days should have been alienated from his sons.

Jefferson told Gallatin, under whose department the job came, that he would like young Harrison to have it. The Treasury Secretary replied: "I certainly cannot object to B. Harrison's appointment if you do not. I know nothing of his qualifications, and you understand how far the humane ground of his appointment may be viewed and avowed in Virginia. Will it produce any bad effect at this critical moment?"[98]

Undeterred by this gentle demurrer from Gallatin, Jefferson proceeded with his plans. The *Spirit of '76*, a Quid paper in Virginia, broke the story to citizens of the commonwealth and sent it on its way through the nation. The Senate refused to confirm the appointment. The President began talking to Senators individually in an effort to change their minds. His persuasiveness did not work. But he did not give up. He wrote Tucker, "If you could find any other unexceptionable character, Republican, who has the same dispositions with Mr. Harrison, and the secret can be kept, the blot may yet perhaps be covered."[99] John Page died while the matter was unresolved.

Even without Senate confirmation, Harrison's commission would be valid through March 3, Jefferson's last day in office. He let it stand and importuned Madison to submit the same appointment when he became President. Despite his dislike of disappointing his friend, Madison refused. But he did choose Thomas Nelson for the position. Five of John Page's children had married children of Thomas Nelson, and even before these matches the two families had been related by blood.[100] Some have wondered whether Nelson, who was approved by the Senate, turned over his earnings to Page's family.

Ironically, in his first term as President, Jefferson had argued that the office of Commissioner of Loans was a sinecure and had supported the efforts of his son-in-law John Eppes to have the position abolished. But perhaps the President used this circumstance to silence his own doubts in offering a solution to Page's problems. If a Commissioner of Loans did little to earn his pay, it might not matter so much who held the position and who reaped the profits. As Jefferson himself admitted in his "Dialogue of Head and Heart," in matters of human sympathy his emotions frequently triumphed over his reason.[101]

He tried to forestall future problems of patronage, preparing a circular letter as a reply to the anticipated deluge of requests:

> The friendship which has long subsisted between the President of the United States and myself gave me reason to expect, on my retirement from office, that I might often receive applications to interpose with him on behalf of persons desiring appointments. Such an abuse of his dispositions towards me would necessarily lead to the loss of them, and to the transforming me from the character of a friend to that of an unreasonable and troublesome solicitor. It therefore became necessary for me to lay down as a law for my future conduct never to interpose in any case, either with him or the heads of departments (from whom it must go to him) in any application whatever for office. To this rule I must scrupulously adhere, for were I to depart from it in a single instance I could no longer plead it with truth to my friends in excuse of my not complying with their requests.[102]

Even aside from long friendship, there were reasons for Jefferson to empathize strongly with Page. The President was deeply in debt and in some danger of losing his own beloved home. On January 23 Jefferson, in a letter to Abraham Venable,[103] referred to "the unexpected difficulties into which I was likely to fall on my winding up my affairs here."

This prospect had caused him to request a relative "to endeavor to procure me the aid of the bank at Richmond." But now, he wrote, "You have been so kind as to interpose and procure for me the sum needed on private loan," which he "infinitely" preferred. "I return to you, my dear sir, my sincere thanks for this friendly relief, and shall ever retain a lively sense of it; and the greater as I should never have thought myself entitled to ask such a favor of you." Jefferson explained that he would have to sell two tracts of land to repay the loan. The sale of "one tract alone is certain, an offer having been made to me for that. Lands are of difficult sale. For that reason I have asked the indulgence of a twelve month certain. The note sent me is for six months, but I presume will be renewable; otherwise I should be forced at its expiration to have recourse to the bank."

On March 4, the day set for Madison's inauguration, Jefferson was touched by the tribute of a delegation of Washington residents who called to express their appreciation of his "mild and endearing virtues." Madison rode to his inauguration accompanied by a military escort. Jefferson rode down Pennsylvania Avenue with his grandson Thomas Jefferson Randolph at his side. Madison looked small and fragile as he took the oath of office.

The new President received well-wishers in his own home because Jefferson had not yet vacated the Executive Mansion. Jefferson seems to have felt no pangs of regret at all about leaving Washington, but he was not yet packed. It took a long time for this prodigious collector to move. He did not leave the city until March 11, a week after the inauguration of his successor.

He was weary as he set out on his journey. The bumps made him conscious of aches that he had not known when he had entered upon the presidency eight years before. And his financial problems gnawed at his peace of mind. But the road led home. At the end was Monticello, of which he once said, "All my wishes end where I hope my days will end, at Monticello."

XI

MEASURE OF A PRESIDENT

JEFFERSON ATTENDED Madison's inaugural ball. There is no indication, however, that he danced. As a college student at William and Mary
he had tripped the hours away with his beloved Belinda, but his
terpsichorean activity had diminished rapidly with the passing years.
At that, he probably felt more like dancing on this evening than he had
in decades, certainly than he had in eight years. Jefferson almost always put on
a cheerful face in public, so successfully that observers often concluded that he
was in a particularly good humor when he was depressed or suffering physical
illness. But lately even Margaret Bayard Smith, the Washington diarist who knew
the President well and observed him closely, was convinced that his spirits rose
as the moment of liberation neared.[1]

Jefferson seemed both relaxed and animated as he talked with John Quincy
Adams while others danced. The ex-President nearing his sixty-sixth birthday
and the forty-two-year-old ex-Senator had a great deal in common. Both were
public men freed from the responsibilities of political office, Jefferson by choice
and permanently, Adams by voter dictation and only temporarily. Both men
loved scholarship and literature more than politics. Affection between the two
had been bred in the days when Jefferson and the Adams family had been close
and the seventeen-year-old John Quincy had followed the Virginian so much
that the senior Adams said the boy seemed as much Jefferson's son as his own.
The tie had survived the strains of politics that had separated Jefferson from
John and Abigail. Indeed, John Quincy had lost his Senate seat by supporting
Jefferson's policies, to the dismay and chagrin of his parents.

The ex-Senator not only read poetry; he had written it. Jefferson asked him
now if he still loved verse. Yes, he said, if it was good poetry. The President said
that he did not now take much pleasure in Virgil, but he did still enjoy Homer.[2]

Only a few months into his first term, Jefferson had replied differently to a
young poet sending his most ambitious production for comment. "Of all men
living," he had said, "I am the last who should undertake to decide as to the
merits of poetry. In earlier life I was fond of it, and easily pleased. But as age
and cares advanced, the powers of fancy have declined. . . . The very feelings to
which it is addressed are among those I have lost."[3] Jefferson's reply to Adams
suggests that, upon leaving office, he regained his sense of the poetry of life.

To be freed from the burden and the concomitant censure was to be relieved. To return to Monticello as his daily home, to his family and as he would soon tell citizens of Albemarle County, "to the scenes of my birth and early life, to the society of those with whom I was raised," was to be renewed. He would also say that his happiness would be "complete if my endeavors to fulfill my duties in the several public stations to which I have been called have obtained for me the approbation of my country."[4] Though Jefferson had unrelenting enemies, he had ample proof of the esteem of most of his fellow citizens. And with his keen sense of history, he must have suspected that his career as diplomat and President would win the praise of posterity.

His service as President was marked by some great disappointments but also by extraordinary achievements. There was far more to comfort than to disturb when he reviewed his public actions of the past eight years.

Most United States Presidents considered great or near great have captivated their fellow citizens with inspiring visions. Day-to-day efficiency in administration has not been nearly so important to their success as the ability to conceive the nation's future in grand, even sublime, terms, and to communicate to their countrymen an intense excitement over the prospect. Abraham Lincoln, a notoriously inefficient office manager who daily overestimated the number of people he could talk with in the available time, energized the nation with a sense of mission. He convinced the people, or in any event enough of them, that the American republic was "the last best hope of earth." He roused them to a high resolve that "government of the people, by the people, and for the people" should not "perish from the earth." As early as 1862, he had summoned them: "We cannot escape history. . . . the fiery trial through which we pass will light us down, in honor or dishonor, to the latest generation." Woodrow Wilson stirred his fellow citizens with the concept of a New Freedom and later imbued them with a mission to "make the world safe for democracy." Franklin D. Roosevelt, with his imagery of a New Deal, lifted his dispirited countrymen with a vision of fresh beginnings. Later he took erstwhile isolationists to a high plateau swept by the winds of history, showed them the nations of the earth in battle array, and in that rarefied atmosphere reminded them, "This nation has a rendezvous with destiny."

Jefferson brought to the presidency this same ability to convey a heart-lifting vision. He had displayed this gift as early as his authorship of the Declaration of Independence in 1776, when he had transformed a bill of complaints into a universal document of human freedom. He set the tone with the opening words, "When in the course of human events . . ." and confirmed it with his reference to "a decent respect to the opinions of mankind." To his presidency he brought an apostolic vision of a people born again. At its beginning, in words reminiscent of St. Paul's declaration "Behold, all things are become new,"[5] he said, "We can no longer say there is nothing new under the sun. For this whole chapter in the history of man is new. The great extent of our Republic is new."[6] He inspired his countrymen and the people of distant lands with a dream of the United States of America as a place where the human race might begin anew in a largely virgin land, preserving the best gifts of the Old World but rejecting the dross of human experience.

Exaggerated by chauvinists and scorned by cynics, the dream nevertheless has survived the generations of distortion. It springs alive in national crises and it feeds the hopes of the downtrodden of five continents.

On the day of his first inauguration Jefferson used the drama of the starkly undramatic to image the nature of his presidency. The long-limbed, loose-gaited man walking from his boardinghouse to the Capitol could have been an aristocrat or a farmer; actually, he was both. But he was also the Chief Magistrate of the republic. Probably no other chief of state in the world would have entered with such deliberate simplicity upon his duties.

The contrast between his approach and the regal rides of his two predecessors increased the drama of the event. Washington had believed that pomp and ceremony were necessary to give a sense of stability to a new nation shaky on its feet. John Adams, though at his core a man of solid values, dearly loved the regalia and trumpery of office. Whatever the disparate motivations of the first two Chief Executives, the pageantry which they chose met the republic's psychological need for a sense of tradition. But Jefferson's dignified simplicity, besides expressing one side of his complex personality and appealing to citizens tired of what they saw as Federalist pretensions, was a reminder for which the nation was ready—a reminder of the republican values expressed in the Declaration of Independence and the Constitution of the United States. The President of the United States, in the future, would not be able to remain at the same time effective and aloof in the fashion of some monarchs.

Because of the incomparable allegiance which Washington commanded, and the inhibited growth of political parties in his administrations, this fact was not then obvious. But the rapid development of partisan politics in Adams' administration suggested this truth to some perceptive minds. By the time Jefferson became Chief Executive it was clear that the President of the United States, unlike other chiefs of state, would serve in a dual capacity that made consistent aloofness impossible. He would have to be both the representative of national sovereignty and the leader of a faction. At crucial moments he would have to stand above the fray as spokesman for all the people, but at others he would have to be a party chief. It was as though one person were to serve simultaneously as King and Prime Minister.

Common sense dictated that Jefferson, as the victor in a heated contest for the Presidency, should attempt to unite the nation by stressing points of agreement rather than of difference and by the exercise of tolerance toward his enemies. Despite its wisdom, such forbearance is beyond the reach of many otherwise intelligent people. The urge toward vengeance is too strong for them. But Jefferson, besides being of a generally benevolent disposition, had arrived long ago at his practical philosophy of "the smooth handle." A great phrase-maker, in his first inaugural address he hit upon the ideal expression of the common interests of the two major parties. By a stroke of genius the phrase used the two labels made odious by partisan strife and returned them to their status as common nouns with appealing connotations. He said; "We are all republicans, we are all federalists."

In his address Jefferson did more than speak soothingly to his opponents at the end of a vicious campaign that had terminated only after a deadlocked electoral college gave way to the House of Representatives, which almost collapsed from weariness after thirty-six exhausting ballots. He assured his opponents that he would not hunt them down, and his promise gained credibility from revelation of the philosophy prompting this generosity. His tolerance extended even to those prominent politicians who had advocated secession of the Northeastern states. "If there be any among us," he said, "who would wish to dissolve this Union or to change its republican form, let them stand undisturbed as monuments of the safety with which error of opinion may be tolerated where reason is left free to combat it." In the same paragraph, in a phrase to be echoed with variations by Lincoln, he declared his own faith that "this government" was "the world's best hope."

A measure of Jefferson's extraordinary success in allaying fears is the fact that Chief Justice Marshall, who had broken off a letter to a friend in order to administer the oath of office to his cousin and fellow Virginian, resumed the note afterwards with a description of the inaugural message as "well-judged and conciliatory"—despite the fact that the first part of his letter had said that the new Chief Executive might bring "much calamity to the country."[7] The effect on those less hardened in skepticism was in its way equally impressive. Jefferson saw the inchoate state of the government as an inspiriting challenge and made others do the same.

One thing that reassured the public was as much a matter of substance as of style—his selection of an unusually able cabinet who for all of his first term and half of his second worked in admirable harmony with him and each other. The pivotal figures were two geniuses, Secretary of State James Madison and Secretary of the Treasury Albert Gallatin. Jefferson did not have that fear of rivalry which causes some executives to surround themselves with mediocrity. Madison and Gallatin were both fountains of diverse knowledge and products of wide experience. The President conferred with each Secretary on many matters outside the purview of his department. Primacy in the cabinet belonged to Madison, not just because of protocol, to which this President paid little attention, but because of his long-standing friendship with Jefferson. Though not quite the polymath that Jefferson was, he was an equally keen and perhaps more precise student of government. His habitual restraint complemented Jefferson's occasional impulsiveness. And, of course, the President sometimes luxuriated in the opportunity to propose outrageous solutions in conferences with his chief lieutenant, knowing that his friend would counsel caution. Many Presidents have lacked so safe an outlet.

Most of Jefferson's problems with the cabinet centered on the post of Secretary of the Navy. This was the one most difficult to fill. Most Republicans opposed significant enlargement of the nation's small fleet, and influential politicians were not eager to head a department that seemed doomed to low status. Only after being turned down by four men did the President find a taker, and he, General Samuel Smith of Maryland, agreed to accept the appointment only until a permanent replacement could be found. The somewhat reluctant successor was the Secretary's brother Robert Smith. A lawyer with no naval experience, he nevertheless seems to have served efficiently for most of Jefferson's presidency. There may be some justice in his friends' contention that Smith's services were underrated by many people because of Gallatin's antipathy for him toward the last. In any event, Robert Smith had outlived his usefulness in the cabinet when, in 1808, he said publicly that Madison was the only member who still supported the President's position on the embargo. When Secretary Smith's brother Samuel, now a powerful United States Senator, worked in league with him and with such congressional leaders as John Randolph to thwart the President's foreign policy, Jefferson, as we have seen, moved quickly and shrewdly to undercut the influence of all three. He showed that a smooth handle could sometimes be an effective stick.

Despite some tension over differences within the cabinet, and with the President himself, toward the latter part of his second administration, Jefferson was entitled to boast (as he did) of the harmony prevalent in the executive branch. The record surpasses that of his two predecessors and of most of his successors. Like Jefferson, Washington had two geniuses in his cabinet, Alexander Hamilton and Jefferson himself, but unlike Jefferson's State and Treasury Secretaries, they could not work in tandem. John Adams had trouble within the executive branch partly because his conscience put him at variance with the numerous extremists in his party and partly because he had a prickly personality. Jefferson's unusual success with his cabinet was due partly to the care with which he selected them and partly to his own tactfulness. Yet, while the department heads were usually supportive of Jefferson, they were by no means "yes" men. He was influenced by their advice, especially that of the two principals.

Though Jefferson was a reformer, he was able to launch his first administration smoothly because he was a pragmatic idealist. Though he was eager for fresh beginnings, he said, "No more good must be attempted than this nation can bear." Besides, while Jefferson advocated measures that most of us would still call progressive, the revolution that he preached was principally of the spirit. He breathed confidence into his fellow Americans and led them into rededication to the ideals that had given impetus to national and individual independence. Who could more appropriately perform this feat than the author of the nation's title deed to freedom?

The changes that Jefferson did effect were facilitated by his practice of playing down his departures from custom. He had mastered this technique as early as 1787, when he submitted to the General Assembly of Virginia his design for the state Capitol, emphasizing its derivation from a classical structure of antiquity and making no mention of his significant alterations in fenestration, columns, and proportions.[8] He knew that to claim credit for originality in public measures, except at a comfortable distance after the fact, was to invite automatic opposition from some quarters.

Another advantage of Jefferson's presidency was that he personally applied to both foreign and domestic affairs the considerable diplomatic talents that he had employed so well as Minister to Paris and Secretary of State. He was one of the most effective diplomats in the Western world in his generation.

One of the great shaping forces of Jefferson's presidency was his realization of the importance of the American West. Ironically, the only other American statesman in national office who had an equal appreciation of Western potential was one of his arch enemies, Aaron Burr. And, whereas Burr apparently saw the West as a future empire with himself as founder of a dynasty, Jefferson saw it as a bulwark to the republic and to the freedoms it espoused.

Several things contributed to Jefferson's interest in the West. One was the fact that he was born on the frontier. Charlottesville, today one of the nation's cultural capitals, was then an expanded trading post on the edge of adventure. His father, an explorer and cartographer of some note, had lived that life of adventure and returned with exciting tales of it. Indian chiefs, as dinner guests at Shadwell, the Jefferson home, had whetted the boy's appetite for information about the West. The same susceptibility to motion sickness that made ocean travel something to be refused except as an inescapable duty also made overland travel over rugged terrain painful to Jefferson, so that only once did he travel more than fifty miles west of his birthplace. But his insatiable curiosity roamed the West for the rest of his life.

Ever mindful of opportunities for his country, Jefferson, as he matured, found patriotic reasons to be concerned about the vast region beyond the Atlantic littoral. Both ego gratification and a concern for preservation of the ideals he deemed essential to democratic government heightened Jefferson's appreciation of the West when its people heartily endorsed him and the candidates of his Republican Party. He also thought the virgin lands of the West presented the best opportunity for the fresh beginning he coveted for America. He planned for the rise there of new states free of the burden of slavery and offering a free education to young people of both sexes and every class.

Considerations of national security and international politics also turned his thoughts westward. He early anticipated that Spain would cede the Louisiana Territory to France and was stirred to action by the threat to the United States implicit in French control of the Mississippi. He recognized that such an eventuality would not only stunt the growth of the American republic but also would make it dependent upon the whims of the dominant power on the European continent. Acquisition of the Louisiana Territory, doubling the size of the United States, at once making the nation's borders more secure and placing within them "more cultivable land" than was available in any other "civilized nation," was made possible by Napoleon's needs and frustrations. But it was realized only through action on Jefferson's part of a scope and daring matched by neither of his predecessors and few of his successors.

In the whole matter of securing and developing the West, Jefferson exhibited the happy combination of contemplation and action that makes him a superb rarity among national leaders in any time or place. The Lewis and Clark expedition, one of history's supreme examples of exploration in the grand tradition, was Jefferson's brainchild. It not only facilitated development of virgin lands as an integral part of the nation but added to the sum of human knowledge.

In his first year as President, Jefferson—as we have seen—dealt with or adumbrated every major initiative of his two administrations. His first year, therefore, provided an introduction to the seven succeeding ones that gives his entire tenure as Chief Magistrate a unity and organization much less often met with in real life than in such dissertations as he delighted to compose for the American Philosophical Society. Between March 1801 and March 1802 he not only anticipated and prepared for the negotiations with Napoleon over Louisiana and began laying the groundwork for the Lewis and Clark expedition but also sent forces to Tripoli to fight Barbary blackmail and terrorism, rejected Adams' "midnight appointments" and began behind-the-scenes management of repeal of the Judiciary Act, besides effecting significant governmental economies representative of the fiscal responsibility that he practiced so consistently in public life and so erratically in private.

Jefferson's boldness and decisiveness in all these undertakings was rendered only a little less obvious by his penchant for behind-the-scenes guidance where feasible. He was an energetic, activist President in all the chief measures of both administrations—so much so that Federalists charged that he was threatening the constitutional division of powers and some Republicans protested that in matters of federal initiative he was "out-federaling the Federalists." Nevertheless, in most instances he showed a scrupulous regard for constitutionalism, saying on such occasions as the Louisiana Purchase that though he must act before explicit authorization he must submit his actions to the Congress for confirmation or rejection. While for many years he had maintained that functions which could be effectively carried out by local and state governments should be left to them, he was no sudden convert to advocacy of a strong federal government. Not only had he long been a philosophical advocate of the doctrine of implied powers, but immediately after the Revolution he had supported the strengthening of the central government and later he had approved the increase in federal authority under the Constitution of 1787. His willingness to make full use of executive power to annex the Louisiana Territory, to explore the West, to challenge the Barbary terrorists, to advance judicial reform, and to impose an embargo on American commerce was consistent with views that he had expressed both privately and publicly for two decades before becoming President.

Unfortunately, Jefferson's scrupulousness in constitutional matters was not flawless. As with virtually every other statesman, however highminded, his perspective on civil liberties yielded to alarm when he thought his country's life was endangered. His countenancing of flagrant violations of individual citizens' rights during General Wilkinson's domination of New Orleans is the darkest spot on his presidency. Another major blemish was his branding Burr a traitor before the former Vice President could be judged by a jury of his peers. The provocation to this unjust and unwise action is understandable in light of the Chief Justice's all too obvious sympathy for the accused. Nevertheless, two great Americans, Jefferson and Marshall, performed below their customary high standards on that occasion and neither's indiscretions can excuse the conduct of the other.

A third, much more venial offense, also mars Jefferson's largely unblemished reputation of rectitude in the presidency. He attempted to provide a sinecure for John Page when his old friend, after a career as one of Virginia's most beloved Governors, was dying in financial distress. The President did try to insure that the public would not have to pay for labors unperformed; he tried to arrange for a relative or friend of Page to carry out the duties for which the former Governor would be paid. Furthermore, Jefferson was motivated by devotion to a faithful friend who, in the President's eyes, had served the commonwealth well and deserved special consideration from its citizens. Also there is no reason to suppose that Jefferson ever would have contrived to secure special benefits for himself in a similar situation. Nevertheless his agonizing sympathy for his old comrade led the President into an attempt smacking of cronyism.

All three of these departures from Jefferson's usually exalted standards occurred in his second term. The attempt to provide for Page has been little noted, but the two greater offenses have caused some historians, most notably Henry Adams, to suggest that the Virginian's second term was a failure. The record does not justify such a conclusion. Like virtually every other United States Chief Executive serving more than one term, Jefferson was less successful in his second. This can happen for a variety of reasons aside from presidential policies and personalities, the most common being that a newly anointed President frequently generates enthusiasm by his very newness and that a second-term President usually is regarded as a lame duck who will soon be shorn of powers to punish or reward. In Jefferson's case the disadvantages were compounded by protracted international stress. Steering a precarious path for peace, he could appear neither as the source of security nor as the embattled defender of his country. Nevertheless, his second administration was one of significant accomplishments. He maintained a course of neutrality between France and Great Britain that bought time for the United States to prepare for combat if war should prove inevitable. He acted with calm firmness in the *Chesapeake* crisis, an event which could have led either to war or meek surrender. The most unpopular part of the President's foreign policy was the Embargo Act, eventually detested not only by New England shippers but also by commercial interests elsewhere along the Atlantic Coast. It must not be forgotten, though, that when Jefferson first initiated the measure it won enthusiastic support in Congress. Most of the wisest Americans then saluted it as a good idea. Some sizeable groups supported it to the last. Indeed, it never excited much ire in most of the South, and it provided a significant stimulus to manufacturing in Pennsylvania and other mid-Atlantic areas, and even in some parts of Connecticut.

If the President had not taken important steps to strengthen the nation while buying time, the accomplishment would have been futile. But he did take such steps.

Although the embargo in the end became self-defeating as it eroded the national economy, some domestic industries flourished in the new freedom from foreign competition, and, overall, Jefferson reduced the national debt and strengthened the republic for future conflicts. More realistically than many leaders of his generation, he perceived that military and naval strength depended on a strong economy.

The most persistent and egregious error about Jefferson's presidency is the belief that he was so prejudiced against military and naval forces that he crippled the defenses of the United States. Many conscientious historians have been deluded in this matter by the compellingly interesting writings of Henry Adams and Theodore Roosevelt. Even some of the third President's stoutest admirers have conceded that, great as his accomplishments were, he should bear a large share of responsibility for American naval weakness in the War of 1812. At the outset of my research, I was among them. But the evidence compelled me to rethink my position. As I indicated in the preceding chapter, it is now clear that in defense, as in other aspects of government, Jefferson chose to exercise influence from behind the scenes, working through trusted legislative leaders. He did not move the nation's defenses ahead as fast as was desirable, but he did carry them as fast and as far as the Congress was willing to go. And that was farther than Congress would have gone without his skilled and persistent maneuvering. Jefferson's role was analogous to that of Franklin D. Roosevelt in dealing with an isolationist Congress before American entry into World War II. Neither President did enough to prepare his country for such involvement, but each made Congress do more than it would have on its own initiative.

Jefferson's second term saw the completion of the Lewis and Clark expedition, which he had initiated, and the beginning of the long process of reaping its bountiful rewards. It also saw, on the President's recommendation, enactment of federal prohibition of slave importations into the United States, a cause he had supported consistently for four decades and a process carried forward by individual states beginning with his own Virginia in 1776. But probably the greatest legacy of his second administration is one eloquently cited by the astute Samuel Eliot Morison: "Accustomed as we now are to revolutionary leaders imposing their policies by rigid tyranny and cruel oppression, we may take inspiration from one who deliberately preferred the slow process of reason to the short way of force. By his forbearance, even more than by his acts, Jefferson kept alive the flame of liberty that Napoleon had almost snuffed out in Europe."[9]

Despite these significant accomplishments, even in the second term, another tenacious misconception about Jefferson's presidency is that it ended in frustration and repudiation. Henry Adams, one of the most brilliant historical writers the United States ever produced and intermittently one of its most insightful, saw the last days as "appalling"—"disaster" amid "mortification such as no other President ever suffered."[10] He wrote, "He who longed like a sensitive child for sympathy and love left office as strongly and almost as generally disliked as the least popular President who preceded or followed him."[11] Adams disliked both Jefferson and his chief lieutenant, Madison, and these aversions deprived him of objectivity. The New England historian was able to re-create with remarkable and engaging fidelity almost every aspect of the Age of Jefferson except the central figure himself. One of the most respected historians of our own time, and one of the most stimulating, Forrest McDonald, echoes Adams' claim. He says, "Jefferson's legacy to his successor was a can of serpents. Jefferson's second term was merely a calamity." He blames Jefferson for the so-called disaster of Madison's first term and cites the "petty bickering" that followed Jefferson's departure, together with the fact that subsequently "Congress split into irreconcilable factions and repeatedly asserted its will against" his successors, as evidence of the "weakness of the Jeffersonian scheme of things."[12] Even if, like Professor McDonald, one remains unpersuaded by Irving Brant's generally convincing reassessment of Madison as a rather able Chief Executive with significant accomplishments, there is still no basis for discrediting Jefferson. The gap left on the horizon by the removal of a forest giant is one evidence of its magnitude. Is Lincoln's presidential stature compromised by the fact that "petty bickering" followed his demise and that the "Congress split into irreconcilable factions and repeatedly asserted its will against" his successor, even to the unprecedented extent of impeaching him?

There is solid evidence that Jefferson at the conclusion of his second administration was not repudiated by the American people. They did not have a chance to vote for or against electors pledged to him, though many shrewd politicians urged him to seek a third term and freely prognosticated a sweeping victory. But the American people did have the opportunity to vote for Jefferson's handpicked successor, his chief lieutenant in the most controversial measures of his tenure. The Jeffersonian triumph was a rout. In a three-way race Madison easily bested his two rivals in state after state, gaining well over twice as many electoral votes as both opponents combined. Jefferson did not delude himself when he told a group of fellow citizens, "On your verdict I rest with conscious security." His remarks could have been addressed with equal validity to the great mass of American citizens.

XII

SHADOWS ON THE MOUNTAIN

FOR JEFFERSON in 1809 the Ides of March held no dread. On March 15, four days after leaving Washington for good, he came home to stay. Monticello's familiar dome was an even more welcome sight than it would ordinarily have been because to reach it he had ridden through one of the worst snowstorms he had ever known.[1] The weather was reminiscent of that in January of 1772, when he and his bride had arrived at the same destination after riding up the mountain through great snowdrifts. They had come late at night, when no ray of light gleamed from any of the plantation's buildings. Monticello was then in an early stage of construction, and a small cottage at the end of what would become the south terrace was the only habitable portion. Here they took shelter and, lacking fire and food, found warmth in wine and each other. Soon the voices of the twenty-eight-year-old husband and his twenty-four-year-old wife blended in a happy song.[2]

Martha's voice had been stilled now for twenty-seven years. Therefore, to the nearly sixty-six-year-old widower the mansion in its handsome symmetry, seen by day, could not hold the promise of delight that he had known as the couple had trudged toward the dark cottage. But Jefferson was habituated to making the best of things. And Monticello was infinitely preferable to Washington. Moreover, it was the place that he loved best, the one to which his thoughts had so often turned longingly amid the stresses of public life, the place where he hoped that his life would end. And though Martha was gone, there were those here who loved him. As a boy in gentler weather he had lain under a tree on this then houseless mountaintop and read and dreamed. It was appropriate that with a kind of classical unity this neoclassical giant, having realized some of those dreams and exceeded others, had come full cycle and returned to the site of his imaginings.

He was still dreaming of the future, still planning and working to make his dreams come true. He had a vision of Monticello surrounded by the most beautifully landscaped acres in America and fields of the most diverse produce. Though winter had not relinquished its icy grip on the land, he was looking ahead to the budding of spring and burgeoning of summer. Through the fury of the snowstorm he had brought some of Richard Fitzhugh's famous Ravensworth peas for planting as soon as the weather permitted. And one of the three lumbering wagons that carried his personal possessions from Washington was loaded with shrubbery from a nursery near the capital. The vehicles—two drawn by six-mule teams and one by four horses—had begun the journey two days ahead of the President but the eager horseman had passed them on the road.[3]

There were also seeds of scholarship to be nurtured in the months ahead. Among some baggage Jefferson had put aboard a ship traveling between a Potomac landing and Rivanna wharf was a trunk holding notes on American Indian vocabularies that he had collected over three decades. His linguistic abilities were considerable, as demonstrated by his facility in French, the rapidity with which he had taught himself Spanish, and the innovations which he had proposed in the teaching of Anglo-Saxon. Jefferson had studied about fifty different aboriginal American tongues, and his researches in anthropology complemented his linguistic research. He had reason to hope that the opus he contemplated might prove the most comprehensive in the field so far.

The day after Jefferson's arrival jarring news broke in upon his happy reunion with family, staff, and friends.[4] The vessel bearing his trunk had run aground in a branch of the Potomac, and his belongings had been transferred to another ship. Somewhere above Richmond the trunk had disappeared. Richmond agents Gibson and Jefferson (partner George Jefferson was the President's cousin) began an anxious search.

Jefferson was worried, but there was still hope the trunk would turn up. Meanwhile, there was much that was pleasant to occupy his attention. Not only were there the plans for further landscaping, but there also were improvements to be made in the house itself. After the master's forty years of building and rebuilding, his home was probably the most beautiful in America. But ornamental balustrades could link dependencies more effectively with the main house. Then there was Poplar Forest, his retreat on his Bedford County estate. The new house there, after almost three years of construction, as architecturally innovative on a small scale as Monticello on a grand one, had already assumed its distinctive shape of a square surrounding an octagon.[5] Anyone unfamiliar with the owner's habit of architectural tinkering after realization of the original concept would have deemed it nearly complete. But Jefferson was capable of continued alterations for more than a decade.

Superior to all these pleasures, however, was delight in his family. Martha Jefferson Randolph, his beloved Patsy, with the six of her eight children still at home, had been at Monticello to welcome him on his return. They expected to stay. Patsy had once assured her father that he was first of all human beings in her affections. Her duty to her husband would come before that to all other people *except* her father.[6] Henceforth she would go back to her own home for brief visits but Monticello would be her headquarters. Her husband, Thomas Mann Randolph, adjusted to the situation. Apparently he usually slept at his father-in-law's home and had breakfast and dinner there, though normally he would spend part of each day on his own estate.[7]

Randolph also adapted with good grace, at least outwardly, to the fact that, although he had been a prominent member of Congress and was often regarded as a future Governor, he still was often introduced as Mr. Jefferson's son-in-law. Though he won recognition for studies in natural history, these were easily eclipsed by Jefferson's contributions. Though he invented an ingenious plow for work on hillsides, it was Jefferson's plow that won an international award at an exposition in Paris. As a planter better able to concentrate on farming than Jefferson was, he had achieved larger yields per acre than the older man but it was the sage of Monticello's agricultural experiments that attracted attention on two continents. Randolph seems to have been sincerely fond of this man who held him in paternal affection and sometimes rescued him from financial difficulties, but his dependence must have been galling to a highly intelligent and ambitious man of forty-two years.

Jefferson thoroughly enjoyed the role of paterfamilias to eight people, and sometimes more.[8] Anne Cary, Martha's oldest child, was now the bride of Charles Lewis Bankhead and lived just a little way down the slope. Sixteen-year-old Jeff was at school in Richmond, but he would be returning to Monticello whenever he could. He was an intelligent boy, but schooling probably would not keep him away as long as his grandfather had expected. Jefferson had wanted him to graduate from his own alma mater, William and Mary, but the youth took little interest in abstract learning. Eight-year-old Francis Eppes, son of the President's deceased daughter, Polly, a much more bookish child, frequently visited his grandfather.

At Monticello now were Ann Cary's four sisters, ages five to twelve, and Jeff's brothers, three-year-old James Madison Randolph and infant Benjamin Franklin Randolph.

Many of Jefferson's neighbors constituted an extended family. He himself took pride in their pride in him. And their pride was immense. A committee representing the citizens of Albemarle had saluted him shortly after his return as "a friend and neighbor as exemplary in the social circle as he is eminent at the helm of state."[9] But the relationship was free and easy. Among them Jefferson was like a son returned to his family after heroic accomplishment. Though convinced that his reputation was well deserved and ready to fight anyone who questioned it, they still remained completely unawed by his presence. Jefferson liked it that way. To the Polish patriot Kosciuszko he wrote: "I talk of ploughs and harrows, of seeding and harvesting, with my neighbors, and of politics too if they choose, with as little reserve as the rest of my fellow citizens, and feel at length the blessing of being free to say and to do what I please without being responsible to any mortal."[10] Note that he discussed politics with his neighbors *if they chose*. It was not his favorite topic.

How did he appear physically to friends and working associates at this juncture of his life? There are various descriptions, none more interesting than those by Edmund Bacon, an acute observer who was Jefferson's valued farm manager at Monticello. "Mr. Jefferson," he wrote, "was six feet two and a half inches high, well proportioned, and straight as a gunbarrel. He was like a fine horse—he had no surplus flesh."[11] For many years people had described him as lean but there had been no emphasis on ramrod erectness. Indeed, Pennsylvania's Senator William Maclay nineteen years earlier had written: "He sits in a lounging manner on one hip commonly, and with one of his shoulders elevated much above the other; . . . his whole figure has a loose, shackling air."[12] Other references from the Washington years suggest a loose-gaited walk and a less than military posture. Did Jefferson slouch in an urban setting and stand straight amid his fields? Or was he careless about posture until he became sensitive to the fact that people might think he looked like an old man?

His principal exercise was a daily horseback ride on his own estate, not in booted elegance and a tailored habit but in overalls.[13] He was an accomplished horseman, and when he was in the saddle his white hair did not keep him from looking younger than he was. His animation in conversation seemed to burn away additional years. Nevertheless, knowing that Jefferson had never been athletically inclined and was not accustomed to physical labor, probably very few people expected an impressive performance when he approached an arm-strength testing machine set up at Monticello. Thomas Mann Randolph had had the satisfaction of besting most people in these trials, even men much younger than his forty-two years. But his nearly sixty-six-year-old father-in-law made a higher score.[14]

But even Paradise had its serpent. Though Jefferson was far happier than during his presidency, he was still worried about his heavy burden of debt. He had had to borrow $8,000, then a considerable sum, to pay bills before leaving Washington. Much larger sums still were owed. He was hopeful, though, that by personal supervision of his estates, he could make them more profitable. He knew, however, that much application would be required. "My whole life," he had recently told his son-in-law, "has been passed in occupations which kept me from any minute attention to [my farms], and finds me now with only very general ideas of the theory of agriculture, without actual experience."[15]

Another worry, starting the day after his return to Monticello, he had at first been able to shove into the back of his mind. But, as time passed, it more frequently moved unbidden to the forefront. The reward offered in May for return of his lost trunk had brought no results. His fears increased that he would never recover the notes he had collected in thirty years of linguistic research. He could not hope to begin again. Without those notes his dreamed-of work could not be executed. In May his cousin George sent him the sad news that, although some of the papers had been found in the James River, only a few legible notes remained. Later both the trunk and its taker were discovered, but nothing could bring back the lost work. In the summer, when the thief was on trial, Jefferson wrote with unconcern, if not with relish, that the man probably would be hanged.[16] The President was so generally tolerant and humane that his rare outbursts of vindictiveness usually caught his friends by surprise.

Despite his frustration and anger over the loss of his notes, Jefferson faced the world in general with good humor in the summer of 1809. Once again, as life burgeoned in the clay soil of his fields, the exuberant green and red of Gauguin succeeded the Corot-like misty green and delicate white tracery of dogwood as predominant features of the landscape. And this time he knew that with the coming of fall he would not have to leave for Washington.

Not that he was tired of everyone in the capital. He corresponded frequently with the President, who was first of all his old friend James Madison. And he kept in touch with Albert Gallatin, who continued as Secretary of the Treasury. He had written a letter to his old maitre d'hotel, Etienne Lemaire, expressing his "affectionate esteem."[17] And in August he was visited by two of his favorite Washingtonians, Mr. and Mrs. Samuel Harrison Smith. Mr. Smith, as editor of the *National Intelligencer*, had long been one of Jefferson's most ardent defenders in every controversy. Soon after the President's departure from Washington an anonymous author had published a two-volume work, *Memoirs of the Hon. Thomas Jefferson*, satirizing him. Harrison wrote a spirited defense, memorable today chiefly because he referred to Jefferson as the "Sage of Monticello,"[18] a term to be used innumerable times by generations of writers.

Mrs. Smith's friendship was a special one, important to him then and to his biographers now. Margaret Bayard Smith was one of Jefferson's devoted admirers and understanding observers. Her journal, published as *The First Forty Years of Washington Society*, is one of the most important sourcebooks on the great man. She had called on Jefferson shortly before he left Washington and, admiring a geranium that he had personally nurtured, asked if she might have it if he did not expect to take it home with him. Her tears, she said, would water it in the absence of "the most venerated of human beings." She would, she promised, visit Monticello in the summer. He sent her the plant with a note saying that it would surely be "proudly sensible of her fostering attentions."[19]

The Smiths' visit in August was for Jefferson a highlight of the season. Mrs. Smith said that his chronological age was made inconsequential by his "activity, strength, health, enthusiasm, ardor, and gaiety."[20] So strong were her "affections" and "veneration" that, on seeing him again, "gentle and kind" as he was, she could not "converse with him with ease." She shared his enthusiasm for the great vistas, waves of mountains fading from dark blue-green into ice blue as they disappeared into the illimitable distance. But she was disappointed in the gardens that he showed with such delight. Terracing was in progress and Jefferson had sowed eighteen squares, but he saw what was to be whereas she saw an unrealized dream. She was struck with the handsome foyer and with the "noble" dome room, strangely "unfurnished and unused," as it might be made the most beautiful room in the house. She was a little disappointed, too, when he showed her his famous library. She was impressed with his ease in reading from books in Anglo-Saxon, Greek, Latin, French, and Italian. And the 20,000-volume collection was certainly one of the largest, most diverse, and most selective private ones on the North American continent. But it was divided among three rooms. The space, she thought, was cut up by too many arches and partitions, so that the library did not seem as large as it really was. Nevertheless, she was thrilled that her hero had admitted her to his "sanctum sanctorum," where "any other feet but his own seldom intrude."

Jefferson was cheered, as almost always, by the company of congenial friends. And the kind of unqualified admiration from the female sex that he had enjoyed, beginning with his sister Jane and extending through the experiences of a lifetime, was both comforting and revitalizing. It was so to an intense degree in his passionate relationships with his wife and, as a widower, with Maria Cosway. But it was true when he was quite innocent of any impulse to seduction, as in a multitude of other friendships or even acquaintanceships with women. And it was certainly true in his association with his adoring daughters. It is fortunate for his happiness that a man so dependent on feminine admiration was always capable of finding it.

He found a quieter kind of comfort in routine, and followed one just as faithfully in retirement as in public life. He habitually rose with the sun if not before, took a walk on the terrace when the sun's first rays were gilding the landscape, and returned to make his own fire in his room.[21] At this time, and for generations to come, Virginia planters had their fires, even in their bedchambers, made by servants. It is surprising that Jefferson, of all people, should have been an exception in this respect. Once, in picturing the attractions of a truly simple life, he had listed as the bare necessities "a very small house, with a table, half a dozen chairs, and one or two servants."[22] Mentally the most industrious of men, he was to an extraordinary degree dependent on the physical labor of others. Perhaps he made his own fire to prolong his privacy. At 9:00 a.m., weather permitting, he began the day's ride over his plantation.

Jefferson was self-consciously agrarian, like Horace at his Sabine farm. He wrote a Washington correspondent that he was "occupied constantly out of doors from an early breakfast to a late dinner every day." He said, "Writing, as with other country farmers, is put off to a rainy day. . . . The total change of occupation from the house and writing table to constant employment in the garden and farm has added wonderfully to my happiness. It is seldom and with great reluctance I ever take up a pen. I read some, but not much."[23]

The internal evidence of Jefferson's correspondence is that even in this first year of retirement he read more than he thought he did. He did, however, cancel subscriptions to all newspapers except local ones. To Levi Lincoln, his former Attorney General, he wrote: "I shall give over reading newspapers. They are so false and intemperate that they disturb tranquility without giving information."[24]

Despite his efforts, Jefferson could not for long shut out the world of politics. And the intrusion did disturb his tranquility.

At first the news was more good than bad. Though the Senate had blocked Madison's choice of Gallatin as Secretary of State, forcing the President to compromise by retaining him as Treasury Secretary, the new administration seemed to be off to a satisfactory start. While Madison was not idolized by the Republicans as Jefferson was, he was not so much hated by the die-hard Federalists as his predecessor. Most Republicans and most Americans not allied with any party seemed to find comfort in expectation of a fairly pedestrian continuation of Jefferson's policies. Federalists were grateful for any dilution of the Jeffersonian essence. Before the end of April, Jefferson had received heartening news from Washington. David Erskine, the young British Minister who liked Americans in general and Jefferson in particular, reported that his Majesty's government would withdraw on June 10, 1809, the hated Orders in Council of 1807 barring all shipping from the coastal trade of France and her allies and prohibiting trade with Continental ports from which the British flag was excluded. The United States had repeatedly protested that these decrees were an infringement of its sovereignty and under Jefferson had introduced the embargo in retaliation. On April 19, in response to the United Kingdom's anticipated removal of the orders, Madison issued a proclamation permitting the resumption of trade with Great Britain.

Jefferson abandoned restraint in his correspondence with Madison far more than with anyone else, but the letter[25] he now wrote his old friend is remarkable even in that freewheeling style. He began moderately enough, citing events as evidencing "the triumph of our forbearing and yet persevering system." Then he yielded to almost unbounded enthusiasm, saying that the new turn in Anglo-American relations insured "peace in your time." The national debt could now be eliminated. Jefferson, who in his last message to Congress had suggested consideration of a federal program of roads, canals, and other internal improvements, and who had long advocated an extensive public school system, said that this happy development would make possible "the noblest application of revenue that has ever been exhibited by any nation." Then he inserted two qualifying sentences: "As to Bonaparte, I should not doubt the revocation of his edicts, were he governed by reason. But his policy is so crooked that it eludes conjecture." Having made these concessions to reason, Jefferson indulged his fancy. He said that the French tyrant ought "to conciliate our good will, as we can be such an obstacle to the new career opening on him in the Spanish colonies. That he would give us the Floridas to withhold intercourse with the residue of these colonies cannot be doubted. But that is no [inducement]; because they are ours in the first movement of the first war; and until a war they are of no particular necessity to us. But, although with difficulty, he will consent to our receiving Cuba into our Union, to prevent our aid to Mexico and the other provinces. That would be [an inducement] and I would immediately erect a column on the southernmost limit of Cuba and inscribe on it a *ne plus ultra* as to us in that direction. We should then have only to include the north [Canada] in our confederacy, which would be of course in the first war, and we should have such an empire for liberty as she has never surveyed since the creation; and I am persuaded no constitution was ever before so well calculated as ours for extensive empire and self-government."

His words foreshadow the orotund oratory of 1840s proponents of Manifest Destiny. They are not what one would expect from the President who, with controlled skill, had guided the nation along a firm but cautious course between war and submission. They were reminiscent, however, of some of the private messages about opportunities for imperial conquest which that same President, his sense of drama and his patriotic acquisitiveness aroused, had sent on the eve of the Louisiana Purchase to the same trusted, circumspect old friend.

The empire of his imagination was dealt a rude blow in August, when he learned that the Erskine agreement, so pleasing to the United States, had been repudiated in London. The British Minister, it turned out, had acted entirely on his own initiative, trusting that he could convince his government to endorse his efforts. The shock was softened only a little by the fact that both Jefferson and Madison had begun to suspect in June that the British course might not be as certain as they had assumed. Madison had the embarrassment of having to issue a proclamation contravening the one with which he had so recently restored trade with Great Britain.[26]

Angry at being taken in, Jefferson wrote Madison: "I look upon all cordial conciliation with England as desperate during the life of the present king. I hope and doubt not that Erskine will justify himself. My confidence is founded in a belief of his integrity."[27] He had no such faith in Foreign Secretary Canning, whom he accused of "unprincipled rascality," or any other member of the ministry in London. He said: "I consider the present as the most shameless ministry which ever disgraced England. . . . In general, their administrations are so changeable, and they are obliged to descend to such tricks to keep themselves in place, that nothing like honor or morality can ever be counted on in transactions with them." He also said: "Should Bonaparte have the wisdom to correct his injustice towards us, I consider war with England as inevitable." American ships would go to France and its dependencies, and the British would seize them. "This will be war on their part and leave no alternative but reprisal. I have no doubt you will think it safe to act on this hypothesis, and with energy." In so saying, Jefferson was dangerously near breaking his self-imposed rule about not advising his successor. He went further. "The moment that open war shall be apprehended from them [the British], we should take possession of Baton Rouge. If we do not, they will, and New Orleans becomes irrecoverable and the western country blockaded during the war."

When the Erskine agreement had been accepted in the United States as a bona fide expression of British policy, some Federalists, while welcoming the development, said that it had been made possible by Jefferson's retirement. But now that the prospect of a firm peace was revealed as a mirage, Federalists blamed Jefferson for the failure. The intraparty opposition was active too. John Randolph of Roanoke seized the occasion to assert: "Never has there been any Administration which went out of office and left the nation in a state so deplorable and calamitous as the last." Even among those disposed to criticize Jefferson, the sweeping "never" must have been deprived of considerable force by the reflection that he had had only two predecessors. Contrasting the two terms of Jefferson, Randolph said, "The lean kine of Pharaoh devoured the fat kine."[28] The mouth had bite in it this time; he introduced a resolution calling for an inquiry into financial transactions in Jefferson's presidency. The resolution passed but with the support of many who had no thought of indicting the ex-President. Even one of Randolph's comrades, Nathaniel Macon, while saying that he believed every administration should be investigated, irritated his colleague by adding, "I feel no hesitation in saying that the nation will never be blessed with such another Administration as the last." The investigating committee eventually made a halfhearted report, which was tabled.

Loyal Republicans, too, had to find a scapegoat. Few would blame Jefferson, and not many more would attack Madison. But the foreigner in the cabinet, Gallatin, had never been very popular with the party's rank and file, or even some of its leaders for that matter. Jefferson had always strongly defended him in his administration. Now Madison defended him too, but the new President was not the popular hero that his predecessor was. Discouraged by attacks from within his own party, in the fall Gallatin wished to resign. Jefferson asked him to remain. "I consider the fortunes of our country," he said, "as depending in an eminent degree on the extinguishment of the public debt before we engage in any war."[29] To enter upon a major conflict without that accomplishment would be to commit ourselves "to the English career of debt, corruption, and rottenness," all ending in revolution. "The discharge of the debt therefore is vital to the destinies of our government, and it hangs on Mr. Madison and yourself alone. We shall never see another President and Secretary of the Treasury making all other objects subordinate to this. Were either of you to be lost to the public, that great hope is lost. I had always cherished the idea that you would fix on that object the measure of your fame, and of the gratitude which our country will owe you."

Jefferson's letter was colored by his long-standing but freshly aroused prejudice against British governments, but it was essentially as a keen analyst and realistic statesman that he wrote. There were none of the self-indulgent transports of his correspondence with Madison.

But his reasonable message provoked an emotional response. Gallatin said that he had entered upon public office principally to reduce the national debt, but the cooperation of the President alone would not enable him to achieve his purpose. "I cannot, my dear sir," he wrote, "consent to act the part of a mere financier, to become a contriver of taxes, a dealer of loans, a seeker of resources for the purpose of supporting useless baubles, of increasing the number of idle and dissipated members of the community, of fattening contractors, pursers and agents, and of introducing, in all its ramifications, that system of patronage, corruption, and rottenness which you so justly execrate."[30] Gallatin continued to complain, but he stayed on.

Jefferson had an artist's imagination, and it apparently enabled him to convince himself that—amid all his concern for international developments and attempts to influence American policies in relation to them—he was living the life of a simple son of the soil. In this same troubled autumn, he wrote his friend Dr. Benjamin Rush, the famous Philadelphia physician and signer of the Declaration of Independence: "A retired politician is like a broken down courser, unfit [for the] turf, and good for little else. I am endeavoring to recover the little [I] knew of farming, gardening, etc. and would gladly now exchange [every] branch of science I possess for the knowledge of a common farmer."[31]

As the term "science" in Jefferson's day embraced all fields of scholarship, he was expressing a willingness to trade all his intellectual acquirements for a mastery of farming techniques. It is difficult to imagine anyone who would be more bereft by such a loss. But Jefferson cherished the image of himself as simple agrarian, a concept fed by both the pastoral idylls of classical literature and his idealistic view of America as a new Eden. He was the most articulate of a host of Virginians who clung to the same ideal. The belief that a countryman is more likely to be a substantial citizen than an urban-oriented person persisted in Virginia well into the twentieth century. Many a resident of Richmond or

Norfolk stressed his rural background as evidence of proper orientation. This credo was especially emphasized by the culturally privileged, including those who, like Jefferson himself, knew their way around Philadelphia, New York, and Paris.

Jefferson emphasized his supposed isolation, telling Rush: "I find I am losing sight of the progress of the world of letters. Here we talk but of rains and droughts, of blights and frosts, of our plows and cattle, and if the topic changes to politics I meddle little with them. In truth I never had a cordial relish for them and abhor the contentions and strife they generate. You know what were the times which forced us both from our first loves, the natural sciences."

He was conversing with such simple farmers as his son-inlaw, whose remarks about his harvest of grain might be interlarded with tales of collecting botanical specimens, or his neighbor James Monroe, with whom he might follow either a furrow in a cornfield or a course of recollection down the Champs Elysées.

Jefferson probably was not deceiving himself when he said he wished that a much larger portion of his life had been devoted to literature and scholarship. During Margaret Smith's visit to Monticello he had expressed that desire and explained why he had not felt free to fulfill it. Presumably Mrs. Smith, worshipful though she was, did not take notes while her host talked, but the quotations that she committed to her journal are consistent with the content and style of his letters. "If his life had not proved to the contrary," she wrote, "I should have pronounced him a man of imagination and taste [rather] than a man of judgement, a literary rather than a scientific man, and least of all a politician, a character for which nature never seemed to have intended him, and for which the natural turn of mind, and his disposition, taste, and feeling equally unfit him. I should have been sure that this was the case even had he not told me so."[32]

But one evening he did tell her. "The whole of my life," he said, "has been a war with my natural taste, feelings, and wishes. Domestic life and literary pursuits were my first and my latest inclinations. Circumstances, and not my desires, led me to the path I have trod. And like a bow though long bent, which when unstrung flies back to its natural state, I resume with delight the character and pursuits for which nature designed me. The circumstances of our country, at my entrance into life, were such that every honest man felt himself compelled to take a part, and to act up to the best of his abilities."

Supporting Jefferson's statement is the fact that several times he had had to be urged by friends, insistently and even reproachfully, to return to, or remain in, public life. Adding to the demands of public duty in his own generation was a strong tradition of public service among the Virginia aristocracy. Few oligarchies in history have placed such strong emphasis upon noblesse oblige, in this case an amalgam of paternalism, ego gratification, and genuine idealism of a high order.

There were still calls on Jefferson, some public and some private, to play an influential role in politics. With the United States beset by crises, foreign and domestic, the Madison administration was divided against itself. The Smith brothers (the Secretary of the Navy and the Senator), as they had in Jefferson's administration, were making trouble for the President by making trouble for Gallatin. The Sage of Monticello had handled them with an adroitness rarely matched by anyone in public life and, even so, had barely bested them. Madison was not faring that well.

The government needed the support of James Monroe, the presidential candidate recently preferred above Madison by a significant number of republicans. Madison wished to bring him into his Administration, suggesting that the administration of Orleans, or perhaps of all Louisiana, might be an appropriate job. Monroe said he was not interested, and Madison appealed to Jefferson to exercise his powers of persuasion.

The ex-President rode over to Highland Track (it was not yet called Ash Lawn) to appeal to Monroe. But the younger man vowed that he would not accept any position in which "he should be subordinate to anybody but the President himself, or which did not place his responsibility substantially with the President and the nation."[33]

A cabinet position was about the only thing answering this description, and every one of those posts was filled. Jefferson tried to feel him out about accepting a military command, but Monroe put an end to that speculation by saying he "would sooner be shot than take a command under Wilkinson."

Jefferson tried to allay fears about dissension in the cabinet by telling prominent Republicans that the disagreements could not be "greater than between Hamilton and myself, and yet we served together four years in that way. We had indeed no personal dissensions. Each of us, perhaps, thought well of the other as a man, but as politicians it was impossible for two men to be of more opposite principles."[34] Jefferson had very humanly forgotten the time when, as Secretary of State, he had complained to President Washington that Treasury Secretary Hamilton was "a man whose history, from the moment at which history can stoop to notice him, is a tissue of machinations against the liberty of the country which has not only received him and given him bread, but heaped its honors on his head." A bit more realistic was Jefferson's explanation to Dr. Walter Jones about the relationships in Washington's official family: "Hamilton and myself were daily pitted in the Cabinet like two cocks." But the public didn't hear it. "The pain was for Hamilton and myself, but the public experienced no inconvenience."[35]

Next to discord in his family, Jefferson hated discord among his friends and in his political party. Now his party was rocked by fierce quarrels among his friends. Senator William Branch Giles of Virginia, his confidant in several crises, was allied with the Smith faction attacking Gallatin. William Duane, editor of the *Aurora* and long loyal to Jefferson, joined in criticism of the Treasury Secretary and was losing his enthusiasm for Madison. The ex-President was trying to retain his friendship with all and make them more tolerant of each other. There was no question, however, in the minds of those closest to Jefferson that in a showdown he would stand with Gallatin and, of course, with Madison.

In the fall of 1808, when Jefferson was visiting the cottage of Mr. and Mrs. Samuel Harrison Smith, Mrs. Smith's reference to the charms of winter caused the President to exclaim: "But you can here form no idea of a snowstorm. No, to see it in all its grandeur you should stand at my back door. There we see its progress—rising over the distant Allegheny—come sweeping and roaring on, mountain after mountain, till it reaches us. And then when its blast is felt, to turn to our fireside, and while we hear it pelting against the window to enjoy the cheering blaze, and the comforts of a beloved family."

In his "Dialogue of Head and Heart" love letter to Maria Cosway twenty-two years before, he had written of Monticello: "With what majesty do we there ride above the storms! How sublime to look down into the workhouse of nature, to see her clouds, hail, snow, rain, thunder, all fabricated at our feet!"[36]

As the autumn of 1809 moved into winter, and 1810 dawned with all its troubles for the republic, Jefferson was forced to the unhappy realization that in retiring from office he had not shed all political cares. However secure a refuge Monticello was from the storms of nature, Mr. Jefferson's mountaintop citadel was not impervious to storms in the affairs of men.

XIII

'DIFFUSION OF KNOWLEDGE'

JEFFERSON WAS still expressing disappointment in his retirement when, on February 26, 1810, he wrote to his old friend General Thaddeus Kosciusko[1]—but this time with two significant differences.

The great Polish patriot had been a prominent officer in the American Revolution, earning by his services the rank of Brigadier General and the officially granted privileges of United States citizenship. Jefferson had always regarded him as a kindred spirit, so much so that he confided to him his fears as well as his hopes. He did not find it necessary to show him only the smiling face that he habitually turned to the public. In another February of doubts and apprehensions, eleven years before, Jefferson had confided his anxiety that the United States might find itself at war with France. "If we are forced into a war," he had written, "we must give up political differences of opinion and unite as one man to defend our country, but whether at the close of such a war, we should be as free as we are now, God knows."[2]

This time the menacing nation was Great Britain, but the problems were much the same. Jefferson referred to "the anxieties which I know you have felt on seeing exposed to the jostling of a warring world a country to which, in early life, you devoted your sword and services when [it was] oppressed by foreign dominion." [3] The ex-President gave a rather too sanguine estimate of the nation's preparedness as a result of measures initiated in his own administration but admitted that the vital harbors of New York and New Orleans were not yet adequately fortified.

Then he confessed a great frustration. "Two measures," he said, "have not been adopted which I pressed on Congress repeatedly at their meetings. The one, to settle the whole ungranted territory of Orleans, by donations of land to able-bodied young men, to be engaged and carried there at the public expense, who would constitute a force always ready on the spot to defend New Orleans. The other was to class the militia according to the years of their birth, and make all those from twenty to twenty-five liable to be trained and called into service at a moment's warning. . . . These two measures would have completed what I deemed necessary for the entire security of our country. They would have given me, on my retirement from the government of the nation, the consolatory reflection, that having found, when I was called to it, not a single seaport town in a condition to repel a levy of contribution by a single privateer or pirate, I had left every harbor so prepared by works and gunboats, as to be in a reasonable state of security against any probable attack; the territory of Orleans acquired, and planted with an internal force sufficient for its protection; and the whole territory of the United States organized by such a classification of its male force, as would give it the benefit of all its young population for active service, and that of a middle and advanced age for stationary defence."

Loyal as ever to Madison, he concluded: "But these measures will, I hope, be completed by my successor, who to the purest principles of republican patriotism, adds a wisdom and foresight second to no man on earth."

There followed paragraphs which Jefferson was embarrassed to write and which A. A. Lipscomb and A. E. Bergh chose to omit from the letter as printed in their twenty-volume edition of Jefferson's writings. The sentences concerned financial arrangements by Jefferson which directly affected Kosciusko. The loan from the Bank of the United States which Jefferson had obtained just before leaving Washington was endorsed by Madison, with John Barnes, a Georgetown factor, as endorser of first liability. Barnes felt insecure with this arrangement, and Jefferson, explaining why he felt driven to the necessity, asked Madison to assume first liability. Barnes now proposed a solution. Jefferson had power of attorney over Kosciusko's investments in the United States, and the Georgetown factor managed them. Some eight-percent certificates in the General's portfolio were about to be retired, and the investment of the earnings was left to Barnes' discretion. Why, he asked, couldn't the capital be loaned to Jefferson at the same rate, eight percent, continuing the same return for Kosciusko and enabling Jefferson to retire the loan from the Bank of the United States. There was no time to lose, and Jefferson, sure that Kosciusko would approve, as indeed he did, jumped at the chance. Nevertheless, he was a little uncomfortable in explaining to his Polish friend after the fact.

Having explained, Jefferson concluded with words that he might not have written or spoken to anyone with whom he would be in frequent face-to-face association except Madison: "Instead of the unalloyed happiness of retiring unembarrassed and independent, to the enjoyment of my estate, which is ample for my limited views, I have to pass such a length of time in a thraldom of mind never before known to me. Except for this, my happiness would have been perfect. That yours may never know disturbance, and that you may enjoy as many years of life, as health and ease to yourself shall wish, is the sincere prayer of your constant and affectionate friend."

The candor and explicitness with which Jefferson confessed his worries was one difference between his admission of disappointment this time and on earlier occasions. But the letter to Kosciusko was even more significant for something else: for its revelation of his consolations, and of one consolation in particular. For though the letter ended on a melancholy note, it first cited some compensations. Chief among these, of course, was his family. His daughter was a devoted and congenial companion. The grandchildren had grown up around him, playing and frolicking about his chair while he caressed them almost unconsciously as he conversed with their elders on a variety of topics. The relationship remained easy and affectionate.

But there was a new source of pleasure, one that he wrote about with quickening excitement: "A part of my occupation, and by no means the least pleasing, is the direction of the studies of such young men as ask it. They place themselves in the neighboring village, and have the use of my library and counsel, and make a part of my society. In advising the course of their reading, I endeavor to keep their attention fixed on the main objects of all science, the freedom and happiness of man. So that coming to bear a share in the councils and government of their country, they will keep ever in view the sole objects of all legitimate government."

The temptation is great to say that Jefferson was at heart an educator. But then one could make an equally good case that he was at heart a writer, a scholar, or an architect. Certainly education was close to his heart. Like Chaucer's clerk of Oxenford, "gladly wolde he lerne and gladly teche." Even in his early years, he had outlined courses of reading for his friends. He had exercised close supervision over the education of his daughters, his nephews, and his grandchildren. "Diffusion of knowledge" was one of his favorite phrases, and he had long been an advocate of measures and institutions to promote that happy process.

As early as 1777–1779, when Jefferson was the most influential member of the Committee to Revise the Laws of the Commonwealth and the principal agent of legal reform in Virginia, he had advocated a detailed plan "for the more general diffusion of knowledge." Part of the plan was a proposal for a system of public education by districts, beginning at the primary level with the sons and daughters of all citizens and extending upward, with free tuition for the most proficient of the poor, to embrace three years of education for some young men at the College of William and Mary.

Jefferson was not content to leave his alma mater unreformed if it was to be the capstone of education in Virginia. He proposed that its two chairs of divinity be eliminated and that chairs be added in law, medicine, history, and modern languages. Both the elimination of the chairs of divinity and the creation of chairs of modern languages were controversial proposals. Jefferson by no means wanted modern languages at the expense of Latin and Greek. Hearing in the 1770s that the classic tongues were "going into disuse in Europe," he said, "I know not what their manners and occupations may call for, but it would be very ill-judged in us to follow their example in this instance."[4] His reforms would make William and Mary even more of a university than it was. The Virginia institution, founded in 1693, was America's second college but its first university by default of Harvard, which, though founded fifty-seven years earlier, eschewed a broad curriculum in favor of concentration on ministerial studies.

Of all his purposes in advocating a comprehensive system of public education, Jefferson said "none is more important, none more legitimate than that of rendering the people the safe, as they are the ultimate, guardians of their own liberty."[5] For this purpose, he thought the most important acquisitions were skill in reading and a knowledge of history. He also said, "The general objects of this law are to provide an education adapted to the years, to the capacity, and the condition of everyone, and directed to their freedom and happiness."

Jefferson was far ahead of even most well-educated Americans in advocating the use of public funds to provide for the enrichment of citizens' lives through acquaintance with art. Not only did he call for a state library—itself a startling innovation—but he wanted it in combination with a gallery of paintings and sculpture. But with the Revolution in progress, and finally with Virginia invaded, the General Assembly did not act in any significant way to advance Jefferson's program for the diffusion of knowledge. Even after the war it was not ready for most of it. As for establishing a state museum of art, no state in the Union was ready for that expenditure of funds until such a structure was completed in 1936, appropriately enough by his own Virginia.

One notes immediately that, while Jefferson's educational scheme called for free college education for young men, it made no similar provision for young women. There was no college for young women, and the public was not prepared to consider the necessity for one, much less to think of making a men's college coeducational. Many citizens were not ready for his plans to provide free education for females at any level. Even in Enlightenment circles in France, with their famous salons presided over by learned women, he was considered a bit peculiar because of the care which he lavished on the education of his daughters. He personally found a woman's charm greatly enhanced by learning. It should not be necessary to point out that in the matter of women's rights Jefferson's stance should be judged by the prevailing standards of his own time, not those of subsequent generations. When he was working on his educational propositions, he enthusiastically and successfully championed a law providing that male and female descendants should share equally in the division of intestate estates.[6]

In the years after the Revolution, Jefferson thought increasingly of designing a public university as the capstone of Virginia's educational system. Establishing such a public institution might be easier than remolding William and Mary, a private one, to his heart's desire. A new university could be more centrally located than the existing one and, perhaps not entirely incidentally, would be nearer Monticello.

When Monroe became Governor, he talked, perhaps at Jefferson's instigation, of the need for a public university. In 1800 Jefferson sought suggestions from two eminent foreigners, Joseph Priestley and Du Pont de Nemours, about the curriculum for such an institution. Even in his busy first term as President, he solicited advice from the Institut National of France and the prestigious universities of Edinburgh and Geneva.

A bill to establish a public university was introduced in the General Assembly in 1806 but was smothered quietly beneath a pile of other legislation. At that time the President revealed to Littleton W. Tazewell his hopes that the curriculum would embrace every branch of learning, with flexibility in each discipline's offerings to meet both advances in scholarship and the changing needs of society. All subjects should be presented "in the highest degree to which the human mind has carried them."[7] Oxford, Cambridge, and the Sorbonne, he said, were a century and a half to two centuries late in matching their curricula to the advances of civilization. But there were teachers in the ancient institutions who should welcome an opportunity to put fresher ideas into practice. He hoped to recruit some of Europe's "first characters" in scholarship. He would leave his own library to such an institution.*

He envisioned the university not as a monolithic structure but as an "academical village." He hoped to foster a true community of scholarship with students' quarters interspersed with the homes of the faculty.

Though Jefferson had the satisfaction as President of founding a school, the academy at West Point, this only whetted his appetite for creation of a broad-based institution of higher learning. In his message to Congress on December 2, 1806, he boldly called upon them to initiate a constitutional amendment to permit establishment of a truly national university. Soon, however, whatever their wishes might otherwise have been, the Congress were too concerned with the receipt of threatening missives and the threat of fatal missiles from foreign nations to consider importing scholars from them. The preservation of national sovereignty took precedence over the founding of a national university.

Jefferson's hopes for such an institution were not crushed. His naturally sanguine disposition and historian's perspective caused him to write Joel Barlow, who cherished similar hopes: "There is a snail-paced gait for the advance of new ideas on the general mind, under which we must acquiesce. A forty years' experience of popular assemblies has taught me that you must give them time for every step you take. If too hard pushed, they balk, and the machine retrogrades."[8]

Whether because of delight in teaching his young neighbors or philosophical resignation to the slow progress of his university project, or for some reason he himself did not know, Jefferson was in a decidedly optimistic mood when he wrote to two friends on March 5, 1810. In a letter to Dr. Walter Jones[9] he conceded that the nation was troubled by some discord at home and by threats from England, the world's greatest sea power, and France, its greatest force on land. But he said of American troubles, "When viewed in comparison to those of Europe, they are the joys of Paradise. . . . and the system of government which shall keep us afloat amidst the wreck of the world will be immortalized in history. We have, to be sure, our petty squabbles and heart burnings, and we have something of the blue devils at times, as to these rawheads and bloody-bones who are eating up other nations. But happily for us, the Mammoth cannot swim, nor the Leviathan move on dry land; and if we will keep out of their way, they cannot get at us. If, indeed, we choose to place ourselves within the scope of their tether, a gripe of the paw, or flounce of the tail, may be our fortune."

He still believed that the embargo had been a wise policy, one that if continued would have kept the United States out of the way of the chief belligerents until they had worn each other out or until it was in a better

---

*The proposals outlined to Tazewell, and other aspects of Jefferson's educational philosophy, are presented in more detail in Chapter XVI of this book.

position to defend its interests. "Our business," he said, "certainly was to be still. But a part of our nation chose to declare against this, in such a way as to control the wisdom of the government. I yielded with others, to avoid a greater evil. But from that moment, I have seen no system which could keep us entirely aloof from these agents of destruction. If there be any, I am certain that you, my friends, now charged with the care of us all, will see and pursue it. I give myself, therefore, no trouble with thinking or puzzling about it. Being confident in my watchmen I sleep soundly. God bless you all, and send you a safe deliverance."

If Jefferson's letter to Walter Jones was optimistic, the one he wrote the same day to Governor John Langdon of New Hampshire was positively ebullient. The first sentence brimmed with his old effusiveness: "Your letter, my dear friend, . . . comes like the refreshing dews of the evening on a thirsty soil." The memory of past tribulations did not depress him. It fed his hopes. "These have passed away, and so, I trust, will those of the present day. The toryism with which we struggled in '77 differed but in name from the federalism of '99, with which we struggled also; and the Anglicanism of 1808 against which we are now struggling is but the same thing still in another form."[10]

He was sure that the United States would emerge safely from its troubles if it would resist the blandishments of the English government. England, he said, "presents the singular phenomenon of a nation, the individuals of which are as faithful to their private engagements and duties, as honorable, as worthy, as those of any nation on earth, and whose government is yet the most unprincipled in this day known."

It is difficult to see how Jefferson found the British government more unprincipled than Napoleon's. But the quotation is important in clarifying what is sometimes cited as a paradox in Jefferson: his frequent condemnation of England despite his strong friendships with English men and women and his belief that three Englishmen—Bacon, Newton, and Locke—were the three greatest figures in modern history. Jefferson's words in this letter make it clear that his quarrel was not with the English people but with their government.

The main trouble with the English government, as he saw it, was that it was headed by an hereditary monarchy. Royalty, he argued, were bred to be unfit for the exercise of power. He gave the recipe:

Now, take any race of animals, confine them in idleness and inaction, whether in a sty, a stable or a state-room, pamper them with high diet, gratify all their sexual appetites, immerse them in sensualities, nourish their passions, let everything bend before them, and banish whatever might lead them to think, and in a few generations they become all body and no mind; and this, too, by a law of nature, by that very law by which we are in the constant practice of changing the characters and propensities of the animals we raise for our own purposes. Such is the regimen in raising Kings, and in this way they have gone on for centuries.

Then he got down to particulars:

STUART'S JEFFERSON   This 1805 portrait by Gilbert Stuart, through United States postage stamps and currency, has become the most familiar likeness of the President. Courtesy of the Colonial Williamsburg Foundation.

POPLAR FOREST   When Monticello was overrun with visitors, Jefferson had to build a retreat from his retreat. Constructed according to his own design, it was on a plantation ninety miles away, near Lynchburg. Photo by Tom Graves, Jr.; courtesy of Central Virginia Images Photography and the Corporation for Jefferson's Poplar Forest.

MARGARET BAYARD SMITH A perceptive chronicler of Washington life, she boasted that Jefferson had admitted her to his "sanctum sanctorum" where "any other feet but his own seldom intrude." Portrait by Charles Bird King. Courtesy of the Redwood Library and Athenaeum, Newport, Rhode Island.

JOHN RANDOLPH This Jefferson cousin was the President's most powerful opponent in Congress, becoming majority leader of the House of Representatives at age twenty-eight. He sometimes entered the legislative chamber in foxhunting togs, followed by his pack of hounds, and gestured with a riding crop as he addressed his colleagues. Portrait by John Wesley Jarvis, 1811. Courtesy of The New-York Historical Society, New York City.

AARON BURR Except for his hypnotically luminous eyes there was nothing unusual about this Jefferson antagonist until he started talking. His unguarded eloquence blew his disguise when he was fleeing the law to avoid trial for treason. Portrait by John Vanderlyn, 1809. Courtesy of The New-York Historical Society, New York City.

JOHN MARSHALL This great Chief Justice dined with Aaron Burr while presiding over his trial for treason. Cousin to Jefferson, he was the principal opponent of the President's attempt to reform the judiciary. In the processs he established the Supreme Court's power to declare an act of Congress unconstitutional. Portrait by John Wesley Jarvis, c. 1825. Courtesy of the Marshall-Wythe School of Law, College of William and Mary.

THE MARQUES DE CASA YRUJO Portraitist Gilbert Stuart captures the arrogance of this Spanish ambassador who imperiled Jefferson's plans for the Louisiana Purchase. The President was in the frustrating position of having an apt reply to the nobleman's charges but being unable to use it. From the private collection of Thomas R. McKean; courtesy of the Philadelphia Museum of Art.

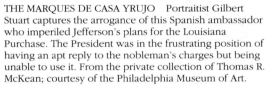

JAMES MONROE Jefferson's protégé's close friendship with his mentor was threatened when the President would not choose him over Madison as his successor. But Jefferson's diplomacy resolved differences and Monroe served as Madison's Secretary of State before succeeding him as Chief Executive with Jefferson's blessing. Portrait attributed to Rembrandt Peale, c. 1820. Courtesy of the James Monroe Museum and Library.

JAMES MADISON   The greatest friend
of Jefferson's mature years, Madison
was his Secretary of State and his
handpicked successor as President. He
also succeeded Jefferson as Rector of
the University of Virginia. Portrait by
Asher B. Durand, 1833. Courtesy of
The New-York Historical Society,
New York City.

JOSEPH C. CABELL   State Senator Cabell was
Jefferson's chief lieutenant in shepherding through
the Virginia General Assembly a bill for the
creation of the University of Virginia. Having
studied first-hand the great universities of Europe,
he afterwards worked knowledgeably and
faithfully to translate Jefferson's dream into reality.
Portrait by Louis M. D. Guillaume. Courtesy of the
Special Collections Department, Manuscripts
Division, University of Virginia Library.

FRANCIS WALKER GILMER   This young man,
whom Jefferson considered the most learned
Virginian of his generation, was sent by him to
Europe to recruit a faculty for the University of
Virginia. He was passionately in love with
Jefferson's granddaughter Ellen Randolph but his
sentiments were not returned and he called her
"the cold nymph of the mountain." Courtesy of the
Special Collections Department, Manuscripts
Division, University of Virginia Library.

ROBLEY DUNGLISON   Named to the first faculty of the University of Virginia, young Dr. Dunglison of Scotland became Jefferson's personal physician and his most frequent dinner guest. Though he became one of the world's most celebrated medical scientists, he said that his most interesting days were those spent with the President. Courtesy of the Special Collections Department, Manuscripts Division, University of Virginia Library.

THE ROTUNDA   Jefferson modeled this "focal building" of the University of Virginia after the Pantheon in Rome. A few days before his death at the age of eighty-three in 1826 he superintended the placement of the last remaining capital to top one of the six classical columns. Courtesy of the Special Collections Department, Printing Services Archive Neg. DS-740140.54, University Archives, University of Virginia Library.

THE LAWN AND ROTUNDA The long vista of Jefferson's "academical village" is one of the world's most famous university settings. In 1976 a jury of the American Institute of Architects adjudged his plans for the University of Virginia the most outstanding architectural designs by an American architect. Courtesy of the Special Collections Department, Printing Services Archive Neg. DS-770031, University Archives, University of Virginia Library.

DR. BENJAMIN RUSH The famous Philadelphia physician and signer of the Declaration of Independence was a friend to whom Jefferson confided religious views that he shared with few people. Telling John Adams of a strange, prophetic dream, Rush effected a reconciliation between him and Jefferson. The Adams-Jefferson correspondence is now a national treasure. Portrait by Thomas Sully, c. 1813. Courtesy of the National Museum of American Art, Smithsonian Institution; lent by Deborah Norris Brock Rush and Lockwood Rush.

CORNELIA JEFFERSON RANDOLPH   Jefferson's elegantly coiffed granddaughter joined him in a rugged horseback ride over the Blue Ridge Mountains. He encouraged her to read the great Latin and Greek classics and all the modern English and French literature and pronounced her one of the "severest students" he had ever known. Terra cotta bust by William Coffee, c. 1819. Courtesy of Monticello, Thomas Jefferson Memorial Foundation, Inc.

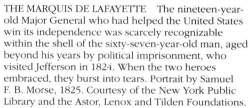

THE MARQUIS DE LAFAYETTE   The nineteen-year-old Major General who had helped the United States win its independence was scarcely recognizable within the shell of the sixty-seven-year-old man, aged beyond his years by political imprisonment, who visited Jefferson in 1824. When the two heroes embraced, they burst into tears. Portrait by Samuel F. B. Morse, 1825. Courtesy of the New York Public Library and the Astor, Lenox and Tilden Foundations.

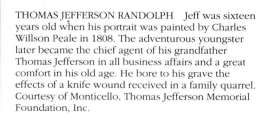

THOMAS JEFFERSON RANDOLPH   Jeff was sixteen years old when his portrait was painted by Charles Willson Peale in 1808. The adventurous youngster later became the chief agent of his grandfather Thomas Jefferson in all business affairs and a great comfort in his old age. He bore to his grave the effects of a knife wound received in a family quarrel. Courtesy of Monticello, Thomas Jefferson Memorial Foundation, Inc.

THOMAS JEFFERSON, 1825   Jefferson understandably looks grim. Sculptor John H. I. Browere almost smothered the eighty-two-year-old statesman in making the life mask from which he modeled this plaster bust. Five years later the artist was charged with graverobbing to make a death mask of another prominent American. Courtesy of the New York State Historical Association, Cooperstown.

WEST FRONT OF MONTICELLO   This idyllic watercolor, commissioned by Jefferson's granddaughter Ellen Wayles Randolph, was painted by Jane Bradick near the time of his death. The little boy with the hoop is Jefferson's grandson George Wythe Randolph, who became the Confederate States Secretary of War. The two young women in the middle ground are the President's granddaughters Mary Jefferson Randolph and Cornelia Jefferson Randolph. Courtesy of Monticello, Thomas Jefferson Memorial Foundation, Inc.

While in Europe, I often amused myself with contemplating the characters of the then reigning sovereigns of Europe. Louis the XVI was a fool, of my own knowledge, and in despite of the answers made for him at his trial. The King of Spain was a fool, and of Naples the same. They passed their lives in hunting, and despatched two couriers a week, one thousand miles, to let each other know what game they had killed the preceding days. The King of Sardinia was a fool. All these were Bourbons. The Queen of Portugal, a Braganza, was an idiot by nature. And so was the king of Denmark. Their sons, as regents, exercised the powers of government. The King of Prussia, successor to the great Frederick, was a mere hog in body as well as in mind. Gustavus of Sweden, and Joseph of Austria, were really crazy, and George of England, you know, was in a straight waistcoat. There remained, then, none but old Catharine, who had been too lately picked up to have lost her common sense. In this state Bonaparte found Europe; and it was this state of its rulers which lost it with scarce a struggle. These animals had become without mind and powerless; and so will every hereditary monarch be after a few generations. Alexander, the grandson of Catharine, is as yet an exception. He is able to hold his own. But he is only of the third generation. His race is not yet worn out. And so endeth the book of Kings, from all of whom the Lord deliver us, and have you, my friend, and all such good men and true, in His holy keeping.

Ironically, Jefferson himself was descended from some famous monarchs, notably King David I of Scotland, Alfred the Great, and Charlemagne.[11] Doubtless he would have seen these great men as examples of what a sovereign could be in the inchoate stages of monarchical government when a King had to be energetic to survive and he would have counted himself fortunate that his line had been saved from degeneracy by losing its thrones.

The most important feature of Jefferson's letter to Governor Langdon, aside from its revelation of his rising spirits, was its style—sinewy, sprightly, and graceful. With Jefferson's retirement, his letters seemed to gain in eloquence. Maybe it was because he had more time for their composition. Maybe it was because, freed from the minutiae of public administration, his literary creativity flourished.

Jefferson's restored optimism was not simply the passing euphoria of a single day. On March 14 he wrote to Abbe Salimankis,[12] thanking him for a pamphlet. "That it contains many serious truths and sound admonitions," he said, "every reader will be sensible. At the same time it is a comfort that the medal has two sides. I do not myself contemplate human nature in quite so somber a view. That there is much vice and misery in the world, I know; but more virtue and happiness, I believe, at least in our part of it; the latter being the lot of those employed in agriculture in a greater degree than of other callings."

But his optimistic expressions could have an acerbic tinge, as in his letter thanking Robert Fulton for the gift of a pamphlet describing his newly invented torpedo. "I am not afraid of new inventions or improvements," he said, "nor bigoted to the practices of our forefathers. It is that bigotry which keeps the Indians in a state of barbarism in the midst of the arts, would have kept us in the same state even now, and still keeps Connecticut where their ancestors were when they landed on these shores."[13]

Correspondence was for Jefferson now almost always an interest but sometimes a burden. From all over the United States and abroad came letters seeking the advice or the endorsement of the Sage of Monticello. Those addressed to the sage, ranging from the practical to the quixotic, were usually more interesting than those addressed to the ex-President. The month of May brought typical variety.

From the trustees for a lottery to benefit East Tennessee College came a request that Jefferson accept tickets to sell in Virginia. He told them, "It would be impossible for them to come to a more inefficient hand. I rarely go from home, and consequently see but a few neighbors and friends, who occasionally call on me. And having myself made it a rule never to engage in a lottery or any other adventure of mere chance, I can, with the less candor of effect, urge it on others, however laudable or desirable its object may be."[14] He then suggested some things for them to consider in building a college. He deplored "the common plan followed in this country, but not in others, of making one large and expensive building." He suggested the construction of buildings linked by barracks of students' rooms "opening into a covered way to give a dry communication between all the schools. The whole of these, arranged around an open square of grass and trees, would make it what it should be in fact, an academical village, instead of a large and common den of noise, of filth, and of fetid air. It would afford that quiet retirement so friendly to study, and lessen the dangers of fire, infection, and tumult."

Obviously, Jefferson had clearly in mind the essential physical design of the university which he longed for in Virginia. His letter to the Tennessee trustees concluded without the slightest hint that they might have been presumptuous in trying to make a ticket salesman of the elder statesman and seer. Instead, he wrote, "I pray you to pardon me if I have stepped aside into the province of counsel." He hoped that they would "pardon the presumption," as he was motivated by the idea his plan would lend itself to piecemeal construction and thus might ease the financial burden of getting started.

A few days later he was writing to James Madison,[15] not about the problems of the presidency but about the importation of merino sheep to improve Virginia flocks. The two friends were importing the rams, some selling for thousands of dollars apiece. Jefferson wrote, "No sentiment is more acknowledged in the family of Agricoltists than that the few who can afford it should incur the risk and expense of all new improvements, and give the benefit freely to the many of more restricted circumstances. The question then recurs, What are we to do with them? . . . that we may have some proposition to begin upon, I will throw out a first idea, to be modified or postponed to whatever you shall think better. Give all the full-blooded males we can raise to the different counties of our state, one to each, as fast as we can furnish them. And as there must be some rule of priority for the distribution, let us begin with our own counties, which are contiguous and nearly central to the state, and proceed, circle after circle, till we have given a ram to every county. This will take about seven years." Jefferson had planned how the generous project could be organized and had calculated how many generations of breeding would be necessary to raise the flocks to the desired level. "There will be danger," he said, "that what is here proposed, though but an act of ordinary duty, may be perverted into one of ostentation, but malice will always find bad motives for good actions. . . . We may guard against this perhaps by a proper reserve, [revealing] our purpose only by its execution."

To G. Voolif, perpetual secretary of the First Class of the Royal Institute of Sciences, of Literature and of Fine Arts, at Amsterdam, Jefferson wrote a letter[16] of appreciation upon being made an honorary member of the organization. He also said he was "duly sensible of the honor done" him "by the approbation which his Majesty the King of Holland has condescended to give to their choice. His patronage of institutions for extending among mankind the boundaries of information proves his just sense of the cares devolved on him by his high station, and commands the approving voice of all the sons of men." Doubtless Jefferson's attitude was softened by the honor and he was habitually effusive in thanking the most humble as well as the most exalted. Besides, he had said that there were exceptions among monarchs. Nevertheless, his language was more that of a courtier than of one who had trenchantly expressed his contempt for royalty.

Later he was writing to Count Pahlen, the newly arrived Envoy Extraordinary and Minister Plenipotentiary of Russia: "I am much flattered by the kind notice of the Emperor, which you have been so obliging as to communicate to me. The approbation of the good is always consoling; but that of a sovereign whose station and endowments are so preeminent is received with the sensibility which the veneration for his character inspires."[17] Even in his letter blasting royalty, he had said: "Alexander . . . is as yet an exception." There was no catering here. Jefferson would have been equally gracious to a praiseworthy serf in the Emperor's dominions.

Writing to Virginia's Governor John Tyler, Jefferson deplored the state of higher education and professional training in the United States. Law studies, he said, definitely had declined. "I still lend my counsel and books to such young students as will fix themselves in the neighborhood." Otherwise they, like others, would obtain only an "elegant digest." He saw too many graduating after an easy beginning and an easy ending, with a light "intermediate course of two or three years." Sarcastically he lamented: "Now men are born scholars, lawyers, doctors; in our day, this was confined to poets."[18]

In answer to an appeal from the Governor, he said: "You wish to see me in the legislature, but this is impossible, my mind is now so dissolved in tranquility that it can never again encounter a contentious assembly."

But he was no longer protesting that he was through with public measures. "I have indeed two great measures at heart, without which no republic can maintain itself in strength. 1. That of general education, to enable every man to judge for himself what will secure or endanger his freedom. 2. To divide every county into hundreds of such size that all the children of each will be within reach of a central school in it."

"Hundred" was an English term designating a county division large enough to have its own court, or "hundred moot." The term had been used in Virginia in 1619, when the first legislative body in English America met at Jamestown.[19] Besides administering public schools, the hundreds envisioned by Jefferson would perform the functions of New England townships. "These little republics," he said, "would be the main strength of the great one. We owe to them the vigor given to our Revolution in its commencement in the Eastern states, and by them the Eastern states were enabled to repeal the embargo in opposition to the Middle, Southern, and Western states, and their large and lubberly division into counties which can never be assembled. . . . Could I once see this I should consider it as the dawn of the salvation of the republic, and say with old Simeon, 'Nunc dimittis, Domine.' "[20]

Jefferson's enthusiasm for this plan accords well with his long-held conviction that government, insofar as possible, should be kept close to the people. But it seems to threaten the significance of the states, and therefore it is strange that it should be advocated by one who, when he said "my country," so often meant Virginia.

After giving his prescription for solving the nation's problems, the ex-President concluded: "But our children will be as wise as we are, and will establish in the fullness of time those things not yet ripe for establishment. So be it, and to yourself health, happiness, and long life."

The flow of Jefferson's sparkling letters on a variety of subjects to correspondents in many parts of the world almost dried up in June. Not until July 16 did he reply to a letter from William Lambert enclosing some scientific treatises on which the writer sought his opinion, together with some papers praising the ex-President's work. After thanking Lambert for the flattering references to himself, Jefferson declined to comment on the scientific papers, saying that he had "no doubt of their accuracy" but his "own familiarity with the subject had been too long suspended to enable [him] to render a critical opinion on them." He apologized for his "late acknowledgement" of Lambert's letter, saying, "An indispensable piece of business, which has occupied me for a month past, obliged me to suspend all correspondence during that time."[21]

His explanation was substantially accurate, but he had not suspended all correspondence on one topic—the one that had dominated his thoughts. His concern began just past mid-May, when he received a disturbing letter from John Wickham, the brilliant Richmond attorney who had been chief counsel for the defense in the trial of Aaron Burr. Wickham said that Edward Livingston of New Orleans had asked him to bring an action against Jefferson in federal court. The attorney said that, whether or not he participated in any subsequent proceedings, professional responsibility required that he institute them.[22]

Despite the fact that he himself was a lawyer, or perhaps because of it, Jefferson always agonized over any threat of a suit. This time his anxiety was increased by the fact that the laconic message gave no particulars of the impending action.

Jefferson had a general idea of what the suit must be about. As President of the United States, he had been indirectly in controversy with Livingston since October 1807, when Secretary of State Madison, acting for the Chief Executive, instructed the United States Marshal of the Orleans Territory to remove squatters from a certain piece of land claimed by the federal government. This tract, running along the Mississippi in New Orleans, was known as the Batture, that being a French word for land formed from a river or other body of water. The Batture was contiguous to land to which Livingston had a clear title, and he claimed it too as his own. The city of New Orleans, on the other hand, claimed that the Batture was in the public domain.

The case was complicated by the prominence and political affiliations of the principal actor on the scene. A member of one of New York State's most prominent families, Livingston had been an outspoken Republican Congressman before being elected mayor of New York City in the same year in which Jefferson became President. He served simultaneously as United States District Attorney for the state of New York. During an epidemic of yellow fever in 1803, he himself, while striving to aid the distressed, became a victim. On recovering his health, he found that a subordinate in the district attorney's office had taken advantage of his absence to steal from public funds.

Believing himself morally, if not legally, responsible, Livingston vowed to make good the government's losses. To this end he surrendered his property in New York, resigned both as District Attorney and as Mayor, and moved to New Orleans to begin life anew.

Before long he attracted a considerable law clientele in his new home and was once again on his way to wealth. He began acquiring property and moved from success to success until he invited controversy by claiming the Batture as part of his lands.

Jefferson, unanimously supported by his cabinet, backed the claim of public domain. Livingston sued the city in the territorial court and won, but Jefferson, advised by Attorney General Caesar Rodney, claimed that the property belonged to the United States government as successor to the French and Spanish crowns, to which it had belonged. The territorial court, he insisted, had no jurisdiction in the case. The President was influenced by Governor Claiborne of Louisiana, who wrote to the Secretary of State: "Mr. Livingston is alike feared and hated by most of the ancient inhabitants. They dread his talents as a lawyer, and hate his view of speculation, which in the case of the Batture was esteemed very generally by the Louisianians no less iniquitous than ruinous to the welfare of the city."[23] Therefore, by Jefferson's orders, when Livingston tried to build a levee and develop the property his workers were chased off.

On March 7, 1808, six days after learning from Claiborne that Livingston's workers had been forced to vacate the Batture, the President referred the matter to Congress.[24] It was, he believed, the appropriate body to deal with questions of United States sovereignty over lands acquired by treaty. Just as in the case of the Louisiana Purchase, Jefferson believed that Congress had the power to disapprove his action. It also had the power to appoint commissioners to study the matter and make recommendations, or indeed to deal with the controversy in any way it saw fit. When Jefferson retired from the presidency, Congress still had not acted. In fact it had not acted when Livingston initiated his suit against Jefferson.

Soon after receiving Wickham's letter at Monticello, Jefferson learned that Livingston was suing him for $100,000 for trespass and damages. A victory for the plaintiff could have meant Jefferson's financial ruin. In these circumstances he did a curious thing: he asked Wickham to be his attorney. The Richmond lawyer declined. Jefferson must have been almost certain he would but perhaps did not want to lose even a remote chance of engaging the foremost attorney in Virginia.

Jefferson then obtained the services of George Hay and William Wirt, who had prosecuted Burr. Brilliant and effectively, even if floridly, eloquent, Wirt had gained in stature since his impressive performance in that celebrated trial. A little later he also engaged Littleton W. Tazewell, an attorney respected throughout Virginia and beyond for both ability and integrity.

When deeply engrossed in the problems of the presidency, especially successive international crises, Jefferson had given little personal study to the complex ramifications of the Batture problem. He had depended on what he was told by those he trusted. Now, however, as the object of a suit threatening both his financial security and his reputation, he became a diligent student of the issues posed.

Governor Claiborne, who liked Jefferson and disliked Livingston, hastened to express his regret that the ex-President's well-earned tranquility had been disturbed by one who apparently was "unprincipled."[25] Gallatin used the same word in conveying his sympathy, calling the plaintiff "an unprincipled and delinquent speculator."[26] The Richmond *Enquirer*, dependably loyal, championed Jefferson; but, even when the charges were accompanied by a vigorous defense, it was painful to have them trumpeted in the press. Hay earnestly sought from Jefferson every scrap of evidence that could be used in his defense. "The subject," he wrote, "is not understood; in fact, it is grossly misunderstood." Such words were painful to the sensitive elder statesman who had hoped to escape public controversies when he left Washington.

Livingston had taken his case to the public by publishing a pamphlet titled *An Address to the People of the United States*. With characteristic thoroughness, Jefferson researched both the legal and historical evidence, drawing on records in Latin, French, and Spanish as well as English. His energy was comparable to that with which almost three decades before he had brought forth a full-scale book, *Notes on the State of Virginia*, in answer to a questionnaire from a French diplomat. Again he produced a book, *The Proceedings of the Government of the United States in Maintaining the Public Right Against the Intrusion of Edward Livingston*. The earlier work has been called "probably the most important scientific and political book written by an American before 1785."[27] The new book served a much narrower purpose.

Livingston issued another pamphlet in reply to Jefferson's 91-page book, charging him with mistranslations and very selective use of the available evidence. Jefferson sought still more ammunition from the State and Treasury departments. He was in an agony of apprehension that, "under the intrigues and urgency of Livingston," Congress might "be induced to take some step which might have an injurious effect on the opinion of a jury."[28] Specifically, he feared that Congress might act to validate Livingston's title. He could not maintain that the legislative branch had no right to act. After all, as President, after instructing a United States Marshal to drive out the "squatters," he had referred the issue to Congress to settle as it saw fit.

He wished to have the Attorney General "attend the case as a public concern, for really it is so. It would be totally unnecessary for me to employ counsel to go into the question at all for my own defense. That is solidly built on the simple fact that, if I were in error, it was honest, and not imputable to that gross and palpable corruption or injustice which makes a public magistrate responsible to a private party. I know that even a federal jury could not find a verdict against me on this head. But I go fully into the question of title because our characters are concerned in it, and because it involves a most important right of the citizens, and one which, if decided against them would be a precedent of incalculable evil." He had escalated to superlatives, as he so often did under stress.

Jefferson feared that he would not receive a fair trial with John Marshall and Cyrus Griffin presiding. The first he had accused of "the base prostitution of law to party passions," the second of "imbecility."[29] Worse, he believed Griffin to be a slavish follower of Marshall. Jefferson wrote Madison that the Chief Justice's "twistifications in the case of Marbury, in that of Burr, and the late Yazoo case show how dexterously he can reconcile law to his personal biases; and nobody seems to doubt that he is ready prepared to decide that Livingston's right to the Batture is unquestionable, and that I am bound to pay for it with my private fortune."[30] Neither Jefferson nor Marshall was at his noblest when describing the other.

The ex-President urged Hay to enter a technical plea that the case was not properly within the jurisdiction of the federal court in Richmond as the land in question was in New Orleans. He hoped on these grounds to have the suit dismissed. At the same time he worried that such a plea would "place everything under the grip of the judge, who in the cases of Marbury and of Burr has given us lessons of the plastic nature of law in his hands."[31] Hay argued with Jefferson that escaping on a technicality would do nothing to clear his record in the public mind, that it might indeed excite suspicion.[32]

By August, however, Jefferson again was desperate enough to suggest reliance on a technicality. He wanted to plead that Livingston, being a citizen of a territory, was therefore not a citizen of a state and hence not within the jurisdiction of a federal court. Reluctantly, Hay agreed to comply with his client's wishes.

By this time Jefferson had sufficiently recovered from his siege mentality to make some of the intellectual sorties in which he delighted. He had found time to translate a chapter of Destutt de Tracy's *Idéologues*, still in manuscript, and send it as a sample to William Duane with the recommendation that he publish the entire work in English. The French Senator's book, Jefferson said a little later, was "the most valuable political work of the present age." Jefferson had corresponded with this libertarian nobleman and admired him. Besides, the subject and character of the work appealed to him. It was a point-by-point discussion of Montesquieu's *De l'Esprit des Lois*, consisting of both endorsements and refutations. This accorded well with the views of Jefferson, who had gone from extravagant admiration of the philosophical classic in early years (including twenty-seven excisions from it in his own twenty-eight-page Commonplace Book) to a pronounced antipathy in later years to some of its Anglophile observations.[33] And Jefferson astutely perceived that Destutt's own book was a future classic. In addition, the circumstances of publication appealed strongly to the pleasure in mystery and innocent intrigue, which was still almost as strong in Jefferson as when he and John Page, both in their teens, had corresponded in a secret code. Because of the political climate in France, it was deemed unwise for Destutt to acknowledge authorship. Instead, the plan was for the book to appear first in English and in the United States, as if it were the work of an anonymous American and only later in France in what purported to be a translation.

He also had the excitement of becoming a great-grandfather, when Anne Cary Randolph Bankhead gave birth to a boy. The event was a reminder of his increasing age but also of the continuity of life.

He continued too to enjoy the role of farmer, even though the acres surrounding Monticello were not nearly so rich in fertility as in beauty. In a letter to Charles Willson Peale,[34] who had now moved out of Philadelphia to enjoy farm life, he said: "I have often thought that if Heaven had given me choice of my position and calling, it should have been on a rich spot of earth, well watered, and near a good market for the productions of the garden. No occupation is so delightful to me as the culture of the earth, and no culture comparable to that of the garden. Such a variety of subjects, some one always coming to perfection, the failure of one thing repaired by the success of another, and instead of one harvest a continued one through the year."

He said too, "But though an old man, I am but a young gardener." He meant of course that despite his advanced years, he had been so distracted by a public career that he had little personal experience in the art and science of cultivating the earth. But the observation was also true in another sense. To gardening he brought a youthful enthusiasm.

The birth of his great-grandchild and the rebirth of the seasons melded in a reassuring reaffirmation of life. There was much hope mingled with a quantum of resignation in the letter he wrote on May 26, 1811, to his granddaughter Anne, who, with little John Warner Bankhead, was visiting her in-laws: "Nothing new has happened in our neighborhood since you left us. The houses and trees stand where they did. The flowers come forth like the belles of the day, have their short reign of beauty and splendor, and retire like them to the more interesting office of reproducing their like. The hyacinths and tulips are off the stage, the irises are giving place to the belladonnas, as this will to the tuberoses etc. As your Mama has done to you, my dear Anne, as you will do to the sisters of little John, and as I shall soon and cheerfully do to you all in wishing you a long, long, goodnight."[35]

The pleasures of gardening, however, were severely curtailed in the troubled summer of 1811 by an attack of rheumatism so severe that he was unable to walk. Pain gripped his back, hips, and thighs. Fortunately, he was without pain or fever as long as he remained still. From Poplar Forest he wrote Dr. Benjamin Rush on August 17 that the ninety-mile ride from Monticello in a hardgoing gig had given him "great sufferings which I expect will be renewed on my return as soon as I am able." By this time he had regained the ability to walk but reported, "A pain when I walk seems to have fixed itself in my hip and to threaten permanence. . . . The loss of the power of taking exercise would be a sore affliction to me. It has been the delight of my retirement to be in constant bodily activity looking after my affairs."[36] Though he did not say so, he must have been caught in a vicious cycle, the stress of his worries intensifying if not triggering his arthritis and the arthritis in turn depriving him of physical exertion to help his nerves.

If Monticello was his retreat from the world, then Poplar Forest was his retreat from Monticello when the world's importunities pursued him even to his mountaintop. He described it to Rush as a place "which I visit three or four times a year, and stay from a fortnight to a month at a time. I have fixed myself comfortably, keep some books here, bring others occasionally, am in the solitude of a hermit, and quite at leisure to [write] to my absent friends."

He had not surrendered his mind to worry during the difficulties of recent months. "Having to conduct my grandson through his course of mathematics, I have resumed that study with great avidity." Obviously, it supplied something most welcome amid the shifting uncertainties of this stage of his life. "We have no theories there, no uncertainties remain on the mind; all is demonstration and satisfaction."

But even this pleasure was sullied by what he perceived as another sign of deterioration. "I have forgotten much," he wrote, "and recover it with more difficulty than when in the vigor of my mind I originally acquired it. It is wonderful to me that old men should not be sensible that their minds keep pace with their bodies in the progress of decay. Our old revolutionary friend Clinton, for example, who was a hero, but never a man of mind, is wonderfully jealous on this head. He tells eternally the stories of his younger days to prove his memory, as if memory and reason were the same faculty. Nothing betrays imbecility so much as the being insensible of it. Had not a conviction of the danger to which an unlimited occupation of the executive chair would expose the republican constitution of our government, made it conscientiously a duty to retire when I did, the fear of becoming a dotard and of being insensible of it, would of itself have resisted all solicitations to remain."

He closed on what seemed a melancholy note of resignation. "The sedentary character of my public occupations sapped a constitution naturally sound and vigorous, and draws it to an earlier close. But it will still last quite as long as I wish it. There is a fullness of time when men should go, and not occupy too long the ground to which others have a right to advance." Meanwhile, he found comfort in friendship, "the true old man's milk and restorative cordial."

Less than a week later Jefferson's supposedly deteriorated mind had produced a new design for an especially precise sundial and had calculated its adjustment for the proper horary lines for latitudinal variations. "The calculations are for every five minutes of time and are always exact to within less than half a second of a degree." He also had a suggestion about the material for the dial. "Slate, as being less affected by the sun, is preferable to wood or metal."[37]

Meanwhile, he continued to view almost every development in light of the judicial threat hanging over him. Not only was he worried about what might happen in the federal court in Richmond, but, even if he should win there, the plaintiff might appeal the case to the Federalist-dominated United States Supreme Court. Accordingly, when Justice William Cushing, a staunch Massachusetts Federalist, died, Jefferson wrote Gallatin: "I observe old Cushing is dead. At length, then, we have a chance of getting a Republican majority in the Supreme judiciary. For ten years has that branch braved the spirit and will of the nation. . . . The event is a fortunate one, and so timed as to be a Godsend to me." A court with a Federalist majority, he insisted, would simply do the will of John Marshall. His "inveteracy is profound, and his mind of that gloomy malignity which will never let him forego the opportunity of satiating it on a victim."[38]

Jefferson suggested that Madison appoint Levi Lincoln as Cushing's successor. He was from the same state and was a true Republican. Even more important, though the ex-President didn't say so, Lincoln had been his own loyal Attorney General and was still his personal friend. Jefferson conceded that Lincoln was no profound interpreter of the law but argued that no lawyer from the Northeast was. "Their system of jurisprudence, made up from the Jewish law, a little dash of common law, and a great mass of original notions of their own, is a thing *sui generis*."[39]

Death removed another Federalist from the bench. This time it was Cyrus Griffin of the federal court in Richmond. Jefferson privately urged Madison to appoint John Tyler. The former Governor of Virginia was an honest and able man, and Madison was happy to comply. This development meant that, when Jefferson's case came before the district court in Richmond, the judge sharing the bench with the Chief Justice would be one of the ex-President's longtime friends and, moreover, one who owed his appointment partly to Jefferson's support. Jefferson does not seem to have seen any contradiction between his rejoicing over this circumstance and his own earlier shock at John Marshall's presiding over the trial of Aaron Burr after having dinner with him. Jefferson was a man of astonishing intellectual fecundity and versatility and a master of logic to boot. But he was much swayed by his emotions. Anyone who tries to fit him to the procrustean bed of the quintessential "Man of Reason" will either quit in frustration or distort the reality of the man beyond recognition.

When Livingston's case came before the federal court in Richmond, Hay reluctantly pleaded, as his employer wished, that the Louisiana territorial resident was not the citizen of a state and therefore was outside the jurisdiction of the court. Tyler wrote an opinion granting the motion and Marshall concurred. So on December 5, 1811, the case was dismissed. Ironically, Jefferson, who had agonized about the matter so long, was being a hermit at Poplar Forest when the case was thrown out. He learned about it on his return to Monticello—twenty-three days later.

He did not relax. Not only as self protection but as a duty to the public, he told Hay, the case should be published to the American people. Otherwise, he said, his fellow citizens would be misled by Livingston's "squalling as if his throat had been cut."[40] Age and retirement, he said, had rendered public controversy even more repugnant than it had formerly been, but the responsibility could not be shirked. He must publish the book that he had prepared as a brief for his lawyers. He was aware that most readers would consider it "unnecessarily erudite and pedantic," but he lacked the energy to produce a more popular version.

His fears on this score were warranted. The work included lengthy quotations in Spanish, French, Latin, and Greek. He sent the manuscript to Ezra Sargeant, of New York, the only printer in the United States he deemed qualified to handle the multilingual assignment. The title was not likely to mislead any potential reader into the belief that a lively popular chronicle awaited him. Jefferson called the work *The Proceedings of the Government of the United States, in Maintaining the Public Right to the Beach of the Mississippi, adjacent to New Orleans, against the Intrusion of Edward Livingston.*

In March 1812 the book was in print and the author sent copies to members of Congress, high-ranking federal officials, and many personal acquaintances—including, strangely enough, Livingston's brother Robert. Wirt, who as Jefferson's attorney was not an unbiased judge, praised the work for its combination of "lightness and solidity. of beauty and power," and pronounced it, "by far the best piece of Grecian architecture that I have ever seen, either from ancient or modern times, "[41] a description which must have appealed strongly to the classically minded author. While some said, as Jefferson himself had, that it was ill suited to general taste, others praised the industry and erudition that had produced it.

Livingston was frustrated by the turn of events. He could bring Jefferson to trial only in a New Orleans court and then, since Jefferson was not a local property owner, only if the ex-President happened to be in New Orleans. Quite apart from the Batture controversy, Jefferson could foresee nothing that would cause him ever to leave Virginia again. He did not propose to go to Washington, much less New Orleans.

Jefferson's emotionalism in fighting the case—even after it had been decided in the court and in his favor—should not blind us to the fact that valid legal issues were involved. The case became recognized by legal experts as "the leading one in the United States for the proposition that actions for trespass to real estate must be brought in the district where the land is located."[42]

Nevertheless, one is inclined to lament the vast amount of talent, energy, and acrimony poured into the dispute by two talented Americans, each intent upon revealing the other as a monster. Jefferson and Livingston, under other circumstances, might have delighted in each other's company. Both were patrician politicians born to privilege but at war with Federalist protectors of privilege. Each was of a generally benevolent cast of mind. Each was a distinguished scholar—Jefferson as one of the greatest polymaths of his time and Livingston as one whose legal writings would become international classics. But Jefferson, distracted by many emergencies amid the pressures of the presidency, dealt from afar, and perhaps superficially, with a local crisis until it became a national cause célèbre. And Livingston, his pride stung and his stubbornness aroused, saw himself as the object of persecution. Each man saw the other as his sworn enemy. Jefferson was unduly sensitive about his reputation because of some of the calumnies circulated during his presidency. Livingston was overprotective of his good name because of the scandal caused by the defalcation of an employee in New York. So these two worthy citizens used their extensive vocabularies to mold epithets attacking each other and diverted their scholarly energies from extensive projects for the public good so that they could concentrate on unremitting war over an issue that might have been settled amicably. When Jefferson had been a member of Washington's cabinet, and the national capital had been in Philadelphia, he had lamented that politics could make good men, including old friends, cross the street to avoid speaking to each other. As he now had helped to prove, it could also lead them to march inexorably, from opposite ends of the same street, on a collision course.

XIV

WAR AND FRIENDSHIP

TIDES OF WAR dashed against American shores by the storms of Europe soon placed in proper perspective the teapot tempest over the Batture. The threatened loss of that celebrated piece of real estate by the federal government to one of its own citizens shrank to insignificance beside the danger that all of New Orleans, and with it control of the Mississippi, might pass to a foreign power. Any perceived danger from Livingston's efforts to build a levee on disputed acreage was dwarfed when the flood tide of war that had engulfed Europe swept toward North America like a tidal wave.

Jefferson's absorption in the smaller conflict kept him from bombarding Madison and Gallatin with advice as he had his attorneys in the Batture case. But in March 1812, with his book about the dispute with Livingston being circulated, he could turn his attention toward the larger threat. He wrote Madison, "Everybody in this quarter expects the declaration of war as soon as the season will permit the entrance of militia into Canada, and although peace may be their personal interest and wish, they would I think disapprove of its longer continuance under the wrongs inflicted and unredressed by England."[1]

Augustus J. Foster, British Minister to the United States, said that to some young Congressmen war was "as necessary to America as a duel is to a young officer to prevent his being bullied and elbowed in society." John Randolph of Roanoke, turning political ornithologist, claimed to have discovered a new species, the "war hawks," readily identifiable by their whippoorwill-like cry, "one monotonous tone—Canada! Canada! Canada!"[2] Generally recognized as the leader of the group was Henry Clay, a Kentucky Congressman born and reared in Virginia. At the start of the 1810–1811 session, at the age of thirty-four, Clay was elected Speaker of the House and thus became the second most powerful man in the federal government. A fervent supporter of Clay's belligerent views was a still younger Congressman, the chairman of the Foreign Relations Committee, twenty-nine-year-old John C. Calhoun of South Carolina. Western Congressmen were strong for war and particularly eager for the conquest of Canada, partly as an expression of national chauvinism and because of the chance to acquire more forest lands for settlement, but even more because of the constant danger of attacks along the frontier by Britain's Indian allies. Clay encouraged these designs on the northern neighbor. "The militia of Kentucky" unaided, he told his followers, were "competent to place Montreal and upper Canada at your feet."

In his message to Congress on April 1, President Madison called for an immediate and general embargo for sixty days. Welcoming the proposal as a move toward war, the House enacted it by a vote of 70 to 41. In the Senate moderate Republicans obtained an amendment extending the embargo to ninety days and comparably, they hoped, increasing the chances of success by diplomacy. The measure became law on April 4, and six days later Congress empowered the President to call up 100,000 militia for six months' service.

On that same day, April 10, by coincidence, British Foreign Secretary Lord Castlereagh dispatched to the President a reiteration that his Majesty's government refused to annul the Orders in Council. Madison accepted the communication as a final confirmation of English intransigence.

Soon, however, with British factories closing, and unemployment and prices soaring simultaneously, both employers and employees in the United Kingdom petitioned Parliament to consider repeal of the orders. Seeing that his hold on office was tenuous at best, Prime Minister Spencer Perceval determined to comply, but on May 11, before he could execute his plan, he was assassinated. The emergency caused a lengthy delay, and a forthcoming suspension of the orders was not announced until June 16. Nevertheless, so it seemed, here was vindication of the foreign policy pursued by Jefferson and Madison.

But on June 1 President Madison told Congress that Great Britain's impressment of United States seamen, disregard of neutral rights and territorial waters, blockade of American harbors, and refusal after all these offenses to repeal the Orders in Council, provided ample grounds for a declaration of war. Three days later the House voted 79 to 49 for war. The more cautious Senate acted more slowly. Finally, though, on June 18, unaware that Britain two days before had announced a decision to lift the hated orders, the Senate voted 19 to 13 for war. On June 19, 1812, the President proclaimed that the United States and the United Kingdom were at war.

Several months before the declaration Jefferson had confided to Madison his anxiety that Congress would not prove adequate to the emergency. He feared that an assembly including a hundred lawyers would never stop talking long enough to do anything.[3] But, except for a transient observation that America's young men had had no military experience and that its experienced men were too old for the strain, he had faith in the soldiers of the United States. Throwing aside the caution that had characterized most of his estimates when he himself was President, he rivaled the optimism of the young War Hawks. On August 4 he wrote to Duane, the editor and publisher, "The acquisition of Canada this year, as far as the neighborhood of Quebec, will be a mere matter of marching, and will give us experience for the attack on Halifax the next, and the final expulsion of England from the American continent."[4]

By presidential appointment, Henry Dearborn, Jefferson's former Secretary of War, had succeeded James Wilkinson as ranking officer in the United States Army, though that flamboyant old survivor had once again emerged, robust and gaudily flourishing, from a well-publicized court-martial. While loyal, dependable, and altogether a big improvement on Wilkinson, Major General Dearborn brought little imagination to his assignment. He was expected to guard the border from the Niagara River to New England and to take Montreal. Dearborn spent much time and energy in ensuing weeks in New England promoting recruitment and trying to persuade the Governors to call out the militia. These Federalist officials were most familiar with Dearborn in his role of Republican politician. In mid-August, Madison wrote Jefferson that "seditious opposition" in two states, Massachusetts and Connecticut, had "clogged the wheels of the war."[5]

Because of these obstructions and delays, the invasion of Canada came through Detroit and was led by William Hull, newly named Brigadier General in command of the Michigan Territory, which he had served as Governor by appointment from Jefferson. Without gaining naval control of Lake Erie, the Americans marched on the British outpost at Detroit, trusting to disgruntled inhabitants of the area to rise in revolt at first sight of a liberating army. The residents showed no such enthusiasm, Hull's forces were trapped, and he surrendered. Roars of outrage rose from all over America, nowhere louder than from a mountaintop in Albemarle County. Jefferson had no mercy on his old appointee. He wrote Madison that "Hull will of course be shot for cowardice and treachery."[6] He wrote another correspondent, "My wonder is that his officers and men permitted themselves to be given up like sheep without even bleating. However we do not know the particulars."[7] Subsequently, a court-martial convicted Hull of cowardice and neglect of duty but did not charge him with treachery. Whether this brave old Revolutionary veteran was the scapegoat for a frustrated nation is still in dispute.

Having vented his spleen, as he could afford to do when he would have no responsibility for seeing that anyone was shot, Jefferson settled back into the comfortable routine of private life. While the Fates were weaving the destiny of nations, his attention was focused on the production of his own looms. Like most plantation owners, Jefferson for years had had spinning and weaving operations on his property. But these had been very limited enterprises, dependent on ordinary spinning wheels and the simplest of looms. Now, with the coming of the War of 1812, home manufacture assumed new importance and the sixty-nine-year-old master of Monticello was in the vanguard of those dealing effectively with the realities of the situation and the opportunities that it presented.[8] On June 28, 1812, he exulted to Kosciusko, "My household manufactures are just getting into operation on the scale of a carding machine costing 60 dollars only, which may be worked by a girl of 12 years old; a spinning machine which may be made for 10 dollars, carrying 6 spindles for wool, to be worked by a girl also; another which can be made for 25 dollars, carrying 12 spindles for cotton; and a loom with a flying shuttle weaving its 20 yards a day. I need 2000 yards of linen, cotton, and woolen yearly to clothe my family, which this machinery, costing 150 dollars only, and worked by two women and two girls, will more than furnish."

Characteristically, Jefferson had meticulously calculated the needs and the possibilities. Equally characteristically, he had called upon someone with expertise, William Maclure of North Carolina. He employed the Carolina weaver to move to Albemarle County, teach Monticello workers the textile arts, and help to set up a small manufacturing center. The operation grew rapidly, turning increasing quantities of flax, cotton, and wool into cloth—enough to take care of his family and his people, as he called the blacks on his farms. He bought the flax, rather than growing it himself, because he believed it depleted the soil, and the soil on his Monticello lands was poor, not nearly so fertile as that of Madison's plantation. Cotton came to him up the James River; most Albemarle planters had concluded years before that its cultivation was not profitable so far north. But the wool came from his own sheep, the stock that he was improving with an infusion of merino, and he took special delight in the fact that his woolen goods were in every sense a home product.

He bought more complicated spinning machines but eventually concluded it made more sense to stick to simple machinery that could be repaired by his own workmen. Of course, he was alert for ways of improving all the machinery to be used. He sketched his proposal for a carding machine consisting of "two circular cards in peritrochio."

By October 11 Jefferson was telling a correspondent: "We shall in all events derive permanent benefits from the war by its giving time for the permanent establishment of our manufactures. . . . High duties," he said, sounding a little like a Federalist, would protect the native industry and "enrich our treasury." He added: "We always manufactured a great deal in this state in the household way, but this was on the old spinning wheel. The introduction of machines into our families is becoming common. Those of six spindles suit the smaller families. I have 36 spindles going myself and shall soon add 18 more. My son-in-law has 40. . . . In a year or two more household manufactures will be so universally established in this state that the British commerce in coarse goods will be completely extirpated, and never more will be of much value to them. . . . I think that this, or one year more, will have raised our stock of sheep to one for every person in the state, which we deem sufficient for our clothing with the aid of our cotton."

The author of the Declaration of Independence was acutely aware that neither that document nor the war that gave it force had guaranteed the economic independence of the United States. But he had never ceased to dream of its attainment.

The textile industry, though it loomed especially large in Jefferson's considerations in 1812, was only one of several on his property. Indeed, the events of 1812 caused the suspension of one type of manufacturing which had once interested him even more than the making of cloth. In 1794, half in self-deprecation but with a great deal of genuine pride, he had boasted to a French correspondent, "I am myself a nail-maker. . . . my new trade of nail-making is to me in this country what an additional title of nobility or the ensigns of a new order are in Europe."[9] Though there was a considerable demand for nails in Albemarle County and elsewhere in central Virginia, the business was ill managed in his absence and collecting money from the retailers became a more than challenging task. Hardly had the enterprise begun to benefit from his personal attention when the War of 1812 cut off shipments of the necessary iron from Pennsylvania and he had to suspend operations for the duration of the conflict.

Like many large plantations, Monticello had long had its own blacksmith shop. This enterprise was alternately a source of satisfaction and of worry. The head blacksmith was a good workman when sober but frequently went on drunken sprees. The talented but troublesome man left in 1807. By that time the smithy had been combined with the nailery and housed in a stone building.[10]

Shoemaking was another activity at Monticello. Some of the leather came from Jefferson's own cattle, and some was purchased from other planters. His instructions to workmen to "Get bark for tanning leather where your next clearing is to be, felling the tree and stripping it clean," suggest that some tanning was done on the plantation. Some leather was used for harnesses and saddles. Apparently the shoes and other leather products were entirely, or at least principally, for the use of those who lived on the plantation.[11]

Monticello had four coal kilns for manufacture of wood charcoal for the blacksmith's shop and for fuel in the mansion. A cord of wood produced about thirty-five bushels of charcoal. The average annual production was 1,043 bushels.[12]

During the War of 1812 Joseph Miller, a British Captain resident in Norfolk, Virginia, was confined to the hills of Albemarle for reasons of security. Jefferson befriended the man and offered the hospitality of Monticello for his whole period of confinement. Miller had been a brewer in London, and Jefferson soon put his guest's skills to use in starting a distillery and teaching some of the plantation workers the processes of malting and brewing.[13] Corn, rye, and wheat grown on Jefferson's lands were the raw materials. The master of Monticello, insofar as his control extended, allowed whiskey to slaves and workmen only on certain occasions, as he believed it disruptive. He himself preferred wines and cider and almost always abstained from hard liquor.[14]

The incident of Captain Miller is reminiscent of Jefferson's experience with the Hessian prisoners of war confined to Albemarle County in the Revolution. He had befriended them and, finding good musicians among them, had organized them into a little orchestra, bringing pleasure both to them and to the residents of Monticello.

There was a mill which seemed to produce more trouble than flour. Jefferson's frustration was increased by the fact that he had studied mills and knew a great deal about them. He had sent out his sketches of mechanisms as an aid to friends in America and Europe. But he had to deal with some recalcitrant mechanisms not so easily altered to meet specifications—human beings considerably less adaptable and efficient than some of those who helped him with other operations.

That mill, which Jefferson called the "manufacturing mill," was strictly a commercial enterprise. Also powered by the Rivanna River were a gristmill, inherited from his father and serving only Jefferson's own family and workers, and a sawmill. Sometimes sudden floods damaged these structures. Vulnerable also were the dams and the locks which Jefferson operated in his canal. Once, just after he had completed a new dam, a big freshet swept it all away. Bacon had the unhappy duty of telling his employer what happened. The heavy downpour did not contribute to the manager's comfort as he rode up the hill in the gray light of early morning to make his report. Years later he recalled, "I never felt worse." Mr. Jefferson, in Bacon's words: "had just come from breakfast. 'Well sir,' said he, 'have you heard from the river?'

"I said, 'Yes, sir; I have just come from there with very bad news. The milldam is all swept away.'

" 'Well, sir,' said he, just as calm and quiet as though nothing had happened, 'we can't make a new dam this summer, but we will get Lewis' ferry-boat, with our own, and get the hands from all the quarters, and boat in rock enough in place of the dam, to answer for the present and next summer. I will send to Baltimore and get ship-bolts, and we will make a dam that the freshet can't wash away.' "[15]

The Rivanna River was far more to Jefferson than a source of power for his mills. He had played beside it as a child, and on its banks he had sung in the "soft summer twilight" with his beloved older sister Jane.[16] When Jefferson, fearful that a friend had given him undue praise in a biographical sketch, set down his own record of services to his country, he listed first in chronological order: "The Rivanna had never been used for navigation; scarcely an empty canoe had ever passed down it. Soon after I came of age, I examined its obstructions, set on foot a subscription for removing them, got an Act of Assembly passed, and the thing effected, so as to be used completely and fully for carrying down all our produce."[17] The Declaration of Independence was next on his list of eleven accomplishments. At that time he had not been President of the United States.

As Edwin Morris Betts said, "By his close association with the river Jefferson knew every bend and every cliff in its course."[18] The Rivanna was only a small river but, whether he was in Williamsburg, Richmond, New York, Philadelphia, or Paris, it ran always through the landscape of his mind.

Sometimes Jefferson had seen the Rivanna overflowing its banks and smashing and swallowing the structures in its path, and he never succeeded in taming it completely. Sometimes in a summer drought most of the bottom would be exposed. Dams, canals, and locks were required to make the river consistently navigable. Jefferson's father, Peter, who was responsible for many improvements benefiting the entire neighborhood, had built a dam and a canal. The son had added others to complete a much more complex system. Down-river was the little town of Milton, which, through the lower Rivanna and through the James River, had regular commerce with Richmond. Jefferson's improvements on the Rivanna made it possible for him to send to Milton canoes or flat-bottomed bateaux laden with the produce of his mills and fields. One such vessel might carry eighty to a hundred barrels of flour or forty to sixty hogsheads of tobacco.[19]

Jefferson's problems with the Rivanna were complicated in 1806 when the

Rivanna Navigation Company was incorporated to open the river to navigation for the approximately six miles between Milton and Charlottesville. If the company was to achieve its purpose a way had to be found through or around a major obstacle: a dam Jefferson had erected at the site of his mills.[20]

Jefferson was cooperative. He not only granted the directors permission to build locks in his canal just above his mills but provided materials for the job. He was surprised when the board, composed of neighbors and friends, asked him to bear the heavy cost of construction and perpetual maintenance. Surprise turned to shock and irritation when they insisted that he was duty-bound to assume the expense.

Nevertheless, he replied diplomatically. "On reading [the directors'] resolution . . . it is a subject of sincere regret that I cannot coincide in their opinion that I am bound to erect a lock and keep it in perpetual repair at the ridge of my rocks on which my dam rests. I regret it the more because I observe it to be an unanimous opinion of the four directors then present, and because it is so possible that my opinion, in opposition to theirs, may be under a bias of interest insensible to myself." Here, of course, was a gentle hint that they might look for the influence of self-interest in their own stand. He was asking them to reconsider because "it is so much a law of reason and right that no decisions shall be conclusive until the parties interested are heard." He added, "I am the more encouraged to do it by a thorough conviction of the disposition of the directors to require from me no unnecessary or unjust sacrifice, and of their desire to hear everything and to do only what, on full discussion, shall appear to be right." Less than two years after Jefferson's retirement to his native county, some of the neighbors who had saluted him as "a friend and neighbor as exemplary in the social circle as he is eminent at the helm of state" were finding his attitude less than exemplary. Many, of course, were still warm in admiration, but for some the friendship could flow smoothly only if the flow of their produce down the Rivanna was uninhibited.

Jefferson, as was his custom, had taken matters by the smooth handle first. His patient and persistent diplomacy appeared to have paid off by 1812. But when the locks did not prove satisfactory, the company petitioned the legislature late in the year to perpetuate their charter and empower the directors to regulate tolls. Jefferson was determined not to be pushed around—especially by people whose interest he had served so well in the past. But though firm, he was still restrained. He said that an article in the Richmond *Enquirer* provided "the first notice I have of a petition to enlarge powers . . . to be exercised almost wholly and exclusively over my property." Such a situation, he said, "cannot fail to be interesting to me. . . . I hope no perpetuity will be established. It is an evil, in all cases, and especially onerous when it affects the public right and use of water courses. Temporary powers, if they prove inconvenient, give opportunities of amendment at every renewal."

Jefferson recalled the trouble and expense he had gone to after a great flood had swept away the mill built by his father. "Though the difficulties of the canal exceeded everything which could have been imagined, I persevered working on it for the years 1776 to 1806 with the intermission of four or five years only while I was in Europe, and here and there a year occasionally at other times, during which time I expended not less than twenty thousand dollars on the canal alone. And since that a great additional expense has been incurred in making it wide enough for the passage of bateaux, in erecting a solid pier head of stone of a sufficient width and height of arch to admit them to enter, and in building a dam of about 400 feet long over a most powerful stream."

Jefferson believed that he was being called upon to surrender his riparian rights after spending a fortune on improvements beneficial to his neighbors as well as to himself. He did not give in. He was prepared to do what he eventually did in 1817, institute a friendly suit in chancery.

Fortunately, amid the straining of old ties of friendship, Jefferson had the pleasure of renewing cherished bonds that had been severed. He had had the pleasure of doing his part in bringing Madison and Monroe together again and, aided by the march of events and each man's sense of enlightened self-interest, had so far succeeded that Monroe was now Madison's Secretary of State. But at the start of 1812 there was another rupture still unhealed between ardent patriots who had been close friends—John Adams and Jefferson himself. Dr. Benjamin Rush of Philadelphia, a firm friend to both men and a fellow signer of the Declaration of Independence, had already begun to address the problem.[21] As far back as the fall of 1809 he had told Adams of a "dream" in which he had seen the two old Revolutionary friends reconciled. In this dream, Adams had taken the first step. Adams replied: "A dream again! I wish you would dream all day and all night, for one of your dreams puts me in spirits for a month. I have no other objection to your dream, but that it is not history. It may be prophecy."

Rush pertinaciously pursued the role of peacemaker. In a letter to Jefferson at the beginning of 1811, he said of Adams, "Tottering over the grave, he now leans wholly upon the shoulders of his old Revolutionary friends." The Hamiltonians, a numerous crew in Adams' own state, were inveterate enemies. These references clearly were calculated to remind the Virginian of the old Revolutionary bonds that had united him with the Massachusetts statesman and of the fact that Adams, like Jefferson, had later warred against the worst excesses of Alexander Hamilton.

Rush told of the pleasure he found in correspondence with the old curmudgeon of Braintree. "His letters glow with the just opinions he held and defended in the patriotic years 1774, 1775, and 1776."[22] Currently Adams was much exercised about banks issuing paper money at interest. Rush, of course, was aware that Jefferson's ire was stirred by the same practice.

Then Rush cast away all subtlety and said: "When I consider your early attachment to Mr. Adams, and his—to you—When I consider how much the liberties and independence of the United States owe to the concert of your principles and labors, and when I reflect upon the sameness of your opinions at present, upon most of the subjects of government, and all the subjects of legislation, I have ardently wished a friendly and epistolary intercourse might be revived between you before you take a final leave of the common object of your affections. . . . Posterity will revere the friendship of the two ex-Presidents that once were opposed to each other. Human nature will be a gainer by it. I am sure an advance on your side will be cordial to the heart of Mr. Adams."

Jefferson replied cautiously that he still esteemed Adams but that he could not be sure that his old companion would not spurn the hand of friendship. The Virginian said that he had not broken the friendship to start with, and he would not be averse to its resumption. His friendly overtures to Mrs. Adams had been rebuffed after she had written him a letter of condolence on the death of his daughter Maria. If the Adamses were not receptive under those circumstances, why should they be now? He enclosed copies of his correspondence with Abigail, saying, "I have never communicated it to any mortal breathing before. . . . Indeed, I thought it highly disgraceful to us both, as indicating minds not sufficiently elevated to prevent a public competition from affecting our personal friendship."[23]

Rush continued to include references to Jefferson in his letters to Adams. Jefferson, happily, did not see one of Adams' replies, one of those in which he dwelt on the American people's failure to appreciate his services and said: "The Declaration of Independence I always considered as a theatrical show. Jefferson ran away with the stage effect of that . . . and all the glory of it."[24]

Late in the year, two of Jefferson's neighbors, John and Edward Coles, called upon Adams in the course of a visit to New England. The conversation quite naturally turned upon Adams' old revolutionary colleague from Albemarle County and the Virginians mentioned Jefferson's great solicitude for Adams' feelings after defeating him in the presidential contest of 1800. The topic was a somewhat touchy one and might have drawn from Adams a caustic comment. Instead he exclaimed, "I always loved Jefferson and still love him."[25]

Sometime later, when the incident was revealed to Jefferson, he melted. On December 5, 1811, he reported the incident to Rush and said: "This was enough for me. I only needed this knowledge to revive towards him all the affections of the most cordial moments of our lives. . . . I knew him to be always an honest man, often a great one, but sometimes incorrect and precipitate in his judgments. . . . But with a man possessing so many other estimable qualities, why should we be dissocialized by mere differences of opinions in politics, in religion, in philosophy or anything else. His opinions are as honestly formed as my own. . . . I wish, therefore, but for an apposite occasion to express to Mr. Adams my unchanged affections for him."

There were still impediments though. "There is an awkwardness which hangs over the resuming a correspondence so long discontinued, unless something could arise which should call for a letter." Would Rush suggest to Adams that he write first? And the wound inflicted by one Adams had cut too deep for reconciliation. "From this fusion of mutual affections, Mrs. Adams is of course separated. It will only be necessary that I never name her."

Rush hastened to tell Adams of Jefferson's affectionate words.

But Adams' reply was disappointing. "I perceive plainly enough, Rush," he said, "that you have been teasing Jefferson to write to me, as you did me some time ago to write to him. . . . Where there has been no war, there can be no room for negotiations of peace. . . . I have always loved him as a friend. If I ever

received or suspected any injury from him, I have forgiven it long and long ago.
. . . But why do you make so much ado over nothing? Of what use can it be for
Jefferson and me to exchange letters? I have nothing to say to him but to wish
him an easy journey to Heaven when he goes. . . . And he can have nothing to
say to me but to bid me make haste and be ready." Then he cracked the door
just a little. "Time and chance, however, or possibly design, may produce ere
long a letter between us."[26]

On New Year's Day, 1812, an appropriate time for beginning anew, Adams
wrote a letter to Jefferson. "As you are a friend to American manufactures under
proper restrictions, especially manufactures of the domestic kind, I take the
liberty of sending you by the post a packet containing two pieces of homespun
lately produced in this quarter by one who was honored in his youth with some
of your attention and much of your kindness." After filling Jefferson in on some
happenings in the Adams family over the years, he concluded: "I wish you, sir,
many happy New Years and that you may enter the next and many succeeding
years with as animating prospects for the public as those at present before us. I
am, sir, with a long and sincere esteem your friend and servant John Adams."[27]

Jefferson hastened to reply without waiting for the arrival of the "pieces of
homespun." After thanking Adams for the anticipated gift, Jefferson launched
into a discussion of the progress of manufactures in Virginia. Then his warmth
came through. "A letter from you calls up recollections very dear to my mind.
It carries me back to the times when, beset with difficulties and dangers, we
were fellow laborers in the same cause, struggling for what is most valuable to
man, his right of self-government."[28] Jefferson probably would not have recalled
so warmly those days of joint labor if he had known that Adams had once
written to Rush: "You should remember that Jefferson was but a boy to me. . . .
I am bold to say I was his preceptor in politics and taught him everything that
has been good and solid in his whole political conduct."[29]

Jefferson rejoiced in the prospects of the republic for which he and his old
friend had worked. "So we have gone on, and so we shall go on . . . prospering
beyond example in the history of man." Not so with France and England. "With
all their preeminence in science [by *science* he meant scholarship of all kinds],
the one is a den of robbers and the other of pirates. And if science produces no
better fruits than tyranny, murder, rapine and destitution of national morality, I
would rather wish our country to be ignorant, honest and estimable, as our
neighboring savages are." A very romantic "noble savage" expression from the
supposed "man of reason"! Ironically, right after his deprecatory reference to
scholarship, Jefferson said that he had given up newspapers to devote more
time to Tacitus, Thucydides, Newton and Euclid.

The Virginian reminded his New England friend that only seven signers of
the Declaration of Independence were still alive. "You and I," he said, "have
been wonderfully spared." He himself enjoyed "remarkable health" for a man
of his years and, though he experienced great difficulty in walking, was still at
home on a horse. He was glad to hear that Adams' legs were better than his
own. He concluded his letter with assurances of "unchanged affection and
respect."

One can imagine the delight with which Rush learned of the exchange between the two old patriots. His prophecy that posterity would cherish their correspondence and "revere the friendship of the two ex-Presidents that were once opposed to each other" was amply fulfilled. To the exchange of letters that then resumed we owe a far more candid and detailed exposition of Jefferson's mature thoughts than we otherwise would have. As for Adams, the man who would otherwise be remembered chiefly as a crabbed hoarder of past glories shines through his epistolary musings as a trenchant observer and devoted patriot who had first won Jefferson's affection in the great days of the Revolution.

XV

'OF CABBAGES AND KINGS'

"**T**HIS IS NO BOOK; who touches this touches a man." What Whitman said of his own work might be appropriately applied to each volume of the letters Jefferson wrote after retirement from the presidency. His correspondents included the principal thinkers, male and female, in the United States and Europe. He dealt with the specialty of each, summoning the lore of multiple languages and drawing on reservoirs of ancient and modern learning in political science, natural science, technology, linguistics, literature, art, history, philosophy, and theology. But the items of his learning are not compartmentalized from each other or from his life. He does not bring them forth from storage smelling of the mothballs of pedantry. His learning is inseparable from his life and part of its excitement. Even when he marshals numerous technical details to support his conclusions, the writing is suffused with the enthusiasms, and sometimes the aversions, of the man. Though a master of syllogisms, he is no logic-chopping machine, no detached embodiment of the Age of Reason. He brings to his discussions the warmth, the weakness, and the surprising, soaring strength of mercurial humanity.

As richly varied as his correspondence is, it has a double-note leitmotif: education and freedom. A concern for one or the other permeated his every major interest. One might almost say a concern for both—because Jefferson saw the two at their best as inseparable. A civilized society could not remain free without widespread education, and higher education could not serve its noblest purposes unless teachers and students were free to follow truth wherever it might lead. His interest in education is manifested in many ways—in his enthusiastic quest for the latest findings of science, his devotion to classical learning, his eager pursuit of a linguistic lead, his anxiety about transmitting to posterity an accurate account of his own times, his advice to the young on study habits and to their seniors on library selections, and especially in his interest in the formal processes of education, a concern that becomes increasingly concrete and particularized.

A request from John Adams for the name of a reliable book on the American Indians brought from Jefferson an analysis of works on the subject by various American and British writers including his personal findings related to their major theses.[1] His consideration of the parallels between the American aborigines and the ancient Hebrews drawn by James Adair led him into an informal discussion of Jewish society in the old kingdoms of Israel. He said that he had been "very familiar" with the Indians in "the very early part" of his life and had "acquired impressions of attachment and commiseration for them which have never been obliterated." He recalled: "Before the Revolution they were in the habit of coming often, and in great numbers, to the seat of our government, where I was very much with them. I knew much the great Outassete, the warrior and orator of the Cherokees. He was always the guest of my father on his journeys to and from Williamsburg."

Jefferson brought forth one of the most vivid impressions of his boyhood: "I was in [Outassete's] camp when he made his great farewell oration to his people the evening before his departure for England. The moon was in full splendor, and to her he seemed to address himself in his prayers for his own safety on the voyage, and that of his people during his absence. His sounding voice, distinct articulation, animated actions, and the solemn silence of his people at their several fires, filled me with awe and veneration, although I did not understand a word he uttered."

Jefferson described both the Cherokees and the Creeks as "far advanced in civilization," and noted "a branch of the Cherokees is now instituting a regular representative government."

These words of praise and understanding hardly prepare the reader for the letter's abrupt conclusion, in which Jefferson prophesies that, although "English seductions will have no effect" on the more advanced tribes, "the backward will yield and be thrown further back. These will relapse into barbarism and misery, lose numbers by war and want, and we shall be obliged to drive them, with the beasts of the forest, into the Stony Mountains. They will be conquered, however, in Canada. The possession of that country secures our women and children forever from the tomahawk and scalping knife, by removing those who excite them and for this possession, orders I presume are issued by this time." When war engaged his emotions, Jefferson had no room for detached observation of his country's enemies, actual or potential.

Late in the year Jefferson received from John Melish, a Scottish-born author and cartographer settled in Philadelphia, his newly published atlas of the United States. The former President said that he had read the book "with extreme satisfaction." He added: "As to the western states, particularly, it has greatly edified me; for of the actual condition of that interesting portion of our country, I had not an adequate idea. I feel myself now as familiar with it as with the condition of the maritime states." It seems ironic that Jefferson, who always placed such trust in the people of the West and who had doubled the size of the nation by westward expansion, should have confessed to such ignorance of the vast area inland from the seaboard. But at this time Jefferson, who was painfully sensitive to any rocking motion on land or sea, had never traveled more than fifty miles over the rugged terrain to the west of his birthplace. Only once would he travel farther westward and then for only seventy-five miles. He studied sedulously the reports of Lewis and Clark and the fossils and other natural history specimens from them which had transformed Monticello's handsome foyer into a museum. But until he read Melish's book he lacked a knowledge of the occupations and achievements of settlers even in Western states just beyond the Atlantic littoral. "I had no conception," he wrote, "that manufactures had made such progress there, and particularly of the number of carding and spinning machines dispersed through the whole country."[2]

Very tactfully, though, Jefferson called attention to one of Melish's comments which disturbed him highly. The Philadelphian had written that the chief difference between the two great political parties in the United States was "whether the controlling power shall be vested in this or that set of men." Jefferson insisted that, while "each party endeavors to get into the administration of the government and exclude the other from power," this motive "is only secondary, the primary motive being a real and radical difference of political principle. . . . The question of preference between monarchy and republicanism, which has so long divided mankind elsewhere, threatens a permanent division here."

He divided Federalists into three classes, depending upon the degree of their adherence to "the English constitution as a model of perfection." He said that some wanted England's constitution "with a correction of its vices. Others, like the late Alexander Hamilton, believed that "a correction of what are called its vices would render the English an impracticable government." They accepted the Constitution of the United States only "as a stepping stone to the final establishment of their favorite model." Much rasher, however, was "a weighty MINORITY . . . of these *leaders*" who, "considering the voluntary conversion of our government into a monarchy as too distant, if not desperate, wish to break off from our Union its eastern fragment, as being, in truth, the hot bed of American monarchism, with a view to a commencement of their favorite government, from whence the other states may gangrene by degrees and the whole be thus brought finally to the desired point."

Altogether, Jefferson's analysis was no more objective than one would expect from the passionate patron saint of one party discussing the shortcomings of its chief opponents. But he did qualify his observations by writing "minority" in capitals for emphasis and underlining "leaders" for the same reason. Generations of historians have criticized Jefferson for saying that Hamilton wished the United States to be a monarchy, but we have the testimony of Hamilton's cherished friend Gouverneur Morris, who, the day before he delivered the eulogy at Hamilton's funeral, confided to his diary, "He was on principle opposed to republican and attached to monarchical government."[3] Jefferson's charge that a minority of Federalist leaders wanted the Northeastern states to secede and form a separate Confederacy was strictly factual. The Essex Junto, a group formed in Essex County, Massachusetts, under the leadership of Massachusetts Senator Timothy Pickering, had advocated this very course and had attracted some support elsewhere in New England as well as in New York and New Jersey.

In words obviously not intended for Adams' eyes, Jefferson told Melish that "Massachusetts, the prime mover in this enterprise," should be "the last state in the Union" to advocate "a *final* separation, as being of all the most dependent on the others. Not raising bread for the sustenance of her own inhabitants, not having a stick of timber for the construction of vessels (her principal occupation), nor an article to export in them, where would she be, excluded from the ports of the other states, and thrown into dependence on England, her direct and natural but now insidious rival?"

Jefferson reiterated that the majority of Federalist leaders did not "aim at separation." He further emphasized regarding the secessionist minority among the Federalist chiefs: "The moment that these leaders should avowedly propose a separation of the Union, or the establishment of regal government, their popular adherents would quit them to a man and join the republican standard; and the partisans of this change, even in Massachusetts, would thus find themselves an army of officers without a soldier."

Though there is no reason to think that Adams ever read what Jefferson said about Massachusetts in this letter, he did soon read two of Jefferson's earlier letters that had been reprinted in a recent work published in London, Thomas Belsham's *Memoirs of the Late Reverend Theophilus Lindsay*. These were confidential communications to Joseph Priestley during Adams' presidency, and one was bitterly critical of Federalist policies. Jefferson realized that his renewed friendship with his revolutionary colleague—doubly precious because it had been resurrected from apparent death—might be freshly imperiled by these revelations. But he did not stoop to insinuate that he had been misquoted. Instead he reminded Adams of its context. "It recalls to our recollection the gloomy transactions of the times, the doctrines they witnessed and the sensibilities they excited. It was a confidential communication of reflections on these from one friend to another, deposited in his bosom, and never meant to trouble the public mind. Whether the character of the times is justly portrayed or not, posterity will decide. But on one feature of them they can never decide, the sensations excited in free yet firm minds by the terrorism of the day. None can conceive who did not witness them, and they were felt by one party only. This letter exhibits their side of the medal. The Federalists no doubt have presented the other, in their private correspondences, as well as open action. If these correspondences should ever be laid open to the public eye, they will probably be found not models of comity toward their adversaries."[4] Probably upon reading these words Adams recalled some letters of his own that he would not want Jefferson to read.

Having made his point, Jefferson used his most tactful diplomacy. He said that there had been nothing of personal animosity in his quoting Adams' words as examples of dangerous Federalist doctrine. "You happen indeed to be quoted because you happened to express, more pithily than had been done by themselves, one of the mottos of the party." He wrapped the pill of instruction in a compliment:

One of the questions you know on which our parties took different sides, was on the improvability of the human mind, in science, in ethics, in government etc. Those who advocated reformation of institutions, pari passu, with the progress of science, maintained that no definite limits could be assigned to that progress. The enemies of reform, on the other hand, denied improvement, and advocated steady adherence to the principles, practices and institutions of our fathers, which they represented as the consummation of wisdom, and acme of excellence, beyond which the human mind could never advance. Although in the passage of your answer alluded to, you expressly disclaim the wish to influence the freedom of enquiry, you predict that that will produce nothing more worthy of transmission to posterity, than the principles, institutions and systems of education received from their ancestors. I do not consider this as your deliberate opinion. You possess, yourself, too much science, not to see how much is still ahead of you, unexplained and unexplored.

Jefferson concluded the letter with appealing warmth:

As to myself, I shall take no part in any discussions. I leave others to judge of what I have done, and to give me exactly that place which they shall think I have occupied. Marshall has written libels on one side; others, I suppose, will be written on the other side and the world will sift both, and separate the truth as well as they can. I should see with reluctance the passions of that day rekindled in this, while so many of the actors are living, and all are too near the scene not to participate in sympathies with them. About facts, you and I cannot differ; because truth is our mutual guide. And if any opinions you may express should be different from mine, I shall receive them with the liberality and indulgence which I ask for my own, and still cherish with warmth the sentiments of affectionate respect of which I can with so much truth tender you the assurance.

Evidently Adams too was unwilling to imperil a great friendship so recently restored. The correspondence between the two patriots continued, sometimes with the warmth of argument but always with the warmth of friendship.

Despite the impediments of war, some of Jefferson's liveliest correspondence was with European intellectuals. He wrote Madame de Tessé,[5] Lafayette's aunt and a friend since Jefferson's days as United States Minister to France. It was the comtesse to whom he once confided that he had been "gazing whole hours at the Maison Carrée like a lover at his mistress" and to whom he had sent many plants after his return to America. "While at war, my dear Madam and friend, with the leviathan of the ocean," he wrote December 8, 1813, "there is little hope of a letter escaping his thousand ships; yet I cannot permit myself longer to withhold the acknowledgement of your letter of June 28 of last year, with which came the memoirs of the Margrave of Bayreuth." He was fully appreciative of "this singular morsel of history which has given us a certain view of kings, queens and princes disrobed of their formalities. It would not be easy to find grosser manners, coarser vices, or more meanness in the poorest huts of our peasantry."

He facetiously proposed that someone write a "Natural History of Kings and Princes" and then turned to beings "of a higher order, the plants of the field." He sought information on the marron or *Castanea sative* which had been imported into France and which he wished to bring to America but had no hope of seeing until the war's end. He burned with curiosity about "the botanical riches which you mention to have been derived to England from New Holland." He wrote enthusiastically about the plants, some "curious, some ornamental, some useful," even some which might "by culture be made acceptable to our tables." He was saving for her "a very handsome little shrub of the size of a currant bush. Its beauty consists in a great produce of berries of the size of currants, and literally as white as snow, which remain on the bush through the winter, after its leaves have fallen, and make it an object as singular as beautiful. We call it the snow-berry bush," but he thought it could be made botanically respectable by calling it "Chionicoccos or Kallicoccos."

About the same time that he wrote to Madame de Tessé he wrote to one of Europe's most versatile geniuses, Baron Alexander von Humboldt.[6] The two men had a great deal in common. Both were statesmen, writers, and scientists. Each was particularly devoted to agronomy and botany, and each was especially fascinated by meteorology and climatic influences on society. Each was an aristocrat who was also a zealous republican. Each was the originator and planner of an historic expedition in the Western Hemisphere and an ardent student of the artifacts brought back. An important difference was that, while the physical part of Jefferson's expedition into the North American West was a strictly vicarious adventure, Humboldt actually trudged through the South American jungles and set a new world record by climbing 18,893 feet toward the summit of Chimborazo. In 1813 Humboldt's fame in Europe was second only to Napoleon's, and Jefferson's fame on that continent was greater than that of any other American. It was extremely unlikely that Humboldt would ever equal Jefferson's reputation as a statesman, but at age forty-four the German Baron had already far surpassed the American as a scientist. All in all, though, if one omitted Humboldt's physical feats, the two Enlightenment giants were well matched in versatility.

Addressing Humboldt as "My Dear Friend and Baron," Jefferson gratefully acknowledged receipt of the German's published notebooks of astronomical observations and South American explanation as well as his two atlases of New Spain. The American lamented that Meriwether Lewis had died before publication of the record of his North American journey and that "the measures taken by his surviving companion, Clark, for the publication, have not answered our wishes in point of dispatch." Not a very swiftly efficient phrase either, but Jefferson was given to circumlocution when criticizing someone he liked.

Of Humboldt's report on the Latin American states, Jefferson wrote: "I think it most fortunate that your travels in those countries were so timed as to make them known to the world in the moment they were about to become actors on its stage." He hazarded a prophecy: "That they will throw off their European dependence I have no doubt; but on what kind of government their revolution will end I am not so certain. History, I believe, furnishes no example of a priest-ridden people maintaining a free civil government. This [a priest-ridden society] marks the lowest grade of ignorance, of which their civil as well as religious leaders will always avail themselves for their own purposes. The vicinity of New Spain to the United States, and their consequent intercourse, may furnish schools for the higher, and example for the lower classes of their citizens." Through these means there might be growth toward democracy but, first, he believed, there would be "military despotisms. The different castes of their inhabitants, their mutual hatreds and jealousies, their profound ignorance and bigotry, will be played off by cunning leaders, and each be made the instrument of enslaving others."

Lest it be thought that Jefferson was a superhuman, always capable of being simultaneously a happy paterfamilias to a numerous brood and a smiling host to a horde of visitors, all without missing a beat in his intellectual contemplations or breaking the rhythm of his writing, we must note what he wrote to another European. He once told M. de Becourt: "I have living with me . . . eight grandchildren, their parents, and other connections making up a dozen at our daily table, and that number generally enlarged by the successive visits of other friends and relations. Quarters so crowded are illy calculated for the quiet or comfort of the aged or the studious."[7]

Nevertheless, information and observations continued to flow copiously from Jefferson's pen. When Dr. Walter Jones invited his criticism of a manuscript history of United States political parties, the elder statesman was stimulated to sound off on the unreliability of newspapers as a guide either to contemporaries or posterity and to produce in the course of his letter the most famous essay ever written about Washington. First he said: "I deplore, with you, the putrid state into which our newspapers have passed, and the malignity, the vulgarity, and mendacious spirit of those who write for them; and I enclose you a recent sample . . . as a proof of the abyss of degradation into which we are fallen. These ordures are rapidly depraving the public taste, and lessening its relish for sound food. As vehicles of information, and a curb on our functionaries, they have rendered themselves useless, by forfeiting all title to belief."[8]

Agreeing with Dr. Jones in attributing the low quality of newspapers in part to "the violence and malignity of party spirit," he opined that the doctor's "succinct, correct, and dispassionate history of the origin and progress of party among us" should "give to posterity a fairer view of the times than they will probably derive from other sources."

Of course, Jefferson could not approach any creative work in literature, architecture, or the art of government without wishing to tinker with it. "In reading it with great satisfaction," he wrote, "there was but a single passage where I wished a little more development of a very sound and catholic idea, a single intercalation to rest it on true bottom." He followed with the nuances that could be added by rewording Jones' statement that "the people ought to possess as much political power as can possibly exist with the order and security of society."

He then said there was no real basis for Jones' fear that Washington's relations with the Federalists would be "a perilous topic." He argued: "You have given the genuine history of the course of his mind through the trying scenes in which it was engaged, and of the seductions by which it was deceived but not depraved."

Jefferson himself had criticized Washington in private correspondence when Hamilton had the first President's ear and Jefferson thought that the great man was squinting toward monarchy. Tattlers were all too willing to carry the former Secretary of State's words to his old chief and give them the worst possible interpretation. Partly because of his own indiscretion, but largely because of the chicanery of others, Jefferson had lost the trust of the man who had been to him a father figure. When Washington died on December 14, 1799, there had been no reconciliation. One can easily imagine the eagerness with which Jones read on after seeing the words "I think I knew General Washington intimately and thoroughly; and were I called on to delineate his character, it should be in terms like these."

Jones became the first reader of a truly classic characterization that deserves to be read in its entirety by every student of the genre and everyone seriously interested in American history. There leaped out phrases that since have been quoted innumerable times: "His mind was great and powerful, without being of the very first order; his penetration strong, though not so acute as that of a Newton, Bacon, or Locke; and as far as he saw, no judgement was ever sounder. It was slow in operation, being little aided by invention or imagination, but sure in conclusion. Hence the common remark of his officers, of the advantage he derived from councils of war, where hearing all suggestions, he selected whatever was best. . . . He was incapable of fear, meeting personal dangers with the calmest unconcern. Perhaps the strongest feature in his character was prudence, never acting until every circumstance, every consideration, was maturely weighed; refraining if he saw a doubt, but, when once decided, going through with his purpose, whatever obstacles opposed."

Jefferson, who had sometimes been angered by Washington's decisions, especially when they had seemed to favor Hamilton over him, now wrote upon reflection after himself having borne the burdens of the presidency: "His integrity was most pure, his justice the most inflexible I have ever known, no motives of interest or consanguinity, of friendship or hatred, being able to bias his decision. He was, indeed, in every sense of the words, a wise, a good, and a great man." Jefferson noted that Washington had a naturally high temper "but reflection and resolution had obtained a firm and habitual ascendancy over it. If ever, however, it broke its bonds, he was most tremendous in his wrath." Jefferson was probably thinking not only of the battle of Monmouth, when the General's soldiers, their ammunition exhausted, had faced the enemy rather than their enraged commander; he was probably thinking also of the cabinet discussion in which he had seen the venerable Chief of State throw his own hat on the floor and "stomp on it."

Jefferson penetrated to the central fact of Washington's greatness and revealed it with uncommon eloquence:

On the whole, his character was, in its mass, perfect, in nothing bad, in few points indifferent; and it may truly be said that never did nature and fortune combine more perfectly to make a man great, and to place him in the same constellation with whatever worthies have merited from man an everlasting remembrance. For his was the singular destiny and merit of leading the armies of his country successfully through an arduous war for the establishment of its independence, of conducting its councils through the birth of a government, new in its forms and principles, until it had settled down into a quiet and orderly train; and of scrupulously obeying the laws through the whole of his career, civil and military, of which the history of the world furnishes no other example.

He obviously was addressing posterity, and with a great need to be believed, when he added, "These are my opinions of General Washington, which I would vouch at the judgment seat of God, having been formed on an acquaintance of thirty years."

In a letter to Dr. Thomas Cooper,[9] Jefferson referred to "the pious disposition of the English judges to connive at the frauds of the clergy, a disposition which has even rendered them faithful allies in practice." To satisfy his correspondent's whetted curiosity, Jefferson sent him some reflections on the subject he had written in his Commonplace Book when he "was a student of the law, now half a century ago." He explained, "They were written at a time of life when I was bold in the pursuit of knowledge, never fearing to follow truth and reason to whatever result they led, and bearding every authority which stood in their way. This must be the apology if you find the conclusions bolder than historical facts and principles will warrant."

Jefferson may have felt that he could not spare the time to reexamine his opinions of a distant day. He had been a long time away from activity in the courts, having spent more time as a student of the law than as a practitioner. But he may have valued the luxury of presenting his views as a young man without having to reveal whether he still held them. The youthful Jefferson had cited the pronouncement of Sir Matthew Hale: "Christianity is parcel of the laws of England." Jefferson argued that this view, so often encountered in judicial rulings, was dependent on the myth that Alfred the Great had based his famous code of laws on Christian doctrine whereas the King himself had declared that they were drawn from the laws "of Ina, of Offa, Athelbert and his ancestors, saying nothing of any of them being taken from the Scriptures."

The truth of the matter is that Jefferson and his ancestor Alfred shared the sensible habit of introducing innovations as if they were at most only slightly altered legacies from the forefathers. Alfred was a loyal Anglo-Saxon and a devout Christian, and in his code of laws as in the epic *Beowulf*, the northern heritage and the Christian culture mixed and mingled. Jefferson, however, was certainly on firm ground in arguing that many English judges had distorted the relationship between Christianity and the common law. They had done so both to bolster the ecclesiastical establishment and to give the law the support of scriptural endorsement.

The young law student had written, "The truth is that Christianity and Newtonianism being reason and verity itself, in the opinion of all but infidels and Cartesians, they are protected under the wings of the common law from other sects, but not erected into dominion over them." Jefferson was not then as tolerant as he would become in matters of religion, but he had embraced the idea, which he would later express in the Statute of Virginia for Religious Freedom, that "error may be safely tolerated where truth is left free to combat it." And he gives an example that foreshadows his later eloquence: "An eminent Spanish physician affirmed that the lancet had slain more men than the sword. Doctor Sangrado, on the contrary, affirmed that with plentiful bleedings, and draughts of warm water, every disease was to be cured. The common law protects both opinions but enacts neither into law."

Dr. John Manners requested Jefferson's opinion on "the comparative merits of the different methods of classification adopted by different writers on natural history." Jefferson said that his opinion was "one which I could not have given satisfactorily even at the earlier period at which the subject was more familiar, still less after a life of civil concerns has so much withdrawn me from studies of that kind."[10] But after this demurrer he did make an effort to answer, beginning with an important reminder that various scientists have issued through the generations but perhaps none more clearly or effectively than the Sage of Monticello.

"Nature has, in truth," he said, "produced units only through all her works. Classes, orders, genera, species, are not of her work. Her creation is of individuals. No two animals are exactly alike; no two plants nor even two leaves or blades of grass; no two crystallizations. And if we may venture from what is within the cognizance of such organs as ours, to conclude on that beyond their powers, we must believe that no two particles of matter are of exact resemblance. This infinitude of units or individuals being far beyond the capacity of our memory, we are obliged, in aid of that, to distribute them into masses, throwing into each of these all the individuals which have a certain degree of resemblance; to subdivide these again into smaller groups, according to certain points of dissimilitude observable in them, and so on until we have formed what we call a system of classes, orders, genera and species."

"In doing this," he said, "we fix arbitrarily on such characteristic resemblances and differences as seem to us most prominent and invariable in the several subjects, and most likely to take a strong hold in our memories. Thus Ray formed one classification on such lines of division as struck him most favorably; Klein adopted another; Brisson a third, and other naturalists other designations, till Linnaeus appeared. Fortunately for science, he conceived in the three kingdoms of nature, modes of classification which obtained the approbation of the learned of all nations. His system was accordingly adopted by all, and united all in a general language. It offered the three great desiderata: First, of aiding the memory to retain a knowledge of the productions of nature. Secondly, of rallying all to the same names for the same objects, so that they could communicate understandingly on them. And Thirdly, of enabling them, when a subject was first presented, to trace it by its character up to the conventional name by which it was agreed to be called. This classification was indeed liable to the imperfection of bringing into the same group individuals which, though resembling in the characteristics adopted by the author for his classification, yet have strong marks of dissimilitude in other respects. But to this objection every mode of classification must be liable, because the plan of creation is inscrutable to our limited faculties."

He made his principal point succinctly: "Nature has not arranged her productions on a single and direct line. They branch at every step, and in every direction and he who attempts to reduce them into departments, is left to do it by the lines of his own fancy. The objection of bringing together what are disparata in nature, lies against the classifications of Blumenbach and of Cuvier, as well as that of Linnaeus, and must forever lie against all. Perhaps not in equal degree; on this I do not pronounce. But neither is this so important a consideration as that of uniting all nations under one language in Natural History. This had been happily effected by Linnaeus, and can scarcely be hoped for a second time. Nothing indeed is so desperate as to make all mankind agree in giving up a language they possess, for one which they have to learn."

There is much more to the letter. Though addressed to a single person, it is actually an essay on classification in natural history which discusses knowledgeably the entire process from the times of Aristotle and Pliny to those of Jussieu, Haüy, and Buffon, noting applications to botany, mineralogy, and zoology. It deserves a place in English-language anthologies of scientific explication.

On April 6, 1814, the abdication of Napoleon left Britain free to concentrate on the North American theater of a war already going badly for the United States. The month before, President Madison had recommended and obtained repeal of the embargo against trade with the enemy. Adequate enforcement had been impossible, and New York and New England contractors had supplied beef and flour to Britain's navy and armies. Violations of the embargo had been a sore point with Jefferson ever since his own presidency, but in this troubled April another subject struck more sparks of ire from him. On Jefferson's instructions, a Philadelphia dealer had paid for a new book to which the Virginian had subscribed, *Sur la Creation du Monde*, by M. de Becourt. Jefferson had assumed, because of the title, the book would be "either a geological or astronomical work." Instead, it turned out to be a philosophical work whose aspersions on religion infuriated many readers. Moreover, the dealer, N. G. Dufief, was investigated for his part in the purchase.

"I am really mortified," Jefferson wrote the unfortunate man, "to be told that *in the United States of America*, a fact like this can become a subject of inquiry, and of criminal inquiry too, as an offense against religion; that a question about the sale of a book can be carried before the civil magistrate. Is this then our freedom of religion? And are we to have a censor whose imprimatur shall say what books may be sold, and what we may buy? And who is thus to dogmatize religious opinions for our citizens? Whose foot is to be the measure to which ours are all to be cut or stretched? Is a priest to be our inquisitor, or shall a layman, simple as ourselves, set up his reason as the rule for what we are to read and what we must believe?"[11]

He added: "It is an insult to our citizens to question whether they are rational beings or not, and blasphemy against religion to suppose it cannot stand the test of truth and reason. If M. de Becourt's book be false in its facts, disprove them; if false in its reasoning refute it. But for Gods's sake, let us freely hear both sides, if we choose. I know little of its contents, having barely glanced over here and there a passage, and over the table of contents. From this, the Newtonian philosophy seemed the chief object of attack, the issue of which might be trusted to the strength of the two combatants; Newton certainly not needing the auxiliary arm of the government, and still less the holy author of our religion as to what in it concerns Him. I thought the work would be very innocent, and one which might be confided to the reason of any man; not likely to be much read if let alone, but, if persecuted, it will be generally read. Every man in the United States will think it a duty to buy a copy, in vindication of his right to buy, and to read, what he pleases."

A book that Jefferson received a little after trying to plow through Bécourt's dissertation kindled his enthusiasm so much that he wrote a lengthy letter to the author. Thomas Law's *Second Thoughts on Instinctive Impulses* arrived just as he was setting out for Poplar Forest, and he carried it with him. In the solitude of that retreat he found ample opportunity to concentrate on its contents. He wrote Law that the work "contained exactly my own creed on the foundation of morality in man."[12] By citing some philosophers and arguing against others, Jefferson bolstered his argument that "the Creator" had made "the moral principle" so much a part of our constitution. Quoting particularly Greek, French, and British writings, he asserted that in most human beings there coexisted with self-love a disposition of kindness toward most of their fellows. "The Creator would indeed have been a bungling artist," Jefferson wrote, "had he intended man for a social animal without planting in him social dispositions. It is true they are not planted in every man, because there is no rule without exceptions; but it is false reasoning which converts exceptions into the general rule. Some men are born without the organs of sight, or of hearing, or without hands. Yet it would be wrong to say that man is born without these faculties, and sight, hearing, and hands may with truth enter into the general definition of man. The want or imperfection of the moral sense in some men, like the want or imperfection of the senses of sight and hearing in others, is no proof that it is a general characteristic of the species."

Late in the twentieth century some prominent scientists would argue that altruism was not only distributed in varying degrees throughout humanity but also through a large proportion of the animal kingdom. Though at Poplar Forest he lacked the resources of the library at Monticello, he quoted exactly or in paraphrase pertinent words from Wollaston, Helvétius, and Lord Kames, and cited the examples of Diderot, d'Alembert, d'Holbach, and Condorcet. He made various arresting comments, among them: "I have observed, indeed, generally, that while in Protestant countries the defections from the Platonic Christianity of the priests [are] to Deism, in Catholic countries they are to atheism." In the end he apologized to Law: "The leisure and solitude of my situation here has led me to the indiscretion of taxing you with a long letter on a subject whereon nothing can be offered you." Jefferson seemed to travel between a surfeit of company at Monticello and a dearth of it at Poplar Forest.

July 5, 1814, was the day after the thirty-eighth anniversary of the Declaration of Independence, so Jefferson was then moved by many memories when he wrote to John Adams.[13] He expressed "great regret" upon learning that his Massachusetts friend had suffered a "serious illness" but cautioned "our machines have now been running for 70 or 80 years, and we must expect that, worn as they are, here a pivot, there a wheel, now a pinion, next a spring, will be giving way; and however we tinker them up for awhile, all will at length surcease motion. Our watches, with works of brass and steel, wear out within that period. Shall you and I last to see the course the seven-fold wonders of the times will take?"

These words of the Sage of Monticello would seem ill calculated to cheer the ailing Sage of Braintree. But Jefferson used his question as a swift and smooth transition to a discussion of some of these "seven-fold wonders," a subject sure to engage the lively interest of his correspondent. First he listed: "The Attila of the age dethroned, the ruthless destroyer of 10 millions of the human race, whose thirst for blood appeared unquenchable, the great oppressor of the rights and liberties of the world, shut up within the circuit of a little island of the Mediterranean, and dwindled to the condition of an humble and degraded pensioner on the bounty of those he had most injured. How miserably, how meanly, has he closed his inflated career! What a sample of the Bathos will his history present! He should have perished on the swords of his enemies, under the walls of Paris."

Quoting verses about a lion that made men tremble even at his dying, Jefferson said: "But Bonaparte was a lion in the field only. In civil life a cold-blooded, calculating unprincipled Usurper, without a virtue, no statesman, knowing nothing of commerce, political economy, or civil government, and supplying ignorance to bold presumption. I had supposed him a great man until his entrance into the Assembly. . . . From that date, however, I set him down as a great scoundrel only. To the wonders of his rise and fall, we may add that of a Czar of Muscovy dictating, *in Paris*, laws and limits to all the successors of the Caesars, and holding even the balance in which the fortunes of his new world are suspended. I own that, while I rejoice, for the good of mankind, to the deliverance of Europe from the havoc which would have never ceased while Bonaparte should have lived in power, I see with anxiety the tyrant of the ocean remaining in vigor and even participating in the merit of crushing his brother tyrant."

Jefferson zeroed in on a field of more immediate concern. "While the world is thus turned upside down, on which side of it are we? All the strong reasons indeed place us on the side of peace; the interests of the continent, their friendly dispositions, and even the interests of England. Her passions alone are opposed to it. Peace would seem now to be an easy work, the causes of war being removed. Her Orders of Council will no doubt be taken care of by the allied powers, and, war ceasing, her impressment of our seamen ceases of course."

A threat remained nevertheless. Jefferson discussed it in a way that might raise the hackles of his sensitive friend. But he undoubtedly felt sure enough of the renewed friendship to be confident that his words were far more likely to produce a temporary irritation than a lengthy rupture. And he could not resist making his point about something that had long rankled. "But," he said after citing the happy prospects of peace, "I fear there is foundation for the design intimated in the public papers, of demanding a cession of our right in the [North Atlantic] fisheries. What will Massachusetts say to this? . . . She chose to sacrifice the liberty of our seafaring citizens, in which we were all interested, and with them her obligations to the co-states, rather than war with England. Will she now sacrifice the fisheries to the same partialities? This question is interesting to her alone: for the middle, the Southern and Western states they are of no direct concern; of no more than the culture of tobacco, rice and cotton to Massachusetts. I am really at a loss to conjecture what our refractory sister will say on this occasion."

Jefferson's next words could have been both reassuring and infuriating: "I know what, as a citizen of the Union, I would say to her. 'Take this question ad referendum. It concerns you alone. If you would rather give up the fisheries rather than war with England, we give them up. If you had rather fight for them, we will defend your interests to the last drop of our blood, choosing rather to set a good example than follow a bad one.' And I hope she will determine to fight for them."

Having indulged himself in this frankness, Jefferson suddenly cited a quotation from the Latin of Virgil and abruptly declared. "Quitting this subject therefore, I will turn over another leaf." He fell at once to lambasting a target farther removed than New England. He said that he had just returned from a five-week stay at Poplar Forest. "Having more leisure there than here for reading, I amused myself with reading seriously Plato's Republic. I am wrong however in calling it amusement, for it was the heaviest task-work I ever went through. I had occasionally before taken up some of his other works, but scarcely ever had patience to go through the whole dialogue. While wading thro' the whimsies, the puerilities, and unintelligible jargon of this work, I laid it down often to ask myself how it could have been that the world should have so long consented to give reputation to such nonsense as this?"

After confessing he could not account for Cicero's eulogies of the philosopher, he concluded: "With the Moderns, I think, it is largely a matter or fashion and authority. But fashion and authority apart, and bringing Plato to the test of reason, take from him his sophisms, futilities, and incomprehensibilities, and what remains? In truth, he is one of the race of genuine Sophists, who has escaped the oblivion of his brethren, first by the elegance of his diction, but chiefly by the adoption and incorporation of his whimsies into the body of artificial Christianity. His foggy mind is forever presenting the semblances of objects which, half seen through a mist, can be defined neither in form or dimension. Yet this which should have consigned him to early oblivion really procured him immortality of fame and reverence. The Christian priesthood, finding the doctrines of Christ levelled to every understanding, and too plain to need explanation, saw, in the mysticisms of Plato, materials with which they might build up an artificial system which might, from its indistinctness, admit everlasting controversy, give employment for their order, and introduce it to profit, power and pre-eminence. The doctrines which flowed from the lips of Jesus himself are within the comprehension of a child; but thousands of volumes have not yet explained the Platonisms engrafted on them: and for this obvious reason that nonsense can never be explained. Their purposes however are answered. Plato is canonized; and it is now deemed as impious to question his merits as those of an Apostle of Jesus."

Adams did not nurse umbrage at Jefferson's aspersions on Massachusetts and his speculations on the course that she might take in the face of British encroachments. With a little snap of irritation he wrote: "The 'refractory Sister' will not give up the fisheries. Not a man here dares to hint at so base a thought." Then he turned to a topic on which the two men agreed. "I am very glad you have seriously read Plato," he said, "and still more rejoiced to find that your reflections upon him so perfectly harmonize with mine. Some thirty years ago I took upon me the severe task of going through all his works. With the help of two Latin translations, and one English and one French translation and comparing some of the most remarkable passages with the Greek, I laboured through the tedious toil. My disappointment was very great, my astonishment was greater and my disgust was shocking. Two things only did I learn from him. 1. that Franklin's ideas of exempting husbandmen and mariners etc. from the depredations of war were borrowed from him. 2. that sneezing is a cure for the hiccups. Accordingly I have cured myself and all my friends of that provoking disorder, for thirty years with a pinch of snuff."

By this time the correspondence with Adams had become the most satisfying that Jefferson conducted. His family were gathered about him at Monticello so there was no need to communicate with them through the mails, and James Madison he saw at intervals. But only by letters could he communicate directly with Adams. And he could discuss with him a far greater range of topics than with most of his friends. Though the New Englander did not share the Virginian's passion for architecture and the fine arts, gardening and natural science, he did share Jefferson's interest in classical studies, law, government, religion, and philosophy. And of course they shared the bond of revolutionary labors and of being the only two people alive able to look back from the perspective of retirement on the experience of being President of the United States.

Another circumstance strengthened the ties between the old patriots. About a year earlier Jefferson had been surprised and excited to notice at the end of one of Adams' letters[14] a postscript in a once familiar hand—that of Abigail. She wrote: "I have been looking for some time for a space in my good husband's letters to add the regards of an old friend, which are still cherished and preserved through all the changes and vicissitudes which have taken place since we first became acquainted, and will I trust remain as long as A. Adams."

Jefferson replied promptly, telling her that he was always interested "in whatever affects your happiness. I have been concerned to learn that at one time you suffered much and long from rheumatism, and I can sympathize with you the more feelingly as I have more of it myself latterly than at any former period, and can form a truer idea of what it is in its higher degrees." He then turned to happier thoughts. "I have compared notes with Mr. Adams on the score of progeny, and find I am ahead of him, and think I am in a fair way to keep so. I have 10½ grandchildren, and 2¾ great-grand-children; and these fractions will ere long become units. I was glad to learn from Mr. Adams that you have a grandson far enough advanced in age and acquirements to be reading Greek. These young scions give us comfortable cares, when we cease to care about ourselves. Under all circumstances of health or sickness, of blessing or affliction, I tender you assurances of my sincere affection and respect; and my prayers that the hand of time and of providence may press lightly on you, till your own wishes shall withdraw you from all mortal feeling."[15]

Ironically, Mrs. Adams' reply[16] began, "Your kind and friendly letter found me in a great affliction for the loss of my dear and only daughter. . . . You, sir, who have been called to separations of a similar kind, can sympathize with your bereaved friend. . . . You called upon me to talk of myself, and I have obeyed the summons from the assurance you gave me, that you took an interest in whatever affected my happiness. 'Grief has changed me since you saw me last, and care-full hours, with time's deformed hand, hath written strange defections o'er my face.' But although time has changed the outward form, and political 'back-wounding calumny' for a period interrupted the friendly intercourse and harmony which subsisted, it is again renewed, purified from the dross."

Though John Adams' letters reveal him to be no less consistent than Jefferson in his unremitting habits of study, the New Englander did not share his friend's passion for devising schemes of formal education. Once, in answer to Jefferson's questions on the subject, Adams wrote: "Education! Oh Education! The greatest grief of my heart and the greatest affliction of my life! To my mortification I must confess that I have never closely thought, or very deliberately reflected upon the subject, which never occurs to me now without producing a deep sigh, a heavy groan and sometimes tears. My cruel destiny separated me from my children almost continually from their birth to their manhood."[17] Later Adams wrote Jefferson: "Education . . . is a subject so vast, and the systems of writers are so various and so contradictory, that human life is too short to examine it; and a man must die before he can learn to bring up his children. The philosophers, divines, politicians and pedagogues who have published their theories and practices in this department are without number."[18]

At last Jefferson perceived that he would find a more interested audience if he directed elsewhere his ideas about public education. He dispatched his concepts to various other people in the United States and Europe and sought their advice. John Adams did send to Monticello two young Bostonians who were eager listeners to Jefferson's theories.[19] The Sage of Braintree provided letters of introduction for George Ticknor and Francis C. Gray, who were on a Southern journey. Just twenty-three years old, Ticknor was especially interested. Jefferson descried in him the future writer, historian, and educator of distinction. Both young men were from High Federalist families, part of the group that regretted Adams had compromised with the Republicans on anything.

Ticknor was prepared to find the Virginia statesman "notional." Nothing changed his mind when the two visitors arrived at Monticello on a rainy Saturday morning in February 1815 and stepped into a handsome foyer transformed into an intellectual warehouse by the predilections of their host. A buffalo head, animal hides, mineral specimens, mastodon bones and tusks, moose and elk antlers, American Indian tomahawks and clothing vied for attention with eight framed maps, a model of the Great Pyramid of Cheops, numerous European paintings, and sculptures by Houdon.[20] It was like a museum of arts and sciences in which, as in the proprietor's mind, there was no rigid separation of categories.

Gray has left a description of the man who welcomed the two Bostonians: "He is quite tall, six feet, one or two inches, face streaked and speckled with red, light gray eyes, white hair, dressed in shoes of very thin soft leather with pointed toes and heels ascending in a peak behind, with very short quarters, gray worsted stockings, corduroy small-clothes [knee breeches], blue waistcoat and coat, of stiff thick cloth made of the wool of his own merinos and badly manufactured, the buttons of his coat and small-clothes of horn, and an under waistcoat flannel bound with red velvet. His figure bony, long and with broad shoulders, a true Virginian."

Though no more favorably impressed than Gray with the homespun portions of Jefferson's wardrobe, Ticknor was struck with the "dignity in his appearance, and ease and grace in his manners." Both were soon won by his charm. Dinner, served at four, brought the family together with their guests, and Ticknor thought the company among the most agreeable he had ever known. The visitors from Boston were greatly entertained by their host's erudition and anecdotal skills, but these they had been led to expect. What amazed them was that the ladies in the family took part equally with the men when the conversations turned to intellectual topics. The talk that began at four o'clock continued until about half past ten.

In such congenial company, amid elegant surroundings, it was hard to realize that the United States was fighting for its life; that the British, after defeating the Americans at Bladensburg, Maryland, on August 24, 1814, had marched unopposed to Washington and set fire to the Capitol, the Executive Mansion, and most of the buildings in the city that President and Mrs. Madison had had to flee. Though the British had promptly withdrawn, because of one of nature's storms rather than the thunder of American artillery, the Chesapeake Bay was still their naval center of operations in the western Atlantic. Earlier they had nearly destroyed the town of Hampton, at the mouth of the James River, and the commander of that expedition had written, "Every horror was perpetrated with impunity—rape, murder, pillage—and not one man was punished."[21] French captives of the English joined in the orgy of destruction.

Jefferson's son-in-law Thomas Mann Randolph had obtained a Colonel's commission and gone to the defense of Richmond. Jefferson had little empathy for him, writing a friend, "Mr. Randolph has been seized with the military fever.

. . . He will be a great loss to his family, and no man in the world a greater one to his affairs."[22] Grandson Jeff had also gone to the defense of the state capital. When Jefferson's grandson-in-law, Charles Bankhead, left soon after, he carried a letter to his Colonel from Jefferson asking him to do what he could for the boy. "If I were able either to walk or ride," the elder statesman said, "I would join them."[23] At age seventy-one an unusually severe onset of rheumatism had deprived him of the ability to mount his horse. He would be able to ride again but his longest walks now and in the future would be to his nearby garden.

Still he led animated conversations at his dinner table and eagerly talked of plans for a state university in Virginia as if oblivious to tragic events downriver on the James. One should not wonder that this could be so. As Governor of Virginia during the Revolution, though forced to flee the invaders, and with Monticello itself violated by the enemy, he had completed his book *Notes on the State of Virginia* and had made plans for a state library and museum.

By the time Ticknor and Gray visited Jefferson in February, he had reason to hope that the worst of the War of 1812 was over. About two months before, James Monroe had let him know that peace negotiations had been resumed and Castlereagh seemed sincerely desirous of a settlement. Colonel Randolph and Jeff had returned home.

But the young visitors still had two occasions during their three-day visit to wonder at their host's apparent equanimity in receiving news that would have brought strong reactions from most people. Now again able to sit his horse, Jefferson had resumed his morning rides. On his return from one, he quietly told Randolph that overnight the dam had been swept away. Their host's manner led his guests to assume that the event was a trivial annoyance. They were surprised on their ride back to Richmond to hear that the damage amounted to $30,000, a huge sum in those days. The Bostonians would have been even more surprised at Jefferson's low-key reaction if they had known the perilous state of his finances. The flour that he had produced the year before was still unsold and deteriorating, his crops had been wiped out by drought, and he was haunted by unpaid notes. He viewed 1814 as his "most calamitous year" in a long time.[24] The visitors had cause for astonishment the night before their departure when they were aroused from bed to hear news brought from Charlottesville by Jeff. General Andrew Jackson had inflicted a monumental defeat on the British at New Orleans. He had lost only eight men killed and thirteen wounded; British losses, killed and wounded, totaled 2,036. When told of the event, Jefferson left his door closed and said that he would learn the details in the morning. Next morning at breakfast, though a newspaper account was available, he had not yet read it. This restraint was the more remarkable because he had earlier confessed anxiety about the course of events in Louisiana.

Ticknor and Gray were impressed with what they took to be Jefferson's remarkable stoicism. One of his greatest biographers wrote: "It would appear that the septuagenarian had learned to maintain his equanimity under virtually any circumstance."[25] But isn't it possible, as subsequent correspondence would indicate, that Jefferson feared the problem of impressment was still unsettled.

And is it not also possible that, while Jefferson was pleased by the American triumph at New Orleans, his pleasure was lessened by the fact that the instrument of victory was Andrew Jackson, who had harangued street crowds in behalf of Aaron Burr when the former Vice President was on trial for treason? Jefferson had a long memory for offenses committed by Burr supporters at that time when the President himself seemed to be on trial. As one who had served under Washington, Jefferson was fully conscious of the role of victories in propelling Generals into high political office.

The Battle of New Orleans was the greatest American land victory of the war and is altogether the most famous event of the contest. It was rendered even more dramatic by the series of American reverses that preceded it. It cut short not only the careers of many obscure men but also took the lives of Major General Sir Edward Pakenham, the British commander, and two of his subordinate Generals. But it affected not one whit the outcome of the war. The battle was fought January 8, 1815. Unknown to the Americans or their British opponents, a peace treaty between the two nations had been signed at Ghent on Christmas Eve. The chief effects of the battle were to inflate American morale, which had sagged after the burning of Washington, and to send General Jackson's reputation aloft on the winds of war, where it inescapably attracted the attention of those interested in presidential politics.

XVI

NO ROYAL ROAD

THE END OF the War of 1812 freed Americans to concentrate on a long-neglected domestic agenda. In Virginia, peace enabled many leaders to think more consistently about something Jefferson had concentrated on amid all the distractions of war, a system of public education for the commonwealth.

"A system of public instruction. . . ," he once wrote, "as it was the earliest so it will be the latest of all the public concerns in which I shall permit myself to take an interest."[1] About the time Jefferson drafted his Statute of Virginia for Religious Freedom, in 1777, he also produced a plan "for the more general diffusion of knowledge." Although not enacted in his lifetime, and never enacted in precisely the terms he advocated, it eventually proved the most seminal proposal in the history of American public education. This was Jefferson's plan for dividing the state into districts and establishing public schools in each. The most elementary education would be provided free for all children whose parents could not afford to pay for their instruction. There would be opportunities at each level for the most promising to move on to the next above until finally at two-year intervals, from each county, one student "of the best learning and most hopeful genius and disposition" would "proceed to William and Mary College, there to be educated, boarded, and clothed three years." As we have seen, he proposed a broadening of the curriculum at William and Mary to make it a more suitable capstone for education in Virginia.[2] What seems elitist today was considered radical in his own time—much too radical for acceptance. But Jefferson had published the major features of his program in the *Notes on the State of Virginia*, which he completed in 1781.

When Jefferson perceived that the legislators of his state were a long way from endorsing a general system of public education, he still clung stubbornly to the idea of a state university and talked it up at every opportunity. In 1800, just before entering upon the presidency, he detected increased interest among some lawmakers and eagerly sought ideas from Joseph Priestley and Du Pont de Nemours as well as from such fellow Virginians as Governor John Tyler. By this time he had decided that the College of William and Mary was not a sufficiently pliant candidate for reform and proposed the establishment of a new university "on a plan so broad and liberal and *modern* as to be worth patronizing with the public support, and a temptation to the youth of other states to come and drink of the cup of knowledge and fraternize with us."[3]

Near the end of Jefferson's first term as President, he responded enthusiastically and in detail to a hopeful letter from Littleton Waller Tazewell: "No one can be more rejoiced at the information that the legislature of Virginia are likely at length to institute a University on a liberal plan. Convinced that the people are the only safe depositories of their own liberty and that they are not safe unless enlightened to a certain degree, I have looked on our present state of liberty as a short-lived possession unless the mass of the people could be informed to a certain degree. This requires two grades of education. First, some institution where science in all its branches is taught, and in the highest degree to which the human mind has carried it. This would prepare a few subjects in every State, to whom nature has given minds of the first order. Secondly, such a degree of learning given to every member of the society as will enable him to read, to judge and to vote understandingly on what is passing. This would be the object of the township schools. I understand from your letter that the first of these only is under present contemplation. Let us receive with contentment what the legislature is now ready to give. The other branch will be incorporated into the system at some more favorable moment."[4]

The letter—a lengthy one—was typical of Jefferson: in its philosophy, and as an instance of his habit of joyfully accepting when he received a portion of what he wanted and of deferring, but not abandoning, his quest for all. He revealed to Tazewell a carefully thought-out plan for organization of the university and even listed in 1-2-3-4 order the steps which the legislature should take.

Jefferson could not dictate to the General Assembly of Virginia. If he could have, his plan for a university would have been adopted much earlier. But during his presidency, besides his influence as Chief Magistrate, he was the leader of the Republican Party, which dominated the General Assembly of Virginia. After his retirement from office, he continued to exert a powerful influence on politics in his state. James Madison, his closest friend, was his handpicked successor as President. Despite all of Jefferson's protestations about this retreat to the mountaintop, he was the sage and the symbol of the Republican Party. And that party controlled politics in Virginia. The justices of the county courts, which in those days also functioned partly as boards of supervisors, were dominant in the informal selection of candidates for the legislature. These justices were mostly Republicans. The legislature still elected the Governor, and the Governor appointed the justices, almost always filling vacancies according to the recommendations of incumbent justices of the court in question.[5]

Alas, national tribulations intervened, and the establishment of a state university was postponed again. But Jefferson continued to work on his plan. Already he had settled upon the idea of an "academical village." He envisioned a lawn flanked by school buildings and professors' houses "connected by covered ways out of which the rooms of the students should open." Such a design would lend itself to graceful growth. The university would not be an imitation of Oxford, Cambridge, or the Sorbonne. Those institutions were "a century or two behind" the needs of the age. The standard curriculum needed to be updated to include multiplying branches of science and new ramifications of philosophy. Courses would be created to meet the special needs of American society. But such updating would not be at the cost of the classics. The great Greek and Roman intellectual masterpieces would be studied in the languages in which they had first appeared.

Jefferson told Tazewell: "Should this establishment take place on a plan worthy of approbation, I shall have a valuable legacy to leave it, to wit, my library, which certainly has not cost less than 15,000 dollars. But its value is more in the selection, a part of which, that which respects America, is the result of my own personal searches in Paris for six or seven years, and of persons employed by me in England, Holland, Germany and Spain to make similar searches. Such a collection on that subject can never again be made."[6]

But the university did not receive that library. The dreamed-of institution was not even immediately in prospect in August 1814, when the British, while putting the torch to most of Washington, burned the Library of Congress. This act infuriated Jefferson more than any other depredation in the capital. He offered his personal collection as the nucleus of a new Library of Congress. It was now a larger and richer collection than nine years before, when he told Tazewell he intended it for the university. Francis Gray, an ardent bibliophile familiar with the best libraries of Massachusetts, had marveled over some of the riches in the collection at Monticello. He was excited over "a black letter Chaucer," a first edition of *Paradise Lost*, and "a fine collection of Saxon and Moeso Gothic books, among them Alfred's translations of Orosius and Boethius." After noting rare or unusual works in French and Italian, he concluded, "Of all branches of learning, however, that relating to the history of North and South America is the most perfectly displayed in this library. The collection on this subject is without a question the most valuable in the world."[7] Examination of the inventory suggests that this was quite possibly an accurate estimate.

Jefferson offered this collection—the work of a half century—with the assurance that he would accept in payment whatever valuation Congress should place on it. His only stipulation was that it be kept as a unit.[8] Congress did not jump at the opportunity. Many were excited by the prospect, but some objected that the library might contain volumes that the national legislators would never need to consult. A few even suggested that the collection might contain information on matters best left alone. But eventually "the commonsense of most" prevailed, and Congress offered the ex-President $23,950. In April 1815 he boxed up his old friends and sent them to Washington.

Jefferson soon had more time to plan his university and bring it near fruition. On March 16 grandson Jeff Randolph had married Jane Hollins Nicholas, daughter of the President's old friend and political ally, Wilson Cary Nicholas, now Governor of Virginia. The young couple lived in Monticello's dome room, with its extremely heavy crown molding and large round windows commanding beautiful views of distant mountains. The apartment was more romantic than convenient, but for the newlyweds romance may have had a higher priority.

Sometime before the end of June, Jefferson gave over the management of his farms to Jeff.

The young man had always been a great favorite with his grandfather. When he was a little boy his venturesome appetite for life delighted his grandsire. When as a ten-year-old he had commandeered the presidential vehicle and visited the Washington Navy Yard, collecting salutes as he went, his shocked mother had reprimanded him severely but his grandfather had been unable to conceal his own amusement. In manhood, he had the large physique of Jefferson's father, Peter Jefferson, and this could only have endeared him more. Freed by this energetic and dependable twenty-three-year-old from the task of wresting a living from the unpromising soil of his Albemarle estates, Jefferson could limit his agricultural activities to horticultural experiments and an occasional intervention when he really wanted to play farmer.

Grandfather and grandson were close. Jeff had accompanied the President on the ride to the Capitol when the reins of government passed to James Madison. The older man had tutored the boy in his schoolwork and had been his moral preceptor. Jeff learned even more by example than by instruction, and we owe to his recollections some significant insights into the statesman's character and personality.

Jeff recorded one incident that in the context of our times smacks of elitism and paternalism but in an earlier day was regarded as evidence of a sensitive and liberal spirit "His manners," the grandson recalled, "were of that polished school of the Colonial Government, so remarkable in its day—under no circumstances violating any of those minor conventional observances which constitute the well-bred gentleman, courteous and considerate to all persons. On riding out with him, when [I was] a lad, we met a Negro who bowed to us. He returned his bow, I did not. Turning to me he asked, 'Do you permit a Negro to be more of a gentleman than yourself?' "[9]

Another of Jeff's anecdotes illustrates Jefferson's sensitivity to the feelings of a member of his own social group. There was a little competition "among the older gentlemen of the neighborhood, in their gardening; and he who had peas first announced his success by an invitation to the others to dine with him. A wealthy neighbor, without children, and fond of horticulture, generally triumphed. Mr. Jefferson, on one occasion had them first, and when his family reminded him that it was his right to invite the company, he replied, 'No, say nothing about it, it will be more agreeable to our friend to think that he never fails.' "[10]

He didn't really see enough of his Albemarle neighbors in these days of world fame. Jeff observed: "It was a source of continued and deep regret to him that the number of strangers who visited him kept his neighbors from him; he said he had to exchange the society of his friends and neighbors for those whom he had never seen before and never expected to see again."[11]

But the elder statesman exuded a generous humanity that made him seem approachable to the humblest of unknowns. Jeff recalled with pride: "His countenance was mild and benignant, and attractive to strangers. While President, returning on horseback from court, with company whom he had invited to dinner, and who were, all but one or two, riding ahead of him, on reaching a stream over which there was no bridge, a man asked him to take him up behind and carry him over. The gentleman in the rear coming up just as Mr. Jefferson had put him down and rode on, asked the man how it happened that he had permitted the others to pass without asking them? He replied, 'From their looks I did not like to ask them—the old gentleman looked as if he would do it, and I asked him.' He was very much surprised to hear that he had ridden behind the President of the United States."[12]

Jefferson's tact made a strong impression on his grandson. "He never indulged in controversial conversation, because it often excited unpleasant feeling [and served no useful purpose]. His maxim was that every man had a right to his own opinion on all subjects and others were bound to respect that right. Hence, in conversation, if anyone expressed a decided opinion differing from his own, he made no reply, but changed the subject. He believed men could always find subjects enough to converse on, [on] which they agreed in opinion, omitting those upon which they differed."[13]

Jeff learned from the elder statesman a lesson in "the management of men" which was as effective in the running of an estate as in the leadership of a cabinet meeting. "He inquiringly followed out adverse opinions to their results, leaving it to their [advocates] to note the error into which it led them, taking up their doubts as important suggestions, never permitting a person to place himself upon the defensive, or if he did [so place himself], changing the subject, so as not to fix him in a wrong opinion by controverting it."[14] Here was the Socratic method made palatable by liberal seasonings of the Earl of Chesterfield and the yet unborn Dale Carnegie.

Jefferson's methods were tempered by his shrewd perceptions of the individuals with whom he dealt. Jeff noted: "With men of fertile and ingenious minds, fond of suggesting objections to propositions stated, he would some-times suggest the opposite of the conclusion to which he desired them to come, then assent to the force of their objections, and thus lead them to convert themselves."[15]

The admiring grandson observed: "His powers of conversation were great, yet he always turned it to subjects most familiar to those with whom he conversed, whether laborer, mechanic, or other; and if they displayed sound judgement and a knowledge of the subject, entered the information they gave, under appropriate heads, for reference, embodying thus a mass of facts upon the practical details of everyday life."[16]

Jeff had a great desire to emulate his grandfather. He recalled with particular pride that the old man's temper, though "naturally strong," was "under perfect control—his courage, cool and impassive—no one ever knew him [to] exhibit trepidation—his moral courage of the highest order—his will, firm and inflexible. It was remarked of him that he never abandoned a plan, a principle, or a friend."[17]

Among the plans that Jefferson never abandoned were those for a state university. Being able to work toward this goal without having his strength drained off by the multitudinous tasks of estate management infused him with the energy of hope and purpose. This positive power was at war with the debilitating effects of age and illness when he wrote John Adams in April 1816, a little before the time that Jeff relieved him of irksome tasks:

> You ask if I would agree to live my 70, or rather 73, years over again? To which I say Yea. I think with you that it is a good world on the whole, that it has been framed on a principle of benevolence, and more pleasure than pain dealt out to us. There are indeed (who might say Nay) gloomy and hypochondriac minds, inhabitants of diseased bodies, disgusted with the present, and despairing of the future; always counting that the worst will happen, because it may happen. To these I say, "How much pain have cost us the evils which have never happened?" My temperament is sanguine. I steer my bark with Hope in the head, leaving Fear astern. My hopes indeed sometimes fail; but not oftener than the forebodings of the gloomy.[18]

Hope was in the head when Jefferson conceived the idea of making a university out of a preparatory school still existent only on paper a decade after its charting. He was made a trustee of the proposed school, Albemarle Academy, in March 1814 and began at once to work for its transformation. Conveniently, the chairman of the board was his nephew Peter Carr. And Carr opened the door to great possibilities when he asked him to outline a plan for the school.

Most of the trustees apparently envisioned a traditional preparatory school. Jefferson obviously was determined to make it into something more and was taking practical steps toward that goal not only before his first attendance of a board meeting, on April 5, but even before his election in March. On January 16, 1814 he had written to the brilliant Professor Thomas Cooper, of Carlisle College, that a university worthy of his talents might be established not far from Monticello.[19] Clearly Jefferson did not hope to use the prospect of another provincial boys' school to lure from Pennsylvania the educator whom he considered America's leading writer on economics. Further evidence of Jefferson's larger ideas came in the fall. Then 147 citizens of Albemarle County, acting independently of the academy trustees, petitioned the state legislature for permission to run a lottery to raise money for purchasing a local tavern to serve as the school building. Word was passed that the scheme was not in accord with Jefferson's ideas and it was dropped.

The shape into which Jefferson was bending the school project was evident on September 7, 1814, when he wrote Chairman Carr: "On the subject of the academy or college proposed to be established in our neighborhood, I promised the trustees that I would prepare for them a plan, adapted, in the first instance, to our slender funds, but susceptible of being enlarged, either by our growth or by accession from other quarters."[20]

He told of his long-cherished hope that Virginia would "make an establishment, either with or without incorporation into William and Mary, where every branch of science [learning] deemed useful at this day should be taught in its highest degree. With this view, I have lost no occasion of making myself acquainted with the organization of the best seminaries in other countries, and with the opinions of the most enlightened individuals on the subject of the sciences worthy of a place in such an institution." He had been struck with the "diversity" of the curricula—"no two alike. Yet I have no doubt that these several arrangements have been the subject of mature reflection by wise and learned men who, contemplating local circumstances, have adapted them to the conditions of the section of society for which they have been framed. I am strengthened in this conclusion by an examination of each separately, and a conviction that no one of them, if adopted without change, would be suited to the circumstances and pursuit of our country. The example they set, then, is authority for us to select from their different institutions the materials which are good for us, and with them to erect a structure whose arrangement shall correspond with our own social condition, and shall admit of enlargement in proportion to the encouragement it may merit and receive."

Jefferson was not only laying the ground for transforming a projected small academy into a great university but was also paving the way for the exercise of originality in its organization. The method was the same that he had used when he played down the original features of his design for the Virginia state Capitol and stressed adherence to the classical style of the Maison Carrée.[21] At his most innovative, he almost always cited a precedent—at least in public projects. In that way he ameliorated the fear of change.

The political leaders of the United States, Jefferson asserted, had a "duty . . . to provide that every citizen in it should receive an education proportioned to the condition and pursuits of his life. The mass of our citizens may be divided into two classes—the laboring and the learned. The laboring will need the first [level] of education to qualify them for their pursuits and duties; the learned will need it as a foundation for further acquirements."

He wrote:

> At the discharging of the pupils from the elementary school, the two classes separate—those destined for labor will engage in the business of agriculture, or enter into apprenticeships to such handicraft art as may be their choice; their companions, destined to the pursuits of science, will proceed to the college, which will consist, lst of general schools; and, 2d, of professional schools. The general schools will constitute the second grade of education.
>
> The learned class may still be subdivided into two sections; 1, Those who are destined for learned professions, as means of livlihood; and, 2, The wealthy, who, possessing independent fortunes, may aspire to share in conducting the affairs of the nation, or to live with usefulness and respect in the private ranks of life. Both of these sections will require instruction in all the higher branches of science; the wealthy to qualify them for either public or private life; the professional section will need those branches, especially, which are the basis of their future profession, and a general knowledge of the others, as auxiliary to that, and necessary to their standing and association with the scientific class. All the branches

then, of useful science, ought to be taught in the general schools, to a competent degree, in the first instance. These sciences may be arranged into three departments, not rigorously scientific, indeed, but sufficiently so for our purposes. These are, I. Language; II. Mathematics; III. Philosophy.[22]

Anyone who doubted that Jefferson used the word *science* in its general eighteenth-century senses to mean scholarship or any branch of study, not just disciplines concerned with measurement or controlled experiments, should be convinced by his denomination of language and philosophy as two of the three principal scientific categories. Certainly the breadth of his definition of science becomes indisputable when he subdivides language into belles lettres, rhetoric, and oratory as well as grammar, and lists the fine arts as sciences.

Jefferson made several striking proposals in regard to the curriculum. One was that historical writings be used as texts in the teaching of both ancient and modern languages, "not as a kindred subject, but on the principle of economy, because both may be attained by the same course of reading if books are selected with that view." He proposed the creation of "a school for the deaf, dumb, and blind" and the institution of night school classes so that education could be pursued by artisans and others whose days were spent in earning a living. The Sage of Monticello drew much of his inspiration from the classical civilization, but he was far ahead of his time in proposing language instruction as an introduction to a foreign culture as well as a foreign tongue, and in his advocacy of education for the handicapped and of adult education.

After listing specific components of the language, mathematics, philosophy, and physics courses, he proposed the creation of professional schools. "At the close" of their undergraduate college course, he explained, "the students separate, the wealthy retiring with a sufficient stock of knowledge to improve themselves to any degree to which their views may lead them, and the professional section to the professional schools, constituting the third grade of education, and teaching the particular sciences which the individuals of this section mean to pursue, with more minuteness and detail than was within the scope of the general schools for the second grade of instruction. In these professional schools each science is to be taught in the highest degree it has yet attained."

He listed three "departments" which he also called "professional schools":

1st Department, the fine arts, to wit: Civil Architecture, Gardening, Painting, Sculpture, and the Theory of Music; the

2nd Department, Architecture, Military and Naval; Projectiles, Rural Economy (comprehending Agriculture, Horticulture and Veterinary), Technical Philosophy, the Practice of Medicine, Materia Medica, Pharmacy and Surgery. In the

3rd Department, Theology and Ecclesiastical History; Law, Municipal and Foreign.

"The gentleman, the architect, the pleasure gardener, painter and musician," he said, would be drawn to the school of fine arts. Though Jefferson's plan as a whole was far more democratic than most schemes of education at the time, in our day there is quaintness in the supposition that nonprofessional interest in the arts would be limited to those labeled gentlemen. William Morris' fight against that supposition seventy years later was thought by many contemporaries to be part and parcel of his radicalism.

"Technical philosophy" would comprise a fourth department. The designation seems strange in a modern age accustomed to associate philosophy almost entirely with speculative studies. In Jefferson's time, however, as in that of the ancient Greeks, philosophy embraced the practical as well as the theoretical. Indeed many writers in the eighteenth century, of which he was a product, used the term chiefly in reference to practical pursuits.

Therefore there was nothing strange in Jefferson's saying that the department of technical philosophy would serve the needs of "the mariner, carpenter, shipwright, pumpmaker, clockmaker, machinist, optician, metallurgist, founder, cutler, druggist, brewer, vintner, distiller, dyer, painter, bleacher, soapmaker, tanner, powdermaker, saltmaker, glassmaker, to learn as much as shall be necessary to pursue their art understandingly, of the sciences of geometry, mechanics, statics, hydrostatics, hydraulics, hydrodynamics, navigation, astronomy, geography, optics, pneumatics, physics, chemistry, natural history, botany, mineralogy and pharmacy." The only strange thing by the standards of the day was that he conceived it the responsibility of an institution of higher learning to offer such instruction and to provide it "wholly at the public expense."

He emphasized: "The school of technical philosophy will differ essentially in its functions from the other professional schools. The others are instituted to ramify and dilate the particular sciences taught in the schools of the [undergraduate level] on a general scale only. The technical school is to abridge those which were taught there too much *in extenso* for the limited wants of the artificer or practical man. These artificers must be grouped together, according to the particular branch of science in which they need elementary and practical instruction; and a special lecture or lectures should be prepared for each group."

Jefferson also called for something akin to the reserve officer training corps of a later day, only the units he envisioned would be intended for military training without regard to whether the participants were preparing to serve as officers or enlisted men.

Jefferson sent Dr. Thomas Cooper a copy of his letter to Carr. The professor was a versatile scholar, and Jefferson solicited his opinion on the proposed curriculum. They agreed on most points, but Jefferson earnestly differed with Cooper's assumption that botany could be omitted from the eleventh grade of education. "Botany," he wrote, "I rank with the most valuable sciences, whether we consider its subjects as furnishing the principal subsistence of life to man and beast, delicious varieties for our tables, refreshments from our orchards, the adornments of our flower-borders, shade and perfume of our groves, materials for our buildings, or medicaments for our bodies." Moreover, he did not think that it was a study to be pursued only by the specialist. He said: "To a country family it constitutes a great portion of their social entertainment. No country gentleman should be without what amuses every step he takes into his fields."[23]

Cooper was getting a little restless at Carlisle. Jefferson did not want him to commit himself to another institution before the projected school in Virginia had a chance to secure his services. Jefferson was recruiting for a university existing only on paper and whose concept had not yet been approved by the board of which he was a member. He made no unauthorized promises but he was recruiting just the same. He did scrupulously send Carr a copy of the letter to Cooper. Of course, the chairman, as Jefferson's devoted nephew, was probably even more strongly influenced by him than any of the other board members. The elder statesman's influence was particularly strong in this project because surely no one else in Virginia had informed himself so well on the subject at hand.

He confided to Cooper, as a presumably sympathetic spirit, something that he apparently did not share with many of his friends: his conviction that the disciplines of theology and medicine would bear watching. Jefferson was a tireless student of religion who had constructed his own edition of the New Testament and he had been a zealous advocate of such medical innovations as inoculation against smallpox, but he thought that the two studies could easily degenerate—one into charlatanry of the mind, the other into charlatanry of the body.

Before the year was out the principal elements of Jefferson's plan had been approved by the board, and the ex-President had been named with his nephew Carr and his son-in-law Thomas Mann Randolph to a committee to petition the legislature for a charter. Not surprisingly, the old statesman wrote the petition himself. The changed nature of the proposed institution and the continued determination to locate it in the Charlottesville area were symbolized in the petition's request that the name be changed from Albemarle Academy to Central College.

Because of one difficulty that Jefferson had not foreseen, the petition was not presented to the legislature of 1814–1815. The document Jefferson wrote was entrusted to Peter Carr for presentation in Richmond. Carr became too ill to take care of the matter. Upon his death on February 18 nobody could find the petition. About a month before Carr's death, fearing that his nephew had not been able to discharge his responsibility, Jefferson had sent his own copy to State Senator Joseph C. Cabell. Apparently it was then too late to accomplish anything in so complicated a matter before adjournment.

Jefferson grieved for his nephew and was deeply disappointed in the delay of action on the college. If anything should happen to him before fruition of his plans for a university the whole scheme might die.

Fortunately, Jefferson won Cabell's support and gained in him an able and active ally. The young man represented Jefferson's own district in the upper house of the General Assembly. To legislative diligence and superior abilities he added the broadening experience of time spent in Europe.

Nevertheless, Jefferson did not relax his own lobbying. He was not only trying to gain a charter for Central College and thus create the nucleus of a university but was also attempting to obtain authorization for the board of the institution to set up elementary schools in Albemarle County and thus provide the nucleus of a full-fledged statewide system of public schools. To finance these developments, he was hoping for the transfer of funds from the State Literary Fund, created by the General Assembly in 1810 under the inspiration of Governor Tyler. The fund was fed by escheats, confiscations, penalties, forfeitures, some fines, and the sale of personal property for nonpayment of taxes. The fund was created for the encouragement of learning. The grand abstraction was given at least one concrete facet the next year when it was provided that, as soon as the size of the fund permitted, schools for the poor should be established in every county.

One legislator who had doubts about some provisions of the educational bill written by Jefferson was Colonel Charles Yancey, who represented Albemarle County in the House of Delegates, lower chamber of the General Assembly. The elder statesman wrote Yancey a long letter[24] advocating "improvements of roads, canals, and schools," but particularly stressing education. "If the legislature would add to [the Literary Fund] a perpetual tax of a cent a head on the population of the State, it would set agoing at once, and forever maintain, a system of primary or ward schools, and an university where might be taught, in its highest degree, every branch of science useful in our time and country; and it would rescue us from the tax of toryism, fanaticism, and indifferentism to their own State, which we now send our youth to bring from those of New England."

Next, introduced by one of Jefferson's most memorable sentences, came one of the most eloquent passages to be found in his writings: "If a nation expects to be ignorant and free, in a state of civilization, it expects what never was and never will be. The functionaries of every government have propensities to command at will the liberty and property of their constituents. There is no safe deposit for these but with the people themselves; nor can they be safe with them without information. Where the press is free, and every man able to read, all is safe."

In his adulthood Jefferson alternated between praising newspapers as bulwarks of freedom and deploring them as disseminators of misinformation. These lines contain one of his more generous estimates. It should be remembered, too, that the concept of a free press embraced not only newspapers but also journals, pamphlets, and books.

Over the rutted and frozen roads of the hill country there came to Monticello on February 16, 1816 the news that the General Assembly had passed the Central College bill in January. Jefferson entered upon a more urgent stage in his efforts to achieve two things: advance as rapidly as practicable the establishment of the college and accelerate its transformation into a university. With careful management and a little luck, the second objective might even overtake the first.

Pacing was essential here, and Jefferson had developed it into a fine art.

When Dr. Cooper had urged him to divest the plan for the college of all features that served no useful purpose and merely compromised with public opinion, he replied: "We cannot always do what is absolutely best. Those with whom we act, entertaining different views, have the power and the right of carrying them into practice. Truth advances and error recedes step by step only; and to do our fellow men the most good in our power, we must lead where we can, follow where we cannot, and still go with them, watching always the favorable moment for helping them to another step."[25]

Not only was Jefferson prepared to be tolerant with those who had not yet caught up with his thought; he also was aware that he did not possess a monopoly of truth, although he doubtless thought that he possessed a larger share than most people. Judge Learned Hand said, "The spirit of liberty is the spirit which is not too sure that it is right." Jefferson had lived long enough, and had grown enough, to find himself in disagreement with some of his former selves. For example, when informed that his strictures against industrial growth in *Notes on the State of Virginia* were still being quoted as policy guides, he wrote Benjamin Austin:[26] "There was a time when I might have been so quoted with more candor, but within the thirty years which have since elapsed, how are circumstances changed! . . . We have experienced what we did not then believe, that there exists both profligacy and power enough to exclude us from the field of interchange with other nations: that to be independent for the comforts of life we must fabricate them ourselves. We must now place the manufacturer by the side of the agriculturist."

While planning the college Jefferson was busy with a number of other intellectual concerns. The appearance of Charles Thomson's synopsis of the evangelists prompted him to confide to the author: "I, too, have made a wee-little book from the same materials which I call the *Philosophy of Jesus*; it is a paradigma of his doctrines, made by cutting the texts out of the book, and arranging them on the pages of a blank book, in a certain order of time or subject. A more beautiful or precious morsel of ethics I have never seen; it is a document in proof that *I* am a *real Christian*, that is to say, a disciple of the doctrines of Jesus, very different from the Platonists, who call *me* infidel and *themselves* Christians and preachers of the gospel, while they draw all their characteristic dogmas from what its author never said nor saw. They have compounded from the heathen mysteries a system beyond the comprehension of man, of which the great reformer of the vicious ethics and deism of the Jews, were he to return on earth, would not recognize one feature. If I had time I would add to my little book the Greek, Latin, and French texts, in columns side by side."[27] He held on to the idea until he found time. "And I wish," he added, "I could subjoin a translation of Gosindi's Syntagma of the doctrines of Epicurus, which, notwithstanding the calumnies of the Stoics and caricatures of Cicero, is the most rational system remaining of the philosophy of the ancients, as frugal of vicious indulgence, and fruitful of virtue, as the hyperbolical extravagances of his rival sects."

Jefferson wrote freely to this distinguished Philadelphian, the former secretary of the Continental Congress, whom he saluted as "my dear and ancient friend." As interesting as the glimpse afforded of Jefferson's intellectual life is the picture that he includes of his corporeal existence:

> I retain good health, am rather feeble to walk much, but ride with ease, passing two or three hours a day on horseback, and every three or four months taking in a carriage a journey of ninety miles to a distant possession, where I pass a good deal of my time. My eyes need the aid of glasses by night, and with small print in the day also; my hearing is not quite as sensible as it used to be; no tooth shaking yet, but shivering and shrinking in body from the cold we now experience, my thermometer having been as low as 12 this morning. My greatest oppression is a correspondence afflictingly laborious, the extent of which I have been long endeavoring to curtail. This keeps me at the drudgery of the writing-table all the prime hours of the day, leaving for the gratification of my appetite for reading, only what I can steal from the hours of sleep. Could I reduce this epistolary corvee within the limits of my friends and affairs, and give the time redeemed from it to reading and reflection, to history, ethics, mathematics, my life would be as happy as the infirmities of age would admit, and I should look on its consummation with the composure of one "*qui summum nec me tuit diem nec optat.*"

His "distant possession" afforded some lengthy vacations from the heavy correspondence with strangers. But an accumulated burden always awaited him. After his return to Monticello on January 11, 1816, he wrote John Adams:[28] "Of the last five months I have passed four at my other domicile, for such it is in a considerable degree. No letters are forwarded to me there because the cross post to that place is circuitous and uncertain. During my absence therefore they are accumulating here and awaiting acknowledgements. This has been the fate of your favor of Nov. 13."

In that letter he seconded Adams' eulogy of the eighteenth century, saying: "It certainly witnessed the sciences and arts, manners and morals, advanced to a higher degree than the world had ever before seen. And might we not go back to the era of the Borgias, by which time the barbarous ages had reduced national morality to its lowest point of depravity, and observe that the arts and sciences, rising from that point, advanced gradually through all the 16th, 17th, and 18th centuries, softening and correcting the manners and morals of man?"

But, as he saw it, some force, perhaps "the terror of monarchs alarmed at the light returning on them from the west and kindling a volcano under their thrones," had brought about "a combination to extinguish that light. . . . Whatever it was, the close of the century saw the moral world thrown back again to the age of the Borgias, to the point from which it had departed 300 years before. France, after crushing and punishing the conspiracy of Pilnitz, went herself deeper and deeper into the crimes she had been chastising. I say France, and not Bonaparte; for although he was the head and mouth, the nation furnished the hands which executed his enormities."

Some of Jefferson's Poplar Forest neighbors would have been surprised to read his comment on Napoleon. Happenings at the home of the county's most famous resident were always the subject of much interest. A little while before, when Jefferson had called in extra workmen for repairs, alterations, and interior finishing, the rumor had spread that he was converting his retreat into a refuge for the exiled French Emperor. Jefferson had long since grown accustomed to wild rumors about himself, but this one astonished even him.

By April 6 Jefferson had completed the first English translation of Destutt de Tracy's *Political Economy*. Ten days later he was reviewing Du Pont de Nemours' proposed constitution for equinoctial republics in the Western Hemisphere. He made an observation that might seem self-evident but that has been ignored through the centuries by many otherwise astute statesmen: that there is no one form of government practicable for all civilized peoples at all stages of their development. Of Du Pont's constitution he wrote: "I suppose it well formed for those for whom it was intended, and the excellence of every government is its adaptation to the state of those to be governed by it."[29]

The sage of Monticello unwittingly revealed a great deal about himself in one observation. Discussing differences between the government proposed by Du Pont and that operative in the United States, Jefferson said: "I acknowledge myself strong in affection to our own form, yet both of us act and think from the same motive; we both consider the people as our children, and love them with parental affection. But you love them as infants whom you are afraid to trust without nurses, and I as adults whom I freely leave to self-government." Jefferson had always been happiest in the role of pater-familias. Now he thought of himself as pater-familias to a nation. Many of his correspondents made it clear that they saw him in the same light.

He called Du Pont's attention to a provision "in the constitution of Spain as proposed by the late Cortes . . . that no person born after that day should ever acquire the rights of citizenship until he could read and write. It is impossible sufficiently to estimate the wisdom of this provision. Of all those which have been thought of for securing fidelity in the administration of the government, constant ralliance to the principles of the constitution, and progressive amendments with the progressive advances of the human mind, or changes in human affairs, it is the most effectual. Enlighten the people generally, and tyranny and oppression of body and mind will vanish like evil spirits at the dawn of day. Although I do not, with some enthusiasts, believe that the human condition will ever advance to such a state of perfection as that there shall no longer be pain or vice in the world, yet I believe it susceptible of much improvement, and most of all, in matters of government and religion; and that the diffusion of knowledge among the people is to be the instrument by which it is to be effected."

Every public matter with which Jefferson was concerned illustrated the importance of education in a free society. His opportunity to advance the cause was increased October 18, 1816, when Governor Nicholas named a Board of Visitors, or governing board, for Central College. Jefferson, because he was in the near isolation of Poplar Forest, did not receive notice of his appointment until the end of the month, but surely he had expected it. The board consisted, besides Jefferson, of James Madison, James Monroe, Joseph C. Cabell, and two less celebrated but able men, General John H. Cocke and David Watson. Certainly no American college or university ever had a more distinguished board. Two members, Jefferson and Madison, combined with international reputations for scholarship the practical experience of having been Chief Magistrates of the republic.

The Visitors obtained their first quorum on May 5, 1817. By that time, Monroe had succeeded Madison as President. Some Northeasterners grumbled about a Virginia dynasty, but Monroe was generally popular. He had carried every state except Massachusetts, Connecticut, and Delaware and had defeated Federalist candidate Rufus King 183 to 34 in the electoral college. Jefferson's influence on the presidency continued undiminished as his protégé succeeded his best friend. But Jefferson and the Republican Party had changed through the years. In his inaugural address the new President called more openly for a navy than either Jefferson or Madison had found practicable, advocated a standing army, and recommended "the systematic and fostering care of the government for our manufactures."

Though Jefferson's official capacity was no different from that of any other member of the Board of Visitors, it was he who issued the call for the first meeting, fearing that if he did not take the initiative matters would continue to drift. The appointed day was April 8, 1817. Jefferson had delayed the meeting a little in the hope that Madison, having retired from the presidency, would be able to attend. But Madison was not able to leave Washington soon enough. Monroe, as his successor, was too busy to leave the capital. Watson's attendance was prevented by illness. Therefore, besides Jefferson, only General Cocke and Senator Cabell were present. As they did not constitute a quorum, they could not act for the entire board. But they did make recommendations for submission at the next meeting.

According to the college's proctor, Alexander Garrett, Jefferson thought the best site for the institution would be on land outside Charlottesville owned by John Kelly. But Mr. Kelly disapproved the former President's political principles and said that he would see him "at the devil" first and that no amount of money could change his mind.[30] In any event, Jefferson was quickly satisfied with another nearby site, this one about a mile west of Charlottesville on land once owned by Monroe.

Even if the three Visitors who met in April could have announced the choice of a site, he would not have favored doing so. Though always concerned with substance, he was always aware of the significance of image in any project requiring public support. He wanted the presence of three Presidents of the United States to dramatize the first official business of the college's board. Securing Madison's attendance, now that he had returned to Montpelier, was easy, but Jefferson had to press Monroe to leave Washington. Neither Cabell nor Watson was able to attend on May 5, but General Cocke was. But most important was the presence of the triumvirate of Presidents—and on a court day when people from all over Albemarle County flocked to Charlottesville. The effect was all that Jefferson could have wished. The *Richmond Enquirer* duly reported that "three men were seen together at Charlottesville (county of Albemarle), each of whom is calculated to attract the eager gaze of their fellow citizens."[31] From Massachusetts John Adams wrote his friend at Monticello: "I congratulate you and Madison and Monroe on your noble employment in founding a university. From such a noble triumvirate the world will expect something very great and very new. But if it contains anything quite original and very excellent, I fear the prejudices are too deeply rooted to suffer it to last long, though it may be accepted at first. It will not always have three such colossal reputations to support it."[32]

Jefferson advanced the work as rapidly as he could while that support was available. Whether he had the formal title or not, he was de facto chairman at the first official meeting. He also recorded the minutes. The board authorized the purchase of about two hundred acres at the site recommended by the conferees of April 8 and the erection of a building on it. They instructed Alexander Garrett to obtain from the proceeds of glebe land sales the sum of $1,500 for land purchase, and also to make up a subscription form for the solicitation of funds. Provision was made for the payment of four annual installments if a subscriber could not conveniently contribute a lump sum. Jefferson, in the course of the meeting, subscribed a thousand dollars and each of the other Visitors present followed suit. Cocke even subscribed a thousand in Cabell's name because he was sure his friend would want to be one of the first contributors. The sum was a generous one for almost anyone in those days. In view of the perilous state of his finances, for Jefferson some would have deemed it foolhardy. But few sacrifices were too great for his university, which, of course, as his friend John Adams and others recognized, was his true goal. As Albemarle Academy while still on paper had been transformed into Central College, that college itself should prove the paper chrysalis of a brilliant university. The minutes referred to the building plans submitted to the trustees of Albemarle Academy "for erecting a distinct pavilion or building for each separate professorship, and for arranging these around a square, each pavilion containing a schoolroom and two apartments for the accommodation of the professor, with other reasonable conveniences." The building to be erected now would be "one of those pavilions." As funds became available, up to ten dormitories would be built on each side.[33]

When the land purchase was made on June 23, the Visitors settled for two noncontiguous tracts. Construction would begin on the smaller of these, a plot of 43.75 acres. The 750-foot-wide open-ended quadrangle originally planned by Jefferson would not fit on this lot, which consisted of a sloping ridge. He reduced the distance between wings to 200 feet.

Jefferson now walked with great difficulty, seldom venturing on foot beyond the gardens of Monticello. But on July 18 the tall, lean, seventy-four-year-old man, his gait even more shambling than when he had been President, personally surveyed the building site. He staked out three terraces. Some historians have expressed surprise that he should have called them squares although they measured 200 by 255 feet.[34] But Jefferson was entirely within the rules of proper nomenclature for large-scale projects. The term square has long been used to designate a large rectangular area such as a city block or a plaza whether or not its sides are of equal length. He staked out a west and an east pavilion on each of the terraces.

Next day he wrote General Cocke, "Our squares are laid off, the brickyard begun, and the leveling will be begun in the course of the week."[35] He invited him to come up to see the work. The General brought Cabell with him. Afterwards Madison was their host for a meeting of the Board of Visitors at Montpelier. There they rejoiced in the news that the subscription campaign was ahead of schedule.

With this encouragement, Jefferson accelerated the planning of buildings and procurement of materials. As the summer progressed, he hired expert Lynchburg masons to work with the brick made from red clay on the building site. They would have the same warm, earthy hue as the ones used in constructing Monticello. He would not trust to native labor for the elaborate classical capitals of the columns. In accordance with the Visitors' instructions, undoubtedly given at his suggestion, he was trying to import a stonecutter from Italy. Writing to Adams on September 8 from Poplar Forest, he complained: "A month's absence from Monticello has added to the delay of acknowledging your last letters; and indeed for a month before I left it our projected college gave me constant employment; for being the only Visitor in its immediate neighborhood, all its administrative business falls on me, and that, where building is going on, is not a little."[36] Only a naive person would believe that Jefferson really wished to shed this responsibility.

In addition to coordinating and supervising the building of the college, Jefferson busied himself in soliciting funds from friends outside central Virginia. Though contributions from Albemarle County had soared beyond expectations, those from outside had been disappointing. Some uncertainty resulted. As Jefferson wrote Adams, it became necessary in planning to provide for "two conditions of things. If the institution is to depend on private donations alone, we shall be forced to accumulate on the shoulders of four professors a mass of sciences which, if the legislature adopts it, should be distributed among ten. We shall be ready for a professor of languages in April next, for two others the following year, and a fourth a year after."[37]

He implied that Adams' friend George Ticknor, who had visited Monticello two years before, could have the first appointment if he wanted it. Jefferson wrote, "How happy should we be if we could have a Ticknor for our first. . . . To this professor, a fixed salary of $500 with liberal tuition fees from the pupils will probably give $2000 a year. We are now on the look-out for a professor, meaning to accept of none but of the very first order."

In his letter to Colonel Charles Yancey in 1816 soliciting legislative support for Central College, Jefferson had proposed a "university where might be taught, in its highest degree, every branch of science [knowledge] useful in our time and country." As he said in that letter, he was interested in efficient mass education because "if a nation expects to be ignorant and free, in a state of civilization, it expects what never was and never will be." But even in the paragraph containing that now famous quotation, he had emphasized the importance of having in the state an institution where each subject would "be taught in its highest degree."[38] This conviction was closely bound up with his social concepts and philosophy of history.

A good index to his views appears in the letter to John Adams in 1813. He says that selective breeding, as advocated by Theognis, "would doubtless improve the human, as it does the brute animal, and produce a race of veritable aristocrats. For experience proves that the moral and physical qualities of man, whether good or evil, are transmissible in a certain degree from father to son. But I suspect that the equal rights of men will rise up against this privileged Solomon, and oblige us . . . to content ourselves with the accidental aristoi produced by the fortuitous concourse of breeders. For I agree with you that there is a natural aristocracy among men. The grounds of this are virtue and talents."[39]

As 1817 drew to an end, Jefferson, as in 1813, was putting great trust in the natural aristocracy to rescue humankind and carry it to new plateaus. He believed that such aristocrats would be more numerous among the advantaged but he insisted that they were to be found in every class of society. In September the *Richmond Enquirer*, edited by one of Jefferson's most loyal admirers, the able Thomas Ritchie, saluted Central College as a "future nursery of Science and of Liberty." Ritchie hailed Jefferson as the principal founder, one who as a young man had fought for liberty and now as an old man labored for its preservation. On October 6 Monroe presided over cornerstone laying ceremonies in which Jefferson, Madison, and the other Visitors participated. This first structure would be a pavilion consisting of an arcade topped by a Doric portico. There would be two front doors, one an entrance to the classroom, the other leading to faculty quarters.

Less than three weeks later Jefferson wrote Cabell that he had to be at the building site every other day to prod the laborers along and that the drain on his energy was proving too great.[40] By mid-November, when freezing temperatures halted masonry work, only the first-story walls of the two-story structure had been erected.

The hiatus in outdoor work did not give him a vacation from labor for the college. His paperwork, which now engaged his time and energy, was made painful by an arthritic wrist, which itself was a reminder of middle-aged folly. Walking in Paris with the young beauty Maria Cosway, he had attempted to leap over a fence. He failed and, instead of impressing her with his agility, fell on his right arm, either breaking or dislocating the wrist so that for many days it pulsed with pain. The details we do not know, because Jefferson refused to discuss them. He was forced to learn to write with his other hand and, when a friend asked what had happened, he wrote, "How the right hand became disabled would be a long story for the left to tell. It was by one of those follies from which good cannot come, but ill may."[41] He later regained the ability to write with his right hand, though he never again had the flexibility desirable for playing the violin really well, and when arthritis crept up on him it seized with special vengeance upon the injured member.

But pain or no pain, he worked on at his drawing table or desk, sometimes sketching architectural plans, sometimes soliciting legislative or individual support for the college and a statewide educational program, sometimes trying to attract distinguished scholars for the faculty.

In September Jefferson had sent Senator Cabell his proposed bill for the establishment of a statewide system of elementary schools. He said that he had deliberately eschewed the "verbose and intricate style" favored by most of his legal brethren but would accept the insertion of a "said" or "aforesaid" between every pair of words, together with every other customary tautology, if they would only enact it into law.[42] In response to a request from Cabell he had followed on October 14 with the draft of a bill embodying his ideas for a system of public education including not only elementary schools but intermediate and higher education as well.

Jefferson's plan was much more modest than that embodied in the bill earlier introduced by Delegate Charles F. Mercer, which had passed the House but had been defeated in the Senate by a tie vote. Though inspired by Jefferson's aspirations for education in Virginia, the bill had departed from the fiscal realism that characterized Jefferson's public plans. It provided for more academies than Jefferson believed to be financially feasible and for four colleges, one of which would be named Jefferson. The scale was so grandiose that Jefferson believed the elementary school system alone would eat up all funds available for public education. As the proposal had failed by only one vote from one of the two houses, Jefferson deemed it urgent that a more practical scheme be laid before the legislature before the earlier one was revived. Except for this necessity, he told Cabell, he would not have pushed himself to submit his own eleven-page draft on October 24.

Jefferson did not easily abandon his goals. He reminded a correspondent[43] that the Jefferson bill for education that he was now proposing in 1817 was essentially the same as the Jefferson bill of 1779. He had "accommodated to the circumstance of this, instead of that, day," making the Literary Fund part of the system and making both preparatory schools and colleges or universities subject to a statewide Board of Public Instruction. But, as in his original proposal, three years of free schooling for all children regardless of the financial status of their families would be offered in one-room log schoolhouses scattered over the Commonwealth. Local taxation would support local schools. Scholarships would be provided at the college and university levels. He proposed these not primarily as a service to the indigent but as a means "to avail the Commonwealth of those talents and virtues which nature has sown as liberally among the poor as [the] rich."[44]

Though Jefferson had said that the state needed a plan less grandiose than Mercer's, and for the most part adhered to this intention, he did emerge with a proposal for nine colleges instead of the four advocated by the Delegate. These, however, would be colleges largely in the old European sense of preparatory schools. Ever grateful to his old teacher, Jefferson asked that one of these institutions be named for George Wythe.

Capping this system would be a university. Jefferson drafted alternative provisions for its location so that Cabell might propose whichever seemed more likely to obtain passage. One said that Central College in Albemarle

County should be made into a university. The other simply called for creation of a university in a healthful part of central Virginia. We can be sure that Jefferson intended, if this more general provision were adopted, to convince those in authority of the centrality and salubrity of the Central College site.

Cabell knew Jefferson too well to take seriously the former President's statement about the bill he had drafted: "Take it and make of it what you can, if [it is] worth anything. . . . I meddle no more with it. There is a time to retire from labor and that time has come with me. It is a duty as well as the strongest of my desires to relinquish to younger hands the government of our bark and resign myself as I do willingly to their care."[45]

Jefferson's weariness, though, was genuine enough. His mind was active and far-ranging, but on foot he shuffled along painfully within ever narrowing confines. He had invented a cane-seat that he carried with him even on short walks in the yard. It was somewhat like a shooting stick with an unfolding canvas seat, only instead of terminating in a spike it unfolded into a tripod.[46]

Other inventions of his contributed to his comfort. Most were improvements on the original creations of others. He may have been the first American to have dumbwaiters in his house; in any event, he had conceived the idea of concealing them in the sides of a fireplace. He could determine wind directions by reading the dial on the ceiling of the entrance hall. There too was the great clock with the hole cut in the floor for its descending pendulum. It was only the most conspicuous of several timepieces that he had had made to his own specifications. One of these was in the kitchen. Jefferson wound it every Sunday. Despite the fact that he was a connoisseur of gourmet cooking, these were the only occasions on which he entered the kitchen.[47]

The invention he most prized of all those that he had improved was the polygraph, which enabled him to make clear copies of all that he wrote simultaneously with the original writing. And it seemed that he was always writing. Besides correspondence with numerous friends and acquaintances on both sides of the Atlantic he answered strangers' queries about the American Revolution, his own presidency, obscure points of legal history, American Indian dialects, several sciences, English literature, and contemporary European sculpture, besides acknowledging gifts of newly published books, aboriginal pottery, and dead animals of unusual appearance. In January 1818 he was busy summarizing the weather records that he had compiled from his own observations and measurements at Monticello augmented by those of friends he had pressed into service in other parts of Virginia. He hoped that similar records were being compiled in other states so that the movements of fronts could be charted as an aid to development of a national system of weather prediction. Always mindful of the historic significance of public actions in which he had played a part, in February he composed an exegesis of confidential papers that he had collected as Secretary of State.

A current event in the same month sharply refocused his attention on a contemporary topic. The bill to establish a state university was passed by the legislature. Of course, the matter had not been far from the front of the old statesman's mind even when he labored over correspondence on other topics and over his records for posterity. A little before Christmas adjournment of the Assembly, he had written Cabell: "Pray drop me a line when any vote is passed which furnishes an indication of the success or failure of the general plan. I have only this single anxiety in the world. It is a bantling of forty years' birth and nursing, and if I can once set it on its legs, I will sing with sincerity and pleasure my *nunc dimittis*."[48]

He was in a race not only with death but also with old age. He would need all his psychic energy to overcome the growing physical disabilities that threatened to prevent him from bringing to fruition the great dream of his youth. Merely that there should be a university was not sufficient. He must remain alive and sufficiently active long enough to guide its growth in the lineaments of greatness.

The bill as enacted differed in important respects from Jefferson's draft.[49] One provision eliminated would have established literacy as a prerequisite to citizenship. He was uncertain about the right of government to compel attendance at school, but he was certain that it had every right to deny suffrage to those who, because of indifference or inability, had not prepared themselves for the exercise of it. Also eliminated as likely to antagonize some potential supporters of a university were Jefferson's references to the need for guarding against clerical influence so as to foster the separation of church and state and to prevent sectarian strife in academe. As for the provisions for public education at the primary level, few of the legislators were ready for so drastic a move. They could afford to educate their own children and did not shirk this responsibility; they felt no obligation to educate the children of those less prosperous or less provident. If instances of neglected talents came to notice in their own neighborhoods they could take care of them with private dispensations of charity. Wholesale provision for education of the young, they believed, would be wasteful in view of the paucity of abilities to be found among the underprivileged.

As enacted, the bill contained the more general of Jefferson's paragraphs regarding location and establishment of the projected university. There was therefore no specific reference to Central College or even to Albemarle County. Of course Jefferson, having suggested to Cabell that such generalities might be necessary, was prepared to work at the conversion of Central College into the university of his dreams.

The lurid criticism in the press to which Jefferson had been subjected in his public career had left wounds unhealed by the more generous balm of praise. His first impulse was to labor for the university in an inconspicuous role. This inclination was reinforced by realization that some of the legislative opposition to the scheme for a university had sprung from fears that it would be shaped by Jefferson and therefore would become a seminary of sedition. "There are fanatics both in religion and politics," he told Cabell, "who, without knowing me personally, have long been taught to consider me as a raw head and bloody bones."[50] He urged that Cabell himself would be a better choice for appointment from the Albemarle-Nelson senatorial district to the 24-member commission to plan the university. Cabell declined appointment. But he accepted Jefferson's argument about himself, writing: "Probably you will not be nominated in consequence of the considerations stated in your last [letter]. Upon that point I consulted some four or five of your intelligent friends, and left the matter in their hands."[51]

Cabell's forecast proved wrong. Jefferson evidently was made to realize that, while some opponents of the projected university were actuated by hostility to him, more were stirred by the threat of strong competition for William and Mary. Governor James P. Preston named him to the commission and he accepted.

One measure of the old statesman's separation from direct personal activity in the politics of his state after so many years of public activity was that he and this Governor had never met. In the thirty-seven years since completion of his own service as Governor, every other holder of the office had been a personal colleague or opponent, several times a relative by blood or marriage, once (in the case of John Page) a friend since boyhood, once (in the case of Monroe) a protégé.

Certainly it was easier for the commission to receive Jefferson's advice face to face and to act with him on the problems of organization than it would have been to receive his instructions by courier from the mountaintop. The counsel for the prosecution in the trial of Aaron Burr had learned painfully that Jefferson was almost constitutionally unable to remain aloof, or even silently watchful, during the unfolding of any matter with which he was deeply concerned. Among those named to this important body were such leaders as Madison and Judge Spencer Roane. Now fifty-six years old, Roane had sat on the Court of Appeals, Virginia's highest court, since the age of thirty-two and for years had dominated its proceedings. His marriage to Patrick Henry's daughter in no way interfered with his allegiance to Republican principles or friendship for Jefferson. Indeed, he had been Jefferson's choice for Chief Justice when Adams beat his successor to the draw by naming John Marshall. The two most prestigious of Jefferson's fellow commissioners would be his allies by personal association and philosophical affinity.

The commission's first meeting was scheduled for Saturday, August 1, at Rockfish Gap, 1,900 feet high on the crest of the Blue Ridge, where an old buffalo path over the mountains had become a gateway to western settlement. Jefferson's love of great vistas must have been satisfied by the magnificent sweep of scenery to both east and west from this height.

His vision of the future of education in the commonwealth was equally sweeping. But like a good pioneer he would lead his followers by easy stages. Freedom of movement was circumscribed by the limited funds available and by the apprehensions of the legislature. Ultimately nothing could be done without their approval. The commission was empowered only to advise the General Assembly. The act creating the commission specified that it should "in all things, at all times, be subjected to the control of the legislature."

Jefferson always did a prodigious amount of homework before presenting anything for the consideration of a committee, commission, or legislative body. As a young Virginia legislator he had literally spent so much time drafting legislation at home that the Sergeant-at-Arms was ordered to compel his attendance at the repetitive debates that distracted from his preparation.⁵² In a broad sense, for three decades he had been doing his homework on education in the commonwealth. But in the spring and summer he worked specifically on a draft that he hoped would be accepted by his fellow commissioners and would appeal in various ways to the House of Delegates, whose membership he had studied closely, albeit mostly at second hand, in recent months. He sought Madison's advice and before the end of June shared his draft with him.

The first question to be considered was the location of the institution. Charlottesville, Staunton, and Lexington all contended for this honor. Far more than local pride fueled Jefferson's efforts to make Charlottesville the choice. Severe arthritis and an increasing general debility justified doubts as to whether he would be able to supervise the building of the university even if construction was in his own neighborhood. He certainly would be unable to if Staunton or Lexington were selected. Jefferson was unwilling to entrust this task to anyone else. Who else had studied so intensively the educational practices of other lands? Who else in Virginia burned with his zeal for the establishment of a great university? A vigorous intellect and a questing spirit still drove the now frail engine of his body. But, as he watched the mental deterioration of some of his contemporaries, he sometimes wondered whether his own intellectual powers would last long enough to guide not only the physical construction of the "academical village" but also the establishment of its curriculum, the hiring of its faculty, and the framing of its governance. Many of the faculty would have to be drawn from overseas and Jefferson's name would be a greater magnet than any other. Above all, in this whole matter of founding a university, Jefferson trusted his own judgment more than that of anyone else likely to be deeply involved in the process.

When Jefferson wrote Adams that he would willingly depart this life if only he could see the university safely advanced, he explained that the fate of this "bantling" was his one remaining worry. Jefferson was able to make this statement because he believed that at least he was making headway against the personal financial problems that for so long had threatened disaster. Although Congress had paid him for his library less than a fifth of its true worth, its sale had enabled him to pay more than half his debt.⁵³

Of course, there were misfortunes reducing this gain. Two successive years of drought had lowered the earnings from his plantations, and his purchase of some farmland had been ruled invalid because the heirs had been minors at the time of the transaction so that he had been required to pay back-rent on what he had believed to be his own and then repurchase it. In April 1817 he informed his Richmond agent that he would be "much distressed" if he could not obtain a bank loan to repay a loan dating from the 1790s. Originally a loan of about $2,000 from an Amsterdam house, it had been refinanced in 1816, and the debt, with interest, now exceeded $6,000. He had promised to pay it off to Leroy and Bayard, the New York firm representing the Amsterdam creditors, in three annual installments beginning in May 1817. The Bank of Virginia discounted a sixty-day note endorsed by Jefferson's Richmond agent, and the first of the annual payments to Leroy and Bayard was made.

All this refinancing increased his interest payments. Then came the news that the note could not be renewed. On his agent's advice Jefferson turned to Wilson Cary Nicholas, president of the Richmond branch of the Bank of the United States.

Nicholas, of course, was an old friend and political ally as well as Jeff's father-in-law. He enabled Jefferson to obtain a loan of $3,000 and assured him that it could be renewed. The notes were renewed but, in order to make his 1818 payment to Leroy and Bayard, he had to appeal to the Bank of the United States for a second loan of $3,000, secured through Nicholas' personal endorsement of the note.

Jefferson apparently had promised himself never to endorse a note, but when Nicholas within a few weeks asked Jefferson to endorse for him two notes of $10,000 each he felt he had no moral right to refuse. Nevertheless, he was troubled by thoughts that he had no right to jeopardize his own family's inheritance.[54]

Before the Rockfish Gap conference, however, Jefferson was able to regard his financial situation with some optimism. He had made the second payment to Leroy and Bayard, and the banks had renewed his loans. His Albemarle wheat crop promised to be so good that he hoped farm earnings would provide the final payment next year to the New York agents. Then he could start paying the banks. Meanwhile he had a little cash-flow problem, enough to necessitate his borrowing a hundred dollars from a Charlottesville merchant to finance the trip to Rockfish Gap. As he prepared to travel with Madison to the conference site, his mind was freed from the energy-sapping worries about personal finances that had plagued him for years. For that changed state of affairs he was profoundly grateful as he prepared for an effort requiring physical stamina and a distraction-free mind.

But on July 30, the eve of his departure, the mails brought him alarming news. There was an announcement from the Bank of the United States that on August 5, four days after the convening of the conference, it would require a curtailment of twelve and a half percent on all notes presented for renewal. For Jefferson, as his agent explained in an accompanying note, the bank's announcement meant that his $3,000 note could be renewed for no more than $2,625. Jefferson replied, "That notification is really like a clap of thunder to me, for God knows I have no means in this world of raising money on so sudden a call."[55]

He signed a blank note and sent it to Jeff for endorsement. The note was to be sent to Jefferson's agent with a note asking him to do what he could. And then this seventy-five-year-old man, crippled with arthritis and plagued by insistent reminders of mortality, not knowing what financial ruin might impend for him or even for the state that he called upon to finance his dream, set forth on the thirty-five-mile journey to the place where he would labor to obtain endorsement of his personal vision.

Apparently he said nothing about his financial troubles to Madison as the two old friends rode to the meeting on the crest of the Blue Ridge. It therefore is not surprising that he confided nothing to the other commissioners. They seem to have found the same optimistic Jefferson that most of them had expected. By unanimous vote they elected him president.

The choice of a site, potentially the most divisive question before the commission, was postponed beyond the first day. But it surely was uppermost in virtually everyone's mind. The site of the meeting itself, far removed from the urban centers that usually housed important deliberations of state, dramatized the issues involved in placement of the university. Rockfish Gap was a famous gateway in Virginia's principal natural barrier between east and west. Tidewater, the portion of Virginia east of the fall line, had dominated its colonial councils. In the early days of the Commonwealth, leadership had spread far enough westward to embrace the Piedmont as well as Tidewater. Population in the large area of Virginia west of the Blue Ridge continued to grow. In 1818 that area was inadequately represented in the state Senate.

Jefferson strongly favored correction of the inequity, but reform was frustrated because, by the very nature of the problem, the group that benefited most from the status quo controlled the chamber called upon to reform itself. Incidentally, as the members convened in Rockfish Gap were appointed from the senatorial districts, they too reflected the imbalance in representation between east and west. One could look both eastward and westward through Rockfish Gap. The meeting place symbolized the existing demographics and an awareness of future probabilities.

The report[56] written by Jefferson before the meeting for submission to his fellow commissioners said that "the governing considerations should be the healthiness of the site, the fertility of the neighboring country, and its centrality to the white population of the whole State." Few accounts of the founding of the university note the emphasis on "centrality to the white population." Actually this was a key point. The commissioners did not think it necessary to state that for the foreseeable future the students would be white; no one then would conceive otherwise. For that reason it would be unfair to use the center of the entire population of Virginia as a basis for location. The black population of the eastern counties was far heavier than that of the western. In fact, the Negro population exceeded the white in some Tidewater counties.

Jefferson emphasized that the three desiderata of healthfulness, fertility, and centrality should be the governing considerations. "For, although the act authorized and required [the commission] to receive any voluntary contributions, whether conditioned or absolute, which might be offered through them to the President and Directors of the Literary Fund, for the benefit of the University, yet they did not consider this as establishing an auction, or as pledging the locations to the highest bidder."

While no action was taken the first day to determine a site, a committee of six—including Jefferson and Madison—was appointed to frame a report on all other items to be considered. Jefferson had already written such a report and obtained Madison's support for it. It only remained for him to convince the other four committeemen. After studying Jefferson's proposal Saturday night and Sunday, they supported it on Monday. This report, containing the plans which we already know from Jefferson's letters to Cabell, Madison, and others, was adopted, with insignificant changes, by the whole commission and signed by each member. In balloting on the site, Staunton received 2 votes, Lexington 3, and Central College 16. Jefferson had obtained everything he had sought. Later one commissioner told Cabell that Jefferson "did not even intimate a wish at any time or in any shape except when his name was called and his vote was given."[57] The incident is reminiscent of the time when a Congressman, emerging from a quiet conversation in which then President Jefferson had converted the legislator to his views, boasted that he truly believed that he could convince the Chief Executive of anything.

On motion of Judge Roane, seconded by General James Breckenridge, the commissioners thanked Jefferson for the "ability, impartiality, and dignity" with which he had served. He was triumphant but exhausted. The General Assembly still had to be convinced, and this task would be harder than persuading the commission, but the unanimity of the commission's support would be a big step toward legislative approval.

Jefferson had made the journey from Monticello to Rockfish Gap in two stages on horseback. One might suppose that a coach would have provided easier transportation, but such was not the case for him. Axled wheels traveled over rough roads with a more exaggerated motion than a rider experienced on horseback. He did not look forward to traveling again by any mode. But travel he must—not immediately to Monticello, however. He rode into the Shenandoah Valley, spent the night in Staunton and from there proceeded to Warm Springs. It was the search for health that carried him to this spot seventy-five miles from Monticello, the farthest west he ever traveled.[58] The curative powers of the springs were celebrated. Jefferson spent three weeks at the baths. His natural desire to find greater comfort and vigor was rendered preternaturally urgent by his intense desire to prepare himself for the educational labors ahead.

At Warm Springs, as almost everywhere else, he was the subject of much solicitous attention. And he enjoyed the company of two men of some sophistication, General Breckinridge and Colonel William Alston, father of the South Carolina Governor who had married Theodosia Burr. Jefferson, for all his declared love of republican simplicity, loved elegance and luxury as much as a senator of the late Roman empire. But this habitually busy devotee of the work ethic was not so constituted as to enjoy the old imperial habit of lounging in hot baths. After a few days he was restless. He told of a new problem in a letter he wrote to Martha on August 21. "I do not know what may be the effect of this course of bathing on my constitution," he said, "but I am under great threats that it will work its effect through a system of boils."[59]

Soon it became obvious that the baths were not effecting a significant improvement in his general health and that the curse of boils carried with it no compensating cure of his pains. The problem was further complicated by the fact that the boils were on his buttocks. The rough motion of travel would have made the long ride back to Monticello an ordeal, but this new affliction could make it a torture. But soon, as he became increasingly ill, he felt that he must return to Monticello without delay. He had traveled to Rockfish Gap and from there to Staunton and Warm Springs on horseback to avoid the disturbing motion of a wheeled vehicle, but now travel in the saddle was impossible. By short stages, he rumbled home over rough roads, losing strength all the way.

One can imagine the relief with which he returned to his own bed. But by now it was clear that his life might be in danger. Undoubtedly he had contracted in the baths an infection that was sapping his vitality. Modern medical science presumes that he had contracted a staphylococcus infection, an affliction that even with modern antibiotics can be life threatening. Admittedly staphylococcus has generally increased in virulence since Jefferson's day because of survival of the fittest among bacteria under attack by antibiotics.

Deprived of the solace of activity by his illness, Jefferson could only lie abed with leisure to contemplate the possibility of his personal financial ruin and, without his guidance, the frustration of his dreams for the university. Threatened with the loss of all his worldly goods and the dissolution of his cherished dream and now "afflicted . . . with loathsome sores," he might have been pardoned for seeing parallels between his suffering and Job's.

Recovery was slow. On October 7 Jefferson wrote John Adams:

> . . . I have been severely indisposed and not yet recovered so far as to sit up to write, but in pain. Having been subject to troublesome attacks of rheumatism for some winters past, and being called by other business into the neighborhood of our Warm Springs, I thought I would avail myself of them as a preventative of future pain. I was then in good health and it ought to have occurred to me that the medicine which makes the sick well, may make the well sick. Those powerful waters produced imposthume, general eruption, fever, colliquative sweats, and extreme debility, which aggravated by the torment of a return home over 100 miles of rocks and mountains reduced me to extremity. I am getting better slowly and, when I can do it with less pain shall always have a pleasure in giving assurances to Mrs. Adams and yourself of my constant and affectionate friendship and respect.[60]

Adams replied on October 20,[61] saying that, on reading in the newspapers that the Virginian had gone to the Springs, he had "anxiously suspected that all was not healthy at Monticello." But now, he said, Jefferson's account of eruptions and sweats had given him hope. He believed that such occurrences "often indicate strength of constitution and returning vigor. I hope and believe they have given you a new lease for years, many years. Your letter, which is written with your usual neatness and firmness, confirms my hopes."

But the letter ended on a far different note. "Now sir, for my griefs! The dear partner of my life, for fifty-four years as a wife and for many years more as a lover, now lies in extremis, forbidden to speak or be spoken to."

Soon the press carried the news of Abigail Adams' death from typhoid fever on October 28. Jefferson's mind must have turned back to the days when he and Adams had both been diplomats in Europe and there had been much visiting. When Jefferson was in Paris and Adams was United States Minister in London, Jefferson and Mrs. Adams had shopped for each other in their respective capitals. Once he had bought her shoes and once silk stockings. She had called him "one of the choice ones of the earth." Writing to him from London about her sadness in leaving Paris, she said she had been sad to leave her garden but added, "I was still more loth on account of the increasing pleasure and intimacy which a longer acquaintance with a respected friend promised," discreetly adding "to leave behind me the only person with whom my companion could associate with perfect freedom and unreserve, and whose place he had no reason to expect supplied in the land to which he is destined."[62] Mrs. Adams had welcomed young Patsy Jefferson to Europe with a mother's warmth even as she reproved her father for not leaving his diplomatic duties to greet her in person.

Much later there had been the time when Abigail had turned on him like a tigress because of her mistaken belief that he had denied a government job to her cub. Political bitterness had separated both Adamses from Jefferson. When correspondence between the two ex-Presidents was resumed through the efforts of Benjamin Rush, Jefferson had assured the Philadelphian that there would, however, never be any resumption of correspondence between him and Mrs. Adams. But eventually she had added a postscript to one of her husband's letters and Jefferson had begun to include messages for her in his notes to John.

The sad news of Abigail's death carried Jefferson back to something antedating mutual experiences in Europe. He was forcibly reminded of his own dear wife's death, which had brought him such misery that his family had feared for his sanity. Jefferson wrote his bereaved friend:

> Tried myself, in the school of affliction, by the loss of every form of connection which can rive the human heart, I know well, and feel what you have lost, what you have suffered, are suffering, and have yet to endure. The same trials have taught me that, for ills so immeasurable, time and silence are the only medicines. I will not therefore, by useless condolences, open afresh the sluices of your grief nor, altho' mingling sincerely my tears with yours, will I say a word more, where words are vain but that it is of some comfort to us both that the term is not very distant at which we are to deposit, in the same cerement, our sorrows and suffering bodies, and to ascend in essence to an ecstatic meeting with the friends we have loved and lost and whom we shall still love and never lose again. God bless you and support you under your heavy affliction.[63]

Some people were already writing off Jefferson himself as practically dead. On November 17 the *Richmond Enquirer* gave the lie to a New York newspaper's report that he was on his deathbed.

In December, Madison called at Monticello to see for himself how his old friend fared and delightedly reported to Monroe that Jefferson had returned to the saddle. He had also returned, insofar as his limited strength permitted, to promoting the university. On November 20 he had sent to the presiding officers of the state Senate and House of Delegates official copies of the Rockfish Gap commission's report. Spearheading the effort in Richmond and keeping Jefferson informed at every turn was Senator Cabell. But Cabell's own health was severely threatened. As a young man he had gone to Europe to recover his health and, though he had led an energetic and useful life ever since, had never been robust. Now he was in pain and weakened by internal hemorrhaging. He felt the need to retire but was determined to remain on duty until the fate of the university was settled. Events in Virginia at this time certainly lent support to the old saying that much of the world's most important work is done by people who do not feel like doing it.

Both houses of the legislature distributed to their members printed copies of the commission's report and Thomas Ritchie published it in toto in the *Richmond Enquirer* with the editorial comment that it bore the marks of Jefferson's "ever-luminous" pen. On December 8 Cabell wrote Jefferson, "All that I can now positively affirm is that the clouds seem to be scattering and the prospect to smile."[64]

If that meteorological metaphor was justified, the Senator must have been describing the calm before the storm. Soon the east-west rivalry that increasingly divided the legislature was causing conflicts over the commission's report. Some supposed proponents of a university were half-hearted at best. Many legislators thought that the existence of William and Mary obviated any need for another state university in Virginia. A bill to provide for such an institution without designating the site drew a tie vote in the House committee. The chairman's vote was decisive, and the bill reported out of committee provided that the university be located at Central College. Before the new year Cabell had almost completely abandoned hope that the General Assembly would do anything for the project. He was making full use of quotations from Jefferson but did not expect them to have a magical effect. "The liberal and enlightened views of great statesmen," he wrote in a message to Monticello, "pass over our heads unheeded like the spheres above."[65]

Jefferson did not despair, but he found the suspense excruciating. On January 19, 1819, he wrote Adams: "We are all atiptoe here in the hourly expectation of hearing what our legislature decides on the report." The legislators, he said, were "a good piece of a century behind the age they live in." Therefore "we are not without fear as to their conclusions. We have to contend with so many biases, personal, local, fanatical, financial, etc., that we cannot foresee in what their combinations will result." [66]

Unbeknown to the anxious man on the mountaintop, Cabell the day before had penned him a letter beginning, "Grateful, truly grateful, is it to my heart, to be able to announce to you the result of this day's proceedings in the House of Delegates."[67] After losing in a last-ditch effort to have references to Central College omitted from the bill, Delegate Briscoe G. Baldwin of Staunton made an eloquent plea for the university that brought tears to the eyes of fellow legislators and contributed to the impressive margin of the victory, 143 to 28. On January 25 the Senate passed the bill, 22 to 1. On that date the University of Virginia was officially chartered.

XVII

'A RACE BETWEEN EDUCATION
AND CATASTROPHE'

"**I**T IS VAIN to give us the name of a university without the means of making it so."[1] So wrote Jefferson to Senator Cabell just three days after passage of the university bill. He had no idea of pausing to celebrate. The great clock of the universe ticked on as inexorably as the great clock of the entrance hall at Monticello, and the old man knew that his time was running out. A battle had been won, but it was only the first major one in what promised to be a long campaign. The $15,000 appropriated by the General Assembly was hardly enough for a stunted beginning. Far larger infusions of cash would be needed to make the university more than an abstraction. The process of financing must be speeded up if the essential momentum was not to be lost—and if something was to be accomplished while Jefferson was still able to direct it.

He pressed Cabell to push for a substantial additional appropriation before the legislature adjourned. But the Senator thought that such an effort would be a mistake at this time, and Jefferson bowed to the judgment of the expert on the scene.

The University of Virginia was chartered. Of course the Governor appointed Jefferson to the Board of Visitors for the new university. Serving with him would be Madison, Cabell, and Cocke. Thus the new board would include the four most valuable members of the commission that had preceded it. Another appointee was General Breckinridge, who as a commissioner had argued the case for Lexington as a university site but afterwards had seconded the resolution praising Jefferson's performance as presiding officer and had provided good company for the former President on the ride to Warm Springs and at the resort. Other members were Chapman Johnson, a prominent and forceful attorney from Staunton, and General Robert B. Taylor, a prominent Norfolk attorney even better known as the able commander of American forces at the battle of Craney Island in the War of 1812. The Governor scheduled the first meeting of the Visitors for March 29.

Jefferson was not willing to lose that much time. But he thought of a perfectly legal way to advance the work in the interim. If the Board of Visitors could not assume its responsibilities before March 29, then the commission could continue to perform its duties in the meantime. Jefferson called a meeting of commissioners for February 23 at Montpelier, Madison's home. Jefferson was there on time. This nearly seventy-six-year-old man who three months before has been believed to be at the point of death kept his engagement by riding on horseback through a snowstorm. General Cocke also made it through the storm and a fourth commissioner, David Watson, granted a proxy to be exercised by the majority present. They approved, in general terms, Jefferson's building plans for the university.[2]

But Jefferson's associates were not rubber stamps. Madison, through the years, had caused Jefferson to modify his views or methods in many enterprises. General Cocke had demonstrated his independence many times, not only in particular groups but in society as a whole. He was a vociferous opponent of slavery, dueling, and the consumption of alcoholic beverages. The "temperance fountain" at his Bremo estate on the James River was a conspicuous symbol of what he hoped to achieve by the legal prohibition of the manufacture or sale of intoxicating liquors.[3] Jefferson's fellow commissioners evidenced their independence when they did not act on his recommendations concerning faculty. The small group conferred informally, and there was no necessity for a formal vote on the proposals. Madison agreed with Jefferson. Cocke didn't. Apparently he believed that some absent commissioners felt the same way. There was no confrontation. Like Jefferson, his associates preferred "the smooth handle."

The disagreement was over Jefferson's insistence that, since Thomas Cooper had been elected to the faculty for Central College, which was to be superseded by the University of Virginia, the university was obliged to appoint him to a professorship. His salary, Jefferson argued, should begin in the spring although the university certainly would not open until a much later date. Jefferson assured them that Cooper could simultaneously teach classics and conduct a school of law.

The inchoate university had no legal obligation to Cooper. Whether it was morally obligated was a moot question. Probably Jefferson felt personally responsible. Apprehensive that the renowned scholar would leave Carlisle for a more satisfying affiliation before he could secure him for Charlottesville, Jefferson had painted for him glowing pictures of the university to be, implying that Cooper himself could be part of the picture.

Quite apart from questions of responsibility, legal or moral, Cocke and others had serious doubts about appointing so controversial a figure to the faculty of a fledgling school struggling to attract public support. Of the richness and variety of his learning there could be little doubt. He was a lawyer, a physician, a chemist, a mineralogist, and an economist. But he was tactless and vociferous in the reiteration of opinions offensive to most people. He was almost fanatical in his opposition to organized religion. He had stirred animosity everywhere he had lived.

Jefferson soon learned that, even if Cabell had been able to attend the meeting at Montpelier, he would not have helped him in the argument over Cooper. Awaiting him on his return to Monticello was a letter[4] from the Senator asserting his conviction that the university had no obligation to employ Cooper and saying that he believed it unwise to hire him anyway. Perhaps he could be appointed eventually as part of a group but naming him by himself in advance of his colleagues would draw undue attention to one likely to make enemies for the school. In any event, he thought that the decision about employing Cooper was one for the Board of Visitors to make, not the commission.

Cabell probably irritated Jefferson a little when he wrote that Cooper "certainly is rather unpopular in the enlightened part of society." The old sage replied: "Cooper is acknowledged by every enlightened man who knows him to be the greatest man in America in the powers of mind and in acquired information, and that without a single exception."[5]

Jefferson was not free of tormenting distractions while he dealt with frustrating problems concerning the university. He was almost constantly threatened by financial ruin, including the loss of Monticello to himself and his descendants. And he had borne the weight of an agonizing family crisis when he rode to the meeting at Montpelier.[6] On February 1 his grandson Jeff had been seriously wounded in a street fight in front of a Charlottesville store. His antagonist was Charles Bankhead, the husband of Jeff's sister Anne Cary Randolph. When Bankhead rushed him with a knife, Jeff sprang back, tripped, and fell. From the ground, as Bankhead moved in on him, young Randolph raised the butt of his riding whip and struck his assailant in the face. Bankhead stabbed Jeff in the hip and left arm. Bleeding heavily, Jeff was carried into the countingroom of the store, where he was attended by four doctors.

After nightfall a messenger brought Jefferson an account of the fight and the news that his grandson lay in the store, too gravely injured to be moved. The old man had returned a little while before from a trip into town. His arthritis was painful and his energies were still low since his nearly fatal illness, so that even that short trip must have been tiring. But he had his horse saddled at once and galloped back down the mountain and the rest of the four-mile way into town, his thoughts as black as the enveloping night. Jeff had always been a favorite with his grandfather and he had come to rely on him to administer his estates while the elder statesman pursued his public projects. He had come to depend on his companionship too. After the young man and his expanding family had moved from the dome room at Monticello into a home of their own across the river, Jefferson had missed them so much that they now were preparing to move into a house only a mile away from him. How cruelly ironic would be the loss of his grandson just when Jefferson had looked forward to having him near him again!

Finding Jeff lying on a pile of blankets, Jefferson knelt at his head and wept. Until this moment the young man had maintained stoic control but now he broke down too. A little later, when Jefferson sent servants to bring him to Monticello on a litter, it was deemed unwise to transport him even by that means. When he was moved two days later, it was only to the nearby home of Alexander Garrett, proctor of Central College. Jeff's wife came to town to nurse, and various young men of the town sat up with him and helped to turn him in the bed.

The physicians feared that Jeff's left arm would be permanently paralyzed but he gradually recovered most of its use, although he always thought of himself as "permanently maimed." After two weeks he was in the saddle again, an important landmark of recovery in those days.

Not so easily healed, however, were the wounds in family relationships, and not just between Jeff and Charles Bankhead either. The cause of the immediate quarrel supposedly was an insulting note from Bankhead to Jeff's wife. But the enmity went back beyond that. Bankhead was an alcoholic of violent temper and his wife Anne Cary, Jeff's sister, was often the victim of his violent rages. Four years before the fight in Charlottesville the fathers of the couple, Thomas Mann Randolph and Dr. John Bankhead, had had to assume Charles' debts and the management of the property on which the young couple lived. For a while Charles had returned to Caroline County, to his father's house and his father's medical ministrations. When he returned to his own home, he seemed a changed man. But one time later, when he and Ann Cary were visiting Monticello, his wrath rose against his wife and she had to flee to the protection of her mother's room. Jefferson wrote to Dr. Bankhead, saying that Charles' family could be safe only if the son returned to his old home where his father could exercise his ascendancy over him.[7] Jefferson, writing an in-law about Charles' violence toward Ann Cary, said that he had "taken for granted that she would fall by his hands."[8]

Charles had been required to post bail immediately after the fight. Jefferson tried to persuade Ann Cary to leave him for the shelter of Monticello, but she remained unswervingly loyal to her spouse. He wrote a letter to Jefferson declaring his great respect for his grandfather-in-law and claiming that he had acted solely in self-defense. The bail was forfeited; Charles Bankhead fled the county. Ann Cary joined him, causing one friend to say she did not see how "a woman of delicacy" could "get into bed with a drunk" and another to observe that she had "always thought there must be something wrong in a woman who could live with such a beast." Jefferson regretted that the young man was not in prison. Martha, Ann Cary's mother, had earlier expressed a harsher judgment. She suggested the hiring of a keeper who would prevent him from harming anyone else but would let him drink himself to death.

About this time news from the public arena disturbed Jefferson, though of course it was not nearly so unsettling as the near tragic event in his own family. But it did deepen his fears that a move toward centralized government and the growth of powerful banking interests, both far removed from the average American citizen, threatened democracy in the United States. On March 6, 1819, in *M'Culloch* v. *Maryland*, the United States Supreme Court unanimously ruled that the act of Congress establishing the Bank of the United States was constitutional but that a tax imposed on the bank by the Maryland legislature was unconstitutional. Chief Justice Marshall, who delivered the opinion, seized upon the occasion to expound his views on the Constitution, especially the doctrine of implied powers. He drew heavily upon Alexander Hamilton's arguments for the constitutionality of the bank expressed in a paper that the Treasury Secretary had written at President Washington's request in 1791. Jefferson at the same time had presented one expressing the view that such an institution would be unconstitutional. Hamilton had prevailed. In his opinion on *M'Culloch* v. *Maryland*, Marshall declared that the powers of the federal government were derived directly from the people, not from the states. The national government, he insisted, was supreme in its sphere of action. "Let the end be legitimate, let it be within the scope of the Constitution, and all means which are appropriate, which are plainly adapted to that end, which are not prohibited, but consist with the letter and spirit of the Constitution, are constitutional."

The argument was akin to that used by Jefferson himself to justify his departure from strict constructionism in the Louisiana Purchase. But he had regarded it as a resort for extraordinary occasions and had stressed that his action could be vetoed by the Congress. He was profoundly troubled because he saw the Supreme Court's ruling as demonstrating that the center of power in the federal government resided in nine people who, so long as they refrained from criminal behavior, were immune to the pleas and protestations of the mass of citizens. He had foreseen the emergence of the Supreme Court in this role. For this reason, he was not shocked or dismayed by Marshall's ruling. But the absence of shock made it no whit less troubling.

Jefferson praised Judge Spencer Roane's published criticisms of the decision but he did not personally involve himself in the controversy. His battles for the university would take all the energy that he could spare.

At the first meeting of the Board of Visitors, March 29, 1819, with all members present, Jefferson was of course chosen rector. He had entertained his fellow Visitors at Monticello the day before and doubtless had used the opportunity to create a climate of opinion favorable to some of his ideas. Habitually he left nothing to chance in matters in which he was deeply concerned. Though a secretary was elected, the official minutes[9] of this meeting are in Jefferson's handwriting.

Despite his colleagues' doubts about appointing Cooper to a professorship, Jefferson was determined that this should be done. He was not prompted by mere willfulness. He believed that the first appointments to the faculty should signal to the world that the university would be a major institution of higher learning, a center of uncompromising scholarship. What better way to accomplish this purpose than by securing the services of the man who, in his estimation, was the preeminent scholar in America? Such a move, followed by the employment of some of Europe's most learned men, should insure both the image and the substance of the new university.

Jefferson compromised to the extent of agreeing that Cooper should not be appointed for the spring term in the immediate offing. But he insisted that he be appointed for the following year and carried his point. In Jefferson's handwriting, the minutes report the decision that Cooper be offered a contract as "professor of chemistry, mineralogy and natural philosophy, and as professor of law also, until the advance of the institution, and the increase of the number of students, shall render necessary a separate appointment to the professorship of law." [10] His salary would be larger than that of other professors, and, like them, he would also be rewarded from the tuition paid by his students. An

interesting sidelight on academic financing in that day is provided by an
exception granted Cooper: "that until he shall have fifty students of chemistry,
the expense in articles consumed necessarily [by demonstrations] in the courses
of chemical lectures be defrayed by the University, not exceeding $250 in any
course."

Jefferson presented to the Visitors his architectural plans for the university.[11]
Not surprisingly, these were a revision of his plans for Central College. After all,
he had planned from the beginning to convert the college into a state university.
Now, instead of six pavilions with connecting dormitories, there would be ten.
There would be four parallel buildings instead of two. The student dining
rooms, which Jefferson called "hotels," and the dormitories would look out
upon the backs of the pavilions, but their rear windows would look out upon
gardens. Cabell suggested that the arrangement would be more pleasing if
gardens were planted between the two rows of buildings and those on the
second row of West Range were built to face outward. General Taylor noted the
good-humored readiness with which the architect accepted these suggestions.
Then Cabell and General Cocke suggested other changes and the old man dug
in his heels. They thought that some of the faculty quarters domestic rooms that
doubled as classrooms might not be large enough. They feared that, being small
and only one story high, the students' rooms in the warmer months would be
much too hot. Charlottesville was not nearly so cool as Jefferson's mountaintop.
A majority of the Visitors agreed with Cabell and Cocke that the flat roofs which
Jefferson envisioned for the West Range were likely to leak.

The rector compromised only so far as agreeing to defer a decision on this
last point until the next meeting of the Visitors. Meanwhile, he would be
working with Cocke, who already had been named with Jefferson to a committee
to superintend construction.

Most of the Visitors apparently knew little about architecture, but Cocke
was no mere novice who knew what he liked.[12] In designing his beautiful
mansion, Bremo, he had sought Jefferson's advice and he had been strongly
influenced by the Jeffersonian version of Palladian. Indeed, in constructing his
horse stalls, he directly copied those at Monticello. And as at Monticello,
depressed passageways linked the main house to its dependencies. But a great
deal of the design apparently was Cocke's own work, and his house is one of
the masterpieces of domestic architecture of nineteenth-century Virginia. Cocke
not only continued to argue for conversion of the dormitories into two-story
structures but made architectural drawings embodying this idea and mailed
them to Jefferson.

Respecting the fact that the Visitors had not yet made a final decision on
West Range but determined to avoid any delay in construction, Jefferson ordered
that excavations begin on the East Lawn. Assuming that the whole appropriation
for 1820 would be available on the first day of the year, Jefferson and Cocke
jointly decided that they would be justified in beginning construction of seven
pavilions rather than only the four so far authorized by the board.

However much he might be troubled by Cocke's independence on some
points, Jefferson was glad to have so capable a colleague to help him superin-

tend the building of the university. Soon, too, there was a new proctor, Arthur S. Brockenbrough, who was well versed in construction. Jefferson completed the East Lawn plans in June and was happy to be able to place them in the hands of one so well qualified.

As if he did not already have enough educational projects to deal with, Jefferson at this time founded a classical private grammar school. If successful, it could help prepare students for the University (In this instance, one should not read "elementary" for "grammar"; the school was a preparatory one). Jefferson had a more personal reason for establishing the academy. One of his grandsons, the studious Francis Eppes, was ready for secondary schooling and Jefferson wanted him to obtain a first-rate education without leaving the state.

Jefferson brought to Charlottesville as the teacher for this school Gerald Stack, an alumnus of Dublin's Trinity College whom Professor Cooper had called the best classics teacher in the nation. He would be the only instructor in the new school and would teach French as well as Latin and Greek.[13] In thus setting up a school, Jefferson was in the tradition of Virginia planters who for generations had built one-room schoolhouses and imported tutors to teach the children of their own families and some neighbors.

As might be expected, however, Jefferson introduced a variation on the usual plan. He persuaded a Frenchman to set up a boardinghouse for the students. The man's nationality was important. Jefferson's idea was that the community of young scholars would be encouraged to speak French in the house where they were fed and domiciled. Thus Jefferson had instigated a forerunner of the "French dorms," "Spanish dorms," and the like, to be found on twentieth-century American campuses.

Francis Eppes' father, John W. Eppes, by then one of Virginia's United States Senators, traveled to Charlottesville when the boy entered the academy. He visited Monticello for the first time in eight years, and the reunion was an emotional one for both him and Jefferson. When Eppes and Thomas Mann Randolph had been in Congress together, both sons-in-law had lived with Jefferson and the three had been quite close. But for some time now Eppes had kept away from the mountaintop because of a disturbing sense of Randolph's brooding hostility.

One of Francis' new schoolmates was Browse Trist, the great-grandson of Elizabeth House Trist, at whose Philadelphia boardinghouse Jefferson and his daughter Patsy had once lived quite contentedly. Jefferson had long maintained a friendship with Browse's mother. After her third marriage Browse and his brother Nicholas had paid a visit to Monticello and remained as parts of the ménage. They and Jefferson's granddaughters, and other young people, danced happily many an evening at Monticello. Sometimes Jefferson longed for quiet, but generally he loved being surrounded by happy youngsters.

They felt great veneration and affection for their host, but some of his eccentricities amused them. At times, from attachment or indifference, he would wear the same garment over and over. If the chosen suit was one of his many dark and sober ones, the repeated wearings attracted little attention. But when he appeared repeatedly in a red vest, the fact was inescapable. More conspicuous still was a pair of bright red knee breeches in which he appeared day after day. Many of his neighbors had never seen anyone else wearing the like, and it seemed particularly strange that a man so little given to gaudiness should have selected such attire. Some learned that the red breeches had been selected for him decades ago when he was United States Minister to France by a member of his staff who deemed them appropriate garb for a diplomat in Paris.[14]

Increasingly, though, Jefferson discarded knee breeches for the full-length trousers then coming into favor. At first the long pants had been workingmen's clothes, but they were becoming popular with all classes. Though Jefferson was much more enthusiastic about mental work than physical labor, it was very much in line with his personal philosophy and habits that he should have embraced a practical garment whose growing popularity symbolized the ascendancy in society of those who did a large share of the world's work.

In July, Jefferson retreated to Poplar Forest, lamenting to Madison that despite his labors in the spring and into early summer, not one brick had been laid upon another at the site of the university.[15] But masons from Philadelphia had been engaged and two stonecutters had been imported from Italy to carve the elegant capitals of the classical columns Jefferson had insisted on.

He had been busy at the drawing board, sketching arches and porticoes, cornices and architraves. The inspiration was classical and Palladian but, as with his design for the Virginia state capitol, he had impressed his own personality upon ancient designs and adapted them to a New World landscape. His substitution of red brick for stone, as in Monticello, gave a warmth to his Palladian adaptations. He united the Doric, Corinthian, and Tuscan orders in a single architectural entity and blended harmoniously distinctive features of the Fortuna Virilis, the Baths of Diocletian, the Theater of Marcellus, and the Temple of Trajan. The last structure's ornate pilasters he chastened "to suit our plainer style, still, however, retaining nearly their general outlines and proportions."[16]

Notwithstanding these plans, the university was altogether on the drawing board and in Jefferson's head. He had to face the fact that it would not open in the spring of 1820.

He was prepared to put some of these worries and frustrations behind him as he settled once again into the slower paced life of Poplar Forest. But the estate there presented its own problems. An illness had spread among the workers and their condition had not been alleviated—indeed may have been worsened—by an inept practitioner of doubtful credentials. His crops had been damaged, first by hail, then by drought. He himself was afflicted by terrible pains in his joints.

In the midst of these difficulties, an old nemesis pursued him to his retreat. When he received a letter from Wilson Cary Nicholas[17] on August 9, he may have felt a twinge of apprehension. It was with some sense of foreboding that he had endorsed two $10,000 notes for Nicholas, but he had felt that he could not refuse the request from a man who had helped him to secure a $3,000 loan. And of course Nicholas' estate supposedly was valued at $350,000 or more. A glance at the letter justified Jefferson's anxiety. It began, "It is with the greatest pain and mortification I communicate to you . . . ," and went on to explain that

Nicholas was at the brink of financial ruin. He had turned over all his property to trustees and was sure that something would be left after all obligations were met. While he thought that he should inform Jefferson of the situation because of his strong obligation to him, he did not see how the circumstances could harm his old friend. He said, "If I am the cause of your being uneasy or being put to inconvenience, I shall never forgive myself."[18]

Two days after receiving the letter, Jefferson replied, "A call on me to the amount of my endorsements for you would indeed close my course by a catastrophe I had never contemplated, but the comfort which supports me is the entire confidence I repose in your friendship to find some means of warding off this desperate calamity."[19] There was nothing angry or peevish in Jefferson's answer, but he was tactfully reminding Nicholas of just how damaging his misfortune could be to his Monticello friend and of the duty to labor to the utmost to prevent a debacle engulfing both of them.

Jefferson wrote to President Monroe, asking him to give Nicholas some government job as the man could no longer buy bread for his family.[20] So great was the fall of this Virginia planter who so recently had been president of the Richmond branch of the Bank of the United States and before that had been Governor of the commonwealth.

After several days Jefferson could empathize, not just sympathize, with Nicholas. The same day that he wrote to Monroe, he wrote his ruined friend, "Your misfortunes are sufficient to humble us all, and to extort the involuntary exclamation of, 'Lord, what are we?' "[21] A week later he wrote: "I know well how apt we are to be deluded by our own calculations, and to be innocently led into error by them."[22]

Soon the bank demanded that Jefferson, because of his liability for Nicholas' debts, provide additional security. The diarrhea that had assailed him in 1774 as he traveled to Williamsburg to present revolutionary resolutions that could have caused his arrest for treason, and in 1801 after he assumed the responsibilities of the presidency, and at various other times of crisis, struck him now.[23] This time the affliction was not a matter of a few days or even several weeks.[24] It was a classic case of what used to be called spastic colitis, nervous diarrhea, or irritable colon but is now more generally known as irritable bowel syndrome. Spasms of the muscle fibers in the wall of the colon caused diarrhea and constipation to alternate in a seemingly unending cycle fraught with pain. His family feared that he was headed for an agonizing death. On top of all this, the pain in his joints was excruciatingly magnified.

Before the physical troubles reached their peak, Monticello's south pavilion caught fire and, with strong winds fanning the blaze, burned to the ground. Then the wind suddenly shifted and carried the fire to the north pavilion. Jefferson ran out to deal with the emergency, slipped, and fell. Fortunately, no bones were broken. Except for the added pain to his joints, he suffered only a skinned shin.

The blaze was extinguished before much harm was done to the north pavilion, but metaphorically Jefferson had to deal with far more fires than he could put out. He was debtor to five banks. To deal with his most pressing financial problem, the one resulting from endorsement of Nicholas' notes, Jefferson took out a blanket mortgage on Monticello and every other acre he owned and then conveyed Poplar Forest to Jeff as trustee for the benefit of the bank. A financial depression descended on the nation and was felt particularly strongly in Virginia, where many great planters were heavily extended. And now, when Jefferson's only hope for financial survival lay in agricultural success, not only did depressed prices make some harvests unprofitable but bad weather severely reduced the yields.

But Jefferson survived and regained his fighting spirit. On November 7 he wrote John Adams, "Three long and dangerous illnesses within the last 12 months must apologize for my long silence towards you."[25] But he said not a word more about his illnesses before launching into a discussion of the nation's financial crisis. "The paper bubble is then burst," he said. "This is what you and I, and every reasoning man seduced by no obliquity of mind or interest, have long foreseen. Yet its disastrous effects are not the less for having been foreseen. We were laboring under a dropsical fullness of circulating medium. Nearly all of it is now called in by the banks who have the regulation of the safety valves of our fortunes and who condense or explode them at their will. Lands in this state cannot now be sold for a year's rent: and unless our legislature have wisdom enough to effect a remedy by a gradual diminution only of the medium, there will be a general revolution of property in this state. Over our own paper and that of other states coming among us, they have competent powers. Over that of the bank of the U. S. there is doubt; not here, but elsewhere. That bank will probably conform voluntarily to such regulation as the legislature may prescribe for the others. If they do not we must shut their doors and join the other states which deny the right of Congress to establish banks, and solicit them to agree to some mode of settling this constitutional question. . . . I do not know particularly the extent of this distress in the other states, but Southwardly and Westwardly I believe all are involved in it."

From the depths of indignation he summoned the energy to demand reform. Though his prejudice against the banks had long been bitter, there was justice in much that he said. The Panic of 1819 was aggravated by unbridled speculation in Western lands, grossly overextended investments in manufacturing, collapse of overseas markets, and commodity inflation, but the greatest factor in precipitating the disaster was the unwarranted expansion of banking and credit in the euphoria after the War of 1812. The Bank of the United States and the state banks were both guilty.

In a letter to Spencer Roane,[26] Jefferson recalled with pride his own earlier efforts toward reform of the government. Roane, under the pseudonym Hampden, suggesting the seventeenth-century foe of tyranny, had written a series of essays criticizing Marshall's opinion in *M'Culloch* v. *Maryland* and restating the states' rights view of the Constitution. Jefferson told Roane that he endorsed "every tittle" of the Hampden papers. He said that they expressed "the true principles of the revolution of 1800," the year of his election to the presidency, and pronounced it "as real a revolution in the principles of our government as that of 1776 was in its form; not effected indeed by the sword, as that, but by the rational and peaceable instrument of reform, the suffrage of the people."

In the midst of Jefferson's troubles there came to him a letter[27] ironic in its message and timing. It was from Maria Cosway, whose golden curls and piquant charm had enchanted him when he first met her in Paris in 1786 and whose departure from him had, in his own words, left him "more dead than alive."[28] She had been living apart from her husband in a Catholic retreat in Italy, but news that he had been paralyzed sent her immediately to his side. She told Jefferson that Angelica Church, another celebrated beauty whose attentions from the Virginian had once annoyed Maria, was now dead. Madame de Corny, another Paris friend, was gravely ill. "Strange changes over and over again, all over Europe," Maria wrote. "You only are proceeding on well."[29]

Jefferson replied much later and then not in the style of the gallant lover of old. He wrote, "Such is the state of our former coterie—dead, diseased, dispersed. . . . Mine is the next turn, and I shall meet it with goodwill."[30]

At that he might outlive his financial resources. Hospitality continued to be a constant drain. Edmund Bacon, his farm manager, said: "He knew that it more than used up all his income from the plantation and everything else, but he was so kind and polite that he received all his visitors with a smile, and made them welcome. They pretended to come out of respect and regard to him, but *I* think that the fact that they saved a tavern bill had a good deal to do with it, with a good many of them. I can assure you I got tired of seeing them come, and waiting on them."[31]

Bacon may have been unduly cynical about the visitors' motives, but he had reason to look on them with a jaundiced eye. He said: "They were there all times of the year; but about the middle of June the travel would commence from the lower part of the State to the Springs, and then there was a perfect throng of visitors. They travelled in their own carriages, and came in gangs— the whole family, with carriage and riding-horses and servants; sometimes three or four such gangs at a time. We had thirty-six stalls for horses, and only used about ten of them for the stock we kept there. Very often all of the rest were full, and I had to send horses off to another place. I have often sent a wagon-load of hay up to the stable, and the next morning there would not be enough left to make a hen's nest. I have killed a fine beef, and it would all be eaten in a day or two. There was no tavern in all the country that had so much company. Mrs. Randolph, who always lived with Mr. Jefferson after his return from Washington, and kept house for him, was very often greatly perplexed to entertain them. I have known her many and many a time to have every bed in the house full, and she would send to my wife and borrow all her beds—she had six spare beds—to accommodate her visitors. I finally told the servant who had charge of the stable, to only give the visitors' horses half allowance. Somehow or other Mr. Jefferson heard of this; I never could tell how, unless it was through some of the visitors' servants. He countermanded my orders."

Meanwhile, a very different diet from that enjoyed by Jefferson's guests was being served in the boardinghouse for students in French at Stack's Academy. Breakfast and supper consisted solely of bread and milk except for the possible substitution of café au lait. Dinner, the middle meal, included both salted and fresh meat and plenty of vegetables. Ordinarily, however, no dessert was served with any meal. Jefferson had instructed Laporte that neither wine nor any other alcoholic beverage should be served, "a young stomach needing no stimulating drinks, and the habit of using them being dangerous."[32] The boys grumbled about the food, as students have for generations, but apparently with more than the usual justification. One day Browse Trist complained that there was a maggot in his food, and Laporte, the proprietor, asked him to leave.

The students conferred, drinking from a potent mixture of wine and whiskey. The combination of juvenile and alcoholic spirits sent seven of them sallying forth into the town, disturbing the peace with a series of antics culminating in the stoning of the Frenchman's residence.

The Frenchman rode up the mountain to inform Jefferson that the students were in rebellion. He also told him that among the seven chief offenders were Browse Trist and Jefferson's grandsons Francis Eppes and Francis' cousin Wayles Baker. What the boys did not know was that the boardinghouse menu had been suggested by Jefferson himself. Browse's initial complaint had caused Laporte to tell him that he would be unwelcome at the boardinghouse. When Jefferson learned of their conduct he told all three boys that they would be unwelcome at Monticello. After a few days Martha appealed to her father in the boys' behalf and he yielded.[33] By that time he may have welcomed her entreaty.

Discipline in the academy itself was not much better than in the boarding-house. Though a conscientious scholar, Gerald Stack did not have the personal forcefulness to demand respect from his young charges. His painful introversion and his awe of Jefferson had caused him to decline a dinner invitation from the great man, but conditions in the school finally got so bad that he called at Monticello to present his resignation. Jefferson talked him out of it and wrote him a letter to help in soliciting students.

Jefferson was catching up with his correspondence during this period when he had recovered sufficiently to be active at his desk but not enough to return to the saddle. His close brush with death had given him ample time and motive to consider his personal philosophy, and this concern was expressed in a letter he wrote to William Short, a protégé and surrogate son, on October 31, just three or four days after he was "able to get on horseback."[34]

Short had written that he now was leading an indolent life and described himself as a disciple of Epicurus. Jefferson replied: "I take the liberty of observing that you are not a true disciple of our master Epicurus, in indulging the indolence to which you say you are yielding. One of his canons, you know, was that 'indulgence which prevents a greater pleasure or produces a greater pain, is to be avoided.' Your love of repose will lead, in its progress, to a suspension of healthy exercise, a relaxation of mind, an indifference to every-thing around you, and finally to a debility of body, and hebetude of mind, the farthest of all things from the happiness which the wellregulated indulgences of Epicurus ensure; fortitude, you know, is one of his four cardinal virtues. That teaches us to meet and surmount difficulties; not to fly from them, like cowards;

and to fly, too, in vain, for they will meet and arrest us at every turn of our road."

Before inditing this paternal reproof, Jefferson wrote: "As you say of yourself, I too am an Epicurean. I consider the genuine (not the imputed) doctrines of Epicurus as containing everything rational in moral philosophy which Greece and Rome have left us. Epictetus indeed, has given us what was good of the stoics; all beyond, of their dogmas, being hypocrisy and grimace. Their great crime was in their calumnies of Epicurus and misrepresentations of his doctrines; in which we lament to see the candid character of Cicero engaging as an accomplice. Diffuse, vapid, rhetorical, but enchanting. His prototype Plato, eloquent as himself, dealing out mysticisms incomprehensible to the human mind, has been deified by certain sects usurping the name of Christians, because, in his foggy conceptions, they found a basis of impenetrable darkness whereon to rear fabrications as delirious of their own invention. These they fathered blasphemously on him whom they claimed as their founder, but who would disclaim them with the indignation which their caricatures of his religion so justly excite."

After briefly reviewing the strengths and weaknesses of several other ancient philosophers and spiritual teachers who had endeavored to reform the faiths of their countrymen, Jefferson said: "But the greatest of all the reformers of the depraved religion of his own country, was Jesus of Nazareth. Abstracting what is really his from the rubbish in which it is buried, easily distinguished by its lustre from the dross of his biographers, and as separable from that as the diamond from the dunghill, we have the outlines of a system of the most sublime morality which has ever fallen from the lips of man. . . . Epictetus and Epicurus give laws for governing ourselves, Jesus a supplement of the duties and charities we owe others."

The closet theologian next revealed that his thoughts on the subject were precise and of long standing. "The establishment of the innocent and genuine character of this benevolent moralist," he said, "and the rescuing it from the imputation of imposture, which has resulted from artificial systems, invented by ultraChristian sects, unauthorized by a single word ever uttered by him, is a most desirable object, one to which Priestley has successfully devoted his labors and learning. It would in time, it is to be hoped, effect a quiet euthanasia of the heresies of bigotry and fanaticism which have so long triumphed over human reason, and so generally and deeply afflicted mankind; but this work is to be begun by winnowing the grain from the chaff of the historians of his life. I have sometimes thought of translating Epictetus (for he has never been tolerably translated into English) by adding the genuine doctrines of Epicurus from the Syntagma of Gassendi, and an abstract from the Evangelists of whatever has the stamp of the eloquence and fine imagination of Jesus."

He said: "The last I attempted too hastily some twelve or fifteen years ago. It was the work of two or three nights only, at Washington, after getting through the evening task of reading the letters and papers of the day. But with one foot in the grave, these are now idle projects for me. My business is to beguile the wearisomeness of declining life, as I endeavor to do, by the delights of classical reading and of mathematical truths, and by the consolations of a sound philosophy, equally indifferent to hope and fear."

His next words belied his declaration of detachment from the affairs of this world. He enthusiastically urged Short to visit Monticello with Correa as a way of rousing himself from apathy and adding "much to the happiness" of his host. And he exclaimed, "Come, too, and see our incipient University, which has advanced with great activity this year. By the end of the next, we shall have elegant accommodations for seven professors, and the year following the professors themselves. No secondary characters will be received among them. Either the ablest which America or Europe can furnish, or none at all. They will give us the selected society of a great city separated from the dissipation and levities of its ephemeral insects."

The affairs of the inchoate institution were soon claiming a large proportion of Jefferson's time and returning energy. On December 1, 1819, he sent his first annual report as rector to the president and directors of the Literary Fund. It was transmitted to Virginia's new Governor, none other than Jefferson's son-in-law Thomas Mann Randolph, who entered upon his duties December 13. The election portended little change in Jefferson's household arrangements at Monticello. Randolph had socialized less and less with the family and Martha expected to spend much more time with her father than with her husband at the Executive Mansion in Richmond.

Randolph transmitted Jefferson's report to the General Assembly. The office of Governor still suffered from the weaknesses built into the state Constitution by a generation that had suffered under colonial exercise of executive power. So the Governor could use some influence, but no direct power, in behalf of the university. But such influence as the Governor had was available to the school and its adherents. More important for the university than his office as Governor was his position as president of the State Literary Fund. Randolph had been active with Jefferson in behalf of Central College, and he was a loyal friend to its great successor.

Jefferson explained in a letter accompanying the rector's report that construction on the site of the university had not proceeded as rapidly as had been anticipated when the document had been adopted at an October meeting of the Visitors. Nevertheless, there were now standing the walls of seven pavilions and thirty-seven dormitories. As defined in the plans, a dormitory was not a large aggregation of students' rooms but quarters suitable for one or two students. More money was necessary to complete these structures and to begin work on others. The report also officially announced the appointment of Dr. Cooper to the university's first professorship. No date had been set for the beginning of his active service. He would remain the sole faculty member until accommodations were ready for others and for the students.

Jefferson was bound to be painfully aware that the financial crisis in the nation, and especially in Virginia, of which he was one of the greatest victims, argued badly for the acquisition of either public or private funds for a new institution. When the legislature received the rector's report from Governor Randolph, the coupling of a request for funds with the announcement that

Cooper had been appointed professor had the deleterious effect that Cabell and Cocke had forecast. In the vanguard of protest were two letters[35] to the General from the Rev. John H. Rice, a prominent Presbyterian minister and personal friend who earlier had saluted Cocke for his part in founding the university. He feared that the appointment of Cooper signaled development of the school along lines subversive to society. He followed the letter with articles in January and February 1820 issues of a publication he edited, the *Virginia Evangelical and Literary Magazine*. One of the articles contained a published quotation from Cooper: "The time seems to have arrived when the separate existence of the human soul, the freedom of the will, and the eternal duration of future punishment, like the doctrines of the Trinity and transubstantiation, may no longer be entitled to public discussion."[36] Cooper was not only denying beliefs cherished by most citizens; he seemed to imply that those who wished to defend them were not entitled to a hearing.

If the Presbyterian clergy became aroused against the university, their opposition could be costly. More than the ministers of any other denomination in the state, they were strong supporters of education. And their influence might be strong with some legislators, especially those from west of Charlottesville, where the Scotch-Irish were a sizable element.

Jefferson reinforced his official report as rector with a letter to Cabell, which the Senator released to the *Richmond Enquirer*. In accordance with Jefferson's wishes, it appeared anonymously, though no informed citizen could have doubted the identity of the author. Cabell omitted from the copy he furnished the newspaper a few sentences that Jefferson had written about Cooper.[37] Obviously Cabell thought that defending the choice of the controversial professor was not so good a strategy as refraining from any unnecessary discussion of his qualifications.

Jefferson's letter was an appeal to state pride and a warning that other states were surpassing the Old Dominion in provisions for higher education. Kentucky, taken from Virginia's side and until recent decades a collection of frontier settlements, was already moving ahead of the mother commonwealth. She had in operation Transylvania University, with fourteen professors and more than two hundred students. Jefferson was writing off his old alma mater, William and Mary, then between periods of greatness. If the General Assembly of Virginia did not support the university being built in Charlottesville, the state's promising young men would have to leave her to complete their formal education. In that case, he would prefer that they go to Kentucky, because that former county of Virginia had "more of the flavor of the old cask." He borrowed a leaf from the notebook of one of his three favorite heroes, Francis Bacon. The seventeenth-century polymath had written, "Knowledge is power." Jefferson wrote, "The efforts now generally making through the states to advance their science [learning] is for power, while we are sinking into the barbarism of our Indian aborigines, and expect, like them, to oppose by ignorance the overwhelming mass of light and science by which we shall be surrounded."

There was enthusiasm for the university in the Senate but a good deal of distrust of the institution in the House of Delegates, where western counties were more heavily represented. Finally, on February 24, 1820, Cabell could tell Jefferson that the legislature had enacted a law authorizing the Board of Visitors to borrow up to $60,000 at an interest rate not exceeding six percent. This was not enough for them to proceed at the pace the rector believed desirable, but it did breathe a little more life into the project.

The anxiety for Virginia expressed in Jefferson's letter about education in the state was inextricably bound up with even deeper worries about the future of the commonwealth and the Union of which it was a founding member. These anxieties were focused by debate when the applications of Missouri and Maine for statehood were before Congress.

It was no accident that, of the twenty-two states then comprising the Union, eleven were slave and eleven free. This balance had been carefully preserved for seventeen years by the alternate admission of slave and free states. As each state was allotted two United State Senators, representation of slave and free states was equal in the upper chamber. In the House, however, where representation was proportionate to population, the more rapid growth of the free states had given them a majority of 105 to 81. Moreover, all prognostications were for an increasing disparity of population between the two groups of states. The slave states now looked to the Senate as their sole protection from the tyranny of a House majority.

The situation would not so seriously have threatened the Union if the principal division had been between slave and free, and states in the two categories had been scattered over a large part of the continent. But the chief differences were economic, and the states were ranged in two geographical groups, the members of each being contiguous. The rivalry was between the industrially dominated society of the North and the predominantly agricultural society of the South. Just as Northeastern politicians had once feared Southern domination unfriendly to industrial development, Southern politicians now feared Northern domination inimical to agriculture. Only the policy of preserving the exact balance in the Senate by alternate admission of slave and free states partly solaced the apprehensions of many Southerners.

Representative James Tallmadge of New York set the scales to trembling when, with statehood legislation for Missouri pending, he dropped into the hopper an amendment prohibiting further introduction of slaves into Missouri and mandating the manumission at age twenty-five of all children born to slaves in Missouri after its admission. If Missouri were to become a state under these provisions and Maine were to be admitted at almost the same time, the Northern states would be destined to have a majority in the Senate as well as the House.

Tallmadge's amendment was carried in the House but defeated in the Senate. When the new Congress convened in December, however, Senator Rufus King of New York insisted that it had the authority to make the prohibition of slavery in Missouri a prerequisite to statehood. Senator William Pinkney of Maryland retorted that, as the Union was composed of equal states, a coalition of states acting through the Congress could restrict the freedom of action of a single state. After much bitter debate in both chambers, Senate and House compromised on a bill admitting Maine as a free state and Missouri as a slave state and prohibiting slavery in the Louisiana Purchase north of latitude 36° 30'. Thus on March 3 the Missouri Compromise became law, satisfying nobody but nevertheless prompting sighs of relief from many practical politicians in both North and South.

Jefferson was alarmed by the whole controversy surrounding the compromise. On his seventy-fifth birthday he confided his fears to William Short.[38] A cycle of conflicts between North and South, he said, would build "such mutual and moral hatred as to render separation preferable to eternal discord." His argument foreshadows Robert E. Lee's in a letter of January 29, 1861: "I can anticipate no greater calamity for the country than a dissolution of the Union. . . . Still, a Union that can only be maintained by swords and bayonets, and in which strife and civil war are to take the place of brotherly love and kindness, has no charms for me."[39] Jefferson saw slavery as exacerbating the differences between North and South, but he did not see it as the sole cause or probably even as the principal one. He said that it was "a hideous evil" and a problem even more sorely felt by Southerners than Northerners because Southerners had to live with it until they could find a "cure." He said that Northerners and Southerners should cooperate to determine a "practicable process" for eradicating this wicked institution.[40]

Jefferson correctly prognosticated forty-one years before the Civil War that when division came the lines would not be drawn strictly between the states where slavery was legal and those where it was not. He correctly predicted that the Potomac River would be the boundary of the contending nations, with Maryland and Delaware, though slave states, remaining in the Union. Indeed, when Abraham Lincoln issued the Emancipation Proclamation he would except both Maryland and Delaware, along with some Virginia counties and cities, from its provisions to avoid offending slaveholders in those areas who were fighting in the federal forces or otherwise supporting the Union Cause. [41] Jefferson also predicted that the Northwest would join the area with which it had the closest economic ties. This prognostication also came true, but not as Jefferson expected. In 1820 the Northwest (today the Upper Middle West) was linked economically with the South because of transportation through the Mississippi and its tributaries. Like virtually everyone else in his day, Jefferson could not foresee that railroad links with the North would supersede water links with the South as the financial lifelines of the Northwest.

He did understand that political strife between North and South was born of conflicting economic interests. Lincoln evidently believed the same thing in September 1861 when he rebuked Union General John C. Fremont and removed him from his post for declaring free the slaves of Missouri rebels and even as late as May 9, 1862, when he dismissed General David Hunter's proclamation of emancipation for slaves in South Carolina, Georgia, and Florida.[42] Like Jefferson, Lincoln abhorred slavery; and like Jefferson, he urged the ending of slavery through a system of financial compensation to the owners; but each statesman realized that the conflict between North and South was a struggle for economic survival and far more complex than war between holy crusaders on one side and unregenerate infidels on the other.

One can easily imagine Jefferson's agitation of spirit when he envisioned the dissolution of the Union. He had no prouder claim to fame than his authorship of the Declaration of Independence. The Fourth of July was the only birthday that he celebrated. He was one of the builders of the nation, not only as a founding father, but when, as President of the United States, he had doubled its size. At seventy-five he was fighting a rear-guard action against Death in his determination to build for Americans a university where they could receive at home under democratic auspices an education rich in the cultural largess of Europe.

Jefferson wrote a particularly eloquent and prescient letter[43] to Congressman John Holmes of Maine, who had presented his state's petition for statehood and had cochaired the conference committee that presented the Missouri Compromise. Holmes sent the ex-President a copy of a letter to his constituents explaining his actions in Congress. Jefferson replied: "I had for a long time ceased to read newspapers, or pay any attention to public affairs, confident they were in good hands, and content to be a passenger in our bark to the shore from which I am not distant. But this momentous question, like a fire bell in the night, awakened and filled me with terror. I considered it at once as the knell of the Union."

Jefferson foresaw a breach of the Union growing out of conflicting economies of North and South with differences heightened and emotionalized by disagreements over how to deal with the problem of slavery and ideological differences over states' rights. The Missouri Compromise gave him little comfort. The fire bell still echoed in his mind. "It is hushed, indeed, for the moment," he said. "But this is a reprieve only, not a final sentence. A geographical line, coinciding with a marked principle, moral and political, once conceived and held up to the angry passions of men, will never be obliterated; and every new irritation will mark it deeper and deeper. I can say, with conscious truth, that there is not a man on earth who would sacrifice more than I would to relieve us from this heavy reproach, in any *practicable* way. The cession of that kind of property, for so it is misnamed, is a bagatelle which would not cost me a second thought, if, in that way, a general emancipation and *expatriation* could be effected; and gradually, and with due sacrifices, I think it might be. But as it is, we have the wolf by the ears, and we can neither hold him, nor safely let him go. Justice is in one scale, and self-preservation in the other."

There was significance in Jefferson's underlining the words *practicable* and *expatriation*.

His record of opposition to slavery was consistent. As a student he had on his own initiative copied into his Commonplace Book the words of historians, jurists, and philosophers inveighing against the institution.[44] In 1774 he proved that his own views coincided with these expressions when, in *A Summary Review of the Rights of British America*, he condemned the slave trade. In 1776 he argued that the Declaration of Independence should carry a commitment to the abolition of slavery. He stressed the anomalous and vulnerable position of those who countenanced slavery while appealing, for justification of rebellion, to a belief in freedom as a God-given right of all people. He was sorely chagrined when planters from the Deep South and New England delegates with slave-trading constituents united to thwart his efforts toward reform.[45] He had rejoiced when his own Virginia became the first state of any kind—either state of the Union or national state—in modern history to outlaw importation of slaves. But he was bitterly disappointed when efforts to abolish bondage in the commonwealth failed by agonizingly narrow margins. As a member of the Continental Congress in 1784, he had proposed an ordinance including the abolition of slavery after 1800 from territories west of the original thirteen states, but this specific provision was deleted by his fellow Congressmen.

In his *Notes on the State of Virginia* he had written one of the most eloquent and insightful denunciations of slavery ever composed, saying, "The whole commerce between master and slave is a perpetual exercise of the most boisterous passions, the most unremitting despotism on the one part, and degrading submission on the other. . . . Indeed I tremble for my country when I reflect that God is just; that his justice cannot sleep forever; that considering numbers, nature, and natural means only, a revolution of the wheel of fortune, an exchange of situation, is among possible events; that it may become probable by supernatural interference!"[46]

But the awareness that made Jefferson consider the size of the black population and fear "a revolution of the wheel of fortune, an exchange of situation," caused him to insist that any measures to eradicate the curse of human bondage be "practicable" and that "expatriation" go hand in hand with emancipation. He feared that some Northern Congressmen would be tempted to make political capital of Southern slavery and thus provoke into defense of the institution many Southerners who now sought a means of ending it. He feared that North and South would be swept beyond a common area of reasonable accommodation. He was afraid that the North, controlling the House of Representatives by the sheer numbers of its electorate, and perhaps destined to control the presidency by the same means, would attempt to impose on the states a simplistic settlement of a complex problem. Many Southerners, then, would be ready to fight for states' rights.

"I regret," Jefferson concluded, "that I am now to die in the belief that the useless sacrifice of themselves by the generation of 1776, to acquire self-government and happiness to their country, is to be thrown away by the unwise and unworthy passions of their sons, and that my only consolation is to be that I live not to weep over it. If they would but dispassionately weigh the blessings they will throw away, against an abstract principle more likely to be effected by union than by scission, they would pause before they would perpetrate this act of suicide on themselves, and of treason against the hopes of the world."[47]

Congressman Holmes shared with friends Jefferson's letter about "a fire bell in the night" and "the knell of the Union." Like many people since, they were deeply impressed by the imagery. They thought that general circulation of such a message from so respected a statesman might have a wholesome influence. Holmes asked Jefferson's permission to publish it.[48]

The old statesman politely refused, saying that, while his opinions might be welcomed by those of kindred views, they would only stir renewed animosity among former enemies. "My time for retiring" he said, "is long since arrived. I feel it most sensibly in all the functions of mind and body; and in nothing more than the wish to pass the remainder of life in tranquility. . . . It was my fortune, good or bad, to be placed at the head of the phalanx which entered first the breach in the federal ramparts, and our opponents, like Nero, wishing for a single neck, chose to consider mine as that of the whole body, and to spend on that all the hackings and hewings of their wrath. Some, I know, have forgiven, some have forgotten me: but many still brood in silence over their angry recollections and why should I rekindle these smoking embers? Why call up from their cerements the ghosts of the dead?"[49]

Once he had retired from public office, he had studiously avoided public controversy. He seemed to feel that, having presented himself as a target of abuse during forty years of service to the people, he had earned a permanent exemption from more of the same. In recent years Jefferson had privately blessed various efforts to eliminate slavery; but, although he believed that freed blacks must be relocated, he had not joined in the work of the American Colonization Society, an organization for emancipation and relocation of which his friend General Cocke was vice president. Jefferson believed that the problem of slavery would not be solved in his time and was loath to sacrifice in the effort whatever serenity might be available to him.

Though he tried to avoid public controversy even in his efforts for the university, telling himself (and for a while convincing Senator Cabell) that it was best for the institution, he nevertheless risked intervention when he believed it necessary. In several observations he anticipated, not quite so pithily, H. G. Wells' comment in 1920 that "human history becomes more and more a race between education and catastrophe." Convinced that his life was drawing to a close, he husbanded his remaining time, energy, and influence for a significant contribution to the winning of that race. Four years before, he had written, "If a nation expects to be ignorant and free, in a state of civilization, it expects what never was and never will be." He still believed that an educated citizenry was essential to survival of the United States. And the matter was of more than national importance. America, as he had indicated in his first inaugural address as President, was a place of new beginnings for the human race. The United States, if it provided its own people the education for full citizenship, could be an example to the world. On October 20, in a letter[50] to Richard Rush, son of his old friend Benjamin Rush and now Ambassador to Great Britain, Jefferson eloquently expressed his mingled anxiety and hope: "We exist . . . as standing proofs that a government, so modeled as to rest continually on the will of the whole society, is a practicable government. Were we to break to pieces, it would damp the hopes and the efforts of the good, and give triumph to those of the bad through the whole enslaved world. As members, therefore, of the universal society of mankind . . . it is our sacred duty to suppress passion among ourselves, and not to blast the confidence . . . that a government of reason is better than one of force."

The new session of Congress that convened November 13 did nothing to strengthen Jefferson's hopes for union with freedom in the United States.

Dominated by Northerners, the House of Representatives denied Missouri's bid for statehood. Officially, the sticking point was a provision of its constitution intended to prevent settlement by free blacks. In principle, this was not very different from Virginia's law enacted in 1806 requiring that freed blacks leave the commonwealth. The acrimony of the debate dramatized the angry opposition of North and South in many matters.

The treaty with Spain, awaiting ratification in Madrid, arranged for purchase of Florida by the United States. This would someday be an additional Southern state. Texas, however, was outside the boundaries of the Louisiana Purchase as defined in the treaty, largely because of Northern unwillingness to press for more Southern territory. But Jefferson foresaw its eventual annexation and predicted that it would someday be the richest state in the Union. Despite the prospect of adding a few more members to the Southern phalanx, demographics doomed the South to subordination or separation. The disparity in population and consequently in congressional representation would grow. In numbers of citizens, an overwhelmingly agricultural region would fall ever farther behind an increasingly urban, commercial, and industrial one.

The day after Christmas, with the troubled year of 1820 drawing to a close, Jefferson wrote several letters in which he said that the concern of too many Northern legislators in the Missouri matter was really one of politics and economics rather than morality and he thought that their holier-than-thou attitude would only inflame Southern resentment and diminish the possibility of effective compromise. To Albert Gallatin he wrote: "Moral the question certainly is not. . . . However, it served to throw dust into the eyes of the people and to fanaticize them, while to the knowing ones it gave a geographical and preponderant line of the Potomac and Ohio, throwing 12 states to the North and East and 10 to the South and West. With these [Northern states] therefore it is merely a question of power, but with this [Southern] geographical minority it is a question of existence. For if Congress once goes out of the Constitution to arrogate a right of regulating the conditions of the inhabitants of the states, its majority may, and probably will, next declare that the condition of all men within the United States shall be that of freedom, in which case all the whites south of the Potomac and Ohio must evacuate their states; and most fortunate those who can do it first." [51]

He foresaw several possible developments in the controversy over Missouri statehood, none of them encouraging. If the Missouri constitutional provision objectionable to the House's Northern majority were expunged and statehood granted, "all will be quieted until the advance of some new state shall present the question again. If rejected unconditionally, Missouri assumes independent self-government, and Congress, after pouting awhile, must receive them on the footing of the original states. Should the Representative[s] propose force, (1) the Senate will not concur; (2) were they to concur, there would be a secession of the members south of the line. . . . What next? Conjecture itself is at a loss. . . . And finally the whole will depend on Pennsylvania. While she and Virginia hold together, the Atlantic states can never separate. Unfortunately in the present case she has become more fanaticized than any other state. However useful where you are [as United States Minister to France], I wish you were with them. You might turn the scale there, which would turn it for the whole."

Even while he wrote in sectional terms about the American crisis, Jefferson was mindful of the international context. He said, "Should this scission take place, one of its most deplorable consequences would be its discouragement of the efforts of the European nations in the regeneration of the oppressive and cannibal governments."

Even so, Jefferson's attitude was not one of unrelieved gloom. "Amidst this prospect of evil," he wrote, "I am glad to see one good effect. It has brought the necessity of some plan of general emancipation and deportation more home to the minds of our people than it has ever been before. Insomuch that our Governor has ventured to propose one to the legislature. This will probably not be acted on at this time. Nor would it be effectual; for while it proposes to devote to that object one third of the revenue of the state, it would not reach one tenth of the annual increase." It was typical of Jefferson to refer to his son-in-law Thomas Mann Randolph impersonally, as the Governor, rather than by name even in a personal letter to his good friend Gallatin. Jefferson tended to draw a veil between his family relations and the outside world. "My proposition," he said, "would be that the holders should give up all born after a certain day, past, present or to come, that these should be placed under the guardianship of the State, and sent at a proper age to San Domingo. There they are willing to receive them, and the shortness of the passage brings the deportation within the possible means of taxation aided by charitable contributions. In this I think Europe, which has forced this evil on us, and the Eastern states, who have been its chief instruments of importation, would be bound to give largely. But the proceeds of the land office, if appropriated, would be quite sufficient."

Obviously Jefferson had thought long and hard about what he wanted to say to Gallatin in this letter. It was in the nature of a valedictory, as indicated by its beginning and end. In the first paragraph he said: "My ill health has long suspended the too frequent troubles I have heretofore given you with my European correspondence. To this is added a stiffening wrist, the effect of age on an ancient dislocation, which renders writing slow and painful, and disables me nearly from all correspondence, and may very possibly make this the last trouble I shall give you in that way." The wrist injury, of course, was the one he had incurred in middle age when he had tried to demonstrate his agility to a young Maria Cosway by leaping over a Paris fence. With increasing frequency, when he was writing on matters of tremendous scope and seriousness, the old pain returned to remind him that he was not a creature of pure reason. Jefferson's last sentence to Gallatin had an air of finality: "God bless you and preserve you *multos años*."

Early in the new year Jefferson was even more pessimistic about the fate of the Union than he had been in the last days of the old. On January 22, 1821, he congratulated John Adams on having "health and spirits enough" to participate in the recent convention to revise the Constitution of Massachusetts. He said that the amendments encouraged "a hope that the human mind will some day get back to the freedom it enjoyed 2000 years ago. This country, which has given to the world the example of physical liberty, owes to it that of moral emancipation also. For, as yet, it is but nominal with us. The inquisition of public opinion overwhelms in practice the freedom asserted by the laws in theory."[52]

Apropos of that problem, he said, "Our anxieties in this quarter are all concentrated in the question, 'What does the Holy Alliance, in and out of Congress, mean to do with us on the Missouri question?'" The Holy Alliance was Jefferson's sarcastic label for Northern politicians and businessmen who, in his view, made capital out of opposition to the South while professing moral inspiration. "The real question," he said, "as seen in the states afflicted with this unfortunate population is, 'Are our slaves to be presented with freedom and a dagger?' . . . Are we then to see again Athenian and Lacedaemonian confederacies? To wage another Peloponnesian War to settle the ascendancy between them? . . . That remains to be seen but not, I hope, by you or me. Surely they will parley a while, and give us time to get out of the way. What a Bedlamite is man!"

As Governor, Thomas Mann Randolph had seen evidence of a change in the attitude of some Virginians toward slavery as a result of Northern attacks on Southern morality. A short while ago there had been a general feeling among leading planters that slavery was an evil to be eradicated by some means. Even those who would not concede it was morally wrong admitted that it was an economic and social plague. Now some were responding to attack with "the new morality which tolerates perpetuity of slavery, and the new doctrine of the civil benefits supposed to be derived from that system."[53]

Jefferson had begun writing his memoirs on January 6. In February, the month in which a Missouri Compromise was attained under Henry Clay's leadership, Jefferson wrote about slavery in his memoirs. The compromise did nothing to lessen his anxiety because, as he wrote Spencer Roane, the agreement had merely "smeared over"[54] the central issue. So Jefferson, in his memoirs, wrote of American blacks: "Nothing is more certainly written in the book of fate than that these people are to be free. Nor is it less certain that the two races, equally free, cannot live in the same government. Nature, habit, opinion has drawn indelible lines of distinction between them. It is still in our power to direct the process of emancipation and deportation peaceably and in such slow degree as that the evil will wear off insensibly, and their place be pari passu filled up by free white laborers. If on the contrary it is left to force itself on, human nature must shudder at the prospect held up."[55]

Bold words. But they were not written for the public in his own time. The introductory sentence was: "At the age of 77, I begin to make some memoranda, and state some recollections of dates and facts concerning myself, for my own more ready reference, and for the information of my family."[56]

Political confusion was increased in the United States at this time by the fact that many of the Federalists were calling themselves Republicans. As Jefferson saw it, they had stolen the name of his party without adopting its principles. He had begun to regard Whig as an appropriate name for his party and he had long referred to the Federalists as Tories. Why not adopt the names used in British politics to separate those who feared the people and those who trusted the people more than they did the magnates? A little later he would argue that such a division would be far safer than one along geographical lines, which might well lead to division into two nations.[57] But he himself would not again play an active role in party politics.

XVIII

BROAD VISTAS

JEFFERSON's political skills, like his architectural abilities, his various learning, and the fruits of his long study of education, were concentrated in behalf of the project that would be his last great contribution to society. Financial panic, political upheaval, even the threat of a dissolution of the Union that he had helped to create and the rapid decline of his own physical powers, could not deflect him from work to advance the university.

Indeed, his country's troubles seemed to him to increase the urgency of provision for such an institution. He linked the two in a letter[1] to a legislator who had been associated with him in the efforts for Central College, General James Breckinridge. "I learn, with deep affliction," he wrote, "that nothing is likely to be done for our University this year. So near as it is to the shore that one shove more would land it there. I had hoped that would be given, and that we should open with the next year an institution on which the fortunes of our country may depend more than may meet the general eye." The rising generation in the commonwealth must deal with the threats to national union and with the protection of Virginia's rights. "These are considerations which will occur to all; but all, I fear, do not see the speck on our horizon which is to burst on us as a tornado, sooner or later. The line of division lately marked out between different portions of our confederacy is such as will never, I fear, be obliterated, and we are now trusting to those who are against us in position and principle, to fashion to their own form the minds and affections of our youth." He argued, "If, as has been estimated, we send three hundred thousand dollars a year to the northern seminaries, for the instruction of our own sons, then we must have there five hundred of our sons, imbibing opinions and principles in discord with those of their own country. This canker is eating on the vitals of our existence, and if not arrested at once, will be beyond memory."

He answered those who said that a state system of primary schools was even more important than a university and that "we cannot give the last lift to the University without stopping our primary schools." There was not enough money for both. Jefferson replied: "Nobody can doubt my zeal for the general instruction of the people. Who first started that idea? I may surely say myself. Turn to the bill in the revised code which I drew more than forty years ago, and before which the idea of a plan for the education of the people, generally, had never been suggested in this state. There you will see developed the first rudiments of the whole system of general education we are now urging and acting on; and it is well known to those with whom I have acted on this subject, that I never have proposed a sacrifice of the primary to the ultimate grade of instruction. Let us keep our eye steadily on the whole system. If we cannot do everything at once, let us do one at a time. The primary schools need no preliminary expense; the ultimate grade requires a considerable expenditure in advance. A suspension of proceeding for a year or two on the primary schools, and an application of the whole income, during that time, to the completion of the buildings necessary for the University, would enable us then to start both institutions at the same time."

That word "time" was very much in Jefferson's thoughts. It was the commodity that he was running out of. He told Breckinridge: "I have brooded, perhaps with fondness, over this establishment, as it held up to me the hope of continuing to be useful while I continued to live. I had believed that the course and circumstances of my life had placed within my power some services favorable to the outset of the institution. But this may be egoism, pardonable, perhaps, when I express a consciousness that my colleagues and successors will do as well whatever the legislature shall enable them to do."

He had suffered other disappointments regarding the university. The two Italian sculptors imported to carve the ornate capitals for the classical columns found that the native stone was not of sufficient quality for that work. Jefferson thought that perhaps they could at least perform the plain work, but they revealed that their experience had qualified them only for the fancy.[2] Despite Jefferson's assurances to Cooper that his appointment to the faculty would be upsetting only to Presbyterians, a not very numerous sect, and would be acceptable to Baptists, Methodists, and Episcopalians, a storm of protest from many quarters soon proved the rector mistaken. The Visitors, anxious about the appointment from the first, were now truly alarmed. Cabell told Jefferson that the payment of a $1,500 advance to Cooper had proved an impediment to funding of the university.[3]

The Senator informed Madison that undoubtedly there would be only two votes among the Visitors, except Jefferson's, to confirm a long-term contract for the controversial scholar—Madison's and his own.[4] The board informed Cooper that delays in the opening of the university and uncertainty about the actual date made it advisable to reconsider his contract but that $1,500 would be regarded as a termination fee. Cooper responded angrily, but the Visitors were taken off the hook when he reported that he had been hired by Columbia College in South Carolina at twice the salary proffered in Virginia and expressed regret that there had been so much trouble because of him.

Jefferson did not accept this result calmly. He insisted that Cooper had "more science in his single head than all the colleges of New England, New Jersey, and I may add Virginia, put together."[5]

Meanwhile Jefferson kept construction going forward even when he could give the workmen only promises instead of cash. Not only had the legislature failed to appropriate sufficient funds, but private philanthropy was discouraged by the publicity about Cooper as well as fears that the institution would never become a reality. General Cocke helped to supervise some of the details of building, and his knowledge of construction and flair for architecture were valuable. But Jefferson rode down from the mountain every day to give the work his personal attention. Walking was increasingly difficult. His "walking-stick chair" no longer provided sufficient support during his frequent rest stops. Even when he walked in the yard at Monticello a servant carried a folding camp stool. The servant, of course, accompanied him with the stool whenever he visited the building site.[6] Despite his feebleness, he would spend hours observing the workmen and telling them what to do.

In April Thomas Sully visited Monticello to paint Jefferson's portrait for the military academy at West Point, established nineteen years earlier during his presidency. Painted about the time of his seventy-eighth birthday, it shows a face marked by time but not ravaged by it. The mouth and jaw are still firm, as in the bust by Houdon and the two presidential portraits by Rembrandt Peale, but there is a newly wistful expression about the eyes. Withal, though, it is a resolute face as well as a sensitive one—the countenance of a man who still dreamed and had not yet put all his projects behind him.

In fact, Jefferson was working so hard for the future that he had no time to record his past. In July 1821 he abandoned the writing of his autobiography. Beginning with his ancestry and birth, before stopping he had carried the narrative to his acceptance of the post of Secretary of State in Washington's cabinet in 1790. It contained interesting information and some striking phrases but, in what amounted to about a hundred printed pages, revealed little of a personal nature.[7]

Jefferson had made his priorities clear in a letter to Cabell about the university: "What service can we ever render . . . equal to this? What object of our lives can we propose so important? What interest of our own which ought not to be postponed to this? Health, time, labor—on what, in the single life which nature has given us, can these be better bestowed than on this immortal boon to our country?"[8]

A shortage of funds continued to plague Jefferson in his personal affairs as well as in those of the university. Wilson Cary Nicholas was now dead and buried in the family cemetery at Monticello. Jefferson could not help wondering whether his own life would end in the same poverty. But, despite Nicholas' role in Jefferson's own misfortunes, the old statesman spoke of his friend sympathetically as a good but unfortunate man. Jefferson had some slight reason for encouragement about his situation. His son-in-law John Eppes loaned him $4,000 in exchange for the transfer of twenty slaves to work on the Eppes plantations. The older man did not believe in selling slaves except for "delinquency or on their own request." But he felt that this case was different. No families would be separated and these people, on young Francis Eppes' coming of age in about two years, would live on one of Jefferson's own plantations, which he would leave to his grandson.[9] The Monticello plantation, despite its poor soil, had become more profitable under the management of another grandson, Jeff. So now Jefferson turned over to him also the management of his Bedford County plantation. Even so, Edmund Bacon, Jefferson's longtime manager, thought his employer's chances of financial recovery were slim at best. Reluctantly, because he was devoted to him, Bacon left in October for opportunities in the West.[10] Jefferson was considerably in arrears in paying Bacon's salary, but the man was confident that his old employer would continue to pay him in installments after his departure. He had learned that Jefferson's word could always be relied on.

A drain on both money and time were the hordes of people for whom Monticello was either a home or a hotel. Fully as much a drain on time and energy were those who stayed away and wrote. His correspondence with his family, with old friends, and with intellectually stimulating acquaintances was a delight. But most of the writing was a chore, especially now that his wrist pained him. Nevertheless, he conscientiously answered everyone who wrote to him. He told one of his favorite correspondents, John Adams, that in 1820 alone he had received 1,267 letters, many "requiring answers of elaborate research, and all to be answered with due attention and consideration . . . . Is this life? At best it is but the life of a mill-horse, who sees no end to his circle but in death."[11]

Despite his talk of finding release in death, Jefferson labored on for the university, supervising construction when it could be done, and at other times drafting architectural plans, elaborating on the curriculum, and considering how to recruit a faculty. What faith sustained him? Most directly involved was his faith in humanity's capacity for progress through education. It not only gave meaning to life and thus afforded him a general inspiration; it also channeled his energies into a specific project in which he believed he could make an important difference.

Over and beyond this belief was a religious faith that he never discussed publicly. At rare intervals he had shared some of its features with a few relatives and such trusted friends as Richard Rush and John Adams. At last, on June 26, 1822, he furnished a compact outline of his creed. It was in a letter to Dr. Benjamin Waterhouse,[12] whose evangelizing for inoculation against smallpox had won Jefferson's enthusiastic support near the beginning of his presidency. Now the elder statesman praised the Boston physician's "denunciation of the abuses of tobacco and wine." Jefferson, of course, used wine in moderation and tobacco not at all. He also seemed drawn to Waterhouse by the doctor's expression of Unitarian sentiments. Jefferson wrote, "The doctrines of Jesus are simple, and tend all to the happiness of man." And then he listed those doctrines as he conceived them:

1. That there is one only God, and he all perfect.
2. That there is a future state of rewards and punishments.
3. That to love God with all thy heart and thy neighbor as thyself, is the sum of religion. These are the great points on which he endeavored to reform the religion of the Jews.

Jefferson invited his correspondent to "compare with these the demoralizing doctrines of Calvin":

1. That there are three Gods.

2. That good works, or the love of our neighbor, are nothing.

3. That faith is everything, and the more incomprehensible the proposition, the more merit in its faith.

4. That reason in religion is of unlawful use.

5. That God, from the beginning, elected certain individuals to be saved, and certain others to be damned; and that no crimes of the former can damn them; no virtues of the latter save.

He asked: "Now which of these is the true and charitable Christian? He who believes and acts on the simple doctrines of Jesus? Or the impious dogmatists, as Athanasius and Calvin? Verily I say these are the false shepherds foretold as to enter not by the door into the sheepfold, but to climb up some other way. They are mere usurpers of the Christian name, teaching a counter-religion made up of the *deliria* of crazy imaginations, as foreign from Christianity as is that of Mahomet. Their blasphemies have driven thinking men into infidelity, who have too hastily rejected the supposed author himself, with the horrors so falsely imputed to him. Had the doctrines of Jesus been preached always as pure as they came from his lips, the whole civilized world would now have been Christian."

Then Jefferson, as he virtually never did in public papers but fairly often did in private communication, made a still more sweeping statement: "I rejoice that in this blessed country of free inquiry and belief, which has surrendered its creed and conscience to neither kings nor priests, the genuine doctrine of only one God is reviving, and I trust that there is not a *young man* now living in the United States who will not die an Unitarian."

Such a fruition, however, was not without danger. "But much I fear," he wrote, "that when this great truth shall be reestablished, its votaries will fall into the fatal error of fabricating formulas of creed and confessions of faith, the engines which so soon destroyed the religion of Jesus, and made of Christendom a mere Aceldama; that they will give up morals for mysteries, and Jesus for Plato. How much wiser are the Quakers, who, agreeing in the fundamental doctrines of the gospel, schismatize about no mysteries, and, keeping within the pale of common sense, suffer no speculative differences of opinion, any more than of feature, to impair the love of their brethren. Be this the wisdom of Unitarians, this the holy mantle which shall cover within its charitable circumference all who believe in one God, and who love their neighbor!"

Jefferson was quite ecumenical. The ceremonies of christening and burial in his family were Anglican. And according to Edmund Bacon he "never debarred himself from hearing any preacher that came along." A particular favorite of his was Mr. Hiter, an itinerant Baptist minister of little formal education but noble character. Jefferson nearly always went to hear him when he preached in the yard of Charlottesville Court House. One day, perhaps when he had visited the building site of the University, Jefferson came up to the scene of the preaching in his overalls, accompanied by his servant bearing the folding camp stool. The man unfolded the chair and the elder statesman joined the impromptu congregation. "After the sermon," Bacon said, "there was a proposition to pass round the hat and raise money to buy the preacher a horse. Mr. Jefferson did not wait for the hat. I saw him unbutton his overalls, and get his hand into his pocket, and take out a handful of silver, I don't know how much. He then walked across the Court House to Mr. Hiter, and gave it into his hand. He bowed very politely to Mr. Jefferson, and seemed to be very much pleased."[13]

Jefferson's health improved early in 1822. He had more energy to devote to the planning and building of the university. One incentive was that his efforts might make it possible for other young Virginians to do what his Francis Eppes could not: "complete his education within the limits of Virginia." He was pleased, however, with some of the opportunities that the boy found in South Carolina, especially that of being one of Dr. Cooper's students. But he was relieved that his grandson had not enrolled at an Eastern (or, as we would say today, Northeastern) college. Before the young man settled on South Carolina's Columbia College, Jefferson wrote to Francis' father about the problem of finding a suitable school. He admitted that some of his ideas were "perhaps illiberal and many of them founded on prejudice," but he must confess to a "decided preference for the Virginia character and principles. All the science in the world would not to me as a parent compensate the loss of that open, manly, character, which Virginians possess and in which the most liberal and enlightened of the Eastern people are deplorably deficient. I have known many of their conspicuous men intimately, and I have never yet seen one who could march directly to his object. Some view at home or at the seat of Government entered all their projects and subjected them continually to the commission of acts which would tinge with shame the face of a Virginian."[14]

Jefferson was a statesman of uncommon integrity, idealism, and dedication, but it is amusing when he criticizes the Northeastern leaders for not marching directly to their objects. He himself often followed subtly circuitous paths to his goals, tempering his approach to the psychology of those with whom he dealt, emphasizing either the freshness or the venerability of his ideas according to the predilections of his audience.

It became apparent in the summer of 1822 that Francis Eppes, who had been an excellent student, was not likely to complete his formal education anywhere. His father had been nearly ruined by a combination of severe health problems and the economic depression afflicting the Virginia plantocracy. There was no more money for Francis to continue his college studies, and he returned to Virginia. Most lawyers then learned their profession by reading under the guidance of an experienced member of the bar. Jefferson suggested that his grandson follow that course and sent him a long list of books from which he could gain a knowledge of the law and its historical context. He thought three years of reading would be necessary to obtain more than the superficial education that enabled so many to qualify. The young man, if he wished, could pursue his studies at Monticello under his grandfather's guidance.[15]

But Francis had his eyes on a more exciting prospect—one likely to slow his studies for a while. He was in love with the beautiful Mary Cleland Randolph and eager to marry her. Jefferson could think of many objections to the plan.

Francis was not yet twenty-one. He had no money of his own, and his father was impoverished. The bride's father was in financial quicksand. Jefferson believed his grandson's age was objection enough in itself. He told John Eppes: "The European period of full age at 25 years is certainly more conformable with the natural maturity of the body and mind of man than ours of 21. The interruption of studies and filling our houses with children are the consequences of our habits of early marriage."[16]

The elder Eppes thoroughly approved of the prospective bride but believed that, under the circumstances, marriage would be unreasonable. Despite his own objections, Jefferson urged Eppes to accept the fact that the problem was not "under the jurisdiction of reason."[17] He himself gave his grandson what he had planned to give him at a future date: Poplar Forest and a thousand acres. Only it was not quite as he had planned. He could give him the use of the property but he could not deed it to him because it was tied up with his obligation for the notes of Wilson Cary Nicholas.

Jefferson was not able to attend the wedding, which was on November 28. On November 12, a rotted step on one of the terraces at Monticello gave way beneath him. His fall broke his left forearm and dislocated the wrist bones. The surgeon who set the bones instructed him to stay at home until Christmas. Gradually it became apparent that he was unlikely ever to regain the full use of his left hand. His right, of course, had never recovered from the accident he had suffered long ago when walking in Paris with Maria Cosway.

Recently he had written Mrs. Cosway in reply to a letter from her. The black border of her stationery signaled the contents of her note. Her husband had died the week before in an apoplectic fit. She took comfort in the fact that his last days had been his happiest. "All my thoughts and actions were for him," she said. "I shall retire from this bustling and insignificant world to my favorite college at Lodi [Italy] as I always intended, where I can employ myself so happily in doing good. I wish Monticello was not *so far*! I would pay you a visit if it was ever so much out of my way, but it is impossible. I long to hear from you—the remembrance of a person I so highly esteem and venerate affords me the happiest consolation. . . ."[18]

Calling her "my dear friend," Jefferson rejoiced that her comfort would be much increased by a change of residence "from the eternal clouds and rains of England to the genial and bright skies of Lodi."[19]

Did Jefferson take at face value her protestations of devotion to the late Richard Cosway? Jefferson had written many a gentle letter of sympathy to bereaved friends, but he sent Mrs. Cosway not one word of condolence. He was content to express his "great pleasure" that her husband's estate was "sufficient to place you in comfort."

Of his own situation, he told her: "My elder daughter, Mrs. Randolph, is well and greets you kindly. She has given me 11 grandchildren of whom 9 live with me, and all make me contented in the prospect of their worth and good qualifications." He said that a visit from Mrs. Cosway to him and his daughter "would be a real beatitude." He was no longer pretending to more youthful vigor than he possessed as he had in his fence-vaulting days in Paris. "I enjoy good health," he said, "though octogenary [actually he was some months short of his eightieth birthday]; but am too weak to walk further than my garden; yet I ride daily and without fatigue."

The most interesting part of Jefferson's letter describes with glowing enthusiasm the project that now claims his energies. "The sympathies of our earlier days," he wrote, "harmonize, it seems, in age also. You retire to your college of Lodi and nourish the natural benevolence of your excellent heart by communicating your own virtues to the young of your sex who may hereafter load with blessings the memory of her to whom they will owe so much. I am laying the foundation of a University in my native state, which I hope will repay the liberalities of its legislature by improving the virtue and science of their country, already blest with a soil and climate emulating those of your favorite Lodi."

After those florid lines, more akin to Maria's usual style than to his own, the congested prose gave way to a torrent of excitement, pride, and quest for approval: "I have been myself the architect of the plan of its buildings and of the system of instruction. Four years have been employed in the former, and I assure you it would be thought a handsome and classical thing in Italy. I have preferred the plan of an academical village rather than that of a single massive structure. The diversified forms which this admitted in the different pavilions and varieties of the finest samples of architecture, has made of it a model of beauty, original and unique. It is within view, too, of Monticello so it's a most splendid object, and a constant gratification to my sight. We have still one building to erect which will be on the principle of your Pantheon, a Rotunda like that but of half of its diameter and height only. I wish indeed you could recall some of your by-past years and seal it with your approbation."

Jefferson had an engraving made of the ground plan for his "academical village" and in November 1822 distributed copies to legislators and others.[20] It showed the four parallel rows of buildings already constructed as well as the Rotunda, still only on the drawing board, which eventually would dominate the long vista between the two central rows. The rector let the public know that only some plastering and the installation of a few classic capitals to be shipped from Italy were necessary to complete the pavilions, dormitories, and hotels. Lack of funds, he said, had prevented the start of construction on the Rotunda. And the Visitors had determined that the university would not open until this building also was ready for use. The plans had impact. Being able to visualize the physical layout made the university seem a much more attainable goal. An article appearing a little earlier in the *Richmond Enquirer* helped to increase interest and pride in the project. Under the pseudonym *Argus*, a visitor to the building site said that the physical plant would equal or excel that of any other educational institution in the United States. He noted fears that the university might turn its students away from religion but expressed his own conviction that Jefferson would not permit such a development.

The rector acted to quell anxiety that the school might promote atheism. In his official report for 1822 he suggested that schools of divinity bordering on the university grounds be established by separate denominations. The presence of the university would attract potential students to these schools. While they would be entirely separate from the larger institution, proximity would make possible some sharing of faculty. Jefferson did not compromise his long-held belief in separation of church and state but everyone would know that, if atheism was to be encouraged at the university, the rector would not invite the various denominations of churchmen to surround the campus with their watchtowers. He explained that the university itself would have no chair of divinity because that would violate both the separation of church and state and the principles of religious freedom. Jefferson was sticking to his tenets and at the same time being a resourceful politician in behalf of the university. In this, as in other instances, he was unswerving in his aim but flexible in his approach.

Early in 1823 prospects for the university brightened. Not only had Jefferson favorably influenced public opinion with publication of his sketches, his invitation to the churches to establish contiguous schools, and a meticulous record of expenditures, but the composition of the newly elected House of Delegates furnished additional reasons for hope. Cabell rejoiced that they were of higher caliber than their immediate predecessors and more disposed to make sacrifices for higher education. A little later he told Jefferson that his invitation to the churches to establish denominational schools had had a marvelous effect on the legislators. No denomination had leaped to accept the offer, but it had "drawn the lightning from the cloud of opposition."[21]

Early in February, Jefferson received word from Cabell that the legislature had authorized the Visitors to borrow $60,000 more from the State Literary Fund. Bursar Alexander Garrett said that Jefferson received the news like a man learning of the birth of his first, long-awaited son.[22]

On March 12, almost exactly a month before his eightieth birthday, he jubilantly told the Visitors that he had ordered construction to begin on the Rotunda.

When they met again on October 6, Jefferson reported that the distinctively round walls of the building were already complete. He would not proceed immediately to cap them with the even more distinctive hemispherical roof. Since its structure would tend to press not only down but outward on the vertical walls, he wanted to give them plenty of time to settle and harden. When warm weather returned, work on the roof could begin. Much more time—probably more than a year—would be necessary to complete the interior with its handsome classical trim. The university, Jefferson said, should be ready to operate as soon as it had a faculty. But there was one big qualification. Most of the appropriations for the university were actually loans. The institution was a heavy debtor. It could hardly repay the loans while meeting operating expenses. If its indebtedness was not dramatically reduced, it might not function for a quarter of a century.

Meanwhile, one of the founders of the University of Virginia was too busy to give much thought to the institution. President James Monroe was deeply involved in knotty problems of international relations, and he turned for advice to one of the world's greatest achievers in the field, his old friend Jefferson. Monroe had written in June about disturbing events in Spain. Ferdinand VII's repudiation of the Constitution of 1812, persecution of its supporters, and reinstitution of the Inquisition had provoked rebellion by liberals who forced the King to pledge that he would henceforth govern in accord with the Constitution's provisions. But royalists rose in his support in various parts of the country and civil war ensued. Ferdinand appealed for help from the Holy Alliance—Russia, Austria, Prussia, and France. The Bourbons had been restored in Paris. In April 1823 French troops invaded neighboring Spain in Ferdinand's behalf. Under the circumstances, Monroe asked, should the United States be content merely to offer the world an example of liberty or should it act in its support?[23]

Though Jefferson bitterly criticized the arrogance of the French attempt to deny the Spaniards their choice of governments, he thought the United States should not deliberately intervene in the quarrels of Europe: "Their political interests are entirely distinct from ours. Their mutual jealousies, their balance of power, their complicated alliances, their forms and principles of government, are all foreign to us."[24] Americans should take advantage of the Atlantic moat that separated them from so much entanglement and strife. Admittedly, isolation was far from complete. Some of Spain's American colonies were revolting against her. But even here he believed that the United States should concentrate on protecting and enlarging freedom at home. "Peace and neutrality seem to be our duty and interest."

Though troubled by the Spanish crisis, he was optimistic about the ultimate fate of liberty in Europe. He wrote to John Adams more philosophically than to Monroe. Adams was not an incumbent President, charged with responsibility and seeking a course of action. Besides, Jefferson's Massachusetts friend was more deeply philosophical than his Virginia protégé.

So to Adams he wrote: "The light which has been shed on mankind by the art of printing has eminently changed the condition of the world. As yet that light has dawned on the middling classes only of the men of Europe. The kings and the rabble, of equal ignorance, have not yet received its rays; but it continues to spread. And, while printing is preserved, it can no more recede than the sun return on his course. A first attempt to recover the right of self-government may fail; so may a 2d. a 3d., etc., but as a younger, and more instructed race comes on, the sentiment becomes more and more intuitive, and a 4th, a 5th or some subsequent one of the ever renewed attempts will ultimately succeed. In France the 1st. effort was defeated by Robespierre, the 2d. by Bonaparte, the 3d. by Louis XVIII and his holy allies; another is yet to come, and all Europe, Russia excepted, has caught the spirit, and all will attain representative government, more or less perfect. . . . To attain all this, however, rivers of blood must yet flow, and years of desolation pass over. Yet the object is worth rivers of blood, and years of desolation, for what inheritance so valuable can man leave to his posterity?"[25]

Later in the year Monroe wrote to Jefferson again about a foreign affairs crisis involving the Holy Alliance and Spain's former colonies in the Western Hemisphere. Efforts to establish and maintain republican governments in the South American countries were constantly frustrated by the ignorance of their populations. In each there was a small, well-educated elite, but there was no large, literate middle group. The Holy Alliance, dedicated to stamping out revolutions, especially republican ones, appeared poised for intervention in Spain's former colonies as earlier in Spain itself. British Foreign Secretary Canning, perceiving that it probably would be easier to discourage the monarchical alliance's intervention than to extirpate it after the fact, proposed to the government of the United States that the two English-speaking nations cooperate to forestall intervention in Latin America by the Continental powers. Monroe wanted Jefferson's opinion. Should the United States join Great Britain in a declaration designed to prevent such a move by the Holy Alliance? Monroe was inclined to think Canning's proposal might have merit.

Jefferson had long distrusted Canning, but he did not think the Foreign Secretary was a fool. He was sure that the Englishman wanted the former Spanish colonies to remain independent, not principally because of a desire to foster the spread of democracy, but because such a situation would be far better for British trade than their return to colonial status. Self-interest insured the sincerity of Canning's proposal. But was it good for the United States? "The question presented by the letters you have sent me," Jefferson wrote, "is the most momentous which has ever been offered to my contemplation since that of Independence. That made us a nation, this sets our compass and points the course which we are to steer through the ocean of time opening on us. And never could we embark on it under circumstances more auspicious. Our first and fundamental maxim should be, never to entangle ourselves in the broils of Europe. Our second, never to suffer Europe to intermeddle with cis-Atlantic affairs. America, North and South, has a set of interests distinct from those of Europe, and peculiarly her own. She should therefore have a system of her own, separate and apart from that of Europe. While the last is laboring to become the domicile of despotism, our endeavor should surely be to make our hemisphere that of freedom."[26]

In reading to this point, Monroe might have supposed that, to avoid European entanglements, Jefferson would oppose Canning's proposal for united action by Great Britain and the United States. But Jefferson drew a different lesson. "One nation, most of all," he said, "could disturb us in this pursuit; she now offers to lead, aid, and accompany us in it. By acceding to her proposition, we detach her from the band of despots, bring her mighty weight into the scale of free government, and emancipate a continent at one stroke, which might otherwise linger long in doubt and difficulty. Great Britain is the nation which can do us the most harm of any one, or all on earth; and with her on our side we need not fear the whole world. With her then, we should most sedulously cherish a cordial friendship; and nothing would tend more to knit our affections than to be fighting once more, side by side, in the same cause."

This was not as much an about-face as it might seem. Jefferson had deeply resented the actions of British governments before the Revolution, during the embargo, and during the War of 1812. But he said during his presidency that, if France or Spain should control the Mississippi River, the United States should "marry itself to the British fleet and nation." He had foreseen that, under certain conditions, an alliance between the American republic and the mother country could be beneficial.

As for the two countries "fighting . . . side by side," he explained: "Not that I would purchase even her amity at the price of taking part in her wars. But the war in which the present proposition might engage us, should that be its consequence, is not her war, but ours. Its object is to introduce and establish the American system, of keeping out of our land all foreign powers, of never permitting those of Europe to intermeddle with the affairs of our nations. It is to maintain our own principle, not to depart from it. And if, to facilitate this, we can effect a division in the body of the European powers, and draw over to our side its most powerful member, surely we should do it."[27]

But he did not believe that fighting would ensue if the United States and Great Britain issued a joint warning. He was "clearly of Mr. Canning's opinion that it will prevent instead of provoking war. With Great Britain withdrawn from their scale and shifted into that of our two continents, all Europe combined would not undertake such a war. For how would they propose to get at either enemy without superior fleets? Nor is the occasion to be slighted which this proposition offers, of declaring our protest against the atrocious violations of the rights of nations, by the interference of any one in the internal affairs of another, so flagitiously begun by Bonaparte, and now continued by the equally lawless Alliance calling itself Holy."

Before proceeding, Jefferson faced up to a central question—about his country's relations with its neighbors and about his own earlier attitude on the subject. In this dedicated libertarian there had long been a streak of imperialism. After discussing the advantages of cooperation with Britain to prevent European conquest of Spain's former colonies, he said: "But we have first to ask ourselves a question. Do we wish to acquire to our own confederacy any one or more of the Spanish provinces? I candidly confess, that I have ever looked on Cuba as the most interesting addition which could ever be made to our system of States. The control which, with Florida Point, this island would give us over the Gulf of Mexico, and the countries and isthmus bordering on it, as well as all those whose waters flow into it, would fill up the measure of our political well-being. Yet, as I am sensible that this can never be obtained, even with her own consent, but by war; and its independence, which is our second interest, (and especially its independence of England,) can be secured without it, I have no hesitation in abandoning my first wish to future chances, and accepting its independence, with peace and the friendship of England, rather than its association, at the expense of war and her enmity."

Jefferson had said years ago that he could not understand a system of morality which, though exacting strictest honesty from an individual in personal dealings, would excuse any amount of deceit in his representation of his government in dealings with other nations. So it was important to him to satisfy his own honor so far as his aspirations for Cuba were concerned, and he deemed it important that the nation do the same. Having done this, he said: "I could honestly, therefore, join in the declaration proposed, that we aim not at the acquisition of any of those possessions, that we will not stand in the way of any amicable arrangement between them and the mother country; but that we will oppose, with all our means, the forcible interposition of any other power, as auxiliary, stipendiary, or under any other form or pretext, and most especially, their transfer to any power by conquest, cession, or acquisition in any other way." He thought it "advisable," inasmuch as the announced policy might "lead to war, the declaration of which requires an act of Congress," that the President lay the case before them for consideration at their first meeting, "and under the reasonable respect in which it is seen by himself."

Monroe sought the advice of Madison, who gave his general approval. And, of course, he discussed the matter at length with his Secretary of State, John Quincy Adams, who urged that the proposed policy be announced unilaterally rather than "to come in as a cockboat in the wake of the British man-of-war." Monroe agreed. Adams, however, thought that the announcement should be made in separate messages addressed to the several European powers. Monroe instead chose to proclaim it in an address to Congress, as Jefferson had advocated. So on December 2, 1823 President Monroe, in his address to Congress, as advocated by Jefferson, published to the world a statement of policy in the Western Hemisphere very much like what Jefferson had approved.

Very few people in the world then, including the most astute observers in Washington, London, Paris, and Vienna, appreciated the significance of the event. Some European politicians were mildly irritated by what they considered American impudence. The chief politicians in Washington and elsewhere in the United States were far more interested in the disruptive presidential candidacies of three of Monroe's cabinet: Secretary of State Adams, Secretary of the Treasury William H. Crawford, and Secretary of War John C. Calhoun.

But Jefferson did see the declaration as "most momentous" and after being "so long weaned from political subjects," was gratified "to contribute still my mite towards anything which may be useful to our country." Encouraged by his success while the Monroe Doctrine was being formulated, Jefferson ventured to do something he had never done before: request the appointment of a friend to an office in the Monroe administration. He asked that, as a personal favor, Bernard Peyton be named postmaster for Richmond, Virginia. President Monroe refused. But Jefferson did not know the fate of his recommendation until August 1824.

XIX

CAPTAIN, DRUMMER, AND FLAGBEARER

T HE SAME SOFTENING toward Great Britain shown by Jefferson in his advice to President Monroe about what would become known as the Monroe Doctrine was shown by him about the same time in a letter[1] to Madison about hiring faculty for the University of Virginia. Jefferson said that the Visitors apparently were unanimous in their belief that an agent should be sent to Britain to secure professors. He had explained a month earlier to the president and directors of the State Literary Fund that efforts to secure several teachers from New England and elsewhere in the United States had proved fruitless, that Virginia alone could not furnish enough instructors of the caliber needed, and that it would not have been moral to "seduce" away from their present employment some reluctant to leave their posts.[2] If the university was to assemble a faculty of sufficient stature, it must look abroad. And the search, he thought, must be conducted principally in Great Britain, among those whose language, traditions, and mores were "our own."

Underlying Jefferson's hostility toward British governments that had deceived him and the British King who had turned his back upon him at a royal reception was a consistent admiration for British tradition. Though he had considered British cabinets among the most perfidious of the eighteenth century, he had said that the British people individually were among the most moral in the world. He was a great admirer of Anglo-Saxon culture in the reign of Alfred the Great and insisted that the Anglo-Saxon language be taught at the university. And of course, for him, the world's three greatest heroes in modern history had long been three Englishmen: Francis Bacon, Isaac Newton, and John Locke.

In his eightieth year, Jefferson was moving closer to his origins. This tendency was reflected not only in the increasing frequency of his favorable comments on the English but in the mounting intensity of expressions of devotion to his native Virginia. One of the most notable examples was the letter in which he told John Eppes that he believed it was desirable to educate the youth of Virginia in the state rather than have them go elsewhere, because he felt that Virginia ways were best. One portion of Jefferson's mind had censored these comments, saying that they probably sprang from prejudice. But there could be no doubt about the leaning of his heart.

At first it was believed that Cabell would recruit professors in Great Britain. He would be ideal for the mission. He was second only to Jefferson himself in the founding of the university. He was broadly educated. He had lived in Europe for several years, spending part of his time analyzing the systems and methods in use at the Continent's most famous institutions of higher learning. Moreover, he was a sophisticated man of the world, having formed friendships with some of Europe's most celebrated geniuses, meeting them both on his own and in travels with Washington Irving.

But Cabell's delicate health and other personal considerations made it seem an unwise undertaking for him, and Jefferson turned to Francis Walker Gilmer, a young man whom he considered the most learned Virginian of his generation. After a lengthy conference with Madison and consultation with Cabell and others, the rector offered Gilmer both the mission to Great Britain and the professorship of law at the university. On December 3 the young man accepted the recruiting job but requested more time to consider the chair of law.[3]

A thirty-three-year-old attorney, Gilmer, like the university's founders, was a man of many talents. While rapidly moving to the forefront of the Virginia bar and winning high praise from such of its longtime leaders as William Wirt, he also gained some prominence as a writer on political theory and pursued a career as botanist that brought him membership in the Philadelphia Academy of Sciences and high praise from Portugal's great Abbé Correa.[4]

Jefferson usually was most comfortable when he could entrust important tasks to qualified persons among old friends or their offspring. Gilmer was the son of old friends and neighbors. Once he had seemed likely to become a member of the Monticello family. He had fallen deeply in love with Jefferson's granddaughter Ellen Randolph. When he discovered that the passion was not mutual, he was plunged into melancholy. Years later he was saddened by regrets about the one he now called "the cold nymph of the mountain," but he maintained an affectionate relationship with her family.

Near the end of the year one of Jefferson's own old friendships was threatened. Had it been destroyed, a deep shadow would have fallen over him at year's end despite his enthusiasm for the Monroe Doctrine and his excited hopes as Gilmer prepared to embark for Europe. E. M. Cunningham published the correspondence between his late father, William Cunningham, and John Adams during the years 1801 to 1812. Some of Adams' letters contained bitter comments he had made about Jefferson when they were political opponents and when the second President was still smarting from his defeat by the third. Before Jefferson had seen the book, he read some of the more opprobrious comments from it in the *Richmond Enquirer*.

Would Jefferson act as if he were unaware of the publication? Or would he be able to resist answering some of Adams' charges? Jefferson chose not to ignore the published criticisms. He wrote: "Crippled wrists and fingers make writing slow and laborious. But, while writing to you, I lose the sense of these things, in the recollection of ancient times, when youth and health made happiness out of everything. I forget for a while the hoary winter of age, when we can think of nothing but how to keep ourselves warm, and how to get rid of our heavy hours until the friendly hand of death shall rid us of all at once. Against this tedium vitae however I am fortunately mounted on a Hobby, which indeed I should have better managed some 30 or 40 years ago, but whose easy amble is still sufficient to give exercise and amusement to an octogenary rider. This is the establishment of a university. . . . But the tardiness with which such works proceed may render it doubtful whether I shall live to see it go into action."[5]

He quickly got down to his main purpose. "Putting aside these things, however, for the present, I write this letter as due to a friendship coeval with our government, and now attempted to be poisoned, when too late in life to be replaced by new affections." He said that the extracts he had seen from the published correspondence were "such as seemed most likely to draw a curtain of separation between you and myself. . . . [But] if there had been, at any time, a moment when we were off our guard, and in a temper to let the whispers of these people make us forget what we had known of each other for so many years, and years of so much trial, yet all men who have attended to the workings of the human mind, who have seen the false colours under which passion sometimes dresses the actions and motives of others, have seen also these passions subsiding with time and reflection, dissipating, like mists before the rising sun, and restoring to us the sight of all things in their true shape and colors."

He concluded: "It would be strange indeed if, at our years, we were to go an age back to hunt up imaginary, or forgotten facts, to disturb the repose of affections so sweetening to the evening of our lives. Be assured, my dear Sir, that I am incapable of receiving the slightest impression from the effort now made to plant thorns on the pillow of age, worth, and wisdom, and to sow tares between friends who have been such for near half a century. Beseeching you then not to suffer your mind to be disquieted by this wicked attempt to poison its peace, and praying you to throw it by, among the things which have never happened, I add sincere assurances of my unabated, and constant attachment, friendship and respect."

Adams wrote a glowing reply.[6] He said he had received Jefferson's letter while he was breakfasting with his family and had asked one of the younger members to read it aloud. Afterwards it was passed around the table, eliciting, Adams said, such comments as: "How generous! How noble! How magnanimous!" Adams himself pronounced it "the best letter ever written."

No matter how close Jefferson felt to Adams, he did not, in discussing his hopes for the university, confide information about Gilmer's trip to Great Britain to recruit faculty. Jefferson and the other Visitors believed that the facts of this trip should be kept quiet as long as possible. They anticipated that a storm of public anger would break around them when it was learned that they had hired foreigners in preference to United States citizens. The decision of the board to employ Americans in two of the eight professorships—law and moral philoso-phy—would do little to mitigate the wave of indignation from New England to Georgia. When Gilmer sailed for Britain in the spring of 1824, he would be on a secret mission.

Even some of those privy to the secret and deeply loyal to the rector were anxious about the plan to recruit so many of the faculty from overseas. An April 1824 meeting of the Visitors, pleading financial problems, voted to defer appointment of a professor of anatomy. Actually, Cocke and Cabell were trying to save the place for an American—any qualified American. They were trying to work out an informal system whereby one United States citizen would be appointed to a professorial post for every one filled by a European, much as the Congress had formerly admitted one free state for each slave state. Jefferson had permitted his colleagues to prevail through their financial arguments. But almost immediately afterward he may have suspected their real motivation. In any event, just two days after the close of the meeting, he sent each of his fellow Visitors his proposal to authorize Gilmer to offer a contract to a professor of anatomy and medicine and asked each to submit his opinion immediately.[7]

Cocke wrote Cabell, "Do save us from this inundation of foreigners if it is possible." The Senator went to Bremo to confer with Cocke. The upshot was that Cabell wrote from there a letter to Jefferson, saying that he would bow to the sage's judgement and adding that it delighted him to please Jefferson "upon any and all occasions." The General concurred in a postscript.[8] On the same day Madison wrote his acceptance of the rector's proposal.[9]

Later that month Gilmer called at Monticello for a briefing and letters of introduction to the American Minister in London and various distinguished scholars. Jefferson gave him a copy of the engraving of his plans for the university. He thought this should be a strong selling point in the interviews. Once, when chided about the cost of construction, he had said that the university could have been housed in log cabins but if so probably would not have attracted the faculty and students desired. He stressed to Gilmer that each prospective professor's character and temperament, as well as his learning, were vital considerations. Each instructor's salary would begin on October 1, or on the day of embarkation if that should be later. The university was scheduled to open February 1, 1825. Gilmer sailed from New York on May 8, 1824, with instructions to report back to the rector every two weeks.

Jefferson's eagerness might be enough to account for the admonition, but there may have been another reason as well. Virtually everyone who knew Gilmer testified to his brilliance, some to his genius.[10] As a student at William and Mary he had been hailed as a prodigy. All over Virginia discriminating people expected from him some monumental work of intellect. At the age of twenty-five, he had published *Sketches of American Orators*, a slender volume of such acute perception that it is still quoted today in scholarly works on the subject. He had so profited from lessons in French from Martha Jefferson Randolph, and had so added to them by his own unaided efforts, that his translations were attracting international attention. Many declared the charm and brilliance of his conversation unsurpassed by that of any other American, and many of his acquaintances entertained audiences by quoting from him. But Gilmer seemed to have little drive. He was a procrastinator. There were signs that he might spend most of his eloquence in conversation when he might be composing for print. Jefferson may have thought it prudent to be in frequent communication with the university's traveling agent.

Jefferson had very practically instructed Gilmer not to waste time trying to entice scholars of international renown to leave their posts at Oxford, Cambridge, or Edinburgh but to pitch his appeal to young instructors who seemed headed for that kind of renown. The first news of success reached the rector on August 6. George Blaetterman, a German linguist then living in London, one of Jefferson's correspondents to whom he had given Gilmer a letter of introduction, had accepted appointment as professor of modern languages. He was pronounced qualified to teach the French, German, Spanish, and Italian languages and modern history, and Jefferson wanted him to teach all five subjects. He also wanted him to teach Anglo-Saxon. The information that Blaetterman had no knowledge of that tongue disappointed Jefferson only slightly. He would not have to teach it the first semester. Meanwhile, he could learn it. Jefferson was quite understanding about the average person's difficulties in learning, but he expected a great deal of anyone who professed to be a scholar. After all, languages were easy. Jefferson once said that, starting with no knowledge of the subject, he had taught himself Spanish in 19 days of his voyage to Europe in 1784.[11]

The rector was now dependent on messages from others to keep track of the university's progress—not only as regarded Gilmer's expedition abroad but also construction in Charlottesville. Between the time of the agent's departure from Monticello and his embarkation in New York, Jefferson had ridden into town to inspect the building site and on the way back had been so overcome with fatigue that he feared he would not reach home. Afterwards he had written to Arthur Brockenbrough, the proctor, asking him to come up to the mountaintop when consultation was necessary.[12]

Even though most of the time now he saw the university's buildings only through his telescope, he was still busy in its behalf. In June and July he spent four hours a day making up a catalog of books to be acquired for its library and by August was devoting full work days to the project. By September 24 he had recorded data on 6,860 volumes and had determined that they would cost $24,000.[13] That sum was not yet available. Ordinarily, such a compilation would have been the work of a committee representing diverse disciplines. In truth, Jefferson was a committee of one representing diverse disciplines.

Jefferson had more architectural plans too. The focal point of his "academical village" was the Rotunda, whose massive dome gave distinction to the architectural grouping. He conceived an idea for making this feature useful as well as ornamental. He proposed that the concave ceiling of the Rotunda "be painted skyblue and spangled with gilt stars in their position and magnitude copied exactly from any selected hemisphere of our latitude. A seat for the operator movable and fixable at any point in the concave will be necessary, and means of giving every star its exact position." He designed machinery for moving the operator. It included a thirty-five-foot-long white oak boom six inches in diameter at the butt and three inches at the small end and weighing about a hundred pounds. He calculated the moving meridian and the method for adjusting to the "zenith distance and amplitude of every star." "Braces of window cord" would be used for "keeping the meridian in its true curve." The operator could ride "to any point of the concave" in "a common saddle with stirrups."[14]

Jefferson wanted the university to have an observatory as well as a planetarium. In fact, it had figured in his early plans and a mountain had been purchased "with a view to the permanent establishment of an observatory with an astronomer resident at it employed solely in the business of observation."[15] Since then Jefferson had come to see the primary need as a structure "for the ordinary purposes of the astronomical professor and his school" and believed that it "should be placed on the nearest site proper for it and the university." Jefferson wrote: "For an Observatory the material attentions are 1. That it be so solid in its construction, with a foundation and walls so massive as not to be liable to tremble with the wind, walking, etc. 2. That it have ample apertures in every direction. 3. That it have some one position perfectly solid which may command the whole horizon and heavens; with a cupola cover, movable and high enough to protect long telescopes from the weather." He realized that many who had visited, or seen pictures of, some of Europe's observatories would be surprised by the ground-hugging structure he had designed. But bringing the observer seventy or eighty feet nearer to an object in stellar space would not significantly increase its visibility. And there were good reasons for keeping close to the ground a building designed to decrease tremors from wind and other causes. "As to height of the building," he explained, "the less the solider. The observatories in the considerable cities of Europe are high of necessity to overlook the buildings of the place. That of Paris is 80 feet high, but so much the worse, if avoidable."

Jefferson was hopeful even though not confident of living to see the university in operation. Then from Scotland on October 5 came a letter that abruptly changed his outlook. Gilmer wrote that his efforts in Edinburgh had met with such frustration that he despaired of securing the services of anyone he would "choose to be associated with." Accordingly he chose not to be a member of the faculty and respectfully declined his appointment.[16] Jefferson admitted to Madison that this "most unwelcome letter" had dashed his hopes and plunged him into one of the deepest sessions of melancholy he had ever experienced. One of his most cherished dreams of half a century had seemed on the verge of realization.

Four days later there was another letter from Gilmer. He did not retract his decision to withdraw from the faculty. But he did say that on his return to England he had signed up a highly regarded young teacher of mathematics, Thomas Hewett Key, master of arts from Cambridge and alumnus of both Trinity College and the medical training program at Guy's Hospital, London. Jefferson liked people proficient in more than one discipline. Through Key, Gilmer had met a respected young classicist from Cambridge. He had found other good possibilities in London.

Jefferson was relieved, but he still wondered who could be found for the professorship he thought he had filled with Gilmer. And most of the other positions were still highly problematical.

Another arrival from Europe diverted Jefferson for a while from a portion of his anxiety about how many professors would be coming. His old friend the Marquis de Lafayette had been invited by President Monroe to visit the United States as a guest of the nation. The French hero arrived in New York on August 15 and began his triumphal tour with a journey to Boston. He wrote Jefferson that he would be in Virginia in October to commemorate the American triumph at Yorktown.

Lafayette wrote before receiving a letter from Jefferson extending the hospitality of the city of Charlottesville in a formal welcome and that of Monticello in a warmly informal one. As Jefferson had expected, the American people responded to the general in a "delirium of joy." It soon became apparent that, as Jefferson said, Lafayette was "making a triumphant progress through the states, from town to town, with acclamations of welcome such as no crowned head ever received."[17] Jefferson had wisely made his invitation flexible: Lafayette was to come when convenient and stay as long as he wished. Amid his progress from city to city through arches of flowers, the Marquis paused in Philadelphia long enough to write Jefferson a note saying that he would be with him within three weeks. The two days allotted for the journey from Yorktown to Charlottesville became two weeks. It became evident that the visit might well extend over more than a year. Jefferson was impatient to see the great friend of the American Revolution, a Major General in the patriot cause at the age of nineteen, an advocate of peaceful revolution in his own country who had aided the Virginian's efforts as American Minister in Paris and in turn had sought his aid in forging a constitution for France. Violent radicals had turned against Lafayette and his health had broken during seven years as a political prisoner. The once glamorous young officer was now a corpulent and feeble man who appeared much older than his sixty-seven years. Madison said that, if he had not been told who he was, he would not have recognized him.

Jefferson's eagerness turned to anxiety in ensuing days as a painful abscess recurred on his jaw, forcing him to take nourishment only through a tube and confining him to his home for a fortnight or longer. He was afraid he might not be well enough to greet his friend properly. At last, when Lafayette arrived in Albemarle County on November 4, Jefferson was much improved but not well enough to join others in greeting him at the county line. The family honors were done by Jeff, who presented the esteemed guest a letter from his host saying that he awaited him at Monticello.

Jeff has given us the best eyewitness description of Lafayette's meeting with Jefferson early in the afternoon on the lawn, a little less than an acre, on the east side of Monticello: "The barouche containing Lafayette stopped at the edge of this lawn. His escort—one hundred and twenty mounted men—formed on one side in a semicircle extending from the carriage to the house. A crowd of about two hundred men, who were drawn together by curiosity to witness the meeting of these two venerable men, formed themselves in a semicircle on the opposite side. As Lafayette descended from the carriage, Jefferson descended the steps of the portico. . . . . Jefferson was feeble and tottering with age— Lafayette permanently lamed and broken in health by his long confinement in the dungeon of Olmutz. As they approached each other, their uncertain gait quickened itself into a shuffling run, and exclaiming, 'Ah, Jefferson!' 'Ah, Lafayette!' they burst into tears as they fell into each other's arms. Among the four hundred men witnessing the scene there was not a dry eye—no sound save an occasional suppressed sob. The two old men entered the house as the crowd dispersed in profound silence."[18]

Not surprisingly, Lafayette found Jefferson "in full possession of all the vigor of his mind and heart." But his observation that his friend was physically "marvelously well" is a testimony to Jefferson's continued ability to mask his illness. At that, while his chronic difficulties continued, he must have been recovering rapidly from his current problem. Besides entertaining Lafayette at Monticello that evening, his host accompanied him when he left for town at ten o'clock the next morning. Another formal welcome awaited the hero at Charlottesville's Central Hotel, where there were more speeches before a reception at which people could shake hands with the Frenchman and apparently with the two local celebrities, Jefferson and Madison. At noon they headed a procession to the university, where about four hundred lucky people would dine with them in the Rotunda. This would be the first public function in the building, which was still not quite complete. Its classical columns were not in place. As the tall, corpulent Lafayette, flanked by the tall, lean Jefferson and the tiny Madison, approached the portico, several hundred ladies on the terraces waved their handkerchiefs in salute in what must have looked like a gesture of enthusiastic surrender. The welcome was primarily for Lafayette, but it was also for the two founding fathers, and it was fueled by all the fires of sentiment for an heroic age whose giants were passing from the scene. The three men mingled with the crowd until three o'clock, when they ascended the stairs to the room just below the dome, where tables were set in three concentric circles.

Small wonder that the dinner lasted about three hours. There were thirteen "regular" toasts on the program, one for each of the thirteen original states, and each called for a speech in response. There was another to "Thomas Jefferson and the Declaration of Independence—alike identified with the cause of Liberty."

Jefferson said that he had neither strength nor voice to reply but had brought a written response which he asked V. W. Southall, the toastmaster, to read for him: "I joy, my friends, in your joy, inspired by the visit of this our ancient and distinguished leader and benefactor. His deeds in the war of independence you have heard and read. They are known to you, and embalmed in your memories and in the pages of faithful history. His deeds in the peace which followed that war, are perhaps not known to you; but I can attest them. When I was stationed in his country, for the purpose of cementing its friendship with ours and of advancing our mutual interests, this friend of both was my most powerful auxiliary and advocate. He made our cause his own, as in truth it was that of his native country also."[19]

As Southall read Jefferson's words, Lafayette grasped his friend's hand and, as the reading continued, sobbed aloud. "His influence and connections there were great. All doors of all departments were open to him at all times; to me only formally and at appointed times. In truth I only held the nail, he drove it. Honor him, then, as your benefactor in peace as well as in war."

When the scheduled toasts were over, some people rose to propose additional ones. For Jefferson, it must have taken the edge off the celebration momentarily when Charles Bankhead, his granddaughter's wayward husband, back from exile, sprang up to insinuate himself into the proceedings. But the old man must have been moved when James Dinsmore, whose woodworking skill adorned the Rotunda and whom he had described in 1803 as "an excellent young man from Philadelphia who has lived in my family as a house joiner five or six years,"[20] raised his glass in tribute to "Thomas Jefferson, founder of the University of Virginia."

Lafayette and his entourage remained at Monticello until November 15. During the ten-day visit there was much talk of old times and of present problems in Europe and America, and an opportunity for Jefferson to take his guest on a tour of the "academical village." The master of Monticello thoroughly enjoyed the occasion and did nobly by the Frenchman who was both a cherished friend and the "Guest of the Nation," but his entertaining almost exhausted his stock of red wine and seriously injured his economy when his finances were critical.

Harassed though he was by debts, Jefferson seems to have been even more concerned with the fate of Gilmer's mission. If it did not succeed, where would the rector find the means and energy to institute another? How long would the opening of the institution be delayed? And might not extended delay prove not only crippling but fatal? He was not only worried that he might not be physically equal to seeing the university through another crisis but was haunted by another anxiety as well. As early as June 1, 1822, he had written John Adams: "I have ever dreaded a doting old age; . . . I dread it still."[21] Those who had to deal with him, whether as allies or opponents, continued to be impressed with his acuity. But in the way of the aged who have become fearful of senility, he exaggerated the significance of minor lapses of memory that in earlier years he would have attributed to concentration on tasks at hand.

With a mixture of eagerness and apprehension, Jefferson opened on November 19 a letter sent by Gilmer from New York. The address instantly revealed that, for better or worse, his recruiting expedition was over. No professors had accompanied Gilmer and there had been doubts of his own safe arrival. Suffering from undisclosed maladies and apparently exhausted by his efforts in Great Britain, he had been ill during the entire voyage of thirty-five days and was now in the care of physicians. But he had secured the services of five teachers who were following close behind him. Two of these, of course, were Key and Blaettermann. There was, as Gilmer had predicted, a young classicist from Cambridge, George Long. A professor of natural philosophy bore the cheerful name of Charles Bonnycastle. And there was a rising star, Dr. Robley Dunglison, professor of anatomy and medicine. Only twenty-six years old, Dunglison had just produced a book, *Commentaries on the Diseases of the Stomach and Bowels of Children*, which promised to make him internationally famous in his profession. He had also earned a reputation as an excellent teacher. His academic credentials included studies in Edinburgh, Paris, and London, and an M. D. degree from Prussia's Erlanger University. Besides his proficiency in his specialties, he was reputed to be "a close student of philosophy and general literature" and a voracious reader in many subjects.

Still vacant were the chairs of natural history and moral philosophy and, unless Gilmer relented, law. Jefferson was now virtually sure that the university would open February 1 as planned, but not quite sure enough to begin registering students for the dormitories.

News of Gilmer's accomplishments in recruiting brought attacks, especially from Northeastern newspapers, which construed the employment of foreigners as a reflection on American scholarship in general and that of Yankee land in particular. Some Virginians were unhappy about it too. Jefferson's taste for Italian architecture and especially for French food had aroused the ire of some of his fellow Americans for decades. Patrick Henry had talked darkly about a man who would "abjure his native victuals," and various Northerners had suggested that such exotic appetites were not consistent with true Americanism. Such people saw Jefferson's importation of scholars as one more manifestation of dangerous xenophilia. It was ironic that Jefferson, who was so eager for young Americans to be educated in their own country and even for young Virginians to be educated in their native commonwealth, should have been accused of trying to subject American students to alien influences.

Jefferson filled both the natural history and moral philosophy posts with American citizens, but with men not likely to placate those who opposed foreigners. For the first he secured Dr. John Patton Emmet, a native of Ireland and son of Thomas Addis Emmet, an Irish rebel who had emigrated to the United States. Dr. Emmet, moreover, was the nephew of Robert Emmet, the revolutionary hailed as a patriot by the Irish but hanged for treason by the British. Were foreign revolutionaries acceptable if they had fought against George III? The answer might depend on the geographical origins or personal predilections of the citizens answering. On Madison's advice, the rector offered the professorship of moral philosophy to George Tucker, a native of Bermuda. Some critics might complain of his Bermudan birth, but Tucker had represented Virginia in Congress and was an integral part of Virginia society. A prominent Richmond attorney, he also had earned a national reputation as a writer, first of all in political philosophy and agrarian economy. He had broadened his fame in 1822 with publication of his *Essays on Subjects of Taste, Morals, and National Policy*. He was a verse satirist as well and had just produced his first novel, *The Valley of the Shenandoah*. Soon it would be followed by *Voyage to the Moon*, a pioneering work of science fiction. He is sometimes included today in specialized courses in American literature.

The university could ill afford any public resentment of the faculty selected.

Some supporters of the College of William and Mary wanted to move the college from Williamsburg to Richmond and add a medical school. The current capital was much larger and livelier than the old colonial one and was also a little more central. The addition of a medical school would make the 131-year-old college a formidable rival of the upstart university in Charlottesville. Besides, location in Richmond would provide many opportunities for courting the legislature when it was in session. A number of William and Mary alumni were members of the General Assembly, and some of them were prone to endorse the proposal to move and enlarge the Williamsburg school. Of course, not all of the alumni felt this way. The three principal founders of the university (Jefferson, Cabell, and Cocke) and its chief recruiter of faculty (Gilmer) were all William and Mary alumni.

Jefferson drafted a counterproposal designed to frighten the petitioners for removal of William and Mary to Richmond. Ominously titled "A bill for the discontinuance of the College of William and Mary, and the establishment of other colleges in convenient distribution over the state," it was designed to appeal to local pride and economic interest in ten districts of the commonwealth. Jefferson had wanted it introduced only as a last resort and was chagrined when rumors of it circulated prematurely and perhaps unnecessarily. In February 1825 Cabell relieved his worries with the news that the petition to relocate William and Mary had been defeated in the House.[22]

Whatever the apprehensions of Virginians, the university was attracting praise from outside the state. George Ticknor, now a Harvard professor and well launched toward fame, had visited Monticello with his wife and Daniel Webster in December and Jefferson had given them a tour of the "academical village." Afterwards Ticknor described it as "a mass of buildings more beautiful than anything architectural in New England, and more appropriate to a university than are to be found, perhaps, in the world."

Blaettermann and Long arrived in Virginia in December. Jefferson described Blaettermann to Madison as "rather a rough-looking German, speaking English roughly, but of an excellent mind and high qualities."[23] Long he saw as "a most amiable man, of fine understanding, well qualified for his department, and acquiring esteem as fast as he becomes known."[24]

Jefferson made no first-hand observations of the rest of the faculty from Europe. They had not arrived in Virginia. Indeed, they had not even been seen anywhere in the United States. They were supposed to have left Britain in October, but the new year dawned with no reports of their arrival in America. Long wrote Gilmer on January 25 that Jefferson was, "like all of us, very uneasy about the delay of our friends." To Cabell, Jefferson wrote: "We are dreadfully nonplussed here by the non-arrival of our three professors. We apprehend that the idea of our opening on the 1st of February prevails so much abroad (although we have always mentioned it doubtfully) as that the students will assemble on that day without awaiting the further notice which was promised. To send them away will be discouraging, and to open a university without mathematics or natural philosophy would bring on us ridicule or disgrace."[25]

Jefferson therefore "published an advertisement stating that, on the arrival of these professors, notice will be given of the day of opening of the institution."

Cabell, who had feared that the missing teachers had perished in a North Atlantic storm, was relieved to learn at the end of January that as of December 5 their ship had not yet sailed. It arrived in Norfolk on February 10, and newsmen boarded it as soon as it came alongside the wharf. Professor Dunglison, as soon as he was ensconced in the Steamboat Hotel, wrote Jefferson of their arrival. The Englishman was surprised by the attention given their coming in Norfolk and later in Richmond. In the capital he was amused to learn that a Mrs. Camp, misunderstanding that "university professors" were the cause of the excitement, had spread the word that the "universal confessors" had arrived.[26]

Jeff Randolph happened to be in Richmond at the time and he changed his plans so as to accompany the professors from Richmond to Charlottesville over bad dirt roads rendered almost impassable by a recent thaw. The prospect of travel over these routes seemed to excite more apprehension than their transatlantic trip. "The accounts which we had of them from the Richmond ladies," said Dr. Dunglison, "were sufficient to intimidate the stoutest hearts."[27] Under these conditions two entire days would be consumed in the 70-mile trip from the capital to the university. "Not infrequently in the course of the day," Dunglison said, "Mr. Randolph left his seat by the driver to prop up the stage when it was likely to be overset; and it may be imagined with what relief we sat down at 10 o'clock by a cheerful wood fire to Mrs. Tinsley's table [halfway between the two cities], after having toiled through roads since 6 o'clock of the morning such as most assuredly we had never witnessed in all our previous experience in England or on the Continent of Europe."

The next day Jeff traveled with them until they were within a few miles of the university, saying then that he could be sure of their safe travel over the short distance remaining. Shortly after he was out of sight, the wheels on one side of the coach sank into a deep hole and the vehicle overturned. Fortunately, the horses stood firm and no one was injured, though the passengers had difficulty extricating themselves. "The accident," Dunglison said, "occurred at a short distance from Moore's Creek, over which there was no bridge, and we were, consequently, compelled to ford it, bearing the ladies over; and such was our unpropitious introduction to the neighborhood of the University. A Roman would have regarded it as a bad omen, and been disheartened. We were not Romans, however, and the affair only excited amusement."[28] They then walked about two miles into Charlottesville, arriving late in the evening and spending the night at the Stone Tavern.

In the morning Jefferson called on them. Dunglison was impressed with the rector's "dignity and kindness" and with the fact that at eighty-two "his intellectual powers [were] unshaken by age." Jefferson sympathized with them over the discomforts of their long voyage and rough trip overland and told of his "great distress" from fear that they were lost at sea. He had "almost given [them] up" when Dunglison's letter with its "joyful intelligence" arrived from Norfolk. On receiving that news, he had released an announcement that the university would open Monday, March 7, 1825.

Soon the professors were occupying their quarters at the university but, as their beds had not yet arrived, they and their wives had to sleep on the floor.[29]

Except for the initial absence of beds, Dunglison and his colleagues found their houses "much better than we had expected to find them." They could have been far more convenient though, he said, "had Mr. Jefferson consulted his excellent and competent daughter—Mrs. Randolph—in regard to the interior arrangements. . . . Closets would have interfered with the symmetry of the rooms or passages, and hence there were none in most of the houses; and in the one which was furnished with a closet, it was told as an anecdote of Mr. Jefferson, that not suspecting it according to his general arrangements, he opened the door and walked into it on his way out of the pavilion."[30]

The Board of Visitors, in a meeting on March 4, just three days before the formal opening, ratified the appointments of Tucker and Emmet. It continued the search for a professor of law.

Finding it so hard to fill the post with any person he deemed qualified, Jefferson thought it was especially desirable to prescribe certain elements of the law curriculum that would serve to counteract any monarchical influences that might be exerted by an unfortunate choice. He feared the consolidationist ideas of some New England pedagogue or "Richmond lawyer." Ironically, his first choice for the position, Gilmer, was a Richmond attorney, but Jefferson was sure of that young man's Republican principles.

In a letter to Madison before the meeting, Jefferson proposed for required reading in the law classes the essays of John Locke, the Virginia Resolutions of 1798, *The Federalist Papers*, and, with no false modesty, the Declaration of Independence. Madison approved most of Jefferson's choices but thought perhaps the Virginia Resolutions of 1798 should not be included, and on this point his opinion carried special weight as he was their author. He did suggest the addition of Washington's first inaugural address and Farewell Address. He agreed with Jefferson that the Visitors should list works deemed important to an understanding of modern democracy but believed that this should be done "without requiring an unqualified conformity to them." Leonard Levy and others have pointed out that, in proposing that the Visitors prescribe certain specific readings for the law courses, Jefferson seemed to depart from his own dictum of December 27, 1820: "This institution will be based on the illimitable freedom of the human mind. For here we are not afraid to follow truth wherever it may lead, nor to tolerate any error so long as reason is left free to combat it."[31]

The charge of compromise is valid, but for proper perspective we must view the action in the context of the times. It was then quite common for schools' governing boards to prescribe quite minutely what was taught in all classes if they wished. By comparison the Visitors of the University of Virginia had acted with restraint—entirely too much restraint in the eyes of many contemporaries.

On March 7, 1825, the university opened. There was no fanfare. It would have seemed inappropriate. The interior of the rotunda was unfinished. In the basement, masons stirred mortar where students would later mix chemicals in the test tubes and retorts; on the first floor, workmen's shouts bounced off walls that would echo to lectures before large classes; and on the top floor, where faculty and students would pore over library tomes, only blueprints were read. Two faculty members had not yet arrived. A third, the professor of law, had not even been engaged. Only about thirty students showed up for the first day. Not until about two weeks later would the number have increased to fifty or sixty. To obtain this many, Jefferson had had to relax his original standards of admission, but he was determined to return to them the following year.

None of these difficulties, however, could negate the fact that Jefferson had won his fight. He had realized his dream of half a century. And to do so he had triumphed over public apathy and public antagonism, a financial panic and a lingering economic depression. He had transcended the ocean barrier that separated America from the great centers of Western learning. He had charmed, cajoled, shamed—and, yes, sometimes tricked— the reluctant into action. He had had the valuable help of able people, especially Cabell, Cocke, and Madison, but he himself had conceived the idea; designed the buildings and grounds and so beautifully integrated them that they became a landmark in the history of landscaping and architecture; personally surveyed the lots and supervised the construction; hired the faculty, and this with a single eye to quality in spite of all the pressures of local loyalties and national chauvinism; composed the curriculum, and it was an innovative one; selected the books for the library in every major category of knowledge; served as rector, presiding always with courtesy and tact but always dominating the proceedings and at the same time, as secretary, recording the actions taken under his guidance, all the while reanimating the flagging spirits of those who labored with him. Meanwhile, he was fighting a great private battle—against financial ruin that could swallow his beloved home, and violence that tore his cherished family, and above all against illness and old age that, crippling his body though not his spirit, threatened to end his life before that of the university had begun.

He had performed the services that an optimist might have hoped to obtain from a highly talented committee with a staff of experts at its command. If Jefferson had perished before accomplishing his goal, there would have been no one so passionately dedicated to complete the work and no one so well qualified as he both to design the physical plant and, from the resources of his richly varied intellect, devise a broad and pioneering curriculum of both arts and sciences.

But the old man did win his series of battles to give Virginia and the world something new in universities, retreating only to retrench and charge again, serving as captain, drummer, and flagbearer of a pitifully outnumbered band of warriors. And the victory he gained was one of the great triumphs of the human spirit.

IMPERILED TRIUMPH

JEFFERSON WAS probably too tactful to say that he had a favorite among the faculty at his university. But the record of dinner invitations to Monticello makes it clear that he did. Soon Dr. Robley Dunglison was dining with Jefferson two or three times a week and was always seated to the left of his host. The variety of the young Scotsman's interests, ranging from science to literature, appealed to the older man. So did his studiousness. Besides, the testimony of his contemporaries suggests that he was an unusually decent person and also one who, like Jefferson, preferred the "smooth handle."

Soon after his arrival in Charlottesville, Dunglison, like Jefferson, received an honorary doctorate from Yale. (Strangely enough, it arrived unceremoniously in the mail and late—because it had been mistakenly addressed to Hampden-Sydney College.) It was not hard to predict even at this stage that Dunglison would become one of the great compilers and organizers of medical knowledge in his century.

He observed both as a friend and a physician the toll of Jefferson's strength exacted by a constant stream of visitors, many of them strangers. He was also aware of the financial strain, which in turn was translated into mental strain. Many American citizens traveled through central Virginia, stopping both at Monticello and Madison's Montpelier, visiting two Presidents on one tour.[1]

One evening as Dunglison and Jefferson sat on the porch, two couples drove up. Though they rode in separate gigs, they comprised one touring party. Dunglison said that it was "evidently the desire of the party to be invited to stay the night. One of the gentlemen came up to the porch and saluted Mr. Jefferson, stating that they claimed the privilege of American citizens in paying their respects to the Ex-President and inspecting Monticello. Mr. Jefferson received them with marked politeness, and told them they were at liberty to look at everything around, but as they did not receive an invitation to spend the night, they left in the dusk and returned to Charlottesville. Mr. Jefferson, on that occasion, could scarcely avoid an expression of impatience at the repeated, though complimentary, intrusions to which he was exposed."[2]

On another occasion, one of Dunglison's colleagues introduced a visiting Rhode Islander to Jefferson. "This person," the doctor said, "did not impress me favorably; and when I rode up to Monticello I found no better impression had been made by him on Mr. Jefferson and Mrs. Randolph. His adhesiveness was such that he had occupied the valuable time of Mr. Jefferson the whole morning and stayed to dinner. . . . Mr. Jefferson was apprehensive that he had said something which might have been misunderstood and be incorrectly repeated. He therefore asked me to find the gentleman if he had not left Charlottesville and request him to pay another visit to Monticello. . . . Mr. Jefferson took the opportunity of saying to me how cautious his friends ought to be in regard to the persons they introduce to him."[3]

Dunglison observed: "In Mr. Jefferson's embarrassed circumstances in the evening of life, the immense influx of visitors could not fail to be attended with much inconvenience. I had the curiosity to ask Mrs. Randolph what was the largest number of persons for whom she had been called on unexpectedly to prepare accommodations for the night, and she replied fifty. . . . I confess I have no sympathy with the feeling of economy—political or social—which denies to the ex-President a retiring allowance, which may enable him to pass the remainder of his days in that useful and dignified hospitality which seems to be demanded by the citizens of one who has presided over them."[4]

Soon the doctor's visits were professional as well as social. On May 11, 1825, Dr. T. G. Watkins, who had been Jefferson's physician and now was preparing to leave the area, recommended that his patient secure the services of Dr. Dunglison. Watkins diagnosed Jefferson as suffering from a urinary stricture and inflammation, apparently produced by enlargement of the prostate gland. In parting, he prescribed castor oil, warm water fomentations, rest, and a bland diet. If the irritability did not abate, he should take at bedtime a half grain of opium with one grain of calomel.[5]

Dunglison paid his first professional call six days later when Jefferson complained of "a condition of great irritability of the bladder under which he had suffered for some time, and which inconvenienced him greatly by the frequent calls to discharge his urine." After examining the patient, Dunglison confirmed Watkins' diagnosis. He employed a different treatment, however, using a bougie, a slender, flexible instrument, to dilate the urethra. Jefferson soon learned to use the instrument himself and obtained substantial relief. Nevertheless, "this condition interfered . . . materially with his horseback exercise to which he had been accustomed on his excellent and gentle horse Eagle."[6]

The young doctor won his illustrious patient's confidence partly by his intelligence and diligence but also by the fact that he made no exaggerated claims for his profession. Once Jefferson told Dunglison, "Time and experience as well as science are necessary to make a skillful physician, and Nature is preferable to an unskillful one."[7] The professor had been told that the rector had "little faith in physic," but Jefferson corrected this impression, saying, "It is not to physic that I object so much as physicians." Dunglison was not at all offended. He knew he had the old man's trust, and he understood his playfulness. When a fellow practitioner was offended by Jefferson's remark that whenever he saw three physicians together he looked for a turkey buzzard,

Dunglison said he knew that Jefferson spoke jocularly, and added, "If the same thing had been said to me, no offense would have been taken."[8]

Later he said: "Whatever may have been Mr. Jefferson's notions of physic and physicians, it is but justice to say that he was one of the most attentive and respectful of patients." He bore suffering inflicted upon him for remedial purposes with fortitude and in my visits showed me by memoranda the regularity with which he had taken the prescribed remedies at the appointed times. From the very first, indeed, he gave me his entire confidence and at no time wished to have anyone associated with me."

Actually, Dunglison's best efforts availed little other than to serve the useful purpose of making his patient more comfortable. This accomplishment may have made Jefferson's health seem better than it was. Alexander Garrett, bursar of the university, wrote General Cocke on June 18: "Mr. J's health is rather better than it has been for some weeks past. Yet his spirits are much worse than I have ever known them. Indeed, it is wonderful that he retains any under the many distressing circumstances under which he now labors."[9]

A tobacco barn and its contents had burned. The lands he planned to sell in Bedford County turned out to be worth half, or less, what he had thought. He now knew that he would not be able to pay all his debts by selling land. He was unable to collect rent on his mill. He had to borrow more money. It seemed increasingly unlikely that he would, as he had hoped, end his days at Monticello unless those days were few indeed.

About the time that Dunglison became Jefferson's doctor a happy event took place at Monticello. Ellen Randolph, the "cold mountain nymph" wooed in vain by Francis Gilmer, had responded warmly to the attentions of a bright young Bostonian, Joseph Coolidge, Jr., nephew of the distinguished architect Charles Bulfinch. They were married on May 27, 1825. Intelligent and articulate, she was one of Jefferson's favorites and frequently his companion at Poplar Forest. He is said to have observed that "if she had been a man, she would have been a great one."[10] The comment is reminiscent of Jefferson's estimate of his beloved sister Jane. According to his family, "He ever regarded her as fully his own equal in understanding."[11]

Not all relationships at Monticello were so happy. Thomas Mann Randolph, after completing his service as Governor of Virginia, was introduced frequently as "Governor Randolph, Mr. Jefferson's son-in-law." But it was seldom necessary to introduce him to anyone. He was becoming more and more a recluse. He entered and exited Monticello at times in the night when no one saw him. His eccentricities had become aberrations. His temper became surly and at times violent. By now Jeff was busy administering his father's affairs as well as his grandfather's, but Thomas Mann Randolph was not grateful. He saw his son as an enemy. Once he tried to stone him in a lonely place, and Jeff had to put spurs to his horse to escape.

These circumstances, painful at best, were made all the more sorrowful for Randolph's family by remembrances of how he had been in earlier days. Professor Tucker, who had known him socially and as a friend to the university, wrote: "One of the most generous, disinterested, and high-minded men on earth, he was gradually transformed into a gloomy, unsocial misanthrope—his proud spirit suffering intensely, but suffering in silence, seeking solace of no one, but showing too plainly the discontent, which secretly preyed on his mind, by the harshness or coldness with which he treated all around him."[12]

Whatever the problems of family conflict or personal illness, Jefferson continued his labors for the university. It had no president, but a chairman of the faculty elected by them with the understanding that there would be rotation in office. However, Professor Tucker, who was chairman, testified that the real power resided in Jefferson. He said: "Everything was looked into, everything was ordered by him. He suggested the remedy for every difficulty, and made the selection in every choice of expedients."[13]

The rector also maintained personal contacts with both faculty and students. Professors and their families were frequent guests, and "every Sunday some four or five of the students dined with him." Apropos of the Sunday dinners, Tucker made a curious observation: "At these times he generally ate by himself in a small recess connected with the dining room; but, saving at meals, sat and conversed with the company as usual."[14] Jefferson was graciousness itself and the most affable of hosts. It has been suggested that he withdrew from his guests at dinner because of his increasing deafness. But this assumption, even though his hearing was impaired, is weakened by the report that he "sat and conversed with the company" afterwards. Could his increasingly severe arthritis have made eating before casual acquaintances an awkward business?

Tucker's report of Jefferson's commanding role in the university's affairs is corroborated by Dunglison, who in the course of his tenure served the institution in two general offices. "It was beautiful," he wrote, "to witness the deference that was paid by Mr. Jefferson and Mr. Madison to each other's opinions. When, as secretary, and as chairman of the faculty, I had to consult one of them, it was a common interrogatory—what did the other say of the matter? If possible, Mr. Madison gave indications of a greater intensity of this feeling; and seemed to think, that everything emanating from his ancient associate must be correct."[15]

"In framing a system of laws for the government of the University, as well as for its course of instruction," Tucker says, "Mr. Jefferson had had almost the sole agency; for though everything was submitted to the approbation of the board of visitors, yet it was rarely that any of them dissented from him, and when it did happen, he was commonly supported by a majority. . . . Thus, believing that the authority of government is often needlessly exerted, and the restraints of law are too much multiplied, he allowed more latitude and indulgence to students than was usual. . . . These liberal and indulgent views well accorded both with the temper of the professors, and their inexperience, and they undertook to conduct a body of youths, by appeals to their reason, their hopes, and to every generous feeling, rather than to the fear of punishment, or dread of disgrace."[16]

Tucker strongly admired Jefferson and had great faith in his wisdom, but he became convinced during the university's first term of operation that "while you may appeal to the generous feelings, and innate love of truth and right in some, you must appeal to the fears of others. If this is not done, the few who can only be kept in restraint by this curb will be vicious and disorderly, and their example and impunity may draw many of the well disposed into the same vortex; and [even] though they did not, they would be sufficient to disturb the tranquility and order that are so essential in such a place, and destroy its good name."[17]

In August, Jefferson was delighted that his experiment in trust seemed to be working. Writing William Short on August 9, he compared the tranquility of the university to that of a convent.[18] Eighteen days later he wrote his granddaughter Ellen Randolph Coolidge: "Our university goes on well. We have passed the limit of 100 students some time since. As yet it has been a model of order and good behavior, having never yet an occasion for the exercise of a single act of authority. We studiously avoid too much government. We treat them as men and gentlemen, under the guidance mainly of their own discretion. They so consider themselves, and make it their pride to acquire that character for their institution. In short we are as quiet on that head as the experience of 6 months only can justify."[19]

He told her also, "Our professors too continue to be what we wish them." He reported that her former suitor Francis Walker Gilmer had after all accepted the chair of law, and added "all is well."

Jefferson's optimistic estimate had included several qualifying phrases, above all the suggestion that six months might be too short a period for conclusive proof that the laissez faire system of governance was successful. His caution was appropriate. Disorders at the university became nightly events. Though Jefferson was minutely informed about matters of finance and curriculum at the institution, the faculty may have spared him reports on student behavior. He not only was not a witness to what happened there at night but had not set foot on the grounds in many days. He had last seen Ellen Coolidge at the time of her wedding on May 27. This particular letter to her was written on August 27, three months later. In it he said: "My own health is what it was when you left me. I have not been out of the house since, except to take the turn of the Roundabout twice; nor have I any definite prospect when it will be otherwise."

Seven months revealed dramatically what six months had not. On September 10 Jefferson wrote each member of the Board of Visitors that ill health would prevent him from traveling even the short distance to the university to attend the regular meeting scheduled for Monday, October 3. He was accustomed to entertaining them at Monticello when they met. This time he proposed to welcome them to his home on Sunday, October 2, and then conduct a working session there the next morning. To give legal force to their decisions, it would be necessary to act upon them in a formal session afterwards at the university.[20] Since all decisions would already have been made, the rector's presence would not be necessary to this work of official enactment.

In anticipating that the business of the board could be transacted in a single morning, Jefferson did not know that General Cocke would pay a two-day visit to the university in the meantime and would be so shocked by the general laxness of student discipline that he would write to Cabell proposing that the problem be brought before the Visitors at their October meeting.

Jefferson did not anticipate one happy development—that his health would improve sufficiently for him to travel to the university after all. But he also did not foresee the extremely unfortunate events of Friday, September 30, and Saturday, October 1. On Friday night a student tossed a bottle and a pack of cards through a window of Professor Long's quarters. This was undoubtedly a symbolic protest of the prohibition against liquor and playing cards that Jefferson had written into the university rules. Jefferson had long abstained from whiskey, and the gambling troubles of his early patron Governor Fauquier and other friends had prejudiced him against card playing. While the university's code was liberal in making each student responsible for policing himself, it was quite strict in its standards of conduct. Having secured attention by his aggressive act, the student cursed foreign professors and said they should be taken to the pump. In this favorite nineteenth-century method of humiliation, the offender's head was held under a pump and he was subjected to an involuntary shower. The student escaped without being identified.

The incident was a small foretaste of what would happen the next night.[21] Sounds of a disturbance on the Lawn, including shouts of "Down with European professors," brought Professors Tucker and Emmet out of their pavilions. They were confronted by fourteen masked students. Emmet snatched at a counterpane in which one young man had wrapped himself and another student threw a brick at him. When Tucker grabbed one student, another struck the teacher with a cane. The two professors found themselves hopelessly outnumbered by a masked mob shouting epithets and howling in derision. When the demand that the young men unmask and reveal their identities brought rude hoots, the teachers withdrew from the field.

The next day, the faculty met with the student body and read a prepared address charging them with various infractions. The faculty demanded the names of the masked rioters of the night before. The students refused to cooperate. On Monday sixty-five students signed a paper condemning Emmet and Tucker for laying hands on two of their members. They also insisted that their teachers were liars.

When the Visitors met on Monday they were confronted not only with this determined opposition from the students but also with the resignations of Professors Long and Key. They were ready to leave not just because of the two nights of rioting but because these were the culmination of a series of disorders. Apparently many of the students drank, gambled, and carried firearms before matriculating and felt no compulsion to change their way of life in an institution that boasted of the freedom it afforded.[22] Obviously the board was not going to be able to dispense with all business in a single morning as the rector had hoped.

The Visitors did decide, as Cocke had wished, that the instructors should call class rolls regularly and, at intervals, report attendance records to parents or guardians. The board also asked the professors to be more diligent in enforcing rules and regulations. The teachers, having been told that individual students would be expected to regulate their own conduct, may not have been certain what role they themselves were to play in discipline. The Visitors were mildly critical of the faculty and more critical of the student body for a schoolboy code that forbade "telling on" any of their classmates. In language that sounds like Jefferson's, the Visitors declared: "This loose principle in the ethics of schoolboy combinations is unworthy of mature and regulated minds."

The next day the rector and Visitors, in session at the university, summoned the entire student body to appear before them. One later recalled: "At a long table near the center of the room sat the most august body of men I have ever seen." There were three Presidents of the United States—Jefferson, Madison, and Monroe—and Senator Cabell, General Cocke, and Chapman Johnson, a prominent attorney and legislator. Jefferson stood to address the students. He looked both venerable and time-ravaged. He began by saying that this was one of the most painful events of his life but then said little more before his voice faltered. His physical constitution was not equal to the stress. He said that he would leave to abler ones the task of saying what he had to say.[23]

The students obviously were moved. They were too when Madison, also enfeebled, addressed them. Johnson, in the full vigor of his courtroom career, spoke energetically to the students about the seriousness of their offenses and called upon those who had rioted to come forward and give their names. Nearly all did, one by one. When Jefferson's own great-great-nephew confessed, the old man found the voice that he had lost. Professor Tucker reported: "The shock which Mr. Jefferson felt when he for the first time discovered that the efforts of the last ten years of his life had been foiled and put in jeopardy by one of his family was more than his own patience could endure, and he could not forbear from using for the first time the language of indignation and reproach."

The great-great-nephew was among several students expelled by the faculty. Lighter punishments were prescribed for others. The students withdrew their petition. The Visitors refused to accept the resignations of Professors Long and Key. As Tucker concluded, "The exercises of the University were resumed . . . under a system liberal without being lax."

While alarming friends of the university and furnishing abundant argument for those who would curtail its funds, the disturbances at the fledgling school had been no more serious than those occurring about the same time at other institutions of higher learning from New England to South Carolina. About a week later Jefferson, in letters to his grandson-in-law Joseph Coolidge and to William Short, predicted that "the vigilance of the faculty and energy of the civil power" would forestall future violence. He thought it was good that the students now knew that the rules would be enforced. Altogether, he was sure, the university was stronger than before.[24]

XXI

THE LAST FOURTH

AS THE UPRAISED mallet fell, a groan escaped from the plaster cast that encased Jefferson's head and neck. Sculptor John H. I. Browere had left the life mask to harden for an hour instead of the expected twenty minutes. Now he was wielding mallet and chisel to free the eighty-two-year-old patriarch from the prison that threatened to smother him.

The life mask almost became a death mask. Jefferson afterwards wrote Madison: I was taken in by Mr. Browere. He said his operation would be of about 20 minutes, and less unpleasant than Houdon's method. I submitted without enquiry, but it was a bold experiment on his part on the health of an octogenary worn down by sickness as well as age. Successive coats of grout plastered on the naked head and kept there an hour would have been a severe trial of a young and hale man. He suffered the plaster also to get so dry that separation became difficult and even dangerous. He was obliged to use freely the mallet and chisel to break it into pieces and get a piece at a time. . . . The family became alarmed. . . . I was quite shaken, and there became real danger that the ears would leave from the head sooner than from the plaster."[1]

Jefferson's family told people what had happened and news of it got into the *Richmond Enquirer*. The sculptor said that his reputation had been injured* and asked Jefferson for a testimonial to offset the harm. The old statesman complied, but to granddaughter Virginia Randolph, Browere was still a "vile plasterer."[2]

The sculptor's procedures on October 15, 1825, did not bring Jefferson's life to a sudden end. But he was chiseling away at that life almost as surely as he was at the plaster. Not Browere alone, but the whole train of artists, memoirists, diarists, inventors, and others who came to Monticello in hopes of receiving some authentic tale of the Revolution or the early republic from his lips, or of perpetuating his likeness for posterity in paint or bronze, or of gaining celebrity status or lasting fame by linking their names with his.

The life mask that Browere made at the expense of Jefferson's comfort and

---

*In 1830 Browere was charged with grave robbing to make a death mask of Rev. Elias Hicks. Justin Kaplan, *Walt Whitman* (New York, 1980), 76.

his family's equanimity is, not surprisingly, severe. The resulting portrait bust shows a man aged but still firm-jawed, with a bold nose and chin. His hair is no longer worn in a queue and is pulled back at the sides, revealing ears strikingly large but close to his skull. There is no hint of a double chin. The neck is thin but not scrawny. The exposed right hand, slender and long-fingered, could be that of a young man. It is the kind of hand popularly regarded as artistic and recalls Rodin's representation of the hand of the Creator.

Jefferson's look of severity doubtless is more representative of the harrowing circumstances of the image-taking than of his typical appearance at this stage of life. Descriptions of him at the time are filled with references to his benevolent expression. There are other evidences of his mellowing. Opposite the marble bust of Jefferson in the entrance hall at Monticello was one of Alexander Hamilton. Professor Tucker said that when any reference to this surprising conjunction was made by the elder statesman's guests he "remarked that they were 'opposed in death as in life,' in a tone and manner that showed that no vestige of ill feeling was left on his mind."[3] Indeed, the professor says that Jefferson was not "slow to acknowledge the virtues and talents of Alexander Hamilton."

Significantly, Jefferson spoke as if he and Hamilton were both now in the realm of the dead. Increasingly, his correspondence referred to his life as a drama ended.

He devoted almost none of his dwindling energy to politics except in behalf of his university. Though he appears to have favored William H. Crawford in the presidential election of December 1824 he issued no public statement on the contest and in 1825 warmly congratulated John Adams on John Quincy's victory. Almost to the end of 1825 he seemed determined to remain aloof from national politics because of his friendship for the Adams family, his reluctance to sacrifice the tranquility of his final days, and his desire to husband his energies for service to the university.

He was moved to break his silence by his perception that the internal improvements program of the Adams administration would violate the states' rights. In a parting message to Congress at the end of his presidency, Jefferson himself had suggested the federal government might strengthen the nation's economy by building bridges, roads, canals, and other aids to communication. But he thought that such a program should be carried out only with proper constitutional safeguards. He believed that under the Adams program these were lacking. He drafted a Virginia protest, which he hoped to have adopted by the General Assembly, but other matters came to the fore. Support for the university was in some jeopardy among the legislators, and Jefferson as rector probably was reluctant to antagonize them on any other matter. Perhaps even more influential was the advice of Madison, whose counsel he sought, that Virginia should not lead the opposition to a program of national improvements. Jefferson himself was mindful that, with the end of the Virginia dynasty in the presidency, the Old Dominion's politicians frequently were viewed as the vanguard of opposition. He abandoned the protest.[4] On New Year's Day 1826, in a letter to William Fitzhugh Gordon, an Albemarle County legislator who had sought his advice about appropriate action on states' rights, Jefferson said: "As to the state of my health. . . . It is now 3 weeks since a reacerbation of my painful complaint [a severe attack of diarrhea and dysuria] has confined me to the house and indeed my couch. Required to be constantly recumbent, I write slowly and with difficulty. Yesterday for the 1st time I was able to leave the house and to resume a posture which enables me to begin to answer the letters which have been accumulating. . . . Weakened in body by infirmities and in mind by age, now far gone into my 83d year, reading one newspaper only and forgetting immediately what I read. . . ."[5]

Though Jefferson was demonstrably weakened physically, most who knew him would have denied that there was a concomitant deterioration mentally. Many visitors in their letters testified to his intellectual vigor. Certainly some who had tried to thwart his designs for the university—even some friendly members of the Board of Visitors who had tried subtly to alter the channels of the institution's development—were aware of his mental agility. It is possible that Jefferson's memory had declined enough for him to be aware of a change but that it was still so superior to that of most people that they would perceive no mnemonic deficiency.

Even more likely, the prospect of financial disaster made it difficult for him to think of matters less personal and less cataclysmic. To paraphrase Dr. Samuel Johnson, when a man knows he is to be ruined, it concentrates his thoughts wonderfully.

On January 2 Jefferson had a cruel reminder of what might happen to Monticello when his son-in-law Thomas Mann Randolph's home, Edgehill, was sold at public auction. Jeff, who had assumed most of his father's debts, was the highest bidder and thus saved the estate for the family. In order to do this, he had to sell some of his own property.

The fate of Monticello might be much worse than that of Edgehill. If it had to be sold at public auction, it was virtually certain that no relative or combination of relatives, however eager to keep it in the family, would be able to meet the purchase price. Keenly able to empathize with his son-in-law, Jefferson wrote[6] urging him not to look back on his misfortune and told him that he was missed at the dinner table and fireside. But Randolph continued to remain aloof, returning to his wife only at night after all others were in bed and leaving early before he was seen.[7] Jeff's purchase of Edgehill deepened his father's hatred for him and he soon forbade the younger sons to visit their older brother. Colonel Randolph told Martha that, if he ever discovered that she had permitted such visits, he would take the boys from her.

Such discord in the family was itself painful to the patriarch who had always found his greatest comfort in a loving home. But Randolph's financial ruin had for Jefferson grave consequences other than the effect on the Colonel's disposition. Jefferson now became the sole support of his daughter and her children at Monticello.

On the night of January 19[8] he was lying awake, tortured by thoughts of the poverty that awaited his family upon his death if not before. Suddenly an idea dawned upon him "like an inspiration from the realms of bliss."[9] At sunrise he could wait no longer and sent for Jeff. The young man must have been surprised by his grandfather's suggestion for a solution to the family's financial problems. Jefferson proposed a lottery. He had long been opposed to all forms of gambling and once had told the promoters of Transylvania University that he did not consider a lottery an appropriate means of raising money for such a purpose. But now he argued earnestly that it was a sensible alternative to his and Jeff's ineffectual efforts to sell land in a region where many formerly prosperous planters were land-poor. They could sell great numbers of low-cost lottery tickets, offering land as the prize. Jeff was immediately persuaded of the efficacy of the plan.

Lotteries were frowned upon by many Virginians as encouraging an immoral desire to get something for nothing. It was argued that they weakened initiative, encouraged idleness, and led people of meager means to gamble away money better spent on the real needs of their families. Therefore any lottery established in Virginia had to be authorized by the General Assembly. Legislators and their constituents were becoming more insistent that any lottery authorized be a special case unlikely to open the door to many other such enterprises.

In the course of the day, Jefferson wrote letters to Senator Cabell and at least four other legislators. He explained to his old friend that Jeff would be talking with members of the Assembly in his behalf. The matter was of "ultimate importance." He wrote a paper headed "Thoughts on lotteries, and on that particularly which is now asked," not for publication but to provide Cabell and other friends with arguments for the establishment of a lottery to benefit the Jefferson estate.[10] Presumably Jeff carried this paper with him.

In it Jefferson argued that while such games of chance as cards and dice were inherently harmful, a lottery might be either injurious or beneficial depending on circumstances and the care with which it was organized to insure fairness. He cited examples from Virginia history of lotteries that he believed had served worthy purposes. He argued that the one he proposed was in this same tradition and pleaded that it was the only means by which he could obtain fair value for his property. A measure of his desperation is the fact that he argued he was entitled to special consideration because of public services, especially to the commonwealth, and then proceeded to catalogue these contributions. He even dropped his habitual facade of modesty, saying that granting him the favor asked could not set a harmful precedent inasmuch as it was not likely that anyone else could match his sixty-four years of service.

Arriving in Richmond and presenting copies of his grandfather's arguments to those friends designated to receive them, Jeff found that they were disturbed by the suggestion. Most thought that it was not a suitable solution to the problems of one of the noblest leaders of the Revolution and feared that it would injure their hero's reputation in his own time and in history. Jeff, however, told his grandfather nothing of these doubts and on January 31, after the old statesman's friends had had time to absorb the initial impact, he was able to report: "We propose on Thursday to ask leave to bring in the bill. Your friends are confident of success. The bill has been drawn in conformity to the opinions of the most zealous and most judicious of your friends. It is drawn with a preamble simply stating the length of your public services. . . . To take away all ground of objection as a scheme to raise money, valuers are appointed to set a fair and liberal value on the property on the usual credit and we are authorized to raise such a sum as will give us the valuation net."[11]

On February 1, Hetty Carr, widow of Jefferson's nephew Peter, wrote to her son that the venerable statesman was "very unwell" and she believed that a defeat for the lottery would kill him. Jefferson was engaged in a life or death gamble of his own with his life's reputation at stake. A rejection by the representatives of his own Virginia would be insupportable.

Jeff was surely aware of this fact, and it is easy to imagine the pain with which he wrote his grandfather on February 3: "You will be disappointed in hearing your bill is not yet before the Legislature. . . . A panic seized the timid and indecisive among your friends as to the effect it might have upon your reputation, which produced a reaction so powerful that yesterday and the day before I almost despaired of doing anything."[12] But he had availed himself of the counsels of Judges Brook, Cabell, Green and Carr of the Virginia Supreme Court of Appeals "and their weight of character and soundness of views, to act upon gentlemen of less experience and decision. They have been again rallied to the charge and are now bold and determined, and assure me they will not again hesitate or look back and feel confident of success; they do not believe that the delay has been injurious. The policy of the state had been against lotteries as immoral and the first view of the subject was calculated to give alarm which it took time and reflection to remove."

After a little discussion of business possibilities, Jeff added: "I do not anticipate [trouble, but] will not be unprepared to meet it. If you will preserve y[our health] and spirits and not suffer yourself to be affected by it, [your grandc]hildren will be so happy in that, that we shall never think of difficulties or loss of property as an evil."

Delegate George Loyall of Norfolk, a Visitor of the University of Virginia, on February 8 formally requested permission of the House to introduce a bill authorizing Jefferson to dispose of property by lottery. His request was tabled by the margin of a single vote. The next day it carried, but by only four votes. If Jefferson's friends were barely able to muster enough votes to permit presentation of the bill, what hope was there for passage of the bill itself?

On the very day that Loyall presented his request to the House, Jefferson wrote Jeff[13] upon learning "there are greater doubts than I had apprehended whether the Legislature will indulge my request to them." He said, "It is a part of my mortification to perceive that I had so far overvalued myself as to have counted on it with too much confidence." Many years ago, at the conclusion of his tenure as Governor, the legislature had called for an inquiry into his conduct of the office. The result had been resolutions of commendation and appreciation, but the earlier action had rankled in his sensitive mind for decades. Now the apparently imminent act of rejection by the same body must have awakened painful memories.

"I see, in the failure of this hope," Jefferson wrote, "a deadly blast of all my peace of mind during my remaining days. You kindly encourage me to keep up my spirits but, oppressed with disease, debility, age, and embarrassed affairs, this is difficult. For myself, I should not regard a prostration of fortune. But I am overwhelmed at the prospect of the situation in which I may leave my family. My dear and beloved daughter, the cherished companion of my early life, and nurse of my age, and her children, rendered as dear to me as if my own, from having lived with me from their cradle, left in a comfortless situation, hold up to me nothing but future gloom. And I should not care were life to end with the line I am writing, were it not that I may yet be of some avail to the family. Their affectionate devotion to me makes a willingness to endure life a duty, as long as it can be of any use to them."

And he added: "Yourself particularly, dear Jefferson, I consider as the greatest of the god-sends which heaven has granted to me. Without you, what could I do under the difficulties now environing me?"

Nevertheless, he did not rail against a malignant fate. Of his financial troubles, he said: "These have been produced in some degree by my own unskillful management, and dividing my time to the service of my country, but much also by the unfortunate fluctuations in the value of our money, and the long continued depression of farming business." He did not refer to the disastrous results of his endorsing notes for Wilson Cary Nicholas.

Despite the gloomy beginning of the letter, a dauntless spirit shines through its last lines: "Perhaps, however, even in this case, I may have no right to complain, as these misfortunes have been held back for my last days, when few remain to me. I duly acknowledge that I have gone through a long life, with fewer circumstances of affliction than are the lot of most men. Uninterrupted health, a competence for every reasonable want, usefulness to my fellow-citizens, a good portion of their esteem, no complaint against the world which has sufficiently honored me, and above all, a family which has blessed me by their affections, and never by their conduct given me a moment's pain. And should this my last request be granted, I may yet close with a cloudless sun a long and serene day of life. Be assured, my dear Jefferson, that I have a just sense of the part you have contributed to this, and that I bear you unmeasured affection."

How many people, if they had lived it, would have described Jefferson's life as one of "uninterrupted health"? If they had overlooked the severe bouts of diarrhea that had plagued him from time to time and in late years the infection caught at the springs, there would still be the excruciating migraine headaches for most of his adult life that had disabled him for long hours and sometimes had afflicted him for a large portion of each day over a period of several weeks. And how many in his situation would have said that their families had "never by their conduct given me a moment's pain"? He must have excluded in-laws from consideration, for Thomas Mann Randolph and Charles Bankhead had certainly caused him much misery.

Jefferson's next letter to Jeff revealed that, while Fate seemed poised to deliver a blow in the Capitol, it had struck under the roof of Monticello itself. Jefferson's granddaughter, Anne Cary Randolph Bankhead, the long suffering wife of Charles Bankhead, had returned to Monticello for the birth of her baby. On February 11, Jefferson wrote his grandson: "Bad news, my dear Jefferson, as to your sister Anne. She expired about half an hour ago. I have been so ill for several days that I could not go to see her till this morning, and found her speechless and insensible. She breathed her last about 11 o'clock. Heaven seems to be overwhelming us with every form of misfortune, and I expect your next will give me the *coup de grâce*."[14]

Dr. Dunglison later reported: "When the announcement was made by me that but little hope remained,—that she was, indeed, moribund, it is impossible to imagine more poignant distress than was exhibited by [Mr. Jefferson]. He shed tears, and abandoned himself to every evidence of intense grief."[15]

Grieving himself, Jeff wrote to comfort his grandfather. After writing of their mutual loss, he told him that the lottery bill was "daily gaining ground."[16] He hoped that it would pass the lower house and was sure it would "pass the Senate by a large vote." He answered his grandfather's talk of a *coup de grâce*: "Preserve yourself for our sakes. If the worst should happen, which I again repeat I do not in the least suppose, neither my mother or yourself can ever want comforts as long as you both live. I have property enough for us all and it shall ever be my pride and happiness to watch over you both with the warmest affection and guard you against the shafts of adversity."

Jeff was generous and devoted, but Jefferson knew that the young man's own business interests were imperiled by his efforts to salvage his father's fortunes. There was no question of Jeff's sincerity, but he might not have much to share. Jefferson, however, would not have disputed Jeff's assertion that his grandfather was "rich" in the "devoted attachment" of his descendants.[17] Another proof of that came from Francis Wayles Eppes, the studious grandson to whom he had given Poplar Forest. Francis wrote to "return . . . with the utmost good will the portion of property which you destined for me, and which I should always have considered as yours. . . . You cannot do me the injustice to suppose that I could consent to retain the smallest portion. . . . Do not therefore, my dear grandfather, form any ill-founded fears on my account, or from any other motive oppose an act which, setting aside its justice, is the necessary consequence of the filial tenderness with which my heart is overflowing. Do not mortify me by refusing that which you own; and which if [you did] not, I should think the same feelings which prompt the son to offer, should compel the father to accept."[18] If Jefferson regarded his grandchildren as his children, they in turn looked upon him as a father. In this instance, he exercised his parental prerogative and refused to accept the return of Poplar Forest.

While the lottery bill was pending, a citizens' meeting in its behalf was held in Richmond and stirred enthusiasm. When the Senate had by only four votes permitted introduction of the bill, a discouraged Senator Cabell had written Jefferson, "I blush for my country, and am humiliated to think how we shall appear on the page of history."[19] Thanking the loyal legislator for his support, Jefferson had said: "I count on nothing now. I am taught to know my standard, and here to meet with no further disappointment."[20] But Cabell now thought Jefferson could count on the legislature.

His optimism was confirmed. On February 20 he was able to report to his old friend that the bill had passed. In the House it won a two-to-one majority. In the Senate the vote was 13 to 4.[21]

Jefferson told Loyall that, thanks to the bill which the Norfolk Delegate had introduced and steered to passage, he would be able to pay all his financial debts. But he said that he had incurred another obligation which he could never repay—the deep debt of gratitude to Loyall and other friends for what they had done for him. Not until Jeff returned from Richmond did Jefferson learn that, under terms of the bill of authorization, the properties offered as prizes in the lottery would not, as he had believed, be restricted to his mills and a thousand acres of land. Monticello itself would be a prize. At this revelation his face was drained of color.[22] News that the beloved home would remain his for life and that his daughter would not have to vacate it immediately after his death mitigated the trauma only slightly. At first he said he needed time to think and to talk with Martha, whose interest was involved. But soon he assented. What else could he do?

Embarrassed by the necessity for resorting to a lottery, Jefferson left all the procedural details to Jeff. Complicated questions arose when citizens of various states, even though in some cases not enthusiastic about a lottery, expressed their eagerness to contribute outright gifts of money as due to one who had served his country well. Such contributions were acceptable, but neither Jefferson nor his grandson wanted to appear to seek them. Also there was the danger that, with two competing plans for Jefferson's relief, both might be aborted.

Resourceful Jeff proposed a practical solution that would have the added advantage of patriotic propulsion. Civic groups interested in helping Jefferson with cash gifts but not in gambling could buy lottery tickets on Jefferson's birthday, April 13, and then publicly burn them on the Fourth of July. It was soon found that the tickets could not be printed and distributed by April 13, but the rest of the plan remained in effect. Jeff set out on a tour of Eastern cities to confer with his grandfather's admirers and help them devise plans. Although the trip was definitely a working one, he did look forward to visiting his sister Ellen Coolidge in Boston and making a side trip to meet John Adams.

On March 16, 1826, a month before his eighty-third birthday and with a sense of mortality weighing heavily on him, Jefferson made his will.[23] Of course, the fate of his legacy was much in doubt. He bequeathed Poplar Forest to Francis Eppes despite that young man's insistence that he could not accept it from the grandfather that he had "held . . . ever in the light of a father."[24] The residual estate he bequeathed in trust to Martha. The three trustees were Jeff; granddaughter Virginia Randolph's husband, Nicholas Trist; and University Bursar Alexander Garrett. The next day Jefferson added a codicil. In it he left a gold-headed walking stick to James Madison, a watch to each of his grandchildren, and his books to the university. He granted freedom to five slaves who had acquired skills that would enable them to support themselves. In so doing, he was relying on the generosity of his creditors not to block this disposal of property on which they would have a claim. He also depended on the sympathy of the legislature, asking it to grant them exemptions from the Virginia statute requiring all freedmen to leave the state within a year of their emancipation. He hoped that they would be given employment at the university and provided that each be given a dwelling convenient to his work. In addition he left Burwell, a glazier by trade but an indispensable factotum at Monticello, the sum of three hundred dollars.

To Jeff, whom he named his executor, he left all his papers except the official ones that he had scrupulously deposited in Richmond and Washington. Besides his farm book and account book, he left a trove of some forty thousand letters. Embracing politics, philosophy, religion, architecture, agriculture, horticulture, several sciences, the fine arts, linguistics, and education, and including letters from the world's greatest thinkers and leaders as well as his communications to them, it touches on almost every aspect of Western civilization in his time. To this day it is unmatched in significance by the correspondence of any other person writing in the English language.

Jefferson was able to preside over the April meeting of the Board of Visitors, but he was so feeble that his colleagues must have wondered if it was the last time. In February, when his physical sufferings were exacerbated by anxiety over the pending bill for a lottery, he had written Madison a letter in which he expressed gratitude for their friendship of half a century and said that Madison would now have to be the chief defender of both the university and republican principles. He said that his friend had been to him "a pillar of support through life. Take care of me when dead and be assured that I shall leave with you my last affections."[25] The context made clear that, in saying, "Take care of me when dead," Jefferson was committing to his comrade the defense of his reputation.

Jefferson visited the university again on May 4 and reexamined the Rotunda before giving Proctor Arthur S. Brockenbrough detailed directions for erection of the columns whose marble bases and capitals had been unloaded on a bank of the Rivanna River after shipment from Italy. When a capital was placed on the southwest column of the portico in June, Jefferson, seated in a chair provided by a student librarian, was watching carefully.[26]

Jeff returned in June from his Northern journey and found his grandfather much worried about Martha. He told his grandson that he saw her dying daily under the burden of her duties and responsibilities and elicited from him a promise, freely given, never to leave her.

Jefferson had said that the Fourth of July was the only birthday that he ever celebrated. The nation was preparing to celebrate it as never before, for this would be its fiftieth anniversary. Even the birth itself had not been so universally hailed because the step to independence had not commanded such universal allegiance. As the author of the Declaration of Independence and America's most celebrated founding father still alive, Jefferson was to be the central figure of the observance. He was invited by the citizens of Washington, D.C., to be part of the program in the nation's capital.

On June 24, suffering from diabetes, urinary infection, diarrhea, and perhaps cancer of the colon,[27] Jefferson wrote what he undoubtedly realized would be his valedictory to the nation. As amid the universal truths of the

Declaration of Independence there were some particulars of the here and now, so his reply to the citizens of Washington necessarily included certain gracious comments solely in response to the invitation of the moment. But like the Declaration it included a message to all peoples in all times. Jefferson said, "It adds sensibly to the sufferings of sickness to be deprived by it of a personal participation in the rejoicing of that day. . . . I should, indeed, with peculiar delight, have met and exchanged these congratulations personally with the small band, the remnant of that host of worthies, who joined with us on that day, in the bold and doubtful election we were to make for our country, between submission or the sword; and to have enjoyed with them the consolatory fact that our fellow citizens, after half a century of experience and prosperity, continue to approve the choice we made."

Then, on the subject of that choice, he addressed the generations of humanity: "May it be to the world what I believe it will be (to some parts sooner, to others later, but finally to all) the signal of arousing men to burst the chains under which monkish ignorance and superstition had persuaded them to bind themselves, and to assume the blessings and security of self-government. That form which we have substituted, restores the free right to the unbounded exercise of reason and freedom of opinion. All eyes are opened, or opening, to the rights of man. The general spread of the light of science has already laid open to every view the palpable truth, that the mass of mankind has not been born with saddles on their backs, nor a favored few booted and spurred, ready to ride them legitimately, by the grace of God. These are grounds of hope for others. For ourselves, let the annual return of this day forever refresh our recollections of these rights, and an undiminished devotion to them."[28]

A day or two earlier Jefferson had written a much more personal note, to Dr. Dunglison, requesting a visit. Heavy rains had flooded Moore's Creek, which always had to be forded in going from the university to Monticello. This delayed communication so that Dunglison did not arrive until the 24th, the same day that Jefferson had composed his reply to the invitation from Washington. Professor Tucker accompanied the doctor. Tucker later wrote of Jefferson: "When he entered the drawing room from his bed chamber, his tottering gait and altered appearance showed us that the attack had been a serious one."[29] As they rode back afterwards, the doctor confided his apprehension that the latest assault would be fatal.

Dunglison returned on the next day and again on the 27th. This time he spent the night and prepared to become a resident of Monticello for as long as he was needed. It was clear to the doctor that his patient indulged no hopes for recovery. "From this time," he noted, "his strength gradually diminished and he had to remain in bed. The evacuations became less numerous but it was manifest that his powers were failing."[30]

On the 27th Jefferson received a message from Henry Lee, son of General Henry (Lighthorse Harry) Lee. The elder Lee had been one of the leading cavalry officers in the Revolution, had been three times Governor of Virginia, and had made the much quoted pronouncement that Washington was "first in war, first in peace, and first in the hearts of his countrymen." Young Henry Lee was gathering material for a second edition of his father's memoirs and particularly sought facts to vindicate his father's record. He sent word that he wished to discuss certain events with Mr. Jefferson. General Lee had been a sincere patriot but so fiery a Federalist partisan that he could not view Jefferson objectively. Without conscious distortion he had publicly maligned the Republican leader. A meeting with General Lee's son might well be stressful for the dying man. Therefore his grandson-in-law, Nicholas Trist, called upon young Lee the next morning and told him that the elder statesman's critical illness would probably make conversation impossible. Trist told him, however, that the family invited him to dine with them either that evening or the next.

But Lee decided to come well before noon, hoping that he would find Jefferson able to talk with him. Martha greeted him, explained that her father's illness would not permit a meeting, and "excused herself to answer a call from the sick room." But she returned to say that her father, on learning that the visitor was in the hall, "insisted that he be shown in."[31]

Jefferson was lying on his alcove bed, his paleness probably emphasized in contrast with the red curtains. But his strong handshake and animated conversation encouraged the visitor to believe that his host might yet recover. As it was, Jefferson would not be able to provide him with certain papers until he was able to be up and around. After some talk of the documents, Jefferson turned the conversation to the destruction caused by a recent freshet of the James River and then, brightening, to the progress of the university. A remark of Lee's caused Jefferson "to smile broadly and then laugh." Then the sick man spoke of the probability of his death "as any man would face the prospect of being caught in a shower, an event not to be desired but certainly not to be feared." When the visitor started to leave, Jefferson insisted that he not let his host's "indisposition" interfere with dinner. But Lee did not remain.[32]

The young man was the older half-brother of Robert E. Lee, then a nineteen-year-old unknown to fame, but his character was quite different from his sibling's. He would earn the nickname "Black-Horse Harry" Lee and thwart a promising political career under Andrew Jackson's sponsorship when he had an adulterous affair with his wife's teenaged sister, who was also his ward. Madison would call him a "vial of rage." Fleeing to Europe, he would blame his troubles on the narrow-minded standards of Virginians and would write one book exalting Napoleon and another traducing Jefferson. This man was the last of the thousands of strangers who visited the master of Monticello.[33]

After this he saw only Dr. Dunglison, the household staff, and his family. Martha wanted to sit with him every night, but much as he valued her company in the day, he would not let her exhaust herself. He would not even permit any of the servants to sit up much beyond their usual bedtime. He would sometimes accept the presence at night of a favorite servant, Burwell, if he would sleep on a pallet or cot, able to rest unless called in an emergency. Friends and neighbors volunteered their services, but his family feared that they would cause him to talk too much. Eventually Jeff and Nicholas Trist insisted on sitting with him. Jeff had grown up loving him. Trist had learned to love him even before marrying into the family.

Jefferson gave Jeff directions regarding personal affairs. He was growing weaker but no longer seemed to feel pain. He himself remarked on his tendency now to revert in thought to the days of the Revolution. He related so many things "in his usual cheerful manner" that Jeff sometimes found himself diverted from the realization that his grandfather was dying. Once Jeff told him that he seemed "somewhat better." Jefferson turned to him and said, "Do not imagine for a moment that I feel the smallest solicitude about the result. I am like an old watch, with a pinion worn out here, and a wheel there, until it can go no longer."[34]

Jeff relates: "Upon being suddenly aroused from sleep by a noise in the room, he asked if he had heard the name of Mr. Hatch mentioned—the minister whose church he attended. On my replying in the negative, he observed, as he turned over, 'I have no objection to see him, as a kind and good neighbor.' The impression made upon my mind at the moment was that, his religious opinions having been formed upon mature study and reflection, he had no doubts upon his mind, and therefore did not desire the attendance of a clergyman. I have never since doubted the correctness of the impression then taken."

At times he gave parting admonitions to members of the family. Once, when Jeff's youngest brother, an eight-year-old, was there, the grandfather turned to Jeff with a smile and said, "George does not understand what all this means."

Jeff says of his grandfather as June passed into July: "He would speculate upon the person who would succeed him as Rector of the University of Virginia and concluded that Mr. Madison would be appointed. With all the deep pathos of exalted friendship he spoke of his purity, his virtues, his wisdom, his learning and his great abilities. And then, stretching his head back on his pillow, he said, with a sigh, 'But ah! he could never in his life stand up against strenuous opposition.' "[35]

In his conversations with Jeff, he was philosophical about even the worst of his calumniators. "He had not considered them as abusing him; they had never known *him*. They had created an imaginary being clothed with odious attributes, to whom they had given his name; and it was against that creature of their imaginations they had leveled their anathemas."

On July 2 Jefferson gave Martha a small jewelry box to be opened after his death. His occasional animation caused his family now and then to indulge the hope that the end might not be as near as had been believed. Nevertheless, when Senator Cabell and another man, not realizing how sick Jefferson was, rode up to Monticello to discuss the business of the university, they were told that he would not be able to see them.

After taking tea at 7:15 on the morning of July 3, he slept most of the day though there were periods of wakefulness. Waking about seven o'clock in the evening, "he seemed to imagine it was morning, and remarked that he had slept all night without being disturbed."[36] Seeing Dunglison, he asked indistinctly in a husky voice, "Ah! Doctor, are you still here? Is it the Fourth?" Dunglison glanced at the tall case clock and answered, "It soon will be."[37]

At eight o'clock he told the family that Mr. Jefferson might be expected to die in any quarter of an hour. When Dunglison roused him at nine o'clock to take his nightly dose of laudanum, Jefferson said, "No, Doctor, nothing more." Without this medicine, his sleep was fitful and more obviously dream-filled. Once he tried to sit up and eerily went through all the motions of writing. It was an exercise in which he had spent untold hours of his life from youth upward. Once, obviously back in the days of the Revolution, he said that the Committee of Safety should be warned.

As the hours passed, his family hoped, as he so evidently did, that he would live to see another Fourth of July. They had no hope that he would live beyond the day but, as Jeff said, "anxiously desired that his death should be hallowed by the Anniversary of Independence."[38]

Once the old man woke and whispered, "This is the Fourth?" Trist, reluctant to tell him that it was not, said nothing, hoping that Jefferson would drift off to sleep or have his attention diverted. But the question came again: "This is the Fourth?" Not wishing to speak the untrue words, Trist merely nodded. Jefferson murmured, "Ah," as "an expression came over his countenance which said, 'Just as I wished.' "[39] Seated on the sofa, close to Jefferson's pillow, Trist looked constantly from the face of the dying man to that of the clock as its hands crept toward midnight.

At last it was in truth the Fourth and Jefferson was still alive. At four o'clock in the morning he waked and asked "in a strong and clear voice" that the servants be brought in. He bade them farewell and then lapsed into silence. At 9:15 a.m. Trist, still seated at the bedside, wrote a member of the family unable to arrive at Monticello in time to talk with Jefferson: "There is no longer any doubt, unless one chance to a hundred thousand, or a million, may be ground for doubt. He has been dying since yesterday morning; and until twelve o'clock last night, we were in momentary fear that he would not live, as he desired, to see his own glorious Fourth. It has come at last; and he is still alive, if we can apply the word to one who is all but dead. He has been to the last, the same calm, clear-minded, amiable philosopher.

"From the first, he considered his case desperate: he knew the truth that the machine was worn out in some of its essential parts, and therefore could not go on. Yet, for the satisfaction of his family, he determined from the beginning to do everything and anything the Doctor recommended. This determination he adhered to with his wonted inflexibility. . . . He has not aroused from his lethargy now for several hours: his pulse is barely perceptible to the nicest touch; and his extremities have the calmness of death."[40]

There is no reason to doubt Trist's devotion to Jefferson, but the style of his letter and its dateline, "His bedside, July 4, 1826" suggest that despite his grief he was self-consciously writing for history.

About 10:00 a.m. Jefferson "fixed his eyes intently" upon Jeff, "indicating some want" which the grandson could not understand. But Burwell, the faithful servant of many years, who had often traveled with Jefferson, knew that his master always slept with his head far more elevated than was the common custom.[41] He propped his head up in its usual position, and Jefferson seemed satisfied. About eleven o'clock the dying man again fixed his eye on Jeff and this time moved his lips. Jeff "applied a wet sponge to his mouth, which he sucked and appeared to relish. This was the last evidence he gave of consciousness. He ceased to breathe, without a struggle, fifty minutes past meridian—July 4, 1826." Jeff closed the dead man's eyes.

When Martha opened the small box that her father had given her two days before his death, she found that he had penned verses concluding:

> Then farewell, my dear, my lov'd daughter, adieu!
> The last pang of life is in parting from you!
> Two seraphs await me long shrouded in death;
> I will bear them your love on my last parting breath.[42]

The "two seraphs" obviously were Martha Skelton Jefferson, his wife, Martha Randolph's mother; and Maria, Martha's sister. Martha was dry-eyed in her grief. Thomas Mann Randolph, who had stayed away from Monticello during Jefferson's last illness, reappeared after his death. He kept urging his wife to give way to tears and, to Dr. Dunglison's annoyance, kept asking him to give her something to induce weeping.[43]

In accordance with Jefferson's wish that his interment be private, no public announcement was made of the time. Yet, also in accordance with his habitual cordiality, it was agreed that no one would be turned away. Bells in Charlottesville had begun tolling on the afternoon of the Fourth and soon virtually everyone knew that Jefferson was dead. Word of the funeral plans spread by word of mouth through the little town and countryside.

Services were set for July 5 at 5:00 p.m. The skies were overcast and some rain was falling. Family and servants bore the wooden coffin from the house across the West Lawn and under the willow trees to the family graveyard. The open grave, dug by Wormeley, the gardener, awaited.

As the family and servants surrounded the spot, Thomas Mann Randolph stood at the head of the grave and Jeff stood at the foot.[44] Facing each other with the grave yawning between them, they seemed to symbolize the division between father and son.

The family had received word from Charlottesville that a procession was forming in town. They acceded to a request that the obsequies be delayed until the procession's arrival. But amid the stress of events, the family failed to tell the Rev. Mr. Hatch of the change, so he began reading the service at the originally scheduled time.

The procession consisted of both university students and townspeople. The students had assembled early in the Rotunda. One man said, "I never saw young men so deeply affected by any circumstance in my life."[45] Undoubtedly the grief of some was exacerbated by recollections of the misery they had brought to their rector by their misbehavior only months earlier. As part of the institution that Jefferson had created, they felt that he was peculiarly theirs.

But when they joined the citizens of Charlottesville, they found that these people believed they had a superior claim to Jefferson. Many of them had known him all their lives. The students had been intent on leading a procession to the grave. The citizens of Charlottesville determinedly claimed the same privilege. The quarrel held them back long past the expected time of departure. When they reached the cemetery, the grave was already being filled in and people were leaving. Some in the procession voiced both disappointment and irritation.[46] An ironic circumstance at the funeral of one who always sought harmony!

Apparently, some students and some citizens, weary with the argument, had detached themselves from the inchoate procession and had climbed the mountain in time for the services. One young man[47] from the university was a dark-haired seventeen-year-old with dark, haunted eyes. A sensitive youth, he reportedly had had no part in the recent riots. Just sixteen days earlier he had been elected to membership in the Jefferson Society, the university's oratorical, debating, and literary club.[48] Here at the grave of the man whom many regarded as the chief American embodiment of the Enlightenment stood Edgar Allan Poe, whom many would hail as the nation's most conspicuous representative of Romanticism. The symbolism is not really as precise as it appears. In truth, Jefferson was at least as much a Romantic as a Man of Reason.

Undoubtedly the two people who missed Jefferson most, although he was mourned by a numerous and most devoted family, were his daughter Martha and his grandson Jeff. The plans to save Monticello for the Jefferson family by lottery or solicitation collapsed with its builder's death. The chief motivation for the efforts ended when it could no longer be his home. After a "decent interval," Martha moved out. Jeff was protective of his mother as he had been of his grandfather. Both mother and son were sources of comfort and strength to other members of the family. Thomas Mann Randolph, long a burden to his wife and son, died about two years after his father-in-law, returning at the last to the gentle disposition that had characterized his early years.

Jeff lived the life of a conscientious, hardworking country gentleman, cultivating his crops and fulfilling many responsibilities, domestic and public. In some moods, Jefferson had said that this way of life might well be the best of all. Ever true to his grandfather's memory, Jeff published in four volumes in 1829 his *Memoir, Correspondence, and Miscellanies from the Papers of Thomas Jefferson*. His little daughter Sarah heard anecdotes about Jefferson as she was dandled on her father's knee, and as a mature woman edited, compiled, and wrote *The Domestic Life of Thomas Jefferson*, a work of great value to biographers and historians ever since.

Jeff's youngest brother, George, who as an eight-year-old could not quite comprehend his grandfather's deathbed admonitions, was a forty-three-year-old Richmond attorney when the Civil War that Jefferson had foreseen shocked America "like a fire bell in the night." He served the Confederate States of America both as Secretary of War and as Brigadier General. Of him Lieutenant General Daniel Harvey Hill would say, "He has no superior as an artillerist in any country."[49]

Probably the friend who most missed Jefferson was James Madison. Their connection had begun when Madison's family had consulted Jefferson regarding the education of their son, then fifteen years old.[50] Jefferson at the time was only twenty-three. With passing years the eight-year difference in their ages had shrunk, and each had consulted the other with great frequency. Each had complete confidence in the other's intelligence, integrity, and goodwill. Madison occupied a special place in Jefferson's life as an intimate friend to whom he could vent extreme opinions and violent personal reactions before issuing statements in public tones of moderation. On receiving news of his friend's death, Madison wrote that in their friendship for half a century "there was not an interruption or diminution of mutual confidence and cordial friendship for a single moment in a single instance." But he was "more than consoled for the loss by the gain to him, and by the assurance that he lives and will live in the memory and gratitude of the wise and good, as a luminary of science, as a votary of liberty, as a model of patriotism, and as a benefactor of the human kind."[51] He succeeded his friend as rector of the university and worked to fulfill Jefferson's hopes for it.

As the one who had cared for Jefferson professionally in his last days with all the affection of devoted friendship, Dr. Dunglison stood in a special relationship to him. He had revered Jefferson for his contributions to liberty and for his intellectual accomplishments, but his heart had been touched particularly by the opportunity of observing him in his home. "It was impossible," he said, "for anyone to be more amiable in his domestic relations."[52] When the furnishings of Monticello were sold at public auction he bid beyond prudence to obtain as a memento the bedroom clock by which Jefferson regularly arose whenever dawn revealed the hands. Nevertheless, his bid was eventually topped by Nicholas Trist. When Dunglison apologized for running the price up, saying that he had not realized he was bidding against a member of the family, Trist said that he had been instructed by Mrs. Randolph to buy the timepiece so that it could be presented to the doctor.[53]

Dunglison left Charlottesville in 1833 for the University of Maryland and about three years later moved to Jefferson Medical College in Philadelphia. Some of his writings became medical classics and he became one of the most renowned physicians in the world, but in his memoirs he seemed to present as the high point of his life the time when he was a member of the first faculty of the University of Virginia and had Thomas Jefferson as a patient and a friend.

With Jefferson's death his cousin Chief Justice John Marshall was now indisputably the most eminent living Virginian. It was inevitable that journalists and others would seek to pry from him some comment on the illustrious dead, but none succeeded. Not until January 20, 1832, did he yield an opinion, and this was in the course of refusing one. To Henry Lee, who was still pursuing his vendetta and had sought information from Marshall, the Chief Justice replied: "I have never allowed myself to be irritated by Mr. Jefferson's unprovoked and unjustifiable aspersions on my conduct and principles, nor have I ever noticed them except on one occasion, when I thought myself called on to do so, and when I thought that declining to enter upon my justification might have the appearance of crouching under the lash, and admitting the justice of its infliction."[54]

News of the Virginian's death brought sadness in other parts of the world. The Marquis de Lafayette, before returning to France, had visited Jefferson once more at Monticello and found him in great pain from his bladder infection. Learning from Dr. Dunglison that gum catheters of a kind more readily obtained in Paris than anywhere else could contribute to the patient's comfort, he shipped some to his friend immediately upon his arrival in the city. Devoted to Jefferson and never one to do things by halves, the general sent a case of one hundred, enough for a small hospital. He was saddened to learn that they had not arrived in time to be of service.[55]

Behind the walls of her convent college in Lodi, Italy, Maria Cosway was anxiously wondering why she had not received an answer to her last latter to Jefferson when she learned of his death. She had had her school's great salon painted with murals representing "four parts of the world and the most distinguished objects in them." The American mural consisted of natural scenery with an indication of the location of the city of Washington. She had "left a hill barren" to accommodate representations of Monticello and the University of Virginia as the most important buildings in the United States outside the capital. She asked for descriptions of the two structures so that they could be reproduced. When she learned from a newspaper that Jefferson was dead, she decided to leave the hill barren forever.[56]

John Adams did not learn of Jefferson's death. The stout-hearted old Yankee had died in Braintree, Massachusetts, on the same day that Jefferson had breathed his last at Monticello. From his deathbed Adams had pronounced, "Thomas Jefferson still survives," not realizing that his friend had died five hours earlier.

Americans in every state of the Union had celebrated the Fourth of July, the fiftieth anniversary of the Declaration of Independence, with no suspicion that its author, whom they toasted, was no longer alive. Then came word to Virginians and to residents of the District of Columbia, and eventually to people all over the Union, that the author of the Declaration of Independence had not only died on the fiftieth anniversary of its adoption but at fifty minutes past the meridian, at about the time that the original document had been presented to the Continental Congress. President John Quincy Adams, who as a boy had followed Jefferson around in admiration, was in the Executive Mansion in Washington contemplating a proclamation or other notice to honor the departed statesman when he learned that his own father had died on the same day. John Adams had not only been a signer of the Declaration; he had served with Jefferson on the committee to prepare it and, more than any other person, was responsible for the selection of the Virginian as author. Cool logician though he sometimes seemed to be, the President asked himself if the hand of God was not in what appeared to be coincidence.[57]

Fourteen years earlier, when Dr. Benjamin Rush was working to bring about a reconciliation between John Adams and Jefferson, he had written the New Englander of a dream in which he had seen the nation moved by the renewed friendship between the two great founders of the republic and had seen a rebirth of patriotism as a result. The prophecy came true. Orators from

Daniel Webster and William Wirt to every courthouse Cicero and district Demosthenes rang all the changes on the theme of unity. For a while, sectional conflicts subsided and Americans once again celebrated their sense of uniqueness among the peoples of the earth. Awestruck but emboldened, they faced the future together strong in the sense of a mystic bond.

No sentiment, however, is universal. An Albemarle County resident who was a zealous Democrat, and who admired Jefferson more than he did any other man of the age, proclaimed that the patriot's death on the half-century anniversary of the nation's birth was an apotheosis raising both Jefferson and his party "one step higher in the temple of fame." Then he was told that John Adams had died on the same day. At first he refused to believe the report. But when the mass of confirmation was too great to be ignored, he exploded that "it was a damned Yankee trick."[58] The incident was the sort of thing that Jefferson might have chuckled over and then quoted to Adams to tease him.

XXII

WHO IS HE?

JEFFERSON WAS spared the knowledge that none of his material legacy to his family would be theirs. But he left to all humanity a vastly larger legacy seemingly impervious to the vicissitudes of worldy fortune. Shortly after Jefferson's death it was pointed out that, although John Adams had literally been in error when he said, "Thomas Jefferson still survives," he had in a larger sense spoken the truth. And the words have remained true to this day, cited amid the national tragedy of the American Civil War, quoted repeatedly in World War I, in the Great Depression, in World War II, and in Europe and Asia in the 1990s as men and women struggled with varying degrees of success to free themselves from oppression. Indeed, in the world at large in 1990, Jefferson became not only the most quoted American but also the most quoted secular figure of any nationality.

We know what he considered the most important elements of his legacy. They mattered so much to him that he had them carved into stone. He wrote his own epitaph and prescribed that it be incised in a block of coarse granite that would not tempt pilferers of marble and other valuable materials:

Here was Buried
THOMAS JEFFERSON
Author of the Declaration of American Independence,
Of the Statute of Virginia for Religious Freedom,
And Father of the University of Virginia

Lest anyone miss the significance of the priority he deliberately assigned these achievements, he explained, "By these, as testimonials that I have lived, I wish most to be remembered."[1]

One of the most notable things about the list is the time span represented. The first accomplishment is the writing of the Declaration of Independence in 1776; the last is the founding of the University of Virginia in 1819 if one goes by the date on the charter or, more realistically, 1826 if one considers all the steps that transformed existence on paper to bricks and mortar reality and full-functioning with a diverse curriculum. As defined by what he considered his greatest achievements, the most important stretch of events in Jefferson's public career extended over a period of fifty years. It began when he was thirty-three years old and ended a few weeks before his death at the age of eighty-three. Almost equally noteworthy is the distribution of achievements on a time line. His second major accomplishment, Jefferson said, was the writing of the Statute of Virginia for Religious Freedom in 1777. As he saw it, two of his three most important contributions were made in successive years and by the time he was thirty-four years old.

Of course, Jefferson arrived at this distribution by omitting some things that most people would have listed: his brilliant service as United States Minister to France, 1785–1789; as first Secretary of State, 1790–1793; and as President, 1801–1809, or, to single out a particular event of his presidency, the Louisiana Purchase in 1803. Nevertheless, the triad that he chose for his epitaph deserves, even apart from inherent merit, special consideration because it was the selection he chose to exalt. The omission of public offices may in part reflect the fact that, while Jefferson was faithful to every public trust, he was not disposed to consider the highest official position in any body politic, whether state or nation, necessarily the noblest occupation to which any citizen was committed. Witness his reminder to the astronomer David Rittenhouse, who was being urged to accept public office, that society had many members fit for political positions but had only one Rittenhouse.

The first two accomplishments—authorship of the Statute of Virginia for Religious Freedom and of the Declaration of Independence—are expressions of a passionate concern, throughout his adult life, for individual liberty. In its argument that matters of religion are for individual decision, the Statute quite obviously voices this fervent faith. Though the Declaration speaks of the freedom of a people and their right to nationhood, it too stresses individualism because it assumes personal access to a higher law independent of the decrees of government.

Less obviously but just as truly related to the theme of individual liberty is Jefferson's role as founder of the University of Virginia. He stressed that people in an advanced society could not be at the same time ignorant and free, and emphasized the value of education as an instrument of freedom. Beyond this utilitarianism, he saw as the chief value of a liberal education its liberating influence on the mind. This was not just a matter of awakening the individual to a concern for civil rights and an awareness of threats to them; it was also a matter of opening new intellectual vistas and thus making possible an expansion of intellect and spirit. The person benefiting from such an education should not only be more sagaciously watchful of governmental encroachment but also more immune to the tyranny of public opinion. And a magnification of vistas should present a liberating increase of options. Jefferson believed that higher education should be dedicated to the "illimitable freedom of the human mind" and that its devotees should not be afraid "to follow truth wherever it may lead." He wished not only to free individual expression from coercive government but also to free thought itself from the limitations of ignorance and the shackles of superstition.

The Statute of Virginia for Religious Freedom and the Declaration of

Independence are both in the stately measures favored for serious discourse in the eighteenth century, but each also has a certain liveliness, pungency, and depth and breadth of view suggesting that the two are works of the same author. Each is an immensely quotable document.

Jefferson was extremely clever in wording the Statute so as to turn the tables upon its chief critics. He knew that to advocate religious freedom in a society accustomed to the partnership of church and state was to invite charges of impiety. He therefore included in the Statute a reminder that "Almighty God had created the mind free; that all attempts to influence it by temporal punishments or burthens or by civil incapacitations, tend only to beget habits of hypocrisy and meanness, and are a departure from the plan of the Holy Author of our religion, who, being Lord both of body and mind, yet chose not to propagate it by coercions on either, as was in his Almighty power to do." He attacked "the impious presumption of legislators and rulers, civil as well as ecclesiastical, who, being themselves but fallible and uninspired men, have assumed dominion over the faith of others, setting up their own opinions and modes of thinking as the only true and infallible, and as such endeavoring to impose them on others."

Few state papers are studded with so many memorable phrases: "Our civil rights have no dependence on our religious opinions, more than on our opinions in physics and geometry. . . . The legitimate powers of government extend to such acts only as are injurious to others. But it does me no injury for my neighbor to say there are twenty gods, or no god. It neither picks my pocket nor breaks my leg." To the assertion that a nonbeliever should at least be restrained from propagating error, Jefferson answered, "Constraint may make him worse by making him a hypocrite, but it will never make him a truer man." He declared faith "that truth is great and will prevail if left to herself, that she is the proper and sufficient antagonist to error, and has nothing to fear from the conflict, unless by human interposition disarmed of her natural weapons, free argument and debate, errors ceasing to be dangerous when it is permitted freely to contradict them."

In chaste eloquence, he wrote: *"Be it therefore enacted by the General Assembly*, That no man shall be compelled to frequent or support any religious worship, place or ministry whatsoever, nor shall be enforced, restrained, molested, or burthened in his body or goods, nor shall otherwise suffer on account of his religious opinions or belief; but that all men shall be free to profess, and by argument to maintain, their opinions in matters of religion, and that the same shall in no wise diminish, enlarge, or affect their civil capacities."

In the end passion breaks through the cool logic of the Enlightenment. So strongly did Jefferson feel about the purposes of the Statute that this master parliamentarian departed from parliamentary practice to add: "Though we well know that . . . to declare this act irrevocable would be of no effect in law, yet we are free to declare that if any act shall be hereafter passed to repeal the present, or to narrow rights hereby asserted . . ., such act will be an infringement of natural right." The body of the statute is addressed to humanity's sense of logic, the addendum to its conscience. In every generation there will be men and women who cannot ignore either.

The Declaration of Independence also is a living document, vital enough still to provoke arguments not only between autocrats and democrats but also among adherents of democracy who debate the meaning of the statement that "all men are created equal." Incidentally Jefferson himself indicated that he meant all human beings were equal in rights and equally entitled to justice whatever their inequalities of mental and physical development and social and economic status.

John Richard Alden said that the document "must remain a great historical landmark in that it contained the first formal assertion by a whole people of their right to a government of their own choice." The elevation and in some instances sublimity of Jefferson's language is worthy of this historic role. The Declaration necessarily includes a catalogue of complaints against King and Parliament, and, not surprisingly, since it was written in the heat of conflict, the list departs at times from judicial objectivity. But whereas most revolutionary papers have breathed hatred like dragon fire when they were not descending to pettiness, this document sounds a note of sublimity in its first sentence: "When in the course of human events it becomes necessary for one people to dissolve the political bands which have connected them with another, and to assume among the powers of the earth the separate and equal station to which the laws of Nature and of Nature's God entitle them, a decent respect to the opinions of mankind requires that they should declare the causes which impel them to the separation."

The Declaration was not a strikingly original document, nor was it intended to be. Indeed, a paper bristling with fresh turns of thought and glittering neologisms would not have served nearly so well. The author's purpose was to produce "an expression of the American mind." This he did in an esthetic and moving blend of the political currency of the time as known to the representatives of the American states in Congress assembled. The thoughts and some of the phrases recall the words of John Locke, Francis Hutcheson, James Wilson, and George Mason. Julian Boyd said of Jefferson's composition: "The greatness of his achievement, aside from the fact that he created one of the outstanding literary documents of the world and of all time, was that he identified its sublime purpose with the roots of liberal traditions that spread back to England, to Scotland, to Geneva, to Holland, to Germany, to Rome, and to Athens. In the fundamental statement of national purpose for a people who were to embrace many races and many creeds, nothing could have been more appropriate than that the act renouncing the ties of consanguinity should at the same time have drawn its philosophical justification from traditions common to all."[2]

The Declaration has inspired friends of freedom even in the land from which it declared separation. Its references to "Life, Liberty and the pursuit of Happiness" and its ringing phrases about the right to revolution against tyranny inspired Antonio de Narino and Francisco de Miranda in their revolts against the Spanish empire in South America and were quoted by Mirabeau in the French Revolution as well as numerous Asian rebels in the twentieth century, besides both rebels and leaders of professedly democratic regimes in Poland, Hungary, Czechoslovakia, and the Soviet Union.

And the Declaration, even in the pastiche portions, is almost entirely the work of Jefferson. His mind imposed unity, and the rhythms of his utterance made the work a euphonious whole. For the most part, the editing of colleagues altered his composition in only minor details. The principal change, deletion of a pledge to abolish the importation of slaves, greatly weakened the document and left it with a logical inconsistency that Jefferson deplored: that of a people simultaneously declaring the inherent right to individual freedom and leaving untouched the institution of slavery. The political influence of slaveowners in the Deep South and slave traders in New England compelled this unfortunate excision.[3]

How true was Jefferson to his own ideals of liberty as expressed in the Statute of Virginia for Religious Freedom and the Declaration of Independence? In the case of religious freedom, the answer is unequivocal. He did not let his personal religious views intrude upon policy. Even apart from his reputation for honor among those who knew him well, there is every reason to believe Jefferson's few detailed expressions of personal faith. Far from indulging in public posturings of piety, he shared these views only with a few relatives and close friends. In his statements on the subject, there was no temptation to play up to a political audience, because the audience was personal and individual. Even charges of atheism, which hurt him politically, could not provoke him to depart from his rule of privacy in such matters. The statements of Jefferson's mature years show him to have been religious though unorthodox. He believed in God and an afterlife, and called himself a Christian although he did not accept the trinitarian concept. But there is no record of his ever having sought to coerce others into agreement with him, and he strongly defended the religious liberties of those to both the left and right of his own position. He invited and energetically supported the candidacy of the highly vocal agnostic Thomas Cooper for the first faculty post at the University of Virginia—unwisely, some would say, because he scared off potential backers of the institution. On the other hand, he also supported out of his own pocket the work of an itinerant Baptist evangelist.

How faithful was he to the ideals of liberty set forth in the Declaration of Independence? Most of Jefferson's public actions are consistent with his famous statement, "I have sworn upon the altar of God eternal hostility against every form of tyranny over the mind of man." There are exceptions.

As Secretary of State and as President, he launched no invasion of Spanish Florida, but he did cast a covetous eye upon it, and this strict republican sometimes indulged in dreams of empire. In his heart, he lusted after this exotic territory.

When he was President of the United States he commented on the trial of Aaron Burr in ways improper while the trial was in progress. He was open to charges that by reiterating his belief in the defendant's guilt he was using his personal prestige and that of his office to influence the outcome. Admittedly, the evidence of the presiding jurist's partisanship must have been signally provoking, but it still does not excuse impropriety on Jefferson's part. Also Jefferson's approval of General James Wilkinson's suspension of civil rights in the New Orleans area does not seem consistent with the President's avowed belief that truth would prevail without the aid of coercion. Yet in so acting in what he believed to be a grave national emergency, he was doing what Washington had done and what Abraham Lincoln, Woodrow Wilson, and Franklin D. Roosevelt would do in similar cases.

He had said of his plans for the University of Virginia: "This institution will be based on the illimitable freedom of the human mind. For here we are not afraid to follow truth wherever it may lead, nor to tolerate any error so long as reason is left free to combat it." Yet, under his leadership, the Board of Visitors dictated certain readings for the school of law and emphasized the need "to pay especial attention to the principles of government which shall be inculcated therein, and to provide that none shall be inculcated which are incompatible with those on which the Constitutions of this State, and of the United States, were genuinely based." But even here, after consultation with Madison, Jefferson tried to have the readings representative of the best in Federalist as well as Republican thought. The first serious problems within the university came not from an abridgement of students' individual rights but from an unwise enlargement of individual liberty among the immature. Jefferson probably spoke truly when he said a few months before his death that students at the University of Virginia enjoyed a "free range of mind" not experienced by their counterparts in any other American institution of higher learning. For this freedom Jefferson, more than anyone else, was responsible.

More people are disturbed by Jefferson's dual role as slaveholder and slavery foe than by any other inconsistency, real or apparent, in his record on civil rights. World literature probably contains no more eloquent attack on slavery than his denunciation of it in *Notes on the State of Virginia* beginning: "The whole commerce between master and slave is a perpetual exercise of the most boisterous passions, the most unremitting despotism on the one part, and degrading submission on the other. . . . And with what execration should the statesman be loaded, who permitting one half the citizens thus to trample on the rights of the other, transforms those into despots and these into enemies, destroys the morals of the one part, and the amor patriae of the other." After an appeal to reason, Jefferson closes his argument with an impassioned outburst: "Indeed, I tremble for my country when I reflect that God is just: that his justice cannot sleep forever: that considering numbers, nature and natural means only, a revolution of the wheel of fortune, an exchange of situation, is among possible events: that it may become probable by supernatural interference! The Almighty has no attribute which can take side with us in such a contest."

Jefferson was Governor of Virginia when he wrote those words. His testimony against slavery was certainly not perfunctory. Since his days as a student at the College of William and Mary he had copied into his Commonplace Book arguments against the institution. In 1776, as we have seen, he wrote into the Declaration of Independence a pledge to abolish the importation of slaves and was chagrined and frustrated when it was excised. He was one of the leaders of opinion who two years later helped to make Virginia not only the first American state but, in the words of J. H. Ballagh, "the first community in the civilized modern world to prohibit the pernicious traffic."[4]

Once, during the Revolution, Jefferson had said of slavery, "It is impossible to be temperate and to pursue this subject." As a young reviser of the laws of Virginia, he had supported a plan to emancipate all slaves born after passage of a proposed act "and further directing that they should continue with their parents to a certain age, then be brought up, at the public expense, to tillage, arts or sciences, according to their geniuses, till the females should be eighteen, and the males twenty-one years of age, when they should be colonized to such place as the circumstances of the time should render most proper, sending them out with arms, implements of household and of the handicraft arts, seeds, pairs of the useful domestic animals, etc., to declare them a free and independent people, and extend to them our alliance and protection, till they shall have acquired strength."

He anticipated the modern reader's indignant question. "It will probably be asked, Why not retain and incorporate the blacks into the state? . . . Deep rooted prejudices entertained by the whites; the thousand recollections, by the blacks, of the injuries they have sustained; new provocations; the real distinctions which nature had made; and many other circumstances, will divide us into parties, and produce convulsions which will probably never end but in the extermination of the one or the other race."

This answer, from which we recoil today, is essentially the same as that later given by Abraham Lincoln. Should we fault Jefferson if on this point in his day he was no more enlightened than the Great Emancipator two generations later?

Jefferson was judged on this issue in the context of his own time by his contemporaries. Many of them, North and South, found him provokingly radical. It is extremely naive for us to judge him in the context of our time.

Jefferson's estimate of the abilities of blacks coincided with that of most educated white men of his day, but it is tempered by a scintilla of doubt reminiscent of Judge Learned Hand's pronouncement that "The spirit of liberty is the spirit which is not too sure it is right." Jefferson said: "The opinion that they are inferior in the faculties of reason and imagination must be hazarded with great diffidence. To justify a general conclusion requires many observations, even where the subject may be submitted to the anatomical knife, to optical glasses, to analysis by fire, or by solvents. How much more then where it is a faculty, not a substance, we are examining; where it eludes the research of all the senses; where the conditions of its existence are various and variously combined; where the effects of those which are present or absent bid defiance to calculation; let me add too, as a circumstance of great tenderness, where our conclusion would degrade a whole race of men from the rank in the scale of beings which their Creator may perhaps have given them."

Jefferson was consistent in statements of opposition to slavery during the period of the Missouri Compromise and into the last year of his life. He was also consistent in his insistence that emancipation must be accompanied by colonization. In his own striking image, the slaveholding society had "a wolf by the ears" and found it difficult to hold on and unthinkable to let go. In his last years, Jefferson would sometimes repeat his antislavery sentiments to correspondents but ask them not to make his statements public. He seemed to feel that he should have earned an exemption from public controversy. Certainly such controversy would be more sensational for him than for many other public men because of the politically inspired stories about his amorous adventures with a slave concubine. And after he became deeply involved in soliciting support for the University of Virginia, he was determined not to become embroiled in unrelated disputes that would make the project vulnerable.

Also, as we have seen, the freeing of his own slaves in the latter part of his life would have been complicated by the Virginia law requiring freed slaves to leave the state. A further complication was that, because of the various mortgages on his property, Jefferson did not have the legal right to emancipate them.

How consistent were Jefferson's actions with the ideals expressed in the Statute of Virginia for Religious Freedom, the Declaration of Independence, and various other public papers that he wrote? Almost perfectly in the case of the first great document. Manifestly imperfectly, but substantially, in the case of the second. Jefferson, John Adams, John Quincy Adams, Theodore Roosevelt, and Woodrow Wilson were all intellectuals who wrote about the ideals of citizenship, but unlike many of their fellow intellectuals they also had the responsibility of administering governments. They put their ideals on record and then, as human actors in the drama of events, had the sometimes uncomfortable experience of being measured against them. Each must have felt like echoing, with a contextual difference, the lament of Job, "My desire is . . . that mine adversary had written a book."

The third contribution Jefferson chose to list on his tomb, the founding of the University of Virginia, was the last great act of his life and the crowning achievement of nearly a half century of thought and activity for the benefit of education. In 1779, at the age of thirty-six, he had introduced bills for the provision of a statewide system of public education and had led in reorganizing the College of William and Mary. In 1795 he had proposed the removal of Geneva professors to America to provide opportunities for them to improve the quality of higher education in the United States. In 1800 he was planning a state university for Virginia and continued afterwards to collect information appropriate to the task. Through his efforts, Virginia's State Literary Fund, a source of money for education, was established. In 1814 he proposed a centrally located state university in Virginia and, while a trustee of Albemarle Academy, worked to transform it into Central College. When that was achieved in 1816, he labored to transform the college into a state university. As we have seen, nobody ever performed personally more functions in the founding of a high quality institution of higher learning than Jefferson did.

While among educational achievements he emphasized only the fathering of the University of Virginia as a major accomplishment, this work was so integral a part of his general scheme of education that his whole approach to the schooling of the citizenry deserves review. His plans of 1777–1779 for the "diffusion of knowledge" proposed free education in the public schools for three years for the capable sons and daughters of all citizens. Small as this now seems, it was then deemed sweeping and radical. At each level above this primary stage, up to and including college, a few of the most promising students whose families were not financially able to provide schooling would be educated completely at public expense. Jefferson personally believed strongly in education for women but his plan did not call for their education at public expense beyond the first three years. To have attempted this reform would definitely have doomed the entire scheme. Contemporary opinion held that making education beyond the primary stage available to those girls whose families could afford it was quite liberal. And many thought that educating either sex at public expense was a waste of money and an infringement of individual rights. Jefferson was considered radical when he argued: "Every government degenerates when trusted to the rulers of the people alone. The people themselves therefore are its only safe depositories. And to render even them safe their minds must be improved to a certain degree."

At that time Jefferson envisioned the College of William and Mary as the "capstone of education" in Virginia. He proposed that its two chairs of divinity be eliminated and called for the addition of chairs of medicine, history, and modern languages. The last addition was considered almost as radical as removal of the chairs of divinity. When Jefferson found that he could not reorganize his alma mater through legislation, he accomplished a partial reformation with the cooperation of its president, Bishop James Madison.

Jefferson's plan for the diffusion of knowledge also called for establishment in Richmond of a state library and state museum of art to serve the public. The museum proposal was so advanced that no state public institution of this kind appeared in the United States until 1936. He would have been disappointed that realization came so late but pleased that it came first in his own Virginia.

Jefferson's founding of the University of Virginia would have been a significant event even if it had only provided a more central and more dynamic alternative to William and Mary at a time when the Williamsburg college was languishing between periods of greatness, and thus had brought new intellectual yeast to the Old Dominion, but it did far more. The rector put into operation in Charlottesville certain reforms that not only benefited the students at the new institution but also inspired emulation at other American colleges and universities.

Notable was his emphasis on languages, not primarily as ends in themselves but as means to other acquirements. He still believed, as he had in the 1770s, that very young people should be introduced to both ancient and modern languages. The early years, he insisted, were high in memory skills but not in judgment, so that they were the ideal time for basic training in languages. In higher education, languages could be avenues to studies involving insight, analysis, and evaluation.

He prized Latin and Greek as portals to the great heritage of Western civilization and deplored evidences of recent neglect of them in Great Britain. He valued Anglo-Saxon as an aid in the study of modern English and of the common law as well as of political institutions derived from Britain. He made the University of Virginia the first institution of higher education in America to include the subject in its curriculum.[5] The *Essay on the Anglo-Saxon Language,* which he wrote in 1818, contained suggestions for effective teaching of the language which were not fully implemented until the twentieth century, when they became standard.[6] He believed that Greek, Latin, and Anglo-Saxon should be taught with the thoroughness with which the classical languages were imparted at William and Mary.

The Rockfish Gap Report, of which Jefferson was the principal author, stresses the importance of modern languages in the curriculum. It "emphasizes the value of French because of its use in the intercourse of nations and as a depository of science, of Spanish because the language in which much early American history was written, of Italian because of fine style and composition, of German because of its scientific value." Jefferson also foresaw the importance of Spanish because of future United States connections with Spanish America.[7] He anticipated modern methods in the teaching of languages when he established for Central College a dormitory in which "the boarders shall be permitted to speak French only, with a view to their becoming familiarized to conversation in that language."[8]

Jefferson introduced interdisciplinary teaching across the curriculum with particular emphasis on languages and history. The study of ancient and modern history went hand in hand with appropriate language study because of his belief that "both may be attained by the same course of reading, if books are selected with that view." He instituted the teaching of the history and geography of a people along with their language. He also insisted that history be "interwoven" with government and law.[9]

While Jefferson designed his university to cultivate the highest intellectual development, insuring that no matter how important it became in training for law, medicine, or other specific professions it would never become a mere trade school, he also advocated vocational training in the broadest sense. He even called for a technical school affording specific instruction for the mariner, carpenter, shipwright, machinist, clockmaker, and practitioner of many another occupation. In his plans for the Charlottesville institution he anticipated the modern community college as well as the university in its broadest sense.

Perhaps the most pioneering of all Jefferson's moves at the University of Virginia was his inauguration of the elective system. He wrote George Ticknor: "I am not fully informed of the practices at Harvard, but there is one from which we shall certainly vary, although it has been copied, I believe, by nearly every college and academy in the United States. That is the holding of students all to one prescribed course. . . ." Surveying the influence of the elective system at Charlottesville, Roy J. Honeywell concluded, "None of Jefferson's ideas gained a wider acceptance in American education."[10]

In 1825 reforms of the academic system at Harvard, advocated by Ticknor after a visit to the University of Virginia and observation of its operations, were adopted with the aid of William Prescott and Judge Story. Among those most influenced by Jefferson's theories were "consideration to a limited extent of the desires of students in arranging their studies" and the "division of classes according to their proficiency." These reforms were successful only in the Department of Modern Languages, which, significantly, was headed by their principal advocate, Ticknor.[11]

Jefferson's experiment in student government at first was not successful in his own university. But after the application of stern justice to the problem of student riots, the university successfully retained many elements of student government, including an honor court,[12] giving the students powers not equal to those exercised by their South American counterparts but nevertheless rare in North America.

Though Jefferson chose not to list performance in public office among the accomplishments incised on his tombstone, most assessors of his career will, of course, consider it essential. A mere catalogue of the positions he held tells little. John Dewey rightly said: "The fact that he occupied certain offices is of little account in itself; comparative nonentities have been foreign envoys and Presidents. The use he made of these positions is what counts, and the use includes not only the political policies he urged and carried through, but even more the observations he made and the reflections they produced."[13]

The value of Jefferson's observations and reflections from various vantage points of public life was the result of his natural acuity, inquisitive mind, diversity of interests, and breadth of learning. Madison, himself the possessor of one of America's great minds, said that Jefferson "would be found to be the most learned man that had ever devoted so much time to public life."[14] The statement is sweeping. One thinks of Marcus Aurelius, Cicero, Alfred the Great, Frederick the Great. For purposes of comparison, the extent of learning must be measured against the amplitude of intellectual resources in a given period; but, all things considered, Jefferson would have been a fit intellectual companion for any of the four.

Queen Christina of Sweden probably was as passionate in the pursuit of diverse learning as any political figure in history, but the "Minerva of the North" did not make as many contributions to knowledge as Jefferson and abdicated after only ten years on the throne. The great polymath Goethe springs to mind but, although he was a statesman, he did not spend enough of his time in political service to meet Madison's criterion. Benjamin Franklin was honored internationally for both learning and statesmanship, but, although he made more important contributions than the Virginian to both science and invention, his scientific studies were not as far-ranging as Jefferson's and he was generally behind him in the humanities and far behind in the arts. Among statesmen of subsequent generations, Jawaharlal Nehru and Winston Churchill loom as examples of intellectual virtuosity but, while the Indian is remarkable for his success in bridging Eastern and Western culture and the Englishman has notable achievements in history, biography, and literature and was a good painter, neither man was responsive to as many intellectual currents as Jefferson.

Certainly Jefferson had greater intellectual sweep than any other President of the United States. Despite the diversity of interests of John Adams, John Quincy Adams, James Madison, Theodore Roosevelt, and Woodrow Wilson, not one of these leaders could match Jefferson's range over law, political philosophy, history, ancient and modern literature, architecture, horticulture, the fine arts, linguistics and etymology, medicine, meteorology, natural history, astronomy, mathematics, anthropology, paleontology, religion, and invention.

Another factor that gave value to Jefferson's observations was the superb organization of his intellect. The foyer at Monticello might be cluttered with a seemingly meaningless array of curiosities that had engaged his attention, and the floor of his study might be covered with books and papers, but his mind automatically classified the vast amount of data that came to it through reading, conversation, and scientific examination. His skill in communicating his observations both evidenced his high competence in organization and increased their value to others.

Jefferson's service as Burgess in a colony notable for its gifted leadership was distinguished. His ready knowledge and eloquent pen quickly won recognition. His legislative services were even more important after the colony became a state. The fact that the House of Delegates several times had to send the sergeant-at-arms to compel his attendance[15] was evidence not of neglect but of diligence. He was assiduously preparing legislation in the quiet of his quarters while fellow legislators wrangled over legal technicalities and rose repeatedly to explain why they differed minutely with a previous speaker or else thought exactly as he did.

Jefferson was not, as his situation might lead some to believe, caught up in clerical aspects of his job while more practical-minded colleagues got results. At thirty-three years of age he was the principal agent of legal reform in Virginia.[16] He chaired the Committee to Revise the Laws of the Commonwealth, which included Edmund Pendleton, George Wythe, George Mason, and, briefly Thomas Ludwell Lee. The task was one of the most monumental ever successfully completed by any legislative committee of any state in the Union. Besides bringing more logical and efficient organization to the law, it infused the criminal code with a more humane spirit. Even apart from his leadership of this able group, Jefferson was incessantly drafting bills dealing with courts of justice, entails, and such controversial subjects as the established church, the importation of slaves, and legislative representation.

In the Congress, though younger than most prominent members, he quickly was welcomed to leadership. He benefited in part from the so-called "Hartford advice" to the New England delegates to push Virginians forward so that their state, the most populous of all and strategically located midway of the Union, would be firmly committed to revolution. But within the Virginia delegation were formidable competitors: Benjamin Harrison, Richard Henry Lee, Thomas Nelson, and George Wythe. Awarding Jefferson so important a chairmanship as that of the committee to prepare a Declaration of Independence was not only a tribute to his literary skills but an expression of confidence in his character and general ability. At the age of thirty-three, he had won the admiration and friendship of John Adams and Benjamin Franklin and was a leader of national prominence.

By contrast, his tenure as Governor of Virginia was not successful. Neither was that of his predecessor, the first Governor of the Commonwealth, Patrick Henry. The state's constitution makers, determined to prevent the executive tyranny from which the colonists had suffered under royal rule, had made the Governor a mere figurehead. Add to this difficulty, in itself sufficient, the fact that Jefferson had the misfortune to fill the office when his state was at war and invaded by the enemy. He was sometimes literally a Governor on horseback, his office in the saddle somewhere between Richmond and Charlottesville. Pitifully few naval vessels of the colony and her sisters opposed the greatest naval power on earth, creating a particularly perilous situation for a state bisected by the Chesapeake Bay and penetrated far inland by some of the greatest rivers on the East Coast. Most of Virginia's fighting men were outside her borders serving with the Continental Army. In such circumstances, no one could have been a successful Governor.

Charges that Jefferson was a cowardly leader because, after expiration of his tenure, he vacated Monticello while Tarleton's British troops were about to ride up the mountain to capture him are too absurd to discuss except for the fact that the matter was raised repeatedly by political opponents. Was the former Chief Executive supposed to barricade himself behind a sofa in the foyer and, with a brace of pistols, several muskets, and a few servants, repel 180 dragoons and 70 mounted infantry? A more valid criticism would be that he lingered too long over breakfast and the packing of his papers after being warned of the danger.

The most remarkable thing about Jefferson's services as wartime Governor was that in that time of crisis, while attending to the minutiae of administration and rising before dawn in the rain-swept darkness to direct emergency preparations and evacuations at ill-defended river landings, he found time to write *Notes on Virginia*, one of the most important books in early American history in terms both of its quality and its influence.

Of the two most significant results of his gubernatorial service, one was negative and one positive. The negative one was the legislature's adoption, when he left office, of a resolution "that at the next session of the Assembly an inquiry be made into the conduct of the Executive of this State for the last twelve months." The investigation culminated in a unanimous resolution that "the Assembly wish . . . in the strongest manner to declare the high opinion which they entertain of Mr. Jefferson's ability, rectitude and integrity, as Chief Magistrate of this Commonwealth, and mean by thus publicly avowing their opinion, to obviate all future, and to remove all former, unmerited censure." Despite the handsome exoneration, Jefferson remained peculiarly sensitive all his life to criticisms of his conduct in office, especially if they came from his home state. The most positive result of his gubernatorial experience was that he had learned the dire effects of executive weakness. A strict constructionist, he had assumed no powers not clearly conferred upon him by the Constitution. Given the circumstances of his service, he could not have had a successful administration, but there had been some occasions when a bolder executive, willing to assume authority not specifically assigned to him, might have been more effective. In any event, the frustrations of Jefferson's tenure as Governor seemed to have convinced him of the importance of creative initiative, and even audacity, in executive leadership.

Jefferson returned to public office after a hiatus in which he suffered the loss of his wife. He was a Congressman again. As chairman of a committee to prepare a plan for temporary government of the Western lands, he drafted the Ordinance of 1784, a document of historic importance. The first territorial ordinance of the United States, it embodied a concept that he had voiced even before the Declaration of Independence: that the states should not subject the Western lands to the same colonial status they themselves had fought to escape. New states organized in the Western territory would be equal partners of those on the Atlantic Seaboard. Adding to the high importance of this document was Jefferson's inclusion of a provision that slavery should not exist in the territories, a proviso retained in the Northwest Ordinance of 1787. This was strong insurance that the states formed from the territory would never know slavery.

The same year that Jefferson produced the Ordinance of 1784 he was appointed by the Congress as a special envoy to Europe to help John Adams and Benjamin Franklin negotiate commercial treaties. His success in this role led to his appointment as United States Minister to France. In this position he followed Benjamin Franklin, whose intellect had captured the admiration of the salons and whose personality had aroused such general enthusiasm that copies of his fur cap were sold as "Franklin hats" in chic Paris shops.

Despite the fact that he had to follow such a man, Jefferson soon became one of the most respected figures in the French capital. His diverse learning drew admiration as he talked knowledgeably with scientists and philosophes about their particular specialties. Also, as a veteran of the American struggle for freedom, he was consulted by Frenchmen eager to expand constitutional liberties in their own country. He became, as any good ambassador should be, a conduit of information between two nations. But he was far more. He was a remarkably keen observer and analyst of what was happening in France, and what was happening in France would shake Europe. Through diplomatic contacts with the monarchy and personal friendship with such of its critics as Lafayette and La Rochefoucauld he knew some secrets of the citadel of royalty and many of the Patriot Party. In 1865 the celebrated French historian Hippolyte-Adolphe Taine, writing from the perspective of three-quarters of a century, said that when Jefferson was in Paris he had evidenced more understanding of what was happening in France than any one of the twelve hundred members of the National Assembly.

Jefferson helped Lafayette compose a French Declaration of Rights based chiefly on George Mason's Virginia Bill of Rights, wisely suggesting that the Marquis delete from his list of man's inalienable rights "property" and "the care of his honor." The Declaration of Rights, as adopted by the French National Assembly, bore the marks of the American experience as transmitted through Jefferson. He wrote Madison: "Our proceedings have been viewed as a model for them on every occasion; and though in the heat of debate men are generally disposed to contradict every authority urged by their opponents, ours has been treated like that of the Bible, open to explanation but not to question." When a quarrel between the two factions of the Patriot Party, the constitutional royalists and the republicans, threatened it with dissolution, Lafayette prevailed upon Jefferson to be host to representatives of the two groups and a compromise was reached. When Jefferson, fearful that he had overstepped the bounds of diplomatic propriety, confessed his possible indiscretion to the French Foreign Minister, that official said: "I already knew everything which had passed. I earnestly wish you would habitually assist at such conferences."

Jefferson's service in Washington's cabinet as first Secretary of State of the United States set a high benchmark for all his successors. He is generally ranked with John Quincy Adams and William Seward as one of the three greatest occupants of that position. All of his steadfastness and adroitness were called for when, with Britain and France at war, French Minister Edmond Charles Genêt used all his wiles and rabble-rousing talents to bring the United States to his government's side as a co-belligerent. He had to thwart all the Frenchman's incendiary schemes without alienating an old ally, now the only other republic in the world. And he also had to steer a neutral course in relations with Great Britain. If the United States, still in its infancy, did become a partner in the war between empires, such involvement might well be fatal to its free institutions.

John Quincy Adams, writing many years later, after he himself had been Secretary of State, said that Jefferson had "triumphantly sustained and vindicated the Administration of Washington without forfeiting the friendly professions of France." He also wrote of the handling of the Genêt crisis, "Mr. Jefferson's papers on that controversy present the most perfect model of diplomatic discussion and expostulation of modern times."[17] Nor has Jefferson had only the chauvinist praise of a fellow American. George Canning, one of Britain's most brilliant Foreign Secretaries, told the House of Commons in 1823: "If I wished for a guide in a system of neutrality, I should take that laid down by America in the days of the Presidency of Washington and the Secretaryship of Jefferson."[18]

Jefferson's position in Washington's cabinet brought him into frequent conflict with Secretary of the Treasury Alexander Hamilton. Adherents of Hamilton's philosophy of a strong centralized government, with emphasis on aid to industry, commerce, and finance, came to be called Federalists. Those who supported Jefferson's concept of states' rights, exalted agriculture, and distrusted the making of money "by shuffling papers" came to be known as Republicans or Democratic-Republicans. The lines were not drawn as unalterably by the two leaders as by many of their supporters. Far from being completely a strict constructionist, Jefferson early in his national career subscribed to a limited doctrine of implied powers.[19]

In his next office, Vice President of the United States, Jefferson was inactive. Probably his chief influence in that position was to increase its insignificance. John Adams, as the first Vice President of the United States, had worried the Senate so much about devising a sufficiently exalted form of address for him that one exasperated member had proposed "His Rotundity." Jefferson, by contrast, had to be persuaded to travel to Washington for his own swearing in. But, however negligent of the office, he was active in politics. He kept hammering away at the Alien and Sedition Acts and other Federalist measures that he saw as threats to civil liberties. Opponents of the Adams administration looked to him for leadership.

And his leadership became a powerful force for change in 1801 when he became President of the United States. But he waged no vendetta against the defeated Federalists. The conciliatory tone of his first inaugural address is exemplified in its most famous passage: "We have called by different names brethren of the same principle. We are all republicans, we are all federalists. If there be any among us who would wish to dissolve this Union or to change its republican form, let them stand undisturbed as monuments of the safety with which error of opinion may be tolerated where reason is left free to combat it." He also quieted fears of revolutionary change, saying on another occasion, "No more good must be attempted than this nation can bear."

Nevertheless, he did dramatize the break with the previous administration. The pomp of Washington's two inaugurations and perhaps even of Adams' oath-taking had answered a public need for ceremonies suggesting continuity and stability, but Jefferson believed that the time had arrived for republican simplicity. His walk to the scene of his own swearing in provided the perfect image to define the quality of change. He also used effective rhetoric to convey the inspiration of his concept of America as "the world's best hope" and as a place of fresh beginnings for all humanity.

The events of Jefferson's two administrations are narrated in detail in the first ten chapters of this volume and analyzed in the eleventh, so there is no need for another detailed discussion. But it is appropriate to evaluate briefly some of the principal features of his presidency.

One of the great secrets of his success as Chief Executive is that he assembled one of the most effective cabinets in American history. The two principal department heads—Secretary of State Madison and Secretary of the Treasury Gallatin—were geniuses who combined a vast store of theoretical knowledge and considerable acquaintance with the workings of practical politics. Furthermore, they were friends with whom the President felt quite comfortable. Jefferson's own gifts were so extraordinary that he had no need to protect his ego by surrounding himself with mediocrity. Other members of the cabinet were less able, but the cabinet as a whole worked in remarkable harmony with the Chief Executive throughout his first term. All but one were supportive throughout his second. But even the two principals, consistently loyal as they were in public, were never mere "yes men" behind the closed doors of the conference room. The effectiveness of the cabinet was due as much to Jefferson's facility for tact as to his wisdom in selecting co-workers.

As we have seen, Jefferson in his first year as President dealt with or adumbrated every major problem of his two administrations. Thus that first year foreshadowed the achievements of the following seven. It was then he prepared for negotiations with Napoleon over Louisiana and for the Lewis and Clark expedition. It was then, too, that he sent forces to Tripoli to fight Barbary blackmail and terrorism. In the same period he began working toward repeal of the Judiciary Act and initiated significant economies in the operation of the federal government.

All of these accomplishments are important, but two of them—the acquisition of the Louisiana Territory and the Lewis and Clark expedition—are of great international significance. The Louisiana Purchase doubled the size of the United States and gave it control of the Mississippi. The Lewis and Clark expedition, besides its immediate and potential practical significance, helped to extend the frontiers of the human mind. These two achievements, taken with Jefferson's outline of the path from territory to statehood in the Ordinance of 1784, are part and parcel of his active appreciation of the significance of the American West. In this he was far ahead of all other American statesmen of his time.

Some have sought to diminish the magnitude of Jefferson's success in acquiring the Louisiana Territory by saying that he had a lot of luck and that even he did not know at the outset of negotiations that his opportunity would be so great. Herbert Bayard Swope once attributed all his success to luck, adding, "and I found that the harder I worked, the luckier I became." Jefferson's years of "homework" on Louisiana, combined with his formidable knowledge of international relations, enabled him to grasp the significance of the chance at hand. That he had the flexibility and the daring to take full advantage of the unexpected magnitude of the opportunity suddenly presented is impressive evidence of the remarkable quality of his leadership.

Despite frequent statements to the contrary, the boldness with which he seized that opportunity was in no way contradictory to the constitutional philosophy he had expressed on previous occasions. We have seen in this volume, and in *Thomas Jefferson: A Strange Case of Mistaken Identity*, that Jefferson had advocated the doctrine of implicit powers about as long as Hamilton had. He had simply called for more safeguards and had maintained that functions that could be effectively performed by state and local governments should be left to them. When Jefferson acted so decisively to acquire Louisiana he risked his own political future, but he did not place at risk the Constitution of the United States. He said in the case of Louisiana that, although he must act before explicit authorization, he must submit his actions to the Congress for confirmation or rejection.

As with virtually all two-term Presidents of the United States, Jefferson's second term was less successful than his first. But it was far from barren of accomplishment. The usual loss of the impetus of newness and the disadvantage of lame duck status as any President enters his second administration were complicated in Jefferson's case by protracted international stress. Steering a precarious path of peace between two mighty belligerents, he bought time to prepare for combat if war should prove inevitable. This policy might have made little sense if—as has been charged by some critics—Jefferson had not used the time to strengthen national defenses. The record traced in this volume shows that, while Jefferson did not augment the nation's military and naval strength as rapidly as the emergency warranted, he did carry the Congress as fast and as far as it would consent to go. Only his skilled and persistent maneuvering made that much possible. Particularly commendable was his leadership in the *Chesapeake* crisis, when his calm firmness avoided both war and meek surrender.

The most unpopular policy of Jefferson's presidency was his sponsorship of the Embargo Act. Enthusiastically supported by Congress when first initiated, it eventually became self-defeating as it eroded the national economy. Hated as it was by New England shippers and by other maritime interests along the Atlantic Coast, it nevertheless inspired little opposition in most of the South and was strongly supported to the last in some other areas. It did provide a significant stimulus to native manufactures in Pennsylvania and other mid-Atlantic states, and even in parts of Connecticut, and thus increased American self-sufficiency when war threatened.

The accomplishments of Jefferson's second term, with the exception of completion of the Lewis and Clark expedition, do not lend themselves to easy dramatization. As Samuel Eliot Morison wisely observed, "We may take inspiration from one who deliberately preferred the slow process of reason to the short way of force. By his forbearance, even more than by his acts, Jefferson kept alive the flame of liberty that Napoleon had almost snuffed out in Europe."[20]

A surprisingly persistent notion is that Jefferson's presidency ended in personal frustration and public repudiation. If we had no other evidence, the many appeals to Jefferson to accept a third term—solicitation from influential individuals and groups—would indicate that the American people were not eager to get rid of him. But there is far more substantial evidence. Madison was Jefferson's handpicked successor. He had been Jefferson's Secretary of State and chief lieutenant. He was intimately associated with every major policy of Jefferson's two administrations. That Madison would continue most of Jefferson's policies was the principal argument of his advocates. It was also the principal argument of his opponents. In the presidential election of 1808 Madison won more than twice as many votes as both of his opponents combined.

Who was Thomas Jefferson? Haven't we really exaggerated the extent to which he is unknowable? The process began when his enemy Alexander Hamilton described him as "paradoxical." It received a scholarly imprimatur in 1891 when Henry Adams wrote: "Almost every other American statesman might be described in a parenthesis. A few broad strokes of the brush would paint the portraits of all the early Presidents with this exception, . . . but Jefferson could be painted only touch by touch, with a fine pencil, and the perfection of the likeness depended upon the shifting and uncertain flicker of its semi-transparent shadows." Of course, we all have trouble in understanding each other and sometimes even in understanding ourselves. And, like most complex people of subtle minds, Jefferson defies simplistic analysis. Like Lincoln and Franklin D. Roosevelt, he compounds confusion by a friendly loquacity that actually reveals few intimate details. But his correspondence, all written by his own hand, is one of the most voluminous in American history. Studied from his letters as a teenager to his writings in his eighty-third year, it is cumulatively informative. Few historical personages from any society have left so complete a daily record of their thoughts and actions over so long a period. Of those few, fewer still have possessed the knowledge and verbal skill to express their thoughts and describe their actions so precisely.

Admittedly Jefferson, because of the immense range of his interests and zealous guardianship of his privacy, is not the most easily understood of public figures. But we have a great deal of information on him from a number of sources, friendly and unfriendly. And what we have directly from him antedates the complex machinery of professional image-making which today distorts the reality of public figures. As challenging a subject as Jefferson is, it is not as hard to assemble some reliable perceptions of him as of major politicians in our own time. Granted, any scholar who thinks that he knows him fully is indulging in self-deception. But, although a multiplicity of intellectual interests is necessary to follow Jefferson's mental adventures, the personality of the third President, while certainly challenging enough, is no more baffling than that of James Madison, John Quincy Adams, Abraham Lincoln, or Franklin Roosevelt.

Understanding Jefferson, though not easy, is made easier by the fact that his private and public images were essentially the same. The public image under consideration is not one distorted by hero worshipers or obsessed enemies or sensation mongers, but the Jefferson revealed by his public words and actions.

Relevant to evaluation of the public man and private man that we know as Thomas Jefferson is a comment by another scholarly, fluent Virginia native who also became President of the United States—and who, incidentally, was an alumnus of Mr. Jefferson's university. At a Jefferson Day banquet in New York City in 1912, Woodrow Wilson said: "Jefferson's principles are sources of light because they are not made up of pure reason, but spring out of aspiration, impulse, vision, sympathy. They burn with the fervor of the heart. . . ."[21]

Wilson, as both a professional historian and a statesman occupying the same high office that Jefferson had held, was able to view his predecessor from a rare vantage. At the time that he made this memorable statement about Jefferson, Wilson was on the threshold of his nomination as President. There is no indication that his eight years in the White House in any way altered the estimate he then expressed. Indeed, his subsequent references to his fellow Virginian indicate that they tended to confirm it. As a scholarly master of logic who often burned with passion behind what he himself called his "Presbyterian face," Wilson felt empathy for the man of fire behind the Enlightenment facade of cool reason.

Jefferson's temperament was that of a passionate artist. Let no one be misled by the fact that he frequently invoked his generation's watchword, *reason*, or that he habitually expressed his thoughts and emotions in the measured phrases and balanced sentences of eighteenth-century literature. He was no more the disciplined slave of reason than an eighteenth-century composer whose emotions tumbled in torrents through the symmetrical sluices of antiphony or an English Renaissance poet whose "muse of fire" burned its way through the ordered framework of a sonnet like flames racing along a gridiron of urban streets.

Jefferson had superior reasoning powers. He used them to organize large bodies of information and to marshal powerful arguments. Few Americans of his time were more adept in the use of classical logic. He was a reasonable man in the sense of one who usually was prepared to reach a sensible accommodation if it did not violate principle and who was not inclined to waste time and energy railing against the inevitable. But he was not obsessed with the pursuit of reason to the exclusion of emotion in making major decisions, personal or public. Sometimes he followed Reason with deadly seriousness in the hope that it would lead him down one path to the truth. But, like many brilliant people, he often enjoyed playing games with his mind. Sometimes he pursued Reason as some of his fellow Virginians pursued the fox, not out of any desire to capture it, least of all to possess it, but for the sheer joy of the chase. Often in a moment of passion Jefferson's initial response to a public issue was florid, hyperbolic, and indiscreet. But, except for a few embarrassing instances, only relatives and trusted friends were privy to these eruptions. As the quieter Madison once explained to Nicholas Trist, there was a tendency in Jefferson, "as in others of great genius, of expressing in strong and round terms, impressions of the moment."[22]

Of course, Jefferson often presented himself in the role of Man of Reason. In the days of his early public career, virtually every self-respecting intellectual on each side of the Atlantic did. They were all sons of the Enlightenment. In the latter part of his career, Romanticism had chased reason into hiding in many parts of Europe, but Old World fashions arrived late in the New World, and America's intellectual societies still were colonies of the European Enlightenment.

There is no reason to doubt the sincerity of Jefferson's belief in his own rationalism. But gifted artists are notoriously blind in categorizing themselves. Among extreme examples is Lord Byron, one of the most conspicuous figures of the Romantic movement, who believed himself a pillar of the Age of Reason's Enlightenment. After all, one does not give allegiance to a school of thought as to a political party and demonstrate loyalty by voting for its official candidates.

Jefferson was a complete, fully rounded person, fully developed both intellectually and emotionally, and both head and heart were influential in his decisions. In some instances he thought that the heart should be dominant. A case in point is his famous "Dialogue of Head and Heart," which constitutes the chief portion of a celebrated love letter to Maria Cosway. Such dialogues were a common literary convention of the time. The arguments used by Head and Heart are both so strong that for a long time the reader is hard pressed to discover which agent has the author's sympathy. Indeed, some historians, after studying the work, have concluded that the Head won the debate and thereby proved Jefferson's conviction that Reason should always dominate. They are determined to fit his philosophy, however mangling the process, to the procrustean bed of his presumably complete surrender to enthroned Reason. They choose to overlook the passage where the Heart says to the Head:

If our country, when pressed with wrongs at the point of the bayonet, had been governed by its heads instead of its hearts, where should we have been now? Hanging on a gallows as high as Haman's. You began to calculate, and to compare wealth and numbers; we threw up a few pulsations of our blood; we supplied enthusiasm against wealth and numbers; we put our existence to the hazard, when the hazard seemed against us, and we saved our country: justifying, at the same time, the ways of Providence, whose precept is, to do always what is right, and leave the issue to Him.[23]

The Heart ascribed to its own influence the movement for American independence, and the Head did not dispute the claim. If Jefferson had believed that the Heart should always be subservient to the Head, would he have offered the declaring and winning of American independence as an example of an action due to the promptings of the Heart rather than the dictates of the Head? Did he believe that American independence was the result of inferior motivation? It is inconceivable that this was the view of the man who asked that his authorship of the Declaration of Independence be inscribed on his tombstone as one of the three principal things for which he wished to be remembered.

Jefferson was avid in the pursuit of truth, and he did not neglect any access to knowledge—sensory, rational, or emotional. He argued that historical examples, in order to improve conduct, must "excite . . . sympathetic emotion." He wrote that great fiction and drama often could be more effective guides to right actions than histories and essays on ethics because the first two more often engaged the imagination and the emotions. He said, "Every emotion of this kind is an exercise of our virtuous dispositions; and dispositions of the mind, like limbs of the body, acquire strength by exercise."

He also believed in an emotional measure of the success of public actions. He subscribed to Francis Hutcheson's belief: "That action is best which accomplishes the greatest happiness for the greatest numbers." And he accepted the statement of Henry Home, Lord Kames: "There is a principle of benevolence in man which prompts him to an equal pursuit of the happiness of all." He agreed with Thomas Reid that, while reason provided the better access to some moral truths, inborn feeling was the superior way to others. Reid asserted: "Moral truths, therefore, may be divided into two classes, to wit: such as are self-evident to every man whose understanding and moral faculty are ripe, and such as are deduced by reasoning from those that are self-evident." This belief made even reason ultimately dependent on inspiration. The advocates of these views were leaders of the Scottish Enlightenment, but their epistemology owed as much to the inspiration exalted by Romanticists as to the reason enthroned by the philosophes.

Emotion entered into many of Jefferson's decisions, sometimes for good, sometimes for ill. Emotion led him to condone violations of civil liberties in General Wilkinson's activities, to speak out unwisely during the trial of Aaron Burr, and to seek an unfortunate public solution to his friend John Page's problems. Sentiment, rather than reason, caused him to build Monticello on a mountain whose poor soil was never capable of supporting him as a plantation should. But sentiment also told him that certain satisfactions made it worth the cost. Emotion brought him into the tangled frustrations of his relationship with Maria Cosway and led him to a satisfying renewal of his old friendship with John Adams. Emotion gave him empathetic understanding of many with whom he worked but also caused him to idealize beyond reality the young students who later rioted at his university. His passion for his country and for liberty infused him with a power, almost always beneficially used, that could not have been generated by the conviction of reason alone.

Jefferson believed that a reliable "moral sense" was implanted in every human being of normal capacity. He believed that was why the jury system generally produced just decisions, even when the jurors were ignorant, if technical knowledge was not essential to an understanding of the case. He personally used reason more than most people and prized it as a God-given agency for the amelioration of human suffering, but, except perhaps as a youthful student, he never believed it could provide all the answers in any matter of human needs and aspirations.

So it is impossible to pigeonhole Jefferson as either a Rationalist or a Romanticist, just as we discovered in *Thomas Jefferson: A Strange Case of Mistaken Identity* that it was impossible to classify him as either liberal or conservative. Even disregarding the shifting meaning of the terms, even within a single lifetime, it still is impossible with any accuracy to pin either label on him. As an almost consistent advocate of individual liberty, he appears liberal. In subscribing to Edmund Burke's opinion that society is a compact among the past, the present, and the future, he was conservative. He was not willing to be consistently wrong to be consistent.

Jefferson, it is frequently said, was paradoxical and therefore complex. This cause and effect explanation has the appeal of simplicity, but perhaps it is too simple. If Jefferson was complex because he was paradoxical, might it not be equally true that he was paradoxical because he was complex? Is there a principle in human personality analogous to Kurt Gödel's Incompleteness Theorem in mathematics with its argument that any formal system must be either incomplete or inconsistent? Of course, finitude is the fate of all human minds. But are those that, in range and sensitivity, approach nearest to completeness (though admittedly light-years from its achievement) inevitably more than ordinarily paradoxical?

Jefferson's sense of place and devotion to his native state were so strong that particular emphasis must be given to his geographical and social background. While he was not typical of the society that produced him, he was representative of it. It was a society that taught that superior advantages of birth, wealth, or talent conferred an obligation of public service. Also, while it had its liars and cheats, it valued integrity more than most societies have. And its ruling class emphasized the importance of knowledge as a prelude to action.

John Dewey has said that "Jefferson was fortunate in his birth and early surroundings, being a product of both the aristocracy of the time and of the pioneer frontier."[24] The circumstances of heredity and environment were calculated to make an intellectually awake person look backward to the heritage of the Old World and forward to the broadening opportunities of the New. Together with his education at the College of William and Mary and later associations with American patriots and European scholars, they tended to develop in him the tension between the pull of the familiar and the lure of adventure which is the principal source of vitality in a society. Jefferson found excitement in the experimental nature of the new republic but preferred for the architectural form of the Capitol "some one of the models of antiquity, which have had the approbation of thousands of years."

Most of Jefferson's paradoxes are not weaknesses but strengths. That is true not only of his idea of drawing nutriment from the past to grow toward the future. It is also true of his being, simultaneously, intensely concerned with his family, his neighborhood, his state, his nation, and the whole civilized world. Ideal citizenship is a matter of concerned loyalty to concentric circles. No President of the United States was ever more devoted to the minutiae of affairs in his own locality and his own state but also none was ever more in tune with all the main currents of the world's thoughts. It is true, too, of his varied responses, some labeled liberal and some conservative, to a lifetime of challenges. These differences result primarily from two things: evolution of his views through experience (as in his altered attitudes toward commerce and industry) and the fact that he was not an ideologue.

Who, then, was Jefferson?

He was, of course, a many-sided genius with a voracious appetite for all knowledge. It is easy to picture his sympathizing with King Alfred's statement that the worst thing of all is not to know. Jefferson took no pleasure in any of the blood sports so popular in his day and appears to have had no interest in any sort of athletic contest, but fields of knowledge were the playing fields of his vigorous intellect. He was a zestful fighter in a lifelong battle with the forces of ignorance.

Though he raged against Benedict Arnold and Aaron Burr, he was almost always good-tempered and courteous. To the world at large he was benevolent, and with family and friends he was loving. He was thoughtful and considerate of almost everyone, delighting loved ones with carefully chosen gifts and individually appropriate remembrances. Contrary to an impression fostered by one of his biographers and followed by nearly all others since, he had a sense of humor that defused exasperations and facilitated social relations. The image of a humorless Jefferson dissolves in the genial warmth of shared amusement exuded by many of his letters. It cannot stand up to his delight in funny passages of *Don Quixote* or his repeated readings of *Tristram Shandy*, which he so frequently took with him in his travels. Then there is the picture of President Jefferson unable to hide his amusement as his daughter Martha scolded little Jeff Randolph for commandeering the presidential coach for an impromptu visit to the Washington Navy Yard. The boy remembered that, while his mother had been upset, his grandfather had thought the juvenile expedition was a great joke. There is Congressman Samuel Mitchill, perhaps a little surprised, reporting after a dinner at the Executive Mansion that the intellectual President could "both enjoy and relate humorous stories as well as any other man." Mitchill had been taken in by a shaggy dog story which Jefferson had narrated with great gravity before arriving at the ridiculous punch line.

Jefferson could enjoy humor even when he was the target. Once Martha, highly indignant, brought him a satire by Thomas Moore of which he was the subject. She was startled when, upon reading it, he "broke into a clear, loud laugh which was instantly contagious."[25] Years later he included some lines from Moore in his deathbed note to Martha. There is Jefferson's note about an unidentified book that he sent on May 10, 1813 from Poplar Forest to Mrs. Trist: "I brought the enclosed book to this place the last fall, intending to forward it to you; but having a neighbor here who loves to laugh, I lent it to him to read; he lent it to another, and so it went the rounds of the neighborhood. . . . I was myself amused by its humor as much as its object would permit me to be; for that is evidently to deride the Republican branches of our government."[26] When Jefferson was on his deathbed, a remark by Henry Lee caused him to "smile broadly and then laugh."[27]

Despite the luxury of his own life, he was ever mindful of the suffering of the poor. His farm manager, Captain Bacon, said that when he tried to curb the volume of Jefferson's goods flowing to the needy, the master of Monticello regularly checked the situation and thwarted his efforts. To strangers in no particular need he was often generous to a fault. Even after his fame drew hordes of tourists to Monticello, he adhered to the rule of Virginia hospitality that forbade turning a visitor from one's door. Hordes of the admiring and the merely curious destroyed the privacy of his home and devoured his substance when he was heavily in debt.

The matter of debt raises another point. Whatever the state of his finances, he could not resist buying books, art, and furniture, and adding to the beauty of his handsome home. Though ironically pictured as a hedonist and libertine by his enemies, he appears to have been more conservative in his behavior with women than most of his male contemporaries. And there is ample evidence that this restraint was not for lack of passionate interest. Out of conviction he eschewed tobacco, followed a sensible diet, and drank only moderately. He could make himself labor at correspondence hour after hour, day after day, even when he had come to regard the work as a form of slavery. Yet he could not restrain himself in spending for excellence. And though he seems to have been almost always considerate of his servants, even refusing to have them sit up with him in his last illness, he was almost totally dependent on personal service. Though no sybarite, he pictured the simple life as lived in a small house with a loving mate, a table, a few chairs, "and one or two servants."

Perhaps the discipline and the zeal were both responsible for his remarkable perseverance. Two impressive examples spring to mind. He argued for standing up to the Barbary pirates when he was a diplomat in Europe and when he was Secretary of State, but could convince neither the great states of Europe nor President Washington. But when he became President he carried out the plan to deal with them he had formulated and never abandoned. As a young legislator, he formulated a plan for a great state university. Through the decades he kept adding to that plan and refining it, always watching for an opportunity to translate it into reality. At last as an octogenarian he conceives the opportunity to convert a provincial secondary academy into the university of his dreams. In the end, though aged and ill, he performs the work of five strong men, five specialists. As he labors to build his university, you can see Death as his implacable antagonist, like the hooded figure in a Medieval morality play or an Ingmar Bergman film. But the old man builds his university.

In this and other efforts he is sustained by a strong faith. He believes in a benevolent God and the moral supremacy of Jesus (though he is not a Trinitarian), and the promise of an afterlife. His religious views are too orthodox for many of his philosophical friends but too liberal for many of his neighbors. No matter. His faith satisfies him. For the most part, he keeps quiet about it but lives by it.

He passionately follows another faith as well. He is a lifelong apostle of liberty.

What lessons may we learn from his example? In personal life, the benefits in accomplishment and in peace of mind to be derived from "taking things by the smooth handle." The reminder that courtesy is not subservience. The realization that industry and perseverance can triumph over a multitude of obstacles. The lesson that time and energy are saved by laying hatred aside.

There are important lessons in public life. He passionately believed that knowledge was better than ignorance and that excellence should be a constant goal. Democracies especially need to be reminded of this lesson, partly because their survival depends on an informed electorate and partly because of a tendency to debase the theory of equality into the supposition that, without striving, we are all noble in our unimproved commonness. Vital, too, is the reminder that, while we should avoid "frequent and untried changes in laws and constitutions, . . . laws and institutions must go hand in hand with the progress of the human mind."

Who was Thomas Jefferson? We should rephrase the question. Who *is* Thomas Jefferson? He is alive to more people today than ever before. Thomas Jefferson, the strange case of mistaken identity, the paradoxical patriot, as definitively American as ever, is also a light to the world. The passionate pilgrim in search of truth and liberty speaks now to men and women in every inhabited continent. In the decade of the nineties, as the world moves toward the twenty-first century, he is the most quoted political leader on this planet.

NOTES

Punctuation and spelling of some quotations from Jefferson and his contemporaries to which notes refer were modified to aid the reader.

"LC" stands for the Library of Congress.

"Arch. Aff. étr." stands for the Archives of the Ministère
des Affaires étrangères, Paris.

CHAPTER I   THE GREAT EXPERIMENT

1. Charles R. King, ed., *The Life and Correspondence of Rufus King*, Vol. 3 (New York, 1971), 461.
2. T. J. to Dr. Joseph Priestley, March 21, 1801; Paul Leicester Ford, ed., *The Writings of Thomas Jefferson*, Vol. 8 (New York, 1892), 22.

CHAPTER II   A REASONABLE REVOLUTIONIST

1. Robert Troup to Rufus King, March 21, 1801; Charles R. King, ed., *The Life and Correspondence of Rufus King*, Vol. 3 (New York: 1971), 454.

2. T. J. to Judge Spencer Roane, September 6, 1819; Paul Leicester Ford, ed., *The Writings of Thomas Jefferson*, Vol. 10 (New York, 1892), 140.

3. T. J. to Dr. Walter Jones, March 31, 1801 (Jefferson Papers, LC microfilm Series I, Doc. 19108, Reel 23).

4. Ibid.

5. T. J. to Thomas Mann Randolph, June 4, 1801 (ibid., Doc. 19390, Reel 23).

6. T. J. to Meriwether Lewis, February 23, 1801 (ibid., Doc. 18766, Reel 22).

7. T. J. to P. G. Muhlenberg, January 31, 1781; Julian P. Boyd, ed., *The Papers of Thomas Jefferson*, Vol. 4 (Princeton, 1950–1982), 487.

8. T. J. to James Monroe, May 29, 1801 (Jefferson Papers, LC microfilm Series I, Doc. 19355, Reel 23).

9. Madison to Charles Pinckney, June 9, 1801; James Madison, *The Papers of James Madison*, Robert A. Rutland and Thomas A. Mason, eds., Vol. 1 (Charlottesville, Va., 1984), 273–279.

10. Secretary of State Madison to William Eaton, May 20, 1801; James Madison, *The Papers of James Madison: Secretary of State Series*, Robert J. Brugger, ed., Vol. 1 (Charlottesville, Va., 1986), 199–201.

11. Hamilton assumed the name of Lucius Crassus (December 17, 1801, issue); *The Works of Alexander Hamilton*, John C. Hamilton, ed., Vol. 8 (New York, 1851), 745–748.

12. Of course the President's House was not yet known as the White House.

13. T. J. to Governor Joseph Bloomfield of New Jersey, December 5, 1801 (Jefferson Papers, LC microfilm Series I, Doc. 20360, Reel 25).

14. T. J. to Elias Shipman and others, July 12, 1801 (ibid., Doc. 19624, Reel 24).

CHAPTER III   THE BATTLE IS JOINED

1. John Taylor to John Breckinridge, December 22, 1801; Albert J. Beveridge, *The Life of John Marshall*, Vol. 3 (New York, 1919), 610.

2. Nathan Schachner, *Thomas Jefferson, A Biography* (New York, 1951), 702.

3. T. J. to John Wayles Eppes, January 22, 1802; ibid., 703.

4. Gouverneur Morris to Robert Livingston, August 21, 1802; Anne Cary Morris, ed., *The Diary and Letters of Gouverneur Morris*, Vol. 2 (New York, 1970), 426.

5. T. J. to Thomas Mann Randolph, February 21, 1802 (Jefferson Papers, LC microfilm Series I, Doc. 20836, Reel 25).

6. T. J. to James Monroe, June 2, 1802 (ibid., Doc. 21290, Reel 26).

7. T. J. to Rufus King, July 13, 1802 (ibid., Doc. 21460, Reel 26).

8. T. J. to J. W. Eppes, January 1, 1802; Schachner, 705.

9. T. J. to Charles Willson Peale, January 16, 1802 (Jefferson Papers, LC microfilm, Series I, Doc. 20680, Reel 25).

10. Account Book.

11. T. J. to Maria Eppes, March 3, 1802 (Jefferson Papers, LC microfilm Series I, Doc. 20875, Reel 25).

12. Martha J. Randolph to T. J., April 25, 1790; Edwin M. Betts and James A. Bear, Jr., eds., *The Family Letters of Thomas Jefferson* (Charlottesville, Va., 1986), 52–53.

13. The peculiarly apt phrase is borrowed from William Manchester's description of Douglas MacArthur's love for his son, *American Caesar* (New York, 1978), 702.

14. T. J. to Thomas Mann Randolph, March 12 and 28, 1802 (Jefferson Papers, LC microfilm Series I, Doc. 20905, Reel 25).

15. Donald Jackson doubts that Lewis was appointed Jefferson's secretary to become a trainee for a Western expedition. Donald Jackson, *Thomas Jefferson and the Stony Mountains* (Urbana, Ill., 1981), 117.

16. T. J. to Messrs. Nehemiah Dodge, Ephraim Robbins, Stephen S. Nelson of The Danbury Baptist Association in the state of Connecticut (Jefferson Papers, LC microfilm, Series I, Doc. 20594, Reel 25). Note misquotation in generally highly reliable Library of America, *Thomas Jefferson: Writings* (New York, 1984), 516, substituting "legislative" for "legitimate."

17. Julian P. Boyd, ed., *The Papers of Thomas Jefferson, 1760–1776*, Vol. 1 (Princeton, 1950), 3.

18. Samuel Latham Mitchill, "Dr. Mitchill's Letters from Washington," *Harper's New Monthly Magazine*, Vol. 5, No. 58 (April 1879), 743–744.

CHAPTER IV   LONELY LABOR AND PUBLIC SCANDAL

1. T. J. to Benjamin Rush, December 20, 1801 (Jefferson Papers, LC microfilm Series I, Doc. 20496, Reel 25).

2. T. J. to Benjamin Rush, February 28, 1803; Paul Leicester Ford, ed., *The Writings of Thomas Jefferson* Vol. 8 (New York, 1892), 220–221.

3. Rush to T. J., March 12 and May 5, 1803; Malone, Vol. 4, 185–186. The meticulous and usually correct Malone mistakenly says that T. J. first experienced diarrhea after becoming President; Dumas Malone, *Jefferson and His Time: Jefferson the President, First Term, 1801–1805*, Vol.4 (Boston, 1970), 186. For information on early attack see Thomas Jefferson Randolph, ed., *Memoir, Correspondence and Miscellaneous from the Papers of Thomas Jefferson*, Vol. 1 (Charlottesville, Va., 1829), 7; and Alf J. Mapp, Jr., *Thomas Jefferson: A Strange Case of Mistaken Identity* (Lanham, Md., and New York, 1987), 79.

4. T. J. to John D. Banks, June 21,1801 (Jefferson Papers, LC microfilm Series I, Doc. 19501, Reel 23).

5. Waterhouse to T. J., October 1, 1801 (ibid., Doc. 20093, Reel 24). Waterhouse to T. J., March 1, 1803 and T. J. to Waterhouse, March 21, 1803; Malone, Vol. 4, 185.

6. T. J. to Constantine de Chasseboeuf, Comte de Volney, May 20, 1802 (Jefferson Papers, LC microfilm Series I, Docs. 21086–88, Reel 26).

7. Thornton to Grenville, Malone, Vol. 4, 96.

8. Joseph Hale to Rufus King, April 13, 1802; Charles Rufus King, ed., *The Life and Correspondence of Rufus King*, Vol. 4 (New York, 1971), 107.

9. W. C. Nicholas to T. J., October 30, 1801 (Jefferson Papers, LC microfilm Series I, Doc. 21914, Reel 24).

10. T. J. to Robert R. Livingston, April 18, 1802 (ibid., Docs. 21077–80, Reel 26).

11. Thornton to Hawkesbury, March 6, 1802; Malone, Vol. 4, 254.

12. Pinchon to Talleyrand, July 22, 1801; Malone, Vol. 4, 252.

13. T. J. to Du Pont, April 25, 1802 (Jefferson Papers, LC microfilm Series I, Docs. 21125–26, Reel 26).

14. Du Pont to T. J., April 25, 1802; Malone, Vol. 4, 257.

15. T. J. to Du Pont, May 5, 1802; ibid.

16. T. J. to R. Livingston, May 5, 1802 (Jefferson Papers, LC microfilm Series I, Doc. 21197, Reel 27).

17. Virginius Dabney, *The Jefferson Scandals* (New York, 1981), 34–35.

18. T. J. to Callender, October 6, 1799; Charles A. Jellison, "That Scoundrel Callender," *Virginia Magazine of History*, Vol. 67 (July 1959), 299.

19. Dabney, 8.

20. T. J. to Monroe, May 29, 1801; Ford, Vol. 8, 61.

21. Mapp, 44–45.

22. T. J. to Robert Smith, 1805; Dabney, 10.

23. Ibid., 10–11.

24. Ibid., 12.

25. Ibid., 13.

26. From "The Embargo" (1808).

27. Mapp, 263–264.

28. Dabney, 26–27; John Chester Miller, *The Wolf by the Ears: Thomas Jefferson and Slavery* (New York, 1977), 162–163; James A. Bear, "The Hemings Family of Monticello," *Virginia Cavalcade*, Vol. 29, No. 2 (Autumn 1979), 85.

29. Malone, Vol. 4, 263.

30. Mrs. William Thornton's diary, September 18, 1802; Malone, Vol. 4, 166.

31. Edward Dumbauld, *Thomas Jefferson, American Tourist* (Norman, Okla., 1946), 239.

32. Du Pont to T. J., February 20, 1802; Dumas Malone, ed., *Correspondence Between Thomas Jefferson and Pierre Samuel Du Pont de Nemours, 1798–1817* (Boston, 1930), 41–43.

33. December 13, 1802; Nathan Schachner, *Thomas Jefferson, A Biography* (New York, 1951), 721.

34. Peachy R. Gilmer, quoted in Richard Beale Davis, *Francis Walker Gilmer* (Richmond, Va., 1939), 373.

35. Margaret Bayard Smith, *The First Forty Years of Washington Society* (New York, 1906), 34.

36. Ellen Randolph Coolidge to Henry Randall, January 15, 1856; Henry S. Randall, *The Life of Thomas Jefferson*, Vol. 3 (Philadelphia, 1865), 102.

37. M. B. Smith, 34.

38. Ibid., 35.

39. Abigail Adams to T. J., July 6, 1787; Julian P. Boyd, ed., *The Papers of Thomas Jefferson*, Vol. 9 (Princeton, 1950–1982), 550–552.

40. Malone, Vol. 4, 172.

41. Second annual message, December 15, 1802 (Jefferson Papers, LC microfilm Series I, Docs. 22071–73, Reel 27).

42. Schachner, 722.

43. Philip Alexander Bruce, "John Randolph," in *Library of Southern Literature*, Vol. 10 (Atlanta, 1907), 4329–4336.

44. Francis Coleman Rosenberger, ed., *The Virginia Reader: A Treasury of Writings about Thomas Jefferson* (New York, 1953), 350–351.

45. T. J. to Gallatin, October 13, 1802 (Jefferson Papers, LC microfilm Series I, Doc. 21825, Reel 27).

46. T. J. to Edward Carrington, August 4, 1787; Boyd, *Papers of T. J.*, Vol. 8, 678–679.

CHAPTER V   WONDERFUL YEAR

1. Manasseh Cutler, *Life, Journals, and Correspondence*, W. P. Cutler and J. P. Cutler, eds., Vol. 2 (Cincinnatti, 1888), 113, 116 ff.

2. Maria Eppes to T. J., January 11, 1803; Edwin M. Betts, ed., *The Family Letters of Thomas Jefferson* (Charlottesville, Va., 1986), 240.

3. T. J. to J. P. G. Muhlenberg, January 3, 1781; Julian P. Boyd, ed., *The Papers of Thomas Jefferson*, Vol. 4 (Princeton 1950–1982), 487.

4. Talleyrand to Guillemardet, May 20 to June 19, 1798; Arch. Aff. étr. MSS. Quoted in Henry Adams, *History of the United States of America During the First Administration of Thomas Jefferson*, Vol. 1 (New York, 1917), 355–357.

5. Portion now Haiti.

6. J. Christopher Herold, *The Age of Napoleon* (New York, 1963), 145.

7. Ibid., 301.

8. Adams, Vol. 1, 383.

9. Ibid., 388.

10. Ibid., 391.

11. Ibid., 392.

12. Ibid., 392–393.

13. Dumas Malone, *Jefferson and His Time: Jefferson the President, First Term, 1801–1805*, Vol. 4 (Boston, 1970), 252.

14. Adams, Vol. 1, 383.

15. Malone, Vol. 4, 293.

16. Livingston to Madison, March 18, 1803; Nathan Schachner, *Thomas Jefferson, A Biography* (New York, 1951), 735.

17. Madison to Livingston and Monroe, March 2, 1803. *American State Papers, Foreign Relations*, Vol. 2, 540–544.

18. T. J. to William Stevens Smith, November 13, 1787; Merrill D. Peterson, ed., *Thomas Jefferson: Writings*, The Library of America (New York, 1984), 911.

19. T. J. to John Bacon, April 30, 1803 (Jefferson Papers, LC microfilm Series I, Doc. 22645, Reel 28).

20. T. J. to Dr. Hugh Williamson, May 30, 1803; A. A. Lipscomb and A. E. Bergh, eds., *The Writings of Thomas Jefferson* (Washington, D.C., 1903), 386.

21. Ibid.

22. Schachner, 737.

23. Ibid.

24. Ibid., 738.

25. Ibid.

26. Herold, 195.

27. Shachner, 738.

28. Source is Lucien's account as given in Th. Jung, *Lucien Bonaparte et ses Memoires*, 121–192, and translated by Adams, Vol. 2, 39.

29. C. L. Lokke, "Secret Negotiations to Maintain the Peace of America," *American Historical Review*, Vol. 49 (October 1943), 55–64. Evidence is in documents in the British Museum and the Arch. Aff. étr.

30. Schachner, 739–740.

31. Adams, Vol. 2, 43–44.

32. Ibid., 43.

33. Schachner, 739–740.

34. Adams, Vol. 2, 58.

35. Talleyrand to Beurnonville, June 22, 1803; ibid., 61–62.

36. Livingston to T. J., June 2, 1803 (Jefferson Papers, LC microfilm Series I, Docs. 22792–93, Reel 28).

37. Account Book summary in Henry S. Randall, *The Life of Thomas Jefferson*, Vol. 3 (Philadelphia, 1865), 21–22, for March 4, 1801–March 4, 1802. See Account Book for March 4, 1803.

38. Paul Leicester Ford, ed., *The Writings of Thomas Jefferson*, Vol. 8 (New York, 1892–1899), 241–249.

39. T. J. to Priestley, January 29, 1804; ibid., 295.

40. Wilson C. Nicholas to T. J., September 8, 1803 (Jefferson Papers, LC microfilm Series I, Docs. 23255–56, Reel 29).

41. T. J. to Wison C. Nicholas, September 7, 1803 (ibid., Docs. 23273–74, Reel 29).

42. T. J. to Madison, October 14, 1803; Ford, Vol. 8, 263.

43. Ibid., 269.

44. T. J. to Benjamin Rush, October 14, 1803; Ford, Vol. 8, 265.

45. Breckinridge and Madison letters; Ford, Vol. 10, 5–8.

46. Schachner, 750–751.

47. T. J. to John Page, November 25, 1803 (Jefferson Papers, LC microfilm Series I, Doc. 23570, Reel 29).

48. See Bernard DeVoto, ed., *The Journals of Lewis and Clark* (Boston, 1953), xv-xvi.

49. Ibid., xv.

50. Ibid., xv-xvi.

51. Ibid., xvi.

52. Ibid., xvii.

53. Ibid.

54. Ibid., xxxi-xxxii.

55. Ibid., Appendix I, 481–487.

56. Lester J. Cappon, ed., *The Adams-Jefferson Letters: The Complete Correspondence Between Thomas Jefferson and John and Abigail Adams* (Chapel Hill, N.C., 1959), 307.

57. T. J., *Notes on the State of Virginia*, William Peden, ed. (Chapel Hill, N.C., 1955), 62.

58. Herold, 119–120.

59. DeVoto, xxvi.

60. Ibid., xliii-xliv.

61. Malone, Vol. 4, 152.

62. Margaret L. Coit, *The Growing Years, 1789–1829* (New York, 1963), 148.

63. Ralph T. Whitelaw, *Virginia's Eastern Shore*, Vol. 1 (Richmond, Va., 1951), 40–41.

64. David John Mays, *Edmund Pendleton*, Vol. 1 (Cambridge, Mass., 1952), 168–169.

CHAPTER VI   PRIVATE LOSS AND PUBLIC TRIUMPH

1. T. J. to Thomas McKean, February 27, 1804: Paul Leicester Ford, *The Writings of Thomas Jefferson*, Vol. 8 (New York, 1892–1899), 292–293.

2. "Draft of the Kentucky Resolutions," Merrill D. Peterson, ed., *Thomas Jefferson: Writings*, Library of America (New York, 1984), 450.

3. T. J. to Judge John Tyler, June 28, 1804; Ibid., 1147.

4. T. J. Memoranda, January 2 and 26, 1804; Ford, Vol. 1, 301–304.

5. Adams to Elbridge Gerry, April 6, 1797; John Adams, *Works*, ed., Charles Francis Adams, Vol. 8 (Boston, 1853), 539.

6. Alf J. Mapp, Jr., *Thomas Jefferson: A Strange Case of Mistaken Identity* (Lanham, Md., and New York, 1987), 354.

7. Noble E. Cunningham, Jr., *The Jeffersonian Republicans in Power: Party Operations, 1801–1809* (Chapel Hill, N.C., 1963), 103–108.

8. Nathan Schachner, *Thomas Jefferson, A Biography*, (New York, 1951), 771–772.

9. T. Pickering to G. Cabot, January 29, 1804; Henry Adams, ed., *Documents Relating to New England Federalism* (1905), 338–342.

10. T. Pickering to R. King, March 4, 1804; Henry C. Lodge, ed., *Life and Letters of George Cabot Lodge* (1877), 447–9.

11. T. J. to Maria Eppes, December 26, 1803 (Jefferson Papers, LC microfilm Series I, Doc. 23659, Reel 29).

12. Martha Eppes to T. J.; Edwin M. Betts and James A. Bear, Jr., eds., *The Family Letters of Thomas Jefferson* (Charlottesville, Va., 1986), 252.

13. Maria to J. W. Eppes, February 6, 1804; Dumas Malone, *Jefferson the President: First Term, 1801–1805*, Vol. 4 (Boston, 1970), 411.

14. T. J. to Maria Eppes, January 29, 1804; Betts and Bear, *Family Letters*, 256.

15. Maria Eppes to T. J., February 10, 1804; ibid., 256.

16. T. J. to Martha Randolph, March 8, 1804, ibid., 259.

17. J. W. Eppes to T. J., March 9, 12, 19, 23, 26, 1804; Malone, Vol. 4, 413.

18. T. J. to J. W. Eppes, March 15, 1804. Henry S. Randall, *The Life of Thomas Jefferson*, Vol. 3 (Philadelphia, 1865), 98–99.

19. T. J. to Madison, April 9, 1804 (Jefferson Papers, LC microfilm Series I, Doc. 24131, Reel 30).

20. T. J. to Madison, April 23, 1804; (ibid., Doc. 24212, Reel 30).

21. T. J. to Maria Jefferson, September 20, 1785. Julian P. Boyd, ed., *The Papers of Thomas Jefferson*, Vol. 8 (Princeton, 1950–1982), 532–533.

22. T. J. to John Page, June 25, 1804; A. A. Lipscomb and A. E. Bergh, eds., *The Writings of Thomas Jefferson*, Vol. 11 (Washington, D. C., 1903), 30–32.

23. Martha Jefferson to T. J., May 31, 1804, Betts and Bear, *Family Letters*, 260.

24. T. J. to J. W. Eppes; March 15, 1804; Randall, Vol. 3, 98–99.

25. T. J. to C. W. Peale (Jefferson Papers, LC microfilm Series I, Doc. 24210, Reel 30).

26. Charles C. Sellers, *Charles Willson Peale, Later Life, 1790–1827*, Vol. 2 (Philadelphia, 1947), 182–184.

27. Alexander von Humboldt to T. J., June 27, 1804; Malone, Vol. 4, 421–422.

28. Mapp, 110; 432–434; Carl Becker, *The Declaration of Independence* (New York, 1940), 135.

29. Adams to T. J., January 22, 1825; Lester J. Cappon, ed., *The Adams-Jefferson Letters: The Complete Correspondence Between Thomas Jefferson and John and Abigail Adams* (Chapel Hill, N. C., 1959), 606–607.

30. T. J. to Abigail Adams, September 25, 1785; Boyd, *Papers of T.J.*, Vol. 8, 548.

31. Abigail Adams to T. J., June 6, 1785; ibid., 198.

32. Ibid.

33. Abigail Adams to T. J., July 6, 1787, ibid., Vol. 11, 550–552.

34. Abigail Adams to T. J., May 20, 1804; Cappon, *Adams-Jefferson Letters*, 268–269.

35. T. J. to J. W. Eppes, June 4, 1804; ibid., 266.

36. Ibid.

37. Ibid.

38. Virginius Dabney, *The Jefferson Scandals* (New York, 1981), 7.

39. Ibid., 13.

40. T. J. to Abigail Adams, July 22, 1804, Cappon, *Adams-Jefferson Letters*, 274–276.

41. Abigail Adams to T. J., August 18, 1804; ibid., 276–278.

42. T. J. to Abigail Adams, September 11, 1804, ibid., 278–280.

43. Abigail Adams to T. J., October 25, 1804, ibid., 280–282.

44. Ibid., 282.

45. Ibid., 268.

46. Mapp, 1–2.

47. Hamilton to James A. Bayard, January 16, 1801; Harold C. Syrett, *Papers of Alexander Hamilton*, Vol. 25 (New York, 1977), 319–320. Also Mapp, 392.

48. T. J. to William Heath, December 13, 1804; Schachner, 791.

49. T. J. to John Taylor, January 6, 1805; Ford, Vol. 10, 124–126.

50. John Adams, *Works*, Vol. 2 (Boston, 1853), 143.

51. Malone, Vol. 4, 465.

52. Schachner, 778.

53. Mapp, 4.

54. T. J. to J. H. Nicholson, May 3, 1803. Ford, Vol. 10, 3–12.

55. Scene based on Henry Adams.

56. *New York Evening Post*, February 6, 1805; quoted in Forrest McDonald, *The Presidency of Thomas Jefferson* (Lawrence, Kans., 1976), 91.

57. Malone, Vol. 4, 470.

58. McDonald, 93.

59. Ibid.

CHAPTER VII   'DESCENT INTO THE MAELSTROM'

1. Dumas Malone, *Jefferson and His Time: Jefferson the President, First Term, 1801–1805*, Vol. 4 (Boston, 1970), 749–50.

2. All quotes from "Second Inaugural"; Merrill D. Peterson, ed., *Thomas Jefferson: Writings*, Library of America (New York, 1984), 518–523.

3. A. J. Foster, *Jeffersonian America* (1954), 15.

4. Nathan Schachner, *Thomas Jefferson, A Biography* (New York, 1957), 641.

5. Library of America, 522.

6. *The Papers of Thomas Jefferson*, second series, *Jefferson's Extracts from the Gospel*, Charles T. Cullen, ed. (Princeton: 1983), 21–22.

7. Ibid., 22–26.

8. Ibid., 25

9. Ibid., 340

10. Priestly's *A Harmony of the Evangelists* was published in Greek 1777 and in English in 1780.

11. T. J. to Adams, October 12, 1813; Library of America, 1301.

12. T. J. to Waterhouse, March 9, 1805 (Jefferson Papers, LC microfilm Series I, Doc. 25743, Reel 32).

13. Waterhouse to T. J., February 20, 1805; Dumas Malone, *Jefferson and His Time: Jefferson the President, Second Term, 1805–1809,* Vol. 5 (Boston, 1974), 21.

14. Forrest McDonald, *The Presidency of Thomas Jefferson* (Lawrence, Kans. 1976), 95.

15. Ibid., 95–96.

16. Henry Adams, *History of the United States During the Administrations of Jefferson and Madison*, Vol. 2 (New York, 1891–1893), 305.

17. T. J. to Madison, April 27, 1804; Schachner, 783.

18. Armstrong to Madison, December 24, 1804; Adams, Vol. 2, 308–309.

19. Henry Adams, Vol., 2, 21–22.

20. Schachner, 799.

21. T. J. to Madison, August 17, 1805; Schachner, 800.

22. Madison to T. J., September 1, 1805; ibid.

23. T. J. to Madison, August 25, 1805 (Jefferson Papers, LC microfilm Series I, Doc. 26568, Reel 34).

24. Clifford L. Egan, "The United States, France, and West Florida, 1803–1807," (*Florida Historical Quarterly*, Vol. 47 (1968–1969), 229–230.

25. Alfred L. Burt, *The United States, Great Britain, and British North America: From the Revolution to the Establishment of Peace after the War of 1812* (New Haven, Conn., 1940), 230.

26. Ibid., 101.

27. *American State Papers: Foreign Relations*, Vol. 2, 778–798, September 1, 1804–September 26, 1805.

28. Monroe to Madison, October 18, 1805; ibid, Vol. 3, 106–108.

29. T. J. to James Madison, October 23, 1805 (Jefferson Papers, LC microfilm Series I, Doc. 26709, Reel 34).

30. Egan, 227–252.

31. Ibid.

32. Ibid., 239.

33. T. J. message to Congress, December 3, 1805 (Jefferson Papers, LC microfilm Series I, Docs. 26944–48, Reel 34).

34. McDonald, 102–104.

35. Adams, Vol. 3, 136.

36. Malone, Vol. 5, 65–66.

37. Ibid., 66.

38. McDonald, 104.

39. Adams, Vol. 2, 141–143.

40. Though drafted by Adams, the resolutions were presented by Samuel Smith.

41. William Duane to T. J., March 12, 1806 (Jefferson Papers, LC microflm Series I, Docs. 27548–49, Reel 35).

42. T. J. to William Duane, March 22, 1806 (Jefferson Papers, LC microfilm Series I, Docs. 27596–99, Reel 35).

43. Malone, Vol. 4, 110.

44. Adams, Vol. 3, 197.

45. Turreau to Talleyrand, May 10, 1806; translated by Henry Adams from original in Arch. Aff. étr., MSS., *History of U. S.*, Vol. 3, 206.

CHAPTER VIII   BUCCANEERS AND REBELS

1. Madison letters to Yrujo, January 15, 1806. Also *Annals of Congress*, (Washington, D.C., 1852–1853), 9th Congress, 1st session, 1221–1224.

2. Ibid.

3. Henry Adams, *History of the United States During the Administrations of Jefferson and Madison*, Vol. 3 (New York, 1891–1893), 188.

4. Ibid.

5. Turreau to Yrujo, February 7, 1806, translated by Henry Adams, Vol. 3, original in Spanish Archives; ibid., 194–195.

6. Dumas Malone, *Jefferson and His Time: Jefferson the President, Second Term, 1805–1809*, Vol. 5 (Boston, 1974), 84.

7. J. Q. Adams to W. S. Smith; John Quincy Adams, *Writings*, W. C. Ford., ed., Vol. 1 (New York, 1914), 139.

8. Adams to Wilkinson, February 4, 1798; John Adams, *Works*, Charles Francis Adams, ed., Vol. 8 (Boston, 1853), 563–564.

9. Turreau to Talleyrand, March 9, 1805; translated by Henry Adams, Vol. 2, 406.

10. The circumstances of Wythe's death are discussed in Julian P. Boyd and W. Edwin Hemphill, *The Murder of George Wythe: Two Essays by Julian P. Boyd and W. Edwin Hemphill* (Williamsburg, Va., 1955).

11. Daveiss to T. J., January 10, 1806 (Jefferson Papers, LC microfilm Series I, Docs. 27210–12, Reel 35).

12. Gallatin to T. J., February 12, 1806 (ibid., Docs. 27401–02, Reel 35).

13. Daveiss to T. J., February 10, 1806 (ibid., Docs. 27393–94, with list Docs. 27395–95a, Reel 35).

14. Forrest McDonald, *The Presidency of Thomas Jefferson* (Lawrence, Kans., 1976), 123.

15. Nathan Schachner, *Thomas Jefferson, A Biography* (New York, 1953), 821.

16. T. J. to Robert Smith, May 19, 1806 (Jefferson Papers, LC microfilm Series I, Docs. 27819–20, Reel 36).

17. Alf J. Mapp, Jr., *Thomas Jefferson: A Strange Case of Mistaken Identity* (Lanham, Md., and New York, 1987), 224.

18. T. J. to George Morgan, March 26, 1807 (Jefferson Papers, LC microfilm Series I, Doc. 29219, Reel 38).

19. Gideon Granger to T. J., October 9, 1806 (ibid., Docs. 28332–34, Reel 38).

20. Henry Adams, Vol. 2, 429–436.

21. Note infelicitous wording by T. J., a rarity with him. T. J. to Samuel Smith, May 4, 1806; Paul Leicester Ford, ed., *The Writings of Thomas Jefferson*, Vol. 8 (New York, 1892–1899), 450.

22. Laussat to Decres, April 8, 1804. Quoted in translation from the Archives de la Marine by Henry Adams, Vol. 3, 298.

23. Ford, Vol. 1, 317–320; for cabinet meetings October 22, 24, 25, 1806.

24. T. J. to Thomas Mann Randolph, November 3, 1806; Malone, *Jefferson and His Time: Jefferson the President, First Term, 1801–1805,* Vol. 4 (Boston, 1970), 245.

25. McDonald, 124.

26. Ibid., 124–125.

27. Wilkinson to T. J., October 21, 1806; Albert J. Beveridge, *The Life of John Marshall*, Vol. 3 (Boston, 1916), 328.

28. Description based on portrait of Wilkinson by Charles Willson Peale, Independence National Historical Park Collection, Philadelphia.

29. McDonald, 125.

30. Wilkinson to T. J., October 21, 1806; Malone, Vol. 5, 249 ("Letters in relation to Burr Conspiracy").

31. Ibid., 259.

32. T. J.'s proclamation, November 27, 1806; Ford, Vol. 8, 481–482.

33. Quoted from testimony of Dudley Woodbridge; Beveridge, *Marshall*, Vol. 3, 311.

34. Ibid., 325–326.

35. Wilkinson to Col. Thomas H. Cushing, Thomas Freeman, and Governor Claiborne; Beveridge, *Marshall*, Vol. 3, 330–331.

36. Henry Adams, Vol. 3, 319.

37. Beveridge, *Marshall*, Vol. 3, 332–333 n2.

38. Ibid., 335–336.

39. Ibid., 336–337.

40. Leonard W. Levy, *Jefferson and Civil Liberties: The Darker Side* (Cambridge, Mass., 1963), 82–83.

41. T. J. to Wilkinson, February 3, 1807 (Jefferson Papers, LC microfilm Series I, Doc. 28925, Reel 37).

42. T. J. to W. C. Claiborne, February 3, 1807 (ibid., Doc. 28926, Reel 37).

43. Levy, 85.

44. Malone, Vol. 5, 261–262.

45. T. J., "Special Message to Congress," January 1, 1807; Ford, Vol. 9, 14–20.

46. Description by Colonel Osmun, quoted in Beveridge, *Marshall*, Vol. 3, 366.

47. Description by John Randolph; quoted in Beveridge, ibid., 369–370.

48. Ibid., 367.

49. Ibid., 368.

50. Ibid., 369.

51. T. J. to Robert Livingston, April 18, 1802 (Jefferson Papers, LC microfilm Series I, Doc. 21126, Reel 26).

52. George Macaulay Trevelyan, *A Shortened History of England* (New York, 1942), 376.

53. Ibid.

54. McDonald, 132–133.

55. T. J. to J. P. G. Muhlenberg, January 1781; Julian P. Boyd, ed., *Papers of Thomas Jefferson*, Vol. 4 (Princeton, 1950–1982), 487–488. The incident is presented in Mapp, *Thomas Jefferson I*, 145–147.

56. Stephen B. Oates, *With Malice Toward None: The Life of Abraham Lincoln* (New York, 1977), 253.

57. McDonald, 129–130.

CHAPTER IX   THE 'LITTLE EMPEROR' AND THE BLIND GIANTS

1. T. J. to Martha Jefferson Randolph, July 6, 1806; Edwin M. Betts and James A. Bear, Jr., eds., *The Family Letters of Thomas Jefferson* (Charlottesville, Va., 1986), 288.

2. T. J. to Martha Jefferson Randolph, October 20, 1806; ibid., 289.

3. T. J. to Jonathan Shoemaker, April 18, 1807; E. M Betts, ed., *Thomas Jefferson's Farm Book* (Charlottesville, Va., 1976), 365–366.

4. Edwin M. Betts and Hazelhurst B. Perkins, *Thomas Jefferson's Flower Garden at Monticello* (Richmond, Va., 1941), 7.

5. Forrest McDonald, *The Presidency of Thomas Jefferson* (Lawrence, Kans., 1976), 130–131.

6. Information on Lewis and Clark expedition derived principally from Bernard DeVoto, ed., *The Journals of Lewis and Clark* (Boston, 1953).

7. Edward Dumbauld, *Thomas Jefferson, American Tourist* (Norman, Okla., 1946), 239.

8. Albert J. Beveridge, *The Life of John Marshall*, Vol. 3 (Boston, 1916), 396.

9. Matthew L. Davis, ed., *Memoirs of Aaron Burr with Miscellaneous Selections from His Correspondence*, Vol. 2 (New York, 1837), 409.

10. Giles to T. J., April 6, 1807 (Jefferson Papers, LC microfilm Series I, Docs. 29264–65, Reel 38).

11. T. J. to William Branch Giles, April 20, 1807 (ibid., Docs. 29321–29).

12. McDonald, 134.

13. Information on Burr's trial is derived from the following sources, other than cited correspondence:

Reports of the Trials of Col. Aaron Burr, on an Indictment for Treason . . . Taken in Shorthand by David Robertson, 2 vols. (New York, 1875).

James Parton, *The Life and Times of Aaron Burr* (New York, 1858), especially 458–512. Much valuable information is included, but the author's bias is indicated by the dedication of his work: "In Memory of Theodosia, the Daughter."

Davis. Important original manuscripts are quoted by Davis but his approach is indicated by his own statement (v-vi) that he had "committed to the fire" all letters "indicating no very strict morality in some of [Burr's] female correspondents." Davis had urged but Burr had "prohibited the destruction of any part of them in his lifetime."

Andrew Jackson, *The Papers of Andrew Jackson*, Harold D. Moser and Sharon MacPherson, eds., and Charles F. Bryan, Jr., asst. ed., Vol. 2 (Knoxville, Tenn., 1984), 164–172, 174–175, 308–309, 398–399.

Henry Adams, *History of the Unites States During the Administrations of Jefferson and Madison*, Vol. 3 (New York, 1891–1893), 441–471.

Beveridge, Vol. 3, 477–529.

14. Parton, 458. Parton prefaces the account: "The story that Colonel Burr, in his later years, used often to tell of General Jackson's mounting the steps of a corner grocery at Richmond, and declaiming furiously against Jefferson for the part he had taken in crushing the expedition and its author, is confirmed by the testimony of the most distinguished of the living public men of the United States." Parton did not otherwise identify the men. He said that the story was told by "the gentleman to the writer."

Failure to find any other confirmation of the anecdote about Jackson is reported in *The Papers of Andrew Jackson*. Dr. Bryan, in a conversation with the author August 3, 1989, said that his studies of Jackson's correspondence led him to believe that the behavior described by Parton would be uncharacteristic of the General.

15. Adams, Vol. 3, 449. For context, see *Reports of the Trials*, Vol. 1, 199, 267–268, 400–401, 480.

16. Parton, 459.

17. T. J. to Hay, June 20, 1807 (Jefferson Papers, LC microfilm Series I, Doc. 29551, Reel 38).

18. The foregoing aspects of Jefferson are presented in Alf J. Mapp, Jr., *Thomas Jefferson: A Strange Case of Mistaken Identity* (Lanham, Md., and New York, 1987)

19. T. J. to William Short, June 12, 1807 (Jefferson Papers, LC microfilm Series I, Doc. 29522, Reel 38).

20. T. J. to Hay, June 19, 1807 (ibid., Doc. 29547, Reel 38).

21. Adams, Vol. 3, 455.

22. T. J. to Wilkinson, June 21, 1807 (Jefferson Papers, LC microfilm Series I, Doc 29560, Reel 38).

23. Adams, Vol. 3, 463–464.

24. T. J. to Hay, August 20, 1807 (Jefferson Papers, LC microfilm Series I, Doc. 29993, Reel 39).

25. Adams, Vol. 3, 462–463.

26. Hay to T. J., August 11, 1807 (Jefferson Papers, LC microfilm Series I, Doc. 29916, Reel 39).

27. Adams, Vol. 3, 463.

28. William Wirt, *The Two Principal Arguments of William Wirt, Esquire, on the Trial of Aaron Burr for High Treason, and on the Motion to Commit Aaron Burr, and Others, for Trial in Kentucky* (Richmond, Va., 1808), 62–65.

29. T. J. to Hay, September 4, 1807; A. A. Lipscomb and A. E. Bergh, eds., *The Writings of Thomas Jefferson*, Vol. 11 (Washington, D.C., 1903), 360.

CHAPTER X   THROUGH THE STORM

1. Dumas Malone, *Jefferson and His Time: Jefferson the President, First Term, 1801–1805*, Vol. 4 (Boston, 1970), 417.

2. Henry Adams, *History of the United States During the Administrations of Jefferson and Madison*, Vol. 4 (New York, 1891–1893), 2.

3. Ibid.

4. John C. Emmerson, Jr., ed., *The Chesapeake Affair of 1807: An objective account of the attack by H.M.S. Leopard, upon the U.S. frigate Chesapeake, off Cape Henry, Va., June 22, 1807, and its repercussions: compiled from contemporary newspaper accounts, official documents, and other authoritative sources* (Portsmouth, Va., 1954), 9–10.

Immaterial differences appear in the text of the order as reproduced in Henry Adams, Vol. 4, 3.

5. Account of the confrontation of *Chesapeake* and *Leopard* based principally on transcriptions of original documents in Emmerson, *The Chesapeake Affair*, 1–207. A good brief account is in Adams, Vol. 4, 4–26.

6. Emmerson, 24–27. Also Thomas J. Wertenbaker, *Norfolk: Historic Southern Port* (Durham, N.C., 1962) 100.

7. Ibid., 101.

8. Emmerson, 44.

9. Ibid., 45.

10. Ibid., 48.

11. Adams, Vol. 4, 25.

12. Ibid., 28.

13. Ibid., 28–29.

14. Emmerson, 52–55.

15. Cabinet memoranda; Adams, Vol. 4, 31.

16. T. J. to John Page, July 9, 1807 (Jefferson Papers, LC microfilm Series I, Doc. 29684, Reel 38).

17. Dumas Malone, *Jefferson and His Time: Jefferson the President, Second Term, 1805–1809*, Vol. 5 (Boston, 1974), 429.

18. Emmerson, 76–77.

19. Ibid., 101–126.

20. Nicholson to Gallatin, July 14, 1807; Henry Adams, Vol. 4, 32.

21. Gallatin to Nicholson, July 17, 1807; ibid., 33.

22. T. J. to Barnabas Bidwell, July 11, 1807 (Jefferson Papers, LC microfilm Series I, Doc. 29701, Reel 38).

23. T. J. to Clinton, July 6, 1807 (ibid., Doc. 29654, Reel 38).

24. Adams, Vol. 2, 34.

25. Turreau to Talleyrand, quoted and translated in Adams, Vol. 4, 35–37.

26. Ibid., Vol. 2, 268–269.

27. Ibid., Vol. 3, 86.

28. Turreau to Talleyrand, translated and quoted in ibid., Vol. 4, 35–37.

29. Erskine to Canning, July 21, 1807; ibid., Vol. 4, 37.

30. Malone, Vol. 4, 453.

31. Ibid., 453–454.

32. J. Christopher Herold, *The Age of Napoleon* (New York, 1963), 184.

33. Madison to T. J., September 20, 1807 (Jefferson Papers, LC microfilm series I, Doc. 30188–89, Reel 39).

34. Humphreys to T. J., September 25, 1809 (ibid., Docs. 30219–21, Reel 39).

35. T. J. to Humphreys, August 11, 1790; Paul Leicester Ford, ed., *The Writings of Thomas Jefferson*, Vol. 6 (New York, 1892–1899), 118–120.

36. This point is made by Forrest McDonald, *The Presidency of Thomas Jefferson* (Lawrence, Kans., 1976), 142.

37. Gallatin to J. H. Nicholson, July 17, 1807; Henry Adams, ed., *Albert Gallatin: Writings*, Vol. 1 (Philadelphia, 1879), 339.

38. T. J. to Thomas Mann Randolph, November 30, 1807 (Jefferson Papers, LC microfilm Series I, Doc. 30506, Reel 39).

39. Gallatin to T. J., December 18, 1807 (ibid., Doc. 30617, Reel 40).

40. Henry Adams, *Gallatin*, Vol. 1, 363.

41. Malone, Vol. 5, 470.

42. Biographical material on Astor derived from *Dictionary of American Biography* and Samuel Eliot Morison, *The Oxford History of the American People* (New York, 1956), 374.

43. T. J. to John Taylor, January 6, 1808 (Jefferson Papers, LC microfilm Series I, Doc. 30732, Reel 40).

44. "An Act for Classing the Militia and Assigning to Each Class Its Particular Duties," draft in Paul Leicester Ford, ed., *The Writings of Thomas Jefferson*, Vol. 8 (New York, 1892–1899), 409–412.

45. "A Bill for Establishing a Naval Militia," ibid., 403–409.

46. T. J. to Jacob Crowninshield, May 13, 1806; ibid., 451–453.

47. T. J. had held these views for a long time. See T. J. to Elbridge Gerry, January 26, 1799; ibid., 328.

48. Malone, Vol. 5, 500.

49. Christopher McKee, *Edward Preble, a Naval Biography, 1761–1807* (Annapolis, Md., 1972), 317–319.

50. Malone, Vol. 5, 499.

51. Julia H. MacLeod, "Jefferson and the Navy: A Defense," *Huntington Library Quarterly*, Vol. 8 (February 1945), 170–173. Marshall Butt, *Portsmouth Under Four Flags* (Portsmouth, Va., 1971), 30–95. Alf J. Mapp, Jr., and Ramona H. Mapp, *Portsmouth: A Pictorial History* (Norfolk, Va., 1989), 86–87.

52. Jefferson used the phrase in persuading his other son-in-law, Thomas Mann Randolph, not to duel with John Randolph in 1806.

53. T. J. to Major Joseph Eggleston, March 7, 1805; Malone, Vol. 5, 566.

54. T. J. to John Norvell, June 11, 1807 (Jefferson Papers, LC microfilm Series I, Doc. 29519–20, Reel 38).

55. T. J. to Governor James Sullivan of Massachusetts, June 19, 1807 (ibid., Docs. 29549–50, Reel 38).

56. T. J. to Dr. Casper Wistar, June 21, 1807; Ford, Vol. 9, 78–85.

57. Sullivan to T. J., June 3, 1808 (Jefferson Papers, LC microfilm Series I, Doc. 31525, Reel 41).

58. Paul C. Nagel, *Descent from Glory: Four Generations of the John Adams Family* (New York, 1983), 90–91.

59. T. J. to Governor Sullivan, July 16, 1808 (Jefferson Papers, LC microfilm Series I, Doc. 31696, Reel 38).

60. Malone, Vol. 5, 534.

61. T. J. to Latrobe, April 22, 1807 (Jefferson Papers, LC microfilm Series I, Doc 29329, Reel 38).

62. T. J. to William Buchanan and James Hay, January 26, 1787; Ford, Vol. 9, 220; T. J. to James Currie, January 28, 1787; ibid.; Alf J. Mapp, Jr., *Thomas Jefferson: A Strange Case of Mistaken Identity* (Lanham, Md., and New York, 1987), 232–233.

63. Jefferson's relationship with Maria Cosway is discussed in Mapp, 235–248.

64. Latrobe to T. J., May 21, 1807; Saul K. Padover, *Thomas Jefferson and the Capital* (1946), 386–387.

65. T. J. to Latrobe, April 25, 1808; ibid., 414–416.

66. T. J. to Martha Jefferson Randolph, January 5, 1808. Edwin M. Betts and James A. Bear, Jr., eds., *The Family Letters of Thomas Jefferson* (Charlottesville, Va., 1986), 319. See also ibid., 317–329.

67. Ibid.

68. T. J. to Martha Jefferson Randolph, December 29, 1807, and January 5, 1808; ibid., 317, 319.

69. Monroe to T. J., May 11, 1782; Julian P. Boyd, ed., *The Papers of Thomas Jefferson*, Vol. 6 (Princeton, 1950–1982), 183.

70. James Monroe to T. J., February 27, 1805 (Jefferson Papers, LC microfilm Series I, Docs. 31055–56, Reel 32).

71. T. J. to Monroe, February 18, 1808 (ibid., Doc. 30989, Reel 40).

72. T. J. to Monroe, March 10, 1808 (ibid., Docs. 31106–07, Reel 41).

73. Monroe to T. J., March 22, 1808 (ibid., Docs. 31184–85; 33211, Reel 41).

74. Gallatin to T. J., August 6, 1808 (ibid., Docs. 31828–29, Reel 41).

75. Monroe to Joseph H. Nicholson, September 24, 1808; Nathan Schachner, *Thomas Jefferson, A Biography* (New York, 1951), 876–877. See also Noble E. Cunningham, Jr., *The Jeffersonian Republicans in Power: Party Operations, 1801–1809* (Chapel Hill, N.C., 1963), Chap. 5.

76. Gilbert Chinard, *Thomas Jefferson: The Apostle of Americanism*, 2nd ed. (Ann Arbor, Mich., 1960), 463.

77. Report of November 13 in diary of Josiah Quincy; Edmund Quincy, *Life of Josiah Quincy* (Boston, 1868), 143.

78. Speech of November 21, 1808. *Annals of Congress*, 10th Congress, 2nd session, 27.

79. Ford, Vol. 9, 213–225.

80. Gallatin's draft; Ford, Vol. 11, 59–62. Also ibid., 58–59n.

81. Ibid., 548–549. Administration, including embargo, praised by New Hampshire Legislature. Malone, Vol. 5, 607.

82. Malone, Vol. 5, 629.

83. Memo, "Conversation with Erskine," November 9, 1808 (Jefferson Papers, LC microfilm Series I, Doc. 32350, Reel 42).

84. T. J. to Randolph, December 13, 1808 (ibid., Doc. 32550, Reel 42)

85. T. J. to Thomas Mann Randolph, January 2, 1809. (ibid., Doc. 32735, Reel 43).

86. T. J. to Dr. William Eustis, January 14, 1809 (ibid., Doc. 32800, Reel 43).

87. Erskine to Canning, December 4, 1808; Malone, Vol. 5, 636.

88. T.J. to Monroe, January 28, 1809 (Jefferson Papers, LC microfilm Series I, Doc. 32910, Reel 43).

89. Ibid.

90. T. J. to Thomas Mann Randolph, February 7, 1809 (ibid., Doc. 32982, Reel 43).

91. Malone, Vol. 5, 649.

92. Short to T. J., May 14, 1784; Boyd, *Papers of T. J.*, Vol. 7, 148.

93. Agnes Rothery, *Houses Virginians Have Loved* (New York, 1954), 174–177.

94. Claude O. Lanciano, Jr., *Rosewell, Garland of Virginia* (Gloucester, Va., 1978), 119–139.

95. T. J. to Page, September 6, 1808 (Jefferson Papers, LC microfilm Series I, Doc. 32028, Reel 42).

96. St. George Tucker to T. J., October 5, 1808. (ibid., Docs. 32174–75, Reel 42).

97. Page to T. J., September 13, 1808, (ibid., Doc. 32060, Reel 42).

98. Gallatin to T. J. October 12, 1808, (ibid., Doc. 32001, Reel 42).

99. T. J. to St. George Tucker, December 8, 1808 (ibid., Doc. 32512, Reel 42). See also related letter, ibid., Doc. 32625, Reel 43.

100. Lanciano, 121.

101. For analysis, see Mapp, 242–247. Complete text, T. J. to Maria Cosway, October 12, 1786; Boyd, *Papers of T. J.*, 443–453.

102. Ford, Vol. 9, 248.

103. T. J. to Abraham Venable; ibid., 240–241.

CHAPTER XI   MEASURE OF A PRESIDENT

1. Margaret Bayard Smith, *The First Forty Years of Washington Society* (New York, 1906), 58–59.

2. J. Q. Adams to Louise Catherine Adams, March 5, 1809; John Quincy Adams, *Writings*, W. C. Ford, ed., Vol. 3 (New York, 1914), 289.

3. T. J. to John D. Banks, June 21, 1802 (Jefferson Papers, LC microfilm Series I, Doc. 19051, Reel 23).

4. T. J., "To the Inhabitants of Albemarle County in Virginia," April 3, 1809; Merrill D. Peterson, ed., *Thomas Jefferson: Writings*, Library of America (New York, 1984), 550.

5. 2 Corinthians 5:17.

6. T. J. to Joseph Priestley, March 21, 1801; Paul Leicester Ford, ed., *The Writings of Thomas Jefferson*, Vol. 8 (New York, 1892–1899), 22.

7. John Marshall to Charles Cotsworth Pinckney, March 4, 1801; *American Historical Review*, Vol. 53, No. 3, 518–520. This same letter is misquoted in Albert Beveridge's famous *Life of John Marshall* (Boston, 1916).

8. Alf J. Mapp, Jr., *Thomas Jefferson: A Strange Case of Mistaken Identity* (Lanham, Md., and New York, 1987), 232–233.

9. Samuel Eliot Morison, *The Oxford History of the American People* (New York, 1965), 376.

10. Henry Adams, *History of the United States During the Administrations of Jefferson and Madison*, Vol. 4 (New York, 1890 copyright or 1917 printing), 463.

11. Ibid., 454.

12. Forrest McDonald, *The Presidency of Thomas Jefferson* (Lawrence, Kans., 1976), 167.

CHAPTER XII   SHADOWS ON THE MOUNTAIN

1. T. J. to Madison, March 17, 1809 (Jefferson Papers, LC microfilm Series I, Doc. 33201, Reel 43).

2. Henry S. Randall, *The Life of Thomas Jefferson*, Vol. 1 (Philadelphia, 1865), 64; Sarah N. Randolph, *The Domestic Life of Thomas Jefferson* (Cambridge, Mass., 1872), 44–45; Alf J. Mapp, Jr., *Thomas Jefferson: A Strange Case of Mistaken Identity* (Lanham, Md., and New York, 1987), 67.

3. Hamilton W. Pierson, *Jefferson at Monticello: The Private Life of Thomas Jefferson* (New York, 1862), 113–116.

4. Isaac A. Coles to T. J., March 13, 1809 (Jefferson Papers, LC microfilm Series I, Doc. 33191, Reel 43); T. J. to J. S. Barnes, August 3, 1809 (ibid., Doc. 33416, Reel 44); T. J. to B. S. Barton, September 21, 1809 (ibid., Doc. 33494, Reel 44).

5. The account is based on the author's examination of the original building and three-dimensional model therein.

6. Martha Jefferson Randolph to T. J., April 25, 1790; Edwin M. Betts and James A. Bear, Jr., eds., *The Family Letters of Thomas Jefferson* (Charlottesville, Va., 1986), 51.

7. Dumas Malone, *Jefferson and His Time: The Sage of Monticello*, Vol. 6 (Boston, 1981), 9.

8. Betts and Bear, *Family Letters*, 8, 15.

9. Malone, Vol. 6, 21.

10. T. J. to Kosciusko, February 26, 1810 (Jefferson Papers, LC microfilm Series I, Doc. 33705–07, Reel 44).

11. Pierson, 78.

12. Edgar S. Maclay, ed., *Journal of William Maclay, United States Senator from Pennsylvania, 1789–1791* (New York, 1890), May 24, 1790, entry, 272.

13. Pierson, 74.

14. Ibid.

15. T. J. to Thomas Mann Randolph, January 31, 1809 (Jefferson Papers, LC microfilm Series I, Doc. 32919, Reel 43).

16. T. J. to J. S. Barnes, August 3, 1809 (ibid., Doc. 33416, Reel 44); T. J. to Dr. B. S. Barton, September 21, 1809 (ibid., Doc. 33494, Reel 44).

17. T. J. to Etienne Lamaire, March 16, 1809; Malone, Vol. 6, 5.

18. *National Intelligencer*, July 19–October 6, 1809; Malone Vol. 6, 25–26.

19. Edwin M. Betts, *Thomas Jefferson's Garden Book* (Philadelphia, 1944), 382–383.

20. Margaret Bayard Smith, *The First Forty Years of Washington Society* (New York, 1906), 80. Other information about the Smiths' visit is from this volume, 65–81.

21. Pierson, 70.

22. T. J. to John Page, February 21, 1770; Julian P. Boyd, ed., *The Papers of Thomas Jefferson*, Vol. 1 (Princeton, 1950–1982), 34–35.

23. T. J. to John S. Barnes, April 27, 1809 (Jefferson Papers, LC microfilm Series I, Doc. 33275, Reel 43).

24. T. J. to Levi Lincoln, March 11, 1809 (ibid., Doc. 33275, Reel 43).

25. T. J. to Madison, April 27, 1809 (ibid., Docs. 33276–77, Reel 43).

26. T. J. to Madison, June 16, 1809 (ibid., Doc. 33347, Reel 43).

27. T. J. to Madison, August 17, 1809 (ibid., Doc. 33430, Reel 44).

28. *Annals of Congress, 1789–1824* (Washington, 1849–1856), 11th Congress, 1st session, Vol. 1. 69.

29. T. J. to Gallatin, October 11, 1809 (Jefferson Papers, LC microfilm Series I, Doc. 33514, Reel 44).

30. Gallatin to T. J., November 11, 1809 (ibid., Docs. 33555–56, Reel 44).

31. T. J. to Rush, September 22, 1809 (ibid., Doc. 33495, Reel 44).

32. Smith, 80–81.

33. T. J. to Madison, November 30, 1809 (Jefferson Papers, LC microfilm Series I, Doc. 33576, Reel 44).

34. T. J. to Joel Barlow, January 24, 1810 (ibid., Doc. 33652, Reel 44).

35. T. J. to Dr. Walter Jones, March 5, 1810 (ibid., Doc. 33718, Reel 44).

36. T. J. to Maria Cosway, October 12, 1786. For an account of the circumstances attending this letter, see the chapter entitled "Head, Heart, and Glands," in Mapp, 235–273.

CHAPTER XIII   'DIFFUSION OF KNOWLEDGE'

1. T. J. to Kosciusko, February 26, 1810 (Jefferson Papers, LC microfilm Series I, Docs. 33705–07, Reel 44).

2. T. J. to Kosciusko, February 21, 1799; A. A. Lipscomb and A. E. Bergh, eds., *The Writings of Thomas Jefferson*, Vol. 10 (Washington, D.C., 1903), 116.

3. T. J. to Kosciusko, February 26, 1810 (Jefferson Papers, LC microfilm Series I, Docs. 33705–07, Reel 44).

4. T. J., *Notes on the State of Virginia*. William Peden, ed. (Chapel Hill, N.C., 1955), 148.

5. Ibid.

6. T. J.'s proposals for educational and other reforms when he was a member of the Committee to Revise the Laws of the Commonwealth are discussed in Alf J. Mapp, Jr., *Thomas Jefferson: A Strange Case of Mistaken Identity* (Lanham, Md., and New York, 1987), 121–122.

7. T. J. to Littleton W. Tazewell, January 5, 1806; Dumas Malone, *Jefferson and His Time: The Sage of Monticello*, Vol. 6 (Boston, 1981), 235.

8. T. J. to Joel Barlow, December 10, 1807 (Jefferson Papers, LC microfilm Series I, Doc. 30573, Reel 40).

9. T. J. to Dr. Walter Jones, March 5, 1810 (ibid., Docs. 33718–19, Reel 44).

10. T. J. to Governor John Langdon, March 5, 1810 (ibid., Docs. 33719–20, Reel 44).

11. On T. J.'s ancestry, see *Burke's Presidential Families of the United States of America*, 128, 611.

12. T. J. to Abbé Salimankis, March 14, 1810 (Jefferson Papers, LC microfilm Series I, Doc. 33726, Reel 44).

13. T. J. to Robert Fulton, March 17, 1810; Lipscomb and Bergh, Vol. 12, 380–381.

14. T. J. to Messrs. Hugh L. White et al. (Jefferson Papers, LC microfilm Series I, Doc. 33765, Reel 44).

15. T. J. to Madison, May 13, 1810 (ibid., Doc. 33777, Reel 44).

16. T. J. to G. Voolif, May 2, 1810 (ibid., Doc. 33758, Reel 44).

17. T. J. to Count Pahlen, July 13, 1810 (ibid., Doc. 33855, Reel 44).

18. T. J. to Governor John Tyler, May 26, 1810 (ibid., Doc. 33799, Reel 44).

19. Alf J. Mapp, Jr., *The Virginia Experiment: The Old Dominion's Role in the Making of America* (Lanham, Md., and New York, 1987), 43.

20. From "Nunc dimittis servum tuum, Domine (Lord, now letteth thou thy servant depart in peace), Luke 2:29.

21. T. J. to William Lambert, July 16, 1810 (Jefferson Papers, LC microfilm Series I, Doc. 33268, Reel 44).

22. John Wickham to T. J., May 16, 1810 (ibid., Doc. 33781, Reel 44).

23. Letter of September 3, 1807, quoted by T. J. in brief on Batture case, Lipscomb and Bergh, Vol. 18, 23.

24. Ibid., 124–127.

25. Claiborne to T. J., June 4, 1810 (Jefferson Papers, LC microfilm Series I, Doc. 33818, Reel 44).

26. Hay to T. J., July 15, 1810; Henry Adams, *History of the United States During the Administrations of Jefferson and Madison*, Vol. 1 (New York, 1879), 488.

27. William Peden, introduction to T. J., *Notes on the State of Virginia*, xi.

28. T. J. to Gallatin, August 16, 1810 (Jefferson Papers, LC microfilm Series I, Docs. 33926–27, Reel 44).

29. T. J. to Tyler, May 26, 1810 (ibid., Doc. 33799, Reel 44).

30. T. J. to Madison, May 25, 1810 (ibid., Doc. 33797, Reel 44).

31. T. J. to Hay, June 18, 1810 (ibid., Doc. 33841, Reel 44).

32. Hay to T. J., July 15, 1810 (ibid., Docs. 33866–67, Reel 44).

33. Mapp, *Virginia Experiment*, 62.

34. T. J. to Charles Willson Peale, August 20, 1811 (Jefferson Papers, LC microfilm Series I, Doc. 34408, Reel 45).

35. T. J. to Ann Cary Randolph Bankhead, May 26, 1811; Edwin M. Betts and James A. Bear, Jr., eds., *The Family Letters of Thomas Jefferson* (Charlottesville, Va., 1986), 394.

36. T. J. to Benjamin Rush, August 17, 1811 (Jefferson Papers, LC microfilm Series I, Doc. 34403, Reel 45).

37. T. J. to Charles Clay, August 23, 1811 (ibid., Doc. 34416, Reel 45).

38. T. J. to Gallatin, September 27, 1810 (ibid., Docs. 33981–82, Reel 45).

39. T. J. to Madison, October 15, 1810 (ibid., Doc. 34008, Reel 44).

40. T. J. to Hay, December 28, 1811 (ibid., Doc. 34535, Reel 45).

41. Wirt to T. J., April 15, 1812 (ibid., Doc. 34774, Reel 45).

42. Malone, Vol. 6, 69.

CHAPTER XIV   WAR AND FRIENDSHIP

1. T. J. to Madison, March 26, 1812 (Jefferson Papers, LC microfilm Series I, Doc. 34747, Reel 45).

2. Samuel Eliot Morison, *The Oxford History of the American People* (New York, 1965), 380.

3. T. J. to Madison, February 19, 1812 (Jefferson Papers, LC microfilm Series I, Doc. 34648, Reel 45).

4. T. J. to William Duane, August 4, 1812 (ibid., Doc. 34920, Reel 46).

5. Madison to T. J., August 17, 1812; James Madison, *Writings*, Gaillard Hunt, ed., Vol. 8 (New York, 1900–1910), 176–177.

6. T. J. to Madison, November 6, 1812 (Jefferson Papers, LC microfilm Series I, Doc. 34999, Reel 46).

7. T. J. to John Hollins, September 16, 1812 (ibid., Doc. 34947, Reel 46).

8. Information on T. J.'s textile manufacturing drawn from letters, notes, and drawings in Edwin M. Betts, ed., *Thomas Jefferson's Farm Book* (Charlottesville, Va., 1976), 464–495.

9. Ibid., 426–453.

10. Ibid., 421–426.

11. Ibid., 453–454.

12. Ibid., 454–455.

13. Ibid., 413–414.

14. Ibid., 414, and Hamilton W. Pierson, *Jefferson at Monticello: The Private Life of Thomas Jefferson* (New York, 1862); Also Sarah N. Randolph, *The Domestic Life of Thomas Jefferson* (New York, 1872).

15. Pierson, 71–72.

16. Henry S. Randall, *The Life of Thomas Jefferson*, Vol. 1 (Philadelphia, 1865), 41.

17. T. J., "A Memorandum: Services to My Country"; Paul Leicester Ford, ed., *The Writings of Thomas Jefferson*, Vol. 7 (New York, 1892–1899), 475–477. The friend was John Beckley.

18. Betts, *Farm Book*, 341.

19. Edwin M. Betts, ed., *Thomas Jefferson's Garden Book* (Philadelphia, 1944), 341.

20. Correspondence and other information regarding Jefferson's problem with the Rivanna Navigation Company were printed in Betts, *Farm Book*, 343–344, 376–398, 400–401, 404–406.

21. L. H. Butterfield, "The Dream of Benjamin Rush: The Reconciliation of John Adams and Thomas Jefferson," *Yale Review*, Vol. 40 (December 1950), 279–319.

22. Rush to T. J., January 2, 1811; John Adams, *The Spur of Fame: Dialogues of John Adams and Benjamin Rush*, John A. Schutz and Douglass Adair, eds. (San Marino, Calif., 1966), 157–158n.

23. T. J. to Rush, January 16, 1811 (Jefferson Papers, LC microfilm Series I, Docs. 34176–78, Reel 45).

24. Adams to Rush, June 21, 1811; Adams, *Spur of Fame*, 182.

25. T. J. to Rush, December 5, 1811 (Jefferson Papers, LC microfilm Series I, Doc. 34511, Reel 45).

26. Adams to Rush, December 25, 1811; John Adams, *Works*, Charles Francis Adams, ed., Vol. 10 (Boston, 1853), 10–12.

27. Adams to T. J., January 1, 1912; Lester J. Cappon, ed., *The Adams-Jefferson Letters: The Complete Correspondence Between Thomas Jefferson and John and Abigail Adams* (Chapel Hill, N.C., 1988), 290.

28. T. J. to Adams, January 21, 1812; ibid., 290–292.

29. Adams to Rush, October 25, 1804; Adams, *Spur of Fame*, 159.

CHAPTER XV   'OF CABBAGES AND KINGS'

1. T. J. to John Adams, June 11, 1812, Lester J. Cappon, ed., *The Adams-Jefferson Letters: The Complete Correspondence Between Thomas Jefferson and John and Abigail Adams* (Chapel Hill, N.C., 1988), 305–308.

2. T. J. to John Melish, January 13, 1813; Merrill D. Peterson, ed., *Thomas Jefferson: Writings*, Library of America (New York, 1984), 1267–1271.

3. Harold Syrett, ed. *Papers of Alexander Hamilton,* Vol. 26 (New York, 1961–1973), 324. This matter is discussed more fully in Alf J. Mapp, Jr., *Thomas Jefferson: A Strange Case of Mistaken Identity* (Lanham, Md., and New York, 1987), 307–308.

4. T. J. to Adams, June 15, 1813; Cappon, *Adams-Jefferson Letters*, 331–333.

5. T. J. to Madame de Tesse, December 8, 1813; Peterson, Library of America, 1314–1316.

6. T. J. to Alexander von Humboldt, December 6, 1813; ibid., 1311–1314.

7. T. J. to M. de Becourt, February 6, 1813 (Jefferson Papers, LC microfilm Series I, Doc. 35105, Reel 46).

8. T. J. to Dr. Walter Jones, January 2, 1814; Peterson, Library of America, 1317–1321.

9. T. J. to Dr. Thomas Cooper, February 10, 1814; ibid., 1321–1329.

10. T. J. to Dr. John Manners, February 22, 1814; ibid., 1329–1333.

11. T. J. to N. G. Dufief, April 19, 1814; ibid., 1333–1335.

12. T. J. to Thomas Law, June 13, 1814; ibid., 1335–1339.

13. T. J. to Adams, July 5, 1814; Cappon, *Adams-Jefferson Letters*, 29.

14. Adams to T. J., July 15, 1813; ibid., 357–358.

15. T. J. to Abigail Adams; ibid., 366–367.

16. Abigail Adams to T. J., September 20, 1813; ibid., 377, 378.

17. Adams to T. J., July 16, 1814; ibid., 438.

18. Adams to T. J., June 19, 1815; ibid., 443.

19. For accounts of visit by Ticknor and Gray, see Francis Coleman Rosenberger, ed., *Jefferson Reader: A Treasury of Writings about Thomas Jefferson* (New York, 1953), 76–85.

20. Ibid., 78, 81–82. Also personal examinations of some relics preserved at Monticello and Frederick D. Nichols and James A. Bear, Jr., *Monticello* (Charlottesville, Va., 1982), 22–26.

21. Virginius Dabney, *Virginia the New Dominion* (Garden City, N.Y., 1971), 206–207.

22. T. J. to Elizabeth Trist, May 10, 1813; *Glimpses of the Past: Correspondence of Thomas Jefferson, 1788–1826*, Vol. 3 Missouri Historical Society (St. Louis, April-June 1936), 120.

23. T. J. to Col. Charles Yancey, August 29, 1814 (Jefferson Papers, LC microfilm Series I, Doc. 35926, Reel 47).

24. T. J. to Archibald Robinson, June 21, 1814; Nathan Schachner, *Thomas Jefferson, A Biography* (New York, 1951), 930.

25. Malone, Vol. 6, 125.

CHAPTER XVI   NO ROYAL ROAD

1. Once, in a more parochial mood, Jefferson listed, as the earliest of his public concerns, the opening of the Rivanna River to navigation; T. J., "A Memorandum (Services to My Country)" (c. 1800), Merrill D. Peterson, ed., *Thomas Jefferson: Writings* The Library of America (New York, 1984), 702.

2. Thomas Jefferson, *Notes on the State of Virginia*, ed. William Peden (Chapel Hill, N.C., 1955), 46, 146–149; Alf J. Mapp, Jr., *Thomas Jefferson: A Strange Case of Mistaken Identity* (Lanham, Md., and New York, 1987), 125–127.

3. T. J. to Priestley, January 18, 1800; A. A. Lipscomb and A. E. Bergh, eds., *The Writings of Thomas Jefferson*, Vol. 10 (Washington, D.C., 1903), 140–142.

4. T. J. to Littleton W. Tazewell, January 5, 1805; Peterson, Library of America, 1149–1150.

5. Virginius Dabney, *Virginia the New Dominion* (Garden City, N.Y., 1971), 203.

6. T. J. to Tazewell, January 5, 1805; Peterson, Library of America, 1152–1153.

7. Francis Coleman Rosenberger, ed., *Jefferson Reader: A Treasury of Writings about Thomas Jefferson* (New York, 1953), 80–81.

8. T. J. to Samuel H. Smith, September 21, 1814 (Jefferson Papers, LC microfilm Series I, Doc. 35970–71, Reel 47).

9. Rosenberger, 64.

10. Ibid., 65

11. Ibid.

12. Ibid.

13. Ibid., 63.

14. Ibid.

15. Ibid.

16. Ibid., 65.

17. Ibid.

18. T. J. to Adams, April 8, 1816; Lester J. Cappon, ed., *The Adams-Jefferson Letters: The Complete Correspondence Between Thomas Jefferson and John and Abigail Adams* (Chapel Hill, N.C., 1959), 467.

19. T. J. to Thomas Cooper, January 16, 1814 (Jefferson Papers, LC microfilm Series I, Docs. 35626–29, Reel 47).

20. T. J. to Peter Carr, September 7, 1814; Peterson, Library of America, 1346–1352.

21. Mapp, 233, 277–278.

22. T. J. to Peter Carr, September 7, 1814; Peterson, Library of America, 1346–1352.

23. T. J. to Thomas Cooper, October 7, 1814 (Jefferson Papers, LC microfilm, Series I, Doc. 36001, Reel 47).

24. T. J. to Col. Charles Yancey, January 6, 1816; Paul Leicester Ford, ed., *The Writings of Thomas Jefferson*, Vol. 10 (New York, 1892–1899), 1–4.

25. T. J. to Thomas Cooper, October 7, 1814 (Jefferson Papers, LC microfilm Series I, Doc. 36001, Reel 47).

26. T. J. to Benjamin Austin, January 9, 1816; Peterson, Library of America, 1369–1372.

27. T. J. to Charles Thomson, January 9, 1816; ibid., 1372–1374.

28. T. J. to Adams, January 11, 1816; Cappon, *Adams-Jefferson Letters*, 458–461.

29. T. J. to Pierre Samuel Du Pont de Nemours, April 24, 1816; Peterson, Library of America, 1384–1388.

30. G. W. Randolph (T. J.'s grandson) to Dr. J. L. Cabell, February 27, 1856. Letter quotes Alexander Garrett; Dumas Malone, *Jefferson and His Time: The Sage of Monticello*, Vol. 6 (Boston, 1981), 255.

31. Ibid., 255. Newspaper's name was changed after September 20, 1815 from *Enquirer* to *Richmond Enquirer*.

32. Adams to T. J., May 26, 1817; Cappon, *Adams-Jefferson Letters*, 516–518.

33. Ibid., 256.

34. For example, Malone, Vol. 6, 259.

35. T. J. to General Cocke, July 19, 1817 (Jefferson Papers, LC microfilm Series I, Doc. 37527, Reel 50).

36. T. J. to Adams, September 8, 1817; Cappon, *Adams-Jefferson Letters*, 519–521.

37. Ibid., 519–520.

38. T. J. to Col. Charles Yancey, January 6, 1816 (Jefferson Papers, LC microfilm Series I, Docs. 36585–86, Reel 48).

39. T. J. to Adams, October 28, 1813; Cappon, *Adams-Jefferson Letters*, 387–392.

40. T. J. to Cabell, October 24, 1817 (Jefferson Papers, LC microfilm Series I, Doc. 37688, Reel 50).

41. T. J. to William Stephens Smith, October 22, 1776; Julian P. Boyd, ed., *The Papers of Thomas Jefferson*, Vol. 10 (Princeton, 1950–1982), 478. What is known of the incident is told in Mapp, 240–248.

42. T. J. to Cabell, September 1817 (Jefferson Papers, LC microfilm Series I, Doc. 37635, Reel 50)

43. T. J. to Correa da Serra, November 25, 1817 (ibid., Docs. 37730–31, Reel 50).

44. Roy J. Honeywell, *The Educational Works of Thomas Jefferson* (Cambridge, Mass., 1931), 26–53.

45. T. J. to Cabell, October 24, 1817 (Jefferson Papers, LC microfilm Series I, Doc. 37688, Reel 50).

46. Hamilton W. Pierson, *Jefferson at Monticello: The Private Life of Thomas Jefferson* (New York, 1862), 74–75.

47. Silvio A. Bedini, *Thomas Jefferson: Statesman of Science* (New York, 1990), 514.

48. T. J. to Cabell, December 18, 1817 (Jefferson Papers, LC microfilm Series I, Doc. 37751, Reel 50).

49. Nathaniel Francis Cabell, ed., *Early History of the University of Virginia, as Contained in the Letters of Thomas Jefferson and Joseph C. Cabell* (Richmond, Va., 1856), 427–432.

50. T. J. to Cabell, February 26, 1818; ibid., 128.

51. Cabell to T. J., March 11, 1919; ibid., 129.

52. Mapp, 129. *Journal of the House of Delegates*, October 7, November 23, December 12, December 14, 1778.

53. Bedini, 440.

54. T. J. to Nicholas, May 1, 1818; Malone, Vol. 6, 303.

55. T. J. to Patrick Gibson, July 30, 1818; ibid., 304.

56. "Report of the Commission Appointed to Fix the Site of the University of Virginia, etc.," Honeywell, Appendix J, 248.

57. J. G. Jackson to Cabell, December 13, 1818; Malone, Vol. 6, 277.

58. Charles A. Miller, *Jefferson and Nature: An Interpretation* (Baltimore, 1988), 15n.

59. T. J. to Martha Randolph, August 21, 1818; Edwin M. Betts, and James A Bear, Jr., eds., *The Family Letters of Thomas Jefferson* (Charlottesville, Va., 1986), 426.

60. T. J. to Adams, October 7, 1818; Cappon, *Adams-Jefferson Letters*, 528.

61. Adams to T. J., October 20, 1818; ibid., 528–529.

62. Mapp, 225–226.

63. T. J. to Adams, November 13, 1818; Cappon, *Adams-Jefferson Letters*, 529.

64. Cabell to T. J., December 8, 1818, Cabell, 137.

65. Cabell to T. J., January 7, 1818; Cabell 146–149.

66. T. J. to John Adams, January 19, 1819; Cappon, *Adams-Jefferson Letters*, 531–532.

67. Cabell to T. J., January 18, 1819; Cabell, 149.

CHAPTER XVII 'A RACE BETWEEN EDUCATION AND CATASTROPHE'

1. T. J. to Cabell, January 28, 1819 (Jefferson Papers, LC microfilm Series I, Doc. 38251, Reel 51).

2. Dumas Malone, *Jefferson and His Time: Jefferson the President, First Term, 1801–1805*, Vol. 4 (Boston, 1970), 366.

3. On Cocke, Virginius Dabney, *Mr. Jefferson's University* (Charlottesville, Va., 1981), 3.

4. Cabell to T. J., February 22, 1819; Francis Nathaniel Cabell, ed., *Early History of the University of Virginia, as Contained in the Letters of Thomas Jefferson and Joseph C. Cabell* (Richmond, Va., 1856), 165–166.

5. T. J. to Cabell, March 1, 1819 (Jefferson Papers, LC microfilm Series I, Docs. 38300–01, Reel 51).

6. Joseph C. Vance, "Knives, Whips and Randolphs on the Court House Lawn," *Magazine of Albemarle County History*, Vol. 15 (1955–1956), 28–35. My account of the altercation and its results is based on Vance's article, which in turn is based on a multitude of primary sources.

7. T. J. to Dr. John Bankhead, October 28, 1815; Malone, *Jefferson and His Time: The Sage of Monticello*, Vol. 6 (Boston, 1981), 159.

8. T. J. to W. C. Nicholas, March 18, 1819; Vance, 28.

9. Minutes of the Board of Visitors of the University of Virginia, March 29, 1819; Cabell, 454 ff.

10. Ibid., 454.

11. Cabell to T. J., April 17, 1819; Cabell, 174–176.

12. I. T. Frary, *Thomas Jefferson, Architect and Builder* (Richmond, Va., 1939), 95–97.

13. T. J. to Madison, July 7, 1819 (Jefferson Papers, LC microfilm Series I, Docs. 38486–87, Reel 51).

14. Jefferson's diplomatic attire was not always so gaudy. In Mather Brown's portrait of him in London he wears sober black.

15. T. J. to Madison, July 17, 1819; Malone, Vol. 6, 370–371.

16. Nathan Shachner, *Thomas Jefferson, A Biography* (New York, 1951), 959.

17. Wilson Cary Nicholas to T. J., August 5, 1819 (Jefferson Papers, LC microfilm Series I, Doc. 38530, Reel 51).

18. Ibid.

19. T. J. to Nicholas, August 11, 1819 (ibid., Doc. 38535, Reel 51).

20. T. J. to Monroe, August 17, 1819 (ibid., Doc. 38540, Reel 51).

21. T. J. to Nicholas, August 17, 1819 (ibid., Doc. 38541, Reel 51).

22. T. J. to Nicholas, August 24, 1819 (ibid., Doc. 32552, Reel 51).

23. Dumas Malone, ed., *Autobiography of Thomas Jefferson* (Boston, 1948), 28; Alf J. Mapp, Jr., *Thomas Jefferson: A Strange Case of Mistaken Identity* (Lanham, Md., and New York, 1987), 78–79.

24. Karl C. Wold, *Mr. President—How Is Your Health?* (St. Paul, Minn., 1948), 30.

25. T. J. to Adams, November 7, 1819; Lester J. Cappon, ed., *The Adams-Jefferson Letters: The Complete Correspondence Between Thomas Jefferson and John and Abigail Adams* (Chapel Hill, N.C., 1988), 546–547.

26. T. J. to Spencer Roane, September 6, 1819 (Jefferson Papers, LC microfilm Series I, Doc. 38568, Reel 51).

27. Maria Cosway to T. J., April 7, 1819; Helen Dupree Bullock, *My Head and My Heart: A Little History of Thomas Jefferson and Maria Cosway* (New York, 1945), 173–175.

28. Mapp, *Thomas Jefferson*, Chap. XIV, "Head, Heart, and Glands," 235–273.

29. Maria Cosway to T. J., April 7, 1819; Bullock, 175.

30. T. J. to Maria Cosway, December 27, 1820; ibid., 175–177.

31. Hamilton W. Pierson, *Jefferson at Monticello: The Private Life of Thomas Jefferson* (New York, 1862), 125.

32. Schachner, 971.

33. Browse Trist to Nicholas Trist, October 19, 1819; Malone, Vol. 6, 372–373.

34. T. J. to William Short, October 31, 1819; Merrill D. Peterson, ed., *Thomas Jefferson: Writings*, The Library of America (New York, 1984), 1430–1433.

35. John H. Rice to Cocke, January 28, 1819 and January 6, 1820; Malone, Vol. 6, 376.

36. Ibid.

37. T. J. to Cabell, January 22, 1820 (Jefferson Papers, LC microfilm Series I, Doc. 38681, Reel 51). Cabell to T. J., February 3, 1820; Cabell, 180–182.

38. T. J. to Short, April 13, 1820 (Jefferson Papers, LC microfilm Series I, Docs. 38773–74, Reel 51).

39. Alf J. Mapp, Jr., *Frock Coats and Epaulets*, 2nd ed. (Lanham, Md., and New York, 1987), 153–54.

40. T. J. to Richard Rush, October 20, 1820 (Jefferson Papers, LC microfilm Series I, Doc. 38994–95, Reel 52).

41. Mapp, *Frock Coats*, 103. Also see the Emancipation Proclamation.

42. Stephen B. Oates, *With Malice Toward None: The Life of Abraham Lincoln* (New York, 1977), 280–284, 324–325.

43. T. J. to John Holmes, April 22, 1820; Peterson, Library of America, 1433–1435.

44. Mapp, *Thomas Jefferson*, 53.

45. Ibid., 53.

46. Thomas Jefferson, *Notes on the State of Virginia*, William Peden, ed. (Chapel Hill, N.C., 1955), 162–163.

47. T. J. to John Holmes, April 22, 1820 (Jefferson Papers, LC microfilm Series I, Docs. 38773–74, Reel 41).

48. Holmes to T. J., June 19, 1820 (ibid., Doc. 38842, Reel 52).

49. T. J. to Holmes, July 8, 1820 (ibid., 38868, Reel 52).

50. T. J. to Richard Rush, October 20, 1820 (ibid., Docs. 38994–95, Reel 52).

51. T. J. to Gallatin, December 26, 1820; Peterson, Library of America, 1447–1450.

52. T. J. to Adams, January 22, 1821; Cappon, 569–570.

53. Randolph to Nicholas Trist, June 5, 1820; Malone, Vol. 6, 341.

54. T. J. to Spencer Roane, March 9, 1821; Paul Leicester Ford, ed., *The Writings of Thomas Jefferson*, Vol. 10 (New York, 1892–1899), 189.

55. *Autobiography of T. J.*, with introduction by Malone, 62.

56. Ibid., 19.

57. T. J. to William T. Barry, July 2, 1822 (Jefferson Papers, LC microfilm Series I, Doc. 39686, Reel 53).

CHAPTER XVIII   BROAD VISTAS

1. T. J. to Breckinridge, February 15, 1821; Merrill D. Peterson, ed., *Thomas Jefferson: Writings*, Library of America (New York, 1984), 1452–1454.

2. Nathan Schachner, *Thomas Jefferson, A Biography* (New York, 1951), 971–972.

3. Cabell to T. J., December 20, 1820; Dumas Malone, *Thomas Jefferson and His Time: The Sage of Monticello*, Vol. 6 (Boston, 1981), 379–380.

4. Ibid., 381.

5. T. J. to J. W. Eppes, June 30, 1820; ibid., 379.

6. Hamilton W. Pierson, *Jefferson at Monticello: The Private Life of Thomas Jefferson* (New York, 1862), 74.

7. Dumas Malone, ed., *Autobiography of Thomas Jefferson* (Boston, 1948).

8. T. J. to Cabell, January 31, 1821 (Jefferson Papers, LC microfilm Series I, Doc. 39197, Reel 52).

9. Schachner, 978.

10. Pierson, 128–129.

11. T. J. to Adams, June 27, 1822 (Jefferson Papers, LC microfilm Series I, Doc. 39682, Reel 53).

12. T. J. to Dr. Benjamin Waterhouse, June 26, 1811; Peterson, Library of America, 1458–1459.

13. Pierson, 74–75.

14. T. J. to J. W. Eppes, June 12, 1820; Schachner, 977.

15. Francis Eppes to T. J., March 22, 1822; T. J. to Eppes, April 9, 1822; and Eppes to T. J., May 13, 1822; Edwin M. Betts and James A. Bear, Jr., eds., *The Family Letters of Thomas Jefferson* (Charlottesville, Va., 1986), 442–445.

16. T. J. to John Eppes, summer 1822; Malone, Vol. 6, 390.

17. Ibid.

18. Cosway to T. J., July 15, 1821; Helen Duprey Bullock, *My Head and My Heart: A Little History of Thomas Jefferson and Maria Cosway* (New York, 1945), 178–180.

19. T. J. to Cosway, October 24, 1822; ibid., 181–183.

20. Malone, Vol. 6, 391–392.

21. Cabell to T. J., February 3, 1823; ibid., 272–273.

22. Alexander Garrett to John Cocke, February 18, 1823; ibid., 394.

23. Monroe to T. J., June 2, 1823 (Jefferson Papers, LC microfilm Series I, Docs. 40059–60, Reel 53).

24. T. J. to Monroe, June 11, 1823 (ibid., Doc. 40067, Reel 53).

25. T. J. to Adams, September 4, 1823; Peterson, Library of America, 1477–1479.

26. T. J. to Monroe, October 24, 1823 (Jefferson Papers, LC microfilm Series I, Doc. 40185, Reel 54).

27. Ibid.

CHAPTER XIX   CAPTAIN, DRUMMER, AND FLAGBEARER

1. T. J. to Madison, November 6, 1823 (Jefferson Papers, LC microfilm Series I, Doc. 40200, Reel 54).

2. Report of October 5, 1824 by T. J.; Nathaniel Francis Cabell, ed., *Early History of the University of Virginia, as Contained in the Letters of Thomas Jefferson and Joseph C. Cabell* (Richmond, Va., 1856), 482.

3. Gilmer to T. J., December 3, 1823; Richard Beale Davis, ed., *Correspondence of T. J. and Francis Walker Gilmer, 1814–1826* (Columbia, S.C., 1946), 81–82.

4. Information on Gilmer is principally from Richard Beale Davis, *Francis Walker Gilmer, Life and Learning in Jefferson's Virginia* (Richmond, Va., 1939).

5. T. J. to Adams, October 12, 1823 (Jefferson Papers, LC microfilm Series I, Doc. 40175, Reel 54).

6. Adams to T. J., November 10, 1823 (ibid., Doc. 40202, Reel 54).

7. T. J. to Visitors, April 9, 1824; Cabell, 302–303.

8. Cabell to T. J., April 16, 1824; Cabell, 303–304.

9. Madison to T. J., April 16, 1824; Dumas Malone, *Jefferson and His Time: The Sage of Monticello*, Vol. 6 (Boston, 1981), 399.

10. Material on Gilmer derived principally from Davis, *Francis Walker Gilmer,* and Davis, *Correspondence.*

11. John Quincy Adams, *Memoirs*, Vol. 1 (Freeport, N.Y., 1969, reprint), 317.

12. T. J. to A. S. Brockenbrough, May 4, 1824; Malone, Vol. 6, 401.

13. T. J. to Madison, September 24, 1824 (Jefferson Papers, LC microfilm Series I, Doc. 40594, Reel 54).

14. T. J., "Planetarium for Dome of the Rotunda, University of Virginia, at and for the College," printed as Document 18 in Silvio A. Bedini, *Thomas Jefferson, Statesman of Science* (New York, 1990), 514–516.

15. Bedini, Document 17, 514.

16. Gilmer to T. J., August 13, 1824; Davis, *Correspondence*, 92–100.

17. Sarah N. Randolph, *The Domestic Life of Thomas Jefferson* (New York, 1872), 389.

18. Ibid., 390–391.

19. Ibid., 391.

20. T. J. to Isaac Briggs, April 20, 1803; Edwin M. Betts, ed., *Thomas Jefferson's Farm Book* (Charlottesville, Va., 1976), 458.

21. T. J. to Adams, June 1, 1822; Randolph, 378–379.

22. T. J. to Cabell, December 1824, and T. J. to Cabell, December 31, 1824; Malone, Vol. 6, 412–413. Dumas Malone's speculation on Jefferson's motives in this instance seems valid, and I have followed it.

23. T. J. to Madison, December 26, 1824 (Jefferson Papers, LC microfilm Series I, Doc. 40735, Reel 54).

24. T. J. to Cabell, December 22, 1824 (ibid., Doc. 40731, Reel 54).

25. Robley Dunglison, "The Autobiographical Ana," Samuel X. Radbill, ed., in *Transactions of the American Philosophical Society*, Vol. 53, Part 8 (1963), 21.

26. Ibid.

27. Ibid.

28. Ibid., 22.

29. Ibid., 22–23.

30. Ibid., 23.

31. T. J. to William Roscoe, December 27, 1820 (Jefferson Papers, LC microfilm Series I, Doc. 39041, Reel 52).

CHAPTER XX   IMPERILED TRIUMPH

1. Robley Dunglison, "The Autobiographical Ana," Samuel X. Radbill, ed. In *Transactions of the American Philosophical Society*, Vol. 53, Part 8 (1963), 26–27.

2. Ibid., 27.

3. Ibid.

4. Ibid.

5. T. G. Watkins to T. J., May 11, 1825 (Jefferson Papers, LC microfilm Series I, Doc. 41002, Reel 55).

6. Dunglison, 26.

7. Ibid.

8. Ibid.

9. Alexander Garrett to General Cocke, June 18, 1825; Dumas Malone, *Jefferson and His Time: The Sage of Monticello*, Vol. 6 (Boston, 1981), 447.

10. Ibid., 456.

11. Henry S. Randall, *The Life of Thomas Jefferson*, Vol. 1 (Philadelphia, 1865), 41.

12. Dunglison, 3.

13. George Tucker, *The Life of Thomas Jefferson*, Vol. 2 (Philadelphia, 1837), 477.

14. Ibid.

15. Dunglison, 34.

16. Tucker, Vol. 2, 479.

17. Ibid., 480.

18. T. J. to William Short, August 1825; Malone, Vol. 6, 464.

19. T. J. to Ellen Randolph Coolidge, August 27, 1825; Edwin M. Betts and James A. Bear, Jr., eds., *The Family Letters of Thomas Jefferson* (Charlottesville, Va., 1986), 458.

20. Circular letter, T. J. to Visitors, September 10, 1825 (Jefferson Papers, LC microfilm Series I, Doc. 41149, Reel 55).

21. Account of disturbance based on Tucker, Vol. 2, 480; Dunglison, 24–25, 29–30; and Virginius Dabney, *Mr. Jefferson's University* (Charlottesville, Va., 1981), 8–9.

22. Dabney, 8.

23. Dunglison, 30 (Quotation from Henry Tutwiler).

24. T. J. to Joseph Coolidge, October 13, 1825, and T. J. to William Short, October 14, 1825; Malone, Vol. 6, 467.

CHAPTER XXI   THE LAST FOURTH

1. T. J. to Madison, October 18, 1825 (Jefferson Papers, LC microfilm Series I, Doc. 41192, Reel 5).

2. Dumas Malone, *Jefferson and His Time: The Sage of Monticello*, Vol. 6 (Boston, 1981), 469–470.

3. George Tucker, *The Life of Thomas Jefferson* (Philadelphia, 1837), 503.

4. T. J. to Madison, December 24, 1825, and enclosure (Jefferson Papers, LC microfilm Series I, Doc. 41267, Reel 55; and T. J. to Madison, January 2, 1826; Paul Leicester Ford, ed., *The Writings of Thomas Jefferson*, Vol. 10 (New York, 1892–1899), 359–360.

5. James A. Bear, Jr., "The Last Few Days in the Life of Thomas Jefferson," *The Magazine of Albemarle County History*, Vol. 32 (1974), 63.

6. T. J. to T. M. Randolph, January 8, 1826 (Jefferson Papers, LC microfilm Series I, Doc. 41300, Reel 55),

7. Ibid., Randolph's note at bottom of T. J.'s letter of January 8, 1826.

8. T. J. to Cabell, January 20, 1826; Nathaniel Francis Cabell, ed., *Early History of the University of Virginia, as Contained in the Letters of Thomas Jefferson and Joseph C. Cabell* (Richmond, Va., 1856), 359. Suggests T. J. got idea on 19th.

9. Martha Randolph to Ellen Coolidge, April 5, 1826; Malone, Vol. 6, 473. Mrs. Randolph seems to be quoting her father.

10. Ford, Vol. 10, 362–372.

11. T. J. Randolph to T. J., January 31, 1826; Edwin M. Betts and James A. Bear, Jr., eds., *The Family Letters of Thomas Jefferson* (Charlottesville, Va., 1986), 466.

12. Ibid., 467.

13. T. J. to T. J. Randolph, February 8, 1826; ibid., 469–470. This letter is somewhat scrambled in the printing.

14. T. J. to T. J. Randolph, February 11, 1826; ibid., 470.

15. Robley Dunglison, "The Autobiographical Ana," Samuel X. Radbill, ed., *Transactions of the American Philosophical Society*, Vol. 53, Part 2 (1963), 34.

16. T. J. Randolph to T. J., February 26, 1826; Betts and Bear, *Family Letters*, 472.

17. Ibid.

18. Francis Wayles Eppes to T. J., February 23, 1826; ibid.

19. Cabell to T. J., February 1826; Sarah N. Randolph, *The Domestic Life of Thomas Jefferson* (New York, 1872), 414.

20. T. J. to Cabell, February 1826; ibid.

21. Ibid., 416.

22. Hetty Carr to D. S. Carr, March 13, 1826; Malone, Vol. 6, 479.

23. T. J.'s will; Ford, Vol. 10, 392–396.

24. Francis Wayles Eppes to T. J., February 23, 1826; Betts and Bear, *Family Letters*, 470–472.

25. T. J. to Madison, February 17, 1826 (Jefferson Papers, LC microfilm Series I, Docs. 41340–41, Reel 55).

26. Malone, Vol. 6, 493.

27. Karl C. Wold, *Mr. President—How Is Your Health?* (St. Paul, Minn., 1948), 31; Dunglison, 32; ibid., n. by Radbill.

28. T. J. to Roger C. Weightman, June 24, 1826; Merrill D. Peterson, ed., *Thomas Jefferson: Writings*, Library of America (New York, 1984), 1516–1517. Note: The phrase "that the mass of mankind . . . grace of God" was inspired by Richard Rumbold's speech from the scaffold in 1685.

29. Tucker, 494.

30. Dunglison, 32.

31. Bear, 67–68.

32. Ibid., 68–69.

33. Douglas Southall Freeman, *R. E. Lee*, Vol. 1 (New York, 1934), 97–98, 115–117; Paul C. Nagel, *The Lees of Virginia: Seven Generations of an American Family* (New York, 1990), 206–230.

34. Randolph, *Domestic Life*, 426–428.

35. Note: Randall, in his valuable biography of Jefferson, quotes Jeff Randolph's account of Jefferson's deathbed conversations but omits this sentence without any indication that anything has been omitted. Henry S. Randall, *The Life of Thomas Jefferson*, 3 Vols. (Charlottesville, Va., 1829).

36. Randolph, *Domestic Life*, 428.

37. Dunglison, 32.

38. Recollections of Nicholas Trist; Randall, Vol. 3, 546.

39. Ibid.

40. Ibid.

41. Randolph, *Domestic Life*, 428. We do not know why Jefferson slept in this posture but, as some people with problems of equilibrium find it necessary for comfort, and as Jefferson suffered from motion sickness, this fact may be the explanation. Heart patients frequently sleep with their heads elevated but Jefferson's habit may have antedated any symptom of cardiac disease.

42. Ibid.

43. Dunglison, 33.

44. Bear, *Last Few Days*, 77–78.

45. Henry Horace Worthington to Reuben B. Hicks, July 6, 1826; Malone, Vol. 6, 498.

46. Bear, *Last Few Days*, 78.

47. Ibid.

48. Pendleton Hogan, *The Lawn: A Guide to Jefferson's University* (Charlottesville, Va., 1987), 128–129, 133–134.

49. Douglas Southall Freeman, *Lee's Lieutenants: A Study in Command*, Vol. 1 (New York, 1942), 18.

50. Randolph, *Domestic Life*, 427.

51. Ibid., 430–431.

52. Ibid., 422

53. Dunglison, 34–35.

54. Albert J. Beveridge, *The Life of John Marshall*, Vol. 4 (Boston, 1916), 579–580.

55. Dunglison, 34–35.

56. Helen Dupree Bullock, *My Head and My Heart: A Little History of Thomas Jefferson and Maria Cosway* (New York, 1945), 186–187.

57. John Quincy Adams, *Diary of John Quincy Adams, 1794–1845*, Allan Nevins, ed. (New York, 1951), 358–360.

58. Randolph, *Domestic Life*, 421n. Sarah N. Randolph, Jefferson's great-granddaughter, says this anecdote "has the advantage over most good stories of being true."

CHAPTER XXII   WHO IS HE?

1. Sarah N. Randolph, *The Domestic Life of Thomas Jefferson* (New York, 1872), 431. T. J. provided against greed but not against souvenir hunting. Visitors chipped away at the original stone until by the 1870s it was "a misshapen column." Ibid., 432.

2. Julian P. Boyd, ed., *The Declaration of Independence: The Evolution of Its Text* (Washington, D.C., 1943), 13

3. More discussion of Jefferson's role in writing the Declaration of Independence is included in Alf J. Mapp, Jr., *Thomas Jefferson: A Strange Case of Mistaken Identity* (Lanham, Md., and New York, 1987), 109–115, 408; Mapp, *The Virginia Experiment: The Old Dominion's Role in the Making of America*, 2nd ed. (Lanham, Md. and New York, 1985), 432–435; and Mapp, "Thomas Jefferson and the Language of Liberty," in Kenneth W. Thompson, ed., *Constitutionalism: Founding and Future* (Charlottesville, Va., 1989), 51–78.

4. Beverley B. Munford, *Virginia's Attitude Toward Slavery and Secession* (Richmond, 1909), 25.

5. Roy J. Honeywell, *The Educational Works of Thomas Jefferson* (Cambridge, Mass., 1931), 113–115.

6. T. J., *An Essay Towards Facilitating Instruction in the Anglo-Saxon and Modern Dialects of the English Language for the Use of the University of Virginia* (New York, 1851). Albert H. Marckwardt and James L. Rosier, *Old English Language and Literature* (New York, 1972).

7. Honeywell, 114.

8. Ibid., 115.

9. Ibid., 123–124.

10. Ibid., 130.

11. Ibid., 130–131.

12. Ibid., 134–145.

13. John Dewey, *The Living Thoughts of Thomas Jefferson* (New York, 1940), 1.

14. Edwin T. Martin, *Thomas Jefferson: Scientist* (New York, 1952), 245.

15. Journals of the House of Delegates, October 7, November 23, December 12, and December 14, 1778; Mapp, *Thomas Jefferson*, 129.

16. Mapp, *Thomas Jefferson*, 120–129.

17. John Quincy Adams, *Parties in the United States* (New York, 1941), 17.

18. Dumas Malone, *Jefferson and His Time: Jefferson and the Ordeal of Liberty*, Vol. 3 (Boston, 1962), 80.

19. Any one-paragraph discussion of the philosophical differences between Jefferson and Hamilton is necessarily superficial. A fuller presentation is in Mapp, *Thomas Jefferson*, 275–343; Albert Fried, ed., *The Jeffersonian and Hamiltonian Traditions in American Politics* (Garden City, N. J., 1968).

20. Samuel Eliot Morison, *The Oxford History of the American People* (New York, 1965), 376.

21. Woodrow Wilson, "What Jefferson Would Do," Francis Coleman Rosenberger, ed., *Jefferson Reader: A Treasury of Writings About Thomas Jefferson* (New York, 1953), 239.

22. Dumas Malone, *Jefferson and His Time: The Sage of Monticello*, Vol. 6 (Boston, 1981), 359.

23. T. J. to Maria Cosway, September 20, 1786; Julian P. Boyd, ed., *The Papers of Thomas Jefferson*, Vol. 10 (Princeton, 1950–1982), 443–444.

24. Dewey, 1.

25. Benson John Lossing, "Tom Moore in America," *Harper's New Monthly Magazine*, Vol. 4 (September 1877), 537–541.

26. *Glimpses of the Past: Correspondence of Thomas Jefferson*, Missouri Historical Society, 1788–1826 (St. Louis, 1936), 120.

27. James A. Bear, "The Last Few Days of Thomas Jefferson's Life," *Magazine of Albemarle County History*, Vol. 32 (1974), 69.

SELECT CRITICAL BIBLIOGRAPHY

WHAT WAS SAID in the introduction to the bibliography of *Thomas Jefferson: a Strange Case of Mistaken Identity* is equally true of this volume. By far the most important sources of information are Jefferson's formal writings, journals and record books, and massive correspondence with men, women, and children on three continents. The originals of these writings are to be found chiefly in the Library of Congress, the Alderman Library of the University of Virginia, the Virginia State Library, the Massachusetts Historical Society, and the Earl Gregg Swem Library of the College of William and Mary. *The Papers of Thomas Jefferson*, published by Princeton University Press beginning in 1950 under the brilliant editorship of the late Julian P. Boyd, who saw the work through its first twenty volumes, and continued under Charles T. Cullen, was the most important source for the earlier volume. Unfortunately, however, the Princeton edition does not cover the years (1801–1826) embraced by *Thomas Jefferson: Passionate Pilgrim*. While that excellent series is occasionally resorted to for flashbacks, the indispensable sources for this period are the microfilms of the Thomas Jefferson Papers in the Presidential Papers, Library of Congress, Washington, D.C.

Next in importance among sources for this volume are *The Domestic Life of Thomas Jefferson*, edited by Jefferson's great-granddaughter Sarah N. Randolph, containing many family reminiscences, and *The Family Letters of Thomas Jefferson*, edited by Edwin M. Betts and James A. Bear, Jr.

The most useful of several good biographies are Henry S. Randall's *The Life of Thomas Jefferson*, almost a primary source because of the author's acquaintance with the subject's relatives and friends; Nathan Schachner's *Thomas Jefferson, A Biography*, illuminated by insights gained from experience of practical affairs as well as scholarship; and Dumas Malone's magisterial six-volume *Jefferson and His Time*, which always deserves respectful consideration even on those points on which one ultimately reaches different conclusions.

I. Jefferson's Writings

Betts, Edwin M., and James A. Bear, Jr., eds. *The Family Letters of Thomas Jefferson*. Charlottesville, Va., 1986.

Betts, Edwin M., ed. *Thomas Jefferson's Farm Book*. Charlottesville, Va., 1976.

———. *Thomas Jefferson's Garden Book*. Philadelphia, 1944.

Boyd, Julian P., ed. *The Papers of Thomas Jefferson*. 20 vols. Princeton 1950–1982. Vol. 21, *Index*, Charles T. Cullen, ed., published 1983. This is by far the most ably and thoroughly edited collection of Jefferson's letters, but at this writing extends only to August 1791. See Cullen below.

Cappon, Lester J., ed. *The Adams-Jefferson Letters: The Complete Correspondence Between Thomas Jefferson and John and Abigail Adams*. Chapel Hill, N.C., 1988.

Cullen, Charles T., ed. *The Papers of Thomas Jefferson*, 2nd series, *Jefferson's Extracts from the Gospel*. Princeton, 1983.

Ford, Paul Leicester, ed. *The Writings of Thomas Jefferson*. 10 vols. New York, 1892–1899. Competently though not always objectively annotated, this collection suffers from large gaps in the correspondence. It is valuable chiefly as a printed source of Jefferson letters after August 1791, the latest date so far covered by the Princeton edition edited by Boyd and Cullen.

Glimpses of the Past: Correspondence of Thomas Jefferson, 1788–1826. Vol. 3. Missouri Historical Society. St. Louis, 1936.

Jefferson, Thomas. *An Essay Towards Facilitating Instruction in the Anglo-Saxon and Modern Dialects of the English Language for the Use of the University of Virginia*. New York, 1851.

———. *Notes on the State of Virginia*. William Peden, ed. Chapel Hill, N.C., 1955.

———. *Thomas Jefferson: Writings*. Merrill D. Peterson, ed. (Library of America). New York, 1984.

Jefferson Papers, Library of Congress, Washington, D. C. Microfilm Series I, Reels 14–56. For those years not yet included in the Princeton Edition, this collection is the essential source. Even for those letters available in the Princeton Edition, the LC collection offers the added testimony of variations in handwriting and of Jefferson's suggestive emendation of his first drafts.

Lipscomb, A. A. and A. E. Bergh, eds. *The Writings of Thomas Jefferson*. 20 vols. Washington, D. C., 1903. These volumes include letters not to be found in Ford and not yet within the compass of the Princeton edition, but annotation is sparse and portions of printed letters are omitted without textual indication of that fact.

Malone, Dumas, ed. *Autobiography of Thomas Jefferson*. Boston, 1948.

———. *Correspondence Between Thomas Jefferson and Pierre Samuel Du Pont de Nemours, 1798–1817*. Boston, 1930.

Mayo, Bernard, ed. *Jefferson Himself: The Personal Narrative of a Many-sided American*. Boston, 1942.

Sawvel, F. B., ed. *The Complete Anas of Thomas Jefferson*. New York, 1903.

II. Contemporary Writings

Adams, Henry, ed. *Albert Gallatin: Writings*, Vol. 1. Philadelphia, 1879.

Adams, John. *The Spur of Fame: Dialogues of John Adams and Benjamin Rush*. John A. Schutz and Douglass Adair, eds. San Marino, Calif., 1966.

———. *Works*. Charles Francis Adams, ed. Vols. 8 and 10. Boston, 1853.

Adams, John Quincy. *Diary of John Quincy Adams, 1794–1845*. Allan Nevins, ed. New York, 1951.

———. *Writings*. W. C. Ford, ed. Vols. 1 and 3. New York, 1914.

American State Papers: Documents, Legislative and Executive. Selected and edited, under the authority of Congress, by Walter Lowrie and Matthew St. Clair Clarke. 38 vols. Washington, D. C., 1832–1861. *Foreign Relations*, Vol. 2.

Betts, Edwin M. "Ground Plans and Prints of the University of Virginia, 1822–1826." *Proceedings of the American Philosophical Society*, Vol. 90 (1946).

Cabell, Nathaniel Francis, ed. *Early History of the University of Virginia, as Contained in the Letters of Thomas Jefferson and Joseph C. Cabell*. Richmond, Va., 1856.

Cutler, Manasseh. *Life, Journals, and Correspondence*. W. P. and J. P. Cutler, eds. 2 vols. Cincinnati, 1888.

Davis, Matthew L. *Memoirs of Aaron Burr with Miscellaneous Selections from His Correspondence*, Vol. 2. New York, 1837.

Dunglison, Robley. "The Autobiographical Ana," Samuel X. Radbill, ed. *Transactions of the American Philosophical Society*, Vol. 53, Part 8 (1963).

Hamilton, John C., ed. *The Works of Alexander Hamilton*. New York, 1851.

Jackson, Andrew. *The Papers of Andrew Jackson*. Harold D. Moser and Sharon MacPherson, eds., Charles F. Bryan, Jr., asst. ed. Vol. 2. Knoxville, Tenn., 1984.

King, Charles R., ed. *The Life and Correspondence of Rufus King*. Vol. 3 and 4. New York, 1971.

Maclay, Edgar S., ed. *Journal of William Maclay, United States Senator from Pennsylvania, 1789–1791*. New York, 1890.

Madison, James. *The Papers of James Madison*. Robert A. Rutland and Thomas A. Mason, eds. Vol. 1. Charlottesville, Va., 1984.

———. *The Papers of James Madison: Secretary of State Series*. Robert J. Brugger, ed. Vol. 1. Charlottesville, Va., 1986.

———. *Writings*. Gaillard Hunt, ed. 9 vols. New York, 1900–1910.

Mason, George. *Papers*. Robert A. Rutland, ed. 2 vols. Chapel Hill, N.C., 1970.

Mitchill, Samuel Latham, "Dr. Mitchill's Letters from Washington," *Harper's New Monthly Magazine*, Vol. 5, No. 58 (April 1879).

Morris, Anne Cary, ed. *The Diary and Letters of Gouverneur Morris*. New York, 1970.

Padover, Saul K., ed. *Thomas Jefferson and the National Capital*. 1946.

Pierson, Hamilton W. *Jefferson at Monticello: The Private Life of Thomas Jefferson*. New York, 1862.

Quincy, Edmund. *Life of Josiah Quincy*. Boston, 1868.

Randolph, Sarah N. *The Domestic Life of Thomas Jefferson*. New York, 1872.

Reports of the Trials of Col. Aaron Burr, on an Indictment for Treason . . . Taken in Shorthand by David Robertson. 2 vols. New York, 1895.

Smith, Margaret Bayard. *The First Forty Years of Washington Society*. New York, 1906.

Syrett, Harold C., ed. *Papers of Alexander Hamilton*. Vol. 25. New York, 1977.

Tucker, George. *The Life of Thomas Jefferson*. Philadelphia, 1837.

III. Secondary Sources

Adams, Henry, ed. *Documents Relating to New England Federalism*. 1905.

———. *History of the United States During the Administrations of Jefferson and Madison*. 9 vols. New York, 1891–1893.

———. *History of the United States of America During the First Administration of Thomas Jefferson*. New York, 1917.

———. *The Life of Albert Gallatin*. Philadelphia, 1879.

Adams, William Howard. *The Eye of Thomas Jefferson*. Washington, D.C., 1976.

American Historical Review, Vol. 53, No. 3, 518–520.

Ammon, Henry. *James Monroe: The Quest for National Identity*. New York, 1971.

Bear, James A., Jr. "The Hemings Family of Monticello." *Virginia Cavalcade*, Vol. 40, No. 2 (Autumn 1974), 75–87.

———. *Jefferson at Monticello*. Charlottesville, Va., 1976.

———. "The Last Few Days of Thomas Jefferson's Life." *Magazine of Albemarle County History*, Vol. 32 (1974).

Becker, Carl. *The Declaration of Independence*. New York, 1940.

Bedini, Silvio A. *Thomas Jefferson: Statesman of Science*. New York, 1990.

Berman, Eleanor Davidson. *Thomas Jefferson among the Arts: An Essay in Early American Aesthetics*. New York, 1947.

Betts, Edwin M. and Hazelhurst B. Perkins. *Thomas Jefferson's Flower Garden at Monticello*. Richmond, 1941.

Beveridge, Albert J. *The Life of John Marshall*. 4 vols. Boston, 1916.

Boyd, Julian P., ed. *The Declaration of Independence: The Evolution of Its Text*. Washington, D.C., 1943.

Bruce, Philip Alexander. "John Randolph," in *Library of Southern Literature*. Vol. 10. Atlanta, 1907.

Bullock, Helen Dupree. *My Head and My Heart: A Little History of Thomas Jefferson and Maria Cosway*. New York, 1945.

Burt, Alfred L. *The United States, Great Britain, and British North America: From the Revolution to the Establishment of Peace after the War of 1812*. New Haven, Conn., 1940.

Butterfield, L. H. "The Dream of Benjamin Rush: The Reconciliation of John Adams and Thomas Jefferson." *Yale Review*, Vol. 40 (December 1950).

Chinard, Gilbert. "Jefferson among the Philosophers," *Ethics*. Vol. 53, No. 4 (July 1943), 255–268.

———. "Jefferson's Influence Abroad," *Mississippi Historical Review*, Vol. 30, No. 2 (September 1943), 171–186.

———. *Thomas Jefferson, the Apostle of Americanism*. Boston, 1929.

———. *Thomas Jefferson: The Apostle of Americanism*, 2nd ed. Ann Arbor, 1960.

Cunningham, Noble E. *In Pursuit of Reason: The Life of Thomas Jefferson*. Baton Rouge, La., 1987.

———. *The Jeffersonian Republicans: The Formation of Party Organization, 1789–1801*. Chapel Hill, N.C., 1957.

———. *The Jeffersonian Republicans in Power: Party Operations, 1801–1809*. Chapel Hill, N.C., 1963.

Coit, Margaret L. *The Growing Years, 1789–1829*. New York, 1963.

Dabney, Virginius. *The Jefferson Scandals*. New York, 1981.

———. *Mr. Jefferson's University*. Charlottesvile, Va., 1981.

———. *Virginia the New Dominion*. New York, 1971.

Dangerfield, George. *Chancellor Robert R. Livingston of New York, 1746–1813*. New York, 1960.

Davis, Richard Beale. *Intellectual Life in Jefferson's Virginia*. Chapel Hill, N.C., 1964.

DeVoto, Bernard, ed. *The Journals of Lewis and Clark*. Boston, 1953.

Dewey, John. *The Living Thoughts of Jefferson*. New York, 1940.

Dumbauld, Edward. *Thomas Jefferson, American Tourist*. Norman, Okla., 1946.

Egan, Clifford L. "The United States, France, and West Florida, 1803–1807." *Florida Historical Quarterly*, Vol. 47 (1968–1969).

Flexner, James Thomas. *The Young Hamilton*. Boston, 1978.

Foster, A. J. *Jeffersonian America*. San Marino, 1954.

Frary, I. T. *Thomas Jefferson, Architect and Builder*. Richmond, 1939.

———. *They Built the Capitol*. Richmond, 1950.

Freeman, Douglas Southall. *R. E. Lee*. Vol. 1. New York, 1934.

Herold, J. Christopher. *The Age of Napoleon*. New York, 1963.

Hogan, Pendleton. *The Lawn: A Guide to Jefferson's University*. Charlottesville, Va., 1987.

Honeywell, Roy J. *The Educational Works of Thomas Jefferson*. Cambridge, Mass., 1931.

Jackson, Donald. *Thomas Jefferson and the Stony Mountains*. Urbana, Ill., 1981.

Jellison, Charles A. "That Scoundrel Callender." *Virginia Magazine of History*, Vol. 67 (July 1959).

Jordan, Daniel P. *Political Leadership in Jefferson's Virginia*. Charlottesville, Va., 1983.

Kallen, Horace M. "The Arts and Thomas Jefferson." *Ethics*, Vol. 53, No. 4 (July 1943), 269–283.

Lanciano, Claude O., Jr. *Rosewell, Garland of Virginia*. Gloucester, Va., 1978.

Lodge, Henry C., ed. *Life and Letters of George Cabot Lodge*. Boston, 1877.

Lokke, C. L. "Secret Negotiations to Maintain the Peace of America." *American Historical Review*, Vol. 49 (October 1943).

Lossing, Benson John. "Tom Moore in America." *Harper's New Monthly Magazine*, Vol. 4 (September 1877).

Lyon, Elijah Wilson. *Louisiana in French Diplomacy, 1759–1804*. Norman, Okla., 1934.

Malone, Dumas. *Jefferson and His Time*. 6 vols. Boston, 1948–1981.

Manchester, William. *American Caesar*. New York, 1978.

Mapp, Alf J., Jr. *Frock Coats and Epaulets: Psychological Portraits of Confederate Military and Political Leaders*. 2nd ed. Lanham, Md., and New York, 1987.

———. "Thomas Jefferson and the Language of Liberty." Kenneth W. Thompson, ed., *Constitutionalism: Founding and Future*. Charlottesville, Va., 1989.

———. *Thomas Jefferson: A Strange Case of Mistaken Identity*. Lanham, Md., and New York, 1987.

———. *The Virginia Experiment: The Old Dominion's Role in the Making of America*. 2nd ed. Lanham, Md., and New York, 1987.

Mapp, Alf J., Jr., and Ramona H. Mapp. *Portsmouth: A Pictorial History*. Norfolk, Va., 1989.

Marckwardt, Albert H., and James L. Rosier. *Old English Language and Literature*. New York, 1972.

Martin, Edwin T. *Thomas Jefferson: Scientist*. New York, 1952.

Mays, David John. *Edmund Pendleton*. Vol. 1. Cambridge, Mass., 1952.

McDonald, Forrest. *The Presidency of Thomas Jefferson*. Lawrence, Kans., 1976.

McKee, Christopher. *Edward Preble, a Naval Biography, 1761–1807*. Annapolis, Md., 1972.

McLaughlin, Jack. *Jefferson and Monticello*. New York, 1988.

Miller, John Chester. *The Wolf by the Ears: Thomas Jefferson and Slavery*. New York, 1977.

Miller, Charles A. *Jefferson and Nature: An Interpretation*. Baltimore, 1988.

Morison, Samuel Eliot. *The Oxford History of the American People*. New York, 1965.

Mott, Frank Luther. *Jefferson and the Press*. Baton Rouge, La., 1943.

Munford, Beverley B. *Virginia's Attitude Toward Slavery and Secession*. Richmond, 1909.

Nagel, Paul C. *Descent from Glory: Four Generations of the John Adams Family*. New York, 1983.

————. *The Lees of Virginia: Seven Generations of an American Family*. New York, 1990.

Nichols, Frederick D., and James A. Bear, Jr. *Monticello*. Charlottesville, Va., 1982.

Oates, Stephen B. *With Malice Toward None: The Life of Abraham Lincoln*. New York, 1977.

Parton, James. *The Life and Times of Aaron Burr*. New York, 1858.

Peterson, Merrill D. *The Jefferson Image in the American Mind*. New York, 1960.

Randall, Henry S. *The Life of Thomas Jefferson*. 3 vols. Philadelphia, 1865.

Randolph, Sarah N. *The Domestic Life of Thomas Jefferson*. Cambridge, Mass., 1872.

Randolph, Thomas Jefferson, ed. *Memoir, Correspondence and Miscellaneous from the Papers of Thomas Jefferson*. 4 vols. Charlottesville, Va., 1829.

Rosenberger, Francis Coleman, ed. *Jefferson Reader: A Treasury of Writings about Thomas Jefferson*. New York, 1953.

Rothery, Agnes. *Houses Virginians Have Loved*. New York, 1954.

Schachner, Nathan. *Thomas Jefferson, A Biography*. 2 vols. New York, 1951.

Sellers, Charles C. *Charles Willson Peale, Later Life, 1790–1827*, Vol. 2. Philadelphia, 1947.

Shepherd, Henry E. "Thomas Jefferson as a Philologist," *American Journal of Philology*. Vol. 3 (1882), 211–214.

Trevelyan, George Macaulay. *A Shortened History of England*. New York, 1942.

Vance, Joseph C. "Knives, Whips and Randolphs on the Court House Lawn." *Magazine of Albemarle County History*, Vol. 15 (1955–1956).

Walters, Raymond, Jr. *Albert Gallatin: Jeffersonian Financier and Diplomat*. New York, 1957.

Whitaker, Arthur Preston. *The Mississippi Question, 1795–1803*. New York, 1934.

White, Leonard D. *The Jeffersonians: A Study in Administrative History, 1801–1829*. New York, 1951.

Whitelaw, Ralph T. *Virginia's Eastern Shore*. Vol. 1. Richmond, Va., 1951.

Wilson, Woodrow. "What Jefferson Would Do." Francis Coleman Rosenberger, ed., *Jefferson Reader: A Treasury of Writings About Thomas Jefferson*. New York, 1953.

Wold, Karl C. *Mr. President—How Is Your Health?* St. Paul, Minn., 1948.

INDEX

About the Author

Alf J. Mapp, Jr. brings to *Thomas Jefferson: Passionate Pilgrim* thirty-five years of experience in making Jefferson and his contemporaries come to life for men and women of our own time. His *Thomas Jefferson: A Strange Case of Mistaken Identity* (published by Madison Books in 1987) won critical acclaim on two continents and was a featured selection of the Book-of-the-Month Club.

He has also written on a variety of other topics, and his diversity of interests has helped him to interpret the many-sided Jefferson. Alf Mapp's writings have circled the globe in nine languages, earning the praise of scholarly critics for their literary quality and fresh insights, and winning the plaudits of the public for their high entertainment value. After 31 years on the faculty of Old Dominion University, he is now Eminent Scholar Emeritus and Louis I. Jaffe Professor Emeritus.

He lives with his wife, Ramona, in Willow Oaks, their home on the Elizabeth River in Portsmouth, Virginia.